An official publication of

THE NEW YORK BOTANICAL GARDEN

FIFTH EDITION

Diseases and Pests of Ornamental Plants

PASCAL P. PIRONE
THE NEW YORK BOTANICAL GARDEN

A WILEY-INTERSCIENCE PUBLICATION

JOHN WILEY & SONS, New York · Chichester · Brisbane · Toronto

Library of Congress Cataloging in Publication Data:

Pirone, Pascal Pompey, 1907–
    Diseases and pests of ornamental plants.

    "A Wiley-Interscience publication."
    Bibliography: p.
    Includes index.
    1. Plants, Ornamental–Diseases and pests.
1. Title.

SB603.5.P57 1978   635.9'2   77-26893
ISBN 0-471-07249-4

Printed in the United States of America

10 9 8 7

PREFACE

Plants are living things and, like all living things, are attacked by many kinds of diseases and pests. These we must combat if we would keep our plants in good health. To help professional and amateur gardeners, arborists, nurseries, landscape architects, floriculturists, greenskeepers, and, in fact, everyone interested in growing plants, is the guiding purpose of this volume. Pursuant to this purpose, the Fifth Edition includes new host genera, identifies new diseases, and recognizes the spread of many known diseases to a wider range of host plants. Up-to-date control measures have been reflected throughout; some new illustrations have been incorporated; and the discussions of fungicides, bactericides, and miticides have been greatly expanded. The standard virus nomenclature is used throughout.

This book describes the diseases, pests, and other troubles that assail nearly 500 genera of ornamental plants grown outdoors, under glass, or in the home. It carefully explains, for each plant, when and how to use the most effective fungicides, insecticides, and other control materials and practices.

The present edition differs sharply from earlier ones, particularly on the kinds and uses of pesticides. On January 1, 1971, New York State banned the use of certain chemical materials, including benzene hexachloride, DDD, DDT, endrin, mercury compounds, selenites and selenates, strobane, and toxaphene—some because they are clear-cut deadly poisons or are not readily biodegradable; others because they enter food and cause or abet various disease conditions in humans and animals. Other states are taking similar measures.

On a national scale, the Environmental Protection Agency has banned the use of Aldrin, Dieldrin, and DDT, and in late December 1975, citing a cancer risk to humans, it banned most uses of chlordane and heptachlor.

Many other substances, though not prohibited, have been severely restricted. In New York State, for example, some materials may be sold, distributed, purchased, possessed, and used only by issuance of *a commercial or purchase permit* for uses listed on the approved label as registered with the N. Y. State Department of Environmental Conservation. Amateur gardeners do not qualify for permits.

Wherever there is a choice, the pesticides least harmful to people, animals, and fish life are recommended in this edition. The relative toxicity of most pesticides is given in the chapter on Control. Although some pesticides have been used improperly or excessively, the fact remains that there is a place for their continued use. This is especially true for ornamental plants. Trees, shrubs, flowers, and lawn grasses are not consumed by people and hence can be sprayed with many of the pesticides that cannot be used safely on food crops.

Earlier editions constantly advocated the burning of diseased or insect-infested materials. With the present restrictions on open burning of refuse, an easy method of disposal is unavailable. Some discarded materials can be buried; most of the remainder can be bagged or placed in the trash can to be carted away.

The organization of this edition closely follows that of its predecessors. Part I provides a foundation for a rational approach to the problem of control. It discusses diseases and pests by symptoms and by causes. It considers bacteria and fungi, as well as insects and other animal pests, and sets forth formulas and general instructions for control. Methods and materials are indeed numerous, and possibly some preparations recommended may not be obtainable in all parts of the country. Furthermore, prices and labor costs may dictate the use of methods other than those described. Nevertheless, it is hoped that the four chapters of Part I will show something of the nature of the enemies of plant life, and why certain methods are applied and certain substances are used.

In Part II, the host plants are arranged alphabetically by their scientific names. The usage of these names follows the well-known works of L. H. Bailey. The common names (as well as scientific names) may be found in the Index at the end of the volume. For each plant are shown the disease or pest symptoms, why they appear, what they indicate, and the most effective means of control. While some plants are subject to many ills, others, as will be noted, are relatively free from trouble, and this information is also highly useful. Since these pages are addressed to scientists as well as to nonprofessional gardeners, the scientific names of fungus parasites and animal pests and the generic names of pesticides (and in some instances the chemical composition) have been included.

PASCAL P. PIRONE

New York City
January, 1978

ACKNOWLEDGMENTS

The First and Second Editions of this book were prepared by Drs. B. O. Dodge and H. W. Rickett. In 1960, I prepared the Third Edition with Drs. Dodge and Rickett and in 1970 became the sole author of the Fourth Edition. As in earlier editions, I have made extensive use of information in books and periodicals too numerous to mention here; these sources are listed in the Bibliography in Appendix B. Special thanks are due to the many companies, institutions, and individuals who contributed illustrations to the book. Specific credits are given in the identifying captions. Those not credited are either New York Botanical Garden illustrations or were taken by the author.

In preparing the Fifth Edition, valuable assistance was given by my eldest son, Thomas Pirone, Professor of Plant Pathology, University of Kentucky, and Professor John Hartman, Extension Plant Pathologist at the same institution; Clark Rogerson, Mycologist, and Herbert Bijur, Director of Special Projects, at The New York Botanical Garden; Dr. George Hepting, United States Forest Service; Richard Weir III, Nassau County (New York) Co-operative Extension Association; Dr. Louis Vasvary, Entomologist, Rutgers University; and the late Herminie B. Kitchen. My special thanks go to my former secretary, Ellen Hayes, who typed nearly all of the new material and to Bernice Winkler, who provided supplementary secretarial help.

Above all, however, I want to express my deep gratitude to my dear wife, Loretta, whose help, encouragement, and care have made easier the preparation of this edition.

P. P. P.

CONTENTS

PART I

DISEASES AND PESTS IN GENERAL

CHAPTER 1.   PLANT DISEASES

Diseases Classified by Symptoms   3

Diseases Classified by Causes   16

Diseases Due to Environmental Conditions or Cultural Practices

CHAPTER 2. BACTERIA AND FUNGI

CHAPTER 3. INSECTS AND OTHER ANIMAL PESTS

CHAPTER 4.   CONTROL

PART II

DISEASES AND PESTS OF PARTICULAR HOSTS

I
DISEASES AND PESTS IN GENERAL

1

PLANT DISEASES

By a "disease" of a plant we mean any condition in the plant that interferes with normal development. Development is normal when it is typical of the particular kind of plant. The growth of the stem, branches, and roots, the unfolding of leaves of a certain shape and size, the formation of characteristic flowers and fruit, the manufacture of pigments, foods, fibers—all these are phases of normal development. If the stem is stunted, if the leaves are curled or mottled or spotted, if the plant wilts, if green color is lacking, if the flowers are of an unusual form or color[1]—if the plant manifests any such abnormalities in its development—it is said to be diseased.

The causes of plant diseases fall into two main groups, parasitic and nonparasitic. Included in the former are bacteria, fungi, nemas,[2] viruses, mycoplasmas, viroids, and insects and related pests. Among the nonparasitic causes are such widely different agents as deficiencies or surpluses of raw food materials, unfavorable water relationships including a lack or an excess of moisture, unfavorable environmental conditions such as extremely low or very high temperatures, chemical substances in the soil or the atmosphere, and mechanical and electrical agents.

Plant diseases may be classified in several ways. They may be grouped according to their causes. On this basis diseases due to nonparasitic causes can be easily separated from those caused by parasites or animal pests. The former are treated in considerable detail later in this chapter, whereas the parasitic causes are described in Chapters 2 and 3. Another useful classification is by symptoms, as with many human diseases.

DISEASES CLASSIFIED BY SYMPTOMS

Physicians are accustomed to classifying human diseases by their effects upon the body. They speak of fevers, colds, boils, gangrene, measles and jaundice as diseases which are recognizable by visible symptoms. Plant diseases may likewise be classified by their symptoms and named accordingly: spots, wilts, blights, rots, cankers, rusts, and so forth. It must be borne in mind, however, that *the same symptoms may be caused by entirely different agents and require entirely different methods of control.* Just as headaches may be caused by intestinal troubles, by eyestrain, or by attacks of parasitic bacteria, so wilting of plants may be the result of bacterial or fungal invasion or lack of water in the soil.

[1] Excepting the effects of alterations in heredity, which reappear in subsequent generations.

[2] These are also known as nematodes or eelworms in many publications. Singular, nema.

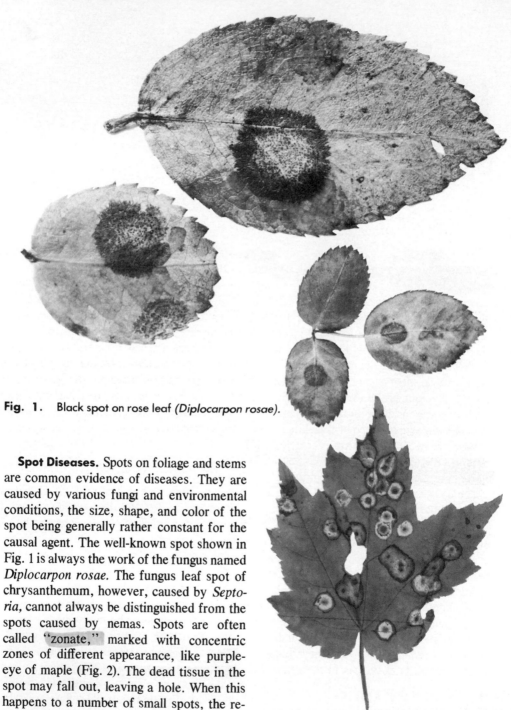

Fig. 1. Black spot on rose leaf *(Diplocarpon rosae)*.

Spot Diseases. Spots on foliage and stems are common evidence of diseases. They are caused by various fungi and environmental conditions, the size, shape, and color of the spot being generally rather constant for the causal agent. The well-known spot shown in Fig. 1 is always the work of the fungus named *Diplocarpon rosae.* The fungus leaf spot of chrysanthemum, however, caused by *Septoria,* cannot always be distinguished from the spots caused by nemas. Spots are often called "zonate," marked with concentric zones of different appearance, like purple-eye of maple (Fig. 2). The dead tissue in the spot may fall out, leaving a hole. When this happens to a number of small spots, the resulting appearance is often known as "shot-hole."

Fig. 2. Leaf spot or purple-eye *(Phyllosticta minima)* on red maple.

Fig. 3.   Anthracnose of *Ficus* caused by *Glomerella cingulata.*

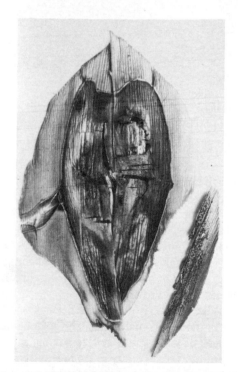

Fig. 4.   Blotch on leaf of *Pandanus pacificus* caused by *Melanconium pandani.* Fruiting bodies of the fungus are visible on the small detached piece.

Brown patch and dollar spot of golf links are to greens what leaf spot diseases are to individual plants. The extension of the disease to many grass plants, with the consequent death of the tops of their leaf blades, results in a large diseased spot.

Anthracnose. This is a term originally associated with diseases caused by a certain genus[3] of fungi. Anthracnose of beans, recognized by the rusty spots on the leaves, pods, and seeds, is well known. Ornamental species of *Ficus* grown as house plants often develop anthracnose areas on the leaves (Fig. 3).

Blotch. If diseased areas of a leaf are irregular in shape and size, the disease is usually called "blotch" rather than spot (Figs. 4 and 203). No definite separation can be made between an extended leaf blotch and blight.

Blight. A blight may be defined as a disease that kills young growing tissues, especially of leaves and twigs, as in Fig. 5. It may extend downward for a long distance in trees. Well-known examples are fire blight of pear

[3] The terms "genus" and "species" are explained in Chapter 2 (page 34).

Fig. 5. Black leg of delphinium *(Erwinia atroseptica).* On the left, the upper part of the plant, the stem blackened; on the right, the stem split to show the destruction of the inner parts.

(a bacterial disease), chestnut blight (a fungus disease), rhododendron and lilac tip blight (both caused by the same fungus), and lilac graft blight (nonparasitic).

Scorch. During very hot weather the sun's rays may cause a browning and shriveling of leaves. It may affect the tips and margins or involve entire leaves. Such symptoms are often called "scorch" or "sunscorch," though they may be due to other conditions or to the effects of a parasite. Even certain types of winter injury are sometimes referred to as "scorch."

Cankers. These are more or less localized diseases, particularly of woody plants. They result in a shrinking and dying of the tissues,

which later crack open and expose the wood underneath. Examples are brown canker of roses, apple nectria canker, chestnut canker, *Phomopsis* canker of delphinium, red-fire canker of amaryllis flower stalk (Figs. 6 and 7). The organisms that cause pear blight live over winter in old cankers caused by the infection of the previous year.

Wilt. Wilting is due to a deficiency of water in the leaves and stems. This may be due to lack of water in the soil, to baking or balling of the soil, to injury to the root system, or to the effects of parasites of various kinds. Sometimes it is difficult to distinguish wilts due to different causes. Wilt of dahlias may be caused by bacteria and by soil-borne

Fig. 6 *(Above, left).* Amaryllis attacked by *Stagonospora curtisii.* The canker at the base causes the abrupt bending of the stem.

Fig. 7 *(Above, right).* Canker on amaryllis stem caused by *Stagonospora curtisii.*

fungi, and by the cracking of the main stem below the soil, caused by strong wind. Aster wilt (Fig. 8) is due to the pink fungus *Fusarium.* Leaves of elm may wilt because of the invasion of the sapwood by the fungus *Ceratocystis ulmi,* the cause of the Dutch elm disease. The fungus *Verticillium* causes wilting of many ornamental species. The wilting caused by such parasites is primarily due to toxins which they produce; later the water-conducting vessels may become plugged by bacterial or fungus growth, or by overgrowth of neighboring cells. Another frequent cause of wilting is a rot of the roots or of the base of the stem, which may be caused by various organisms (Fig. 9).

Damping-off. Certain fungi, which most frequently attack seedlings, kill the tissues of stem and root near the ground line; this causes the plants to fall over. A number of species of fungi common in the soil of propagating beds cause damping-off; the best known are species of *Pythium, Pellicularia* (*Rhizoctonia*), *Fusarium,* and *Botrytis.* *Pythium* usually invades the cells themselves, causing them to collapse and exude their juices.

Rots. Any organism which causes the disintegration of living cells of plants in large numbers may cause a rot. Familiar examples of rot diseases are canna bud rot, caused by a bacterium; crown and rhizome rot of delphin-

Fig. 8. Aster wilt; China aster *(Callistephus)* attacked by *Fusarium oxysporum* var. *callistephi*.

ium (Fig. 10), iris, and aconite; a dry rot caused by a fungus, *Sclerotium;* and *Botrytis* rhizome rot and bacterial soft rot of iris, wet and foul-smelling.

Stunts. Stunting of a plant may be due to a large number of causes, including parasitic and nonparasitic agents. Dahlia stunt may be due to attacks by aphids or leaf-hoppers or by viruses, or to lack of proper nutrients in the soil.

Gummosis. This term is used to designate the exudation of sap (including latex or gum) which breaks out to the surface. Such discharges may be due to the attack of a parasite, often in another part of the plant. The peach borer, working in the crown, may cause gummosis of trunk and branches.

Oedema. When the relations of the plant with water are abnormal, as under conditions of exceptional humidity, small masses of tis-

Fig. 9. Collapse of begonia due to stem rot caused by *Pythium*.

sue may expand and break out on the surface, causing a watery swelling or gall (Fig. 11). Frequently the exposed surface becomes rusty in color so that the lesion may be mistaken for a rust caused by a fungus. Oedema is a nonparasitic disease.

Rusts. While the home gardener may refer to any disease which causes reddish-brown spotting, such as anthracnose of beans, as a rust, it is more correct to confine this term to diseases caused by fungi of the order Uredinales in the Basidiomycetes (Chapter 2). Hollyhock rust, snapdragon rust, carnation rust, cedar-apple rust are among the best-known rusts of ornamentals. The rust fungi are obligate parasites; they must develop on living hosts, and have not as yet been propagated in culture or on decaying substances. One research worker claims he has grown the rust *Gymnosporangium juniperi-virginianae* on ar-

tificial food, but this has not been corroborated by other workers.

Smuts. The black smut pustules that break out on ears of corn and the heads of other cereals are recognized by the masses of black powdery spores. Many smut fungi enter the plants in the seedling stage and develop with the plant as it grows until blossom time; they are systemic. Corn smut, dahlia leaf smut, violet smut, and the smut of *Erythronium*, however, are localized.

Mildews. Powdery mildews are fungi that grow superficially on the leaves and stems of their hosts, causing the grayish fungus layer seen in Fig. 12. As a rule only their haustoria (sucking organs) penetrate the cells (Fig. 13). The downy mildews, on the other hand, invade the hosts deeply; only those structures of the fungi which bear the spores[4] can be seen on the surface of the host. Downy mildew is most obvious after cloudy, moist nights, or on plants protected from air currents. Under such conditions the spore-bearing stalks grow out through the pores (stomata) of the leaves (Fig. 47) and the spores of the fungus are shed into the dew or raindrops clinging to the leaves.

Galls. The swellings called "galls" have many causes. Some are caused by insects which lay their eggs in a leaf or stem and stimulate the tissues to abnormal development. Mossy-rose gall (Fig. 14), oak galls, witch-hazel galls, the cockscomb galls of elm leaves, the midrib galls of ash (Fig. 15), the flower galls of the same tree (Fig. 136)—all these are familiar examples of galls caused by insects or mites. Root galls or root-knots are frequently caused by a common species of nema, *Meloidogyne incognita*. They should be distinguished from nodules on the roots of leguminous plants such as honey locust, Japanese pagoda tree, silk tree, and wisteria, caused by beneficial bacteria. In fact some nonleguminous plants such as alder, *Casuarina*, Russian-olive, and sweet gale also have

[4] For the meaning of this term, see pp. 32 and 36

Fig. 10. Base of delphinium plant attacked by root rot; the light-colored objects are the sclerotia of *Sclerotium delphinii.*

Fig. 11. Oedema on leaf of *Eranthemum,* caused by over-watering or by a very humid greenhouse.

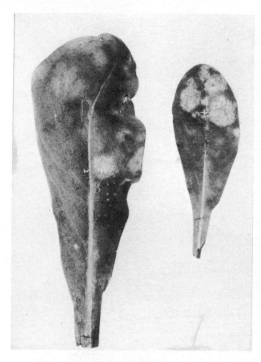

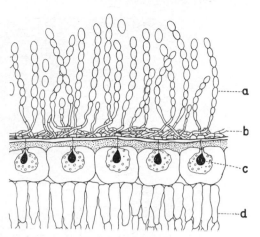

Fig. 13. Powdery mildew *(Sphaerotheca pannosa)* on rose. At *(a)* are the conidia of the fungus, borne on hyphae which rise from the mycelium *(b)*. The mycelium sends haustoria *(c)* through the cuticle into the epidermis of the rose leaf. Below the epidermis are shown a few of the interior cells of the leaf *(d)*.

Fig. 12. Powdery mildew *(Erysiphe polygoni)* on leaves of calendula.

Fig. 14 Mossy-rose gall on rose stem, caused by the gall wasp *Diplopepis rosae.*

Fig. 15. Midrib-gall on ash leaflet, caused by the gall midge *Contarinia canadensis*.

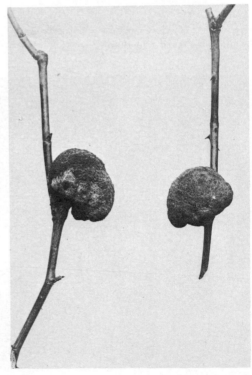

Fig. 16. Telial sori of apple rust (*Gymnosporangium juniperi-virginianae*).

Fig. 17. Crown gall of rose, caused by the bacterium *Agrobacterium tumefaciens*.

nodules on their roots. The function of these nodules, however, is not clearly understood. Cedar-apples, which in the spring develop long golden or rusty horns (Fig. 16), are caused by the invasion of cedar leaves by the rust fungus *Gymnosporangium.* Crown gall of roses (Fig. 17) and many other plants is a familiar abnormal growth caused by a bacterium. It frequently causes the death of the host. Because of the extensive development of abnormal tissue and the general appearance of the overgrowths, they are often spoken of as "plant cancers"; they have no actual relation to cancers of animals.

Witches' Brooms. The development of large numbers of accessory shoots characterizes the diseases known by this name. Such growths are one symptom of aster yellows, which is caused by a mycoplasma-like organ-

Fig. 19. Witches' broom *(Gymnosporangium ellisii)* on southern whitecedar *(Chamaecyparis thyoides).*

ism. Ordinarily, however, witches' brooms are more familiar on woody plants. The cherry witches' broom (Fig. 18) is caused by a fungus belonging to the Ascomycetes. Blackberry witches' broom is caused by a rust fungus which also prevents the development of blossoms; the whole plant is affected systemically—roots, crown, stems, and leaves. Redcedars develop "birds' nest" witches' brooms due to another rust fungus

Fig. 18. Witches' broom on Japanese cherry, caused by *Taphrina cerasi.*

Fig. 20. Witches' broom on southern whitecedar, in closer view.

Fig. 21. Mosaic of dahlia.

Fig. 22. Aster yellows, a disease caused by a mycoplasma-like organism.

Fig. 23. Stunting of dahlia caused by a virus.

(*Gymnosporangium*), and whitecedar forms such overgrowths when attacked by still another species of this genus (Figs. 19 and 20). Some witches' brooms are believed to be caused by mycoplasma-like organisms.

Mosaic. The effects of viruses and related organisms in plants often appear as a mottling of the leaves; they are marked with a pattern of light and dark areas forming a "mosaic" (Fig. 21). Such symptoms are frequently associated with curling of the leaves and with other abnormalities of growth, as shown in Figs. 22 and 23.

Chlorosis. This term, which literally means "becoming green," was first applied

Fig. 24. Chlorosis of *Dicentra,* a disease caused by lack of some substance in the soil.

to certain human diseases, the symptom of which is the appearance of a greenish hue of the skin; in plants whose normal color is green, it means a whitish or yellowish discoloration. It may be caused by mineral deficiency (Fig. 24) or by viruses.

DISEASES CLASSIFIED BY CAUSES

Diseases Due to Environmental Conditions or Cultural Practices

Mineral Deficiencies. All plants need a balanced diet to do well. Those grown in soil which lacks one of the so-called major elements, nitrogen, phosphorus, or potash, or one or more of the essential minor elements such as iron, boron, or magnesium will not be normal.

The foliage of rhododendrons, mountain-laurel (Fig. 25), and andromeda may turn yellow (chlorotic) because of a lack of available iron, which may, in turn, be due to excessive lime. This commonly occurs when these acid-loving plants are planted near a cement wall. Many trees, including pin oaks, cottonwood, boxelder, and sweetgum also become chlorotic because of the unavailability of iron. Incorporating a so-called iron chelate into the soil or spraying it on the leaves helps to overcome such a deficiency.

Plants grown in soil devoid of all traces of boron are stunted as if affected by a virus; this may be accompanied by some wilting. A trace of boron is the remedy for this disease.

Chemical Injuries. Faulty application of nitrate, potash, or acid or alkaline fertilizers often brings on symptoms similar to those caused by parasitic organisms. If an excess of sodium nitrate is applied during dry weather the foliage at the tops of the plants becomes brown and appears scorched.

Careless use of weed killers may result in severe damage or even death of trees and shrubs. Weed-killing materials containing the hormones 2,4-D and 2,4,5-T should be used with extreme care. The hormones are extremely difficult to remove from a spray tank. Hence a special sprayer should be available for applying such materials.

Calcium chloride applied along country roadsides to keep down dust can damage tree roots when washed into the soil. Salt scattered over sidewalks or city streets to melt ice or prevent water from freezing also causes severe damage to plants growing nearby. The salty water is either swept or splashed into the open soil areas near the plant roots.

Trees and shrubs growing along large bodies of salt water are often injured by wind-blown salt spray. During hurricanes the spray can actually damage foliage 50 miles from the body of salt water. Smoke emanating from chimneys of manufacturing plants, apartment house incinerators, and other instruments of combustion, including automobiles, contains ingredients which are harmful to vegetation.

The three major pollutants released by manufacturing plants are sulfur dioxide,

Fig. 25.   Chlorosis of mountain-laurel due to a deficiency of iron.

fluorine compounds, and the smog typical of urban areas. Maple and other broadleaved trees exposed to sufficiently high concentrations of sulfur dioxide show ivory-white markings, mostly between the main veins, whereas Douglas-fir and ponderosa pine exhibit a reddish discoloration of the needles followed by a shriveling of the affected tissues.

Fluorine compounds are even more toxic to vegetation than sulfur dioxide. The leaves of gladioli, peach, prune, and conifers are extremely sensitive to these compounds. Damage by sulfur dioxide and fluorine can be reduced by installing equipment to trap the harmful gases, or by installing extremely tall chimneys so that the smoke is well diluted before it reaches susceptible plants.

High concentrations of ozone formed by photochemical reactions involving nitrogen dioxide, certain hydrocarbons, or other air chemicals cause so-called smog damage. Such damage can be prevented by spraying susceptible plants with ascorbic acid (vitamin C), sold under the trade name Ozoban, before or during a smog attack, or periodically during the season when smog damage is apt to occur.

The solid residue of smoke and soot may also damage plants, particularly evergreens, in large cities. It coats the leaves and screens out the light, thus reducing the leaves' capacity to manufacture food.

Spray Injuries. As a rule the insecticides and fungicides recommended in this book are safe to use on ornamental plants. Under certain conditions, however, some plants may be severely damaged by spray materials. Injury is most apt to occur on tender, succulent growth or when the soil is dry and the plants are in a wilted condition.

Wettable powders in water are usually safer than sprays made from emulsifiable liquid concentrates. The former leave more prominent residues, however. Bordeaux mixture and other copper fungicides applied dur-

Fig. 26. Lily leaves injured by spraying with nicotine sulfate in a hot greenhouse.

ing cool, damp weather may cause a burning or spotting of some kinds of leaves. Those of oak, apple, and rose are among the most susceptible.

The application of so-called dinitro compounds and sulfur when the air temperature is above 85°F. may result in severe damage to flowers and leaves of many plants.

The leaves of such evergreens as *Cryptomeria,* Douglas-fir, hemlock, and yews may be injured by some kinds of dormant oil sprays.

In the greenhouse *Sedum, Sempervivum,* and other succulents may be damaged by organic phosphate sprays such as malathion and parathion. The leaves of lilies are gray-

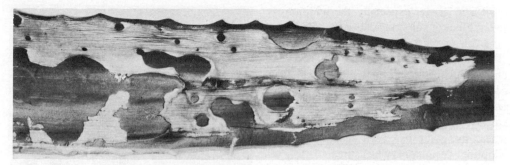

Fig. 27. Physiological disease of the leaf of *Furcraea*; cause not certainly known, but the symptoms are similar to those which result from excessive application of nicotine fumes or from lack of water.

spotted by the faulty use of nicotine sprays (Figs. 26 and 27).

Fume Injury. Many kinds of ornamental plants in greenhouses are burned by faulty applications of fumigants such as hydrogen cyanide and tobacco fumes. Greenhouse paints that contain phenyl mercury compounds to prevent mildewing of the sash produce the same toxic effects.

Lightning Injury. Hundreds of shade and ornamental trees are struck by lightning in the United States every year. The amount and type of damage vary from little or no permanent damage to complete shattering of the tree. Tall trees or those growing in open areas are most likely to be struck. Elm, maple, oak, pine, poplar, spruce, and tuliptree are most commonly hit, whereas beech, birch, and horse-chestnut are rarely struck. A qualified arborist should be consulted on how to handle a lightning-struck tree. Valuable trees growing in locations favorable for strikes can be adequately protected at comparatively small cost by the installation of lightning-protection equipment.

Other Electrical Injuries. Wires carrying electric current may also cause some injury to trees. Suitable nonconductors should be placed over wires passing in the vicinity of trunk and branches. Outdoor evergreens bedecked with lights at Christmas time can be damaged if too many poorly placed bulbs or worn equipment is used.

Mechanical Injuries. Hailstones may completely defoliate trees and shrubs or shred the leaves sufficiently to check growth sharply. The trunks and larger branches of trees may be damaged by motor vehicles, by children, and even by thoughtless adults. The lawnmower, carelessly used, causes severe damage to the inner bark and cambium at the base of tree trunks. Such injuries should be treated as soon as possible after they occur. Wires used to support newly transplanted trees should be covered with a piece of old garden hose, or some other suitable material to prevent girdling. So-called girdling roots which grow closely appressed to the main trunk also account for weakening and premature death of some trees. Such roots should be severed at the point where they are strangling the tree trunk.[5]

Mechanical injury by tractors and bulldozers during house construction also accounts for the rapid decline and death of trees. The heavy machinery compacts the soil, thus making conditions unfavorable for normal root development.

Old trees are extremely sensitive to any changes made around their roots. Hence a

[5] For a more detailed discussion of girdling roots, see *Acer*.

change in grade, especially the addition of several feet of soil, may cause the tree to die in 1 to 4 years. Before any grades are changed around large trees, the homeowner or building contractor might well call in a competent professional arborist for suggestions on preventive measures. An ·arborist can also advise on ways to reduce the damage where the grade has been changed without adopting precautionary measures.

Digging a cellar near large trees not only results in cutting away many valuable roots but also changes the water table for the remaining roots. The combined effect may cause death of the tree.

Sunscorch. New growth of ornamental hemlocks, hydrangeas, and wisterias may become badly scorched by the sun's rays when the temperature exceeds 90°F. in the shade. The leaves of many deciduous trees, particularly Japanese maples and horse-chestnut, may be scorched on warm, windy days, when water is lost more rapidly than it can be replaced through the roots.

Scorch in particularly valuable trees can be prevented, or at least reduced, by spraying the leaves with Wilt-Pruf NCF, a liquid plastic material, before the usual scorching period arrives.

Winter Injury. Despite their dormant condition, trees frequently suffer severely during the winter. This is especially true of trees growing in poorly drained soils or in exposed, wind-swept areas. The maturity of the wood is another factor that governs the ability of a tree to withstand low temperatures. Trees fed with excessive amounts of high-nitrogenous fertilizers, or those making considerable growth in late fall, are most commonly injured.

Another type of winter injury, purely mechanical, is caused by excessive loads of ice or snow. The weight of the ice-coated twig shown in Fig. 28 was about 40 times that of the twig alone after the ice had melted; the effects of such loads are illustrated in Fig. 29.

Fig. 28. An ice-laden branch; the ice was found to increase the weight of the branch approximately 40 times.

Frost cracks, longitudinal separations of the bark and wood, are another phase of winter injury. Such cracks appear principally on the south or west sides of the trunk and are most common on Norway maple, elm, horse-chestnut, linden, oak, planes, and flowering cherries.

Injury to such plants as rhododendron (Fig. 206), azalea, mountain-laurel, holly, pines, spruces, and firs is rarely caused by excessive cold during the winter. The damage is caused, rather, by excessive and rapid fluctuations in temperature or by late spring freezes after the plants have resumed activity. Plants growing in sunny protected areas are frequently subject to this type of injury. Injury on broad- and narrow-leaved evergreens growing in unfavorable locations can

Fig. 29. Damage caused by an excessive load of ice.

be reduced by spraying with an antitranspirant such as Wilt-Pruf NCF or by providing some sort of windbreak.

Injury Due to Conditions Indoors. Housewives often complain that the leaves of begonias, rubber plants, primulas, and other plants become spotted, turn brown, and finally fall. They assume that some fungus is responsible. The leaves have probably fallen because of a diseased condition, but the disease is caused not by a parasite, but a sudden change of light intensity and lack of nutrients when the plant is actively growing.

Plants that are not acclimated to reduced light tend to lose many leaves when brought from a greenhouse or outdoors into a house, apartment or florist shop. *Ficus benjamina* is especially sensitive to leaf drop, particularly if this plant has been grown outdoors in Florida.

House plants should be given as much light as possible unless they are of the type such as African-violet, rubber plant, and dracaenas that does not thrive in strong sun. They should not be overwatered, should be fed only when making active growth. The container in which they are growing should always have a drainage hole at the bottom. The average home is much too dry for fungus diseases to develop on house plants. It is ideal, however, for the development of certain insects such as scales, mealybugs, and aphids, as well as the pests known as spider mites or red spiders.

Diseases Due to Parasites and Pests[6]

Bacterial Diseases. Many ornamental plants suffer from diseases caused by bacteria. The foul-smelling soft rot of iris rhizomes, bacterial leaf spot of carnation, twig blight of ornamental hawthorn, black twig

[6] These organisms are described and classified in Chapters 2 and 3.

blight of lilacs, and leaf spot (Fig. 30) of geranium are familiar examples. Bacteria may enter the plant through the stomata, water pores, wounds, or lenticels.[7] They are unable to penetrate directly through the walls of the epidermal cells. About 1880, Burrill first proved by inoculation that bacteria may cause plant diseases. He showed that the bacterium *Erwinia amylovora* causes a blossom and twig blight of pears, apples, and other pomaceous trees (Fig. 31). Crown gall of various plants and scab of gladiolus are other common bacterial diseases of ornamentals.

Fungus Diseases. Most of the parasitic diseases of plants are caused by fungi. Powdery mildews of rose, lilac, dahlia, chrysanthemum, phlox, and other ornamentals (Figs. 12 and 32) may be recognized by the white, light gray, or slightly brownish growth of the fungus over the surface of the leaf. Black spot of roses (Fig. 1), known by the irregular radiating lines which extend from the margin of the spot, is caused by a fungus that grows beneath the cuticle of the leaf. The Dutch elm disease and chestnut blight, two very destructive diseases of trees, are due to fungus parasites living in the sapwood or beneath the bark (Fig. 33). Practically every species of ornamental plant is more or less subject to attack by parasitic fungi, some of which cause little damage, while others may kill the plant outright.

Virus Diseases. Among the most destructive diseases of ornamentals are those caused by viruses. Viruses are ultramicroscopic and are chemically composed of protein and nucleic acid. They can be purified and crystal-

[7] Stomata (singular, stoma) are minute openings in the outer layer (epidermis) of leaves and stems through which the inner tissues communicate with the air outside. Water pores are structures through which drops of water are exuded. Lenticels are small swellings or blisters in bark through which inner living tissues reach the outside air. Stomata and lenticels are commonly but mistakenly called "breathing-pores." Plants do not "breathe" (inhale or exhale).

Fig. 30. Bacterial leaf spot *Xanthomonas pelargonii* on a geranium leaf. (New Jersey Agricultural Experiment Station)

Fig. 31. Fire blight canker of pear caused by the bacterium *Erwinia amylovora*. (Cornell Extension Bulletin)

Fig. 32. Powdery mildew *(Sphaerotheca pannosa* var. *rosae.*

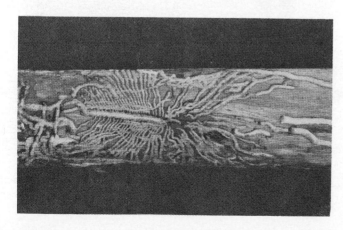

Fig. 33. Tunnels of the smaller European elm bark beetle *(Scolytus multistriatus)* which carries the fungus responsible for the Dutch elm disease.

lized like many chemical compounds. Yet viruses are subject to mutation and other variations usually associated only with living things.

Certain types of dahlia stunt, ringspot of dahlias, nasturtium mosaic, and yellow stripe of narcissus are among the well-known diseases due to viruses.

Though many virus diseases eventually kill infected plants, that which affects *Abutilon striatum* var. *thompsonii* is beneficial, for it results in a beautiful variegation of the leaves, which otherwise appear to be perfectly healthy. Branches occasionally appear with normally green leaves; these are free from the virus and can be propagated to yield virus-free plants. The variegated plants are really diseased, for they do not develop normally. The "breaking" of tulips is caused by two viruses. This was considered desirable because of the resulting beauty of the blossoms, but growers have found that plants so infected gradually degenerate.

Mycoplasma-like Organisms. These organisms, intermediate between bacteria and viruses both in size and other properties, have recently been implicated as plant pathogens. Aster yellows and several of the witches' brooming diseases, previously thought to be caused by viruses, are now believed to be caused by these organisms. Among the reasons for this belief is that the symptoms are suppressed by antibiotics and that the organisms have long resisted isolation and visualization.

Viroids. This class of pathogens was recognized only very recently and thus far has been found only in plants. Viroids are very small molecules of infectious ribonucleic acid. They are about 50 times smaller than typical plant viruses and lack a protein coat. Nonetheless they are rather easily spread by propagating and cultivating procedures as well as in vegetatively propagated material. Chrysanthemum stunt and chrysanthemum chlorotic mottle, formerly thought to be

Fig. 34.   Nema disease of fern leaves.

Fig. 35.   Resistance of chrysanthemums to the foliar nema. The plants in the background are of a resistant strain; those in the foreground were susceptible and badly injured.

caused by viruses, have been shown to be caused by viroids.

Nemas. These microscopic eelworms, more commonly known as nematodes, feed in the intercellular spaces and cause disintegration of the cells. They enter the plant through wounds, stomata, or water-pores (the method of entrance depending on the species). Various nemas cause swelling of the stems, irregularities in branching, deformation of the leaves, suppression of blossoms, and galls on the roots. Leaf nemas attack ferns (Fig. 34), chrysanthemums (Figs. 35 and 118), begonias, dahlias, and many other ornamentals, causing brown or blackish areas between the veins.

Mites. These small animals injure plants by sucking the juice from the tender growing points and leaves. The commonest are the spider mite[8] (Fig. 36), the cyclamen mite, and the broad mite. Greenhouse plants are especially subject to attack. Delphinium "blacks" (Fig. 37) is due to a mite that causes an abnormal development of the leaves and blossoms, a dwarfing of the inflorescence, and a blackening of the tissues.

Insects. The injuries caused by insects are often not thought of as diseases. Such leaf-eating insects as the Japanese beetle may, however, cause the stunting or death of a plant by devouring large parts of the leaves in which food is made (Fig. 38). Wireworms

[8] The adults of some strains of this mite are orange-red in color and are referred to as red spiders or red spider mites.

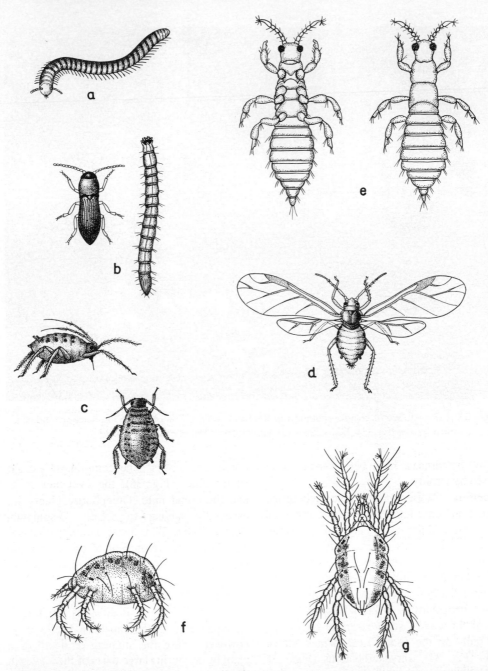

Fig. 36. Various arthropods. *(a)* Millipede. *(b)* Wireworm, the adult of the larva at the left *(Agriotes)*. *(c)* Corn root aphid *(Brachycaudus)*, wingless females. *(d)* Corn root aphid, winged female. *(e)* Iris thrips *(Iridothrips iridis)*, seen from below and from above. *(f)* Immature stage of two-spotted or red spider mite *(Tetranychus urticae)*. *(g)* Mature stage. (From various authors)

Fig. 38. The characteristic work of Japanese beetles *(Popillia japonica)* on rose leaves.

Fig. 37. Blacks of delphinium, caused by the cyclamen mite *Steneotarsonemus pallidus.*

feed on the roots and stems just under the surface of the soil and cause a complete failure of plant development. Other types of injury due to insects, such as the effect on rose buds of an infestation of thrips, or the galls caused by aphids on witch-hazel leaves, are more like the prevailing concept of diseases. The depredations of insects frequently open the way to parasitic fungi that do not penetrate uninjured surfaces. The Dutch elm disease is caused by a fungus which is carried to new hosts by bark beetles. Aphids, leafhoppers, and other insects distribute viruses.

All the above diseases may be classified also by the extent of the invasion of the diseased areas. Diseases may be local, such as many spot diseases, anthracnose, rots, galls, or cankers. Or they may be due to parasites that invade practically all parts of the host, as for example, the orange rust of blackberries, *Sempervivum* rust, anther smut of *Dianthus.* Such diseases are systemic. In the first two of the latter group, at least, the fungus gains entrance through the young shoots or young growth and invades the crown, and from this the mycelium extends downward into the roots and upward into the leaves. It is probably the same with anther smut. In all three diseases the affected plants seldom bloom normally. Very few plants recover from virus diseases. In this they differ from virus diseases of human beings, recovery from which, in these days of scientific medicine, is common.

2

BACTERIA AND FUNGI

BACTERIA

Bacteria are among the smallest living organisms that can be seen with the aid of a microscope. They are so small that as many as 25,000 individual bacteria can be laid side by side within an inch. They are classified in three groups according to their shape; spherical bacteria are cocci, spirally curved bacteria are spirilla, and rod-shaped or oval bacteria are bacilli.[1] Almost all bacteria lack the green coloring, chlorophyll, present in most plants; consequently, they live either as parasites on living plants or animals or as saprophytes causing the decay, putrefaction, or fermentation of nonliving organic materials.

The minute spherical bacteria of the coccus group cause many diseases of human beings and animals. Common boils, pneumonia, and septic sore throat are caused by species of this group. Only one or two plant diseases have been reported to be caused by cocci, and even these organisms may really be very short bacilli.

Most spirilla are saprophytes. Diseases caused by this group of bacteria are more or less limited to animals, including human beings. Asiatic cholera is due to a short spiral type, a species of *Vibrio*.

Practically all the several hundred bacterial diseases of plants are caused by bacteria

[1] Singular, "coccus," "bacillus," "spirillum."

which have a rod-shaped body and belong to the bacillus group. The bacilli vary greatly in length. Some are very short and at first sight may be mistaken for cocci. Others are club-shaped and are placed in the genus *Corynebacterium.* By soaking hay in warm water for a few hours, quantities of the saprophytic bacteria that cause decay of vegetable matter may be obtained. These are very long and can be easily seen with a low magnification. They move about rapidly and irregularly by means of "flagella" (also called "cilia"). These are very delicate hair-like appendages which lash to and fro in a fluid and so propel the organism. Some kinds of rod-shaped bacteria have only one or more flagella at one or both ends (Fig. 39). Others have several distributed over their surface. All presently known plant parasitic bacteria are single-celled plants.

Under certain conditions bacteria reproduce themselves very rapidly simply by dividing in two (fission). This may happen every hour, so that within a single day there would be 17 million descendants of one bacterium, if all survived! Certain bacteria also produce spores within themselves. These are very minute bodies which continue to live a long time even in the absence of water or at temperatures which would kill other organisms. Under suitable conditions the spores germinate and begin a new generation. Some investigators claim to have observed sexual fusion

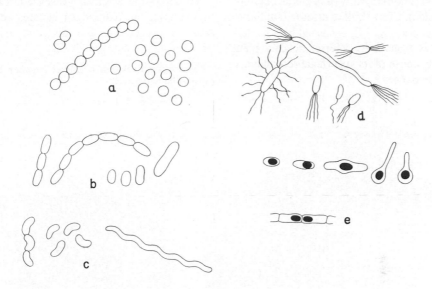

Fig. 39.   Bacteria. At the left are the three types: *(a)* coccus; *(b)* bacillus; and *(c)* spirillum. At *(d)* are various bacteria stained to show the flagella. Bacteria that have formed spores appear at *(e)*; the spores are the black bodies. (After Heald)

of bacteria, but this has not yet been generally accepted; it is quite likely that such a method of reproduction will eventually be recognized.

Bacteria were known for a number of years before it was discovered that they are capable of causing plant diseases. Pear blight had been known for many years as a destructive disease, but it remained for Burrill to prove that it was caused by *Erwinia amylovora*. One has only to puncture a young pear twig with a needle that has been dipped in a culture of this species to realize how rapidly these minute organisms can cause the death of plant tissues. If a young plant of *Delphinium ajacis* is sprayed with a suspension of certain bacteria, within a few days it collapses, turns brown, and appears rotted; in a week it is dead. Some bacteria enter the stomata of leaves or the lenticels of stems. Others enter the roots by way of injured root-hairs or through wounds. Some bacteria collect in the air spaces within leaves and cause a blackening of the leaf which ends with its death. Bacteria may enter the water-conduct-

ing vessels of the roots or stems, cutting off the water supply and causing a wilt. Wilt of dahlias is caused by certain bacteria that live in the soil. The foul-smelling rhizome-rot of irises is caused by bacteria, which can enter the iris leaves or rhizome only through a wound; holes made by the young grubs of the iris borer or of the Japanese beetle or injuries caused during cultivation furnish opportunities for the bacteria to enter the soft tissues.

Several hundred well-known diseases of economic plants and ornamentals are due to bacteria, and are among the very destructive diseases of such plants. They are somewhat difficult to recognize because the symptoms resemble those due to other agents or conditions. For example, a dahlia whose stem has been cracked below the ground by a strong wind wilts in the same way as a dahlia whose water-conducting system is invaded by bacteria. The invasion of the leaves of ferns and chrysanthemums by eelworms (nemas) produces symptoms (Figs. 34, 40, and 118) like those caused by bacteria on other plants, such as the spots on geranium leaves shown in Fig. 30. Figure 3 shows a bacterial blight of *Delphinium.* Crown gall, a disease familiar to all gardeners (Fig. 17), is caused by a bacterium. It is sometimes referred to as a plant cancer because of its superficial resemblance to human cancer.[2]

To determine whether a disease is caused by bacteria, the pathologist isolates any organisms present in the diseased tissues,

[2] There is no relation whatever between crown gall and human cancer

Fig. 40.   Nema disease of bird's-nest fern, *Asplenium nidus.*

grows them in pure culture,[3] then inoculates the suspected ones into healthy plants; if the same diseased condition results from the inoculation, it is probably caused by the species of bacteria used. Further tests of the same kind are necessary to confirm the conclusion.

Some kinds of bacteria require air for normal development, while others live and thrive in the absence of free oxygen. Bacteria are spread through the soil by flowing water, by small animals, and by cultivation. Insects also are important in the distribution of these organisms; for example, the iris borer (*Macronoctua onusta*, Fig. 41) carries on or in its body the bacteria that cause the soft rot disease of the iris leaves and rhizomes which it invades.

Bacterial diseases are controlled by much the same methods as those caused by fungi, which are treated below.

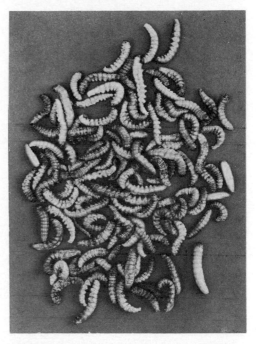

Fig. 41. Iris borers, caterpillars of *Macronoctua onusta*.

FUNGI

A fungus is a plant that lacks the green pigment, chlorophyll, present in most plants, and the conductive tissues found in ferns and seed-plants. Most fungi are formed of more or less branched threads. The individual threads are called "hyphae," and the entire mass of connected threads that make up the vegetative body of a fungus is a "mycelium." The threads of many fungi are composed of fundamental structural units, cells, found generally in plants and animals. Other fungi, such as the yeasts, resemble the bacteria in being composed of single separate cells. Most fungi are rather small and insignificant in appearance, but some have fruiting bodies as much as 2 feet in diameter and 50 pounds or more in weight. Such common fungi as molds, mildews, and mushrooms are familiar to most persons. The fungi that cause diseases of plants live usually within the tissues

of the host plants, and their presence may be difficult to detect without a microscope; commonly only their fruiting structures appear on the surface of the diseased parts. Some parasitic fungi, however, such as the powdery mildews, grow on the surface of the host and are easily visible as a whitish, fluffy growth (Fig. 32).

The threads (hyphae) of many fungi are divided by cross-walls into distinct cells arranged end to end. This is true, for instance, of the powdery mildews and the rust fungi. Such hyphae are spoken of as "septate" (Fig. 42). The threads of other fungi are non-septate, lacking cross-walls (Fig. 43). Examples of these are the common mold *Rhizopus* which causes so much decay and "leak" of strawberries and other fruit in transit, the species of *Pythium* which cause damping-off, and the water molds *Saprolegnia* and *Achlya* which kill goldfish and other fish.

Fungi reproduce in many ways, which may

[3] A pure culture is one from which all other species are rigorously excluded.

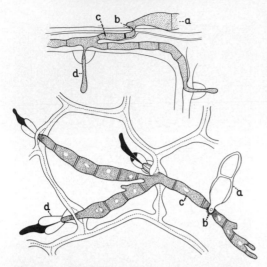

Fig. 42. Black spot *(Diplocarpon rosae)* invading a rose leaf. *(Top)* The process is shown in vertical section; *(bottom)* in surface view. The spore *(a)* forms a tube *(b)* which penetrates the cuticle. From this develops a hypha *(c)*, which grows horizontally between the cuticle and the epidermis of the leaf. Here and there this hypha sends down haustoria *(d)* into the cells of the epidermis. (After Aronescu)

be discussed under two heads: asexual and sexual reproduction. Asexual reproduction is comparable to the propagation of a plant by cuttings. Most frequently it occurs through the separation of minute fragments of the mycelium into "spores." The manner in which these are formed differs in different species. The spores may be contained in special structures such as "sporangia" (Fig. 43), "pycnidia" (Fig. 44), and "acervuli" (Fig. 45); or they may develop without an enclosing structure of any kind, in which case they are usually known as "conidia" (Figs. 46 and 47). Many species form spores in chains at the tips of hyphae; such spores may be named conidia or "oïdia" (Figs. 13 and 46). Some fungi form asexual spores within or upon specialized masses of tissues often visible to the naked eye; these are discussed below under the ascomycetes. Most fungi are propagated very rapidly by means of their asexual spores.

In most cells of plants nuclei may be seen. Each nucleus is a center of activity of the cell and highly important in development and the

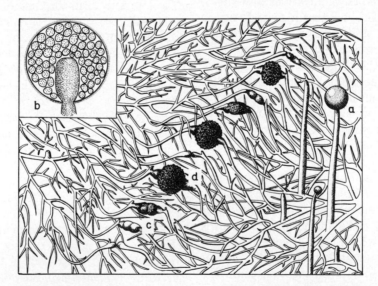

Fig. 43. Part of the mycelium of a fungus, *Mucor mucedo,* greatly magnified. At *(a)* a sporangium, shown more highly magnified and in sectional view at *(b)*. At *(c)*, the gametangia, shown in the process of uniting to form the zygospores *(d)*. (*a, c,* and *d* after Buller)

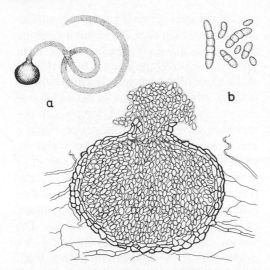

Fig. 44. A pycnidium (in sectional view) of *Stagonospora curtisii,* which causes diseases of narcissus and amaryllis. At *(a)* is a pycnidium from which the spores are emerging in a coiled tendril. At *(b)* are a few spores, highly magnified.

regulation of form. At some time in the normal life of a fungus two nuclei come together and unite. This is called "fertilization" (syngamy), and has been referred to as sexual reproduction. The structures formed in connection with these nuclear fusions have been called "sexual fruiting bodies." Further details of the types of structures involved in sexual reproduction of fungi are given below in the treatment of the several groups.

Classification and Naming of Plants

Though scarcely any two living plants are exactly alike, it is possible to arrange them by their resemblances in the groups called species.[4] Each species is named by two words, the first always written with an initial capital; in this book and in most scientific writings the names of species are printed in *italic.* Several species have been mentioned by name in the

[4] The singular of this word is also "species," not "specie." The plural of "genus" is "genera."

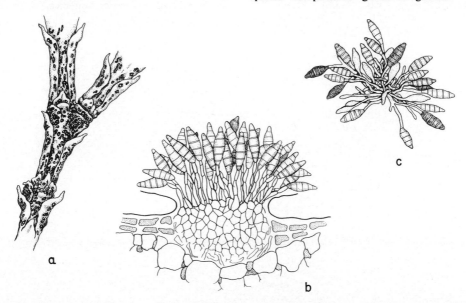

Fig. 45. Spore formation of *Coryneum berckmanii,* which causes a blight of arborvitae. *(a)* The spore pustules on the host. *(b)* Section through a spore pustule or acervulus. *(c)* A cluster of spores more highly magnified; each spore consists of several cells, and is attached to a hypha. (After Milbrath)

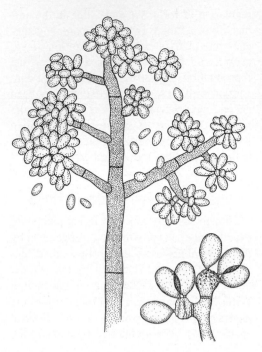

preceding pages: *Erwinia amylovora* and *Delphinium ajacis* on page 29, *Mucor mucedo* on page 32. Similar species belong to the same genus; the name of the genus is the first word of the name of the species. *Delphinium* is the genus to which the species *D. ajacis,*[5] *D. nudicaule,* and many others belong. Close observation may reveal the existence within a species of several groups distinguishable by small differences; such groups are known as subspecies, varieties, or forms. In such categories belong many kinds of plants familiar to gardeners.[6] Genera are classified in larger groups: families, orders, and classes. The classes of fungi (e.g., Zygomycetes) are treated below, and numerous genera (e.g., *Rhizopus*) are mentioned as examples.

[5] Note that in naming a species the genus name may be thus abbreviated when the reference is clear.

[6] Note, however, that many persons really mean species when they speak of "varieties."

Fig. 46. Formation of conidia by *Botrytis* growing on peony. (After Smith)

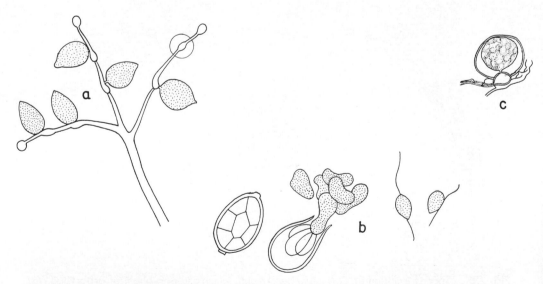

Fig. 47. Spores of *Phytophthora.* (a) Conidia. (b) Zoospores formed by germination of conidia; flagella are visible on those at the extreme right. At (c) the formation of the oospore is illustrated (see Fig. 48).

The Groups of Fungi

Zygomycetes. Fungi are usually classified by their so-called sexual fruiting bodies. The Zygomycetes include species whose reproductive structure is formed by a union of two equal bodies (gametangia), called "zygospores." The method of reproduction of one of these fungi is shown in Fig. 48. Another example is the common fruit mold or "leak" fungus, *Rhizopus*. The asexual spores of these fungi are developed in sacs called "sporangia," also shown in Fig. 43. These are small round structures, usually borne on stalks, and formed in large numbers over the surface of the mold; each may contain hundreds of spores, which are liberated by the disintegration or bursting of the outer covering.

Oömycetes. These include many more species of plant parasites. The sexual reproduction of most of these fungi, illustrated in Fig. 47, involves the union of two unequal cells, the larger one called the "oögonium," and the smaller the "antheridium." A small tube from the antheridium penetrates the oögonium, and fertilization is thus effected.

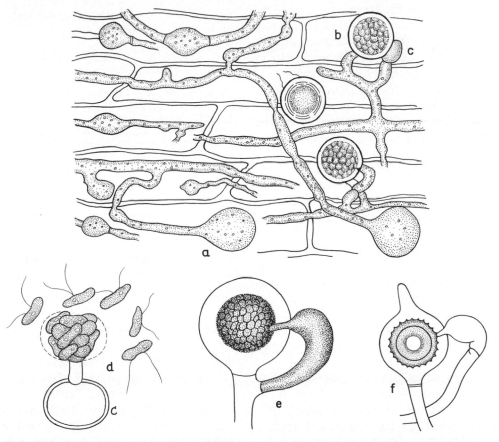

Fig. 48. Reproduction in *Pythium*. Above is the mycelium growing and reproducing among the cells of the host. (*a*) Sporangium. (*b*) Oogonium. (*c*) Antheridium. (*d*) Zoospores formed by the sporangium. (*e*) Penetration of oogonium by antheridium. (*f*) Union has occurred; the oospore lies within the oogonium. (Adapted from De Bary)

The resulting spore, the oöspore, usually has a thick wall and can endure unfavorable conditions of temperature and moisture. Asexual reproduction occurs by means of spores called "zoöspores" (Figs. 47 and 48), each of which has two flagella (cilia). This suggests that these fungi are at home in the water. Potato blight is spread very rapidly by the zoöspores shown in Fig. 47, which swim in water (rain or dew) on the surface of the leaves. Such diseases as calla lily root rot, damping-off of seedlings (especially in greenhouses), a twig blight of lilac and rhododendron, and bleeding canker of dogwood and maple, are caused by Oömycetes. Some of these organisms live for many months in the soil. Others survive during the winter mostly as oöspores developed in old plant tissue. It is necessary to know such facts in order to devise proper methods for their control.

The Zygomycetes and Oömycetes are often considered together as the Phycomycetes. They are all characterized by mycelia that have few or no cross-walls, but the two groups may be only distantly related.

Chytridiales. These are organisms of uncertain classification. They include a number of species that cause plant diseases, but few that affect ornamental plants. Potato wart is caused by a member of this group. The chytrids have no true mycelium, but certain species form growths that approach one; these outgrowths lack cross-walls. Asexual propagation is by means of zoöspores. A few species develop structures corresponding to oöspores. These features have suggested that species of the group belong to the Oömycetes.

Ascomycetes. This large group of fungi includes both simple and complex forms, many of which cause diseases of plants. The yeasts, which are the smallest and simplest fungi,[7] belong in this group. Everyone is familiar with the industrial yeasts used by bak-

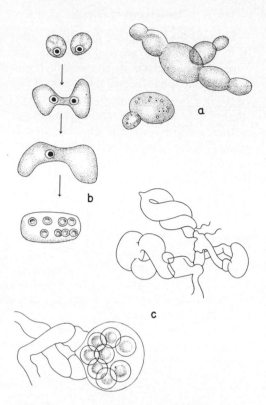

Fig. 49. Yeasts. At *(a)* budding is illustrated. The figures at *(b)* show the union of yeast cells and the formation of spores in the ascus that results from the union. At *(c)* is shown the sexual reproduction of an ascomycete with threads; the tips of the threads conjugate and form an ascus, in which eight spores develop. (*b* after Guilliermond; *c* after Eidam).

ers and brewers; many species are also found wild. Details of the life of yeasts are illustrated in Fig. 49. In most species each plant is a single cell. It reproduces asexually by a process known as budding. Certain species develop hypha-like growths which may be composed of several short cells. Sexual reproduction in yeasts comes about through the union of two individual cells or buds, which is followed by the union of their nuclei. The fusion-nucleus divides, the two nuclei so

---

[7] Unless the bacteria are considered fungi.

formed divide again, and in some species these four may again divide. About these nuclei walls appear, so that the original cell will now contain four or eight spores; this spore-sac is an "ascus." The methods by which spores are formed in the sporangia of the Phycomycetes and in the asci of the Ascomycetes are among the distinctive features of the two groups. In the sporangia of the Phycomycetes spores are formed by a progressive division of the protoplasm into fragments, each containing one or more nuclei. In the asci of the Ascomycetes each nucleus forms a beak from which a system of rays extends; these rays mark the limits of the spore which contains the nucleus. Considerable protoplasm remains unused in the formation of the ascospores.

Yeasts cause a few minor diseases of economic plants but no important diseases of ornamentals. They are found in the slimy flux from injured trees and cause the discharge to ferment.

Other members of the Ascomycetes have a septate mycelium. Asexual propagating bodies are formed in a great variety of ways, the feature common to all being that fragments of special branches of the mycelium, each containing one or more nuclei, are cut off and liberated. The asexual spores of the powdery mildews are borne in chains; they are known as conidia or oïdia (Fig. 13). If a mildewed rose is shaken in the morning after a calm night, a cloud of these white spores may be seen floating in the air. Each one of these minute bodies is a potential source of infection. If an aster that has been killed by the aster wilt fungus (*Fusarium oxysporum* var. *callistephi*) is pulled up, a rose-colored layer is seen on the base of the stem and the crown; this is composed of millions of spores (conidia), each crescent-shaped and divided by one or more cross-walls. The fungus (*Guignardia aesculi*) that causes leaf blotch of the horse-chestnut forms its spores in bodies called "pycnidia." These are small

pear-shaped, dark-colored fruiting structures, just visible to the naked eye as black dots on the leaf. Within them are many round spores which ooze out from the opening at the top. In some species of fungi the spores are exuded from the pycnidia in long tendrils (Fig. 44a). Such spores are washed away by rains and carried to new leaves or branches by wind, rain, birds, and insects. The conidia of some fungi are formed, without an enclosing layer, on fertile pads called acervuli (Fig. 45b). The method by which a spore of one of these fungi, *Diplocarpon rosae*, penetrates its host is shown in Fig. 42.

The sexual stage of the more complicated Ascomycetes usually involves distinct fruiting bodies called "ascocarps." These are composed largely of sterile tissue which grows from the mycelium and in which nutrients accumulate. In the ascocarps are formed the asci, specialized spore-sacs like those of yeasts. The nutrient substances of the ascocarp are partly used in the development of the asci.

For many years it was believed that fertilization or syngamy (union of two nuclei) occurs at the initiation of the ascocarp, and furnishes the stimulus which causes the development of the fruiting body. It is true that certain processes occur at this time which may be compared with the sexual processes of other organisms, but recent work on the genetics of these fungi has furnished evidence that the actual union of nuclei occurs only in the asci themselves, after the ascocarp has developed.

In some kinds of Ascomycetes, such as *Pyronema,* oögonia and antheridia are formed by the same mycelium. Many Ascomycetes, however, are heterothallic; that is, they are of two "sexes" (generally called "plus" and "minus" races), and fertilization depends upon the bringing together, in a common protoplasm, of two nuclei of opposite "sex." Nuclei are brought together in several different ways. When two races of opposite "sex" of *Gelasinospora tetrasperma* or *Neurospora tetrasperma* are grown together so that hyphae of both can come together, openings are formed in the hyphae at the points of contact and through these openings nuclei of one race migrate into the cells of the other. Nuclei multiply by division, and by further openings which appear in cross-walls of the hyphae the nuclei may migrate from cell to cell. The asci are formed at the curved tips, known as croziers, of special hyphae in the fruiting bodies. Each cell of these hyphae contains nuclei of the two "sexes," and in each ascus two nuclei of opposite "sex" unite. In *Neurospora sitophila* (Fig. 50) very small conidia (microspores or spermatia) are formed in special containers; also larger conidia which develop in chains; either of these can fertilize certain receptive hyphae which protrude from the very young ascocarps.[8]

[8] Pioneer work on the cytology and genetics of *Neurospora* was done by the late Dr. B. O. Dodge, the author's predecessor, at The New York Botanical Garden. This was followed by the work of other geneticists that resulted in the discovery of the chemical affinities of chromosomes and genes. For their part in these researches Drs. G. W. Beadle, J. Lederberg, and E. L. Tatum received a Nobel prize in 1958.

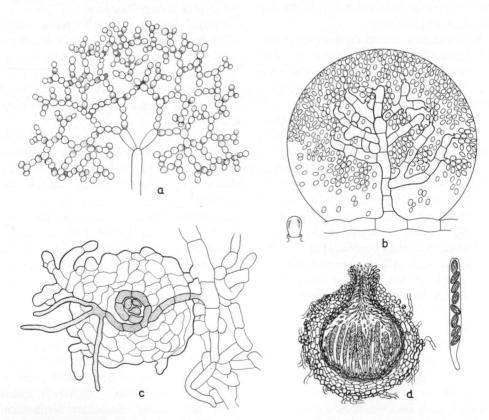

Fig. 50. Reproduction of an ascomycete, *Neurospora sitophila*. *(a)* Conidia. *(b)* Microspores (spermatia) in drop of liquid; at the left is a single microspore more highly magnified. *(c)* Young ascocarp. *(d)* Mature ascocarp (perithecium), shown in section so that the asci may be seen within; at right a single ascus more enlarged, containing eight ascospores.

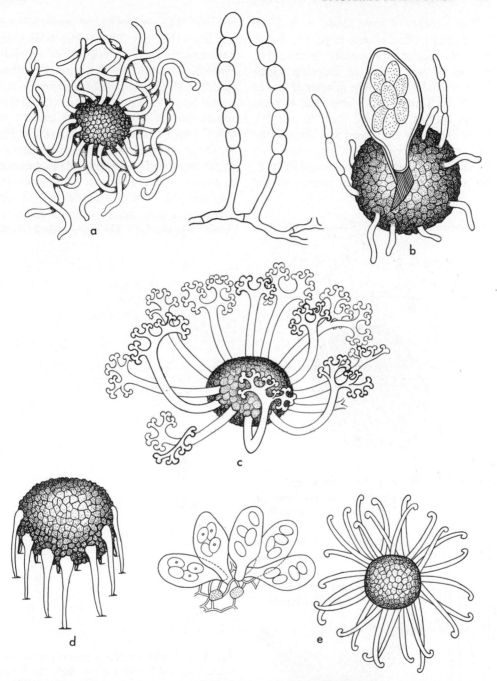

Fig. 51. Perithecia of powdery mildews. *(a) Erysiphe. (b) Sphaerotheca;* its ascus, containing eight ascospores, is being discharged. Between *(a)* and *(b)* is a bit of mycelium bearing two chains of conidia. *(c) Microsphaera. (d) Phyllactinia. (e) Uncinula.* Between *(d)* and *(e)* is a group of its cour-spored asci. (After Tulasne)

The ascocarp of some kinds, such as the morels and truffles, is quite large, but among parasitic species it is usually minute. The number of asci within an ascocarp varies from one to hundreds. The number of spores within each ascus is variable, but is commonly four or eight (see Figs. 50 and 51). Some ascocarps are closed and liberate the asci and spores within them only when they break open at maturity. Such ascocarps, often called "perithecia," are formed by the

powdery mildews familiar on leaves of roses and lilacs (Fig. 51). The perithecia of many Ascomycetes such as *Neurospora sitophila*, *Endothia parasitica* (which causes chestnut blight), and *Cryptosporella umbrina* (which causes brown canker of roses) discharge their spores through special openings called "ostioles"; such a perithecium is shown in Fig. 50. Other ascocarps are more or less fleshy. Those developed on mummified peaches may be an inch or more in height. As they develop they take the form of a funnel or disc supported by a stalk. Such ascocarps are often called "apothecia." They are characteristic

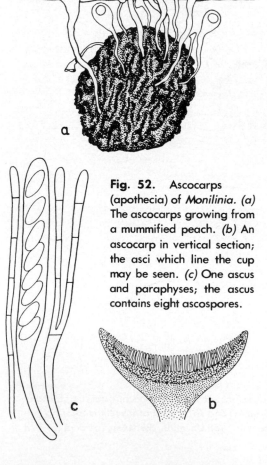

Fig. 52. Ascocarps (apothecia) of *Monilinia. (a)* The ascocarps growing from a mummified peach. *(b)* An ascocarp in vertical section; the asci which line the cup may be seen. *(c)* One ascus and paraphyses; the ascus contains eight ascospores.

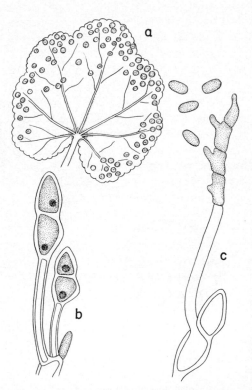

Fig. 53. Hollyhock rust fungus (*Puccinia malvacearum*). *(a)* Pustules on a leaf. *(b)* Teliospores from a pustule; each is composed of two cells. *(c)* Germination of a teliospore; the lower cell has formed a basidium, by which four sporidia have been developed. (Adapted from various authors)

of the species of *Monilinia* (Fig. 52) which cause the well-known brown rot of stone fruits, dry rot of gladiolus, and stem rot of many ornamentals. The form and color of the ascocarp, the characters of the asci, the ascospores and other features, are used in distinguishing the species of Ascomycetes.

Basidiomycetes. Like the preceding, this group is characterized by a special type of reproductive structure. The characteristic spore-forming structure is the "basidium." This is a cell within which two nuclei, often contributed by different parental races, may unite. The fusion-nucleus divides, much as that of an ascus does, until several are present, usually four; these become the nuclei of the spores. The basidium differs from an ascus in developing its spores externally, as small projecting buds into which the nuclei migrate. (Figs. 53 and 59). Usually four spores are formed on each basidium; in some species only two are formed, and in others more than four. The basidium of most of the larger forms is composed of only one cell (Fig. 59); that of the so-called lower forms, such as the smuts, rusts, and tremellas, may have a number of cells, generally four (Fig. 53).

The three more important groups into which Basidiomycetes are commonly divided are the smuts, Ustilaginales; the rusts, Uredinales; and the mushrooms, Agaricales and other orders.

The spores of smuts (Ustilaginales), within which the nuclei unite, are usually massed in blackish pustules known as "sori." The smuts of corn and other grains are familiar examples. Very few diseases of ornamental plants are caused by members of the smut group; the smut of violets and the anther smut of pinks are not uncommon.

The pustules or sori in which the spores of rust fungi (Uredinales) are born very often have a rusty appearance. Gardeners often refer to any disease of the foliage as rust if it causes a brown or rusty spotting of the leaves. Plant pathologists, however, use the term "rust" only for the diseases caused by members of the second group of Basidiomycetes.

Some of the rust fungi, such as *Puccinia malvacearum,* which causes hollyhock rust, have a comparatively simple life history. The parasitic mycelium growing in the leaves of the host forms spores in small pustules which break out to the surface. These spores are called "teliospores"; each is composed of two cells surrounded by rather thick walls. They are shown in Fig. 53. Each cell of the spore is the seat of a nuclear union, the two nuclei having been derived from the same mycelium. The teliospores germinate in the pustules in which they have been formed. Each cell forms a four-celled basidium (Fig. 53c); each of these cells forms a basidiospore or "sporidium." The sporidia are easily detached and blown around, and reinfect the younger leaves of the host. Each forms a mycelium which rapidly penetrates the tissues of the host, and within a week or so new pustules may appear.

Puccinia helianthi, which causes sunflower rust, has a more complicated life history. The teliospores, which live through the winter on parts of plants infected the previous year, germinate during early summer. They form the same type of four-celled basidia (also called "promycelia"), which in turn form sporidia. The sporidia infect the new leaves. From this mycelium a structure arises which is known as a "pycnium" or "spermatogonium," a small flask-shaped body whose opening projects through the surface of the leaf. Within the pycnia spores are formed, called "pycniospores" or "spermatia." These are extruded through the opening into a drop of nectar which is formed there. The nectar is water containing a sweetish substance attractive to insects. Certain hyphae also arise within the pycnium and extend through the opening into the drop of nectar and somewhat beyond it; these are known as "flexuous hyphae" (see Fig. 54).

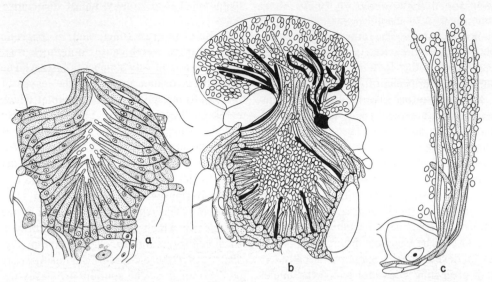

Fig. 54. Spermatogonia and receptive hyphae of a rust fungus. *(a)* Young spermatogonium. *(b)*Spermatia exuded from spermatogonium in a drop of liquid. *(c)* Flexuous hyphae with spermatia adhering. (After Allen)

This rust fungus, like so many other fungi, is heterothallic; two mycelia belonging to two distinct races are necessary for the completion of sexual reproduction. A mycelium which has grown from a single sporidium is unable to complete the life history of this species; only if the nectar of two pycnia which can be traced to sporidia of the two "sexes" is mixed can the life cycle continue. When this occurs the spermatia from a pycnium of one "sex" come in contact with the flexuous hyphae of a pycnium of the other "sex"; the nuclei migrate from the spermatia into the flexuous hyphae; and a structure is formed which contains in its cells two nuclei of opposite "sex." From this structure eventually arise new spore-bearing structures, called "aecia."

The aecium when mature is a cup-shaped body which opens to the exterior through the epidermis of the leaf. A cluster of aecia of another rust is illustrated in Fig. 55 (see also Fig. 56). The bottom of the cup is occupied

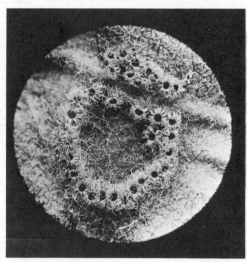

Fig. 55. Cluster-cups (aecia) of the cedar rust fungus *Gymnosporangium juniperi-virginianae)* on apple.

by a layer of somewhat elongated cells each containing two nuclei. Each of these basal cells divides and redivides so as to form a chain of cells (Fig. 57); these are the aeciospores. Like the cells from which they have been formed, each contains two nuclei, of the two "sexes." They are carried by the wind or by insects to other leaves and form hyphae which penetrate the stomata and cause new infections.

The mycelia formed from the aeciospores develop new pustules which contain still another type of spore. These are called the "urediniospores"; they are also called "summer spores" or "repeating spores," since they are formed usually throughout the

summer and cause new infections of the same type as that from which they arise. These spores cause the rapid and wide distribution of the disease in summer. The powdery, reddish pustules in which they are formed are responsible for the designation of such diseases as "rust."

Toward autumn the teliospores are formed, from the same mycelia, in dark brown or blackish pustules. In each of the two cells of a teliospore the two nuclei unite. These two nuclei can be traced back through

Fig. 56. Rust (caused by *Uromyces ari-triphylli*) of Jack-in-the-pulpit. On the left, diseased leaf and spathe; on the right, portion of a leaflet much enlarged, showing the aecia which have not yet broken open. (Right-hand photo, curtesy of S. M. Pady)

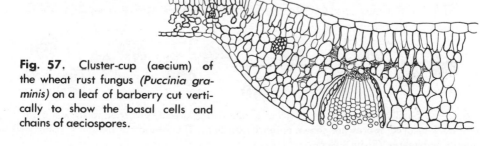

Fig. 57. Cluster-cup (aecium) of the wheat rust fungus *(Puccinia graminis)* on a leaf of barberry cut vertically to show the basal cells and chains of aeciospores.

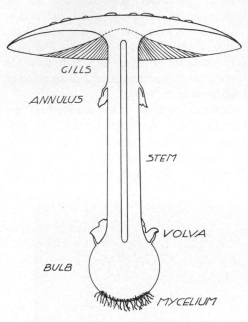

GILLS

ANNULUS

STEM

VOLVA

BULB

MYCELIUM

Fig. 58. Common mushroom illustrated diagrammatically to show the parts.

the long and complicated life history to the migration of nuclei which occurred in the drop of nectar at the opening of a pycnium. Only in the teliospore is syngamy completed with the union of nuclei. The discovery that these rust fungi are heterothallic is quite recent. The fact has practical importance, for we now understand that the rust fungi may easily hybridize in nature and so form new races. New races so formed may be able to infect plants which are resistant to the parental races of the rust fungi.

The sunflower rust fungus forms therefore five kinds of spores: teliospores, basidiospores, pycniospores, aeciospores, and urediniospores. The fungus that causes the common rust of wheat has the same five spore types, but in addition its life cycle is complicated by the fact that it requires two distinct hosts. The uredinial and telial stages occur on wheat, the aecial and pycnial stages on barberry. Such a parasite is called "heteroe-

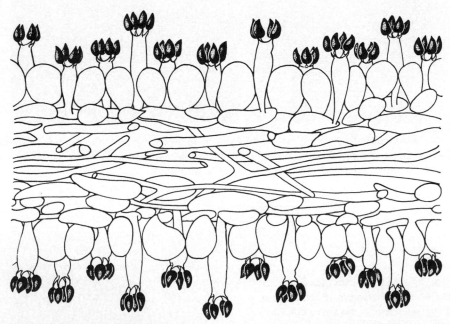

Fig. 59. Small portion of a single gill of a mushroom, greatly enlarged to show the basidia; four dark-colored spores are shown on each basidium. The interior of the gill is composed of interlaced hyphae. (From Buller)

cious"; the two kinds of hosts are spoken of as alternate hosts. Many such parasites are troublesome in gardens. The cedar-apple rust is a good example. The aecial stage of this fungus is found on the foliage of apple trees and related plants such as flowering crabs and hawthorns. Bright yellow or orange spots appear on the leaves. The spores developed in these spots are distributed by the wind. If they reach a redcedar, they germinate and the hyphae from them penetrate the leaves. The mycelium so formed later causes the formation of brown applelike galls, some of them an inch or more in diameter. The development of these galls and the maturing of the fungus within them require nearly two years from the time of infection. During warm, moist, rainy weather in May long bright orange-colored tendrils or "horns" grow out from the galls (Fig. 16); these horns are composed of teliospores and their stalks, which elongate greatly, especially in moist weather. The teliospores develop the basidia. The basidiospores from the cedar in turn reinfect the leaves of apple. The cedar and the apple are alternate hosts.

It is important to the gardener to know such facts as these in order to understand why it is sometimes necessary to destroy redcedar in the vicinity of commercial apple orchards or ornamental crabs and hawthorns. Quarantine regulations in certain regions require the destruction of the common barberry in order to prevent an epidemic of wheat rust. The currant and gooseberry are alternate hosts of the white pine blister rust. It would be difficult now to re-establish new forests of white pine where currants and gooseberries are allowed to grow wild and where the disease has occurred.

The mushrooms and puffballs are classed in the Agaricales and other orders. In this group the mycelium is often marked by what are called "clamp connections." These resemble both in structure and function the croziers of the Ascomycetes; i.e., they are means by which nuclei of opposite "sexes"

are brought together. The nuclei descended from these unite in the basidia (just as in the Ascomycetes the nuclei unite in the asci). The basidia of the Agaricales are grouped in a layer known as the "hymenium" on special structures such as gills or teeth, or in pores; or those of puffballs are borne more or less irregularly in a ball-like fruiting body covered with a protecting layer (peridium). A section through a common mushroom is shown in Fig. 58, and a portion of a gill more highly magnified in Fig. 59. In other species, such as that which causes the root rot of potato and many ornamental plants (*Pellicularia filamentosa*) and the pinkster gall (*Exobasidium vaccinii*) (see Figs. 60 and 61) the basidia are borne more or less superficially and not protected by much sterile tissue. The basidia of all these are one-celled. The fruiting bodies of many species of mushrooms have stalks which raise the spore-bearing parts in the air; the stalks are terminated by caps of various sizes, shapes, and colors. The shoestring or honey mushroom, *Armillaria mellea,* causes a very destructive root rot of maples, apples, and other deciduous trees. The reproductive structures of many wood-destroying fungi, however, do not develop stalks, but arise from the sides of trees or stumps as brackets and are called conks.

Fungi Imperfecti. As has been mentioned above, there is always in the life cycle of a fungus a stage, referred to as the sexual stage, during which nuclear union occurs; this is also called the "perfect" stage. This stage of many fungi, however, has not yet been discovered, the asexual stage being the only one now known. Such species of fungi, which are easily recognized by their vegetative characteristics and spore forms, are grouped together as the "imperfect" fungi or Fungi Imperfecti. Many of the fungi that cause diseases of ornamentals are classed in this group. The pink mold that causes aster wilt, a species of *Fusarium,* is an example. The perfect stages of certain other species of *Fusarium* are known. The *Septoria* that

Fig. 60.   Pinkster gall on azalea, caused by *Exobasidium vaccinii*.

Fig. 61.   Flower gall of rhododendron, caused by *Exobasidium vaccinii*.

causes leaf spot of chrysanthemums must be classed as an imperfect fungus until its sexual stage is discovered.

The imperfect fungi are subdivided into three groups according to the type of fruiting structure connected with their asexual spores; these groups are the Sphaeropsidales, the Melanconiales, and the Moniliales.

In the first group the fruiting structures are pycnidia (Fig. 44). They are often dark brown or black in color, more or less pear-shaped, and those of some species have a definite opening called an ostiole through which the spores are discharged in characteristic fashion. The spores are borne on short stalks from a special tissue called the "sporogenous layer." During wet weather or other moist conditions, the spores are forced out of the opening by the swelling of the gelatinous substance around them, appearing in long coiled tendrils. The pycnidia of the species of *Septoria* that causes leaf spot of chrysanthemums (Fig. 62) are very frail structures without a definite opening. The spores of this fungus are long, thin, and septate.

The fruiting bodies of the second group, Melanconiales, are formed of mats or pads of fertile tissue on which the spores are borne, never completely enclosed by sterile fungus tissue. These structures are acervuli. The anthracnose fungi, such as the species of *Gloeosporium* (Fig. 63), are classified here. Anthracnose of *Opuntia,* one of the most serious diseases of this plant in nature, develops immense quantities of beautiful crescent-shaped spores; these ooze out through the opening made by the cracking of the epidermis of the host, which at first covers the fruiting body. The anthracnoses of sycamore, maple, violet (Fig. 64), and goldenrod are examples of diseases of ornamental plants in which the fungus fruiting body is an acervulus.

The third group, Moniliales, lacks definite fruiting bodies; the spores are variously borne on specialized branches, which may

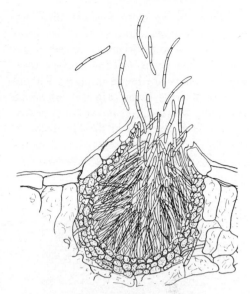

Fig. 62.   Pycnidium of *Septoria.*

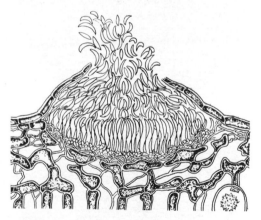

Fig. 63.   Acervulvus of *Gloeosporium* bearing crescent-shaped spores.

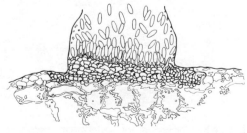

Fig. 64.   Acervulvus of another species of *Gloeosporium.*

sometimes be so close together that they more or less simulate an acervulus. The powdery mildews were originally placed in the group (in the genus *Oidium*) because their asexual spores are borne in chains without protecting sterile tissue (Fig. 13). *Monilinia fructicola,* which causes brown rot of peaches, was first classified in the Moniliales as *Monilia fructicola* because its asexual spores are borne in bead-like chains. Later when its sexual stage was found, it was placed in the genus *Sclerotina,*[9] and finally in the genus *Monilinia.* The species of *Fusarium,* such as that which causes aster wilt, develop their spores almost anywhere on the vegetative mycelia. The fungi of this genus are distinguished by the form and color of their spores and by the number of cells which these contain.

Certain fungi are not known to produce any spores whatever. They are propagated largely by means of pads called "sclerotia" or by fragments of the mycelium that are broken off and dispersed by water, wind, or other agents; these are shown in Figs. 10 and 65. *Sclerotium rolfsii* and *S. delphinii* were originally so classified; it is now known that at least the former has a perfect stage, a fungus named *Pellicularia rolfsii.* It should be understood that some species of fungi now classed among the "imperfects" will ultimately be found to be connected either with some ascomycete, basidiomycete, or phycomycete. In others, the connecting "perfect" stage may be extinct, or that stage may never have existed.

Actinomycetes. Such growths as those which cause potato scab and lumpy jaw of cattle, and the common mold-like growths that develop on heating manure piles and on old dry herbaceous debris, are sometimes classed among the fungi and at other times among the bacteria. The late Dr. Selman Waksman, world-famous microbiologist, considered the Actinomycetes closely related to the true bacteria. Medical men usually group them among the bacteria as a special group, the Actinomycetes. Such difficulties serve to emphasize that classifications are merely artificial means of helping us to group organisms, the better to describe them and understand them.

Myxomycetes. Another group that illustrates the same point includes the slime molds. Some biologists classify them as ani-

Fig. 65. Sclerotia of *Sclerotium delphinii* (bottom) and *Pellicularia rolfsii* (top), growing in agar plates.

[9] This genus may be transferred to *Whetzelinia* some time in the future.

mals (Mycetozoa) while other classify them as fungi (Myxomycetes). Club root of cabbage and other members of the mustard family is caused by a species at one time grouped among the slime molds. "Flowers of tan," a yellowish, slimy, gelatinous growth that develops on sawdust piles and grass lawns in the summer, is another example of the Myxomycetes. Later this mass of jelly-like substance becomes transformed into purplish, dry structures which contain vast quantities of spores. As these spores germinate they form amoeba-like cells which have the power of motion; this has suggested the inclusion of the organisms in the animal kingdom. However, the zoöspores of the fungi that cause damping-off and the late blight of potatoes, and those of the downy mildews also have the power of locomotion, as do the male gametes of mosses and ferns; such organisms are not for that reason called animals. There are no serious diseases of ornamentals caused by Myxomycetes, though dying leaves that are covered with their fruiting structure are often erroneously said to have a disease caused by these organisms.

3

INSECTS AND OTHER ANIMAL PESTS

The largest group of the animal kingdom is the Arthropoda. It includes the Crustacea (crabs, lobsters, sowbugs), the Arachnida (spiders, scorpions, mites), and the Insecta (also known as Hexapoda) (flies, grasshoppers, aphids, butterflies, beetles, bees, ants, and a host of others). A few kinds of crustacea and arachnids and many kinds of insects prey upon ornamental plants and cause great damage to them. Larger animals may also injure plants.

INSECTS

The insects include more species than all other groups of animals and plants together. For a thorough treatment it is necessary to consult the works of entomologists; in this book it is possible to give only a very brief survey of the principal kinds and their characteristics.

The body of an arthropod is composed of a number of more or less similar segments arranged in a series. Some of the segments bear jointed legs.[1] The body of an adult insect is composed of three usually plainly visible parts: head, thorax, abdomen (see Figs. 36, 66, 71). Each of these is composed of several

segments, which may or may not be apparent. On the head is a pair of antennae, which are sense organs. The thorax bears three pairs of legs[2] and usually one or two pairs of wings.

An insect develops in a complex series of stages. The young offspring are often quite unlike the adult. The immature grasshopper (the nymph) resembles the adult in a general way, but lacks wings. At each successive stage in development it resembles the adult more closely; the "metamorphosis" is said to be "gradual." Thrips, aphids, and many other pests of plants have a gradual metamorphosis, which is illustrated in Fig. 67. Most insects have a more complex life history. The egg laid by the female develops into a "larva," a wingless wormlike caterpillar or grub (Figs. 68 and 69) which often feeds on foliage or other plant parts and increases rapidly in size. As it grows it periodically casts its skin. After this period of growth the insect becomes a "pupa," a comparatively inactive and helpless body usually enclosed in some kind of cocoon (Figs. 70, 71, 72). In this stage the body structure is reorganized, and finally the "imago" or adult insect emerges. This sequence is spoken of as "complete metamorphosis." It is illustrated in Figs. 70 and

---

[1] The word "arthropod" means "jointed foot." "Insect" may be translated "in segments."

[2] Hence the name "Hexapoda," "six-footed."

Fig. 66. Carpenter ant.

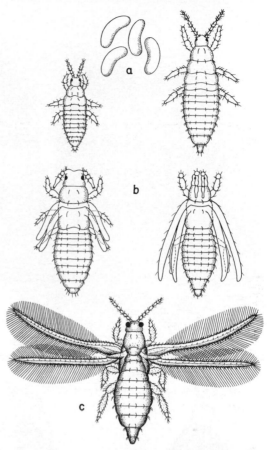

71. The following are the most familiar groups of insects and include those that are most injurious to ornamental plants:

Orthoptera (Grasshoppers, Locusts). They may have two pairs of wings, of which the fore wings are somewhat thicker and cover the hind wings when these are at rest. Their mouthparts are formed for chewing. The metamorphosis is gradual. This group has furnished the tremendous clouds of insects at times so destructive to crops in the central United States and in parts of Asia and Africa.

Fig. 67. Gradual metamorphosis of thrips. *(a)* Eggs. *(b)* Nymphs; four stages known as instars. *(c)* Adult. (From Moulton)

Fig. 68. American dagger moth caterpillar *Acronicta americana.*

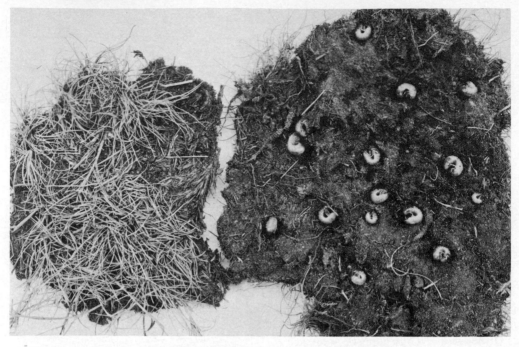

Fig. 69. Grubs of Japanese beetles in sod.

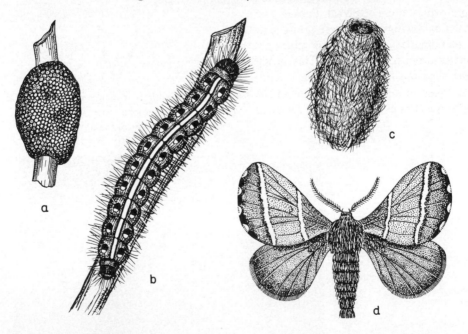

Fig. 70. Complete metamorphosis of *Malacosoma americanum,* the eastern tent caterpillar. *(a)* Egg cluster, attached to twig. *(b)* Larva. *(c)* Pupa case. *(d)* Adult (imago). (Adapted from Lutz)

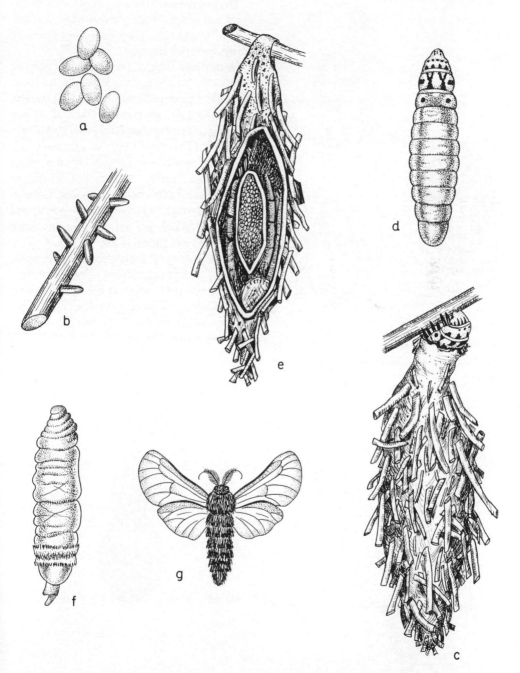

Fig. 71. Complete metamorphosis of the bagworm, *Thyridopteryx ephemeraeformis.* *(a)* Eggs. *(b)* Young larvae, in cases, attached to twig. *(c)* Full-grown larva, moving with its case. *(d)* Full-grown larva removed from its case. *(e)* Larva case in winter condition, cut open to show the pupa case and eggs within. *(f)* Adult female, wingless. *(g)* Adult male moth. (After Felt)

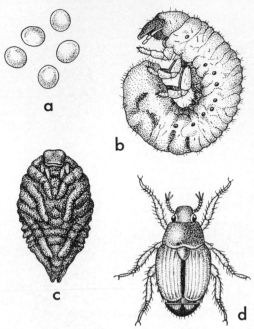

Fig. 72. Japanese beetle *(Popillia japonica).* *(a)* Eggs. *(b)* Larva (grub). *(c)* Pupa. *(d)* Adult beetle. (U.S. Department of Agriculture circular)

Thysanoptera (Thrips). These minute insects are often wingless even when mature. (Figs. 36 and 67). They rasp the tissues of plants and suck the sap.

Hemiptera (Bugs). They have two pairs of wings, the fore wings thickened at the base. They also have piercing and sucking mouthparts. Examples are lace bug (Fig. 73), chinch bug (Fig. 74), plant bugs (Fig. 75), and waterboatmen. (The word "bug" is of course colloquially applied to insects of the other groups also, such as cockroaches, which are Orthoptera, June bugs, which are Coleoptera, mealybugs, which are Homoptera, and to animals which are not even insects, such as the sowbugs shown in Fig. 76.)

Homoptera (Leafhoppers, Whiteflies, Aphids, Mealybugs, Scales). These are characterized by four wings (or none) and mouthparts adapted to piercing and sucking. Like the preceding orders, they have a gradual metamorphosis. The aphids (Figs. 36 and 77)

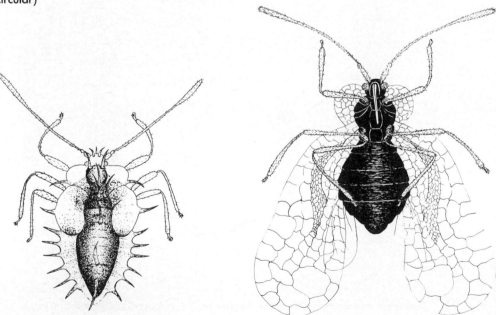

Fig. 73. *(Right)* Lace bug *Stephanitis rhododendri)* seen from below, the proboscis folded back along the body. At the left is an immature individual, seen from above.

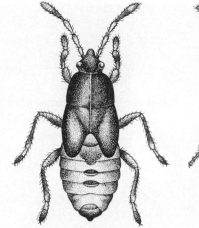
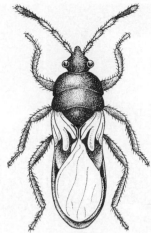

Fig. 74. Chinch bug *(Blissus leu-copterus)*. At the left, immature form with rudimentary wings; at the right, a mature bug. (U.S. Department of Agriculture)

Fig. 75. Tarnished plant bug *(Lygus lineo-laris)*.

Fig. 76. Pillbug *(Armadillidum vulgare)* and sowbug *(Porcellio laevis)*.

Fig. 77. White root-aphids *(Brachycaudus* sp.) on a root of *Centaurea*.

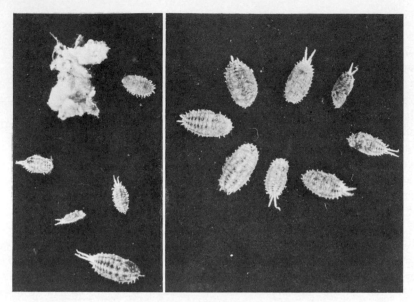

Fig. 78. Mealybugs. An egg mass appears at the upper left.

Fig. 79. Cottony-cushion scale *(Icerya purchasi)*; an example of what can be accomplished by hand-picking. The minute bodies are eggs and young insects.

have a complex method of reproduction which involves the production of a series of generations without fertilization; some of the broods so formed may be wingless, others winged (Fig. 36). The winged generations may migrate to a different host plant; for example, the rose is an alternate host for the potato aphid. Many aphids and the mealybugs (Fig. 78) and scale insects (Fig. 79) cover themselves with a white waxy secretion, under which the young may develop. Some members of this group cause the formation of galls by depositing their eggs in the tissues of the host. The secretion of the honey-dew by aphids and scale insects may result in the growth of a black unsightly mold on the surfaces of leaves and stems. Besides the damage which they do directly, many of these insects are responsible for great loss

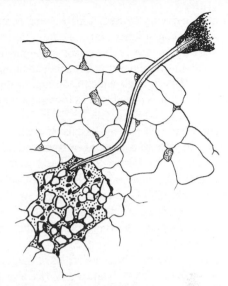

Fig. 80. Beak of an aphid inserted into plant tissues; it reaches the phloem, the food-conducting tissue of the vascular bundle.

Fig. 81. Carpenter ants *(Camponotus pennsylvanicus)* and bronze birch borers *(Agrilus anxius)*.

through carrying viruses, which cause some of our most destructive plant diseases. Figure 80 shows how the proboscis of an aphid is inserted into plant tissue and reaches the conductive cells through which food and water pass; the virus is introduced as food is sucked out.

There are two principal kinds of scale insects, the armored and the unarmored (or soft scale). The former are covered with a hard chitinous material much like that of a turtle. The young (or crawler stage) of the unarmored types usually emerge about two weeks earlier in the spring than do the armored crawlers.

Ground Pearls. These are scales or mealybugs which secrete a white waxy sac about their bodies giving them the appearance of small pearls. They cause irregular dead patches in turf. No effective control is available.

Coleoptera (Beetles). The adults of this very large order are characterized by the fore wings that form hard and usually shining wing-cases which cover the hind wings when at rest (Figs. 36 and 72). They have chewing

Fig. 82. Spotted cutworm (*Amathes c-nigrum*) in amaryllis flower.

mouthparts, and some, such as the Japanese beetle, do extensive damage by feeding on foliage. Their larvae are commonly called grubs. Some grubs live in soil and may do

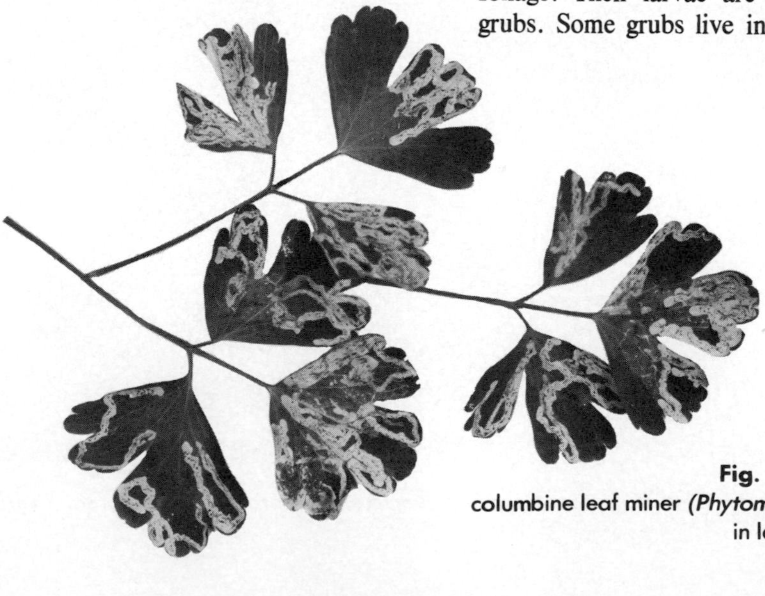

Fig. 83. Work of the columbine leaf miner (*Phytomyza acquilegivora*) in leaves of Aquilegia.

Fig. 84. Bagworm (*Thyridopteryx ephemeraeformis*) on juniper *Juniperus*).

much damage by feeding on the roots of plants (Fig. 69). Many are borers in the stems of plants; the azalea borer and the bronze birch borer (Fig. 81) are the larvae of beetles. Borers often open the way for the invasions of fungi. The elm bark beetle carries the fungus which causes the Dutch elm disease. Wireworms also are larvae of beetles.

Lepidoptera (Butterflies, Moths). The name refers to the dust-like scales which cover their wings and bodies. The adults of these familiar insects are not particularly injurious to vegetation. They feed, by means of sucking mouthparts, largely on the nectar of flowers. Their eggs may often be found attached in masses to leaves and stems (Fig. 70). Their larvae, commonly called "caterpillars," are often destructive. The ravages of cutworms (Fig. 82), tent caterpillars (Fig. 70), leaf rollers, and leaf tiers are familiar to everyone. The American dagger moth caterpillar is shown in Fig. 68. Other caterpillars live as miners within leaf blades (Fig. 83), or as borers within stems (iris borer, Fig. 41; peach borer and leopard moth borer). Some Lepidoptera form gall-like protective structures; the bagworm of evergreens (Fig. 84) is a familiar example. The life history of the latter is shown in Fig. 71.

Diptera (Flies). This group is characterized by a single pair of wings (Fig. 85). It includes many of the most familiar insects that plague us, such as mosquitoes and gnats, horse flies and deer flies, and the common house flies. The mouthparts are adapted to sucking, often also to piercing. In general the flies are not so troublesome to plants as to animals, but the group includes such well-known pests as the rose midge (Fig. 85). The larvae of some Diptera are leaf miners (the boxwood miner). A few species cause galls.

Fig. 85. Rose midge, *Dasineura rhodophaga*. (*Illinois Natural History Survey*)

Hymenoptera (Bees, Wasps, Ants). The sawflies also belong in this order; among them is the elm leaf miner shown in Fig. 86. Hymenoptera are four-winged and many are armed with a poisonous sting. They include the social insects, which form large and complex colonies of many individuals. As is well known, many of these insects are beneficial to plants as pollenizers; Ichneumon wasps (Fig. 87) parasitize the bagworm (*Thyridopteryx ephemeraeformis*) and so aid in the control of this pest. The giant hornet, however, may damage boxwood, lilac, rhodedendron, and other shrubs by girdling the twigs and trunks. Ants are troublesome in various indirect ways. Some species of Hymenoptera cause plant galls.

Fig. 86. Work of the elm leaf miner (*Fenusa ulmi*) in elm leaf.

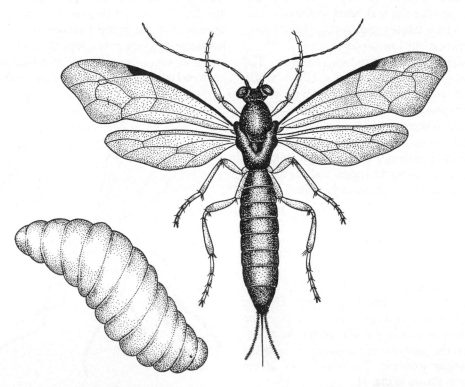

Fig. 87. Ichenumon wasp parasitic on the bagworm; larva at left, more highly magnified. (*Illinois Natural History Survey*)

INSECT PESTS OF GENERAL OCCURRENCE

In this book most of the insect pests are discussed, as are the fungi, under the hosts which they infest (see Part II). Many insects, however, may be described as general pests, not limited to particular species of plants. These are briefly treated in this chapter.

Ants. Ants do not usually attack ornamental plants directly but may indirectly cause considerable damage. They live often in large communities which inhabit ant hills or other dwellings, and have developed interesting social habits often compared with those of man. Among the most remarkable of their activities is the use which some species make of certain aphids. These they carry out and place on the leaves of plants to feed, much as man pastures his herds of domestic animals. The ants gather and feed on the secretions of the aphids. The aphids, of course, may cause considerable damage to plants, and in their excreta sooty molds may obtain a foothold. Certain types of diseases and pests are therefore controlled by destroying the ants. This is usually done by means of ant baits and ant sprays or dusts containing Diazinon, Dursban, or Cythion. Carpenter ants (Fig. 66) weaken trunks of trees by excavating large tunnels in the heartwood, as shown in Fig. 81. In tropical countries leaf-cutting ants may attack ornamental plants.

Termites. These insects are usually associated with damage to wood in buildings. They are occasionally found in decaying wood of live trees. Once they become established in a tree, their feeding is not confined to decaying wood; they also feed on sound heartwood and sapwood. Termites may also infest the roots of annual and perennial ornamental plants. See *Chrysanthemum,* in Part II.

Aphids. Aphids are among the most familiar and troublesome plant pests. Many species affect particular plants; a few of general occurrence are described here.

The potato aphid, *Macrosiphum euphorbiae,* and a related species, *M. rosae,* attack roses early in the spring and the former migrates during the summer to other plants, such as potato, aster, cosmos, dahlia, gladiolus, hollyhock, iris, sweet pea, zinnia, and shepherd's purse. They lay eggs here and there on the tip ends of rose bushes—dark, shining, green-black eggs which live over winter. Pruning of roses in the fall or spring destroys the eggs except on climbers. Spraying of climbers and bush roses with oil, dormant strength, destroys the egg, lime sulfur mixture will destroy some of the least resistant eggs; but since the eggs are difficult to kill, one must also use summer sprays containing malathion.

Root aphids (*Brachycaudus* spp.) attack the roots of many ornamentals including aster, browallia, buttercup, calendula, cosmos, dahlia, primrose, and sweet pea.

Some species live during early summer on such host plants as fir, then migrate or are carried by ants to the roots of other plants as *Centaurea* (Fig. 77). In the fall the ants gather the eggs and keep them over winter, tenderly caring for them, and in the spring take the eggs or young up to the stems and leaves of plants. Root aphid control largely depends on getting rid of ants by applying Diazinon to infested areas.

Plant Bugs. The tarnished plant bug (*Lygus lineolaris*) is a light brown insect, variously spotted, about one-quarter inch long (Fig. 75). It is very destructive to China asters and damages many kinds of ornamentals. It punctures the terminal shoots below the flower buds and injects a poison which usually causes the flowers to droop and die. A Sevin spray is effective in controlling this pest.

The orange-colored or reddish nymphs of the four-lined plant bug (*Poecilocapsus lineatus*) are marked by black dots on the body and later with yellow stripes on each side of the wing pad. The mature insects are yellowish-green with four black stripes down the wing covers. They usually feed on the topmost leaves and cause an irregular bronze spotting. They may be controlled by sprays containing Sevin.

Mealybugs. Mealybugs are among the most troublesome greenhouse and garden pests; one kind is illustrated in Fig. 78.

The citrus mealybug (*Planococcus citri*) found commonly on greenhouse and garden plants, is broadly elliptical in shape, with short bristles or filaments all around the margin. The body is covered with a waxy, mealy substance. The juice of the body is grayish-green in color. The female deposits about 300 eggs in a compact, cottony, waxy sac. The eggs hatch in about ten days, after which the young crawl about over the plants. The young are at first smooth, later developing the leg-like marginal filaments.

A second kind of mealybug (*Pseudococcus longispinus*) that attacks ornamentals is confined in the northern states to greenhouses, although common in gardens and orchards in the southern states. This long-tailed mealybug is covered with a mass of woolly substance, and does not move about so readily as the short-tailed species. It is easily distinguished by its two long and two somewhat shorter appendages. When crushed its body exudes a reddish juice. The female does not lay eggs, but produces nymphs.

Another mealybug (*Pseudococcus fragilis*) also commonly called the citrophilus mealybug, recently has become a serious pest on many trees and shrubs in California.

There are many other kinds of mealybugs, some of which infest the underground parts of trees, shrubs, and flowers. These are discussed under the specific hosts in Part II of this book. Mealybugs were formerly difficult to control. Organic phosphates such as malathion now control them very effectively. Special precautions and practices are discussed later.

Beetles. The Japanese beetle (*Popillia japonica*, Fig. 72) is one of the most serious pests of roses. It rarely appears until after the period of peak bloom of hybrid teas has passed, usually about mid-June or later. The introduction of floribunda roses, which bloom through the summer, has increased the damage by these pests. The beetles may appear in great numbers in July and August. They can be readily distinguished from other beetles by their iridescent bluish-green bodies and streaked gray-brown wing-cases. When approached they are apt to drop down under the foliage and fly away. As many as 50 adults may be found on one rose bloom. As long as blooms are present these insects seem not to feed on foliage. Other plants seriously damaged are elms, lindens, sassafras, grapes, hollyhocks, dahlias, and zinnias. The characteristic work of this pest on a rose leaf is shown in Fig. 38.

The adult beetles lay their eggs in the lawn and other grassy places during July and August, the eggs soon hatch, and the grubs begin to feed on grass roots. Where 25 or more grubs can be taken out of a square foot of lawn, as shown in Fig. 69, the turf will certainly be destroyed. Application of Diazinon at the recommended concentration will control the grubs.

For infested hybrid tea roses in small home gardens, handpicking, which consists in knocking the beetles into a can containing kerosene and water, is one practical means of control.

Sprays containing Sevin,[3] Diazinon, or methoxychlor will control the adult beetles feeding on rose leaves and flowers. They should be applied several times at 7- to 10-day intervals, starting in early July when the beetles first appear.

Repeated use of Sevin on roses and on trees and shrubs may result in heavy infestation of spider mites. Where such a possibility

---

[3] Trade names begin with a capital letter; common names usually do not.

exists, it is wise to include a miticide with the Sevin spray. Among the most effective mite killers are chlorobenzilate, Kelthane, Meta-Systox R, and Tedion.

Milky disease spore powder, prepared under license of the United States government and sold under the name Doom, contains spores of a bacterium that parasitizes and destroys Japanese beetle grubs. A pound can of the spore dust will treat about 4000 square feet of lawn area. The powder is sifted directly on the grass at 3-foot intervals in rows 3 feet apart at any time of the year. The spores live in the soil indefinitely but infect the grubs primarily in the spring and fall. Several years are usually necessary for the bacterial population to become large enough to reduce the grub population appreciably.

The brown Asiatic beetle (*Maladera castanea*) prefers the leaves of China asters to those of many other plants. It feeds on the foliage at night, and when day comes buries itself in the soil near the base of the plant or in the vicinity. Spraying the plants once or twice with Sevin is sufficient.

The white grugs of these beetles, like those of the Japanese beetles, are common and destructive pests in sod. Control of these larvae is described under *Gramineae* (Part II).

Wireworms are the larvae of snapping or click beetles (*Agriotes* spp.). These are an inch or so long and rather blunt-ended (see Fig. 36). Some of them have a long, shield-like head which is capable of snapping so as to jerk the insects into the air. Some fall on their legs, some on their backs; the latter snap again. The larvae are hard-shelled, wiry, smooth, and shining, from yellow to brown in color, and live in the soil, some species spending several years in the larval stage. They feed on the roots, bulbs, and crowns of plants and are especially destructive to germinating seeds. They are controlled in greenhouses by pasteurizing the soil and outdoors by treating the soil with Diazinon or Dursban.

Smoky-brown cockroaches (*Periplaneta fuliginosa*) are troublesome because of their tendency to feed on seedlings and succulent plants. They are established in greenhouses where gardeners leave the remains of their lunches in the refuse pile. Organic phosphate sprays or aerosols containing malathion provide excellent control. Baygon, Diazinon, and Dursban are also effective.

Leafhoppers. More than 2000 species in this family are injurious to trees, shrubs, and other cultivated plants. The aster leafhopper, *Macrosteles fascifrons,* attacks a large number of annual and perennial plants. Among the most common on shade and forest trees are: Japanese maple leafhoppers (*Japanus hyalinus*) on Japanese and Norway maple, and *Idiocerus scurra* on hawthorn, poplar, and willow.

Whitefly (*Trialeurodes vaporariorum*). This pest infests a large number of ornamental plants especially fuchsia, lantana and coleus. The recently developed synthetic pyrethroid, Resmethrin, used at the rate of 1 teaspoonful to a gallon of water gives excellent control. It is also available in aerosal cans under the name Pratt Whitefly Spray.

Borers. Any insect that feeds inside the roots, trunks, branches, or twigs of a tree is known as a borer. The borer is usually in the larval or worm stage, although some beetles, which are the adult stage of certain insects, also may bore into the tree.

Eggs are deposited in the bark crevices and scar tissue or, in a few instances, below the bark surface, by the adult during spring, summer, or fall, depending on the species. Tiny larvae hatch from the eggs and penetrate the bark. Once they are below the surface, they cannot be controlled by the ordinary poisons used for leaf-chewing insects.

Many borer infestations can be prevented by improving, when feasible, any unfavorable conditions around the trees. Proper fertilization, adequate watering during dry spells, periodic spraying for leaf-chewing insects and blighting fungi, and pruning infested or weakened branches are recommended. All bark wounds should receive immediate treatment to facilitate rapid healing and thus reduce the amount of scar tissue.

Borer infestations, which are common in recently transplanted trees, can be materially lessened by placing a barrier over the trunk and larger limbs immediately after the trees have been set in their permanent location. Newspaper, wrapping paper, burlap, or specially prepared kraft crepe paper is used. The last, also known as Tree Wrap, is now employed most extensively because it provides greater protection, is applied more easily, and is neater in appearance than the other materials. The crepe paper consists of two layers cemented together by asphaltum and is sold in 4- and 6-inch widths, wound in bolts of 25 or more yards. It is wrapped around the tree in much the same way as surgical bandage is applied, at an angle that permits sufficient overlap to make a double thickness. Binder twine is wound in the opposite direction to hold the paper in place. Both the twine and the paper remain in place for about 2 years before disintegrating. This is long enough to provide protection during the most susceptible period.

The method used to control borers already established depends upon the part of the tree infested and the species of borer involved. Twig and root borers are controlled by pruning and destroying infested parts or by spraying or injecting certain chemicals into the unpruned infested parts.

Application of insecticides to the bark during the adult's egg-laying period or before the eggs hatch and the borers enter the bark is standard procedure for controlling trunk and branch borers. Among the most generally used materials are malathion, and methoxychlor.

The bark on the main trunk and larger branches can be sprayed or painted with the solution. Unless one is also trying to control leaf-infesting insects, it is not necessary to spray the leaves with borer-controlling materials. Three or four applications at weekly to 10-day intervals may be necessary with some borers to provide protection over the entire egg-laying period. Details on these applications are given later under the different trees susceptible to borers.

Borers that make galleries that lead to the bark surface (sawdust-like frass is a telltale sign) can be controlled by injecting a toxic paste into the holes and then sealing them with a small wad of chewing gum, grafting wax, or putty. These pastes are sold under such trade names as Bor-Tox, Borer-Kil, and Borer-Sol.

Of course, some borers inside the tree can be killed by crushing them with a flexible wire inserted into the opening, or after probing for them with a sharp knife.

Cutworms. Cutworms are the larvae of moths such as *Peridroma saucia* and *Agrotis ipsilon.* The eggs are laid on grass or weeds, and the worms which hatch from them burrow underground. They feed during the night at the surface, cutting off the plants at or near the ground or damaging them so that they soon wilt and die. They also crawl up the plants and devour portions of the leaves and flowers, as shown in Fig. 82. When cold weather comes, they burrow into the soil and spend the winter there. When fully grown they form pupae in the soil. The moths emerge during June, July, and August. Cutworms are extremely troublesome pests because of their nocturnal habits and because they sever the stems of so many plants, killing far more than they can possibly consume. Plants may be protected from them by poison baits as well as sprays containing Diazinon, Dursban, Dylox, Proxol, or Sevin.

The control of cutworms is varied according to the particular species doing the damage.

MISCELLANEOUS ANIMAL PESTS

Mites. The pests hitherto described are all insects, by far the most important group of arthropods. The mites, which are extremely serious pests, are not true insects but belong to the Arachnida or spiders. The best known of the mites is the two-spotted mite, widely known as red spider, illustrated in Fig. 36. This pest, which infests a great variety of plants, is favored by warm, dry conditions such as those often found in greenhouses. Like other spiders, the mites have eight legs. They feed usually on the under side of the leaves by means of sucking mouthparts. Every gardener is familiar with the pale spots on the upper side of the leaves caused by the attacks of red spider. The eggs and the mites themselves are usually covered with a delicate web, which protects them more or less from contact sprays. Since this is a so-called dry-weather pest, abundant watering of plants during dry weather is helpful. Aramite, chlorobenzilate, Dimite, Kelthane, and Ovotran are among the most commonly used mite-killing materials. They should be used as directed on the container. Sevin will not control these pests. In fact, where it is applied frequently, mites will actually increase in number. The reason is believed to be that the Sevin kills off many of the natural parasites that infest mites. With the reduction of natural parasites, the mites then live longer and develop more prolifically.

With frequent use of miticides, mites become resistant to them. Such mites can be controlled either by practicing a sequence of closely timed treatments of an effective substance, or of different effective substances, or by using a combination of two or more of these. Commercial growers faced with the problem of resistant mites should call on their state entomologist for help. He can suggest procedures and combinations for controlling resistant strains.

In recent years mites have become major pests on outdoor plants, particularly on evergreen trees and shrubs and many deciduous ornamentals. Red spider mites and other species are discussed under the hosts they infest.

Sowbugs and Pillbugs. These animals (Fig. 76) represent the remaining large group of the arthropods, the Crustacea. They are related to the crabs, lobsters, and crayfish. The Crustacea are typically aquatic animals, and, though the sowbugs do not live in water they prefer moist environments and are frequent in or near rotten wood.

While these animals usually feed on manure and decaying vegetables, they frequently injure the stems and roots of plants and occasionally feed on the foliage. They are often destructive in greenhouses, feeding on roots of many plants. *Armadillidium vulgare* rolls itself into a ball when disturbed, while *Porcellio laevis* seeks a hiding place. They may be controlled by protecting woodwork against decay so as to reduce their hiding places, and by drenching the soil in greenhouse benches with a mixture of one pound of 50 per cent wetable methoxychlor powder in 33 gallons of water, or by treating infested areas with 5 per cent Sevin dust. Other effective materials are Baygon and Diazinon.

Millipedes. These are members of still another group of arthropods. They feed on manure and other organic materials in soil, being active mostly at night. They do not ordinarily attack living plant tissues unless other food is scarce, but, as is shown in Fig. 88, they may occasionally cause serious damage by feeding on the roots, especially of greenhouse plants. They are primarily destructive to seedlings and help to spread organisms which cause disease. Dusting the surface heavily with either Diazinon or Sevin will control millipedes.

Fungus Gnats. The larval stage of the little black fly (*Sciarid*), that swarms around plants, eats feeder roots and chews larger roots and even below surface stems of most house plants. Drenching the soil with a solution of Diazinon, diluted as directed by the manufacturer, will control this pest.

Psocids. These are tiny, soft-bodies insects with either four wings or none at all. They

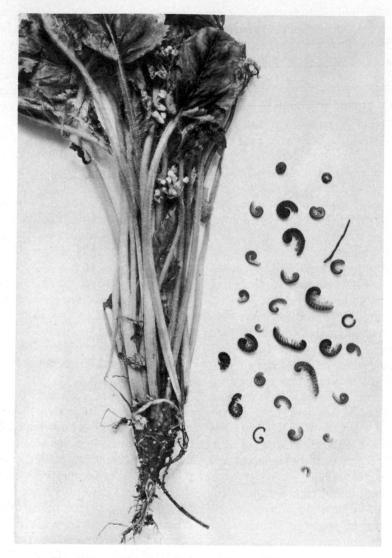

Fig. 88. Millipedes *(Orthomorpha gracilis)* on *Primula.*

feed upon molds and hence abound in damp places such as terrariums, plant containers, and greenhouse benches. They do no harm to plants. If necessary, they can be controlled by dusting the soil or container surfaces with a 2 per cent Diazinon powder.

Garden Symphylan (*Scutigerella immaculata*). This centipede-like pest chews the

smaller roots of many kinds of house, greenhouse, and outdoor plants. It can be eradicated from infested greenhouse soils with malathion.

Nemas.[4] In the early days of zoology, all animals with a worm-like appearance were

4 See footnote 2, page 50.

classed together as the Vermes (worms). We now know that some of these so-called worms are the larvae of butterflies or moths, others the grubs of beetles or the maggots of flies. Besides these, however, there are many animals which are "worms" throughout their life history. These are now classed in several groups, most important of which are the Annelida or segmented worms, of which the earthworm is an example; the Platyhelminthes, or flatworms, which include the tapeworms; and the Nemathelminthes, or roundworms.

In the last-named group are the nemas, the minute eelworms which are extremely abundant in the soil and some of which cause destructive plant diseases. Though the nemas which parasitize plants are minute (barely visible with the naked eye), they are complex organisms with mouthparts, gullet, intestines, and reproductive organs (Fig. 89). In some species the females lay eggs, in others the young develop to some extent before being liberated from the body of the parent. Several hundred species have been described, many of which live on organic remains in the soil and are beneficial in helping to return such debris into a form usable by plants. Other species are parasitic on plants and animals. Parasitic nemas enter plants through wounds, through the delicate root tips, and through the stomata of the leaves, pushing in between the cells and living on intercellular substances and on cell contents.

Nemas are classified according to their feeding habits. The parasitic forms usually feed on living plants and animals whereas the "free-living" types may also feed on decaying organic matter.

Some of the parasitic forms feed on the insides of plants, as for example, the southern root-knot nema *Meloidogyne incognita*, which usually enters the root tips and becomes established in one region of the root, and the various stem and bulb nemas. These are known as endoparasitic nemas.

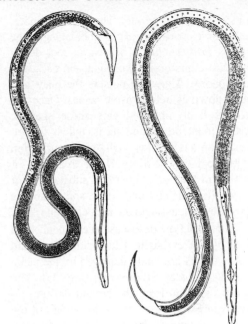

Fig. 89. Nemas, greatly enlarged; *Ditylenchus dipsaci, the* stem and bulb nema. (After Marcinowski)

In northern gardens the common rootknot nema is usually destroyed by excessively low winter temperatures, but it does survive and becomes a serious pest of greenhouse plants.

The northern root-knot nema *M. hapla* is more winter-hardy and is common on all types of crops in the northern United States and Canada.[5] Among the ornamental plants known to be susceptible to this species in the cooler regions of the country are *Abelia grandiflora, Berberis thunbergii, Chrysanthemum morifolium,* clematis, dahlia, delphinium, forsythia, gladiolus, hydrangea, *Ilex crenata,* lavender, *Muscari botryoides, Nandina domestica,* pachysandra, peony, *Papaver* sp., *Pelargonium hortorum, Philadelphus,* rose, *Sinningia (Gloxinia) speciosa,* marigolds, verbena, viola, *Vinca minor,* and *Weigela.*

Meadow (or lesion) nemas constitute an-

[5] This species, rather than *M. incognita*, may be involved on northern-grown plants mentioned in other parts of this book.

other important group. They are elongate, more or less cylindrical pests belonging to the genus *Pratylenchus*. They cause root decay and are common on boxwood, pin oak, iris, and peony. They live outside the plant and are known as ectoparasitic nemas. Once the soil is badly infested with these species, crops must be rotated on it, unless the infested area is small enough for pasteurization with heat or chemicals. Heat treatment of soils and the use of chemical substances for controlling nemas and other soil-inhabiting pests are discussed in the next chapter.

The third type of disease due to nemas is a leaf blotch or blight. Chrysanthemums and other plants are badly damaged by the nema *Aphelenchoides ritzema-bosi* (Fig. 35). The worms emerge from the ground or from already infested leaves on the lower part of the stem and swim up the stem in a film of water. They move out along the leaf stalks and enter the stomata of the leaves. Infestation is possible only when the plants have been wet by rain, sprinkling, or syringing. Control, therefore, involves watering the soil so as to avoid wetting the foliage.

To reduce further the chances of spreading this nema, take cuttings from the tips of healthy plants. Mulch the soil around established plants with peat moss in the spring as soon as the soil has warmed up. Such a mulch provides a barrier between the infested soil and a new crop of leaves above. Many years ago Drechsler and others showed that the nema population is probably reduced by natural biological control. Several soil fungi attack nemas by entangling them in the fungal mycelia; one such mechanism is referred to sometimes as a "lasso mechanism." The root-knot nema and perhaps other parasitic nemas are probably among those that are thus reduced in numbers.

Other nemas invade stems and cause various abnormalities. The most common of these is *Ditylenchus dipsaci,* which infests such plants as *Narcissus, Phlox,* and *Digi-*

talis. As a result of infestation by this parasite, the stems may increase in size and develop abnormal leaves, the blades being much reduced or swollen. Infested plants usually fail to flower. Control involves the destruction of infested plants and pasteurization of the soil. Crop rotation is often necessary for perennials.

Earthworms. In general the presence of earthworms is thought to benefit plants. In their feeding they tunnel in the soil, break it up, and help to keep it aerated and in fine texture. It should be noted that certain plants grow very much better in pots where earthworms are present. Occasionally, however, when they become very numerous, they may do some damage to the roots of plants, particularly in greenhouses. Diazinon provides some control when applied twice at 2-week intervals.

Slugs and Snails. Slugs and snails are members of still another group of animals, the Mollusca. This group includes oysters, clams, and octopuses. Their soft bodies are usually protected by a shell, composed either of a pair of valves like those of an oyster, or of a spiral case like that of a snail. Many mollusks, however, lack shells; among these are the slugs which often cause much damage to garden plants. Slugs usually hide during the day and feed by night on the foliage. They exude slime which hardens and leaves a plainly visible trail behind them.

Figure 90 shows the spotted garden slug (*Limax maximus*) at work. At maturity it reaches 4 inches in length and 1/2 inch in diameter. It is marked by numerous, black, elongated spots on the back and sides. It lays its eggs late in the autumn in groups of 30 to 50; the eggs are covered with a yellowish slime which hardens around them. Working the soil in the spring may destroy dormant slugs and their eggs. One control measure involves dusting slug-infested areas with a 15 per cent metaldehyde dust, or spraying with a 20 per cent metaldehyde liquid, as directed

Fig. 90. Spotted garden slug *(Limas maximus)* feeding on dahlia.

by the manufacturer. The application should be made twice with a 2-to-3 week interval.

Mesurol and Zectran will also control slugs and snails. The former is sold under the name Ortho Slug-Geta. These, as well as metaldehyde, should *never* be used on or near plants grown for food.

Stale or fresh beer placed in shallow saucers in early evening will attract slugs, which then drown in the liquid. The pear slug (Fig. 91) is the larval stage of a sawfly.

Moles. Though the blind mole (*Scalopus acquaticus*) destroys many grubs and the pupae of many insects, the unsightly ridges that it causes are undesirable in the garden and lawn. The breaking of the sod and the consequent drying of the roots damage the grass and ornamental plants in the vicinity. Limited

Fig. 91. Pear slug (*Caliroa cerasi*) feeding on leaves of *Prunus*.

areas can be kept free of moles by burying an 18-inch-high strip of ¹/₂-inch hardware cloth in an upright position.

Mice and Rats. Pine mice are said to follow in the burrows of the blind mole and feed on the roots and rhizomes of plants, bulbs, and seeds of various sorts. Delphinium plants encountered by moles often die from having the crown eaten out. It is said that this is done by pine mice using the moles' runways. Perhaps the moles do the damage while feeding on wireworms and millipedes at the base of the plants. Mice in mole runs can be easily controlled by using ready-prepared mouse bait available in hardware and seed stores.

A bait containing 2 per cent zinc phosphide in cracked-corn mix has found favor with orchardists and nurserymen in rural areas to control meadow mice in the fall. The phos-phide is very poisonous and hence must be handled with great care. The danger to wildlife other than mice from this bait is said to be very low.

Warfarin and Fumarin are anticoagulants used to control rats and mice. They cause death by producing internal hemorrhages.

Rabbits. These animals can be troublesome in gardens. They not only chew the leaves of ornamentals, like pansies, tulips and iris, but by chewing the tree bark at the base they severely damage or even kill dogwood, apricot, Chinese elm, Douglas-fir, firethorn, swamp and scarlet maples, peach, pear, Austrian and Scots pines, and Norway spruce.

A 3-foot-tall cylinder of hardware cloth or window screening placed around the trunk with the lower end inserted an inch or so below the surface provides some protection. Susceptible, dormant deciduous trees and shrubs can be protected by painting or spraying the trunks to a height the rabbits can reach with Arasan 42-S, made by the duPont company; M-S Ringwood Repellent, made by Medical Service Corporation, Chicago, Illinois; with TAT-GO, made by the O. E. Linck Company, Clifton, New Jersey; or RE-PEL, made by the Leffingwell Company, Brea, California.

Deer. These aniamls also cause much damage by feeding on trees and shrubs. Valuable plants can be protected by spraying them with chemical substances which make leaves and bark distasteful to the animals. These are sold under the trade names Arasan 42-S, Magic Circle Deer Repellent, REPEL, and TAT-GO.

Birds. Repellents are available which drive birds away or discourages them from roosting. Among these are Avitrol, Bird Stop, and Red Shield Crow Repellent.

4

CONTROL

CULTURE

In this chapter we can touch only briefly on the proper culture of plants, a subject that requires a manual of its own. The abnormalities caused by improper culture often resemble diseases caused by fungi; the recognition of the cause often suggests the remedy. For example, a water-soaked appearance of stems and their subsequent blackening and collapse may be due to an excess of nitrate in the soil as well as to invasion by soil fungi. The yellowing of plants, "chlorosis," may be due to a deficiency of iron, calcium, or magnesium, as well as to virus diseases. Such troubles may be avoided by proper attention to the soil. A well-known disease of *Ficus elastica* and *F. lyrata* is caused by growing a plant recently obtained from the florist in the excessively hot, dry air of a modern residence. Such conditions are almost unavoidable in many houses, and the only means of preventing the disease is to acclimate the plant by gradually reducing the temperature and increasing the moisture in the air. Plants may be injured by excessive light or shade; again the identification of the cause of the trouble suggests an obvious remedy. Tender plants may suffer from sunscorch in very hot dry weather. It is not true, however, that plants are injured by watering in hot sunny weather.[1]

Sprays, dusts, and fumigants may cause damage to plants, the effect varying with the conditions. Figure 26 illustrates the effect of excessive applications of a nicotine spray. The application of sulfur dust may cause severe burning in hot dry weather, while Bordeaux mixture cannot be used on roses in cool, wet weather without risk of injury. The parasitic organisms that attack plants have received so much attention in recent years that many growers of plants have forgotten that many of their troubles are due to other causes. Not only are faulty cultural practices bad in themselves, but they often lead to later infestation by insects and fungi. It is well known that the common damping-off so destructive in seedbeds is largely dependent on humidity. Adequate ventilation in greenhouses as well as in seed-pans is essential in the prevention of many of the troubles of plants. Proper spacing of the seedlings is also important in controlling such diseases.

SANITATION

Sanitation means providing conditions conducive to health. Since so many plant diseases are caused by parasitic organisms, sanitary conditions are generally thought of as those that reduce the sources of infection.

---

[1] It was thought that the drops of water concentrate the rays of the sun so as to cause an excessive rise in temperature; but it has been shown that the drops of water on the leaves can only focus the sun's rays at a point far beyond the leaf that carries the drop.

Sanitary measures involve: (a) the use of seeds, bulbs, and cuttings only from healthy parents, (b) disinfection of seeds and bulbs, (c) pasteurization of infested soil, and of compost if this is derived from diseased plants, (d) precautions against the transfer of bacteria, fungus spores, insect eggs, and other disease carriers on the tools used in cultivation and on hands and clothing, (e) pruning of diseased parts and disposal of refuse, (f) rotation of crops.

As an example of the importance of sanitation an actual experience is described by Dr. B. O. Dodge. A plot of ground that had been in rough grass for 40 years was dug up, fertilized, and prepared for growing various kinds of annuals as a test garden. Among the plants grown were a variety of *Delphinium ajacis*, some varieties of stock (*Matthiola*), and African marigold (*Tagetes erecta*). During the latter days of July several delphinium plants wilted and died as a result of a root rot caused by a species of *Pythium*; stocks that had reached the height of about six inches suddenly turned brownish, withered, and died from a *Fusarium* root rot; and marigold plants here and there also wilted and died from what appeared to be a *Fusarium* disease which entered through the root system.

The introduction of these diseases into this soil could have come about in several ways. First, and most likely, compost which was introduced with some richer soil to bring up the fertility may have been formed from plants which were infected by one or more of these fungi; the fungi persisted as saprophytes in the compost pile perhaps for a year or more. Another possibility is that the soil used in seed-pans or for growing cuttings of other species in the same plot contained these soil root rot fungi, having obtained them with compost or on tools or seeds. A third possibility is that gardeners in weeding and cultivating plants in nearby borders where these diseases were present could have carried over the spores or mycelia on their shoes or garden tools. However, the chances for such distribution of three different soil organisms in this small new planting could not have been very great. The point which must be emphasized is that it should be a rigid practice not to throw diseased plant parts in piles for composting unless these are restricted for use where soil fungi are of no consequence, as for certain shrubs or trees, or unless the compost pile is thoroughly pasteurized.

Use of Healthy Seeds, Bulbs, and Cuttings. It is well known that the fungi and bacteria which cause so many diseases are propagated by extremely minute spores (Chapter 2). These spores adhere very easily to the surfaces of seeds and other plant parts. Seeds obtained from a hollyhock infected by rust will almost certainly carry on their surface (or on leaf fragments mixed with them) the spores of the rust fungus, and the new plants obtained from such seeds may become badly infected when they are very young. Similarly, bulbs and cuttings, if taken from diseased parents, are very likely to carry the spores and mycelia of fungi, infective virus, or nemas. Lily and dahlia mosaic viruses are very often present in the bulbs and roots purchased from seedsmen. Black spot and brown canker of roses are often found on new plants purchased for the home garden. The diseases may thus be propagated with the host plants.

Disinfection of Bulbs. The surface of bulbs of Easter lily, daffodil, iris and tulip and of gladiolus corms can be protected against *Penicillium* and *Fusarium* fungi by immersion for 15 to 30 minutes in a warm dip (80 to 85° F.) containing 2 tablespoonfuls of Benlate per gallon of water. The treated bulbs should be dried before storage.

Arasan 50-Red will control basal rot and decay of gladiolus corms. The corms can be treated any time after they are dug and dried. They should be coated with the Arasan 50-Red by shaking in a paper bag or similar container, or by dipping in a suspension containing 3 ounces of the chemical per gallon of water for 5 minutes or so. The suspension should be agitated frequently. The corms should be dried before storage.

Gladiolus corms can also be soaked prior to planting in Dowcide B which is effective in controlling certain corm-borne fungi.

Disinfestation of Tools, Hands, and Clothing. Fungus spores, bacteria, and insect eggs may be transferred from infected plants or soil to clean plantings by the tools used in cultivation, or even by the clothing and hands of the gardener. Proper sanitation means the preventing of such contamination, just as in human medicine it means the utmost cleanliness in the use of surgical instruments, dressings, etc. Tobacco mosaic, for example, may be spread by persons weeding seed beds if they smoke or chew tobacco which was obtained from infected plants. The bacterium which causes the foul-smelling soft rot of iris, *Erwinia carotovora,* may be very easily carried into clean soil. Tools may be disinfected by dipping them in 70 per cent denatured alcohol, in a 5 per cent formalin solution, or in Physau 20 or LF solution as recommended by the manufacturer.

Pasteurization of Soil. Many diseases are caused by organisms which may live for considerable periods in the soil. Infestation of the soil may become so severe as to make it impossible to grow certain species there unless it is first pasteurized. All plant parasitic organisms can be destroyed by heating the soil to 180°F. for 30 minutes. Pasteurization, also frequently referred to as sterilization, may be accomplished in a number of ways. In large commercial plantings, pipes are laid in the soil through which steam is introduced to destroy harmful fungi, nemas, insects, and weed seeds.[2]

[2] A most comprehensive discussion of steaming soils with different equipment is in "The U. C. System for Producing Healthy Container-Grown Plants," *Manual 23,* K. F. Baker, ed., University of California, Berkeley, California, 1957.

Commercial florists, nurserymen and large-scale amateur gardeners who have need for large amounts of fungus-, insect-, and weed-free soil can use any one of several electric soil pasteurizers. Information on their manufacture is available from state plant pathologists. An automatic soil pasteurizer known as the "Roto Therm" is also available. This compact machine not only pasteurizes soil quickly and efficiently, but can also be used to disinfest pots, to screen soil, and, in an emergency, to provide heat for a small greenhouse.

Small lots of soil can be heated in the kitchen oven. The soil should be moist but not wet before the heat treatment.

Treatment with steam is faster, easier, and cheaper than most chemical treatments (described below), provided no expensive outlay for a boiler is required. Moreover, its effectiveness can be assessed almost immediately. It also permits treatments within a foot or so of living plants without danger of harming them.

Hot water is occasionally used by some commercial growers to disinfect soils. This method is less effective in destroying parasitic organisms and frequently leaves the soil in very poor condition because of the puddling effect. It is best used to control harmful organisms in sand cutting-benches.

Chemicals. Many kinds of chemical substances are available for disinfesting soils. For the average grower, these are more practical than applying heat. Chemicals are more effective when the amount of soil to be treated is relatively small, and when they do not have to penetrate large soil masses.

As a rule such fungi as *Armillaria, Fusarium,* and *Verticillium* are more difficult to eradicate than are insects, nemas, and most weed seeds. The grower must be sure the chemical selected will do the job it is intended for.

For the most efficient use of chemicals, the soil must be in good tilth, free of lumps or clods, and have a temperature between 65° and 75°F. After treatment the soil must be thoroughly aerated before planting. The residual effect of some chemicals is short-lived; in others 3 or more weeks must elapse before it is safe to plant.

FUNGICIDAL SOIL DRENCHES[3]

Fungicidal soil drenches are supplemental to a thorough soil pasteurization and sanitation program described earlier. They are also helpful in preventing recontamination.

Dexon will prevent and control *Pythium* when used as a post-plant drench. For potted plants, it is mixed in water at the rate of 8 oz. in 100 gallons and 8 oz. of the diluted mixture is applied to each 6 in. pot. For bench and field plants, it is diluted at the rate of 24 oz. per 100 gallons of water and applied to 400 sq. ft. of bed. A second application may be made 2 to 4 weeks later if necessary.

Cover mixing pail with black cloth and apply immediately upon mixing since Dexon deteriorates upon standing in solution and exposed to light.

PCNB (Terraclor) is used to control *Pellicularia* (*Rhizoctonia*), *Sclerotinia,* and *Sclerotium*), not *pythium.* The 75% wettable powder is mixed at the rate of 24 oz. in 100 gallons of water and applied at the rate of 1 pint per square ft. or 100 gallons to 800-1000 sq. ft. Do not repeat the application.

Dexon plus PCNB (Terrachlor) will control *Pellicularia* (*Rhizoctonia*) and *Pythium.* Eight oz. of Dexon and 4 oz. of PCNB (Terrachlor) are mixed into 100 gallons of water and 8 ounces of this mixture is added to each 6 in. pot. For bench and field crops 1 lb. of Dexon and 8 oz. of PCNB (Terraclor) is mixed in 100 gallons of water and this amount

applied to 400 sq. ft. of bed. As already mentioned the mixing pail should be covered with black cloth and the material applied immediately.

Benlate will prevent *Cylindrocladium* blight of azalea, *Ascochyta* ray blight of chrysanthemum, *Thieleviopsis* root rot of poinsettia, and *Fusarium* of aster and carnation. The Benlate 50% wettable powder is mixed at the rate of 24 ounces per 100 gallons of water and one pint of this mixture is applied to each square foot of soil.

A mixture of captan, 50% W P and Ferbam W P will control *Fusarium roseum* on carnations. Eight ounces of each are mixed in enough water to distribute over 1000 sq. ft. of soil.

Thiabendazole (Mertect) is effective against the black root rot of poinsettia caused by *Thielaviopsis.* Three pounds of the 60% wettable powder is mixed in 100 gallons of water and applied at the rate of 1 pint per sq. ft.

Truban 35% W P controls the water molds *Pythium* and *Phytophthora.* For bedding plants it is mixed at the rate of 4 to 6 oz. per 200 gallons of water and this amount is applied to 800 sq. ft. of packs.

For most applications the Truban is mixed at the rate of 4 to 8 oz. in 100 gallons of water and this amount applied to 400 sq. ft. of bed area. The treatment may be repeated in 8 weeks if necessary. The safety margin between effective dose and phytotoxicity is slim; do not overdose. Trial treat a few plants of each kind to determine safety prior to treating large areas.

Formaldehyde[4] has long been used as a soil fumigant. It is used as a soil drench at the rate of 1 pint of commercial formaldehyde (37 to 40 per cent) in 6¼ gallons of water.

---

[3] Material on Fungicidal Soil Drenches taken from Cornell Recommendations for Commercial Floriculture Crops. 1974 Revision. New York State College of Agriculture and Life Sciences. Ithaca, N. Y.

[4] Formaldehyde is a gas, and it is generally available only in the 40 per cent solution known as "Formalin." Whenever formaldehyde is mentioned in this book, it refers to the commercial solution.

The diluted mixture is then used at the rate of ½ gallon per square foot of soil. After treatment the soil is covered for 24 hours to confine the fumes and allow them to act on the harmful organisms.

Formaldehyde fumes are very toxic to living plants. Hence it should only be used in greenhouses or other areas free of plants. The fumes are also highly irritating to persons. Vents and doors should be wide open during application in greenhouses. As with most fumigants, a period 10 to 14 days must elapse before it is safe to plant in treated soils.

A simple method for disinfesting in one operation the seeds, the soil, and the pots or seed-flats in which they are sown is given by Guterman and others as follows: Place a bushel of the prepared soil on a bench. To 2½ tablespoonfuls of Formalin add six times as much water and sprinkle the solution on the soil, which should then be thoroughly mixed and placed in seed-pans or flats. Some seeds may be sown immediately, but it is safer to wait 24 hours. The soil should be thoroughly watered after sowing.

Occasionally captan, ferbam, or thiram, 1 tablespoon per gallon of water, used at the rate of ½ to 1 pint per square foot, is applied to check the advance of soil-infested fungi. Before soaking the infested area with the fungicide, remove the diseased plants and the soil within a foot or so.

A number of substances, particularly volatile substances that liberate heavy poisonous gases, are used to combat certain pests in the soil. Such gaseous poisons are considered under *Fumigants* on page 89. They are useful chiefly against grubs and other larvae, and nemas.

Paradichlorobenzene, long used to control clothes moths in homes, is occasionally still used as a control for certain plant pests, particularly the peach borer. Details on control with this material are found under *Prunus persica.*

Chloropicrin ("tear gas") still holds an important place among soil disinfectants. When properly applied it destroys a large proportion of the organisms in the soil, also weed seeds; it has the virtue of being a fungicide as well as an insecticide. It also avoids puddling and caking of the soil, and leaves no harmful residue. It is unfortunately rather expensive, and this fact and the special apparatus needed for its use may make it impracticable for the home gardener. For professional gardeners and those in charge of large estates who grow plants in large quantities either outdoors or under glass, chloropicrin has advantages over formaldehyde and other soil disinfectants. The instrument for applying it is called an "injector" or "applicator." It should be adjusted to drop 2 or 3 ml. of liquid when it is tripped; the stop plate should be adjusted to allow a penetration of 3 to 6 inches or even more, depending on the material to be pasteurized. For ordinary soil infestations, the plot should be marked off in squares, the lines 10 to 12 inches apart each way. The injector is thrust into the soil at the points where the lines cross on one line and midway between the points on the next, and so on, thus "staggering" the injections and securing even distribution. The soil should be thoroughly watered after the application, and the plot covered with a tarpaulin or plastic sheeting. After about 10 days the soil may be dug up and aired for a day or two before being planted.

When pouring the liquid from the cylinder into the applicator, one should be careful that the gas formed cannot flow in the wind and injure plants growing nearby.

It is a common practice to gather dead or dying asters, snapdragons, pinks, delphiniums, and other plants from the borders and throw them onto the compost pile, where the fungi often present in such plants may continue to grow and the eggs of nemas remain dormant and living for some time. Such compost may be easily freed from undesirable organisms by a single application of chloropicrin.

Certain chemicals are effective in reducing parasitic nemas on such plants as azalea, camellia, gardenia, rose and others. Among these are Nemagon, Fumazone, Nemafume. These are used at the rate of 6.2 oz. of active ingredient per 1000 sq. ft. Follow the manufacturer's directions carefully.

HOT WATER DIPS FOR INFESTED PLANTS

Hot water dips are frequently employed to rid plants and cuttings of mites, nemas, and other pests (Fig. 92). The chief difficulty is the maintenance of the water at the proper temperature during the treatment, particularly if special equipment for regulating the temperature is unavailable. To avoid excessive cooling of the water, the plants are first immersed for a short time in a preliminary bath of warm water; this serves to heat up the plants and their containers without risk of injury. Preheating is especially important if the plants are in large pots. To maintain the treatment water at the desired temperature, provide another vessel of water heated to a higher temperature, and add this as required to the tub in which the plants are being treated. Avoid pouring the hot water on the leaves, and constantly stir the water in which the plants are immersed. A good standard thermometer which registers up to 50°C. (122°F.) is a necessity.

The temperature most commonly used is 43°C. (109°F.). However, the temperature and time necessary to kill the pest without injury to the host must be determined by experiment; since they vary with different hosts and different pests, so that it is impossible to give general directions. It has been found that the foliage of tender plants such as the ferns is seriously damaged by a temperature of 43°C. (109°F.); only slight damage results from exposure for 15 minutes to 40°C. Varie-

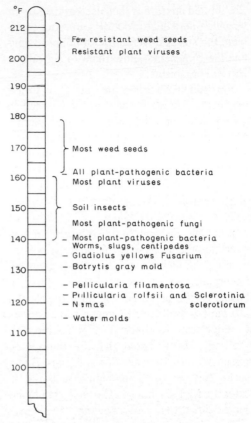

Fig. 92. Temperatures required to kill fungi and other harmful plant pests. Most of the temperatures indicated are for a 30-minute exposure under moist conditions. (Adapted from California Agricultural Experiment Station Extension Service Manual 23)

ties of *Crassula* infested by mites are readily freed by the hot water treatment at 43°C., and many of the mites are destroyed even at 40°C.

To free roots from the root-knot nema (*Meloidogyne incognita*), select one plant for trial. Having picked off as many galls as possible, preheat the roots for 5 minutes in water at 30° to 35°C. (85° to 95°F.); then immerse them for ½ hour in water heated to 45°C. (113°F.). After lifting the plant from the bath, place it on a drainboard and shower it with cool water. The plant should be observed through several days for signs of injury. Foliage of most plants will be killed at such high temperatures. A higher temperature, 48°C. (118°F.), applied for half an hour, kills more root nemas; but each variety of plant must be tested to determine the injury which may be caused by such treatment. For the root nema of black locust nursery stock, it has been reported that a heat of 118° to 120°F. for 30 minutes gave the best results. A mobile unit for treating plants to control nemas is shown in Fig. 93. Among other ornamental plants successfully treated with hot water are Chinese evergreen (*Aglaonema*), *Aloe*, begonia, caladium, and *Dieffenbachia*. The treatment is discussed under each host in Part II of this book. Washing with cold water is

especially helpful if high temperatures and long treatments have been used. Smith recommends shading the plants for a day or two after treatment. He also suggests the use of slatted trays, on which a number of pots can be lifted from the hot water and which can be tilted to ensure quick draining.

For the treatment of narcissus bulbs infested with bulb flies, it is necessary to keep the bulbs at 43° to 44°C. (109° to 111°F.) for 2½ hours. Some growers use a chamber in which the air can be maintained automatically at such temperatures by means of a thermostat. Such equipment of course obviates much of the inconvenience of the hot water treatment. The bulbs should not be packed tightly together, and the air in the

Fig. 93. Mobile unit for treating plants with hot water to control root-infesting nemas. (Photo Dahlgren Studio, Winter Haven, Florida, and State Plant Board of Florida)

chamber should be kept in constant circulation. Large bulbs should be treated for 3 or 4 hours.

Disposal of Refuse. Familiar as they are with the many fungi and pests which cause them trouble, gardeners often do not realize that all these kinds of organisms remain alive also during the winter. Like the plants which they attack, they are usually in a dormant condition at this season. By knowing the places that afford shelter we may often destroy them and so prevent trouble the following season. This is particularly true of many fungi and insects that spend the winter on or in old leaves and other garden refuse, including compost piles. Such common pests as thrips, chinch bugs, and cutworms live during the winter in piles of old leaves. Destruction of such trash is obviously important in preventing the infestation of young plants in the spring. The same is true of many fungi. Fungi which parasitize leaves usually form spores, many of which may adhere to the leaf surface and remain alive even after the leaf and the fungus mycelium within it have died. For this reason fallen sycamore leaves and twigs affected by the sycamore blight and rose leaves with black spot should be carefully raked up and placed in trash cans to be carted away to the city dump. Burning has been recommended in the past but this practice is now prohibited in most communities.

Such generally destructive fungi as the species of *Fusarium,* and *Botrytis,* which attack many plants, also spend the winter sheltered in rubbish heaps, in old leaves, mulch, and the like.

It is obvious that similar precautions should be taken in the disposal of diseased parts which are removed from living plants. Cankered rose stems, diseased peony leaf stalks, mildewed leaves of all sorts, and all such infected parts should be carted away or buried.

If diseased plant parts have been thrown onto the compost pile, this must be pasteurized by one of the methods described earlier for pasteurizing soil.

Control of Weeds. Sanitation also involves the control of weeds, for many weeds are hosts to fungi and insects that attack ornamental plants. Destruction of such weeds removes a source of infection. The mycoplasma-like organism that causes aster yellows, for instance, attacks many wild and cultivated members of the same family and is carried by leafhoppers from them to the garden. The hollyhock rust fungus lives also on other members of the mallow family, including several weeds. Many pests, such as the cyclamen mite, live and breed on wild hosts as well as on cultivated ones, and the destruction of weeds reduces their population.

Many cultivated plants infected with systemic diseases either do not blossom at all or fail to mature their flowers and fruits normally. For this reason they should be considered weeds, and uprooted and discarded. When infection is more local, as in certain wilts, blights, and root and stem rots, there may be partial recovery and some development of blossoms or fruits; but such plants should be discarded because of the danger of spreading the disease to nearby plants. Plants infected with a mycoplasma or virus disease especially should be rogued as early as possible because insects carry both from infected to healthy plants. China asters suffering from yellows harbor the leafhoppers that spread the disease. Destruction of infected plants and of all weeds in the vicinity that are hosts of the leafhoppers materially lessens the spread of the disease. Tulips showing the effects of *Botrytis,* the gray mold that prevents opening of the flowers, should be rogued. For taking out infected bulbs a cylindrical digger may be used which removes also the contaminated soil immediately around the bulb. When dahlias show the effects of stunt, mosaic, or any other virus disease, they should be immediately destroyed, roots and all. They may develop flowers of some value the first year after infection, but are certain to "run out" and serve as a source for the rapid spread of the disease. Some dahlias are rather tolerant of mosaic and stunt; such varieties should not be grown with those that are less tolerant.

The term "roguing" is not applied to pruning out or cutting away diseased branches or cankered parts. Individual leaf stalks of *Paeonia* affected by basal rot due to *Botrytis* should be pulled out and placed into the trash can, but it is unnecessary to rogue the plants. *Sempervivum,* however, with rusted leaves and an abnormal growth of leaves and stems should be rogued, since this rust is systemic and infects roots, crown, offshoots, and leaves. Careful roguing of infected plants as soon as they appear is essential to prevent the gradual spread of the disease throughout the planting.

Rotation of Crops. Rotation of crops is a standard farm practice which often has no relation to plant disease. It may, however, be very useful to gardeners, particularly when it is impossible to pasteurize soil. When soil is badly infested by the aster wilt fungus, it may be planted to something else, and the asters planted in a place not previously used for asters. A 3- or 4-year plan of rotation is advisable for ornamental borders.

RESISTANCE

The use of varieties of plants resistant to particular diseases has proved to be a very satisfactory method of control. For example, several species or cultivars of flowering crabapples are unusually resistant to the four most common diseases of this host, fire blight, cedar-apple rust, powdery mildew, and scab. These include "Adams," *baccata jackii,* "Beauty," "Beverly," "Centennial," "Goldfinch," *halliana parkmani,* "Pink

Spires," "Royalty," "Snow Drift," "White Angel," and "Winter Gold." Varieties of carnations, of chrysanthemums, of snapdragons, and of hollyhocks have been developed which are more or less immune to the particular rusts that infect these species. Varieties of China aster may be obtained that are resistant to the aster wilt. There are degrees of resistance to certain diseases, some varieties being completely immune, others partially susceptible. Losses due to some animal pests also may be avoided by the use of resistant plants. Fig. 35 shows the value of races resistant to nemas.

On the other hand, progress with this method of control is rendered difficult by the large number of varieties of fungi that may infect a given host. During the past 50 years many races of wheat resistant to rust have been developed by plant breeders; several of these races apparently lose their resistance after their introduction. It is now realized that this apparent loss of resistance is due to infection by new races of wheat rust fungus, which is continually undergoing changes by mutation and natural hybridization. A race of the rust found in Minnesota and unable to infect a new hybrid wheat may be quite different in this respect from another race of the same species of fungus from New York or from Texas. Some fungi are apparently so variable in their pathogenicity that we cannot be sure that our new resistant varieties will not encounter new races of the parasites to which they are not resistant. Fortunately it seems that many of the fungi which cause diseases of ornamental plants are fairly stable and our resistant varieties continue to be immune to such diseases. The grower, therefore, should use resistant varieties whenever they are obtainable, without fixing his faith on the ultimate outcome of this method of control. In other words, keep a good stock of insecticides and fungicides on hand, and sprayers and dusters in good working order.

POISONS

The killing agents used to combat and destroy fungi and animal pests include sprays, dusts, and fumigants. In general they differ from drugs and other substances used in human medicine in that they are applied chiefly to the surfaces of the diseased or infested organisms. Many destructive insects, since they live and work on the surfaces of the plant that they infest, may be destroyed or repelled by poisons (solids, liquids, or gases) applied externally. Even wood-boring larvae come to the surface at some time or develop from eggs laid on the surface. Parasitic fungi, on the other hand, live and grow chiefly within their hosts and cannot usually be destroyed without injury to the living tissues which surround them. The control of diseases caused by fungi, therefore, depends largely upon preventing their entrance into the host; the surfaces of plants are sprayed or dusted with substances which destroy the spores of fungi or prevent their germination. Some fungi, for example the familiar powdery mildews, are superficial, and their mycelia may be killed without damage to the host. Fungi and animals in the soil are controlled by gases (fumigants) which penetrate the minute spaces between the soil particles.

Materials to be used for combating fungi and animal pests must be poisonous to the parasites but harmless (or nearly so) to the parts of plants with which they come in contact. The use of sprays by inexperienced workers often causes more damage than the parasites (see Figs. 26 and 27). In temperate regions plants regularly undergo a dormant period during which growth ceases and they may lose their leaves. At such times they are less apt to be injured by poisons, and sprays may be applied in strengths that would be injurious during the growing season. We speak, therefore, of "dormant" sprays and "summer strength" sprays. Dilutions should vary also with the pest in question; the lowest

concentration that will kill is the most desirable.

A great variety of substances has been used for combating fungi and animal pests. Naturally, those that are best adapted for one region may not be so useful in another place. Effectiveness of a spray or dust varies with the climate, and expense (often a limiting factor in control) varies with the availability of the ingredients.

Experimentation with fungicides and insecticides continues and may be expected to develop new and valuable poisons. In recent years many new preparations have come on the market. Until they have been used for some time and under various conditions, it is impossible to say whether or not they are superior to some of the well-known older products. *In using any commercial preparations, old or new, it is important to take great care to follow the printed directions on the label.*

Where specific commercial products are mentioned by their trade names in subsequent pages, it is not to be understood that I recommend them to the exclusion of other similar materials. They are simply representative and in most places readily available products.

Relative Toxicity—LD₅₀

The term "LD$_{50}$" stands for "lethal dose required to kill half (50 per cent) of a group of test animals." The dosage is expressed as a ratio: the amount of pesticide, in milligrams, per 1000 grams of body weight of the test animal concerned (usually rats). For example, an LD$_{50}$ of 5 is a dosage of 5 milligrams per 1000 grams of body weight. Since for all pesticides the lethal dose is expressed in standard form, comparison among dosages states, in effect, their relative toxicity. Note, however, that an LD$_{50}$ of 4 is not lower, but higher, than an LD$_{50}$ of 5: the lower the dosage (that is, the LD$_{50}$ value), the more toxic is the pesticide.

An LD$_{50}$ value of 5 or less will kill most animals. For man, pesticides with an LD$_{50}$ value of 500 and above are relatively safe; a probable lethal dose of these would -range from one ounce to one pint or one pound.

Fungicides

Acti-dione, * also known as cycloheximide, is an antibiotic which controls the powdery mildew of roses and phlox, cedar-apple rusts, azalea petal blight, and rust and leaf spot of lawn grasses. (3 - 2 - (3,5 - dimethyl - 2 - oxocyclohexyl) - 2 - hydroxyethyl - glutarimide.[5] LD$_{50}$: 133.[6]

Acti-dione PM. * is a special formulation of Acti-dione that contains a safener to prevent leaf injury when used to control powdery mildew of roses, phlox and other ornamentals.

Agrimycin. * See *Streptomycin.*

Agri-Strep. * See *Streptomycin.*

Allisan. * See *Botran.* *

Ammoniacal copper carbonate is another useful fungicide for greenhouse plants tolerant to copper. It is sold as Cal-Cop 10,* a dark-blue liquid containing 10 per cent copper.

Anilazine. See *Dyrene.* *

Arasan. * See *Thiram.*

Arasan 50-Red. * See *Thiram.*

Banrot * is used as a soil drench to control several soil-inhabiting parasitic fungi. Ethazol, methyl thiophanate.

Basicop. * See *Bordeaux mixture.*

Benlate * is widely used to control fungus diseases of roses, flowers and other ornamental plants, shade trees and lawn grasses. Methyl 1 - (Butylcarbamoyl) - 2 - benzimidazole - carbamate. LD$_{50}$: 10,000.

---

* The asterisk indicates a registered (i.e., proprietary) trade name.

---

[5] For most of the materials listed, the chemical name, where known, is given.

[6] The term "LD$_{50}$" is explained in the paragraphs immediately preceding. The LD$_{50}$ value is not in all cases available.

Benomyl. See *Benlate.* *

Bordeaux mixture is one of the oldest and still one of the most useful fungicides. The killing principle in the spray, after it is made up and ready for use, is a mixture of certain salts of copper. It is prepared by mixing copper sulfate (blue vitriol) and hydrated lime in various proportions. The formula 4-4-50, for instance, means that 4 pounds of copper sulfate and 4 pounds of hydrated lime are used with 50 gallons of water. The above proportions are so generally useful that this may be considered a standard mixture. It has been found, however, that the amount of lime may be considerably reduced. For example, 2-1-50 or even 3-1-50 has been found satisfactory for certain plants, and the residue does not spot the foliage so badly. Certain plants are rather susceptible to burning by lime.

For preparing small quantities of Bordeaux, the following procedure is suggested: Dissolve 4 ounces of copper sulfate crystals in 1 gallon of water. Then dissolve 2 ounces of hydrated lime in 2 gallons of water. Finally, add the copper sulfate solution to the lime water. This makes 3 gallons of approximately a 4-2-50 Bordeaux.

Mixing the two solutions together forms an insoluble or "fixed" gelatin-like copper precipitate. When it dries on the leaves, it forms a membranous coating which clings. Since the adhesiveness is lost if the mixture stands too long, Bordeaux mixture should always be fresh when used.

Wherever Bordeaux mixture is mentioned in this book as a disease-preventing material, one may safely substitute one of the so-called fixed coppers.

Among the fixed coppers on the market are Basic Copper Sulfate,* Tribasic Copper Sulfate,* Basi-Cop,* Microcop,* Copper 53 Fungicide,* and T-B-C-S 53.

Other copper fungicides are sold as Bordo,* Bordo-Mix,* C-O-C-S,* Kocide 101,* Miller 658,* Ortho Copper Fungicide* and Coprantol.*

One objectionable feature of Bordeaux mixture and other copper compounds is that they may cause some injury to plants when used during cool, wet weather.

Bordo.* See *Bordeaux mixture.*

Bordo-Mix.* See *Bordeaux mixture.*

Botran,* also known as Allisan* and by the common name dicloran, is especially effective against species of *Botrytis* on ornamental plants. 2,6-Dichloro-4-nitroanaline. LD_{50}: greater than 5000.

Brassicol.* See *PCNB.*

Bravo* is effective in controlling several fungus diseases of turf grasses. Tetrachloroisophthalonitrile. LD_{50}: 10,000.

Caddy.* See *Cadmium chloride.*

Cadminate.* See *Cadmium succinate.*

Cadmium chloride is used to control certain fungus diseases of turf grasses. 20.1% equivalent to 12.3% cadmium.

Cadmium succinate is also used to control diseases of turf grasses. 60% cadmium succinate (29% metallic basis).

Calcium polysulfide. See *Lime Sulfur.*

Cal-Cop 10.* See *Ammoniacal copper carbonate.*

Captan,* also sold under the name Orthocide,* is effective in preventing many foliage diseases including black spot of roses and apple scab. cis - N - (Trichloromethyl) thio - 4 - cyclohexene - 1 - 2 - dicarboximide. LD^{50}: 9000.

Carbamate.* See *Ferbam.*

Chem-Bam.* See *Nabam.*

Chem Neb.* See *Maneb.*

Chem Zineb.* See *Zineb.*

Chloroneb. See *Demosan.**

Chlorothalonil. See *Bravo.**

COCS.* See *Bordeaux mixture.*

Copper 53 Fungicide.* See *Bordeaux mixture.*

Coprantol.* See *Bordeaux mixture.*

Coromate.* See *Ferbam.*

Cuprocide.* See *Bordeaux mixture.*

Cycloheximide. See *Acti-dione.**

Cyprex,* commonly known as dodine, is

effective against the leaf blight of sycamores and black walnuts. n-Dodecyguanidine acetate. LD_{50}: 1000.

Daconil 2787.* See *Bravo.**

Demosan,* also known as chloroneb and Tersan SP,* is a fungicide which controls stripe smut of grasses. 1,4 - Dichloro - 2,5 - dimethoxybenzene. LD_{50}: over 11,000.

Dichlone. See *Phygon.**

Dicloran. See *Botran.**

Difolatan* is effective against anthracnose of Sycamores and London plane trees. Cis - N - (1, 1, 2, 2 - Tetrachloreoethyl) thio - 4 - cyclohexene - 1 - 2 - dicarboximide. LD_{50}: 6200.

Dinocap. See *Karathane.**

Dithane D-14.* See *Nabam.*

Dithane M-22.* See *Maneb.*

Dithane M-45* is effective in preventing many fungus diseases of ornamentals. Eighty per cent coordination product of zinc ion and manganese ethylene bisdithiocarbamate. LD_{50}: 8000.

Dithane Z-78.* See *Zineb.*

Dithiocarbamates. See *Dithane* M-22, Dithane* M-45, Ferbam, Fore,* Maneb,* and Zineb.*

Dodine. See *Cyprex.**

Dowicide B* is effective in controlling some diseases of gladiolus bulbs. Sodium 2,-4,5-trichlorophenate 85%.

Dyrene,* also known as Kemate* and anilazine, controls leaf spot of gladiolus and several diseases of turf grasses. 4,6 - Dichloro - N - (2 - chlorophenyl) 1,3,5 - triazin - 2 - amine. LD_{50}: 2710.

Ferbam, also sold under the name Fermate,* Karbam Black,* Carbamate,* Coromate,* and Vancide FE,* is one of the first so-called carbamates to be marketed. It controls the cedar rust disease of crabapples and is very effective when used alone or in a combination spray to control black spot of roses. Ferric dimethyl dithiocarbamate. LD_{50}: 17,-000.

Folpet. See *Phaltan.**

Fore* is a special formulation of Dithane M-45,* for use in controlling fungus diseases of turf and many leaf diseases of ornamentals including holly, horse-chestnut, roses, and others. LD50: greater than 8,000.

Formaldehyde, also known as Formalin, is occasionally used to control soil-borne fungus parasites. It is highly toxic to vegetation and hence should be used only in soils bare of plants.

Funginex,* also known as triforine, has recently been found to be very effective in the control of black spot, powdery mildew and rust of roses. (N, N'[1,4 - piperazinedil - bis - (2,2,2 - trichloroethylidene)] - bis - Formamide).

Fungo* 50, is effective in controlling several fungus diseases of turf grasses. Dimethyl 4,4 - o - phenylenebis 3 - thioallphanate. LD50: 8000.

Karathane,* also known as dinocap and Mildex,* is used to control powdery mildew on many ornamental plants. It also controls several species of mites. 2,4 - Dinitro - 6 - octyl - phenylcrotonate, 2,6 - dinitro - 4 - octyl - phenylcrotonate, and nitro octyl-phenols (principally dinitro). LD50: 980.

Karbam Black.* See *Ferbam.*

Kemate.* See *Dyrene.**

Koban* is used to control the turf diseases caused by species of Pythium. 5 - Ethoxy - 3 - trichloromethyl - 1,2,4 - thiadiazole.

Kocide 101.* See *Bordeaux mixture.*

Lime sulfur is effective in controlling powdery mildews on many ornamental plants. It also helps to combat infestations of spider mites. In concentrated form it is used during the plants' dormant period to destroy overwintering stages of aphids, mites, and scale insects. As a dormant spray it is diluted 1 part of the concentrated lime sulfur in 8 or 10 parts of water. Lime sulfur should not be used near buildings, walls, trellises, etc., because it will stain such objects. It can be diluted 1 part in 50 parts of water and used as a spray during the growing season. Lime sulfur

is also available as a dust. Neither the dust nor the spray should be used when the air temperature is above 85°F. Calcium polysulfide.

Maneb, also sold as Dithane M-22,* Manzate,* and Chem Neb,* is effective in combating leaf spot diseases of ornamental trees and of turf grasses. Manganese ethylene bisdithiocarbamate. LD50: 6750.

Manzate* 200 Fungicide, also sold as Dithane M-45,* is a coordination product of zinc ion and manganese ethylene bisdithiocarbamate, effective in the control of certain diseases of apples, crabapples. LD50: 8,000.

Metam. See *Vapam.**

Microcop.* See *Bordeaux mixture.*

Mildex.* See *Karathane.*

Miller 658.* See *Bordeaux mixture.*

Nabam, also sold as Dithane D-14* and Chem Bam,* is occasionally used to control certain fungus diseases of ornamental plants. Disodium ethylene-1, 2-bisdithiocarbamate. LD50: 395.

Natriphene* is used to control fungus and bacterial diseases of orchid seedlings. Sodium salt of o-Hydroxyphenyl.

Orthocide.* See *Captan.,*

Ortho Copper Fungicide.* See *Bordeaux mixture.*

Oxycarboxin. See *Plantvax.**

Parnon* is a long-lasting fungicide that is effective against powdery mildew of roses and zinnias. a, a - Bis (4 - Chlorophenyl) - 3 - pyridine methanol. LD50: 5000.

Parzate.* See *Zineb.*

PCNB, sold under the trade name Terraclor,* is used as a soil drench and has been found especially effective against fungi that form the tough, resting bodies known as "sclerotia." It is most effective against *Pellicularia (Rhizoctonia), Sclerotinia, Sclerotium, Plasmodiophora,* and *Botrytis.* Used at the rate of 1 tablespoon per gallon of water, this material has checked the damping-off disease on many kinds of greenhouse plants. It is not effective against the water molds

Pythium and *Phytophthora,* however. Pentachloro nitrobenzene. LD$_{50}$: 12,000.

Phaltan,* also sold under the common name folpet, is used to control certain fungus diseases of fruit trees, black spot and mildew of roses, and many others. It is one of the carbamate fungicides presently available that will control powdery mildew. N-(Trichloromethylthio) phthalimide. LD$_{50}$: greater than 10,000.

Phygon,* also sold as dichlone, is used to treat seeds for damping-off control and as a foliage spray. 2,3 - Dichloro - 1 - 4 - napthoquinone. LD$_{50}$: 1300.

Physan 20* is a general purpose disinfectant for algae, bacteria, fungi and viruses. It is especially useful in growing and maintaining orchids in greenhouses. LD$_{50}$: 3625.

Phytomycin.* See *Streptomycin.*

Piperalin. See *Pipron.**

Pipron,* also known by the common name piperalin is effective in combating powdery mildew of catalpa, chrysanthemum, dahlia, lilac, phlox, rose and zinnia. 3-(2-Methyl piperidino) propyl 3,4-dischlorobenzoate.

Plantvax,* also known by the common name oxycarboxin, is effective in controlling rust diseases, especially of crabapples and hawthorns. 5,6 - Dihydro - 2 - methyl - 1,4 - oxathin - 3 - carboxanilide - 4,4 - dioxide. LD$_{50}$: 2000.

Polyram,* controls fungus disease on many ornamental plants. A mixture of ethylene bis (dithiocarbamate) zinc and (dithiobis (thiocarbonyl)-iminoethylene) bis (dithiocarbamate) zinc. LD$_{50}$: over 10,000.

Potassium permanganate is occasionally used in propagating benches to control damping-off of seedlings or cuttings and for sterilizing propagating knives and other tools. KMn$_{04}$.

Streptomycin, also known as Agri-Strep,* Agrimycin 17,* and Phytomycin,* is effective in controlling diseases such as fire blight of pear and apple, walnut blight, and bacterial blight of begonia.

Sulfur has long been used to control many plant diseases such as powdery mildews. It also controls spider mites. See *lime sulfur* for details.

T-B-C-S53.* See *Bordeaux mixture.*

Termil* is a special formulation of Bravo* designed to vaporize without breaking down when heated to a temperature of 600-800 degrees F. for "Thermal dusting" to control gray mold (*Botrytis*) on many greenhouse plants. Tetrachloro isophthalotrile as tablet (90 per cent).

Tersan SP* controls some diseases of turf grasses. 1,4 - Dichloro - 2,5 - dimenthoxybenzene. LD$_{50}$: over 11,000.

Tetramethylthiuram disulfide. LD$_{50}$: 780.

Thiram, available as a seed protectant under the name Arasan* and Arasan 50-Red,* as a turf fungicide as Tersan 75,* and as Thylate* to control rust and scab of crabapples and other diseases, is widely used for these purposes.

Thylate. See *Thiram.*

Triazine,* See *Dyrene.**

Tribasic Copper Sulfate.* See *Bordeaux mixture.*

Triforine. See *Funginex.**

Tutane* is used to prevent *Botrytis* flower rot of chrysanthemum and gladiolus during transit and storage. 2-Aminobutane. LD$_{50}$: 350.

Vancide FE.* See *Ferbam.*

Zineb, also sold as Parzate* and Dithane Z-78,* is used as a preventive fungicide for anthracnose of plane trees and other fungus diseases. Zinc ethylene bisdithiocarbamate. LD$_{50}$: more than 5200.

Bactericides

Most of the various organic and inorganic materials mentioned above are not very effective in combating bacterial diseases. Bordeaux mixture and the fixed copper compounds are fairly effective, but some of the antibiotics are even more so.

The bacterial disease of hawthorn, mountain-ash, pear, and other members of the rose family, fire blight, can be controlled with streptomycin or mixtures of this antibiotic and another one known as Terramycin.* Antibiotics for bacterial plant disease control are sold under such names as Bacticin,* Agrimycin,* Agristrep,* and Phytomycin.*

Insecticides

Agritol,* See *Bacillus thuringiensis.*

Akton* is a nonsystemic insecticide that gives excellent control of chinch bugs and sod webworms in St. Augustine turf. 0-2-chloro-1 (2,5-dichlorophenyl) vinyl phosphorothioate. LD$_{50}$: 146.

Aminocarb, sold under the trade name Matacil,* will control the spruce budworm, jack pine budworm, and other pests. (4-Dimethyl amino)-m-tolyl methylcarbamate. LD$_{50}$:600.

Amiphos* controls aphids, mites, and scales on many ornamental plants. 0,0 - Dimethyl - S - 2 - (acetylamino) ethyldithiophosphate. LD$_{50}$:500.

Appex.* See *Gardona.**

Bacillus thuringiensis, sold under such trade names as Agritol,* Bakthane L69,* Biotrol,* Dipel,* Larvatrol,* and Thuricide,* is a microbe which, as an insecticide, is effective in the control of many kinds of caterpillars. It is harmless to humans and pets.

Bakthane L69.* See *Bacillus thuringiensis.*

Baygon,* also known as Propoxur,* is a carbamate insecticide used to control chinch bugs and sod webworms in lawns. It is also effective in controlling cockroaches. 2-(1-methylethoxy) phenol methylcarbamate. LD$_{50}$:1000.

Biotrol.* See *Bacillus thuringiensis.*

Carbaryl. See *Sevin.**

Carbofuran. See *Furadan.**

Carbophenothion. See *Trithion.**

Ced-O-Flora,* made with petroleum distillates, soap and cedar and hemlock oils, is effective in combating mealybugs and spider

mites on many house plants. It is used at the rate of one part in 25 parts of water.

Chlordane is a stomach and contact poison which is extremely effective against soil inhabiting pests such as ants, Japanese beetle grubs, chinch bugs, sod webworms, and termites. In some areas its use is restricted to control of ants and termites. In others, chlordane is banned as a foliage spray. Sixty per cent octochloromethanohydroindane. LD$_{50}$: 475.

Chlorophos. See *Dipterex.**

Cygon,* also known as dimethoate and Rogor,* is effective in controlling mealybugs on yews, and other insects. It should not be used on Chinese holly, chrysanthemums, and Easter lilies. Some varieties of azalea, fern, gloxinia, hydrangea, Schefflera and African violets may also be injured. Use only on those plants recommended by the manufacturer. 0, 0 - Dimethyl S - (N - methylcarbamoylmethyl) phosphorodithioate. LD$_{50}$: 215.

Cythion,* a premium grade malathion, is recommended for controlling sucking insects on indoor plants. Its odor is less offensive than that of ordinary malathion.

DDVP. See *Vapona.**

Diazinon,* also sold as Spectracide,* controls soil insects such as wireworms and root worms as well as turf pests such as chinch bugs and many insects infesting ornamental plants. It may injure gardenia, hibiscus, pilea, and stephanotis. 0,0 - diethyl 0 - (2 - isopropyl - 4 - methyl - 6 - pyrimidinyl) phosphorthioate. LD$_{50}$: 76-108.

Dibrom,* also known as naled, is effective against many pests including bagworms. 1,2 - Dibromo - 2,2 - dichloroethyl dimethyl phosphate. LD$_{50}$: 430.

Dichlorovos. See *Vapona.**

Dimethoate. See *Cygon.**

Dipel.* See *Bacillus thuringiensis.*

Dipterex,* also known under the common names trichlorfon and chlorophos and the trade names Dylox* and Proxol,* is a phosphate insecticide which is very effective in the control of the omnivorous leaf roller, *Platynotus stultana,* and many other caterpillars and turf grass insects. Some carnations, chrysanthemums and zinnias may be damaged by this insecticide. (2,2,2 - trichloro - 1 - hydroxy - ethyl) phosphonate. LD$_{50}$: 2000.

Dormant oil sprays. Petroleum oils, properly prepared, are used to control many pests that live through the winter on the buds, twigs, and trunks of trees and other woody plants. These are applied in the spring just before new growth begins and when the air temperature is 45°F. or above. Only one application per season is recommended.

Oils having a 60-70 viscosity[7] rating are known as "superior" oils. These are safer to use than oils having a viscosity of 90 to 120.

Some oil sprays having a viscosity of 90 or more are not safe on beech, black walnut, Japanese maple, hickory, sugar maple, and walnut. In certain seasons they may also damage evergreens such as *Cryptomeria,* Douglas-fir, the true firs (*Abies*), junipers, *Retinospora,* Japanese umbrella pine, and yews. Lime sulfur solution is much safer for these plants.

Dursban* is effective in combating chinch bugs, sod webworms, and Japanese beetle grubs in turf grasses, and ants, earwigs, centipedes and millipedes. 0,0 - Diethyl - 0 - (3,5,6 - trichloro - 2 - pyridyl) phosphorothioate. LD$_{50}$: 500.

Dylox.* See *Dipterex.**

Endosulfan. See *Thiodan.**

Ethion controls mites, leafhoppers, thrips and foliar-feeding larvae on a wide variety of ornamental plants. It also controls scales and mites on ornamentals when combined with "superior" type, 60-70 seconds, low-viscos-

[7] Viscosity is measured by taking a small sample of oil and allowing it to flow through a special device. The flow rate is measured in seconds of time. A 60 to 70 second oil flows more rapidly than a 90 to 120 second oil, which makes it safer to use. Other factors which govern the safety of an oil are its purity and its degree of paraffinicity.

ity oils. 0, 0, 0, 0' - Tetraethyl - S, S' - methylene bisphosphorodithioate. LD$_{50}$: 96.

Furadan,* also known by the common name carbofuran, is effective in controlling strawberry and black vine weevils on *Taxus.* 2, 3 - Dihydro - 2,2 - dimethyl - 7 - benzofuranyl methylcarbamate. LD$_{50}$: 10,500.

Gardona* is very effective in controlling caterpillars such as the juniper webworm and gypsy moth. Phosphoric acid, 2 - chloro - 1 - (2,4,5 - trichlorophenyl) vinyl dimethyl ester. LD$_{50}$: 4000-5000.

Guthion* is used by some professional arborists, nurserymen, and foresters to control a wide variety of insects on shade trees and ornamentals. It is not recommended for home gardeners' use. 0, 0 - Dimethyl S - [4 - oxo - 1,2,3 - benzotriazin - 3 (4H) - yl) methyl] phosphorodithioate. LD$_{50}$: 13-16.4.

Imidan* controls many chewing insects including gypsy moth caterpillars and elm spanworms, and a wide variety of sucking insects. N - Mercaptomethyl) phthalimide S(0,0 - dimethylphosphorodithioate. LD$_{50}$: greater than 500.

Larvatrol.* See *Bacillus thuringiensis.*

Malathion, one of the most widely used organic phosphate insecticides, controls a wide variety of pests including aphids, scale crawlers, mealybugs and many chewing insects. A premium grade of malathion, sold under the trade name Cythion,* is less odorous than the regular product. Malathion injures some crassulas, some cacti, ferns, petunias, sweet peas, violets, gloxinias, some red carnations and some rose varieties. 0, 0 - dimethyl phosphorodithioate of diethylmercaptosuccinate. LD50: 1375.

Matacil.* See *Aminocarb.*

Mesurol,* provides control of many species of insects infesting ornamental trees and shrubs. It is also highly effective against slugs and snails attacking ornamental plants. 3,5 - Dimethyl - 4 - (methylthio) phenol methyl carbamate. LD$_{50}$: 130.

Metaldehyde, like Mesurol* and Zectran,* controls slugs and snails in the garden or greenhouse. It may injure *Cattleya* and *Phalaneopsis* orchids. Metacetaldehyde. LD50: 630.

Meta-Systox R* renders plants toxic to aphids, leafhoppers, leafminers mites, whiteflies and many other pests. It may injure some chrysanthemums and Easter lilies. S- 2-(Ethylsulfinyl) ethyl 0,0 - dimethyl phosphorothioate. LD50: 56-65.

Methoxychlor is an insecticide with long residual action used to control elm bark beetles which spread the Dutch elm disease fungus, and many kinds of borers. 1,1,1 - Trichloro - 2,2 - bis (p - methoxyphenyl) - ethanol. LD50: 6000.

Morestan,* also known as Forstan,* controls mites and their eggs, pear psylla and powdery mildew. It may injure some roses. 6 - Methyl - 1,3 - dithiolo]4,5 - b] quinoxalin - 2 - one. LD50: 2500-3000.

Naled. See *Dibrom.**

Nialate.* See *Ethion.*

Nicotine sulfate, also sold as Black Leaf 40,* is a contact insecticide highly effective against aphids and other sucking insects. It is highly toxic if swallowed, inhaled or spilled on the skin. The usual dilution is 1 teaspoon and 1 ounce of soap per gallon of water. Forty per cent (1,3-methyl-2-pyrrolidyl) pyridine. LD50: 50 to 60.

Orthene* is effective in controlling aphids, bagworms, cankerworms, gypsy moths, and many other insect pests. 0,S-Dimethyl acetylphosphoramidothioate. LD50: 950.

Oxamyl. See *Vydate.**

Piperonyl butoxide is a synergist used in aerosols with rotenone and pyrethrins. 80 per cent (butycarbityl) (6 - propylpiperonyl) ether and 20 per cent related compounds. LD50: 11,500.

Pirimor* is a quick-acting insecticide for the control of the green peach and the chrysanthemum aphids on chrysanthemums grown in greenhouses. 5,6 - Dimethyl - 2 - dimethylamino - 4 - pyramidinyl dimethyl - carbamate. LD50: 147.

Prolate. See *Imidan.**

Propoxur. See *Baygon.**

Proxol.* See *Dipterex.**

Pyrethrum is obtained from flowers of a species of chrysanthemum grown in central Africa and Ecuador. Pyrethrin 1, pyrethrin 2, cinerin 1, and cinerin 2. LD50: 1000.

Resmethrin, also known as SBP-1382* and Synthrin,* is a 10 per cent synthetic pyrethroid effective against many household and greenhouse insects, particularly whiteflies. An aerosel formulation of resmethrin is sold as Pratt Whitefly Spray. (5 - Benzyl - 3 - furyl) methyl - 2,2 - dimethyl - 3 - (2 - methylpropenyl) cyclopropane carboxylate. LD50: 4240.

Rogor.* See *Cygon.**

Rotenone is an insecticide extracted from derris and cubé roots grown in Peru. It is moderately toxic to animals and highly toxic to fish. LD50: 300-1500.

Sabadilla, obtained from the seeds of the plant *Schoenocaulon officinale* grown in Venezuela, is used as a contact poison for insects infesting food plants.

SBP 1382.* See *Resmethrin.*

Sevimol* is a formulation of Sevin* in molasses which adheres to sprayed foliage better than Sevin used alone.

Sevin,* known under the common name carbaryl, is widely used to control many insects infesting ornamentals. Repeated use will result in an increase in spider mite populations. It is also toxic to bees and will defoliate Boston ivy and Virginia creeper vines. 1 - Naphthyl N - methyl carbamate. LD50: 500.

Spectracide.* See *Diazinon.**

Supracide 2E is a recently introduced insecticide-miticide that is effective against certain pests infesting nursery-grown trees.

Synthrin.* See *Resmethrin.*

Thiodan,* also known as endosulfan, is effective against many insects that infest trees and greenhouse-grown ornamental plants. It will also control black vine and strawberry weevils, but its use is restricted to registered, certified applicators. Thiodan injures some geranium and chrysanthemum varieties. Hexachlorohexahydromethano - 2,4,3 - benzodio xathiepien - 3 - oxide. LD$_{50}$: 74-130.

Tricarnam.* See *Sevin.**

Trichlorfenson.* See *Ovex.*

Trichlorfon.* See *Dipterex.*

Trithion,* also known as carbophenothion, is useful in the control of many insects and mites infesting ornamentals. S - ((p - Chlorophenylthio) methyl) 0, 0-diethyl phosphorodithioate. LD$_{50}$: 32.2.

Thuricide.* See *Bacillus thuringiensis.*

Vapona,* also known as DDVP and dichlorvos, is used as a contact and stomach poison, and also in resin strips suspended in greenhouses to control certain pests of ornamentals. 2,2 - Dichlorovinyl 0,0 - dimethyl phosphate. LD$_{50}$: 56-80.

Volck* oils are refined grades of petroleum oils often referred to as white oils. These are used in commercial greenhouses and outdoors as summer sprays. They are usually safer to use than most other petroleum oils.

Vydate* controls nemas on Rieger begonias. Methyl - N', N' - dimethyl - N - [methylcarbamoyl) oxy] - 1 - thiooxamimidate.

Zectran,* also known as mexacarbate, is effective against a wide range of insects infesting shade trees, flowers and shrubs, and snails and slugs attacking non-food plants. 4 - Dimethyl amino - 3,5 - xylyl N - methyl - carbamate. LD$_{50}$: 19.

Miticides

Because spider mites are rarely controlled with ordinary insecticides, special materials known as miticides or acaricides are used to combat them. Following are those most widely used.

Acaraben.* See *Chlorobenzilate.*

Aracide.* See *Aramite.**

Aramite,* also sold under the names Aracide,* and Niagaramite,* is an excellent mite killer for use on ornamental and non-food plants. It is compatible with sulfur and with the most commonly used insecticides and fungicides. It should not be used with lime or other highly alkaline materials or with Bordeaux mixture. 2 (P - tert - Butylphenoxy) - 1 - methylethyl - chloroethyl sulfite. LD$_{50}$: 3900.

Arathane.* See *Karathane.**

Chlorfenson. See *Ovotran.**

Chlorobenzilate is very effective against mites infesting ornamental plants. Ethyl 4,4 - dichlorobenzilate. LD$_{50}$: 940

Difenson. See *Ovotran.**

Dimite* kills all stages of mites including the eggs on ornamental plants and shade trees. 4,4 - Dichloro - *a* - methylbenzhydrol. LD$_{50}$: 926.

Kelthane,* known under the common name dicofol, is an extremely effective, widely used miticide. 1 - 1 - Bis (chlorophenyl) - 2,2,2 - trichloroethanol. LD$_{50}$: 809.

Niagaramite.* See *Aramite.**

Omite* is a miticide that is very effective in controlling several species of mites which infest fruit trees. It does not harm beneficial insects like bees. 2 - (p - tert - Butylphenoxy) cyclohexyl - 2 - propynyl sulfite. LD$_{50}$: 2200.

Ovex. See *Ovotran.**

Ovotran,* also known by the common names ovex, difenson and chlorfenson, kills all stages of mites including the eggs. It is toxic to the leaves of some ornamentals early in the growing season. Read the directions carefully prior to using it. p-Chlorophenyl p-Chlorobenzene sulfone. LD$_{50}$: 2050.

Pentac,* is an excellent miticide recommended only for greenhouse floral crops. It may harm the leaves of chrysanthemums. Decachlorobis (2,4 - cyclopentadien - 1 - yl). LD$_{50}$: 3, 160.

Plictran,* controls plant-feeding mites resistant to many other miticides. Tricyclohexyltin hydroxide. LD$_{50}$: 540.

Tedion V-18,* also known as tetradifon, is an excellent miticide for ornamental plants. It does not kill beneficial insects and is harmless to most foliage but may injure some roses. S - p - Chlorophenyl 2,4,5 - trichlorophenyl sulfone. LD$_{50}$: 14, 700.

Tetradifon. See *Tedion V-18.**

Fumigants

Fumigants are poisonous liquids and gases that are used either in the atmosphere surrounding plants or in the soil or other growing media. Most of those that are useful against insects, nemas, and other pests are dangerous also to man, and fumigation must not be undertaken save by trained and experienced persons with proper equipment. The greenhouse or container to be fumigated must be carefully closed so that the poisonous fumes do not escape into the surrounding air or into neighboring greenhouses. The volume (cubic feet) of the space to be treated must be known or measured to the accuracy needed to determine the proper dose. In addition, precautions must be taken against entry by persons unwarned that fumigation is in progress. To minimize the danger, fumigation is best done at night.

Aerosols, available through florists' supply houses and some garden supply shops, contain many different kinds of effective fumigants. The turn of a valve releases the active material for spraying slowly through the greenhouse. Fumigating a large greenhouse takes only a few minutes and is far more effective and safer for the plants than were the older treatments.

A number of organic substances that give off heavy poisonous gases when exposed to air are used for controlling insects, weeds, nemas and some parasitic fungi in the soil.

Following are some of the more widely used fumigants for combatting pests that attack plants either above or below ground:

Bladafume,* also known as Sulfotepp, is used in commercial greenhouse formulations for control of aphids, spider mites, whiteflies and thrips. 0,0,0,0 - Tetraethyl dithiopyrophosphate. LD$_{50}$: 7-10.

Bromofume.* See *Ethylene dibromide.*

Bromomethane. See *Methyl bromide.*

Chloropicrin, also known as Larvacide,* is sometimes used as a soil fumigant to control nemas, soil-infesting parasitic fungi, insects and weed seeds. It is only used on soils free of plants, never near growing plants, because it is highly phytotoxic. Trichloronitromethane.

Dasanit* controls root-knot nemas on boxwood and Japanese holly as well as some soil infesting and leaf-chewing insects. 0,0 - Diethyl - [4 (methylsulfyl) phenyl] phosphorodioate. LD$_{50}$: 2-10.

D-D Mixture.* See *Propylene dichloride.*

Dexon* controls several soil borne parasitic fungi such as *Pythium* and *Phytophthora.* Sodium [4 - (dimethylamino) phenyl] diazene sulfonate. LD$_{50}$: 100.

Dibromochloropropane, also sold as Nemagon* and Fumazone* is a nemacide that can be used around the roots of living plants such as boxwood that are infested with nemas. 1,2 - Dibromo - 3 - chloropropane. LD$_{50}$: 180.

EDB.* See *Ethylene dibromide.*

Ethylene dibromide is an excellent soil fumigant to control soil insects and nemas. It is available in garden supply stores under such names as E D B,* Bromofume,* Dowfume* W-85, Pestmaster* E D B 85, and Soilbrom-86.* Plants should not be set out in treated soil until 3 weeks after treatment.

Dowfume W-85.* See *Ethylene dibromide.*

Fumazone.* See *Dibromochloropropane.*

Larvacide.* See *Chloropicrin.*

Metam. See *Vapam.**

Methyl bromide, also known as bromomethane, is occasionally used as a soil fumigant to control insects, weed seeds, nemas, and certain parasitic fungi. It is highly toxic and must be handled with great care. CH_3Br. LD_{50}: 9.

Mobilawn,* is used to control non-cyst-forming nemas infesting boxwood, Japanese holly, and many other woody plants without harming the plants. It is also used to control lawn chinch bugs on St. Augustine grass, and nemas on African violets. 0 - 2,4 - Dichlorophenyl 0, 0 - diethyl phosphorothioate. LD_{50}: 270.

Mocap* has been found to be effective in controlling the root-knot nemas *Meloidogyne incognita* and *M. javanica* on boxwood and Japanese holly. 0 - Ethyl S, S - dipropyl phosphorodithioate. LD_{50}: 61.5.

Mylone* is a soil fumigant used prior to planting to control certain fungi, nemas, weeds, and soil insects. Tetra hydro - 3,5 - dimethyl - 2H - thiadiazine - 2 - thione. LD_{50}: 500.

Nemafume.* See *Dibromochloropropane.*
Nemagon.* See *Dibromochloropropane.*
Nicofume.* See *Nicotine.*

Nicotine is one of the most generally used fumigants. Commercial preparations such as Nicofume,* which contain free nicotine, are commonly used. This material comes in cans under pressure and is vaporized by opening the can and setting fire to its contents. Several other effective fumigants also come in cans and are used in the same way. LD_{50}: 3-30.

Paracide.* See *Paradichlorobenzene.*

Paradichlorobenzene, also known as PDB and Paracide,* is a fumigant used to control peach tree borers. 1,4 - Dichlorobenzene.

PDB. See *Paradichlorobenzene.*

Pestmaster.* See *Methyl bromide.*

Pestmaster EDB 85.* See *Ethylene dibromide.*

Propylene dichloride, sold under the trade name D-D* Mixture, controls some soil insects and the peach tree borer. 1, 2 - Dichloropropane. LD_{50}: 2000-4000.

SMDC. See *Vapam.**
Soilbrom.* See *Ethylene dibromide.*
Sulfotepp. See *Bladafume.**
Telone.* See *Dichloropropane.*
Terraclor.* See *PCNB.*

Terrazole,* also known as Truban,* controls the *Pythium* and *Phytophthora* fungi. 5 - Ethoxy - 3 - trichloromethyl - 1,2,4 - thiadiazole. LD_{50}: 2000.

Truban.* See *Terrazole.**

Vapam,* also sold as SMDC, VPM and Metam, is used as a general-purpose fumigant to control soil fungi, nemas, and weed seeds. Sodium N - methyldithiocarbamate. LD_{50}: 820.

VC-13 Nemacide.* See *Mobilawn.**

VPM. See *Vapam.**

Systemics

Systemics are substances that can be absorbed through either the roots or leaves of plants and translocated in the sap stream in sufficient amounts to kill insects and related pests feeding or breeding in the plants. What they actually do, then, is kill insects, nemas, and other pests from the inside of the plant rather than from the outside, as do conventional sprays. Systemics are more efficient than chemicals sprayed on the leaves because they spread through the plant as it grows, and do not wash off in rainy weather. Likewise, they present little or no danger to nearby wildlife, unless the plants are eaten. They are now being used primarily by commercial arborists, nurserymen, and professional flower growers on *non-food* crops, though a few can be used on non-bearing fruit trees. Following are the most frequently used materials:

Cygon.* See *Dimethoate.*

Demeton, also sold under the name Systox,* is used as a soil drench to control aphids and mites of ornamentals. It is extremely toxic and should only be used by professional growers. 0,0 - diethyl S - [2 - (ethylthio) ethyl] phosphorothioate mixture with 0, 0 - diethyl S - [2 - (ethylthio) ethyl] phosphorothioate. LD50: 2.5-12.

Dimethoate, also known as Cygon,* (described earlier under *Insecticides*), also has systemic action. When sprayed on azaleas, camellias, and gardenias, enough of it enters the leaves to become toxic to lace bugs, leaf miners, mites, scales, and whiteflies. Sucking insects and mites on narrow-leaved evergreens and on birch, boxwood, and holly can also be controlled with this material. It should be used, however, only on those plants listed on the container. Some plants are damaged by its use. LD50: 215.

Disulfoton. See *Di-Syston.**

Di-Syston,* also known as disulfoton, will control sucking insects, mites, and some chewing insects on birch, holly, mimosa (*Albizia*) and roses. It is available in both granular and liquid forms or impregnated on fertilizer. 0,0 - Diethyl S - [2-(ethylsulfinyl) ethyl] phosphorodiothate. LD50: 192-235.

Mertect. See *Thiabendazole.* Mertect 140 F* is a flowable form of thiabendazole.

Meta-Systox R,* is a systemic insecticide-miticide that is applied to soil around certain plants and renders them toxic to sucking pests as aphids, leafhoppers, scales, whiteflies, and mites. S - [2 - (Ethylsulfinyl) ethyl] 0, 0 - dimethyl phosphorothioate. LD50: 56-65.

Plantvax, also known as Oxycarboxin, (mentioned earlier under insecticides), is a systemic fungicide capable of eradicating the rust fungus from greenhouse-grown carnations. LD50: 2000.

Pyroxychlor* is a newly developed systemic fungicide effective in controlling the water mold fungus *Phytophthora palmivora* when applied as a drench to rooted and unrooted cuttings or as a foliar spray to rooted cuttings of *Dieffenbachia picta.* 2 - Chloro - 6 - methoxy - 4 - (trichloromethyl) pyridine.

Systox.* See *Demeton.*

Thiabendazole, also sold as Mertect* and Tobaz,* is an effective systemic fungicide for controlling certain turf diseases, decay of bulbs and corms of ornamental plants. 2 - (4 - Thyazolyl) - benzimidazole. LD50: 3100.

Tobaz.* See *Thiabendazole.*

SPREADERS

Among the spray ingredients most confusing to gardeners are the so-called wetters and stickers. Their purpose is to help suspend the material in the spray solution, or to improve the wetting of the leaves by the spray, or both.

The inclusion of a commercial or home made spreader-sticker is suggested for sprays to be applied on plants with glossy foliage such as holly, iris, rhododendron, and mountain-laurel.

Commercial spreaders that assure a uniform deposit of insecticide or fungicide to plant surfaces are Triton B-1956, Triton X-100, soap, and certain widely available synthetic detergents such as Dreft, Tide, and Vel. Common materials that enable pesticides to adhere more tenaciously to plant surfaces include casein, powdered skim milk, wheat flour, soya flour, and fish oils. Spreader-stickers are also available under many brand names including DuPont Spreader-Sticker, Filmfast, Nu-Film, Ortho Dry Spreader, and Spray Stay. Most of the ready-made spreader-stickers are used at a dilution of 1 to 1000 or 1/4 teaspoon per gallon of spray. Spreaders such as Dreft or Vel are used to about 1/3 teaspoon per gallon. One tablespoon of wheat flour added to each gallon of spray makes an effective sticker.

Compatibility of Sprays. Some spray materials may be safely combined with others to control fungus or bacterial diseases and insects in a single operation. Because improper mixing of these materials may cause injury to the sprayed plants or reduce the efficiency of one or several of the materials in the mixture, one must know which materials are compatible with each other.[8]

APPLICATION EQUIPMENT

Good equipment for applying insectides and fungicides is absolutely essential. This holds true whether one grows only a few house plants or acres of trees, shrubs, and herbaceous plants.

[8] An excellent spray compatibility chart is available from the Meister Publishing Co., Willoughby, Ohio, for a small charge.

Sprayers. There is a type and size of sprayer to fit every need. These range from small atomizers suitable for a few house plants to power sprayers capable of delivering 50 or more gallons of spray each minute to tall tree (Fig. 94).

The most practical small sprayer for persons with only a few plants is a brass, copper, or stainless steel hand-sprayer of one pint or one quart capacity.

Electric sprayers similar to paint sprayers, with capacities ranging from 1 pint to 3 quarts, are most useful in greenhouses. These are powered by a rotary fan air compressor, fan, or electric vibrator, and are rather expensive.

Fig. 94.   Small power sprayer, excellent for shrubs and low-growing trees.

Compressed-air sprayers of 1½- to 5-gallon capacity have been popular with owners of small gardens with a few low-growing trees and shrubs. Pressures ranging from 30 to 50 pounds are built up by pumping a rod up and down by hand.

Knapsack sprayers ranging from 2 to 6 gal-lons in capacity are strapped on the operator's back. Pressure is maintained by pumping a lever with one hand while spraying with the other.

"Trombone" or slide sprayers discharge a continuous spray at pressures up to 180 pounds. These have a smooth, double action

Fig. 95. The author is using a "Trombone" sprayer in his experimental greenhouse at The New York Botanical Garden.

pump which works both on the in and out strokes much as a trombone does (Fig. 95). They are relatively inexpensive and are among the most reliable kinds.

Bucket pump sprayers are small, powerful brass pumps of the plunger type, capable of developing pressures up to 250 pounds. Most of these produce a continuous, high-pressure spray.

Wheelbarrow, cart, and barrel sprayers have capacities ranging from 7 to 50 gallons and pressures ranging up to 250 pounds. These are most useful for larger gardens and for greenhouses.

Garden hose jar-sprayer attachments are affixed to the garden hose, and the water pressure does the work. Dilute the insecticide concentrate in the jar as directed by the manufacturer, then turn on the water and spray as directed. If properly used and if the right pesticide is available these save much time and energy.

Power sprayers of 10- to 50-gallon capacities are excellent for commercial greenhouses and larger properties. They are operated by one- or two-cylinder pumps which deliver from 1 to 5 gallons of spray per minute at pressures ranging from 20 to 400 pounds. Power sprayers, ranging in capacity from 100 to 1000 gallons, are available for large acreages and very tall trees. Such machines are expensive and are owned principally by commercial arborists and park and shade-tree departments which do considerable shade-tree work (Fig. 96).

Mist Blowers. The newest type of pesticide applicators are so-called mist blowers or air-sprayers which use blasts of air to propel the insecticide or fungicide in liquid form (Fig. 97). There are several sizes and types of mist blowers on the market. Some are better adapted for watershed, park, and forest plantings. Small mist blowers which can be carried on the back, like knapsack sprayers, are also available.

Dusters. For applying pesticides in dry form, many highly efficient applicators are available. These come in a number of general types, including sifter-top cans, plunger dusters, bellows blowers, knapsack-bellows, rotary hand dusters, and compressed-air dusters. Perhaps the most popular and inexpensive type is the small plunger-type duster of 1 pint capacity. Another small rotary duster, the "Midget," is made of rustproof metal, weighs only 1 1/4 pounds, and is capable of throwing an 8-foot dust cloud with one turn of the crank. Another small hand duster, the "Pistol Grip," can be operated with one hand. The "Champion," a bellows-type hand duster that is light in weight and easy to operate, works with as little as 1 teaspoonful or as much as 8 pounds of dust.

Power dusters with capacities of 60 to more than 200 pounds of dust are available for estate and orchard use.

Measuring Apparatus. A set of standard spoons is handy for measuring materials. They are more satisfactory than the ordinary kitchen spoons, which vary greatly in size.

Every gardener should have on hand two or three sets of small scales for weighing ingredients. A "letter balance" for weighing mail, graduated from 1/4 ounce up to 4 ounces, is very useful. A spring balance for weighing up to 4 pounds and another for weighing up to 25 pounds will suffice. Platform scales are available for weighing large amounts. For measuring liquids a series of standard containers should be available. Containers holding 1/2 pint, 1 pint, 1 quart, 1 gallon, and 5 gallons can be very easily assembled and kept for this purpose. *Do not use for household purposes vessels that have been used for mixing or measuring poisons.* In some states it is illegal to use cream and milk bottles for such purposes, but they may be used to measure and mark other containers.

There is generally too much guesswork in mixing fungicides and insecticides.

Although it is a very simple matter to assemble an outfit for measuring and weighing

Fig. 96.   A 400-gallon-capacity hydraulic sprayer, ideal for spraying very tall trees.

materials for plant protection in the home garden, it is rare to find such equipment where it is most needed. In measuring water, many persons take the first pail at hand and guess that it holds 3 gallons, though in reality it may hold only 2.

Care of Equipment. Many complaints are made that fungicides or insecticides do not control plant diseases and pests. Most frequently this is due to faulty equipment or to faulty operation of good equipment. Whether one uses a small sprayer or a power outfit it is important to avoid introducing dirt and other material likely to clog the nozzle. The effi-

Fig. 97. Rotomist mist-blower, a machine developed for applying insecticides to trees and shrubs with a minimum of water and with great speed. (John Bean Division, Food Machinery and Chemicals Corp.)

ciency of the sprayer is measured by the fineness and force of the spray it will provide. When pressure sprayers are being filled, it is a common practice to lay the plunger cylinder on the ground or lawn. Dirt or grass fragments become attached to it and are carried into the container, to clog the nozzle later when pressure is applied. The spray from such a nozzle is neither fine nor strong, for all the pressure is used up in forcing the spray past the obstructing fragments. Spray nozzles are often provided with a screen which can be cleaned by unscrewing the cap. Since there are usually two or three gadgets in the nozzle, the inexperienced user is apt to misplace them in reassembling the parts, and the machine will not give a satisfactory spray even though clean.

Dusters of the hand plunger type are sometimes provided with a rubber washer. The makers recommend the use of graphite for lubricating the steel rod and plunger, to prevent them from squeaking and sticking. The use of oil ruins the machine.

Sulfur left in the container of a fan duster is apt to cake and clog the outlet. When this happens, the mechanism for regulating the output of such a duster will not work properly. All the contents should be removed from this type of duster after use, especially in damp weather.

BIOLOGICAL CONTROL[9]

Biological control of insects includes the use of parasites, predators, and bacterial and

[9] *Biological Control of Plant Pests,* an excellent 98-page booklet, is available from the Brooklyn Botanic Garden, Brooklyn, New York, for a small charge.

virus organisms. More broadly, it also includes the use of sterilizing agents, attractants or lures, and microbial insecticides.

At human instigation, insects are now fighting other insects in more than 200 cases in 65 countries around the world. In 23 areas in the Pacific, there are 123 more or less successful cases of biological control of insect pests by imported natural enemies. Over the past 80 years, more than 650 parasites and predators have been imported into the United States to control some of the major introduced pests.

The principal of biological control is by no means new. Thousands of years ago the Chinese controlled caterpillars and other pests in their citrus trees by placing bamboo poles between the trees to serve as bridges for the movement of the ant *Oecophylla smaragdina,* which preyed upon the undesired organisms.

In recent times, the outstanding example of biological control was the introduction of the Vedalia lady bird beetle, *Rodolia cardinalis,* from Australia in 1887 into citrus orchards in California to control the cottony-cushion scale, *Icerya purchasi.* Within two years of its release into the orchards, the larval and adult stages of this predator had annihilated the cottony-cushion scale, a pest that threatened to wipe out California's citrus industry.

Use of Disease Organisms

Some insects can be controlled by means of pathogenic bacteria. Best known to home gardeners in the eastern United States is the use of so-called spore dust in lawns to control the grub stage of the Japanese beetle. This dust, sold under the trade name Doom, contains a hundred million spores per gram of two species of bacteria, *Bacillus popilliae* and *B. lentimorbus,* which infect the grubs, causing their demise. Moreover, millions of additional bacteria are released from each dead grub to infect any live grubs that re-

main. This treatment is specific for Japanese beetle grubs and does not control other turf-infesting grubs.

Another approach to biological control involves the use of a so-called microbial insecticide made from a specific bacterium, *Bacillus thuringiensis.* In the strictest sense, the use of this material is not biological control but control with a chemical toxin synthesized by bacteria. This product is sold under the trade names Thuricide 90 T Flowable, Agritol, Dipel, and Bakthane L69, all of which affect only the leaf-chewing larvae of butterflies and moths (cabbage looper, tomato and tobacco hornworms, gypsy moths, and spring and fall cankerworms). When a caterpillar eats 40,000 to 80,000 live spores of the *B. thuringiensis*-sprayed leaf, it is poisoned by the toxic crystals produced by the bacteria during spore production. The principal formulations of *B. thuringiensis* are a dust-containing 5 billion spores per gram of product, and a wettable powder containing 15 billion spores per gram of product. *Bacillus thuringiensis* is said to be harmless to all forms of life other than harmful insects; it does not harm crops; it leaves residues that are nontoxic to humans, animals, and beneficial insects.

Insect viruses are also being tested as a means of controlling cabbage loopers and corn earworms. One of these, the polyhedral virus, has been especially effective in controlling the looper in commercial cabbage plantings. The virus contained in one diseased cabbage looper is sufficient to infect more than a billion healthy worms. Two species of pine sawflies have also been controlled with virus-containing sprays.

Sterilizing Agents

Another approach to insect control is the causing of sterility in the male of the species. One of the chief ways of doing this is by exposure to gamma radiation. The outstanding example in which this method was used was on the screwworm, a serious pest of livestock. This pest was completely eradicated from the island of Curaçao and later from the southeastern United States by the release of massive numbers of male screwworm flies that had been sterilized by gamma radiation. Native female screwworm flies mating with sterile males produced no offspring, thereby leading to the eventual annihilation of the population. At the present time, livestock losses in the Southwest due to this pest have been sharply reduced by this method.

Inasmuch as elaborate and expensive equipment is required to rear and sterilize large numbers of insects for release in the field, certain chemicals have been developed that produce sterility in native insect populations at a relatively small cost.

Among the most effective chemosterilants developed thus far are the aziridinyl compounds, which affect the genetic material in the insects' reproductive organs. Only one of the two mates need be affected to abort the resulting fertilized eggs. Apholate, Tepa, and Metepa are the three most effective chemosterilants presently available and have been very effective in controlling house flies when used in baits. When Tepa was applied on one of the Florida keys, egg hatch of house flies was reduced by 90 per cent in one week, and fly density was reduced to zero in four weeks.

However, because of the possibility of harmful effects on humans and beneficial animals (including insects), the widespread use of chemosterilants is not recommended. HMPA and HMM are two dimethylamino derivatives that show much promise in sterilizing male house flies. These are less toxic than the aziridinyl compounds.

Sex Attractants

Still another approach to insect control is by means of sex attractants or sex lures. These are chemicals that attract males to areas where poisonous baits are placed. The use of such an attractant was instrumental in wiping out the oriental fruit fly on Rota, a Pacific island 37 miles north of Guam. The chemical methyl eugenol, which attracts oriental fruit fly males, lured the flies to an insecticide placed in areas away from crops. With the annihilation of males, reproduction ceased, and the species was effectively eradicated.

A synthetic lure for attracting male gypsy moths, Disparlure, is used in Federal and State programs to determine the presence and population of the pest. Also available are sex lures for monitoring the population of codling moth (Pherocon CM); oblique-banded leafroller (Pherocon OBLR); oriental fruit moth (Pherocon OFM); red-banded leafroller (Pherocon RBLR) in orchards. A sex attractant has also been found for elm bark beetle.

Unfortunately, only a few of the thousands of pests that affect plants can be controlled completely by biological means.

For a long time to come, man-made, usually chemical, insecticides will continue to play the major role in the war on insects infesting commercial crops, with an assist, of course, from biological control.

Appendix A

UNITS OF MEASUREMENT

Weight

For weighing out materials referred to in Chapter 4 it is customary to use the avoirdupois system, in which:

16 ounces (oz.) = 1 pound (lb.).

For conversion between systems:

1000 grams (g.) = 1 kilogram (kg.).

For conversion from one system to the other:

1 ounce = approximately 29 grams.
1 kilogram = approximately 2 pounds 2 ounces.

Volume

In the United States liquids are measured as follows:

80 drops = 1 teaspoonful (tsp.) or approximately 1/6 fluid ounce.
3 teaspoons = 1 tablespoonful (tbs.) or approximately 1/2 fluid ounce.
2 tablespoons = 1 fluid ounce (fl. oz.)
8 fluid ounces = 1 cup.
2 cups = 1 pint (pt.) or 16 fluid ounces.
2 pints = 1 quart (qt.) or 32 fluid ounces.
4 quarts = 1 gallon (gal.) or 128 fluid ounces.

In the metric system:

1000 milliliters (ml.) = 1 liter (l).

Milliliters are also generally known as cubic centimeters (cc.).
To convert from one system to the other:

1 liter = approximately 1 quart 1 fluid ounce.
1 fluid ounce = approximately 30 milliliters.

How To Calculate Small Amounts of Pesticides

Since commercial insecticide preparations vary in bulk per unit weight, no exact figures can be given for use in small sprayers. A rule of thumb is: 1 pound of wettable powder per 100 gallons is approximately equal to 1 level tablespoon per gallon. One pint of liquid insecticide per 100 gallons is equal to 1 level teaspoon per gallon. 3 pints (1 1/2 quarts) of liquid insecticide per 100 gallons is equivalent to 1 level tablespoon per gallon.

Length

Inches may be compared with centimeters by the accompanying diagram (Fig. 98).

10 millimeters (mm.) = 1 centimeter (cm.)
100 centimeters = 1 meter (m.)

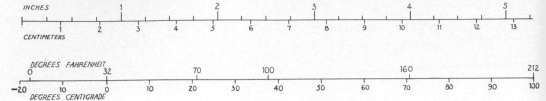

Fig. 98. Common units of measurement.

To convert:

1 inch = approximately 25 millimeters.

1 meter = approximately 1 yard 3 inches.

Temperature

Degrees Centigrade (°C.) may be compared with degrees Fahrenheit (°F.) on the scale shown in Fig. 98. The freezing point of water under standard conditions is 0°C. or 32°F.; the boiling point is 100°C. or 212°F.

To convert degrees Fahrenheit to degrees Centigrade, use the following formula: °F. = (9/5)°C + 32. To convert degrees Centigrade to degrees Fahrenheit, use the following formula:

$$°C. = (5/9) (°F. - 32)$$

Appendix B

SELECTED BIBLIOGRAPHY

Abstracts of Mycology. Philadelphia: Biosciences Information Service of Biological Abstracts. Issued monthly.

Agricultural Chemicals. Caldwell, N.J.: Industry Publications, Inc. Issued monthly.

American Nurseryman. Chicago: American Nurseryman Publishing Co. Issued semimonthly.

American Rose Magazine. Shreveport, La.: American Rose Society, Inc. Issued monthly.

ANDERSON, ROGER F. *Forest and Shade Tree Entomology.* New York: John Wiley and Sons, Inc. 1960.

BAILEY, L. H. *Manual of Cultivated Plants,* rev. ed. New York: The Macmillan Co., 1949.

BAKER, W. L. *Eastern Forest Insects.* U. S. Dept. Agr. Forest Service. Misc. Publ. 1175. Feb. 1972.

Bergey's Manual of Determinitive Bacteriology. 8th ed. Baltimore: Williams and Wilkins Co. 1974.

BILLINGS, SAMUEL C., Chairman. *Consolidated List of Approved Common Names of Insecticides and Certain Other Pesticides.* Entomological Society of America, College Park, Md., 1970.

BILLINGS, S. C. *Pesticide Handbook-Entoma.* 26th ed. College Park, Md.: Entomological Soc. of America. 1975-1976.

BLICKENSTAFF, C. C., Chairman. *Common Names of Insects.* College Park, Md.: Entomological Society of America. 1970.

BORROR, DONALD J. and RICHARD E. WHITE. *A Field Guide to the Insects of North America.* Boston: Houghton Mifflin Company, 1970.

BORROR, DONALD J, and DWIGHT M. DE LONG. *An Introduction to the Study of Insects.* 3rd ed., New York: Holt, Rinehart & Winston, 1971.

BOYCE, J. S. *Forest Pathology,* 3d ed. New York: McGraw-Hill Book Co., 1961.

CANNON, JR., W. N. and D. P. WORLEY. *Dutch Elm Disease Control: Performance and Costs.* U. S. Forest Service Research Paper NE-345. 1976.

CARTER, J. C. *Illinois Trees: Their Diseases.* Urbana, Ill.: Illinois Natural History Survey Circular 46, 1955.

Cornell Guide to Safe Pest Control Around the Home. Miscel. Bul. 74. Ithaca, N.Y.: 3rd. rev. Dec. 1975.

Cornell Recommendations for Commercial Floriculture Crops. Rev. ed. Ithaca, N. Y.: 1974.

Cornell Recommendations for Commercial Production and Maintenance of Trees and Shrubs. Ithaca, N.Y.: Cornell Miscellaneous Bulletin, rev. March, 1974.

Cornell Recommendations for Turfgrass. Ithaca, N.Y.: 1976. Feb. 1976.

COUCH, H. B. *Diseases of Turf Grasses.* New York: Van Nostrand Reinhold Co., 1962.

DIMOCK, A. W. *Gardener's ABC of Pests and Disease.* New York: M. Barrows & Co., 1953.

DOWSON, W. J. *Plant Diseases Due to Bacteria,* 2d ed. Cambridge, England: Cambridge University Press, 1957.

ESSIG, E. O. *Insects and Mites of Western North America,* rev. ed. New York: The Macmillan Co., 1958.

Farm Chemicals Handbook. Willoughby, Ohio: Meister Publishing Co., 1970.

FELT, E. P. *Plant Galls and Gall Makers.* Reprint. New York: Hafner Publishing Co., 1965.

FELT, E. P. and RANKIN, W. H. *Insects and Diseases of Ornamental Trees and Shrubs.* New York: The Macmillan Co., 1932.

FORSBERG, J. L. *Diseases of Ornamental Plants.* University of Illinois Special Publication No. 3. Rev, 1975.

GRAHAM, FRANK, JR., *Since Silent Spring.* Boston: Houghton Mifflin, 1970.

Grounds Maintenance. Intertec Publ. Corp. Overland Park, Missouri. Issued monthly.

Guide to Chemicals Used in Crop Protection, 5th ed. London, Ontario: Canada Department of Agriculture Publication 1093, 1968.

HARDING, W. C., JR., and JOHNSON, W. T. *Insects of Ornamental Trees and Shrubs.* College Park, Md.: Maryland Extension Service Bulletin 169, 1960.

HEADLEY, J. C. and J. N. LEWIS. *The Pesticide Problem: An Economic Approach To Public Policy.* Baltimore: Johns Hopkins Press, 1967.

HEPTING, GEORGE H. *Diseases of Forest and Shade Trees.* U. S. Dept. Agr. Forest Service. Agriculture Handbook. 386. July 1971.

Horticulture Magazine. Boston: Massachusetts Horticultural Society. Issued monthly.

Important Forest Insects and Diseases of Mutual Concern to Canada, the United States and Mexico. Ottawa, Canada: The Queen's Printer and Controller of Stationery, 1967.

JOHNSON, W. J., and LYON, H. H. *Insects that Feed on Trees and Shrubs.* Ithaca, N.Y.: Cornell Univ. Press. 1976.

Journal of Arboriculture. International Soc. of Arboriculture (formerly International Shade Tree Conference). Urbana, Ill.: Issued monthly.

Journal of Economic Entomology. College Park, Md.: Entomological Society of America. Issued quarterly.

KREITLOW, K. W., and JUSKA, F. W. *Lawn Diseases.* Home and Garden Bulletin 61. Washington, D.C.: U.S. Govt. Printing Office, 1963.

MACALONEY, H. J., and EWAN, H. G. "Identification of Hardwood Insects by Type of Tree Injury." U. S. Forest Research Paper LS-11, 1964.

MALLIS, E. *Handbook of Pest Control,* 4th ed. New York: MacNair-Dorland Co., 1964.

Nassau Living. Garden City, N.Y.: Nassau Co., N. Y., Cooperative Extension Service Association. Issued monthly.

NICHOLS, L. P. *Tree Diseases.* State College, Penna.: Penn State University Extension Service Circular 85, 1965.

NICHOLLS, RICHARD. *The Plant Doctor.* Philadelphia: Running Press, 1975.

PEACE, T. R. *Pathology of Trees and Shrubs.* London: Oxford University Press, 1952.

Pesticide Directory. Farm Chemicals. Willoughby Ohio: Meisster Publ. Co., 1974.

Phytopathology. St. Paul, Minn.: American Phytopathological Society. Issued monthly.

PIRONE, P. P. *Tree Maintenance,* 4th ed. New York: Oxford University Press, 1972.

Plant Disease Reporter. Washington, D.C.: U.S. Govt. Printing Office. Issued monthly.

Plant Virus Names. Phytopathological Papers No. 9. Kew, Surrey, England: Commonwealth Mycological Institute, 1968.

PYENSON, LOUIS. *Keep Your Garden Healthy.* New York: E. P. Dutton & Co., 1964.

Review of Applied Mycology. Kew, Surrey, England: Commonwealth Mycological Institute. Issued monthly.

Rutgers, The State University. 1976. *Pesticides for New Jersey.* Extension Service College of Agricultural and Environmental Science, New Brunswick, N.J., 1976.

SCHREAD, JOHN C. *Control of Scale Insects and Mealybugs on Ornamentals.* Conn. Agr. Exp. Sta. Bul. 710. New Haven, Conn. 1970.

————.*Leaf Miners and Their Control.* 19 pp. Conn. Agr. Exp. Sta. Bul. 693. 1971.

SHARVELLE, E. G. *Chemical Control of Plant Diseases.* College Station Texas: University Publishing, 1969.

SHURTLEFF, M. C. *How To Control Plant Diseases in Home and Garden,* 2d ed. Ames, Iowa: Iowa State University Press, 1966.

SMITH, F. F. *Controlling Insects of Flowers.* U.S. Dept. of Agriculture Information Bulletin No. 237. Washington, D.C.: U.S. Govt. Printing Office, 1962.

Suggested Guide for the Use of Insecticides. Agriculture Handbook No. 331. Washington, D.C.: U.S. Govt. Printing Office, 1967.

Trees Magazine. Olmsted Falls, Ohio: Scanlon Publishing Co. Issued bi monthly.

Weeds, Trees and Turf. Cleveland, Ohio: Harvest Publishing Co. Issued bi-monthly.

WELLMAN, F. L. Plant Diseases: An Introduction For The Layman. Garden City, N.Y.: Natural History Press, 1971.

WESTCOTT, CYNTHIA. *Gardener's Bug Book,* 4th ed. Garden City, N.Y.: Doubleday & Co., Inc. 1973.

WESTCOTT, CYNTHIA. *Plant Disease Handbook,* rev. 3rd ed. New York: Van Nostrand Reinhold Co., 1971.

WESTCOTT, CYNTHIA, and NELSON, PETER K., 5th ed. "Biological Control of Plant Pests," *Plants and Gardens,* XVI, No. 3, 1960. Brooklyn, N.Y.: Brooklyn Botanic Garden.

WESTCOTT, CYNTHIA, and WALKER, J. (eds.). *Handbook on Garden Pests.* Special printing of *Plants and Gardens,* XXII, No. 1. Brooklyn, N.Y.: Brooklyn Botanic Gardens, 1966.

WILSON, BILLY R. (ed.). *Environmental Problem: Pesticides, Thermal Pollution, and Environmental Synergisms.* Rev. ed. Philadelphia: J. B. Lippincott, 1971.

Yearbook of Agriculture, 1952: Insects. Washington, D.C.: U.S. Govt. Printing Office.

Yearbook of Agriculture, 1953: Plant Diseases. Washington, D.C.: U.S. Govt. Printing Office.

II

DISEASES AND PESTS
OF PARTICULAR HOSTS

ABELIA[1]

This ornamental shrub has very few diseases and insect pests. A leaf spot caused by a species of the *Cercospora* fungus was reported on *Abelia chinensis* in 1957. A species of *Oidium* causes powdery mildew. In Texas the fungi *Phymatotrichum omnivorum*, *Pythium* sp., and *Pellicularia filamentosa*, cause root rots. The leaves may become chlorotic when plants are grown in alkaline soil. Unless planted in sheltered, well-drained sites, the tops may be damaged by the low temperatures of northern winters.

The northern root-knot nema, *Meloidogyne hapla*, also occurs on this host.

ABIES (FIR)

Diseases

Needle and Twig Blight (*Rehmiellopsis balsameae*). The needles of the current season's growth of balsam fir turn red and shrivel when affected by this disease. Colorado, alpine, noble, and Fraser firs are also attacked but less frequently. The fungus *Cenangium abietis* occasionally attacks firs but is most common on pine.

Control: In ornamental plantings, prune and destroy infected twigs and then spray with a copper fungicide 3 times at 12-day intervals, starting when the new growth begins to emerge from the buds.

Leaf Cast (*Bifusella abietis*, *B. faullii*, *Hypodermella mirabilis*, *H. nervata*, *Lophodermium autumnale*, and *L. lacerum*). Needles turn yellow, then brown, and drop prematurely when attacked by any one of these fungi. Elongated black bodies appear along the middle vein of the lower leaf surface. Spores shot from black fruiting bodies in summer to young leaves germinate and penetrate the new growth.

Control: Copper sprays as suggested for needle and twig blight will control leafcast.

Rusts (*Milesia fructuosa*, *Hyalospora aspidiotus*, *Uredinopsis mirabilis*, *U. osmundae*, *U. phegopteris*, *Pucciniastrum pustulatum*, *P. goeppertianum*, *Melampsora abieti-capraearum*, *Caeoma faulliana*, *Peridermium ornamentale*, and *Melampsora cerastii*). Most of these rust fungi attack forest firs and are seldom found on ornamental specimens.

Control: Measures to control rusts are rarely adopted because the fungi do not cause much damage. Most of the rusts listed above have alternate hosts which are needed to complete the life cycle of the fungus. The elimination of the alternate host will result in nearly complete disappearance of the fungus. A rust expert must be consulted for the name of the alternate host before any eradicatory steps are taken. Periodic applications of sulfur sprays during the summer will also control rusts but these are not practical for large trees.

Cankers (*Cylindrocarpon* sp., *Cytospora pinastri*, *Cryptosporium macrospermum*, *Scoleconectria balsamea*, and *S. scolecospora*). Occassionally sunken dead areas on the trunk and branches of firs in ornamental plantings result from infection by one of the several fungi listed. On balsam fir, the fungus *Aleurodiscus amorphus* forms narrowly elliptical cankers with a raised border on the main trunk of young trees and centering around a dead branch.

Control: Sanitation, avoidance of bark injuries, and fertilization to maintain the trees in good vigor are suggested.

Shoestring Root Rot and **Wood Decay.** Caused, respectively, by the fungus *Armillaria mellea* and by fungi belonging to the genera *Fomes*, *Polyporus*, *Lenzites*, and *Stereum*.

Control: No completely effective control is known. Avoid bark injuries and keep the

---

[1] The host plant is listed under the botanical name of the genus. The common name follows in parenthesis. Where the botanical and common name are the same, only one is given.

trees in good vigor by watering and fertilization when needed.

Insects

Balsam Twig Aphid (*Mindarus abietinus*). This greenish aphid covered with white wax feeds on the young shoots of white and balsam firs, as well as spruce. The needles bend, turning their lighter sides upward. Severe infestations may kill the shoots. The pest hibernates on the shoots in the egg stage.

Control: Spray with malathion or Meta-Systox R in late April and repeat in mid-May if necessary.

Balsam Gall Midge (*Dasineura balsamicola*). Small, subglobular swellings at the base of the leaves are caused by this midge.

Control: Spray the newly developing leaves in late April with malathion.

Bagworm (*Thyridopterix ephemeraeformis*). This caterpillar builds around itself an elongated sac, 2 or 3 inches in length, out of pieces of leaves of its host plant. If the host is a narrow-leaved evergreen, the bag looks as though it were shingled loosely with little sticks. The larva increases in size, enlarging the bag. The adult stage is a moth. The pest overwinters in the egg stage in the old female bags. Various stages in the life of the insect are shown in Figs. 72 and 84.

Control: Hand-pick and destroy bags in winter. Spray with Diazinon, Dipterex, malathion, or Sevin when the young worms first appear. The time of this appearance varies from May 1 to June 1, depending on the locality.[2] Spray 7 to 10 days later if live bagworms are still present.

Caterpillars. Several kinds of caterpillars

feed on the needles of firs. These are the larval stage of the hemlock looper moth, the spotted tussock moth, the balsam fir saw fly, the Zimmerman pine moth, and the pine butterfly.

Control: Spray with *Bacillus thuringiensis* or Sevin when the caterpillars are young.

Spruce Spider Mite (*Oligonychus ununguis*). This is one of the most important pests of evergreen trees. The tiny $1/64$ inch long, sap-sucking pest turns the leaves of firs and junipers yellow, those of arborvitae brown, spruce gray, and hemlock nearly white. In very severe infestations it produces a fine silken webbing over the leaf surfaces. The young are pale green; the adult female is greenish-black (Fig. 183). Winter is passed in the egg stage on the twigs and needles. Depending on the locality and the weather, eggs hatch in April or May and complete a generation in 4 or 5 weeks. Spider mites cause most damage in hot, dry seasons.

Control: Spray with 1 part concentrated lime sulfur in 10 parts of water or with "superior" type dormant oil before growth begins in spring. Or spray in mid- or late May with chlorbenzilate, Kelthane, or Meta-Systox R to kill the young mites of the first generation. Repeat later in the season if necessary. Because of their staining properties, lime sulfur sprays should not be used on trees near white-painted objects.

Scales. Several kinds of scale insects, including the oystershell and pine needle scale, infest firs.

Control: Spray with lime sulfur as for spider mite, or with malathion or Sevin during May and June to control the young crawler stage.

---

[2] Unless specifically noted otherwise, the dates mentioned in the rest of this book for appearance of symptoms and time of control apply to the latitude of New York City. Spray schedules for more southerly points will vary from 1 to 3 weeks earlier and for more northerly areas, 1 to 2 weeks later.

Other Pests

Dwarfmistletoe (*Arceuthobium campylopodium*). In California this mistletoe is a widespread serious pest of red fir (*Abies magnifica*) and white fir (*A. concolor*).

Control: In valuable trees, remove dwarf-mistletoe by pruning.

Balsam Woolly Aphid (*Adelges piceae*). This introduced aphid is becoming increasingly prevalent in the Northeast. It attacks twigs and buds and causes dieback of twigs and treetops.

Control: Spray with malathion when aphids become plentiful.

Spruce Budworm. See *Picea.*

ABUTILON (FLOWERING MAPLE)

Diseases

Mosaic (*Abutilon mosaic virus*).[3] This virus disease causes a variegation of the leaves, to which the value of *Abutilon striatum* var. *thompsonii* as an ornamental is due. This is a systemic disease which can be propagated by grafting. Occasionally a branch outgrows the virus and thenceforth appears perfectly normal. In Brazil the whitefly, *Bemisia tabaci,* was found capable of transmitting the virus to hollyhock, peanut, lentil, white lupin, and potato.

Control: Control measures are not practical because the propagator wants to retain the virus which causes the unusual chlorotic mottling of the leaves.

Stem Rot (*Macrophomina phaseoli*). The lower stems may occasionally be attacked by this fungus which is much more destructive on herbaceous ornamentals.

Control: Soils infested with this fungus should be pasteurized with heat, or treated with the chemical PCNB (Terraclor).

Rust (*Puccinia heterospora*). This rust is widely distributed in the South, from Florida to Arizona, on hollyhock, mallow, and *Malvaviscus,* as well as on *Abutilon.*

[3] The names of the viruses discussed in this book follow those in *Plant Virus Names,* Phytopathological Papers No. 9, issued in June, 1968, by the Commonwealth Mycological Institute, Kew, Surrey, England.

Control: Sulfur dusts or sprays will control this rust.

Leaf Spots. A number of leaf spotting fungi also occur on this host. These are discussed under *Althaea.*

Insects and Other Pests

Abutilon Moth (*Anomis erosa*). This caterpillar feeds also on hollyhocks, hibiscus, and other members of the mallow family. It resembles the cabbage measuring-worm.

Control: Young caterpillars are killed by 1 per cent rotenone dust or with Sevin.

Greenhouse Whitefly (*Trialeurodes vaporariorum*). Plants of *A. grandiflorum* in the greenhouse are subject to heavy infestation of whitefly; this is followed by a heavy growth of the fungus *Hormodendrum* on the honeydew.

Control: See *Fuchsia.*

Fuller Rose Beetle (*Pantomorus cervinus*). This grayish-brown weevil, $1/3$ inch long with a short, broad snout and a white diagonal stripe across each wing cover, feeds at night on the leaves of a wide variety of plants. In the North it is primarily a greenhouse pest, whereas in the South it also chews the outdoor foliage of acacia, apple, apricot, avocado, azalea, begonia, camellia, canna, cape jasmine, carnation, chrysanthemum, cissus, citrus, deutzia, dracaena, fuchsia, gardenia, geranium, golden-glow, hibiscus, lilies, oak, palm, peach, pear, penstemon, persimmon, plum, plumbago, primrose, rose, scabiosa, and vinca.

The larval stage feeds on the roots of berry bushes and young citrus trees, sometimes causing the leaves to turn yellow.

Control: Dust the soil and base of the plant with 2 per cent Diazinon powder to control the adult weevils, which must crawl up the plants because they have no wings for flying.

Imported Long-Horned Weevil (*Calomycterus setarius*). A grayish-black weevil with unusually long antennae and a body about ³/₈ inch long feeds on the leaves and blossoms of ornamental herbaceous and woody shrubs. It chews irregular areas in the leaf margins which resemble those produced by the Fuller rose weevil. In the northern states the adults emerge in late June and are abundant in July and August. Eggs are laid in sod in late summer and the grubs stay in the soil until the following June. The adults are wingless but manage to crawl into homes and vehicles, onto food and people, besides infesting food plants.

Control: Dust with Diazinon powder in the vicinity of the favorite food plants.

Scales. Three species of scales infest flowering maple: black araucaria, lesser snow, and the soft scale.

Control: Spray with malathion or Sevin when the young scales are crawling about.

Nemas (*Meloidogyne incognita* and *M. hapla*). Root-knot nemas attack the flowering maple as they do many other greenhouse plants. For control, see Part I, Chapter 3.

ACACIA

Diseases

The fungus diseases of *Acacia* are not important. A twig canker caused by *Nectria ditissima* and *Fusarium lateritium* (*Gibberella baccata*) has been reported from California. Leaf spotting by the fungus *Physalospora fusca,* a species of *Cercospora,* and the alga *Cephaleuros virescens* occasionally develops in the South. In California powdery mildew caused by the fungus *Erysiphe polygoni* is common. Root and trunk rots caused by the fungi *Phymatotrichum omnivorum, Armillaria mellea, Clitocybe tabescens,* and *Fomes applanatus* have been reported from the South and the West.

Control: [4]

[4] Where no control measures are noted, they may be given under more favored hosts, or the disease or pest may not be important enough to warrant control measures, or control measures are not known.

Insects

Cottony-Cushion Scale (*Icerya purchasi*). This "ribbed scale bark-louse," which has been a serious pest of *Acacia, Citrus,* and other plants in California, has been troublesome in greenhouses in the eastern states for a number of years. The mature insect (Fig. 79) has a ribbed, cottony covering through which may be seen its soft body, sometimes ¹/₄ inch long. The white, fluted mass that extends from the scale is composed largely of eggs covered by a protecting waxy mass. The scale itself is much smaller and is usually inconspicuous. At an earlier stage the scale is greenish and not contained in a woolly excretion. In Fig. 99 it is shown on *Nerium* (oleander). Several other species of scale occasionally infest *Acacia.* These are: California red, which is round and reddish in color; greedy, a small gray species; oleander, a pale yellow kind; and San Jose, which is small and gray with a nipple in its center.

Control: Malathion sprays or aerosols are

Fig. 99. Cottony-cushion scale *(Icerya purchasi)* on oleander *(Nerium).* Young stages are visible on the leaves.

effective against the crawler stage of scale insects.

Caterpillars (*Argyrotaenia citrana* and *Sabulodes caberata*). The former, a dirty-white, brown-headed caterpillar, webs and rolls the leaves of many trees and shrubs on the West Coast. The latter, a yellow to pale pink or green caterpillar, with yellow, brown, or green stripes on the sides and back, also feeds on a wide variety of plants in the same region.

Control: Spray with *Bacillus thuringiensis,* Diazinon, or Imidan when the caterpillars are young.

ACALYPHA (COPPER-LEAF)

Diseases

Leaf Spots (*Cercospora acalyphae, Phyllosticta* sp., and *Ramularia acalyphae*). Three fungi occasionally spot the leaves of *Acalypha.*

Control: Leaf spots rarely cause enough damage to warrant control measures.

Red Leaf Gall (*Synchytrium aureum*). Reddish galls develop on the leaves of this host as well as on delphinium, geum, goldenglow, marsh-marigold, and violet.

Control: Pick off and destroy the infected leaves.

Mildews. Downy mildew caused by *Plasmopara acalyphae* and powdery mildew by *Erysiphe cichoracearum* have been reported from Wisconsin.

Control: Copper sprays will curb the former, and sulfur or Karathane sprays will control the latter.

Other Diseases. Among other fungus diseases of copper-leaf are root rots caused by *Clitocybe tabescens,·Pellicularia filamentosa,* and *Phymatotrichum omnivorum,* and a dieback caused by *Botryosphaeria dothidea.*

Oedema (Nonparasitic). Greenhouse acalyphas are subject to oedema, especially if too heavily watered or in a very humid environment. The intumescences, rust-colored spots, are composed of much elongated cells of the tissues of the leaf.

Control: Avoid overwatering and improve the ventilation.

ACANTHOPANAX (FIVE-LEAF ARALIA)

A fungus leaf spot caused by a species of *Alternaria* has been reported from Missouri, and root rot by *Phymatotrichum omnivorum* from Texas. The four-lined plant bug *Poecilocapsus lineatus* makes dark, depressed spots in the terminal leaves.

ACER (MAPLE)

Fungus and Bacterial Diseases

Anthracnose (*Gloeosporium apocryptum*). In rainy seasons this disease may be serious on sugar and silver maples and on boxelder and to a lesser extent on other maples. The spots are light brown and irregular in shape. They may enlarge and run together, causing the death of the entire leaves. Leaves partially killed appear as if scorched. Another anthracnose, *Gnomonia veneta,* more frequently found on sycamores, attacks maples also.

Control: Spraying 3 times at 2-week intervals with a copper fungicide or with zineb, starting when the leaves begin to unfurl in spring, will provide control.

Leaf Spot (Purple Eye) (*Phyllosticta minima*). The spots are ¼ inch or more in diameter, more or less irregular, with brownish centers and purple-brown margins (Fig. 2). The black pycnidia of the fungus develop in the center of the spots. This disease is most severe on red, sugar, and silver maples but also occurs on Japanese, Norway, and sycamore maples.

Control: Spray with zineb 3 times at 2-week intervals starting when the leaves are unfolding from the buds.

Tar Spot (*Rhytisma acerinum*). Street maples are seldom infected with this fungus, but red maples in forests may be prematurely defoliated. The spots are irregular, shining black tar-like discolorations up to $\frac{1}{2}$ inch in diameter, developed on the upper side of the leaves. The dark color is due to the masses of brown or black mycelium.

Control: Rake up and discard the leaves in fall. If necessary spray with a copper fungicide or ferbam when buds are opening and, when severe, repeat several times at 2-week intervals.

Other Fungus Leaf Spots. *Rhytisma punctatum* causes a minute black spotting on many species of maples. It is rare in the East but rather prevalent on the Pacific Coast. A number of other leaf spots that occur occasionally are caused by fungi belonging to the genera *Cercospora, Septoria, Cylindrosporium, Monochaetia,* and *Cristulariella.*

Control: Spray as for tar spot.

Bacterial Leaf Spot (*Pseudomonas aceris*). In California, the leaves of Oregon maple (*A. macrophyllum*) may be spotted by a bacterium. Spots vary from pin-point dots to areas $\frac{1}{4}$ inch in diameter. They first appear as though water-soaked and are surrounded by a yellow zone; later they turn brown and black.

Control: Preventive sprays containing a copper fungicide applied in early spring should control this organism.

Leaf Blister (*Taphrina sacchari*). The lesions produced by this fungus are circular or irregular in shape, pinkish or buff on the underside, and ochre or buff above. Sugar and black maple are most susceptible. Blistering, curling, and blighting of other species of maple are produced by different species: *Taphrina lethifer* affects mountain maple; *T. aceris,* Rocky Mountain hard maple; *T. dearnessii,* red maple; and *T. carveri,* silver maple.

Control: Leaf blisters on valuable specimens can be prevented by applying dormant lime sulfur, ferbam, or ziram spray just before growth starts in spring.

Fig. 100. A maple tree affected by the wilt disease caused by the fungus *Verticillium albo-atrum.* (Oxford University Press)

Powdery Mildew (*Uncinula circinata* and *Phyllactinia corylea*). These mildews, which are rarely serious, can be controlled by spraying with wettable sulfur or with Karathane.

Wilt (*Verticillium albo-atrum*).[5] The external symptoms of this disease are the sudden wilting and dying of leaves on individual limbs, particularly on one side of the tree, and a reduction of the size of the leaves, which turn yellowish (Fig. 100). Infected

[5] Some investigators claim that the fungus *Verticillium dahliae* causes wilt, on the basis that it forms small black fruiting bodies (sclerotia) in laboratory culture whereas *V. albo-atrum* does not. This difference is not enough, however, to designate it as the causal fungus.

Fig. 101. Discoloration of sapwood, caused by the wilt fungus *Verticillium albo-atrum*. Discolored area is olive-green. (Bartlett Tree Research Laboratory)

trees may die slowly (over a period of several years) or suddenly (within a few weeks) depending on the extent and number of internal infections. An olive-green discoloration may develop in the sapwood (Fig. 101). This is more likely to be present in the roots and trunk base than in the branches. Because several other fungi are known to cause discoloration of the sapwood, positive diagnosis of wilt can be made only by culturing discolored sapwood tissue in the laboratory. The disease does not spread rapidly from tree to tree. Infection takes place most commonly through the roots because the fungus lives in soil. Some infections take place aboveground through wounds caused by insects or by pruning and from wind-blown spores. In a recent survey in New Jersey the silver maple was found to be most frequently infected, with Norway, red, and sugar maple next.

Control: Trees showing general and severe infection by the wilt fungus cannot be saved. Recently infected trees exhibiting wilt on a few branches can be saved by liberal applications of a high nitrogenous soluble fertilizer early in the growing season. The heavy fertilization apparently stimulates leaf growth, which in turn enables the rapid formation of a thick layer of sapwood which seals in the infected parts beneath. Many cases of recovery have been noted after such a treatment.

Bleeding Canker (*Phytophthora cactorum*). This highly destructive disease was first reported from the New England States centering around Rhode Island. The author found the first case of this disease in New Jersey in October, 1940. The following kinds of trees are known to be susceptible: Norway, red, sycamore, and sugar maples as well as birch, elm, horse-chestnut, linden, oak, sweetgum, willow and American beech.

Oozing of sap from fissures overlying cankers in the bark is the most characteristic external symptom. Infected inner bark, cambium, and sapwood develop a reddish-brown necrotic lesion, which commonly has an olive-green margin. A secondary symptom, the wilting of the leaves and dying back of the branches, is due to a toxic material secreted by the causal fungus. The severity of the disease is in some way associated with hurricane damage.

Control: Mildly infected trees have been known to recover without any special treatment. No cure is known once a tree is heavily infected. Injection of various dyes and other chemicals into the trunk have not given consistently beneficial results.

Basal Canker (*Phytophthora cinnamomi*). The author determined that many Norway and other species of maple died in New Jersey some years ago from the effects of basal canker. The leaves of the infected trees are smaller and fewer and the crown is thinner. Cankers at the base of the trunk near the soil line are the most definite symptoms. The inner bark, cambium, and sapwood of the cankered areas are reddish-brown. Discoloration of the sapwood occurs mostly on the surface just below the bark. Trees that are completely girdled die. This may be easily confused with the bleeding canker disease.

Control: No effective control measures are known. Diseased trees should be removed and destroyed. New plantings of Norway maples should be made in well-drained soils, high in organic matter. Frost cracks and mechanical injuries near the base of the trunk should be properly treated and dressed, and trees fertilized and watered to maintain good vigor.

Nectria Canker (*Nectria cinnabarina*). Cankers appear on twigs and branches, and occasionally develop on the trunks to such an extent as to cause the death of the trees. Reddish fungus fruiting bodies develop in large numbers. Although the fungus is most common on maples and lindens, it attacks a wide variety of other hardwood trees. Another fungus, *Nectria ditissima,* causes the development of irregular cankers, accompanied by the formation of thick calluses, which later

become diseased and leave an open wound. Cankers should be cut out well beyond the diseased areas and the wounds protected by a good tree paint. The vigor of the trees should be increased by fertilization.

Boxelder and red and sugar maples occasionally show another type of canker, which differs strikingly from that produced by either of the nectria fungi. The cankers are irregularly circular and contain broad, slightly raised concentric rings of callus tissue. The cankered tissue is firmly attached to the wood with heavy, white to buff, fan-shaped wefts of fungus tissue under the bark near the margins. Tiny black fungus bodies are present in the centers of the old cankers. The fungus responsible for this type of canker is known as *Eutypella parasitica.* Other cankers may be caused by the following fungi: *Botryosphaeria dothidea, Cytospora* sp., *Fusarium solani, Nectria, galligena, Phomopsis acerina, Physalospora obtusa, Septobasidium fumigatum,* and *Valsa sordida.*

Control: Cankers on trunks can rarely be eradicated by surgical methods once they have become very extensive. Those on branches can be destroyed by removing and discarding the affected members. Removal of dead branches, avoidance of unnecessary injuries, and maintenance of trees in vigorous condition by fertilization and watering are probably the best means known of preventing canker formation.

Ganoderma Rot (*Ganoderma lucidum*). Rapid decline and death of many trees growing along city streets were found by the author to be due to this fungus. It forms large reddish fruit bodies with varnish-like coating at the base of the infected tree or on its surface roots (Fig. 102). Red maple and Norway maple appear to be most susceptible.

Control: No control is known for diseases of this type. Planting trees in deep, fertile soil, avoiding bark and root injuries, proper fertilization and watering will reduce chances of infection.

Fig. 102. *Ganoderma lucidum* fruiting at the base of a dying Norway maple.

Sapstreak (*Ceratocystis coerulescens*). This killing disease of sugar maples was first described by Dr. George Hepting of the U.S. Forest Service from North Carolina in 1944. It has since been reported from New England and the lake region of the Midwest. Typical symptoms include thinning crowns with undersized chlorotic foliage, followed by death of the tree. Sapstreak also affects tuliptree in woodlands.

Control: No effective control has been developed.

Trunk Decay. In New England sugar maples tapped for their sap are subject to a serious trunk decay caused by the fungus *Valsa leucostomoides.* In longitudinal section the affected areas appear as truncated cones with pale yellow centers bordered by deep olive or greenish-black streaks.

Control: Tap holes should be sprayed or painted with a fungicide at the time the spiles are pulled. The trees should be tapped on the diagonal or up and down the butts.

Physiological Disease

Maple Decline. Weakening and death of sugar maples along heavily traveled highways in the northeastern United States has been attributed to excessive use of salts (sodium and calcium chlorides) during the winter months.

Some recent studies at the University of Massachusetts revealed that a deficiency of nitrogen may also be involved in maple decline.

Girdling Roots. Many trees, particularly Norway, sugar and silver maples, are weakened and some are killed by the growth habit of certain of their roots. Such roots grow closely appressed to the main trunk or large laterals in such a way as to choke the members surrounded, much as does a wire left around a branch for a number of years. The choking action restricts the movement of nutrients in the trunk or in the strangled area of the large roots. When a large lateral root is severely girdled, the branches that depend on it for nutrients commonly show weak vegetative growth and may eventually die of starvation. If the taproot of a tree is severely girdled, the main branch leader may die back. As a rule, trees affected by girdling roots do not die suddenly, but become progressively weaker over a 5- or 10-year period despite good pruning and feeding practices.

Girdling roots which develop below ground level can often be detected by examining the trunk base. If the trunk ascends straight up from the ground, as it does when a soil fill has been made, or is slightly concave on one side, instead of showing a normal flare (swelling) or buttress at the soil line, then one can suspect a girdling root. Of course, digging the soil alongside the trunk should reveal whether the strangling member is present.

Trees growing along paved streets always suffer more from girdling roots than do those in open areas, and middle-aged or old trees more than younger ones.[6]

Treatment for Girdling Roots. If the girdling root has not yet seriously impaired the tree's chances of recovery, it should be severed with a chisel and mallet at its point of attachment to the trunk or large lateral root. A few inches should be cut from the severed end to prevent its reuniting with the member from which it was severed. Then the cut surfaces, on the trunk or main root and on the severed root itself, should be painted to hinder insect and fungus invasion. Finally the soil is replaced in its original position. If the tree has been considerably weakened, judicious pruning should be practiced and some good fertilizer applied.

Insects and Mites That Attack Leaves

Besides the leaf-eating insects described

[6] For details on how girdling roots develop and how they can be prevented from developing, refer to *Tree Maintenance*, 4th Ed. by P. P. Pirone, Oxford University Press, New York.

below, there are several others that attack maple leaves. These include the elm sawfly, *Cimbex americana;* brown-tail moth, *Nygmia phaeorrhoea;* gipsy moth, *Porthetria dispar,* in certain eastern states; white-marked tussock moth, *Hemerocampa leucostigma;* American dagger moth, *Acronicta americana* (Fig. 68); saddled prominent caterpillar, *Heterocampa guttivitta;* and the oriental moth, *Cnidocampa flavescens.* These are readily controlled by spraying with *Bacillus thuringiensis,* Imidan, Sevin, or methoxychlor. The cankerworms, *Paleacrita vernata* and *Alsophila pometaria,* also known as inch worms and measuring worms, and bagworms, *Thyridopteryx ephemeraeformis,* are also controlled in this way.

Forest Tent Caterpillar (*Malacosoma distria*). These caterpillars, bluish with a row of diamond-shaped, white spots along the back, feed individually on leaves of maple, birch, oak, and poplar, but do not form a tent in the forks of smaller branches as do the eastern tent caterpillars (*Malacosoma americanum*), which have a white stripe down the back. The egg masses look the same, about ½ inch long, completely surrounding the twig, and having a brown, varnished appearance. If possible these should be destroyed.

Control: Spray with *Bacillus thuringiensis,* Dylox, methoxychlor, or Sevin.

Greenstriped Mapleworm (*Anisota rubicunda*). These caterpillars are pale yellowish-green, 1½ inches long, with large black heads; the stripes along the back are alternately pale yellowish-green and dark green. The insects prefer the red and silver maples.

Control: They can be easily controlled by spraying in mid-June and mid-August with Sevin, or a mixture of malathion and methoxychlor.

Maple Leaf Cutter (*Paraclemensia acerifoliella*). Much defoliation of sugar maple and beech trees results from the work of this small caterpillar, which is about ¼ inch long. It cuts out small sections of the leaves and forms a case in which it hides while it feeds. It skeletonizes a ringlike portion, the center of which may fall out. Rake up and destroy all leaf litter in fall to kill the hibernating pupa, or apply Sevin to the foliage.

Japanese Leafhopper (*Orientus ishidae*). These insects cause a characteristic brown blotching with a bright yellow margin, which merges the green part of the leaf. See under *Corylus*.

Leafhopper (*Alebra albostriella*). The Norway maple may become seriously infested with these yellowish leafhoppers; they also cause swellings on the twigs by depositing eggs under the young bark.

Control: Spray in early spring with Sevin.

Leaf Stalk Borer (*Nepticula sercoptera*). Though these small borers more commonly infest the fruit of Norway maples, they may attack the leaf stalks in June. The borers tunnel in the stalks causing a black discoloration about ½ inch from the base. The lower end of the stalk is somewhat enlarged. These borers occasionally cause severe defoliation. The adult is a minute moth with spine-like hairs on the surface of its wings.

Control: Spray with a dormant miscible oil in early spring to destroy the cocoons. If this is not done, spray with methoxychlor in the latter part of May.

Petiole Borer (*Caulocampus acericaulis*). This yellowish, smooth sawfly larva causes leaf fall of sugar maple. It tunnels in the upper end of the leaf stalk about ½ inch from the blade. The leaf blades fall off in May and June and sometimes the leaf stalk itself falls. Only the leaves of the lower branches are usually seriously infested.

Control: Malathion or methoxychlor sprays as the leaves open in May may help to control this pest.

Bladder-Gall Mite (*Vasates quadripedes*). The upper surfaces of maple leaves are often covered with small, green, wart-like galls, which later turn blood-red. These are caused by the feeding of this mite. If the galls are very numerous, the leaves become deformed.

Control: Spray with dormant oil plus ethion in late April. Kelthane spray in the spring when the buds show green color and again 2 weeks later should also protect the foliage.

Ocellate Leaf Gall (*Cecidomyia ocellaris*). These galls are less than ½ inch in diameter, with cherry-red margins; they are easily confused with the purple-eye leaf spot. They occur on red maple but are usually not injurious. The little maggots, which may be seen at the center of the spot, soon drop off. Little damage is done.

Other Galls. Other maple galls are caused by other mites (*Phyllocoptes aceris-crumena*, and *Eriophyes acericola*). The galls are about ⅕ inch long, tapering at both ends (fusiform). They develop on the upper side of the leaf and when numerous render the foliage unsightly. Spray with lime sulfur at blossom time, or with Kelthane in early June.

Several other species of *Eriophyes* and *Phyllocoptes* produce large blotches along the veins or between them. Brilliant purple, red, or pink minute blister-like or pile-like growths are due to the mites. A dormant strength lime sulfur spray just before leaf buds open, or a Kelthane spray when the buds show green color, is recommended for these mites.

Norway-Maple Aphid (*Periphyllus lyropictus*). The leaves of Norway maple are subject to heavy infestation by these hairy aphids, which are greenish with brown markings. Like other aphids, they secrete large amounts of honeydew. The leaves attacked become badly wrinkled, discolored, and reduced in size. Defoliation may follow. Several other species, including *Drepanaphis acerifoli, Periphyllus aceris,* and *P. negundinis,* also occur on maples. Spray in early summer with malathion, being careful to cover the underside of the leaves.

Boxelder Bug (*Leptocoris trivittatus*).

The leaves of boxelder are injured by the sucking of young bright red bugs. The adult stage is a stout, ¹/₂ inch long, grayish-black bug with three red lines on the back. All stages of this pest are clustered on the bark and branches in the early fall.

Control: Spray bark with Sevin when clusters of bugs appear in late May or early June. Because this bug feeds on seeds of pistillate (female) trees, one should plant only staminate (male) trees. To control this pest when it comes indoors, spray or paint with methoxyclor or Cythion into cracks and surfaces where the bugs hide.

Maple Trumpet Skeletonizer (*Epinotia aceriella*). Red and sugar maple leaves are folded loosely by small green larvae which develop inside a long trumpet-like tube.

Control: Methoxychlor, Sevin, or Diazinon sprays applied in mid-July will control this pest.

Scale Insects

Maple Phenacoccus (*Phenacoccus acericola*). The leaves of sugar maple may be covered on the under side by the cottony masses that envelop the females in July, as is well shown in Fig. 103. The males collect in the crevices of the bark and give it a white, chalky appearance. There are several generations a year. Predacious insects feed on the eggs of this scale.

Control: Spray with Diazinon or malathion in spring just as the buds burst. Repeat the spray in early August.

Cottony Maple Scale (*Pulvinaria innumerabilis*). Silver maples are especially susceptible to infestation by this scale. Smaller branches are often covered with large white cushion-like masses. The scale itself is brown, from ¹/₈ to ¹/₄ inch in diameter; the whole mass is about ¹/₂ inch in diameter. The cottony mass may contain as many as 500 eggs in June. The young move out and infest the leaves; later they migrate to the branches, being found especially on their undersides.

Fig. 103. Maple phenacoccus (*Phenacoccus acericola*) on sugar maple leaf.

Control: Spray with lime sulfur in early spring when the trees are dormant. Malathion or Sevin sprays may be applied during midsummer when the young are crawling.

Other Scales. Several other scales attack maples. Among them are the terrapin scale (*Lecanium nigrofasciatum*), gloomy scale (*Chrysomphalus tenebricosus*), and Japanese scale (*Leucaspis japonica*). These may be controlled by spraying with dormant miscible oil, or lime sulfur. The latter is safer. Malathion, Diazinon, or Sevin are most effective when the young scales are crawling.

Wood Borers

Limbs infested with borers are the first to break after a heavy snow storm or after they have been coated with ice (Figs. 28 and 29). Five or six species of wood-boring insects infest maples.

Flatheaded Borer (*Chrysobothris femorata*). Trees in poor vigor are attacked by this light yellow larva, 1 inch long, which builds flattened galleries below the bark, often girdling the tree. The adult is a dark coppery-brown beetle, ¹/₂ inch in length, which deposits eggs in bark crevices in June and July. The pest overwinters underneath the bark in the larval stage.

Control: Increase the tree's vigor by feeding and watering, or protect recently transplanted trees with crepe wrapping paper. Spray the trunk and branches with methoxychlor in mid-May and repeat twice more at 2-week intervals. Borers active in the trees can be killed by inserting a flexible wire into the borer holes.

Sugarmaple Borer (*Glycobius speciosus*) becomes evident through the occurrence of dead limbs among leafy branches or by dead areas on the branches and trunks.

Control: Methoxychlor spray applied to the trunk and branches in mid-August will control this pest.

Pigeon Tremex (*Tremex columba*) bores round exit holes about 1/4 inch in diameter. The larvae usually attack trees which are in a dying condition because of the attacks of fungi or other species of borers.

Control: Insert Bortox into the burrows and seal the openings.

Leopard Moth Borer (*Zeuzera pyrina*). This brown-headed borer is white or slightly pinkish and marked by blackish spots on the body. Full-grown borers may be 3 inches long and nearly 1/2 inch in diameter. They winter in the tunnel they make. Besides their cylindrical burrows they make wide cavities which so weaken the limbs that they break off very readily. Soft maples are especially susceptible.

Control: Preventive treatments include spraying the trunk and main branches with methoxychlor in late May and repeating four times at 2-week intervals. On valuable young trees that are already infested, the boring caterpillars can be killed by inserting into their tunnels a flexible wire or pastes containing nicotine or a few drops of carbon disulfide, and then sealing the openings with putty or chewing gum.

Metallic Borer (*Dicerca divaricata*). The larvae of these brass- or copper-colored beetles frequently invade the limbs of peach, cherry, beech, maple, and other deciduous trees. The beetles live 2 or 3 years as borers in the trees and lay their eggs in August and September. The adults have been known to cause much defoliation.

Control: Infested limbs should be cut and discarded to destroy the grubs before the adult beetles emerge to lay their eggs.

Twig Pruner. (*Elaphidionoides villosus*). This pest attacks many shade and fruit trees in addition to oaks, cutting off twigs which fall to the ground. The larvae are found inside the fallen twigs in July.

Control: Gather and destroy the fallen twigs in July, August, and early September; otherwise the larvae will overwinter in them.

Carpenter Worm. See *Robinia*.

Linden Looper. See *Tilia*.

Whitefly. See *Abutilon*.

Other Pests

Squirrels. The red squirrel (*Tamiasciurus hudsonicus*) bites the bark of young red and sugar maples to drink the sap that flows from the wounds. Cankers develop as a result of fungi which enter the wounds made by the squirrels' teeth.

Nemas. Dieback of sugar maples in woodland areas of Wisconsin has been associated with heavy infestations of several species of root nemas. In Massachusetts the dagger nema *Xiphinema americanum* is associated with a decline of sugar maples.

Control: Controls have not been developed.

ACHILLEA (YARROW)

Diseases

Crown Gall (*Agrobacterium tumefaciens*). This disease, more common on members of the rose family, occasionally occurs on *Achillea*.

Control: Discard infected plants. Set new plants in steam-pasteurized soil.

Powdery Mildew (*Erysiphe cichoracearum*). A white coating occasionally develops on the leaves.

Control: Karathane or wettable sulfur sprays will curb this disease.

Stem Rot (*Pellicularia filamentosa*). A decay of the stem base results from invasion by this fungus, more popularly known as *Rhizoctonia solani*.

Control: Use clean plants in steam-pasteurized soil or in soil treated with PCNB (Terraclor).

Rust (*Puccinia millefolii*). This disease is of rare occurrence.

Control: Spray with a ferbam-sulfur mixture.

ACONITUM (MONK'S HOOD)

Diseases

Crown Rot (*Sclerotium delphinii*). This fungus also attacks delphinium and certain other garden plants. It causes both crown and root rot of *Aconitum*. The fungus enters the crown at the soil line and invades the main roots. It causes black streaks in the water-conducting regions of the stems and the roots. The plants turn yellow, wilt, and fall over. For control see under *Delphinium*.

Stem Rot (*Sclerotinia sclerotiorum*,[7] *Pellicularia filamentosa* and *Botrytis* sp.). These fungi occasionally cause stem decay.

Control: Infested soils should be discarded and replaced with fresh soil, or they should be steam-pasteurized or treated with one of the chemicals discussed in Chapter 4.

Wilt (*Verticillium albo-atrum* and *Cephalosporium* sp.). These fungi are frequently associated with the wilt disease. The former causes drying of leaves, poor flowers, and a

blackening of the vascular tissues in the stem. The latter produces somewhat similar symptoms except that general wilting does not occur until blossoming time. The two causal organisms can be differentiated only by laboratory isolation tests.

Control: Same as for stem rot.

Bacterial Leaf Spot (*Pseudomonas delphinii*). This bacterial parasite occasionally attacks *Aconitum*. See under *Delphinium* for control measures.

Rust (*Puccinia recondita* var. *agropyri*). See *Aquilegia*.

Insects

Four-Lined Plant Bug (*Poecilocapsus lineatus*). Dark, depressed spots in the leaves are produced by this insect.

Control: Spray with Sevin when the young nymphs appear.

Larkspur Leaf Miner (*Phytomyza delphinivora*). Tan to brown blotches in the leaves are caused by the larval stage of this small fly.

Control: Remove and discard infested leaves. Spray with Diazinon or malathion in spring when the flies are about.

Cyclamen Mite (*Steneotarsonemus pallidus*). This mite deforms the leaves and flowers on *Aconitum* as well as many other plants.

Control: Spray the young plants with Dimite or Kelthane early in the growing season and repeat several times at 10-day intervals.

ACTINIDIA (SILVER-VINE)

While this host is not usually attacked by pests and diseases in propagating beds, a damping-off of young plants by *Pellicularia filamentosa* is occasionally injurious. *Actinidia* is sometimes badly infected with the powdery mildew fungus, *Uncinula necator*. To prevent its spread, spray with Karathane or wettable sulfur.

[7] See footnote page 48

The greenhouse orthezia, *Orthezia insignis*, sometimes infests this vine. Spray with malathion or Sevin in the spring when the young scales are crawling about. Silver-vine is very attractive to cats and is often destroyed if not protected by screens. Cat-repelling materials, available in garden supply stores, are also effective.

AESCULUS HIPPOCASTANUM (HORSE-CHESTNUT)

Diseases

Leaf Blotch (*Guignardia aesculi*). This fungus disease is very serious in nurseries, where it often causes complete defoliation of the stock. The spots may be small or so large they include nearly all the leaf. At first they are merely discolored and water-soaked in appearance; later they turn a light reddish-brown with a very bright yellow marginal zone. When the whole leaf is infected it becomes dry and brittle and usually falls. The small black specks seen in the center of the spot are the fruiting bodies of the imperfect stage of the fungus. The leaf stalks are also attacked. This leaf blotch is very similar to scorch, often seen on shade trees along streets and in city parks. The two diseases can be distinguished by the small, black, pimple-like fruiting bodies on the leaf blotch caused by the fungus. The fungus lives over winter on the old leaves where it has produced its perfect stage. The ascospores are the means by which the fungus is spread in the spring. The first signs of infection may not appear until some time in July.

Control: Old leaves under diseased trees should be raked up and destroyed in fall. In the spring trees should be given a dormant spray of commercial lime sulfur. This kills the ascospores that may have lodged in the crevices of the bark and on the buds, and at the same time may destroy certain scale insects that infest the horse-chestnut. Spray with Cyprex, Fore, or zineb 2 to 4 times at 10-day intervals starting after the buds open. The total number of applications is governed by the weather. The disease is always more severe during very wet springs.

Leaf Spot (*Septoria hippocastani*). Small brown circular spots occasionally develop on the leaves of this host. The slender spores may be seen when the fruiting structures are observed under the microscope.

Control: The sprays recommended for leaf blotch will also control this fungus.

Powdery Mildew (*Uncinula flexuosa*). This disease is prevalent in the Middle West, where the undersides of leaves frequently are covered with white mold. The fruiting bodies of the winter stage of the fungus appear as small black dots over the mold.

Control: Spray trees with wettable sulfur or Karathane a few times at weekly intervals starting when the mildew appears.

Wound Rot (*Collybia velutipes*). The fungus enters through wounds and destroys the wood, later forming clusters of mushroom-like fruiting bodies. It is one of the fungi which may be found during the winter months still attached to the trees. The fruiting bodies have dark brown, velvety stalks.

Control: Remove limbs that have been killed by this rot, and cover the cut surface to prevent the entrance of spores into the wound.

Anthracnose (*Glomerella cingulata*). Terminal shoots become blighted down to several inches below the buds. Diseased tissue is shrunken and the epidermis and young bark are ruptured; pustules are formed containing the pink spores of the anthracnose.

Control: Spray with Fore or ziram as for leaf blotch.

Canker (*Nectria cinnabarina*). This disease is said to attack the branches and to cause much defoliation of old trees.

Control: Remove and destroy diseased branches. Spray 2 or 3 times at 10-day intervals with ziram, starting when the new growth appears.

Other Diseases. Horse-chestnut is susceptible to two stem diseases: wilt caused by *Verticillium albo-atrum* and bleeding canker by *Phytophthora cactorum.* These are discussed under more favored hosts.

Leaf Scorch (Nonparasitic). Some horse-chestnut trees are susceptible to nonparasitic leaf scorch. The scorching of leaves usually becomes evident in July or August. First the margins of the leaves become brown and curled. Within 2 or 3 weeks the scorch may extend over the entire leaf. Some claim that scorch is more prevalent in dry seasons, but serious injury also has been observed in wet seasons. Trees that are prone to scorch will show symptoms every year regardless of the kind of weather.

Control: Prune susceptible trees and provide them with good growing conditions. Feed and water when necessary. The application of an antidesiccant such as Wilt-Pruf NCF or Foli-Guard after the leaves are fully expanded may be helpful.

Insect Pests

Walnut Scale (*Quadraspidiotus juglansregiae*). This is a round saucer-shaped scale with a raised point in the center; it is about $1/16$ inch in diameter. Certain trees are more susceptible than others to infestation by this scale. The main trunks are most seriously attacked. Several layers of the scales collect in cracks and under the bark. They winter in a half-grown stage.

Many other scales also attack horse-chestnuts. Among these are the cottony maple, maple phenacoccus, oystershell, Putnam, and scurfy scales.

Control: In spring when the temperature is well above freezing and while the tree is still dormant, spray with miscible oil, Malathion and Sevin are also effective in late spring and early summer when the young scales are crawling about.

Comstock Mealybug (*Pseudococcus com-*

stocki). This small, elliptical, waxy-covered insect attacks umbrella catalpa primarily, but it is also found on apple, boxwood, holly, horse-chestnut, magnolia, maples, osage-orange, poplar, and Monterey pine. After hatching in late May, the young crawl up the trunk to the leaves, where they suck out the juices and devitalize the tree. Twigs, leaves, and trunks may be distorted as a result of heavy infestations. The eggs winter in bark crevices or in large masses hanging to the twigs.

Control: Malathion or Sevin sprays in May and June are effective in controlling the crawler stage of this pest.

White-Marked Tussock Moth (*Hemerocampa leucostigma*). Among the caterpillars that infest park and streetside trees will be found the tussock moth caterpillar, recognizable by its red head and its yellow body with black marks and four tufts of hairs. The mature caterpillars are from $1/2$ to 2 inches long. Late in summer, after the caterpillars have stopped feeding, they may be found crawling rapidly over the limbs and trunks toward the places where they pupate. The egg masses, which live through winter, are $1/2$ inch long and are covered with a white frothy substance. The young hatch in May and can do considerable damage before they are discovered. There are usually two generations a year.

Control: During the days when they are feeding, the caterpillars can be controlled by spraying the trees with *Bacillus thuringiensis,* Dylox, methoxychlor, or Sevin. The egg-masses are plainly visible and can be collected and destroyed in the fall and winter.

Japanese Beetle (*Popillia japonica*). During the bright hot days of July and August the leaves of the horse-chestnut are the preferred food of the Japanese beetle, especially the leaves at the top and on the south side of the tree. The attacks are more or less sudden and the top of the tree may quickly appear scorched. The large veins of the leaves are about all that is left after the beetles have done their work.

Control: Early in July when the beetles become numerous, spray with Diazinon, methoxychlor, or Sevin, as recommended by the manufacturer.

Bagworm. See *Abies.*

Flat-Headed Borer. See *Acer.*

AGAVE (CENTURY PLANT)

Diseases

Anthracnose (*Glomerella cingulata*). This disease appears as circular depressed dark-colored spots up to 1 inch in diameter bordered by a raised ring. The spots may run together so that the entire leaf may be destroyed.

Control: Remove affected leaves and destroy them to prevent further spread of the disease. Spray plants with a copper fungicide to which a sticker-spreader has been added.

Leaf Spot (*Coniothyrium concentricum*). This fungus causes characteristically zoned light grayish-brown spots, reaching 1 inch or more in diameter. On them in concentric rings are large numbers of small black fruiting bodies, in which are formed the light brown spores that spread the disease. Large portions of the leaves may be destroyed. Another species, *C. agaves,* also causes a blotching and spotting of *Agave* leaves.

Control: The same as for anthracnose.

Leaf Blight (*Botrytis cinerea* and *Stagonospora gigantea*). These fungi occasionally cause complete blighting of leaves following overwatering and chilling.

Control: The same as for anthracnose.

Insects

Scales (*Aspidiotus nerii, Aonidiella aurantii,* and *Pinnaspis strachani*). These three scales frequently infest the century plant.

Control: Occasional applications of nicotine sulfate sprays will control the crawler stage of these pests.

Other Insects. The stalk borer *Papaipema nebris,* the larval stage of the yucca moth *Tegeticula yuccasella,* the dracaena thrips *Heliothrips dracaenae,* and the yucca weevil *Scyphophorus yuccae,* occasionally attack the century plant.

Control: Nicotine sulfate sprays applied when the insects are in their vulnerable stages should provide control.

AGERATUM (MIST FLOWER)

Diseases

Root Rot (*Pellicularia filamentosa* and *Pythium mamillatum*). The former fungus causes a root and stem rot of *Ageratum* in the East and Middle West, the latter a root rot in California.

Control: Use clean soil or treat infested soil with steam.

Rust (*Puccinia conoclinii*). This disease has been reported from several southern states. It is of minor importance.

Insects and Related Pests

Corn Earworm (*Heliothis zea*). This common pest of the vegetable garden is also injurious to a number of ornamental plants. The larvae feed on the foliage and buds and tunnel into the stems.

Control: Spray with a mixture of Sevin and Kelthane. The latter material is included to curb mites.

Tobacco Budworm (*Heliothis virescens*). Tiny rusty to green, striped caterpillars eat holes in buds and unfolded leaves of *Ageratum* and many other garden and ornamental plants.

Control: Same as for corn earworm.

Greenhouse Leaf Tier (*Udea rubigalis*). These caterpillars tie leaves together with strands of silk and then feed inside the tied leaves.

Control: Spray with Sevin before the caterpillars have the protection of the tied leaves.

Greenhouse Whitefly (*Trialeurodes vaporariorum*). *Ageratum* is particularly subject to great damage by this sucking insect, which also secretes masses of honeydew.

Control: See *Fuchsia.*

Cyclamen Mite (*Steneotarsonemus pallidus*). In propagating houses young cuttings are very susceptible to attacks by these mites.

Control: Mites may be controlled by spraying with any good miticide such as Dimite or Kelthane. Aerosols containing effective miticides are also available. Some miticides are not safe on all crops. Check with the label or the manufacturer before using them on a large scale.

AGLAONEMA (CHINESE EVERGREEN)

Diseases

Leaf Spot and Leaf Blight (*Xanthomonas dieffenbachiae* and *Erwinia carotovora* var. *aroideae*). In Florida the former causes a leaf spot followed by a blight. The latter then enters to cause complete collapse of the leaves.

Control: No controls have been developed, but copper fungicides or antibiotics might help to keep this disease under control.

Soft Rot (*Erwinia chrysanthemi*). A soft rot of leaves of *Aglaonema pictum* occurs in Florida nurseries.

Control: Measures to combat this disease have not been developed.

Root and Stem Rot (*Pellicularia filamentosa* and *Pythium splendens*). These two fungi are frequently responsible for a root and stem rot of this host, particularly in the South.

Control: Set healthy plants in clean or pasteurized soil. Old canes that are to be used for propagation and that are suspected of harboring the causal fungi should be dipped in hot water at 120°F. for 30 minutes, then cooled and planted.

Anthracnose (*Colletotrichum* sp.). This disease was found for the first time in the United States in 1957 on greenhouse-grown *Aglaonema* in the state of Washington.

Control: Avoid excessive and frequent wetting of the foliage. Spray with a copper fungicide, if necessary.

Nemas (*Pratylenchus musicola*). Eelworms commonly infest the roots of Chinese evergreens in Florida.

Control: A nemacide such as Mobilawn or Nemagon is suggested for trial by commercial growers.

AILANTHUS (TREE-OF-HEAVEN)

Diseases

Wilt (*Verticillium albo-atrum*). This is the most destructive disease of this host. Young trees in parks and ornamental plantings wilt, the leaves turn yellow and fall prematurely, and the tree then dies.

Control: No effective control of the disease on this host has been developed.

Shoestring Root Rot (*Armillaria mellea*). This disease is second in importance as a killer of *Ailanthus.* It enters through the roots or through injuries at the trunk base.

Control: No control measures are known.

Leaf Spots (*Cercospora glandulosa, Phyllosticta ailanthi,* and *Gloeosporium ailanthi*). Leaves are spotted by these fungi.

Control: Control measures are never undertaken for leaf spots on this host.

Twig Blight (*Fusarium lateritium*). A blighting of twigs may occur during very rainy springs as a result of infection by this fungus. The perfect stage of this fungus is *Gibberella baccata.*

Control: No control measures are necessary.

Other Diseases. Other fungus diseases causing dieback or cankers of *Ailanthus* include *Botryosphaeria dothidea, Cytospora* *ailanthi, Coniothyrium insitivum, Nectria coccinea, Physalospora obtusa,* and *P. rhodina.*

Insects

Cynthia Moth (*Samia cynthia*). The larvae of this moth can completely defoliate a tree-of-heaven in a few days. Mature larvae are 3½ inches long, light green, and covered with a glaucous bloom. The adult moth is beautifully colored and has a wingspread of 6 to 8 inches. A crescent-shaped, white marking is present in the center of each of the grayish-brown wings.

Control: Spray with methoxychlor or Sevin in June when the caterpillars begin to chew the leaves.

Ailanthus Webworm (*Atteva punctella*). Olive-brown caterpillars with five white lines feed in webs on the leaves in August and September. Adult moths have bright orange forewings, with four cross-bands of yellow spots on a dark blue ground.

Control: Spray with methoxychlor or Sevin when the young larvae appear in August.

Other Insects. Among other caterpillars which attack this host, particularly in cities, are the fall webworm, *Hyphantria cunea,* and the white-marked tussock moth, *Hemerocampa leucostigma.* Another species, the pale tussock moth, *Halisidota tessellaris,* attacks a wide variety of deciduous trees. These are controlled with methoxychlor or Sevin sprays.

Oystershell scale and citrus whitefly occasionally infest *Ailanthus.* Their controls are given under more favored hosts.

AJUGA (BUGLE-WEED)

Crown Rot (*Sclerotium delphinii*). This is the only serious disease of this host. It is especially destructive in plantings set in poorly drained sites. Large patches may be destroyed within the first few warm, humid days of spring (Fig. 104). The causal organ-

Fig. 104. Crown rot *(Sclerotium delphinii)* in a bed of *Ajuga.*

ism and its control are discussed in greater detail under *Delphinium.*

ALBIZIA (SILK TREE)

Diseases

Wilt (*Fusarium oxysporum* var. *perniciosum*). Silk tree, *Albizia julibrissin,* also known as mimosa, is subject to this highly destructive disease which is extremely prevalent from Maryland to Florida and along the Gulf Coast into Louisiana. The author was first to find it in New Jersey some years ago and at the New York Botanical Garden more recently. Symptoms of the disease are rather striking. The leaves wilt, tend to hang down from the twig, and become dry and shriveled, although they may remain green or yellowish for some time. Later the leaves fall and the branch dies. Brown discoloration is evident in the sapwood. The same discoloration is found in trunks and branches even before the leaves wilt. Discolored areas may appear as complete rings. Large numbers of spores are formed in lenticels on the trunk and branches of affected trees, at times even before actual wilting of the leaves occurs. Such spores may account for widespread outbreaks of the disease.

The causal fungus can be carried over in seed collected from diseased trees.

Control: Dead and dying trees should be cut down and destroyed to avoid the spread of the disease. Some nurseries offer wilt-resistant clones of mimosa, developed by U.S. Department of Agriculture pathologists. Two such clones are sold under the names Tryon and Charlotte. The former has light-colored flowers, and the latter, deeper red ones.

Other Fungi. Several other fungi are reported on this host. *Nectria cinnabarina* causes dieback and canker; *Coniothyrium insitivum* and a species of *Phomopsis* damage the twigs; and *Thyronectria austroamericana* is weakly pathogenic to twigs. The last is more destructive to honey locust. *Ganoderma curtisii* is associated with a root rot of this host.

Insects and Other Pests

Webworm (*Homadaula anisocentra*). The larvae of this pest appear on the foliage in early spring. They are also highly destructive to honey locust. The larvae are $3/5$ inch long when full grown and are gray-brown, sometimes pinkish, with five narrow white lengthwise stripes. At first they feed together in a web, but later spread throughout the tree, tying the leaves in conspicuous masses and skeletonizing them. When mature, they drop to the ground on silken threads and spin cocoons in various kinds of cracks and crevices. The moths, gray with a wingspread of about $1/2$ inch, appear in June to lay eggs on the silk tree flowers and leaves.

Control: When the young caterpillars are just beginning to feed, spray with Sevin or Diazinon. The spraying must be repeated several times, because there are as many as 4 generations of this pest in some areas.

Lesser Snow Scale (*Pinnaspis strachani*). This white, semitransparent scale occasionally infests silk trees in addition to avocado, citrus, hackberry, palms, and other trees and shrubs in the deep South.

Six other species of scales infest *Albizia*.

Control: Spray with malathion, Meta-Systox R, or Sevin when the young are crawling about.

Other Insects. Blister beetles and mealybugs also infest this host.

Nemas (*Meloidogyne arenaria* and *Trichodorus primitivus*). The former, known as the peanut root-knot nema, causes small knots or galls on silk trees in the South. The latter, known as the stubby root nema, infests *Albizia julibrissin* roots in Maryland and azaleas in California.

Control: See nemas in Chapter 3.

ALETRIS (STAR-GRASS)

A leaf spot caused by the fungus *Gloeosporium aletridis* and rust by *Puccinia aletridis* are the only diseases recorded on *Aletris*. Neither is destructive enough to require control measures.

ALLIUM (ONION)

Bulb Rot (*Sclerotium cepivorum*). *Allium unifolium* and other ornamental species of this genus are subject to a bulb rot caused by *Sclerotium cepivorum.* The rot resembles that of *Galanthus* caused by *Botrytis galanthina.* The flower stalk fails to develop and the shoot and bulb become covered with a white mold. When bulbs of *Allium* are planted in pots, the tips of the first leaves become yellow and finally brown. The bulbs and root system are eventually covered with a mat of mycelial growth, on which appear small black sclerotia, each the size of a pinhead or smaller. Sclerotia can be easily observed under a hand lens.

Control: Select bulbs on which no sclerotia are visible. Rogue all plants that show any sign of the disease. Destroy decaying bulbs. It is important not to throw infected parts in the compost pile, for the parasite can remain alive in such debris and infect other plants of *Allium* and other genera; *Galanthus, Scilla,* and *Sternbergia* may be susceptible.

ALNUS (ALDER)

Fungus Diseases

Leaf Curl (*Taphrina macrophylla*). The leaves of red alders grow to several times their normal size, are curled and distorted, and turn a decided purple when affected by this disease. Infection is apparent on the leaves as soon as they appear in the spring.

The other species, *T. amentorium, T. occidentalis,* and *T. robinsoniana,* are known to cause enlargement and distortion of the scales of female catkins. These project as curled, reddish tongues, which are soon covered with a white glistening layer of fungus tissue.

Control: Spray the trees in late fall or while they are still dormant in the spring with lime sulfur. This will destroy most of the spores, which overwinter in the bud scales and on the twigs, and which are largely responsible for early infections. Sprays are suggested only for valuable specimens.

Powdery Mildew. Several species of powdery mildew fungi attack the female catkins of alder. The most common, *Erysiphe aggregata,* develops as a white powdery coating over the catkin. Two other species, *Microsphaera alni* and *Phyllactinia corylea,* occur less frequently.

Control: These fungi rarely cause enough damage to warrant control measures. Where justified, Karathane sprays will give control.

Canker. A number of fungi cause cankers and dieback of the branches. Among the most common are *Nectria coccinea, Solenia anomala,* and *Physalospora obtusa.* Trunk cankers may also be caused by *Diatrypella oregonensis, Hymenochaete agglutinans,* and *Didymosphaeria oregonensis.*

Control: No simple control measures are known. Cankered branches should be pruned to sound wood and the trees fed and watered to increase their vigor.

Leaf Rust (*Melampsoridium hiratsukanum*). Some damage is done to alder leaves by this rust, which breaks out in small yellowish pustules on the leaves during the summer. The leaves later turn dark brown. It is suspected that the alternate host of this rust is a conifer. The disease is never severe enough to justify control measures.

Insects

Woolly Alder Aphid (*Prociphilus tessellatus*). The downward folding of leaves, in which are found large woolly masses covering bluish-black aphids, is typical of this pest. Eggs are deposited in bark crevices and pass the winter in these locations. Maples are also infested by this species.

Control: Malathion or Meta-Systox R sprays when the young begin to develop in spring give excellent control.

Alder Flea Beetle (*Altica ambiens*). The leaves are chewed during July and August by dark brown larvae with black heads. The adult, a greenish-blue beetle ⅕ inch long, deposits orange eggs on the leaves in spring.

Control: Sevin sprays when the larvae begin to feed will control this heavy feeder.

Alder Lace Bug. (*Corythucha pergandei*). This species infests not only alder, but occasionally birch, elm and crabapple.

Control: Spray with malathion or Sevin in late spring.

Alder Psyllid (*Psylla floccosa*). This sucking insect is common on alders in the northeastern United States. The nymphal stages produces large amounts of wax. When massed on the stems, the psyllids resemble piles of cotton.

Control: Spray with malathion when the nymphs or adults are seen.

ALOE
Diseases

Root Rot (*Pythium ultimum*). In California this disease is especially serious on young nursery-grown plants of *Aloe variegata.*

Control: Clean debris from infected plants. Then kill the fungus by immersing the plants in hot water at 115 degrees F. for 20 to 40 minutes, depending on the size of the plants. Replant treated plants in clean soil.

Insects

Scales (*Aonidiella aurantii, Aspidiotus nerii, Coccus hesperidum,* and *Saissetia hemisphaerica*). Four species of scale are known to infest this host.

Control: Spray weekly with nicotine sulfate and soap or Sevin until the infestation is cleaned up. Malathion sprays will also control the crawling stage of scales, but they sometimes damage succulent plants.

ALOYSIA[8] (LEMON-VERBENA)
Diseases

Leaf Spots (*Cercospora lippiae* and *Cylindrosporium lippiae*). The former fungus is rather prevalent over the country, the latter has been reported only from Texas.

Control: Leaf spots on this host are rarely serious enough to warrant control measures.

Other Diseases. Lemon-verbena is also subject to anthracnose caused by *Sphaceloma lippiae,* black mildew by *Meliola lippiae,* blight by *Pellicularia rolfsii,* and root rot by *Phymatotrichum omnivorum.*

The only other problem on this host is the southern root-knot nema, *Meloidogyne incognita.*

ALSINE—see ARENARIA

ALTERNANTHERA[9]

Leaf Blight (*Phyllosticta amaranthi*). This fungus has been reported to cause a blight on leaves which makes them curl up and fall away, leaving the stems bare. In mild cases brown spots appear on one side of the leaf.

Control: Spraying with a copper fungicide or with sulfur has been suggested.

Root Rot (*Pellicularia filamentosa*). Cuttings and young plants grown in the greenhouse are sometimes attacked by this fungus.

Control: Use steam-pasteurized soil or treat soil with PCNB (Terraclor).

Wilt (*Fusarium oxysporum*). This disease is known to cause a wilt of garden varieties of *Alternanthera.* For control, see *Callistephus.*

[8] Formerly Lippia.
[9] Formerly known as Telanthera.

Southern Root-Knot Nema (*Meloidogyne incognita*). This nema attacks plants in greenhouses in the northern states and outdoor plants in the southern states.

Control: See Chapter 3 for control measures.

ALTHAEA (HOLLYHOCK)

Fungus Diseases

Anthracnose (*Colletotrichum malvarum*). This disease has been very destructive to hollyhocks, sometimes destroying most of the crop. Seedlings are especially susceptible, and plants in greenhouses are the most subject to the disease; high temperature and humidity favor the parasite. It attacks the lower part of the stem and invades the roots. See under leaf spots for effects on the foliage of older plants.

Control: Spray the plants with Benlate after periods of wet weather. Clean culture includes the destruction of any wild mallows in the vicinity which are found to harbor this disease.

Rust (*Puccinia malvacearum*). Several species of the mallow family are subject to infection by rust parasites and may limit the use of hollyhocks as ornamentals. Leaves, stems, bracts, and other green parts are subject to infection. Small brown spots about the size of a pinhead develop on the under sides of leaves and are seen on the upper sides as larger, bright yellow or orange spots with reddish centers. The spots may be so numerous as to run together and thus destroy large portions of the leaf, which later fall out. During rainy weather or when nights are dewy, the rust pustules (Fig. 105) are often ash-gray in color.

Fig. 105. Hollyhock rust pustules, caused by *Puccinia malvacearum*, on the lower surface of a hollyhock leaf.

Control: Remove and destroy the first leaves on which the rust is evident. Frequent spraying of the plants with wettable sulfur, zineb, or Fore is effective. Two or three applications a week may be necessary, since new leaves develop rapidly, and it is essential to have a fungicide present on these new leaves as early as possible. Seedlings should be thoroughly sprayed with zineb, Fore, or wettable sulfur as soon as infection is detected. Unless the treatment is continued after the seedlings have been planted out, later infection will be serious. As soon as the flowering season is over, the plants should be cut back to the base and the old parts destroyed, all fragments of leaves and fruits that may have harbored the rust being carefully gathered. Evidently the rust fungus can live over on these fragments, since young seedlings developed in cold frames are very often heavily infected.

Leaf Spots (species of *Cercospora, Ascochyta, Phyllosticta,* and *Alternaria*). Several species of fungi cause spotting of the leaves. The *Cercospora* leaf spots (*C. althaeae*) are more or less angular grayish spots, scattered irregularly over the leaf. The dead tissue often falls out, leaving a sort of "shot-hole" effect. With a hand lens one can usually see the very small fruiting bodies of the fungi which cause these leaf spots. Anthracnose (*Colletotrichum malvarum*) may attack all parts of seedlings in the greenhouse, often causing great losses.

Control: These parasitic fungi live over winter on plant parts infected the previous season; unless such debris is removed and destroyed, the fungus develops in the spring and continues the infection. Spraying the plants with Bordeaux mixture or Fore is an effective control against leaf spots.

Stem Rot. See *Viola.*

Insects and Related Pests

Potato Leafhopper (*Empoascus fabae*). This leafhopper causes injury similar to leafhopper burn on dahlias and potatoes. The leaves curl upward at the tips and large areas become brown and dried out; at first a yellow band borders the brown area. Half of the leaf may be killed. The insect is wedge-shaped, light green, about $1/8$ inch long. It feeds on the under sides of the leaves.

Control: As soon as the first symptoms appear, spray the plants with a Sevin-Kelthane mixture.

Japanese Beetle (*Popillia japonica*). In the regions subject to infestation by this insect, hollyhocks are the plants most often attacked during the blooming season.

Control: See *Aesculus.*

Abutilon Moth (*Anomis erosa*) also infests hollyhocks. See *Abutilon.* If leaf-eating caterpillars are troublesome, spray with Sevin.

Hollyhock Leaf-Skeletonizer (*Bucculatrix thurberiella*). The larval stage of this small, tan and gray moth completely skeletonizes leaves of ornamental hollyhocks and malvas in California.

Control: Spray with Diazinon, methoxychlor, or Sevin when the larvae begin to feed.

Two-Spotted Mite (*Tetranychus urticae*). This parasite is the most serious pest of hollyhock, often causing the leaves to become spotted, dried out, and unsightly during the flowering season.

Control: Use a good mite killer such as chlorobenzilate, Kelthane, Meta-Systox R, or Tedion from time to time to keep this pest under control. The spray should be directed to the lower leaf surface.

Stalk Borer. See *Lilium.*

ALYSSUM—see LOBULARIA

AMARANTHUS (AMARANTH)

Diseases

White Rust (*Albugo bliti.*). The disease is called white rust because of the blister-like white pustules which develop on the leaves and because the spores of the fungus are arranged in chains as in the cluster-cups of true rust (Fig. 55). The pustules change to reddish-brown when mature. The flowers and stems are dwarfed and distorted. The fungus is carried to a new generation within the seed coats.

Control: Destroy all infected plants and debris at the end of the season. Change the location of the plantings. Spray with a copper fungicide during the growing season as needed.

Viruses. A number of viruses can affect *Amaranthus.* The beet curly top virus is the most important.

Control: Rogue out and destroy all plants with virus diseases.

Aster Yellows. This disease, apparently caused by a mycoplasma-like organism, affects *Amaranthus.*

Control: The leafhopper vectors should be controlled with insecticides, and diseased plants should be removed and destroyed.

Insects

Harlequin Bug (*Murgantia histrionica*). This flat, 3/8-inch-long, black bug with bright red markings feeds on a wide variety of food and ornamental plants.

Control: Spray with rotenone or Sevin.

Carrot Beetle (*Bothynus gibbosus*). The bluish-white larvae of this beetle occasionally feed on the roots of *Amaranthus.*

Control: Control measures are rarely attempted.

Cottony-Cushion Scale. See *Acacia.*

AMARYLLIS

Fungus Diseases

Leaf Scorch (*Stagonospora curtisii*). The leaves and flowerstalks of amaryllis attacked by this fungus are characteristically bent or deformed at the point of attack (Fig. 6). Diseased flower stalks and basal leaves have at first small red raised or lacerated spots in longitudinal lines (Fig. 7). Dark brownish-red, discolored spots also develop on the flowerparts and bulb scales. The flower stalks of severely infected plants dry up without producing flowers. With the aid of a hand lens, reddish-brown pycnidia (Fig. 44) can be seen in the diseased area. The spores are at first one-celled but later may develop cross-walls so that the mature spores in nature and especially in culture may have three or four cells, a condition characteristic of this genus. Any injury to amaryllis seems to result in a characteristic reddening of the plant tissues, and does not necessarily indicate the presence of a parasite. Any bruise that exposes the tissues to the air will be followed by a reddening of the surface. *Stagonospora* infects *Narcissus* also, but does not result in the appearance of a red color in this host.

Control: As the leaves and flower stalks push up among the bulb-scales they may become slightly injured and so furnish a point of ready entrance for the fungus, the spores and fruiting bodies of which are probably carried on the bulb. Since the fungus may be present in the dormant bulbs, the disease will appear in the leaves and flower stalks that arise from such bulbs. Badly infected bulbs should be discarded. The disease is more apt to develop in moist weather and under humid conditions; hence the air in the greenhouse should be kept dry and the plants should not be syringed or too heavily watered. Plenty of light should be provided; the temperature in forcing houses should be kept as low as possible. Remove infected leaves and bulb scales.

Amaryllis grown outdoors in the South can be protected from leaf scorch by spraying with zineb, ferbam, or captan about 6 times, starting with the small leaf stage and ending at bloom time.

Mosaic (*Cucumber mosaic virus*). The leaves at first have an indefinite yellow mottling which later becomes more pronounced. Red streaks may appear on infected plants

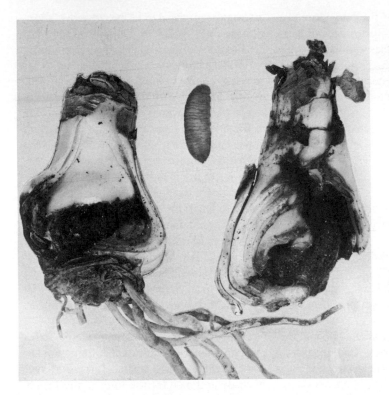

Fig. 106. Work of the larvae of the narcissus bulb fly *(Merodon equestris)* in amaryllis bulbs. A single larva is shown enlarged between the two bulbs.

from secondary causes. Plants become more stunted each year, the leaves, flowers, and bulbs being much reduced in size.

Another virus, tomato spotted wilt, has been reported from Texas and California.

Control: Since these are systemic diseases, it is advisable to destroy all infected plants.

Blight (*Botrytis cinerea*). This disease occurs chiefly on outdoor plants after they have been chilled.

Control: Pick off badly infected leaves and destroy them. Spray with captan to prevent additional infections.

Bulb Rots (*Pellicularia rolfsii, Rhizopus stolonifer,* and *Armillaria mellea*). Bulbs and roots are occasionally rotted by one of the three fungi listed.

Control: Discard diseased bulbs together with the soil immediately surrounding them. Treat soil with steam or a suitable chemical as described in Chapter 4.

Insects and Other Animal Pests

Narcissus Bulb Fly (*Merodon equestris*) and **Lesser Bulb Fly** (*Eumerus tuberculatus*). Apparently sound bulbs may harbor the larvae of bulb flies without showing much decay. On closer inspection the centers of the bulbs may be found badly eaten out. The root plates are destroyed so that the bulbs are worthless. Many infested bulbs, however, may be recognized by the holes which lead to the exterior (Fig. 106). The larvae of the lesser bulb fly may reach ½ inch long; they are marked by a horny outgrowth from the rear end and two small wart-like growths on either side. In one bulb there are usually only one or two larvae of the narcissus bulb fly, but there may be as many as 20 or more larvae of the lesser bulb fly.

Several stages of *Merodon equestris* are shown in Fig. 107.

Control: See *Narcissus.*

Fig. 107. Narcissus bulb fly *(Merodon equestris),* found singly in amaryllis bulbs (adult on top, larvae and pupae beneath).

Bulb Scale Mite (*Steneotarsonemus laticeps*). Members of the Amaryllidaceae are subject to diseases that result in the development of dark reddish spots on the leaves and bulb scales and on the flower stalks. At least one of these red diseases on hybrid varieties of amaryllis is caused by the bulb scale mite, which is too small to be visible except with the aid of a hand lens.

Control: After the bulbs have been dried immerse them in water at 110°F. for 1½ hours; except for larger bulbs, this will be sufficient to kill the mites. Allow the bulbs to cool gradually, because quick cooling may retard growth.

Thrips (*Heliothrips haemorrhoidalis, Taeniothrips simplex*). Several species of thrips occasionally attack amaryllis either in greenhouses or in the field. The gladiolus thrips *T. simplex* do most injury to buds and flowers, causing them to remain closed or to open irregularly.

Control: See *Gladiolus.*

Potato Aphid (*Macrosiphum euphorbiae*). This species attacks amaryllis under field conditions.

Control: Spray with malathion, Meta-Systox R, or Sevin when aphids become abundant.

Two-Spotted Mites (*Tetranychus urticae*). This spider mite occasionally infests the foliage.

Control: See *Althaea.*

Spanish Moth Caterpillar (*Xanthopastis timais*). This brown or black smooth-bodied caterpillar with cream-colored stripes feeds on amaryllis, narcissus, lily, and tuberose leaves along the East coast from Maine to Florida. Because the cream-colored bands around its body look like convict stripes, this pest is also known as the convict caterpillar.

Control: Spray with Sevin when the caterpillars are small.

Black Blister Beetle (*Epicauta pennsylvanica*). In the southern states this beetle feeds on the flowers of amaryllis. The insects sometimes appear in great numbers and do much damage.

Control: In limited areas the plants may be covered with cheesecloth, or they may be sprayed with Sevin.

Mealybug (*Planococcus citri*). These well-known pests of greenhouse plants sometimes infest amaryllis bulbs and leaf bases.

Control: Examine each bulb and remove the insects with a toothpick or some other small instrument. Dusting the bulbs with methoxychlor powder is also helpful.

Spotted Cutworm (*Amathes c-nigrum*). The flowers of amaryllis may be destroyed by the feeding of these cutworms, which climb the plant at night and eat holes at the base and in the segments of the flower (Fig. 82). The larvae are about 2 inches long when full grown and stretched. They are a pale or dirty tan with diagonal marks on the side toward the rear. The cutworms pupate and develop into moths in a comparatively short time. In greenhouses individual worms placed in confinement form a pale orange pupa within 9 days. The pupae turn dark reddish-brown within 2 weeks. A brownish-gray moth with

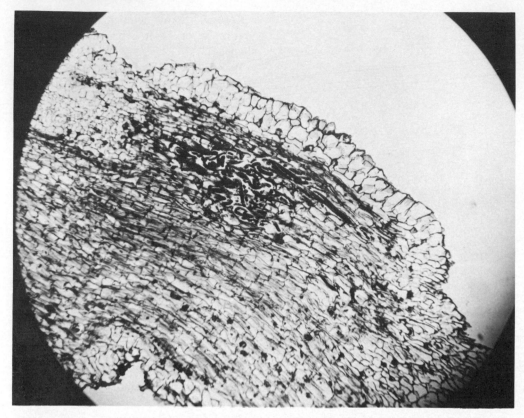

Fig. 108. Longitudinal section through amaryllis root, showing nemas in developing lesion. (Dr. Wray Birchfield)

oval markings of a clear or light gray color on the front wings and hind wings emerges within the next week or two.

Control: Scatter the specially prepared cutworm bait sold in garden supply stores, or dust the soil with Diazinon, or spray the plants with Sevin.

Lesion Nema (*Pratylenchus scribneri*). This nema causes great damage to field-grown amaryllis in Florida. Red spots or lesions on the roots followed by progressive disintegration of the root system are the most common symptoms (Figs. 108 and 109).

Control: See under nema control, Chapter 3.

Stem and Bulb Nema. See *Hyacinthus.*

AMELANCHIER (SERVICE-BERRY)

Fungus and Bacterial Diseases

Rust (*Gymnosporangium* spp.). Service-berry, also known as June-berry and shad-bush, is host of several rusts of the genus *Gymnosporangium,* of which the alternate hosts are the redcedar, the common juniper, and the southern whitecedar. The rust attacks the leaves and fruits of the service-berry, occasionally causing some defoliation and destruction of the fruit. The cluster-cup stage, referred to as the roestelial stage, is characteristic of each species; see Fig. 57. *Gymnosporangium biseptatum* causes the formation of characteristic horned galls on

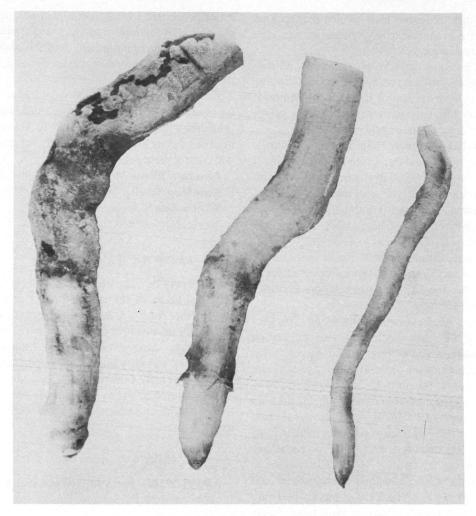

Fig. 109. Roots of amaryllis infested with Scribner's-lesion nema. (Dr. Wray Birchfield)

the under side of the leaves; from these protrude the long aecial structures. Spores from these in turn infect the southern whitecedar; the infection causes long spindle-shaped galls on the leaves and trunks, in which the fungus lives until the branches or trees die (see under *Chamaecyparis*). Provided that infected cedars are near, weather conditions largely determine to what extent the service-berry becomes infected.

Service-berries planted near common juniper heavily infected with *G. clavariaeforme* have been known to remain free from the rust for 6 successive years. Evidently this was because the time of ripening of the spores on juniper did not coincide with the period when the fruits and leaves of the service-berry were in a susceptible condition.

G. nidus-avis is rather destructive to the redcedar, causing the development of large witches' brooms which involve the trunk as well as branches; it may do some damage also to the service-berry.

Control: Eliminate, if practicable, all red-cedars (junipers) within a mile radius, or spray with ferbam or thiram 4 or 5 times at 7-day intervals starting when orange gelatinous masses first appear on redcedars.

Witches' Broom (*Apiosporina collinsii*). The fungus penetrates into the growing point and thereby stimulates many new shoots to develop and form characteristic witches' brooms. The leaves are usually covered with a heavy coating of black mold. Cut off and destroy the brooms.

Leaf Blight (*Diplocarpon theumenii*). Only occasionally is service-berry attacked by this fungus. It is more serious on hawthorn and apple. See *Crataegus.*

Fire Blight (*Erwinia amylovora*). This bacterial disease, which is serious on certain hawthorns and other pomaceous trees, occasionally occurs on service-berry. See under *Crataegus* for control.

Mildews (*Erysiphe polygoni, Phyllactinia corylea,* and *Podosphaera oxyacanthae*). These three species of powdery mildew fungi can be controlled with sulfur or Karathane sprays.

Fruit Rots (*Monilinia amelanchieris* and *M. fructicola*). The fruits of service-berry are rotted in rainy seasons by these fungi. Infections on particularly valuable specimens can be prevented by periodic applications of captan or wettable sulfur sprays.

Insects and Related Pests

Leaf Miner (*Nepticula amelanchierella*). Broad irregular mines, especially in the lower half of the leaf, result from infestation by the larvae. For control see under *Betula,* leaf miner.

Borers. A number of borers including the lesser peach tree (*Synanthedon pictipes*), apple bark (*Synanthedon pyri*), roundheaded apple tree (*Saperda candida*), and the shothole (*Scolytus rugulosus*) occasionally attack service-berry.

Control: Keep trees in good vigor by feeding and watering. Spraying the trunk and branches with methoxychlor at 2- to 3-week intervals during late spring and early summer will control these borers.

Pear Leaf Blister Mite. See *Sorbus.*
Pear Slug Sawfly. See *Prunus.*
Willow Scurfy Scale. See *Salix.*

AMORPHA (FALSE INDIGO)

Plants may be completely defoliated by the uredinial stage of the rust *Uropyxis amorphae.* Other fungus diseases which occur occasionally on this host are leaf spots (*Cylindrosporium passaloroides* and *Diplodia amorphae*), powdery mildew (*Erysiphe polygoni*), and twig canker (*Cytospora amorphae*). Control measures are not practiced for these. Sulfur or ferbam sprays will control rust.

AMPELOPSIS—see PARTHENOCISSUS

ANACARDIUM (CASHEW NUT)

In the southern states *Pellicularia rolfsii* causes a wilt or blight and *Asterina carbonacea* causes a leaf spot. These diseases are relatively unimportant.

ANAGALLIS (PIMPERNEL)

A leaf spot caused by the fungus *Septoria anagallidis* occasionally causes some damage. The aster yellows disease occurs on the West Coast. A nema belonging to the genus *Meloidogyne* attacks the roots of *Anagallis.*

ANAPHALIS (EVERLASTING)

Diseases

A leaf spot caused by *Septoria margarita-ceae* has been reported in the northern parts of the United States and a rust *Uromyces amoenus* in several western states.

ANDROMEDA[10] (BOG-ROSEMARY)

Bog-rosemary is subject to black mildew caused by the fungus *Asterina clavuligera,* gall by *Exobasidium vaccinii,* powdery mildew by *Microsphaera alni* var. *vaccinii,* rust by *Chrysomyxa cassandrae,* and leaf spots by *Rhytisma andromedae* and *Venturia arctostaphyli.*

Control: None is destructive enough to warrant control measures.

ANEMONE (WINDFLOWER)

Leaf Spots. A large number of leaf spotting fungi occur on both cultivated and wild species of *Anemone.* Among the most common are *Phyllosticta anemones, P. anemonicola, Cercospora pulsatillae, Cercosporella filiformis, Didymaria didyma, Ramularia ranunculi, Septoria anemones,* and *S. punicea.*

Control: Valuable plants can be protected by periodic applications of copper fungicides.

Rhizome Rot (*Pellicularia rolfsii* and *Sclerotium delphinii*). A decay of the rhizomes followed by death of the plant may be caused by these soil-infesting fungi.

Control: Dig up and destroy diseased plants as well as the soil immediately surrounding them. Treat remainder of soil with heat or chemicals as described in Chapter 4.

[10]Most of the horticultural plants formerly referred to *Andromeda* are now placed under *Pieris.*

Collar Rot (*Botrytis cinerea*). Occasionally this fungus results in extensive destruction of plants by rotting the crowns.

Control: Same as for rhizome rot.

Spot Disease (*Synchytrium anemones*). The flowers become discolored in spots, dwarfed and distorted, and fall. The leaves and stems also are spotted.

Control: Discard badly infected plants or remove spotted flowers and leaves.

Downy Mildew (*Plasmopara pygmaea*). The fine white mildew covers the under surface of the leaves. Plants become discolored. Stamens abort.

Control: The same as for the preceding disease.

Rust (*Tranzschelia pruni-spinosae*). This is a systemic disease which stimulates the anemone to abnormal development early in the spring. The alternate host is *Prunus.*

Control: Infected plants should be dug up and destroyed. This rust rarely occurs on anemone if cherry and other species of *Prunus* are not grown in the vicinity.

Other Rusts. Several other species of rust infect anemone. *Tranzschelia fusca* causes a thickening and paling of the leaves and crown; brown pustules develop on the under sides of the leaves. This fungus winters in the rhizome. Other species are *T. cohaesa, T. suffusca, T. tucsonensis,* and *Puccinia recondita* var. *agropyri.*

Smut (*Urocystis anemones*). Dark brown powdery pustules appear on swollen regions of the leaf stalks and leaf blades. They break the epidermis and scatter their spores, which are united in balls. This smut winters in the root stalk.

Control: Diseased leaves should be taken off and placed in the trash can. Use only sound root stalks from disease-free plants for propagation.

Virus. A virus disease, mosaic has been reported on Japanese anemones. Infected plants should be rogued out and destroyed.

Insects and Other Pests

Aphids (*Myzus ornatus* and *M. persicae*). The first-named of these aphids has caused damage, especially to double varieties. Flowers were streaked or "broken" as a result of the attacks by these aphids.

Control: Spray either with malathion or Sevin.

Black Blister Beetle (*Epicauta pennsylvanica*). The leaves and flowers of Japanese anemones are favored by this beetle.

Control: Spray with Sevin.

Cutworms (*Agrotis* spp.) Large patches of anemone are destroyed as a result of injury by cutworms.

Control: Dust the soil surface with Diazinon or spray the plants with Sevin.

Fern Nema (*Aphelenchoides olesistus*). *Anemone japonica* is especially susceptible to infestation by this eelworm. It also infests many other species of plants. Dark brown or blackish blotches occur on the leaves as a result of infestation. For control see *Chrysanthemum.*

Stem and Bulb Nema (*Ditylenchus dipsaci*). Leaves, flower stalks, and stems may be infested by this nema, which is more serious on phlox and certain other garden plants. For control see *Phlox.*

ANGELICA

Diseases

Leaf Spots. The following fungi are known to cause spotting of leaves of this host: *Cercospora thaspii, Fusicladium angelicae, Gloeosporium angelicae, Phyllosticta angelicae, Piggotia depressa, Ramularia angelicae,* and *Septoria dearnessii.*

Control: The leaf spotting fungi are rarely severe enough to warrant control measures.

Rusts. Several species of rust fungi affect *Angelica: Puccinia angelicae, P. ellisii, P. ligustici,* and *P. poromera.* These diseases occur primarily on wild plants and rarely attack the few cultivated angelicas.

ANTHURIUM

Anthracnose (*Gloeosporium minutum*). This fungus disease is occasionally found in greenhouses. It causes the formation of more or less circular spots, frequently along the veins of the leaves. The spots run together and form brown areas, up to 1 inch in diameter, with a brownish-yellow margin. The diseased tissue dries up and falls out.

Control: Avoid wetting the foliage when watering. Where the disease is prevalent, spray with wettable sulfur. Badly infected leaves should be removed and destroyed.

Anthracnose (*Colletotrichum* sp.). This anthracnose, which is especially prevalent in very moist greenhouses, is readily distinguished from that caused by *Gloeosporium* by the black bristles which develop in the acervuli (spore pustules). If water is allowed to remain on the leaves, the development of this leaf blotch is favored.

Control: Leaves or parts of leaves marked by these spots should be removed and destroyed. Spraying with a fungicide is usually undesirable for such ornamental foliage.

Spadix Rot (*Colletotrichum gloeosporioides*). A spadix rot of field-grown anthuriums in Hawaii in 1959 resulted in considerable loss in the field and in transit.

Control: Maneb or dodine sprays will control this disease.

Leaf Spot (*Cephaleuros parasiticus*). This is one of the few plant diseases caused by an alga, a plant which in some ways resembles a fungus but possesses chlorophyll and makes at least a part of its own food. It causes rather dark gray spots, $1/2$ inch in diameter, to develop along the main veins of this host. The affected veins become corky. The algal threads develop on the spots when the air is very moist.

Control: Apply a dilute copper spray.

Insects and Other Pests

Scales. Seven species of scale insects infest *Anthurium:* boisduval's, brown soft, dictyospermum, fern, green shield, hemispherical and proteus.

Control: Malathion or Sevin sprays will control the crawler stage of these scales.

Mealybugs and Mites. The former are controlled with malathion sprays, the latter with Kelthane.

ANTIRRHINUM (SNAPDRAGON)

Fungus Diseases

Rust (*Puccinia antirrhini*). This fungus causes one of the most serious diseases of snapdragons in gardens and greenhouses. The leaves, young stems, and calyx are subject to attack; the brown pustules of uredospores, which break out in large numbers, are surrounded by a yellowish area of leaf tissue. Plants wilt and die very quickly. The full life history of the fungus is not known; it is assumed that there is an alternate host. Infected plants bloom prematurely and have only small flowers, or they may be killed early in their growth.

Control: Since the fungus is not carried in the seeds (though spores may adhere to fragments of the seed pods), propagation from seeds is preferable to the use of cuttings. If the latter method is used, healthy plants should be selected. The disease is also spread from plant to plant by insects, which carry the uredospores; the control of insects therefore helps to control rust. Plants should be spaced so that they have plenty of air, and watering of the foliage should be strictly limited. Since the uredospores germinate very rapidly at low temperatures, infection is most likely in cool conditions. Most growers find that if they keep the temperature of the greenhouse above 70°F. for several days and not below 60°F. at night, they can control

rust. Where watering or splashing of the foliage is unavoidable, it is necessary to spray the plants once a week with a mixture of sulfur and zineb, or Fore. The leaves must be thoroughly coated with the fungicide for best results. Where insecticidal sprays are to be used, it is wise to include zineb or maneb in the mixture.

Rust-resistant varieties should be used when snapdragons are grown outdoors.

Anthracnose (*Colletotrichum antirrhini*). This disease is most serious in greenhouses during the fall and spring. In gardens it is most likely to occur in late summer. The leaves and stems of plants of all ages are attacked. The spots on the older stems are sunken, oblong in shape, from pale yellowish-green to gray in color with a narrow brown border. Spore pustules appear later as minute black pimples in the spots. Under a microscope dark brown hairlike out-growths are visible on these pustules.

Control: Spray with zineb, maneb, or captan. Take cuttings only from healthy plants. When watering plants, avoid wetting the leaves.

Blight (*Phyllosticta antirrhini*). This is a disease of garden plants which occurs most frequently in June and July. Cream-colored or light-brown circular spots appear on the leaves, sometimes surrounded by circles of other colors. The small black fruiting bodies of the fungus develop on the upper surfaces of the leaves at the centers of the spots. Ash-gray spots covered with the black pycnidia develop on stems. These spots enlarge rapidly and turn dark brown. If the spots entirely encircle the stem, the plants wilt and may die.

Control: All parts of the plants in diseased beds should be removed and destroyed at the end of the season. Spray with zineb, maneb, or captan as for anthracnose. Keep leaves dry; space plants more widely.

Gray Mold (*Botrytis cinerea*). Individual branches and flower stalks may be attacked by the gray mold, which causes a wilting of the flower spikes and the development of light brown areas on the stems at the base of the flower clusters. The fungus enters the plant through the blossom parts and grows down into the stem, forming cankered areas. Infection has been shown to take place through the glandular hairs. Under moist conditions the spores of the fungus may develop in light brown or gray masses. When the foliage of the plants is too wet as a result of syringing or the application of insecticides against thrips, this mold does considerable damage. Infected plants break over about 2 feet from the ground.

Control: In the greenhouse, avoid excessive humidity by using heat, ventilation, and forced air movement. Cut off and destroy infected flower stalks as soon as they are detected. Keep greenhouse and garden plantings free from debris, for the fungus can live as a rot fungus under such conditions and its spores may be thence blown to living plants. A Benlate or zineb spray after the plants have been cut back to force a second growth will be helpful.

Powdery Mildew (*Oidium sp.*). Largely confined to greenhouse-grown snapdragons, this mildew forms a white powdery coating on both leaf surfaces and young stems.

Control: Spray with Benlate or with Karathane.

Wilt (*Verticillium albo-atrum*). This soilborne fungus, which frequently causes wilting of various ornamental and economic plants has also been reported as causing wilt of snapdragon. It often occurs when snapdragons are planted in old chrysanthemum soil which has not been pasteurized (see Chapter 4).

Root Rot (*Pellicularia filamentosa*). A loss of 80 per cent mature plants through this fungus has been reported from Texas. The plants suddenly wilted and died. Another root rot reported from the southern states is caused by the well-known *Phymatotrichum omnivorum.*

Control: Avoid heavy watering. Apply a soil fungicide such as Terraclor, or a mixture of Dexon and Terraclor.

Crown Rot (*Pellicularia rolfsii*). This fungus is another that attacks the roots and crowns of many economic plants in the southern states.

Control: The same as for root rot.

Stem Rot (*Sclerotinia sclerotiorum*). Sunken water-soaked regions appear on the stem, which soon collapses. Under moist shady conditions, the plants become completely covered with a fluffy white mycelium. The inflorescence becomes pale and wilts, and the flowers collapse. As the disease spreads downward, the whole plant may wilt. Flat, irregular sclerotia may be found inside the stems; they reach 1/4 inch in length, and turn black with age. These bodies carry the fungus through unfavorable conditions and in May develop the ascocarps. From the latter, spores are discharged and float through the air or are carried to the blossoms by bees and mites. Infection of the blossoms occurs through the stigmas; the fungus penetrates and grows downward rather rapidly.

A similar disease is due to *Phytophthora cactorum* and *P. parasitica.*

Control: Remove plants and infested soil from the benches as soon as the symptoms appear. Pasteurize the soil that is to be used for planting.

Leaf Spot (*Cercospora antirrhini*). Previously reported only from Guatemala, this leaf spot was found in Florida in 1958. Spots are circular, 0.5 to 5 mm. in diameter, dingy gray to white.

Control: No control measures have been developed but it is likely that dithiocarbamate sprays will be effective.

Downy Mildew (*Peronospora antirrhini*). This mildew can cause a serious damping-off of snapdragon seedlings or a sharp checking of growth in the terminal shoots.

Control: Spray young plants with a copper fungicide.

Insects and Other Animal Pests

Aphids (*Aphis gossypii*). This insect is often troublesome in greenhouses and gardens. It feeds on the under sides of the leaves and on the tender tip ends. The peach aphid *Myzus perslcae* can produce virus-like symptoms—leaf discoloration and distortion—on some greenhouse-grown snapdragons.

Control: Malathion sprays are effective against aphids.

Greenhouse Leaf Tier (*Udea rubigalis*). The larvae of this insect eat out irregular areas on the leaves and web parts of the leaves together. In greenhouses, where they are apt to be more troublesome than in gardens, several generations are produced during the summer months. They are less troublesome in winter.

Control: Since this insect feeds on many garden plants and on weeds of all sorts, destruction of weed hosts is helpful. Before the leaves have become rolled or tied, spray with Sevin.

Caterpillars. Those of the yellow woollybear *Diacrisia virginica* and the stalk borer *Papaipema nebris,* among others, are troublesome to snapdragons.

Control: The same as for the greenhouse leaf tier.

Two-Spotted Mite (*Tetranychus urticae*). In dry seasons this pest may be very abundant and injurious.

Control: See *Althaea.*

Cyclamen Mite (*Steneotarsonemus pallidus*). See *Cyclamen.*

Red-and-Black Stink Bug (*Cosmopepla bimaculata*). This small red-and-black bug is nearly ¼ inch in length. It attacks snapdragons as well as many other plants.

Control: Spray with Sevin.

Verbena Bud Moth (*Endothenia hebesana*). The larvae of this insect feed on the flower buds, stalks, and seeds. They are sometimes very serious. For further details see under *Iris.*

Control: If the young insects are present before the blooming season, they can be controlled by spraying with Sevin.

Southern Root-Knot Nema (*Meloidogyne incognita*). Occasionally the roots of young seedlings in small pots may be so seriously infested that plants become stunted. This is not a common trouble of snapdragon, however.

APLOPAPPUS (GOLDEN WEED)

In the western states this host is subject to powdery mildew (*Erysiphe cichoracearum*) and to rust (*Puccinia grindeliae*). Valuable specimens subject to these diseases should be sprayed with wettable sulfur.

AQUILEGIA (COLUMBINE)

Diseases

Leaf Spots (*Ascochyta aquilegiae, Cercospora aquilegiae,* and *Septoria aquilegiae*). In rainy season three different fungi are capable of causing spots on the leaves of columbine.

Control: The causal fungi overwinter in old infected leaves. Such leaves should be collected and destroyed at the end of the growing season. This practice usually suffices to keep leaf spots under control although a Benlate or captan spray can be used where circumstances require it.

Crown Rot (*Sclerotinia sclerotiorum* and *Pellicularia rolfsii*). These fungi cause a crown and stem rot which is followed by a drying and wilting of stems and leaves. The whole plant finally dies. Large, flat, black sclerotia, or small, round ones, the size of mustard seeds, are often visible in the decayed stems. The same fungi attack a wide variety of herbaceous ornamental plants.

Control: Remove and destroy infected plants and the soil immediately adjacent to them. Before replanting in the same place, pasteurize the soil. Thorough cultivation around the plant, which allows the soil to dry out completely, prevents the spread of the fungus.

Root Rot (*Pellicularia filamentosa, Phymatotrichum omnivorum,* and *Pythium mamillatum*). Decay of roots may result from invasion by any of these three fungi.

Control: No effective controls are known. Avoid planting in infested soils.

Rust (*Puccinia recondita* var. *agropyri*). This rust also occurs on aconite, anemone, clematis, and delphinium. Its alternate stage occurs on native grasses.

Control: Valuable specimens can be protected with wettable sulfur sprays.

Mosaic (Cucumber mosaic virus). This virus stunts columbines, prevents flowering, and causes a conspicuous leaf mottling.

Control: Rogue out and destroy infected plants. Control aphids with malathion sprays. Avoid planting columbine near other hosts susceptible to cucumber mosaic.

Insects

Aphids (*Pergandeidia trirhoda*). This small, cream-colored, rather flat aphid feeds on the young branches and on the undersides of the leaves in late summer. Other species which attack columbine are *Aphis spiraecola* and *A. gossypii.*

Control: Excellent control of aphids is obtained by spraying with malathion.

Columbine Skipper (*Erynnis lucilius*). This is a greenish caterpillar, nearly an inch long, with a black head. It feeds exclusively on columbine leaves, which it rolls up when not feeding.

Control: Rotenone or Sevin sprays will control this pest.

Columbine Borer (*Papaipema purpurifascia*). The young larvae attack the leaf stalks in May and bore downward in the stems to the ground. They finally attack the roots.

Control: Thorough raking of the soil in early spring destroys many of the eggs, which are laid directly on the ground. Sevin sprays applied when the young larvae are about to enter the leaf stalks also provide control.

Columbine Leaf Miner (*Phytomyza acquilegivora*). The work of this insect is easily recognized because of the very striking white winding markings readily visible on the infested leaves; see Fig. 83.

Control: Pick off infested leaves as soon as they are discovered. In the fall all plant remains should be removed and discarded. Spray with malathion or Meta-Systox R in the spring before the white markings become prominent.

ARABIS (ROCK CRESS)

Diseases

Club Root (*Plasmodiophora brassicae*). This fungus, which causes abnormal overgrowths on the roots of many members of the cabbage family, was formerly classified as a slime-mold. Today mycologists classify it as one of the Chytridiales.

Control: Do not replant *Arabis* in infested soil. The soil fumigant PCNB (Terraclor) has proved effective in controlling the same disease on cabbage and might be worth trying in beds of *Arabis* infested with the fungus.

Downy Mildew (*Peronospora parasitica*). A light gray, powdery fungus growth develops on the undersides of the leaves and over the young stems, causing some distortion and swelling of infected parts. The prompt removal of infected plants is advisable and an application of a fungicide containing copper may be necessary.

White Rust (*Albugo candida*). This fungus causes a light yellowish discoloration of the leaves, which later turn brown in spots. The fungus breaks out, usually on the underside of the leaves, in white pustules. In these the spores are borne in rows much as are the aecial spores in true rust pustules. Badly infected plants may die. The parasite attacks many other members of the cabbage family.

Control: Remove and discard infected plants and all debris in autumn. Avoid growing *Arabis* near other crucifers which harbor the disease. Plants may be sprayed with a copper fungicide.

Leaf Spot (*Septoria arabidis*). Small brown spots may develop on the leaves during rainy weather.

Control: Control measures are seldom adopted for this disease. A copper fungicide can be applied where the disease is prevalent.

Insects

Lily Aphid (*Neomyzus circumflexus*). The only insect that commonly attacks *Arabis* is the crescent-marked lily aphid. This yellow and black species also attacks many other kinds of ornamental plants both in greenhouses and outdoors.

Control: Spray with malathion as soon as any aphids are seen.

ARAUCARIA (NORFOLK ISLAND PINE)

Diseases

Blight (*Cryptospora longispora*). The lower branches are attacked first, and the disease gradually spreads upward. As the entire branch becomes infected, the tip end becomes bent. The limbs die and then break off at the tip ends. Plants 5 or 6 years old are soon killed by this disease.

Control: The infected branches should be pruned off and destroyed as soon as discovered. Seeds of *Araucaria excelsa* imported from Norfolk Island Territory frequently harbor the causal fungus. Hence they are dipped in sulfuric acid by plant quarantine inspectors before being released to nurserymen.

Bleeding Canker (*Botryodiplodia theobromae* and *Dothiorella* sp.). Two fungi are associated with this disease on the Island of

Hawaii, where the Norfolk Island Pine is grown for Christmas trees or is used as a windbreak and as an ornamental.

Control: Control measures have not been developed.

Crown Gall (*Agrobacterium tumefaciens*). This host has been proved experimentally to be susceptible. A typical gall is smooth and up to 1 inch in diameter.

Control: Prune infected branches.

Insects

Mealybugs (*Pseudococcus aurilanatus, Planococcus citri,* and *Pseudococcus ryani*). The first species listed is the golden mealybug; the second, the citrus mealybug; and the third, the Cypress mealybug. All are serious pests of the Norfolk Island pine in California.

Control: Spray with malathion, Meta-Systox R, or Sevin whenever mealybugs are seen.

Scales. Five species of scales are known to attack this host: araucaria (*Eriococcus araucariae*), pure white, feltlike, oval sacs enclosing bodies and eggs of females; black araucaria (*Chrysomphalus rossi*), an almost black species resembling the Florida red scale; chaff (*Parlatoria pergandii*), a circular to elongate, smooth semitransparent, brownish-gray kind; Florida red (*Chrysomphalus aonidum*), an armored, small, $1/12$ inch, circular, reddish-brown to nearly black scale; and soft (*Coccus hesperidum*), a flat, soft, oval, yellowish-brown, $1/8$-inch-long species.

Control: Repeated applications of malathion or Sevin will control scales. These are especially effective against the crawling stages.

ARBUTUS (STRAWBERRY-TREE)

Diseases

Leaf Spots. (*Septoria unedonis* and *Elsinoë mattirolianum*). The former fungus produces small brown spots on leaves of *Arbu-*

tus unedo in the Pacific Northwest, and the latter a spot anthracnose in California.

Control: If only a few plants are involved, pick off the infected leaves; if necessary, spray with wettable sulfur.

Crown Gall (*Agrobacterium tumefaciens*). This bacterial disease occurs occasionally on strawberry-tree in California and Connecticut.

Control: Remove and destroy infected parts.

Insects

California Tent Caterpillar (*Malacosoma californicum*). This species occasionally feeds on the leaves of strawberry-trees in California. It makes large tents in the trees like those of the eastern tent caterpillar.

Control: Spray with *Bacillus thuringiensis,* Dylox, methoxychlor, or Sevin when the caterpillars are small.

Scales (*Saissetia oleae, Hemiberlesia rapax,* and *Coccus hesperidum*). These three species of scales—black, greedy, and the brown soft, respectively—are known to attack strawberry-tree in the West.

Control: Spray with malathion or Sevin from time to time to control the young crawler stages of these pests.

ARCTOSTAPHYLOS GLAUCA (MANZANITA)

Diseases

Leaf Galls (*Exobasidium oxycocci* and *E. vaccinii-uliginosi*). Reddish leaves and shoot hypertrophy result from infection by the former fungus. Leaf galls and witches' broom are caused by the latter.

Control: Remove and destroy infected portions. Spray with a copper fungicide early in the growing season.

Leaf Spot (*Cryptostictis arbuti*). This leaf spot rarely becomes serious enough to warrant control measures.

Rust (*Pucciniastrum sparsum*). This rust has been reported from the Pacific coast. It rarely causes any appreciable damage.

Insects

Leaf Gall Aphid (*Tamalia coweni*). In the West numerous green or reddish roll-galls on leaves of manzanita are produced by this dark green to black aphid.

Control: Valuable specimens should be sprayed with malathion or Sevin before galls develop.

Western Tussock Moth (*Hemerocampa vetusta*). The larval stage of this pest feeds on the leaves and fruits of a large number of fruit and ornamental trees on the Pacific coast.

Control: Same as for california tent caterpillar. See *Arbutus.*

Scales (*Lepidosaphes camelliae* and *Coccus hesperidum*). See *Arbutus.*

Whiteflies (*Aleuroplatus coronatus, Aleyrodes inconspicua,* and *A. iridescens*). Three species of whitefly attack manzanita in the West.

Control: See *Fuchsia.*

ARCTOSTAPHYLOS UVA-URSI (BEARBERRY)

Diseases

Black Mildew (*Asterina gaultheriae*). A blackish coating of the fungus forms on the leaf surfaces. Another species, *A. conglobata,* has been reported from Maine.

Control: Sprays containing a dilute copper sulfate will control this fungus.

Leaf Galls (*Exobasidium vaccinii* and *E. uvae-ursi*). The former causes bladder-shaped galls and red leaf spots and the latter leaf galls and hypertrophy of shoots.

Control: Pick off and destroy infected

parts. Severe infections can be avoided by applying a copper fungicide early in the growing season.

Rust (*Chrysomyxa arctostaphyli*). Bearberry in the Rocky Mountain states and Alaska is occasionally affected by this rust.

Control: Control measures are rarely practiced.

ARCTOTIS (AFRICAN DAISY)

A fungus leaf blotch caused by a species of *Cercospora*, a root rot by *Phymatotrichum omnivorum,* and root-knot caused by the nema *Meloidogyne incognita* are the principal pests of this plant.

Control: The *Cercospora* leaf blotch can be controlled by periodic applications of a copper fungicide. The root rot fungus and the root-knot nema can be controlled by soil pasteurization as described in Chapter 4.

ARDISIA

A leaf spot caused by the alga *Cephaleuros virescens,* crown gall by *Agrobacterium tumefaciens,* and root-knot by the nema *Meloidogyne javanica* occur on *Ardisia* in Florida. This host is also subject to the hemispherical scale *Saissetia hemisphaerica.* A copper fungicide will control the alga. The control of crown gall and nemas is more difficult. Malathion or Sevin sprays will control the young crawler stage of the scale.

ARENARIA (SANDWORT)

Certain species of this genus are subject to a leaf spot caused by the fungus *Hendersonia tenella,* a powdery mildew caused by *Erysiphe polygoni,* an anther smut by *Ustilago violacea,* and to three rusts, *Puccinia arenariae, P. tardissima,* and *Uromyces silenes.*

Control: Control practices are rarely employed to combat any of these fungus diseases.

ARGEMONE (PRICKLY-POPPY)

Downy Mildew (*Peronospora arborescens*). Leaves, buds, and capsules of prickly-poppy are affected by this mildew. A light gray mold develops on the undersides of leaves. On the upper surface yellow to brown blotches eventually turn dark.

Control: Remove and destroy infected plants. Use clean seed.

Leaf Spots (*Alternaria lancipes, Gloeosporium argemonis,* and *Septoria argemonis*). These three fungi cause leaf spotting in the Middle West and South. A rust caused by *Aecidium plenum* occurs in Texas.

Control: As a rule no control measures are necessary for leaf spot and rust diseases on this host.

ARISAEMA (JACK-IN-THE-PULPIT)

Diseases

Rust (*Uromyces ari-triphylli*). This plant, now often grown in moist places in rock and wild flower gardens, is subject to a systemic rust disease which causes a yellowing and dying of leaves and spathe. Such plants seldom flower normally or produce seed. The roots are apparently not invaded by the fungus. It is believed that the germinating spores of the fungus may infect young shoots but cannot reach the corms, which are deeply imbedded in the ground. The light lemon-yellow pustules which bear the aeciospores are rather conspicuous (see Fig. 56). The mycelium of the fungus invades all parts of the plants, even the young ovary and ovules. The disease is evidently spread by the seed, which carries the mycelium.

Control: Since this is a systemic disease, spraying with a sulfur fungicide does not prevent the extension of the disease in a plant already infected, but might prevent its spread to healthy plants. Diseased plants should be pulled up and destroyed.

Blight (*Streptotinia arisaemae*). A leaf and stalk blight is common in the East and Middle West.

Control: Valuable plantings can be protected by periodic applications of ferbam spray.

Leaf Spots (*Cladosporium* sp. and *Volutella* sp.). These two fungi occasionally spot jack-in-the-pulpit leaves. No controls are required.

ARISTOLOCHIA (BIRTHWORT)

Leaf Spots (*Botrytis cinerea, Cercospora guttulata, C. serpentariae, Gloeosporium* sp., *Ovularia aristolochiae,* and *Phyllosticta aristolochiae*). Six fungi are known to cause leaf spots on this host.

Control: Spray several times at 2-week intervals with 2 level tablespoons of captan per gallon of water, starting when the leaves are ¼ inch long.

ARNICA

Two leaf spots caused by the fungi *Ovularia hughesiana* and *Phyllosticta arnicae,* two powdery mildews by *Erysiphe cichoracearum* and *Sphaerotheca humuli,* and two rusts by *Puccinia arnicali* and *Uromyces junci* have been reported on this host. Control measures are rarely practiced for these diseases.

ARONIA (CHOKEBERRY)

Diseases

Blight (*Erwinia amylovora*). This bacterium commonly affects most pomaceous trees and shrubs. It is rarely serious enough on chokeberry to warrant control measures. Pruning and destroying infected branch tips usually suffice.

Leaf Spots (*Ascochyta pirina, Cercospora mali, C. pyri, Mycosphaerella arbutifolia,* and *Phyllosticta arbutifolia*). Five species of fungi cause leaf spotting of chokeberry.

Control: Valuable specimens subject to heavy infections by any of these fungi can be protected by periodic applications of a copper fungicide.

Twig and Fruit Blight (*Monilinia fructicola*). Affected parts are covered with a gray, powdery mold, the spores of which are borne in monilioid chains. The ascocarpic stage develops in the spring on fruits which have been slightly buried in the ground during the winter. A similar blight of service-berry is said to be caused by a closely related species.

Control: If this disease becomes a factor in ornamental plantings the fallen fruit should be either buried deeply or gathered and destroyed. Spraying the plants with captan or Benlate after petal fall would be of some benefit.

Rust (*Gymnosporangium fraternum*). Infected leaves, fruits, and stems develop gall-like overgrowths which bear the long, horny aecial cups. These split open and scatter their spores widely during the summer. The spores are carried to the alternate host, southern whitecedar; upon its leaves are formed brown rust pustules which bear the telial stage of the parasite. The rust is unknown on *Aronia* in the absence of the cedar, and is of little importance in ornamental plantings except where the southern whitecedar is also grown. Three other species also occur on this host: *G. clavariaeforme, G. clavipes,* and *G. davisii.*

Control: Frequent spraying with ferbam or thiram should provide control.

Insects

Roundheaded Apple Tree Borer (*Saperda candida*). The only serious insect pest of chokeberry, this borer also infests many other ornamental and fruit trees.

Control: Spray the trunk and lower branches 3 times at 2-week intervals with methoxychlor starting the first week in June in the latitude of New York.

ARUNCUS (GOAT'S-BEARD)

A leaf spot caused by *Ramularia ulmariae* has been reported from the state of Alaska, and a leaf spot by a species of *Cercospora* and a stem canker by *Leptosphaeria arunci* from Oregon. These are not serious enough to warrant control measures.

ASCLEPIAS (BUTTERFLY-WEED)

Diseases

Leaf Spots (*Cercospora asclepiadorae, C. clavata,* and *Phyllosticta tuberosa*). Three fungi cause leaf spotting of the butterfly-weed. Control measures are not usually adopted.

Rusts (*Puccinia bartholomaei, P. vexans,* and *Uromyces asclepiadis*). As with leaf spots, control measures are rarely undertaken.

Mosaic (Cucumber mosaic virus). This widespread virus occasionally infects the butterfly-weed. Remove and destroy infected plants.

Insects

Aphids (*Aphis gossypii* and *A. nerii*). The former is very dark green but varies to yellow-green, brown, or black; the latter is a pretty yellow-and-black species.

Control: Spray valuable specimens with malathion or Sevin when the aphids are noticed.

Other Insects. Occasionally other insects infest this host: the argus tortoise beetle, *Chelymorpha cassidea;* the larva of the monarch butterfly, *Danaus plexippus;* the serpentine leaf miner, *Liriomyza brassicae;* San Jose scale, *Quadraspidiotus perniciosus;* and the Western flower thrips, *Frankliniella occidentalis.*

Control: Spray with malathion when any of these pests appear on butterfly-weed.

ASPARAGUS (ASPARAGUS-FERN)[11]

Diseases

Blight (*Ascochyta asparagina*). The branches becomes dry and drop off. The plants are often killed down to the crown by a severe attack.

Control: Florida growers use a spray containing 2 pounds of 65 per cent zineb in 100 gallons of water at weekly intervals in summer to control this disease and another they call "rust."

Root Rot (*Fusarium moniliforme*). This soil-borne fungus attacks the roots and basal shoot buds, causing a serious rot. Root rot may be avoided by care in watering and the use of pasteurized soil.

Crown Gall (*Agrobacterium tumefaciens*). The galls, formed at the base of the stem, are thick, fleshy, irregular clumps developed from secondary sprouts. As on other hosts, they may become up to 2 inches in diameter. They are somewhat pale green in color.

Control: Remove and destroy the galls. Do not propagate from infected stock. Do not replant in the same soil without first steam pasteurizing the soil. Dipping stem bases in streptomycin or 30 per cent Clorox solution may help.

Yellows (Physiological Disease). A physiological disease, chlorosis, leads to final bleaching out of most of the green color.

Control: Reduce watering to the least amount necessary to prevent drying.

Insects

Asparagus-Fern Caterpillar (*Spodoptera exigua*). This caterpillar, green above and yellow underneath, with a dark stripe on the back and yellowish stripes on each side, also feeds on corn, cotton, peas, and peppers in

---

[11] "Asparagus-fern" of florists is not a fern but species of *Asparagus,* a genus of flowering plants (usually *A. plumosus nana* or *A. sprengeri*).

Florida and on cotton and other plants in California.

Control: Spray with Sevin when the caterpillars are small.

Onion Thrips (*Thrips tabaci*). This species is reported to attack *A. sprengeri*, causing the "leaves" (which are really branches) to curl and become deformed. The silvery or glassy appearance characteristic of the work of thrips serves to suggest their presence. Brown, corky spots develop later.

Control: Propagate by using only divisions from uninfested plants. Malathion sprays are usually effective.

Asparagus Beetles (*Crioceris duodecimpunctata* and *C. asparagi*). The grubs of these beetles feed on the scale leaves and shoots, occasionally denuding the plant.

Control: Spray with Sevin.

Garden Fleahopper (*Halticus bracteatus*). The adults are small black bugs $1/12$ inch long. When disturbed they jump like flea beetles. This insect, however, feeds by sucking the juices after piercing the epidermis. Whitish or yellowish areas develop on the leaves. Heavy infestations result in stunting of plant growth.

Control: Since this fleahopper breeds on many weeds, clean cultivation of garden space outside the greenhouse should be practiced. Sevin sprays are also effective.

Variegated Cutworm (*Peridroma saucia*). The caterpillars, about 2 inches long, climb the plants and clip the stems just below the buds. They also cut off young plants near the ground.

Control: Apply Diazinon to the soil prior to planting, or spray the plants with Sevin when they are set out.

Two-Spotted Mite (*Tetranychus urticae*). The leaves lose their green color and are covered with mealy webs when this mite infests asparagus-fern.

Control: Spray with chlorobenzilate.

Scales (*Saissetia oleae, S. coffeae, Parlatoria pergandii, Pinnaspis strachani, Aspidi-*

otus destructor and *A. nerii*). Six species of scales occasionally infest this host.

Control: Spray with malathion or Sevin to control the crawler stage.

ASPIDISTRA

Diseases

Leaf Spots (*Colletotrichum omnivorum* and *Ascochyta aspidistrae*). The former fungus produces large whitish spots with brown margins on the leaf blades and leaf stalks. The latter produces large, irregular, pale spots on the leaves. The fungus *Labrella aspidistrae* causes a leaf blight.

Control: None of these diseases is of great importance. The application of a fungicide is seldom necessary for their control, if infected leaves are removed and destroyed. While the plants need an abundance of water, root rots sometimes develop from overwatering and cause a yellowing of the leaves.

Chlorosis. Yellowing and dying of leaves may result from bringing these shade-loving plants into too strong a light.

Insects

Scales (*Aonidiella aurantii, Pinnaspis aspidistrae,* and *Chrysomphalus aonidum*). Three species of scale attack *Aspidistra*.

Control: Spray with malathion or Sevin from time to time until the infestation is cleaned up.

Spider Mites. These pests occasionally infest *Aspidistra*. Spraying with Kelthane will control them.

ASTER (PERENNIAL ASTERS)

Diseases

Leaf Spots (*Alternaria* sp., *Ascochyta compositarum, Cercospora asterata, Cercosporella cana, Discosphaerina pseudimantia, Leptothyrium doellingeriae, Ovularia asteris,*

O. virgaureae, Phyllachora asterigena, Ramularia asteris, Septoria asteris, and *S. astericola*). Perennial asters are subject to a great number of leaf spotting fungi.

Control: Spray at weekly to 10-day intervals with a sulfur or copper fungicide particularly in rainy seasons.

Downy Mildew (*Basidiophora entospora*). This mildew is prevalent in the Middle West and South.

Control: Spray with a copper fungicide when a downy mold first appears on the lower leaf surfaces.

Powdery Mildew (*Erysiphe cichoracearum*). In the vicinity of New York, this powdery mildew develops about the middle of September on asters grown close together in ornamental plantings, particularly on the lower half of the plant where moisture is more abundant.

Control: Spray thoroughly with wettable sulfur or Karathane once or twice at weekly intervals starting as soon as the whitish coating of the fungus is visible.

Rusts (*Coleosporium solidaginis, Puccinia asteris, P. extensicola* var. *asteris, P. grindeliae, P. stipae, Uromyces compactus,* and *U. junci).* Many species of rust fungi infect asters. The alternate hosts of the first one listed above are two- and three-needle pines. The alternate hosts of the others are various species of grasses and sedges.

Control: Valuable plantings can be protected by periodic applications of sulfur sprays. Removal of the alternate host, if practicable, will also help.

Insects

Aphids (*Macrosiphum artemisiae* and *M. asterifoliae*). These species develop in clusters on the flower stems or the undersides of the lowermost leaves.

Control: Spray with malathion, Meta-Systox R, or Sevin.

Japanese Beetle (*Popillia japonica*). Asters are a favorite host of this pest.

Control: See *Aesculus.*

Chrysanthemum Lace Bug (*Corythucha marmorata*). The leaves and stems of certain hardy asters, especially in rock gardens, are attacked by this pest, which also attacks chrysanthemums, goldenrod, and scabiosa.

Control: Spray with Diazinon, malathion, or Sevin, directing the spray primarily to the lower leaf surfaces.

Stalk Borer. See *Lilium.*

ASTILBE

Few diseases affect this host. A powdery mildew caused by *Erysiphe polygoni* and wilt by a species of *Fusarium* have been reported. The former is controlled by spraying with wettable sulfur or with Karathane; the latter, by setting healthy plants out in clean, or pasteurized, soil. The Japanese beetle (*Popillia japonica*) is the only insect pest of importance. It descends on the flowers and leaves of *Astilbe* in great numbers. Control measures are given in Chapter 3.

AUCUBA

Diseases

Leaf Spot (*Phyllosticta aucubae*). After infestation by scale insects and primary fungus parasites, several fungi, including species of *Alternaria* and *Pestalotia,* attack *Aucuba* secondarily. *Phyllosticta aucubae* is the primary parasite responsible for many natural infections. Brown or black zonate spots develop mostly along the margins of the leaves. In serious cases much defoliation occurs. The black pycnidia or fruiting bodies of the fungus exude yellowish spores either in droplets or long tendrils. These spores are splashed by rain or by watering the plants, so that the disease may spread rapidly.

Control: The control of this disease calls for a combined scale insect and fungus control. If the scale is not present, spray with a copper fungicide that does not leave a heavy, unsightly residue. If scale is present, combine the copper spray with malathion or Sevin.

Gray Mold (*Botrytis cinerea*). When humidity is high, healthy twigs may become infected by this fungus. Invasion takes place either through the nectary or through some mechanical injury to the cuticle. The disease has not been found in nature and is of little importance where proper cultural conditions are maintained. The dark or blackish sclerotia are formed by this fungus at the lower ends of twigs, while the spores develop near the top.

Anthracnose, Wither Tip (*Colletotrichum gloeosporioides*). Spots develop on leaves and flowers and cankers form on the stems, causing a general wilt of the tip end of the branches.

Control: Pick off infected leaves and prune back tip ends. Spray with Bordeaux mixture or wettable sulfur.

Frost Injury. Young leaves suffer from spring frosts in the southern states. In the northern states, the older leaves will turn brown in winter unless the plants are well protected. Such injury is frequently mistaken for a disease caused by a fungus.

Insects

Yellow Scale (*Aonidiella aurantii*). This yellow strain of the California red scale is especially serious on *Aucuba* since it opens the way for invasion by leaf-spotting fungi.

Control: Spray with malathion or Sevin at the time when young are crawling about.

Aphid (*Macrosiphum aucubae*). This green species occasionally infests *Aucuba.*

Control: Spray with malathion when the aphids are seen.

AZALEA—see RHODODENDRON

AZARA

In the southern states and in California these evergreens are occasionally affected by the stem rot fungus, *Pellicularia rolfsii.*

Control: Destroy infected plants. Set new plants in uninfested soil.

BACCHARIS (GROUNSEL-BUSH)

Black Mold (*Dimerosporium baccharidis*). While a score or more fungi have been found in America on dead and dying plants of this genus, they are mostly secondary rather than primary parasites. The black mold may lead to a smothering of greenhouse varieties in the southern states.

Rust (*Puccinia baccharidis*) is rather common in the southern and western states.

Control practices for diseases of this host are rarely adopted.

BAMBUSA (BAMBOOS)

Diseases

In the northern states bamboos are not subject to many fungus diseases. From Florida come reports of a rather serious leaf spot caused by a species of bacterium which sometimes leads to partial defoliation. A leaf spot caused by the fungus *Cylindrosporium bambusae* has been recorded from Georgia and a smut, *Ustilago shiraiana,* from the South and the West Coast. Another fungus, *Melanconium bambusae,* causes a black spotting of the leaves. If these diseases become serious, all can be controlled by spraying with copper fungicides.

Rust due to *Puccinia phyllostachydis* is occasionally found on the feather bamboo. Other rusts found on bamboo leaves in the South are *Puccinia ignava* and *P. melanocephala.*

Insects

Aphid (*Myzocallis arundinariae*). This aphid is common on bamboo leaves in California.

Control: Spray with malathion, Meta-Systox R, or Sevin when the insects become abundant.

Cottony Bamboo Scale (*Antonina crawi*). These narrow purplish-red scales, up to one-quarter inch in length, covered with masses of white cottony material, may be densely crowded in the leaf axils of the bamboo canes. This pest was introduced into California from the Orient.

Control: Spray with malathion, or with a white summer oil such as Volck. If the latter is used, the plants should be syringed with water from the hose the next day.

Bamboo Powder-Post Beetle (*Dinoderus minutus*). Those who use oriental bamboo canes for supporting plants in greenhouses or in gardens should be familiar with the work of the bamboo powder-post beetle. Eggs or larvae are frequently found inside the imported canes. The larvae feed on the inside of the cane and completely destroy the wood, leaving a very fine powder frass. The larvae pupate, and the beetles emerge some time in early spring. They are little brown beetles, from ½ to ⅕ inch in length, with rough ridges or striations.

Control: Kiln drying at a temperature of 180°F., or steaming in a saturated atmosphere for 1½ hours at 135°F. will control this pest in infested canes. Small bamboo objects should be treated with paradichlorobenzene, as for the brown powder-post beetle.

Brown Powder-Post Beetle (*Lyctus brunneus*). This insect is cosmopolitan and frequently occurs in bamboo art goods and Mah Jongg sets that are imported from China and Japan.

Control: Enclose infested materials with paradichlorobenzene in an airtight container for a week or two. The fumes of this chemical will penetrate the infested material and kill all stages of the pest.

BAPTISIA (FALSE INDIGO)

Leaf Spots (*Cercospora velutina, Marssonina baptisiae, Septoria baptisiae,* and *Stagonospora baptisiae*). Four fungi have been recorded as causes of leaf spots on this host.

Control: Where control measures are necessary, a copper fungicide is suggested.

Powdery Mildews (*Erysiphe polygoni* and *Microsphaera alni*). White powdery coating of the leaf surfaces is caused by one of the two fungi listed. The former is more prevalent.

Control: Spray with wettable sulfur, or Karathane.

Rust (*Puccinia andropogonis* var. *onobrychidis*). This rust is rarely destructive.

BEGONIA

Fungus, Bacterial, and Virus Diseases

Blotch (*Botrytis cinerea*). Occasionally under unfavorable greenhouse conditions this gray mold develops on the leaves and flowers and causes a well-marked blotch. Leaves and flower parts become brown and die.

Control: Pick off and discard all diseased leaves and destroy badly infected plants. Avoid syringing plants; provide good ventilation. Spray with Benlate, Botran, or with zineb as recommended by the manufacturer.

Leaf Spots (*Cercospora* sp., *Gloeosporium* sp., *Penicillium bacilosporium,* and *Phyllosticta* sp.). Four species of fungi cause leaf spots on this host.

Control: Destroy badly infected leaves and spray as for leaf blotch.

Powdery Mildews (*Oidium begoniae* and *Erysiphe cichoracearum*). Begonias are frequently attacked by powdery mildew fungi. Occasionally the leaves and the leaf and flower stalks become marred by whitish or brownish spots of the mycelium.

Control: When mildews appear spray with Karathane, Acti-dione PM, or wettable sulfur, as recommended by the manufacturer.

Bacterial Leaf Spot (*Xanthomonas begoniae*). A rather widespread leaf spot disease of tuberous begonia is caused by this bacterium. The spots are at first small and blister-like, appearing transparent by transmitted light. They later enlarge and run together, causing a blotched appearance. A slimy substance containing great numbers of bacteria oozes from the broken lesions and dries characteristically. The water-conducting vessels may be invaded by the organism, so that the entire plant collapses. Heavy infection of leaves may cause much defoliation.

Control: Plant parts which show limited infection should be cut off and discarded. Disinfect the pruning knife with 70 per cent denatured alcohol before using it again. Heavy infected plants should be removed, with the earth attached to the roots, and destroyed. The spread of the disease can be prevented by repeated spraying with copper fungicides. The greenhouse should be well ventilated so as to reduce the humidity. Plants should be well spaced. Avoid syringing, especially when the temperature is high. Propagate with cuttings from sound plants only. Avoid the use of soil that has not been pasteurized. Rieger Elatior begonias are particularly susceptible, and symptoms appear as yellowish-green spots at leaf margins.

Crown Gall (*Agrobacterium tumefaciens*). While certain species of begonia, such as *B. lucerna*, are said to be immune to the crown gall organism, possibly because of the plants' high acidity, this organism has been reported to attack other varieties and cause the typical swellings on the crown and lower stem parts.

Control: Cut away and destroy infected parts. Dip the remainder in a solution of streptomycin as directed by the manufacturer for crown gall control.

Root Rot (*Thielaviopsis basicola*). Seedlings and young plants are occasionally attacked by this soil fungus which causes roots to turn black and decay.

Control: Steam-pasteurize the soil in seedbeds where the disease has occurred.

Stem Rot (*Pythium ultimum*). A black stem rot may cause much damage in begonia houses and garden plantings. It may also invade the crown and cause a soft rot and the collapse of the stalks, as illustrated in Fig. 9.

Control: Plants attacked by this *Pythium* should be removed and immediately destroyed, since the disease spreads rapidly wherever plants are syringed. The fungus spreads also through the soil; infested soil should not be used for replanting unless it is first pasteurized. Crowding of plants should be avoided. Drench localized disease spots with Dexon.

Damping-off (*Pythium debaryanum* and *Pellicularia filamentosa*). Seedlings and young plants propagated from leaves are frequently attacked by these fungi. They cause a damping-off and rotting of the seedlings, and also attack leaf stalks and cause the leaf blades to rot, so that many of the cuttings are killed.

Control: Pasteurize the soil and provide well-aerated and well-lighted benches. Avoid crowding the seedlings and cuttings. Use seeds and leaves from disease-free plants. The seeds, seedbeds, and soil can all be treated at once by the use of formaldehyde. (See page 00.)

Viruses. The tomato spotted wilt has been reported in certain species of begonia. In some cases the leaves are deformed with a marked stunting and bronzing of the plants. Typical ringspots may also develop. Spotted wilt is spread by thrips.

Aster Yellows. This leafhopper-borne disease, apparently caused by a mycoplasma-like organism, has been reported to affect begonia.

Control: Remove and destroy infected

plants. Control insect vectors with insecticides.

Insects and Other Animal Pests

Thrips (*Heliothrips haemorrhoidalis* and *Hercinothrips femoralis*). Several species of thrips have been reported as destructive to begonia. Their feeding may result in the development of irregular reddish-brown lines on the upper sides of the leaves or more or less extended rusty brown spots on the undersides, especially along the main veins. The epidermis may become thickened and corky (but this may be due also to other causes). The leaves may become deformed. The leaf stalks and stems also are attacked. The silvery color of the undersides of the leaves, which characterizes the work of thrips, is occasionally evident. It is difficult to be sure that the injury is due to thrips unless the insects are actually observed at work.

Control: Spray the plants with malathion 2 or 3 times at weekly intervals before blooms appear.

Mealybugs (*Pseudococcus longispinus* and *Planococcus citri*). Begonia is among the many greenhouse plants subject to attack by mealybugs. These pests can become extremely troublesome and difficult to eradicate completely if overlooked for too long a period. Their eggs are deposited in difficult-to-reach places and hence are protected from chemical sprays.

Control: Malathion or Sevin sprays applied 2 or 3 times at 7- to 10-day intervals will give good control.

Greenhouse Whitefly (*Trialeurodes vaporariorum.*

Control: See *Fuchsia.*

Cotton Aphid (*Aphis gossypii*). This species of aphid causes serious injury to greenhouse begonia if it is not controlled before the plants come into blossom.

Control: Spray with malathion or Sevin perferably before blossoming time.

Black Vine Weevil (*Otiorhynchus sulcatus*). Tuberous begonia and cyclamen are sometimes attacked by the larvae of this beetle. Roots are often completely destroyed. The plants wilt and die. This pest, however, is far more destructive to the roots of woody plants like rhododendrons, hemlock, and yews.

Control: See under *Taxus* for the latest control methods.

Orange Tortrix (*Argyrotaenia citrana*). This insect occasionally attacks garden begonias. It rarely becomes serious enough to warrent Diazinon or Imidan sprays.

Mites (*Steneotarsonemus pallidus* and *Polyphagotarsonemus latus*). The cyclamen mite and the broad mite cause a stunting of the young growth and curling of the leaves. Occasionally the two-spotted mite *Tetranychus urticae* infests begonia leaves.

Control: Occasional spraying with Dimite or Tedion will keep these pests under control.

Scales (*Chrysomphalus aonidum* and *Howardia biclavis*). The Florida red scale and the mining scale infest begonias in the warmer parts of the country.

Control: Spray with malathion or Sevin to control the crawler stage of these scales.

Leaf Nema (*Aphelenchoides olesistus*). This nema causes irregular brown blotches on the leaves. The blotches increase in size until the leaves curl up and drop off. The plant becomes stunted and unsightly. The nemas pass part of their lives in the soil, and healthy plants transplanted into infested soil soon acquire them.

Control: Prune off and destroy all infested parts of the plant. Destroy the entire plant if badly infested. Pasteurize the soil and disinfest the benches before planting the next crop. Only cuttings from disease-free plants should be used for propagation. Space the plants so that the leaves do not intermingle. Avoid syringing, since nemas swim up the stems and infest the leaves through the stomata only when the plants are wet. Extensive experiments have been carried on to determine to what extent the hot-water treatment can be used on begonia to control eelworms. Begonias in small pots can be submerged for 1 minute at 120 to 121°F. or for 3 minutes at 117 to 119°F.

Southern Root-Knot Nema (*Meloidogyne incognita*). When plants are infested with this nema the tops become stunted and will not grow normally, regardless of the cultural treatment. On tuberous begonias the root galls may become as large as hazelnuts.

Control: Pasteurize infested soil with steam or an appropriate chemical. Soak infested tuberous begonia tubers while dormant in hot water at 120°F. for 30 minutes. Cool and plant in clean soil.

Physiological Disease

Corky Scab. This disease also known as **Oedema,** appears as light brown corky growths on the undersides of the leaves and along the stems. It is thought to be due to high humidity and overwatering in cloudy weather. Peperomias are extremely subject to the same disease.

BELAMCANDA (BLACKBERRY-LILY)

Scorch (*Didymellina macrospora*). The upper parts of the leaves turn brown and wither in summer because of numerous circular spots, which may coalesce. The imperfect stage of this fungus is *Heterosporium iridis.* The same fungus also causes a serious leaf spot of iris. A species of *Alternaria* has also been reported as the cause of a leaf spot on *Belamcanda* in the Middle West.

Control: Spray 2 or 3 times during the growing season with either a copper or a sulfur fungicide.

BELLIS PERENNIS (ENGLISH DAISY)

This host is subject to few diseases and to no insects of importance. A blight caused by the fungus *Botrytis cinerea* has been reported from Alaska. Leaf spots caused by *Septoria bellidis* and a species of *Cercospora,* and root rots caused by *Pythium mastophorum* and *Phymatotrichum omnivorum,* are other fungus diseases of English daisy. Aster yellows, caused by a mycoplasma-like organism, also infects this host occasionally.

BERBERIS (BARBERRY)

Bacterial and Fungus Diseases

Bacterial Leaf Spots (*Pseudomonas berberidis*). The common barberry has been reported subject to infection by this bacterium, which attacks the leaves. The infected areas are at first rather small, irregular, dark green, and watersoaked; later they become purple-brown. Leaf stalks and succulent shoots are subject to attack. When year-old twigs are attacked the buds do not develop the following spring, and if twigs are girdled a blight results.

Control: Prune and destroy affected parts. Spray with a copper fungicide, or with streptomycin, 2 or 3 times at 10-day intervals beginning when new leaves appear.

Anthracnose (*Gloeosporium berberidis*). Broad, nearly circular, brown spots with reddish margins develop on the upper sides of the leaves. This unimportant disease may be controlled by spraying with a copper fungicide if necessary. A purple leaf spot caused by *Phyllosticta asiatica* has also been reported on the Asiatic barberry.

Root Rots (*Pythium debaryanum* and *Phymatotrichum omnivorum*). The former fungus causes a root rot of *Berberis gracilis* in California; the latter has been reported from Texas.

Control: Use clean soil or pasteurize infested soil.

Rust (*Puccinia graminis*). This fungus causes a bright orange-colored spotting; it is not important on barberry and results in the loss of leaves only under heavy infection.

However, the presence of rust on common barberry is a menace to wheat and other cereals grown nearby. In some states the laws require the destruction of common barberry on this account. Interstate movement of certain barberries is under quarantine. State departments of agriculture will provide rules and regulations regarding shipment of barberries. The fungus does not attack Japanese barberry. Another rust, *Cumminsiella sanguinea,* occurs in the northern plain, Rocky mountain, and Pacific coast states.

Wilt (*Verticillium albo-atrum*). This soil-inhibiting fungus causes a brown discoloration of the water-conducting tissues. The leaves become brown or reddish, shrivel, and finally fall. Entire plants may eventually die.

Control: Remove and discard infected plants and the soil immediately surrounding them. Replace with clean soil and replant with healthy stock.

Mosaic (Cucumber mosaic virus). A strain of this virus produces a mosaic pattern of reddish blotches on the leaves of *Berberis thunbergii.*

Control: Remove and destroy infected plants.

Insects and Other Animal Pests

Barberry Aphid (*Liosomaphis berberidis*). This small greenish-yellow plant louse infests the leaves and shoots of barberry.

Control: Spray with malathion, Meta-Systox R, or Sevin.

Barberry Webworm (*Omphalocera dentosa*). The caterpillars, about 1/2 inch long, are black with white spots. They web together the leaves and tips of shoots. They attack both the common and the Japanese barberry.

Control: Spray with Sevin when the caterpillars appear.

Scale (*Lecaniodiaspis* sp.). Rather convex reddish-brown soft scales occur in considerable numbers on barberries at times.

Control: Spray with miscible oil while the plants are dormant in early spring, or with malathion, Meta-Systox R, or Sevin during the growing season.

Northern Root-Knot Nema (*Meloidogyne hapla*). This species may infest the roots of barberry in the northern United States.

Control: See Chapter 3.

Japanese Weevil. See *Ligustrum.*

BERCHEMIA (RATTAN-VINE)

The rattan-vine is one of the alternate hosts of the oat rust (*Puccinia coronata*). Other fungus parasites are *Glonium curtisii* and *Valsa berchemiae.* They are unimportant.

BETULA (BIRCH)

Fungus Diseases

Leaf Spots (*Gloeosporium betularum* and *Cylindrosporium betulae*). The former fungus produces brown spots with a dark brown to black margin. The latter forms smaller spots with no definite margin.

Control: Gathering and destroying fallen leaves usually suffices for practical control. A copper fungicide may be used in late spring as a preventive.

Leaf Blisters (*Taphrina bacteriosperma, T. carnea,* and *T. flava*). The first and second species listed produce red blisters and curling of the leaves on many of the birch species. The latter forms yellow blisters on gray and canoe birch.

Control: Gather and destroy all fallen leaves. Spray with lime sulfur or ferbam just before buds open in spring.

Leaf Rust (*Melampsoridium betulinum*). Leaves of seedlings and of mature trees are sometimes attacked by a rust which causes spotting and defoliation. The rust pustules are bright reddish-yellow. The spores from these pustules carry the infection from leaf to leaf. The alternate or sexual stage causes a blister rust on larch. In mixed forest plantings both hosts may be seriously injured. In ornamental plantings the disease rarely becomes destructive enough to warrant special control measures.

Canker (*Nectria galligena*). Black, paper, sweet, and yellow birches are particularly susceptible to this disease, depicted in Fig. 110. The fungus attacks the branches near the forks and causes very irregular swellings which crack open and expose the wood. As the parasite spreads, a thick callus develops at the border of the canker. These rolls of callus indicate that the tree is overcoming the infection. Successive rings of callus may be visible. Cankers on trunks cause a flattening and bending of the trunk at the canker. When trunks are girdled, death results.

Control: In thick stands it is advisable to remove trees with trunk infections. Trees having cankers or galls on the branches may be saved by pruning out and destroying the cankers. Since the cankers originate on young growth, inspection of the plantings and early destruction of the cankered young trees are advisable. Trees in ornamental plantings should be fed and watered to keep them in good vigor.

Line Pattern Mosaic (Apple mosaic virus). Decline, dieback, and death of both white and yellow birches in forest plantings may be virus-induced. White birch in ornamental plantings may also be affected but to a lesser extent.

Yellow to golden line and ringspot patterns on the leaves are the most striking symptoms.

Control: Control measures have not been developed.

Dieback (*Melanconium betulinum*). Trees weakened by drought may be attacked by this fungus which causes a progressive dieback of the upper branches. Infestations of the bronze birch borer mentioned below may cause similar symptoms, however.

Control: Prune affected branches to sound wood, and fertilize and water heavily to help revitalize the tree.

Fig. 110. Nectria canker on birch trunk. (Bartlett Tree Research Laboratory)

Wood Decay. A number of wood-decay fungi attack birches. One, *Polyporus betulinus,* attacks dying or dead birches and produces shelf- or hoof-shaped, gray, smooth, fungus bodies along the trunk. Others, such as *Torula ligniperda, Fomes fomentarius, F. igniarius, F. applanatus, Poria laevigata,* and *P. obliqua* are associated with decay of living trees.

Control: Wood decays cannot be checked once they have become extensive. Avoidance of wounds and maintenance of the trees in good vigor by fertilization are the best preventive practices.

Other Fungus Diseases. Birches are subject to several other fungus diseases: powdery mildews caused by *Microsphaera alni* and *Phyllactinia corylea,* leaf spots by *Gloeosporium betulae-luteae* and *Septoria betulicola,* and stem cankers by *Physalospora obtusa* and *Diaporthe alleghaniensis.*

Insects and Related Pests

Aphids (*Euceraphis punctipennis* and *Calaphis betulaecolens*). The former, known as the European birch aphid, is yellow and infests cut-leaved and other birch varieties. The latter, the common birch aphid, is a large green species which produces copious quantities of honeydew followed by sooty mold.

Control: Spray thoroughly with Diazinon, Cygon, or malathion as soon as these aphids appear.

Witch-Hazel Leaf Gall Aphid (*Hormaphis hamamelidis*). This insect, which causes the formation of cone galls on witch-hazel, migrates from this host to birches in summer. It feeds on the undersides of the leaves and resembles nymphs of whiteflies.

Control: Spray with malathion or Meta-Systox R when aphids are present.

Birch Skeletonizer (*Bucculatrix canadensisella*). The lower leaf surface is chewed and the leaf is skeletonized and may turn brown as a result of feeding by this skeletonizer, a yellowish-green larva, 1/4 inch long. The adult moth has white-lined, brown wings with a spread of 3/8 inch.

Control: Spray the upper and lower sides of the leaves with Sevin or Diazinon about mid-July.

Birch Leaf Miner (*Fenusa pusilla*). Gray, canoe, and cut-leaf birches are especially susceptible to attacks by the leaf miner, a small, white worm which causes leaves to turn brown in late spring or early summer (Fig. 111). The adult is a small black sawfly which overwinters in the soil as a pupa. The first brood begins to feed anytime from very early to late May, depending on the season and the location of the trees. The first brood causes most damage because it attacks the tender spring foliage. Other broods hatch

during the summer, but these cause less damage because they do not attack mature foliage but confine their feeding to leaves on sucker growths and to newly developing leaves in the crowns of the trees.

Control: Diazinon, malathion, Meta-Systox R, or Sevin sprays will control the ta-Systox R, or Sevin sprays will control the birch leaf miner. The first spray should be applied about May 1. If the spring is a cold one, the first application can be delayed a week or so. For best control, two additional applications should be made at 10-day intervals after the first. To control the second brood of leaf miners, spray again about July 1 and July 10.

In commercial nurseries, a soil application in April of a systemic insecticide such as Di-Syston gives good control.

Bronze Birch Borer (*Agrilus anxius*). Varieties of birch grown in parks as ornamental shade trees, especially where the soil is poor, and trees grown elsewhere under adverse conditions, become prey to this borer. The grub is from 1/2 to 1 inch long, flat-headed and light-colored (see Fig. 81). The adult stage is a beetle, 1/2 inch long. The beetles, which feed on foliage for a time, deposit their eggs in slits in the bark. The borers make flat, irregular, winding galleries just beneath the bark of the main trunk. Heavy infestations usually kill the trees.

Control: Spray the trunk and branches thoroughly and the leaves lightly in early June and twice more at 2-week intervals with methoxychlor as directed by the manufacturer. Dimethoate (Cygon 2E) at the rate of one quart per 100 gallons of water applied to the trunk and branches in early June and again 3 weeks later also provides good control. Keep trees in good vigor by feeding and watering when needed.

Seed Mite Gall (*Eriophyes betulae*). Another conspicuous gall on paper birch and other species is caused by the seed mite. The galls are about 1 inch in diameter, made up of

Fig. 111. Blotches in leaves made by the birch leaf miner *Fenusa pusilla.*

many adventitious branches and deformed buds. They may resemble witches' brooms.

Control: This pest is never serious enough to require control measures.

Linden Looper. See *Tilia.*

BIGNONIA (CROSSVINE)

Diseases

A leaf spot caused by the fungus *Cercospora capreolata,* a blight by a species of *Botrytis,* and black mildew by the fungi *Dimerosporium tropicale* and *Meliola bidentata* are the more common diseases of this host.

Control: Spray with Bordeaux mixture or any other copper fungicide if any of these diseases should become troublesome in ornamental plantings.

Insects and Other Animal Pests

Mealybug (*Planococcus citri*). This insect is troublesome in southern gardens and in northern greenhouses.

Control: Spray with malathion.

Greenhouse Whitefly (*Trialeurodes vaporariorum*). This pest occurs indoors in the North and outdoors in the South.

Control: See *Fuchsia.*

Scales (*Ceroplastes cirripediformis, Saissetia hemisphaerica,* and *Pinnaspis strachani*). Three species of scales may infest this host.

Control: Spray with malathion, Meta-Systox R, or Sevin.

Southern Root-Knot Nema (*Meloidogyne incognita*). This nema is occasionally troublesome.

BISCHOFIA

Algal Spot is one of the few diseases of plants caused by an alga, *Cephaleuros virescens.* It is prevalent only in moist warm climates, or on slow-growing plants in overly moist greenhouses.

BIXA (ANNATTO-TREE)

Besides algal spot (*Cephaleuros virescens*), other leaf spots caused by *Cercospora bixae* and *Phyllosticta bixina* are reported on this host.

BOERHAAVIA (SPIDERLING)

White Rust (*Albugo candida*). This fungus has been reported from many southern states. See under *Arabis.*

Other Diseases. Among the other diseases of this host, all reported from Texas, are a bacterial leaf spot caused by *Xanthomonas campestris,* two fungus leaf spots caused by *Ascochyta boerhaaviae* and *Cercospora boerhaaviae,* and root rot by *Phymatotrichum omnivorum.*

BOUGAINVILLEA

Diseases

Leaf Spot (*Cercospora bougainvilleae*). This serious leaf spot was first reported from Florida in 1962. Spots are 1 to 5 mm, in diameter with depressed tan to light brown cen-

ters. It is considered to be one of the most important diseases of Bougainvillea.

Control: Copper A or maneb sprays applied when the disease is first observed and continued several times at 10- to 14-day intervals will control this leaf spot.

Other Diseases. Another leaf spot caused by the fungus *Cladosporium arthrinioides* occurs in Texas, and an undetermined virus disease has been reported from Florida.

Insects

Bougainvillea Caterpillar (*Asciodes gordialis*). This 1-inch-long caterpillar frequently infests this host.

Control: During the warmer parts of the year in the South spray every 2 weeks with Sevin.

Other Insects. The greenhouse orthezia (*Orthezia insignis*) and nine species of scales —brown soft, cottony-cushion, cyanophyllum, Florida red, hemispherical, latania, mining, pustule, and quahog-shaped—infest bougainvillea.

Control: In the South, summer oil sprays will control these pests. In greenhouses in the North, malathion sprays will control the crawler stage of scales.

BOUSSINGAULTIA (MADEIRA-VINE)

The southern root-knot nema (*Meloidogyne incognita*) may retard the growth of this host in the southern states.

BOUVARDIA

Rusts (*Puccinia bouvardiae* and *P. lateritia*). These two rusts have been reported from the southern states. They are rarely serious enough to justify fungicidal applications.

Foliar Nema (*Aphelenchoides ritzemabosi*). The leaves are blotched and the flower clusters are deformed and dwarfed. See under *Chrysanthemum*. The Southern root-knot nema (*Meloidogyne incognita*) also has been reported to do some damage.

BOWLESIA

Bacterial Leaf Spot (*Pseudomonas bowlesiae*). Irregular water-soaked spots, nearly black, and surrounded by a reddish-brown zone, are caused by this bacterium. When the petioles are infected the leaves droop and wither. No control has been recommended.

BRASSAIA (SCHEFFLERA)

This plant, more commonly called schefflera, is grown outdoors in the warmer parts of the country where it is subject to a leaf spot caused by a species of *Alternaria* and to root-knot caused by the nema *Meloidogyne incognita* var. *acrita*.

Leaf Drop. When grown as house plants, scheffleras are readily harmed by overwatering. Too much or too frequent watering causes root rot, followed by premature leaf drop.

BROUSSONETIA (PAPER-MULBERRY)

Canker (*Fusarium solani*). This disease was first found in Ohio in 1965. Branch dieback results from cankers produced by this fungus, which also infects cottonwood, red oak, and sweetgum.

Control: Prune infected branches. Keep trees in good vigor by feeding and by watering during dry spells.

Root Rot (*Phymatotrichum omnivorum*). This root rot, common on many plants in the southern states, has been reported from Texas on paper-mulberry.

Other Diseases. Among the other diseases reported from the southern states are a dieback and canker caused by the fungus *Nectria cinnabarina*, a leaf spot by *Cercosporella*

mori and *Corynespora cassiicola*, a mistletoe disease by *Phoradendron flavescens*, and root-knot by the nema *Meloidogyne incognita*.

Insect

White Peach Scale (*Pseudaulacaspis pentagona*). See *Prunus persica.*

BROWALLIA

The only diseases reported on this host are smut caused by the fungus *Entyloma browalliae*, spotted wilt by the tomato spotted wilt virus, and wilt by a species of *Fusarium*.

Among the insects which infest *Browallia* are the western aster root aphid *Anuraphis middletoni* and the aster leafhopper *Macrosteles fascifrons*.

The root aphid can be controlled by wetting the soil in the vicinity of infested plants with a dilute solution of Diazinon or malathion. The leafhopper can be controlled with Diazinon, Meta-Systox R, or Sevin sprays.

BUDDLEJA (BUTTERFLY-BUSH)

Diseases

Root Rot (*Phymatotrichum omnivorum*). This fungus has caused serious losses on butterfly-bush in Texas.

A sooty mold caused by the fungus *Cladosporium heugelinianum,* and a stem canker by *Phomopsis buddlejae,* have also been reported on butterfly-bush.

Insects and Related Pests

Checker Spot Butterfly (*Euphydryas chalcedona*). The caterpillar stage of this butterfly is large, bluish-black with small orange markings. It feeds on aster, chrysanthemum, penstemon, veronica, and other plants, in addition to butterfly-bush.

Control: Spray with Sevin when the caterpillars are small.

Japanese Beetle (*Popillia japonica*). *Buddleja* is a favored host for this pest.

Control: See *Althaea.*

Banded Greenhouse Thrips (*Hercinothrips femoralis*). This species occasionally infests this host. Malathion or Cygon sprays will control it.

Southern Root-Knot Nema (*Meloidogyne incognita*). This soil-inhibiting nema occasionally infests butterfly-bush. Controls are outlined in Chapter 3.

BURSERA (GUMBO-LIMBO)

Sooty Mold (*Fumago vagans*). A heavy growth of this sooty mold develops on the plant as a result of infestation with the brown soft scale (see below). The results are sometimes very serious.

Control: Spray with malathion or Sevin to control the scale insect which secretes the substance on which the sooty mold fungus lives.

Other Disease. In the deep South, branches of this host may be killed by the fungus *Physalospora fusca.*

Control: Prune infected branches.

Insect

Brown Soft Scale (*Coccus hesperidum*). This scale insect, which often remains inconspicuous because of its tendency to assume the color of the twigs or leaves upon which it is feeding, does great damage to greenhouse plants. The lower sides of the leaves are sometimes heavily infested with the light green scales, which often choose the petioles or twigs and the upper parts of the trunk on which to develop their mature stages. The scales are arranged longitudinally along the smaller branches and main stem. They are very flat and thin, more or less transparent. Though the young are usually sluggish, not migrating far from the mother scale, they do travel to the leaves above. This scale is said to be a general feeder, attacking many plants in the greenhouse and also tropical fruit outdoors.

At least six other species of scale may infest Gumbo-Limbo.

Control: Spray the plants with malathion, Meta-Systox R, or Sevin every two weeks until all the young scales are destroyed.

BUXUS (BOXWOOD)

Fungus Diseases

Canker (*Pseudonectria rousseliana*). The first noticeable symptom of this destructive disease of boxwood is that certain branches or certain plants in a group do not start new growth so early in the spring as do others, nor is the new growth so vigorous as that on healthy specimens. The leaves turn from normal to light green and then to various shades of tan. Infected leaves turn upward and lie close to the stem instead of spreading out like the leaves on healthy stems. The diseased leaves and branches show small, rosecolored, waxy pustules, the fruiting bodies of the *Volutella* stage of the fungus. The bark at the base of an infected branch is loose and peels off readily from the gray to black discolored wood beneath. Infection is frequently found to take place at the bases of small dead shoots or in crotches where leaves have been allowed to accumulate. A species of *Verticillium* is occasionally associated with the dieback of twigs. The fungus *Nectria desmazierii,* whose imperfect stage is known as *Fusarium buxicola,* is also capable of causing canker and dieback of boxwood.

Control: Dead branches should be removed as soon as they are noticeable, and cankers on the larger limbs should be treated by surgical methods. The annual removal and destruction of all leaves that have lodged in crotches are recommended. Four applications of a copper fungicide or lime sulfur have been shown to be very effective in preventing canker. The first should be made after the dead leaves and dying branches have been removed and before growth starts in the spring; the second, when the new growth is half completed; the third, after spring growth has been completed; and the fourth, after the fall growth has been completed. The boxwood should be fed with occasional applications to the soil of well-rotted cow manure, or commercial fertilizers, and ground limestone.

Blight. Several fungi are associated with the blighting of boxwood leaves. The most common are *Phoma conidiogena* and *Hyponectria buxi.* The exact role of these fungi in this disease complex is not clear.

Control: The fungicides recommended for canker control will also control blight.

Leaf Spots (*Macrophoma candollei, Phyllosticta auerswaldii, Fusarium buxicola,* and *Collectotrichum* sp.). Leaves turn straw-yellow and are thickly dotted with small black bodies, the fruiting structures of the first fungus listed above. The others also cause leaf spotting. All are apparently limited in their attacks to foliage weakened by various causes.

Control: Leaf spot may be controlled by shaking out all fallen and diseased leaves from the center of the bush and destroying them. All dead branches in the center of specimen plants or hedges should be removed to allow better aeration. An application of a copper fungicide before growth starts in the spring is beneficial. This spray will discolor the foliage, but the unsightly effect is soon hidden by new growth.

Root Rot (*Phytophthora cinnamomi*). "Off-color" foliage followed by sudden wilting and death of the entire plant is characteristic of this disease. Yews, rhododendrons, and a large number of other woody ornamental plants are also subject to this disease.

Another species, *P. parasitica,* also causes a root rot and blight of boxwood.

Paecilomyces buxi was found to be associated with boxwood decline in Virginia.

Control: Infected plants cannot be saved. Steam-pasteurize infested soil and replant with healthy specimens.

Nonparasitic Diseases

Winter Injury and Sun Scald. Most boxwood troubles in the northeastern United States are due to freezing and sunscalding, which primarily injure the cambium of unripened wood. Several distinct types of symptoms are exhibited by winter injury. Young leaves and twigs may be injured when growth extends far into fall or begins too early in spring. Leaves may turn rusty brown to red as a result of exposure to cold, dry winds during winter. A dieback of leaves, twigs, and even the entire plant may occur on warm winter days when the aboveground tissues thaw rapidly and lose more water than can be replaced through the frozen soil and roots. Another type of winter injury is expressed by the splitting and peeling of the bark. The bark becomes loosened and the stems are entirely girdled, resulting in death of the distal portions.

Control: Fertilizers should be applied in late fall, preferably, or very early in spring. Adequate windbreaks should be provided during winter, especially in the more northern latitudes. In the latitude of New York City spraying with Wilt-Pruf NCF on a mild day in December, and again on a mild day the following February will provide as much protection from winter winds as do burlap windbreaks. A heavy mulch consisting of equal parts of leaf mold and cow manure should be applied to prevent deep freezing and to aid in supplying water continuously.

Insects

Mealybugs (*Pseudococcus comstocki* and *Rhizoecus falcifer*). The former, known as the Comstock mealybug, attacks many hosts including catalpa, holly, horsechestnut, maple, pine, and poplar. It is one of the few species capable of wintering outdoors. The latter, the ground mealybug, feeds on the roots of many shrubs and trees.

Control: Cygon, malathion, or Sevin sprays applied to the leaves and stems will control the Comstock mealy bug. A dilute solution of Diazinon applied to the soil around the base of the boxwood should control the ground mealybug.

Scales. Five species of scales, California red, cottony maple, cottony-cushion, lesser snow, and the oystershell, may infest boxwood.

Control: Spray with a dormant "superior" oil to control overwintering scales. Where infestations are heavy, follow with a spray containing malathion, Meta-Systox R, or Sevin when the young are crawling about in May and June.

Boxwood Psyllid (*Psylla buxi*). Terminal leaves are cupped and young twig growth is checked by the boxwood psyllid, a small, gray, sucking insect covered with a cottony or white, waxy material. The adult is a small green fly with transparent wings having a spread of $1/8$ inch.

Control: Spray in mid-May and again two weeks later with Diazinon, malathion or Sevin.

Boxwood Leaf Miner (*Monarthropalpus buxi*). Oval, water-soaked swellings on the lower leaf surface result from the feeding inside the leaves by the leaf miner, a yellowish-white maggot, $1/8$ inch long. The adult is a tiny midge, $1/10$ inch long, which appears in May.

Control: When the adult midges are seen in late May (about the time the weigelas are in full bloom) spray the boxwood leaves with Diazinon, Cygon, malathion or Sevin.

Giant Hornet (*Vespa crabro germana*). The bark is occasionally stripped from the branches by the giant hornet, which has a 1-inch wing expanse and dark orange markings. The pests nest in trees, in buildings, or underground.

Control: Locate the nests and blow Diazinon powder into the openings. Apply a Diazinon or Sevin spray in mid July to the trunk and branches of trees subject to bark-tearing by this pest. Repeat the application in early August.

Boxwood Webworm (*Galasa nigrinodis*). This pest chews leaves and forms webs on boxwood.

Control: Spray with malathion, Meta-Systox R, or Sevin when the young larvae begin to feed.

Other Pests

Nemas (*Pratylenchus pratensis*). Leaf-bronzing, stunted growth, and general decline of boxwood may result from invasion by meadow nemas. These are tiny, eel-like worms, $3/10$ to $7/10$ of a millimeter long, which are visible only through a microscope. Invaded roots soon die and the plant forms lateral roots above the invaded area. These laterals in turn are infested. Repeated infestations and lateral root production result in a stunted root system resembling a witches' broom. Even heavy rains may fail to wet such densely woven root-bundles. Boxwoods are also subject to several other parasitic nemas including the southern root-knot nema *Meloidogyne incognita,* various ring nemas *Criconema, Criconemoides, and Procriconema,* and the spiral nema *Helicotylenchus.*

Control: Several chemicals are available for controlling ectoparasitic nemas such as *Pratylenchus pratensis,* which live outside the roots. These include Nemagon and Mobilawn, which are used as soil drenches around old, infested boxwood. The treatment must be repeated each year for several years before good control is achieved. It must be supplemented by shearing and fertilization to stimulate root activity.

Endoparasitic nemas such as the root-knot nema *Meloidogyne incognita,* which live inside the roots of boxwood, have been controlled with Dasanit or Mocap.

The life of infested but untreated plants may be prolonged by providing good care and by soaking the soil thoroughly during dry spells. Before boxwood is replaced in infested soil, the planting site should be fumigated with any one of several materials available for that purpose. Plant pathologists at state experiment stations will advise on selection and use of fumigants.

Boxwood Mite (*Eurytetranychus buxi*). A light mottling followed by brownish discoloration of the leaves is caused by infestations of eight-legged mites, about 1/64 inch long when full grown. Winter is passed in the egg stage. The eggs hatch in April and the young mites begin to suck out the leaf juices. By June or July, considerable injury may occur on infested plants. As many as six generations of mites may develop in a single season.

Control: The dormant oil spray recommended for scales will destroy many overwintering mites. Cygon, Diazinon, Kelthane, or Tedion applied during May and June will also control mites.

CACTACEAE[12] (CACTI)

Bacterial and Fungus Diseases

Crown Gall (*Agrobacterium tumefaciens*). The crown gall organism is known to attack the giant cactus, *Carnegiea gigantea,* forming galls on segments and roots. The aerial galls sometimes attain a diameter of more than 2 feet. The root galls are spongy, sometimes nearly a foot across, and 7 or 8 pounds in weight.

Control: Crown galls on aerial parts have been successfully cut out without destruction

[12] This is the name of the family to which all true cacti belong. Commonly cultivated genera are *Cereus, Zygocactus, Opuntia;* the last is treated separately in this book.

of the plant. If the bacteria are known to be present in the plantings, wounding of ornamental cacti should be carefully avoided. For the prevention of root galls the crown should be soaked in a solution of the antibiotic, streptomycin. Soil contaminated with bacteria should not be used for propagation.

Wilt (*Pythium debaryanum*). This disease has been known to spread rapidly from plant to plant, causing a brown spotting and wilting which begins at the base and extends upwards.

Control: Avoid overwatering and excessive humidity over a long period. Use clean soil for propagating plants.

Fusarium Wilt (*Fusarium oxysporum*). This disease affects *Cereus.* The symptom is a soft, black rot which begins at the tips of the plants and spreads downward. Plants in hot beds under glass may be badly infected. No control has been suggested.

Leaf Spot and Blight (*Fusarium oxysporum*). In Florida Christmas cactus, *Zygocactus truncatus,* is affected by the same fungus that causes wilt of *Cereus.* A water-soaked rot, often with a reddish border, develops at the soil line. Orange to brown spots may develop on the flat, jointed stems.

Control: Infected plants cannot be cured. Cuttings treated with thiabendazole, Benlate, Daconil, or Tersan OM should be completely protected from infection.

Stem Rot (*Helminthosporium cactivorum*). This is a very rapidly developing rot, which begins with well-defined yellow lesions that later become dark brown. Entire plants collapse and die within 2 to 4 days. The fungus enters older plants through the stomata or wounds; in young plants it may penetrate directly through the epidermis. See Figs. 112 and 113.

Control: Spray every 10 to 14 days with captan containing a small amount of a spreader-sticker. Rogue out badly diseased plants and use steam-pasteurized soil to start new plants.

Fig. 112. Top rot on *Cephalocereus tetetzo* and bottom rot on C. *mezcalaensis,* caused by the fungus *Helminthosporium cactivorum.* (Dr. Kenneth Baker)

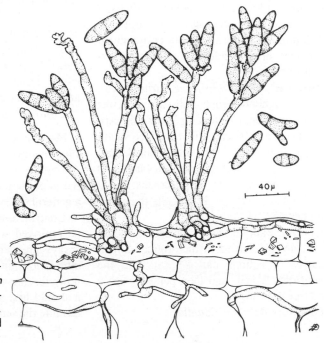

Fig. 113. Conidia and coni-diophores of *Helminthosporium cactivorum* arising from stro-matic masses in host tissue. (From Durbin, Davis, and Baker)

Pad Decay (*Aspergillus alliaceus*). Stem and branch decay of several species of cacti are caused by this fungus, which thrives under high temperatures. The spores, yellow in mass, germinate and gain entrance through wounds.

Control: Avoid wounds. Cut out and destroy diseased parts.

Slimy Collar Rot (*Phytophthora cactorum*). This fungus causes a black, slimy, soft collar rot at the base of the plant. The disease is particularly troublesome on species of *Cereus*. The fungus invades the soil in the vicinity of the plant for the depth of an inch or two.

Control: No effective control is available.

Soft Rot, Gray Mold (*Botrytis cinerea*). Cactus segments, particularly those of *Cereus*, are discolored, and the upper surface rots gradually and collapses. The tissues undergo a slimy disintegration. The gray mold develops over the surface of the diseased parts under moist conditions and develops the black sclerotia which propagate the disease.

Control: Infected parts should be removed and destroyed, and in greenhouse culture the ventilation and watering should be regulated to provide drier conditions. Captan sprays may also help.

Bacterial Blight (*Erwinia carnegieana*). This is a highly destructive disease affecting the giant cactus, *Carnegiea gigantea,* in Arizona. The causal bacteria first produce small, circular, light spots with water-soaked margins. The tissues underneath turn black. As the spots enlarge, the tissue cracks and a brown liquid oozes out. Eventually the entire plant decays.

Control: Badly diseased specimens should be cut up and buried in the ground. Small, localized infections can be cut out, the wound disinfected, and then painted with a good tree dressing.

Fusarium Rot. See *Opuntia.*

Physiological Diseases

Bud Fall. Premature dropping of buds and stunting of the plants have been reported as caused by bad cultural conditions. These may involve lack of nourishment, an excess of nitrogenous fertilizers, drying of the soil, and the use of very cold water for syringing.

Corky Scab. Irregular rusty or corky spots are seen on stems of many species of cacti, especially species of *Opuntia.* The shoots may be thickly covered with these spots, only young growth being free of them. Severe attacks may destroy entire shoots. Milder attacks decrease the production of flowers. The cells of the epidermis dry, and the epidermis breaks open and curls; the corky overgrowth then may be seen from below.

Control: The disease may be prevented by increasing the light and decreasing the humidity. Some cacti, however, are injured by overexposure to sunlight.

Glassiness. This disease is evidenced by dark green translucent spots. A slight pressure on one of these crushes the epidermis, and the tissue beneath rapidly turns black. Severe attacks may kill the shoots above the spots. Mild attacks cause the development of corky layers or spots which cut off the diseased tissue. Bacteria and fungi often enter and cause the decay of the segments.

Control: The same as for corky scab.

Mealybugs (*Pseudococcus longispinus, Planococcus citri*). These sucking insects are among the worst pests of cacti. By extracting the juice they cause extensive yellowing and a general sickly condition of the host.

Control: Small numbers of mealybugs may be removed with a small brush. Malathion sprays are very effective against mealybug infestations on cacti. A few species of cacti, however, are sensitive to this material; hence it should first be tried on a small scale to determine the sensitivity of the plants at hand.

Ground Mealybug (*Rhizoecus falcifer*). This root-parasite lives chiefly on the terminal or outer roots of potted plants. It secretes masses of fibrous wax like that of common mealybugs, but less compact. In these masses the eggs are laid. Infestation may cause the death of the plant. The tulip bulb aphid (*Dysaphis tulipae*) and other species may also infest cacti and cause serious damage.

Control: Wet the soil with a dilute solution of malathion made from the emulsifiable concentrate. Repeat within 2 weeks if necessary.

Cactus Scale (*Diaspis echinocacti*). This species is very common on cacti grown as house plants, and on outdoor species in the Southwest. The female scales have a gray, circular covering; the males are white and slender. The infestation at times may be so heavy as to completely encrust the entire surface of the cactus. Among other species of scales which occasionally attack cacti are: greedy, *Hemiberlesia rapax*, lesser snow, *Pinnaspis strachani*; and oleander scale, *Aspidiotus nerii*.

Control: Malathion as prescribed for mealybugs is very effective against the crawler (young) stage of scales but will not affect adult females, which are stationary and protected by a waxy covering. Cacti that can tolerate malathion should be sprayed every few weeks until the scale infestation is cleaned up. Those that cannot tolerate malathion should be sprayed with nicotine sulfate or Sevin.

Two-Spotted Mite (*Tetranychus urticae*). Cacti infested with mites have an ashy, yellowish, or even whitish appearance. A hand lens will easily reveal the presence of these pests.

Control: See *Althaea.*

CAESALPINIA—see POINCIANA

CALADIUM

Diseases

Tuber Rot. Several organisms cause rotting of caladium tubers: the bacterium *Erwinia carotovora*, which produces a soft, slimy decay; the fungus *Pellicularia rolfsii*, which also attacks a wide variety of other plants; *Botryotinia ricini*, which is also an important parasite of the castor-bean *Ricinus communis*; and the fungus *Rhizopus nigricans*, which also causes a decay of sweet potatoes; the fungus *Fusarium solani* which causes a dry, chalky rot during storage.

The chalky rot caused by *Fusarium solani* can be controlled by dipping tubers in Benlate, or dusting propagative pieces or whole tubers with Benlate.

Control: Store and ship tubers properly so as to avoid high humidities and overcrowding. Florida and California growers should not grow caladiums on ground previously cropped to castor bean. Florists and home gardeners forcing caladiums should provide good ventilation and should not overwater the plants. Dormant tubers infected with some of the parastic fungi, particularly *Pellicularia rolfsii*, can be dipped in hot water at 122°F. for 30 minutes, then cooled and planted in clean soil. Tubers infected with the bacterial soft rot do not respond to this treatment.

Leaf Spot (*Gloeosporium* sp.). This disease has been found on caladium but it is not serious enough to require control measures.

CALCEOLARIA

Fungus and Virus Diseases

Stem Rot (*Sclerotinia sclerotiorum*). The stems of infected plants become dry, the tip regions wilting. A felt of mycelium and numerous black sclerotia are visible. The foliage of such plants wilts severely and in it are irregular decaying spots. It has been shown that the sclerotia which are formed in the greenhouse develop the ascocarpic stage which carries the spores, and the fungus is consequently spread from plant to plant by syringing. Furthermore, the mycelium develops in soil and cinders; this is another means by which the disease spreads.

Root Rot (*Pythium ultimum* and P. *mastophorum*). The roots and lower stems are invaded by these soil-infesting species particularly when young plants are over-watered or overcrowded.

Basal Rot (*Phytophthora cactorum*). The plants are attacked at the base by this fungus, which causes them to wilt and die. This disease occasionally causes much damage in plantings.

Wilt (*Verticillium albo-atrum*). This fungus has been recorded from New York and Washington on calceolaria.

Control: The four diseases listed above are difficult to control once they get started. Avoid overwatering. Provide good drainage, light, and air. Use a light soil for starting seedlings. Treat infested soils either with steam or chemicals as described in Chapter 4.

Virus (Tomato spotted wilt virus). This virus produces stunting of the plants and a striking yellowish mosaic pattern on the leaves accompanied by leaf distortion. Flowers are marked with pale red or yellow rings.

Control: Destroy diseased plants. Control sucking insects with malathion sprays. Take cuttings from virus-free stock plants.

Insects and Other Pests

Greenhouse Whitefly (*Trialeurodes vaporariorum*). This and several species of aphids, among which are *Myzus persicae, Neomyzus circumflexus,* and *Arcythosiphon pelargonii,* may infest calceolarias.

Control: See *Fuchsia.*

Foliar Nemas (*Aphelenchoides olesistus*

and *A. ritzema-bosi*). These leaf-infesting nemas enter the leaves through the stomata and feed on the tissues between the veins. Their depredations result in conspicuous brown areas. The same species attack ferns and other plants.

Control: Since the eelworms swim in the film of water on the surface of the stems of plants and move from leaf to leaf when the plants are wet, one should avoid unnecessary syringing.

Foliar-infesting nemas on some ornamentals can be controlled by frequent sprayings with parathion. Unfortunately this chemical is so dangerous to handle that it is not recommended for amateur gardeners.

CALENDULA (POT MARIGOLD)

Diseases

Leaf Spot (*Cercospora calendulae*). This is probably the most serious fungus disease of calendula. In some fields 50 per cent of the plants have been destroyed. The symptoms are leaf spots, which later run together. Since the disease progresses rapidly, the entire plant may be destroyed early in the season. Almost all varieties of calendula are subject to attack, though plants less than a month old appear to be immune. The fungus is said to enter the host through the stomata.

Other leaf spotting fungi which occasionally affect this host are *Colletotrichum gloeosporioides* and a species of *Alternaria.*

Control: Spray with wettable sulfur or a copper fungicide, beginning when the plants are fairly young so as to prevent the disease from becoming established. Repeat at weekly intervals for 4 or 5 times.

Smut (*Entyloma calendulae* and *E. compositarum*). Pale yellow spots which turn brown to black, $1/4$ inch in diameter, develop on the leaves of calendulas grown in the West.

Control: Gather all infected plants and discard them in the fall, being careful to rake up all pieces of leaves and other debris. It may be advisable to change the location of the plantings and to spray the plants with a copper fungicide.

Stem Rots (*Pellicularia filamentosa* and *Sclerotinia sclerotiorum*). These fungi attack calendulas primarily in the southern states.

Control: Avoid planting in infested soil.

Leaf Blight (*Botrytis cinerea*). This is one of the fungus diseases of calendula that occurs sporadically under moist weather conditions. As a rule it is not serious.

Black Mold (*Fumago* sp.). This mold, which develops on honeydew secreted by various sucking insects, has been reported as doing some damage in greenhouses through cutting off the light from the leaves.

Control: Spray with malathion, Meta-Systox R, or Sevin to control the aphids and scale insects, and other pests that shed so-called honeydew.

Rust (*Puccinia flaveriae*). This rust attacks calendulas in the Middle West and in Texas.

Control: Ferbam sprays will control this disease.

Powdery Mildews (*Erysiphe cichoracearum* and *E. polygoni*). The whitish mycelium of these fungi covers the leaves of plants grown under excessively moist and drafty conditions in greenhouses. See Fig. 12. Circular spots ¼ and ½ inch in diameter first appear. They are irregularly scattered, but later the whole plant becomes involved, and finally withers and dies.

Control: Spray with Karathane or with wettable sulfur. Avoid using these materials during high temperatures or when the plants are blooming, and follow other precautions printed on the package.

Viruses. The cucumber mosaic virus and the tomato spotted wilt virus occur on *Calendula*.

Control: Rogue out and destroy infected plants. Control sucking insects with malathion, Meta-Systox R, or Sevin sprays.

Aster Yellows. This mycoplasma-caused disease also affects *Calendula*.

Control: Same as for viruses.

Insects and Other Animal Pests

Black Blister Beetle (*Epicauta pennsylvanica*). This beetle attacks calendulas year after year in certain gardens during the early part of August.

Control: Effective control is possible by spraying with either methoxychlor or Sevin. Once the beetles appear in summer, the applications must be made weekly because the insects continue to come in swarms.

Greenhouse Whitefly (*Trialeurodes vaporariorum*). This host is among many that are attacked by the greenhouse whitefly. See *Fuchsia*.

Cabbage Looper (*Trichoplusia ni*). The very active green larvae, about 1½ inches long, with white stripes on each side of the body, feed on calendula under glass and in the garden. They eat the foliage and buds.

Control: Sevin sprays provide good control if applied when the larvae are young. Sprays of polyhedrosis virus are also effective.

Yellow Woollybear (*Diacrisia virginica*). The foliage of calendula is sometimes seriously damaged by this caterpillar, which is very hairy and yellow with black lines.

Control: Sevin sprays are effective.

Painted Lady Butterfly (*Vanessa cardui*). The caterpillars of this insect feed on the foliage of calendula, occasionally doing considerable damage. They tie the leaves together in unsightly bunches.

Control: Same as for the yellow woollybear.

Other Pests. Calendulas are also subject to infestation by several species of aphids, by cutworms, leafhoppers, mealybugs, thrips, tarnished plant bugs, and the root-knot nema. Control these in the same way as on other more favored ornamentals.

CALLIANDRA

The roots of the Surinam calliandra in Florida may be rotted by the fungus *Clitocybe tabescens*. In Arizona the rust fungus *Ravenelia reticulatae* occurs on false mesquite. The green peach aphid, *Myzus persicae*, attacks the powder-puff tree, *Calliandra inaequilatera*, when this beautiful tree is grown in northern greenhouses. The aphids are frequently held in check by the parasitic braconid wasps. The wasps thrust their eggs into the abdomens of the aphids. There, after the eggs hatch, the little grubs feed on the body content. The parasite punctures a hole in the under side of the aphid and fastens it to the leaf; the aphid then swells up and turns brown and the skin becomes tough and leathery. When the wasp is about to emerge it cuts a round hole in the body of the abdomen, sometimes leaving a hinge-like portion which holds the lid-like cover in place. The aphids are also controlled by syrphid flies, the sluglike larvae of which feed on the aphids. Ladybugs also are natural enemies of these insects. Aphid infestations that are too heavy to be controlled by natural parasites can be handled with malathion sprays.

CALLICARPA (BEAUTY-BERRY)

Diseases

Leaf Spots (*Atractilina callicarpae*). The spots are irregular, rustlike, very numerous, but scattered. The spindle-shaped, septate, colorless conidia are borne on fertile hyphae gathered together to make a stalk; the leaf spot caused by the fungus *Cercospora callicarpae* may cause complete defoliation of plants in Florida.

Control: Spray frequently with wettable sulfur.

Black Mold (*Meliola cookeana*). This fungus is superficial, the black mycelium growing all over the surface of twigs and leaves.

Control: Spray with malathion, Meta-Systox R, or Sevin to control the insects that secrete honeydew, on which the black mold lives.

Other Diseases. *Botryosphaeria dothidea, Coniothyrium callicarpae, Nectria cinnabarina,* and *Physalospora obtusa* attack the stems of this host.

Control: Cut out and destroy infected parts.

CALLISTEPHUS (CHINA ASTER)

Diseases

Wilt (*Fusarium oxysporum* var. *callistephi*). Except for aster yellows, wilt is the most common and most serious disease of China aster. Depending on the condition of the roots of the young plants when they are set out in the borders, the disease may appear within a week or may not develop until the plants are fully grown. If plants are infected when they are young, all their leaves wilt together, as in Fig. 8; their roots usually appear more or less rotted. If the plants are not seriously infected until blooming time, they wilt less suddenly, the leaves at first becoming pale yellowish-green and the lower leaves wilting first; the feeding roots are usually thoroughly decayed. If the base of the stem is examined at this time, a thin coating of pale pink or rose-colored spores may be seen, especially at or just below the soil level. The spores are very characteristic both in color and in their microscopic characters; they are more or less sickle-shaped and have several cross-walls.

Control: Infested soil should be steam-pasteurized or treated with one of the appropriate chemicals described in Chapter 4. In addition, avoid bringing in soil on tools or shoes from beds previously infested with the wilt fungus. Avoid throwing into the compost pile the debris of plants killed by wilt; the fungus can live several years in such refuse. Infested compost may be used under trees and shrubs away from susceptible China asters.

Benomyl soil drench gives excellent *Fusarium* control at rates given on the label.

Wilt-resistant China aster seed is also available from the larger seed companies. Although no lot of seed is completely immune, most of the seeds can be expected to produce good blooms even when planted in infested soil.

Root Rot (*Phytophthora cryptogea*). The symptoms are like those caused by the wilt fungus. Stems and roots appear water-soaked and black from the soft rot. The rot is more pronounced and lacks the pink coating of spores characteristic of plants infected by wilt.

Control: Wilt-resistant asters are not resistant to the root rot fungus. If possible, asters should not be planted in a garden plot which has shown the disease in previous years. If it is necessary to continue to use the same beds, the soil should be treated with Dexon or Truban, and the same precautions taken as for aster wilt.

Rust (*Coleosporium solidaginis*). The symptoms are similar to those on goldenrod, which is also attacked by this fungus. The leaves, especially those of young plants, become spotted with bright yellowish-orange spores which break out on the lower surface. This parasite is generally uncommon except where pine rust prevails.

Control: Spray with maneb or zineb several times early in the growing season.

Stem Rot (*Pellicularia filamentosa*). This fungus causes a stem rot of older plants and a damping-off of seedlings.

Control: Use clean soil, or pasteurize infested soil with heat, or treat it with PCNB (Terraclor).

Other Diseases. Many other fungi attack China asters. *Phomopsis callistephi* causes cankers on the lower parts of the stem and complete collapse of the distal portion; it does not affect the roots. The gray mold *Botrytis cinerea* may develop under cool, moist conditions. It has been known to cause or accompany a blossom blight. A downy mildew, *Basidiophora entospora,* occurs in Texas and Florida. Leaf spots are caused by *Ascochyta asteris, Septoria callistephi,* and *Stemphylium callistephi.*

Aster Yellows. Competing with wilt for first place among aster troubles is the aster yellows disease, caused by a mycoplasma-like organism. The first sign of infection is the pale yellowish tinge of the leaves. Usually adventitious shoots develop more or less of a witches' broom, as is seen in Fig. 22. The blooms that may develop to any extent are off-color, the rays being usually yellowish-green. The plants do not die, like those infected with wilt and root rot, but continue to be a source of the disease for neighboring plants. This organism is not seed-borne and does not persist in the soil. It lives from season to season on various perennial hosts such as the common daisy, *Chrysanthemum leucanthemum; Erigeron* spp.; plantain, *Plantago major;* and gaillardia.

Control: The causal organism is carried from plant to plant by the aster leafhopper *Macrosteles fascifrons.* This is a common leafhopper of gardens, feeding on many other plants besides asters, and also capable of transmitting the mycoplasma-like organism to many of them. Best control is obtained by growing plants in screened enclosures having cloth with 22 threads per inch. Screens should be installed as soon as plants are set out and the plants should be sprayed with Diazinon, malathion, or Meta-Systox R to kill any leafhoppers present at the start.

Viruses. The tomato spotted wilt and the beet curly-top viruses also affect China aster.

Control: Remove and destroy infected plants and control sucking insects with Diazinon, malathion, or Meta-Systox R.

Insects and Other Pests

Leafhopper (*Macrosteles fascifrons*). This pest has already been discussed under aster yellows because of its importance in spreading that disease. It overwinters in rye, barley, and possibly other plants.

Control: Diazinon, Meta-Systox, or Sevin sprays are effective in combating this pest.

Corn Root Aphid (*Aphis maidiradicis*). This species, which is pale-grayish, is a serious pest of China aster. The aphids feed in large numbers on the roots. Yellowing, dwarfing, and wilting of the plant follow. These plant lice are attended by small brown ants (*Lasius alienus*), which carry them around from plant to plant. In return the aphids give copious honeydew, upon which the ants feed.

Control: Treat the soil with Diazinon before setting out susceptible plants. The soil around already infested plants can be treated with a dilute solution of malathion made from the emulsifiable concentrate, or with Diazinon.

Potato Aphid (*Macrosiphum solanifolii*). This aphid, which attacks many other species of garden plants other than potatoes, also attacks the leaves, stems, and blossoms of asters.

Control: Malathion, Meta-Systox R, or Sevin sprays will control this pest.

Asiatic Garden Beetle (*Maladera castanea*). The brown Asiatic beetle prefers the leaves of China asters to those of many other plants. It feeds on the foliage at night and, when day comes, buries itself in the soil near the base of the plant or in the vicinity.

Control: These beautiful brown beetles can be seen flying about at night if one searches with a flashlight. Spraying the plants once or twice with Sevin is sufficient. Diazinon applied to the soil will destroy the larval stage of this pest.

Black Blister Beetle (*Epicauta pennsylvanica*). This is a long black beetle about 1/2 inch in length. It owes its name to the fact that it produces blisters on the human skin when crushed in the hand. The adults appear about the middle of June and feed on the foliage and flowers, often completely destroying the plants. Other kinds of garden plants commonly attacked are clematis, chrysanthemum, and zinnia.

Control: Sprays containing methoxychlor or Sevin are effective.

Japanese Beetle (*Popillia japonica*). The adult stage is oval, about 1/2 inch long, metallic green with coppery wing covers. It feeds on about 280 kinds of shade, ornamental, and fruit trees; shrubs, annuals, perennials, and some vegetables. The beetles feed from late June to October. The grub stage feeds on the roots of lawn grasses in spring and late fall.

Control: See lawn grubs, under *Gramineae*.

Tarnished Plant Bug. (*Lygus lineolaris*). This is a light brown insect, variously spotted, about 1/4 inch long; it is shown in Fig. 75. It is very destructive to China asters. It punctures the terminal shoot below the flower bud and injects a poison which usually causes the flower to droop and die.

Control: Apply a methoxychlor or Sevin spray each week during the period adults are about.

Other Insects. Leaf rollers, mealybugs, and beetles, which are common on a number of garden plants, also attack asters occasionally. These are discussed elsewhere.

Two-Spotted Mite (*Tetranychus urticae*). These tiny pests frequently infest China asters. They are especially serious where methoxychlor sprays have been used frequently.

Control: See *Althaea*.

Southern Root-Knot Nema (*Meloidogyne incognita*). Asters are among the plants susceptible to this nema. Infested plants have many spindly shoots and the leaves are dwarfed. The roots of such plants have tiny galls or knots on them.

Control: See Nemas, Chapter 3.

CALLUNA (HEATHER)

Diseases

In the northwestern United States, the leaves and stems of heather may be infected by the fungus *Pseudophacidium callunae*.

Insects and Related Pests

Japanese Beetle (*Popillia japonica*). During July and August, when heather in eastern rock gardens is in full bloom, Japanese beetles may be attracted to the plants in large numbers. They feed upon the blooms and green parts and do considerable damage.
Control: See *Aesculus.*

Two-Spotted Mite (*Tetranychus urticae*). Certain prostrate varieties of heather in rock gardens, even when not sprayed with methoxychlor, may be severely damaged by this mite.
Control: Spray with Aramite, Dimite, Kelthane, Ovotran, or Tedion in May and June.

Oystershell Scale (*Lepidosaphes ulmi*). Heather is subject to infestation by this scale, which also attacks a wide variety of woody plants.
Control: Spray with malathion, Meta-Systox R, or Sevin in late June to control the crawler stage.

CALONYCTION (MOONFLOWER)

Diseases

Rust (*Coleosporium ipomoeae*). This rust occurs on moonflower leaves in the southern United States. The alternate hosts are species of *Pinus.*
Control: Valuable specimens can be protected by occasional applications of wettable sulfur sprays.

White Rust (*Albugo ipomoeae-panduratae*). This disease has been reported from Florida. It rarely requires control measures.

Insects and Related Pests

Argus Tortoise Beetle (*Chelymorpha cassidea*). This tortoise-shaped, yellow to bright red beetle with black spots and its yellow larval stage eat holes in the leaves.
Control: Spray with Sevin when the pests begin to feed on the leaves.

Mealybugs (*Planococcus citri* and *Pseudococcus longispinus*). Two species of mealybug occasionally infest moonflower.
Control: Spray with malathion when the pests appear.

Other Insects. The greenhouse orthezia, *Orthezia insignis,* and the greenhouse thrips, *Heliothrips haemorrhoidalis,* occasionally infest this host. Malathion sprays will control these pests.

Fern Nema (*Aphelenchoides olesistus*). Badly infested moonflower leaves either turn brown in spots bounded by veins, or are entirely killed; the dead leaves dry out and hang on the plant. The variegated varieties appear to be much more susceptible.
Control: Pick off and destroy infested leaves as soon as they appear.

CALOTROPIS PROCERA (MILKWEED)

Leaf Blotch (*Cercospora calotripidis*). Circular water-soaked lesions a quarter inch or more in diameter are formed on the leaves. Later these spots become covered with the dark olive spores of the fungus. Complete defoliation may result from heavy infection. The fungus enters through the stomata.
Control: Pick off and destroy infected leaves as soon as they are discovered and remove all debris from infected plants.

Leaf Blight (*Cephaleuros parasiticus*). The epidermal cells are attacked by this alga, which spreads rapidly over the leaf and causes it to blacken and die.
Control: Remove diseased leaves. Heavy infestations may be controlled with copper or sulfur sprays.

CALYCANTHUS (ALLSPICE)

The Carolina allspice *Calycanthus floridus* is subject to the following fungi which cause twig and branch cankers: *Botryosphaeria dothidea, Cytospora laxa, Nectria cinnabarina,* and *Physalospora obtusa.* The crown gall disease caused by the bacterium *Agrobacterium tumefaciens* has been found in Mississippi and New York.

Control: Prune and discard infected twigs and branches.

CAMELLIA JAPONICA AND C. SASANQUA (CAMELLIA)

Fungus and Algal Diseases

Spot Disease (*Pestolotia guepini*). More or less irregular round blotches run together, causing a silvery appearance of the upper surface of the leaves. The diseased area is sharply marked off from the healthy portion. The pycnidia or fruiting bodies of the fungus are visible as black dots. Leaf fall sometimes results. Several other fungi produce leaf spotting: *Phyllosticta camelliae, P. camelliaecola,* and *Sporonema camelliae.* A species of *Sphaceloma* causes scabby spots on the leaves.

Control: Collect and destroy all diseased leaves. Spray larger plantings with some fungicide, such as Bordeaux mixture, if spotting of the foliage is not objectionable; otherwise spray the plants with wettable sulfur.

Black Mold (*Meliola camelliae*). The abundant black fungus growth of the *Fumago* stage covers the leaves and twigs of this host. The ascospores are brown, each provided with several cross-walls.

Control: Spray with malathion to control insects such as aphids and scales which secrete the substance on which this fungus grows. Promptly pick off and destroy infected leaves and discard all debris from infected plants.

Leaf Gall (*Exobasidium camelliae*). The leaves and stems of new shoots are thickened and distorted by this fungus.

Control: See under *Rhododendron,* azalea gall.

Leaf Spot (*Cercospora theae*). This leaf spot, first reported from Louisiana, develops under conditions of overcrowding, partial shade, and high humidity of a lath house.

Control: No controls have been developed.

Flower Blight (*Sclerotinia camelliae*). This blight is confined to the flowers which turn brown and drop. It occurs in the Pacific Coast states and gulf and other southern states from Texas to Virginia. All species and varieties of camellias appear equally susceptible to this blight.

Another flower-blighting fungus, *Sclerotinia sclerotiorum,* has been reported from North Carolina. A bud and flower blight is occasionally caused by *Botrytis cinerea,* particularly after the plants have been subjected to frost.

Control: To control the *Sclerotinia camelliae* blight, pick off and discard all old camellia blossoms before they fall. Ferbam, or sulfur, or Fore sprays help to prevent infection. Infections can also be prevented by placing a 3-inch mulch of wood chips or other suitable material around the base of each plant. Such a barrier will prevent the fungus bodies in the soil beneath from ejecting their spores into the atmosphere and onto the leaves. Soils heavily infested with sclerotia (which later produce ascocarps) may be treated with ferbam or captan. PCNB (Terrachlor) provides even more effective control but must be used in soils free of plants.

No special controls have been developed for the *Botrytis* bud and flower blight, or for *Sclerotinia sclerotiorum.*

Canker (*Glomerella cingulata*). A canker and dieback of camellias is widespread and frequently destructive in the southern states. It also occurs on greenhouse-grown plants in the North. The fungus enters only through wounds. In nature, the usual entrance points are scars left by the abscission of leaves in spring.

In Florida a species of *Phomopsis* also causes somewhat similar symptoms.

Control: Prune and destroy cankered twigs. Where the cankers occur on the main stem of large plants, surgical removal of the diseased portions should be attempted, followed by use of a tree paint containing a fungicide. Copper fungicides applied periodically to the leaves and stems may help to prevent new infections.

Root Rot (*Phytophthora cinnamomi*). This disease is common not only on camellia but also on avocado, maple, pine, and rhododendron as well as many other woody plants. Excessive moisture and poor soil drainage favor its development.

Control: Improve drainage. Drenching soil around living plants with either nabam or zineb may help. Infested soil free of plants may be treated with Dexon, Truban, or Terrazole.

Leaf Blight (*Cephaleuros virescens*). The epidermal cells are attacked by this alga, which spreads rapidly over the leaf and causes it to blacken and die.

Control: Remove diseased leaves. Badly infested specimens may be sprayed with a copper fungicide.

Virus Diseases

The virus diseases of camellia are not well understood. Leaf and flower variegation is presumed to be due to a virus inasmuch as the condition was transmitted by graftage from variegated *Camellia japonica* to uniformly green varieties of *C. japonica* and *C. sasanqua*. Some yellow variegation, however, may be due to genetic changes rather than virus infection. Such variegations usually follow a uniform and rather typical pattern which is more or less similar on all leaves. The author has observed many greenhouse-grown camellias in the North with typical ringspot patterns in the leaves. The symptoms caused by camellia yellow mottle virus are illustrated in Fig. 114.

Control: Plants suspected of harboring a virus should be discarded, or at least isolated from healthy plants.

Physiological Diseases

Bud Drop. Camellias grown in homes, in greenhouses, and even outdoors frequently lose their buds before opening, or the tips of the young buds and edges of young petals turn brown and decay. See Fig. 114.

Bud drop from indoor-grown plants usually is due to overwatering of the soil or to some other faulty environmental condition such as insufficient light, excessively high temperatures, or a pot-bound condition of the roots. Bud drop in the Pacific Northwest may result from a severe frost in September or October, severe freezing during the winter, or an irregular water supply. In California it may result from lack of adequate moisture.

Chlorosis may be caused by deficiency of some elements in the soil.

Oedema. Frequently brown, corky, roughened swellings develop on camellia leaves grown in greenhouses. The condition is associated with overwatering of the soil during extended periods of cloudy weather.

Sunburn. This condition appears on leaves as faded green to brown areas with indefinite margins. It occurs on the upper exposed sides of bushes, particularly those transplanted from shaded to very sunny areas.

Salt Injury. Camellias cannot tolerate high soil salinity even though they grow best in the acid soils and temperate climate of our Eastern and Gulf Coast areas. Salt levels above 1800 parts per million in the soil solution were fatal to camellias in greenhouse tests conducted at the Virginia Truck Experiment Sta-

Fig. 114. Yellow mottle and bud drop of *Camellia*.

tion in Norfolk. Azaleas were found to be equally susceptible to high salt concentrations.

Insects and Other Animal Pests

Tea Scale (*Fiorinia theae*). The most serious pest of outdoor camellias in the South, this scale also infests greenhouse-grown camellias in the North as well as ferns, palms, orchids, figs, and several other plants. It can be distinguished superficially by its oblong shape and the ridge down the center parallel to the sides.

Control: Spray with malathion or Sevin to control the young crawling scales. Repeat the treatment at 2-week intervals for heavily in-

fested plants. In the South, Florida Volck and similar oil emulsions are quite effective on outdoor plants. Oil sprays should not be applied when the temperature is above 85°F., but malathion and Sevin may be applied at any time.

Florida Red Scale (*Chrysomphalus aonidum*). This scale insect, common on citrus and occasionally found on iris and other plants in the greenhouse, has been found to live on camellia leaves. The scale is dark brown and more or less circular. It is easy with a needle to remove the scale; this exposes the very light yellow body of the insect, firmly attached to the leaf by its sucking organ. The leaf shown in Fig. 115 was photographed after several of its scales had been

Fig. 115. Florida red scale on *Camellia.*

thus removed; the insects appear as white spots.

Many other species of scales infest camellias. They include black, California red, camellia, chaff, cottony taxus, degenerate, Florida wax, glover, greedy, hemispherical, latania, Mexican wax, oleander, oystershell, peony, and soft scale. Two other scales known as the camellia parlatoria and the olive parlatoria also attack this host.

Control: Same as for tea scale.

Mealybugs (*Planococcus citri* and *Pseudococcus longispinus*). These two white insects are usually found in the leaf axils and shoot buds.

Control: Spray with malathion or Cygon.

Weevils (*Otiorhyncus sulcatus* and *O. ovatus*). The black vine weevil and the strawberry root weevil feed on the leaves. The larval stages of these pests feed on the roots and the base of the stem much as they do on azaleas and yews.

Control: See *Taxus.*

Fuller Rose Beetle (*Pantomorus cervinus*). This snout-beetle occasionally infests camellias, roses, palms, and many other plants.

A number of other beetles also infest this host. The most common are rhabdopterus, flea beetle, and the grape colaspis.

Control: Diazinon or Sevin sprays will control the various kinds of beetles.

Thrips. The browning of the tips of buds, followed by decay and dropping, has frequently been found to be due to the attacks of a species of thrips. This should be clearly distinguished from the bud drop caused by overwatering (see above).

Control: Spray with Cygon or malathion.

Spotted Cutworm (*Amathes c-nigrum*). This cutworm has been found feeding on the blasted buds of camellias in the greenhouses. Apparently it is able to climb up among the branches, leaves, and flower buds. A similar cutworm is shown in Fig. 82.

Control: See variegated cutworm under *Cineraria.*

Other Insects. A great number of other insects infest camellias both in greenhouses, homes, and outdoors. These include the following aphids: black citrus, melon, green peach, and ornate. Also the following caterpillars which chew the leaves: omnivorus looper, orange tortrix, and western parsley. The fruit tree leaf roller and the greenhouse leaf tier also chew the leaves and roll or tie them together. The greenhouse whitefly is common on greenhouse-grown plants.

Control: Most of these pests can be easily controlled with malathion. The caterpillars can also be controlled with Sevin.

Root-Nema (*Meloidogyne incognita*). Camellias are unusually resistant to root-knot nemas, although the pests have been recorded on camellias in Texas. Another species of nema, *Hemicriconemoides gaddi,* has been reported on the roots of camellia in Louisiana.

Control: See Chapter 3.

CAMPANULA (BELLFLOWER)

Diseases

Crown Rot (*Pellicularia rolfsii*). This serious disease, which may kill many plants, develops under moist soil conditions where the temperature is above 60°F.

A grayish-white discoloration of the stem that results in its decay and falling over is caused by the fungus *Sclerotinia sclerotiorum.*

Control: Soil-infesting organisms can only be controlled with heat or chemicals as described in Chapter 4.

Leaf Spots (*Cercoseptoria minuta, Phyllosticta alliariifoliae,* and *Septoria campanulae*). Spotting of leaves may be caused by any one of the fungi listed above.

Control: Copper fungicides applied periodically will prevent infections.

Rust (*Coleosporium campanulae*). The under sides of the leaves become covered with orange-colored or reddish-brown pustules; the leaves dry and the plants are stunted. This rust has the aecidial (alternate) stage on pine needles, where it develops yellowish-orange-colored blister pustules.

Two other rusts occur on this host: *Aecidium campanulastri* and *Puccinia campanulae.*

Control: Valuable plantings may be protected by periodic applications of wettable sulfur sprays.

Powdery Mildew (*Erysiphe cichoracearum*). Bellflower is occasionally affected by this fungus, which produces a white coating on the leaves.

Control: Spray with Acti-dione PM, Benlate, or Karathane.

Root Rot (*Pellicularia filamentosa* and *Fusarium* sp.). These fungi have been reported to cause a root rot in the East and Middle West.

Control: Refer to Chapter 4.

Aster Yellows. This disease has been recorded on *Campanula* from Pennsylvania.

Control: Remove and destroy affected plants.

Insects and Other Animal Pests

Foxglove Aphid (*Acyrthosiphon solani*). This green aphid sucks the leaf juices from a great number of plants besides bellflower.

Control: Spray with malathion when aphids first appear.

Onion Thrips (*Thrips tabaci*). This rasping-sucking pest also attacks a great number of other plants.

Control: Malathion sprays are effective.

Slugs. Several kinds of slugs may chew bellflower leaves during the night. Dusting the area lightly with 15 per cent metaldehyde dust, or spraying with 20 per cent metaldehyde liquid, as directed by the manufacturer, provides excellent control of these pests.

Zectran and Mesurol are also very effective. None of these should be used on or near plants grown for food.

Slugs are always most destructive in shaded gardens, and during rainy seasons.

CAMPSIS (TRUMPET-CREEPER)

Diseases

Blight (*Mycosphorella tecomae*). Small angular brown spots, which run together, develop on plants east of the Mississippi River and in the South.

Control: This disease is rarely serious enough to warrant control measures.

Leaf Spots (*Phyllosticta tecomae, Septoria tecomae, Cercospora duplicata,* and *C. langloisii*). Four fungi have been reported as the cause of leaf spotting.

Control: Same as for blight.

Powdery Mildews (*Erysiphe cichoreacearum* and *Microsphaera alni*). A white coating on the leaves is the characteristic symptom of powdery mildews.

Control: Spray with Acti-dione PM, Benlate or Karathane when necessary.

Insects

Planthoppers (*Metcalfa pruinosa* and *Anormensis septentrionalis*). White flocculent strands concealing young greenish insects, which jump when disturbed, are common on trumpet-creeper and many woody and herbaceous plants.

Control: Damage by these pests is never serious enough to warrant control measures.

Other Insects. The scale known as olive parlatoria and the citrus whitefly occasionally infest this host.

Control: Valuable specimens may be sprayed with malathion.

CANNA

Bacterial and Fungus Diseases

Bud Rot (*Xanthomonas* sp.). The bacterium that causes bud rot of canna enters through the stomata of young leaves and flower buds, usually before they have opened. As the leaf unfolds, numerous spots are visible which enlarge and run together along the veins, sometimes giving the leaf a striped appearance. The spots may at first be whitish, but soon turn black. Infected flower buds may turn black and die before opening. The disease may progress down the leaf stalk and kill the young stem and buds. If older leaves are infected, the diseased area spreads slowly, forming irregular, yellowish spots with water-soaked margins. The bacteria live through the winter on the rootstocks. The disease occurs early in the season on young plants in hot-houses and gardens.

Control: Use only healthy rootstocks for propagation. Suspicious ones should be dipped into a streptomycin solution before planting. Streptomycin bud and leaf sprays might also help. Avoid overwatering, overcrowding, and poor ventilation.

Rust (*Puccinia thaliae*). This rust has been reported from several midwestern and southern states. It also infects the edible canna, *Canna edulis,* in Florida.

Control: Control measures are rarely necessary although frequent sulfur sprays will control this disease.

Other Fungus Diseases. A stem rot caused by *Pellicularia rolfsii* in Florida, a rhizome rot by a species of *Fusarium* in several eastern and midwestern states, and a leaf spot by a species of *Alternaria* in the Middle West and South, are other fungus diseases occasionally reported on cannas.

Virus and Mycoplasma Diseases

Mosaic (Canna mosaic virus). This virus has been reported on *Canna generalis, C. in-*

dica, and *C. glauca.* The virus can be transmitted by the following insects: *Aphis gossypii, A. maidis, Macrosiphum euphorbiae, Myzus circumflexus,* and *M. persicae.* The popular red-flowered ornamental variety, The "President," is immune to this virus.

Aster Yellows. A mycoplasma-like organism dwarfs plants and causes an irregular, diffuse, dull yellowing of young leaves, which turn brown with age.

Control: Rogue and destroy plants known to be infected. Spray with malathion, Meta-Systox R, or Sevin to control the insect vectors.

Insects

Japanese Beetle (*Popillia japonica*). This is the most serious pest of ornamental cannas in the New York metropolitan area. The adult beetles begin to feed on the young leaves and flower buds around the end of June.

Control: Repeated applications of sprays containing methoxychlor, or Sevin are needed to keep this pest from doing serious damage. Where Sevin is used, it may be necessary to include a mite killer such as Kelthane in order to keep down the mite population. At the peak of the beetle season it may be necessary to spray the plants twice a week to provide adequate protection. Other beetles, such as the Fuller rose and the spotted cucumber beetle, which occasionally feed on cannas can also be controlled by the spray mentioned above.

Yellow Woollybear (*Diacrisia virginica*). This pest does much damage to cannas by eating large holes in the leaves. The holes are sometimes arranged side by side across the leaf. The caterpillar, about 2 inches long, is covered with fine yellowish and brownish hairs. Other caterpillars which feed on cannas are the saddleback and the corn earworm. The larger canna leaf roller *Calpodes ethlius,* the lesser canna leaf roller *Geshna cannalis,* and the greenhouse leaf tier *Udea*

rubigalis complete the list of leaf-eating caterpillars.

Control: If only a few caterpillars are present, they may be destroyed by handpicking. Sprays containing Sevin will also control all sorts of caterpillars.

Scales (*Hemiberlesia lataniae* and *Diaspis bromeliae*). The former, latania scale, is small, gray, and convex in shape; the latter, pineapple scale, is white and gray in color.

Control: Spray with malathion or Sevin from time to time in late spring and early summer to control the crawling stages of these pests.

CARAGANA (PEA-TREE)

Among the relatively few fungus diseases reported on this host are a leaf blight caused by a species of *Ascochyta* in Ohio; a root rot of seedlings by *Pellicularia filamentosa* in North Dakota; a blight of the seed pods by *Botrytis cinerea* in Massachusetts; and a leaf spot by *Phyllosticta gallarum* in Alaska. The hairy root disease caused by the bacterium *Agrobacterium rhizogenes* occurs in the Middle West. These diseases rarely become severe enough to require control measures.

CARICA (PAPAYA)

Diseases

Leaf Spots (*Mycosphaerella caricae, Phyllosticta papayae,* and *Pucciniopsis caricae*). Three fungi cause leaf spotting of papayas in Florida. The last is the most serious of the three.

Control: Spray with Bordeaux mixture or some other copper fungicide.

Other Diseases. A flower blight caused by *Choanephora americana* in Florida, and fruit rots by species of *Diplodia* and *Fusarium* have been reported from Texas and California.

A serious fruit, leaf, and stem rot caused by *Colletotrichum gloeosporioides* occurs in

Florida and Texas. Three virus diseases are reported from Florida: distortion ringspot, faint mottle ringspot, and mild mosaic. The tobacco ringspot virus is suspected as a cause of *Carcia* decline in Texas.

Control: Copper fungicides will probably control the fungi which infect the leaves. The virus diseases are more difficult to control.

CARNEGIEA—see CACTACEAE

CARPINUS (HORNBEAM)

Diseases

Leaf Spots (*Clasterosporium cornigerum, Gloeosporium robergei, Gnomoniella fimbriella, Phyllosticta* sp., and *Septoria carpinea*). These five fungi cause leaf spotting of hornbeam.

Control: Leaf spots are rarely serious enough to warrant control measures. Copper or ferbam sprays are effective in preventing heavy outbreaks.

Cankers (*Pezicula carpinea, Solenia ochraceae,* and *Nectria galligena*). These three species of fungi frequently cause bark cankers, sometimes leading to severe dieback of branches.

Control: Badly cankered trees cannot be saved. Prune out twigs and branches of mildly infected ones. The use of copper sprays may also be justified in some situations.

Twig Blight (*Fusarium lateritium*). In the South this fungus causes a twig blight on hornbeam. The sexual stage of this fungus is *Gibberella baccata.*

Control: Prune and destroy infected twigs on valuable ornamental specimens.

Other Diseases. The felt fungus *Septobasidium curtisii,* occurs on a number of trees in the South. The felt is purplish-black and covers the insect it parasitizes.

Insects

Maple Phenacoccus (*Phenacoccus acericola*). Although this scale is more common on sugar maple, it occasionally infests hornbeam, where it forms large white cottony masses on the lower leaf surfaces.

Control: See *Acer.*

CARTHAMUS TINCTORIUS (SAFFLOWER)

Diseases

Rust (*Puccinia carthami*). This is the most important disease of safflower in the United States, particularly in California, where it is grown as an oilseed crop. Attempts to develop rust-resistant strains have not been successful because the fungus forms new races which infect safflower strains previously resistant. The rust fungus is carried with the seed.

Control: Safflower seed should be soaked for 30 minutes in a solution containing 20 parts of Acti-dione per million parts of water. This treatment gives complete control of rust without impairing germination and seedling growth. Safflowers grown as ornamentals can be protected from rust with wettable sulfur sprays.

Anthracnose (*Gloeosporium carthami*). This disease has been reported from Indiana and several southern states. Control measures are rarely necessary.

Leaf Spots (*Septoria carthami* and *Alternaria* sp.). Occasionally these fungi occur on safflower. Controls are unnecessary.

Powdery Mildews (*Oidium* sp. and *Erysiphe* sp.). The first was found in Arizona in 1960 and the second in Utah in 1961 on greenhouse-grown safflowers.

Control: Karathane or Benlate sprays are effective against powdery mildews.

Wilt (*Sclerotinia sclerotiorum*). Leaves become yellowish, wither, and dry up. A white mycelial growth develops around the crown at soil level, and here rather large black sclerotia, irregular in shape, may be developed. Similar sclerotia may be found inside the stems.

Control: Destroy all infected plants together with the immediately surrounding soil.

Other Diseases. Safflower is susceptible to another wilt caused by *Verticullium alboatrum* and to mosaic caused by the cucumber mosaic virus. The former can be transmitted through the seed.

Control: Ways to control wilt and mosaic have not been developed.

CARYA (HICKORY)

Diseases

Leaf Spots. Several leaf spotting fungi occur on hickory. Of these, *Gnomonia caryae* is the most destructive. It produces large, irregularly circular spots, which are reddish-brown on the upper leaf surfaces and brown on the lower. The margins of the spots are not sharply defined, as are those of many other leaf spots. The minute brown pustules on the lower surfaces are the summer spore-producing bodies. Another spore stage develops on dead leaves and releases spores the following spring to initiate new infections. The fungus *Monochaetia monochaeta* occasionally produces a leaf spot on hickory but is more prevalent on oaks. The fungus *Marssonina juglandis* also attacks hickory but is more destructive to black walnut. Two species of *Septoria*, S. *caryae* and S. *hicoriae,* also cause spots on hickory.

Control: Gather and destroy leaves in fall to kill the fungi they harbor. To protect valuable specimens spray the leaves with maneb or zineb when the leaves open, when half-grown, and again after they are full-grown.

Canker. Several canker diseases occasionally occur on hickory. These are associated with the fungi *Strumella coryneoidea, Nectria galligena,* and *Rosellinia caryae.*

Control: Prune dead or weak branches and paint the wounds with a good dressing. Avoid bark injuries and keep the trees in good vigor by fertilizing, and by watering during dry spells. Keep borer and other insect infestations under control.

Witches' Broom (*Microstroma juglandis*). This fungus, which causes a leaf spot of butternut and black walnut, is capable of causing a witches' broom disease on shagbark hickory. The brooms, best seen when the trees are dormant, are composed of a compact cluster of branches. Early in the growing season the leaves on these branches are undersized and curled, later they turn black and fall.

Control: No effective control measures have been developed, but a dormant lime sulfur spray, followed by ferbam or ziram sprays during the growing season, is suggested.

Crown Gall (*Agrobacterium tumefaciens*). This bacterial disease occurs occasionally on hickory.

Control: Prune and destroy infected twigs and branches.

Powdery Mildews. Two fungi, *Phyllactinia corylea* and *Microsphaera alni,* cause mildewing of leaves.

Control: Control measures are rarely adopted.

Insects and Related Pests

Hickory Leaf Stem Gall Aphid (*Phylloxera caryaecaulis*). Hollow, green galls in June, which turn black in July, on leaves, stems, and small twigs of hickory are caused by the sucking of this small louse. In June the insides of the galls are lined with minute shiny lice of varying sizes. Galls range in size from a small pea to more than $1/2$ inch in diameter.

Control: A dormant spray in late spring just as new growth begins should destroy many overwintering lice. Diazinon, malathion, or Meta-Systox R sprays early in the growing season and repeated several times at 2-week intervals also give good control. Sprays are not effective once the galls begin to develop.

Hickory Bark Beetle (*Scolytus quadrispinosus*). Young twigs wilt as a result of boring by the bark beetle, a dark brown insect $1/5$ inch in length. The bark and sapwood are mined, and the tree may be girdled by the fleshy, legless larva $1/4$ inch long. The larvae overwinter under the bark.

Control: Spray the foliage with Sevin when the beetles appear in July. Remove and destroy severely infested trees, and peel the bark from the stump. Increase the vigor of weak trees by fertilization and watering.

Pecan Cigar Casebearer (*Coleophora laticornella*). The leaves are mined, turn brown, and fall when infested by the pecan cigar casebearer, a larva $1/5$ inch long, with a black head. The adult female is a moth with brown wings that has fringed hairs along the edge of a spread of $2/5$ inch. The larvae overwinter on twigs and branches in cigar-shaped cases, $1/8$ inch long.

Control: Spray with malathion or Sevin as soon as the leaves are fully developed.

Painted Hickory Borer (*Megacyllene caryae*). The sapwood of recently killed trees is soon riddled by painted hickory borers, creamy white larvae that attain a length of $3/4$ inch. The adult beetle is dark brown, has zigzag lines on the back, and is $3/4$ inch long. Eggs are deposited in late May or early June.

Control: Remove and destroy dead trees immediately. Inject a nicotine paste such as Bortox into the tunnels of live trees and then seal the openings with chewing gum, grafting wax, or putty. Spraying the bark with methoxychlor in early June might also help. Thiodan will also control this borer but its use is restricted to professional arborists and nurserymen in some states.

Twig Girdler (*Oncideres cingulata*). Twigs girdled by this pest, a larva $1/2$ inch long, are then broken off by the wind and fall to the ground. The adult is a reddish-brown beetle $3/4$ inch long. The larvae overwinter inside the twigs on the ground.

Control: Gather and discard severed branches and twigs in the autumn or early spring.

June Bugs (*Phyllophaga* spp.). The leaves may be chewed during the night by light to dark brown beetles, which vary from $1/2$ to $7/8$ inch in length. The beetles rest in nearby fields during the day. The larva is $3/4$ to 1 inch long, white, and soft-bodied with a brown head. Three or more years are required for completion of the life cycle of most of the species.

Control: See lawn grubs, under *Gramineae.*

Caterpillars. The leaves of park trees may be chewed by one of the following caterpillars: hickory horned devil, red-humped, walnut, yellow-necked, and white-marked tussock moth.

Control: All caterpillars are readily controlled with Sevin sprays.

Scales. Three species of scales—grape, obscure, and Putnam—occasionally infest hickories.

Control: Spray with malathion or Sevin during late spring and early summer, or with lime sulfur just before growth starts in spring.

CARYA ILLINOENSIS (PECAN)

Diseases

Brown Leaf Spot (*Cercospora fusca*). This leaf spot is common throughout the pecan-growing areas in the South. Downy spot, caused by the fungus *Mycosphaerella caryigena,* also occurs in the same localities.

Control: Spray with a low-lime Bordeaux mixture as recommended by the plant pathologist in the state where trees are affected.

Scab (*Cladosporium effusum*). This is one of the most destructive diseases of pecans in the Southeast. The fungus attacks leaves, shoots, and nuts.

Control: Dyrene, Benlate, or Dodine sprays will control this disease. The local state plant pathologist at the State College of Agriculture can provide details on dilution and timing.

Crown Gall (*Agrobacterium tumefaciens*). The roots of young pecan trees may be infected by this bacterial disease. Occasionally older trees in orchards are also infected.

Control: Remove galls from roots of young, infected trees. Then try dipping the roots for an hour in a solution containing 400 parts of Terramycin in 1 million parts of water, or treat with Bacticin as recommended by the manufacturer.

Other Diseases. Pecans are subject to a number of diseases that infect other species of *Carya*. They are not treated in detail here because the pecan is not an important ornamental.

Insects

Borers. A large number of borers infest pecans. Following are the most important: dogwood, flatheaded apple tree, pecan, pecan carpenterworm, shothole, twig girdler, and twig pruner.

Control: As with borers on other trees, keep ornamental trees in vigorous condition by feeding and watering. Particularly valuable ornamental specimens can be protected from most borers by spraying the trunk and branches with methoxychlor at the time the insects are most vulnerable. State entomologists will provide information on concentrations and application dates.

Caterpillars. The caterpillars that feed on hickory also attack pecans.

Control: See *Carya*.

Other Insects and Related Pests. Many species of scales and aphids infest pecan. Two species of mites—hickory and avocado red—also attack the leaves. These are controlled with the sprays recommended for the same pests on other trees.

CASSIA (SENNA)

Diseases

Few diseases affect this host. A branch dieback caused by the fungus *Diplodia natalensis,* two root rots by *Phymatotrichum omnivorum* and *Clitocybe tabescens,* and the southern root-knot nema *Meloidogyne incognita* occur on senna in the Deep South.

Control: Control measures are not usually adopted.

Insects

The eggplant lace bug, *Gargaphia solani,* and two species of scales, the lesser snow, *Pinnaspis strachani,* and the brown soft, *Coccus hesperidum,* occasionally infest this host.

Control: Spray valuable plants with malathion.

CASTANEA (CHESTNUT)

Diseases

Blight (*Endothia parasitica*). This is the disease that has practically destroyed the chestnut in most of the United States. It may appear as a twig and branch blight which descends rapidly into the trunk. Infection of other branches occurs rapidly until the whole tree is diseased. Cankers also develop from the base of the shoots which grow from the roots of trees, the tops of which have been destroyed by the disease. The pycnidia of the parasite break through the bark of the canker and exude long coiled tendrils of amber-colored spores which are distributed by insects and birds and wind or rainstorms. The ascocarpic stage develops later. The ascocarps have long necks by which the spores are able to emerge through the bark. Although blight is essentially a disease of the American chestnut, it also occurs commonly on the chinquapin, *Castanea pumila.* The causal fungus has been found growing on red maple, shagbark hickory, and staghorn sumac, and on dead and dying white, black, chestnut, and post oaks.

Control: Although many suggestions and recommendations have been published, none has proved effective in controlling chestnut blight. Persistent efforts have been made to find some chemical that when injected into the tree would check the development of cankers. Numerous claims for such chemicals have been advanced, but the author is unaware of the existence of any really effective material at the present time.

Some recent research at the Connecticut Agricultural Experiment Station indicates that cankers can be restricted and caused to heal by the introduction of a weak (hypovirulent) strain of *Endothia parasitica* into the canker.

After 40 years of research in this country, no American chestnut has been found with sufficient resistance to be of practical value. Large blight-free American chestnuts were known to exist in 36 states in 1957. Only time will reveal whether any of these are definitely resistant.

When research scientists finally realized that the chestnut blight fungus was uncontrollable, substitutes were sought. The answer seemed to be the introduction of Asiatic chestnuts which were known to be resistant to blight. Although a few of these chestnuts were introduced as long ago as 60 years, the greatest numbers were introduced in the late 1920's. But their introduction has resulted in the appearance of other diseases, such as the blossom-end rot of the nuts caused by the fungus *Glomerella cingulata* and twig canker, discussed below.

Asiatic chestnuts (*C. japonica* and *C. mollissima*) are now widely available from many nurseries. Most of them are best suited for ornamental plantings and nut production, rather than as forest trees. Many have a shrub-like growth habit, with multiple trunks arising near the ground level. They do not grow so tall and straight as the American chestnut and cannot compete in wooded areas when interplanted with other trees. The varieties of *C. mollissima* that are best for orchard cultivation are Abundance, Kuling, Meiling, and Nanking.[13]

Twig Canker of Asiatic Chestnuts (*Cryptodiaporthe castanea*). This fungus, together with several others, is associated with a blighting of twigs of Asiatic chestnut species. The twig blight can be highly destructive to species that are quite resistant to chestnut blight.

Control: Twig blight is most prevalent on trees in poor vigor. Maintaining good vigor will do much to ward off attacks. Planting sites should be carefully selected, and fertilization and watering practiced to ensure vigorous growth. All unnecessary injuries to the trees should be avoided, since the causal organisms penetrate and infect most readily through bark wounds. Trees should be carefully inspected in early summer, when symptoms are most apparent, and affected twigs should be pruned to sound wood and destroyed. Large cankers on the trunk or larger branches should be removed by surgical methods.

Other Disease. The fungus *Monochaetia kansensis* causes a leaf spot of *Castanea mollissima* in Kansas.

---

[13] For a small charge, the Superintendent of Documents, U.S. Government Printing Office, Washington, D.C. will send on request Farmer's Bulletin 2068, "Chestnut Blight and Resistant Chestnuts." The Connecticut Agricultural Experiment Station, New Haven, Connecticut, also has an excellent publication on the same subject, Bulletin 657.

Insects

The insect pests which attack American chestnut are of no importance because of the destruction of the trees by blight.

Weevils (*Curculio carytrypes* and *C. sayi* and *Cyrtepistomus castaneus*). Three species of weevils, native to the United States, may seriously damage the nuts of the Asiatic species of chestnuts.

Control: Spray the trees with methoxychlor before the weevils lay eggs in August. Treat the soil beneath Asiatic chestnut trees with Diazinon in the spring to kill the larval stage. Nuts harvested from infested trees which have not been treated as described above should be enclosed with methyl bromide in a tight container for 3 hours.

CASTILLEJA (PAINTED-CUP)

This host is subject to two mildew fungi, *Erysiphe polygoni* and *Sphaerotheca humuli* var. *fuliginea,* and three rust fungi, *Cronartium coleosporioides, Puccinia andropogonis,* and *P. castillejae.*

CASUARINA EQUISETIFOLIA (AUSTRALIAN-PINE)

In Florida this tree is subject to a root rot caused by *Clitocybe tabescens* and to a species of root-knot nema. In California it is subject to the shoestring root rot fungus *Armillaria mellea.*

CATALPA

Diseases

Leaf Spots (*Phyllosticta catalpae, Alternaria catalpae,* and *Cercospora catalpae*). Brown spots on the leaves are caused by these three species of fungi. The first-mentioned is illustrated in Fig. 116. Injury by the catalpa midge (discussed below) and infec-

tion by bacteria are believed to increase the tree's susceptibility to leaf spots.

Control: Gather and destroy the leaves in the fall. Spray valuable susceptible trees 3 times with a copper fungicide: first, as the leaves unfurl, then when the leaves are half-grown, and again when they are fullgrown.

Powdery Mildews (*Microsphaera alni* var. *vaccinii* and *Phyllactinia corylea*). Two species of fungi produce mildew of catalpa leaves.

Control: Spray valuable trees with either Benlate or Karathane.

Wilt (*Verticillium albo-atrum*). This disease is most destructive to catalpas planted along city streets. A brownish discoloration of the sapwood is the most prominent symptom.

Control: Heavy applications of a high nitrogenous fertilizer sometimes enable infected trees to put a new ring of summerwood and springwood outside the infected area, and the trees may then recover.

Wood Decays (*Polyporus versicolor* and *P. catalpae*). Two fungi cause heartwood decay in catalpas. The former is most serious in western catalpa, *C. speciosa.*

Control: Avoid wounds, inasmuch as the spores of both fungi enter through bark injuries. Keep the trees in good vigor by fertilizing and watering.

Other Diseases. Among other diseases of Catalpa are twig dieback, caused by *Botryosphaeria dothidea,* root rot by *Armillaria mellea* and *Phymatotrichum omnivorum,* and canker by *Physalospora obtusa.*

Insects

Comstock Mealybug (*Pseudococcus comstocki*). Distorted growth of twigs, limbs, and trunk may be produced by the sucking of this small, elliptical, waxycovered insect. The leaves may be covered with black sooty mold, which develops on so-called honeydew

Fig. 116. Leaf spot of catalpa caused by the fungus *Phyllosticta catalpae.*

secreted by this pest. Winter is passed as eggs in masses of white waxy secretions on the bark.

Control: Before the buds open, spray with 1 part concentrated lime sulfur in 10 parts of water, or with winter-strength miscible oil. A malathion, Meta-Systox R, or Sevin spray applied to the trunk and branches in late spring and again in early summer will provide additional control.

Catalpa Midge (*Cecidomyia catalpae*). Leaves are distorted, and circular areas inside the leaves are chewed, leaving a papery epidermis, as a result of infestation by tiny yellow maggots. The adult, a tiny fly with a wingspread of $1/16$ inch, appears in late May or early June to lay eggs on the leaves. Winter is passed in the pupal stage in the soil.

Control: Cultivate the soil beneath the trees to destroy the pupae, and spray in late May with malathion.

Catalpa Sphinx (*Ceratomia catalpae*). Leaves may be completely stripped from a tree by a large yellow and black caterpillar, the sphinx, which attains a length of 3 inches. The adult female is a grayish-brown moth with a 3-inch wingspread. The winter is passed as the pupal stage in the ground.

Control. Spray the foliage with Sevin early in May and again in mid-August.

CATHARANTHUS ROSEUS (PERIWINKLE)

Periwinkle, formerly known under the botanical names of *Lochnera rosea* and *Vinca rosea,* is subject to a leaf rot caused by the fungus *Phytophthora colocasie,* rust by *Coleosporium apocynacearum,* a root nema *Meloidogyne* sp., the cucumber mosaic virus, and aster yellows. It is also susceptible to five other viruses as demonstrated in experimental tests.

Control: These diseases are rarely serious enough to justify control practices.

CEANOTHUS AMERICANUS (NEW JERSEY TEA)

Diseases

Leaf Spots (*Cercospora ceanothi* and *Phyllosticta ceanothi*). The leaves of New Jersey tea are occasionally spotted by these fungi.

Control: Controls are rarely practiced.

Powdery Mildew (*Microsphaera alni*). In late summer and fall the leaves of this host are coated by this fungus.

Control: Same remark as for leaf spots.

Other Diseases. The western species of *Ceanothus* are subject to several leaf spots including *Septoria ceanothi, Cylindrosporium ceanothi,* and the *Cercospora* that affects New Jersey tea. A rust fungus, *Puccinia tripsaci,* the root rot fungus *Armillaria mellea,* and the crown gall bacterium *Agrobacterium tumefaciens,* are other organisms that affect this host.

CEDRUS (CEDAR)[14]

Diseases

Tip Blight (*Diplodia pinea*). Cankers and dieback of branch tips are caused by this fungus, formerly known as *Sphaeropsis ellisii.*

Control: Same as for tip blight of *Pinus.*

Root Rots (*Armillaria mellea, Clitocybe tabescens,* and *Phymatotrichum omnivorum*). These fungi are associated with root and trunk decay of cedars.

Control: No effective, practicable control measures are known.

Insects

Black Scale (*Saissetia oleae*). This dark brown to black scale is primarily a pest of citrus on the west coast. It attacks a wide variety of trees and shrubs in the South and West, including the Deodar cedar, *C. deodara.* Besides extracting juice from the plant, it secretes on the leaves and stems a substance on which the sooty mold fungus grows.

Control: Malathion or Sevin sprays when the young are crawling about in May and June are effective.

Deodar Weevil (*Pissodes nemorensis*). This brownish, snouted weevil feeds on the

---

[14] Plants commonly called cedar belong to several genera. See *Juniperus, Thuja, Chamaecyparis.* The cedars referred to in this section are *Cedrus atlantica, C. deodara,* and *C. libani.*

cambium of leader and side branches of Deodar, Atlas, and Lebanon cedars. It deposits eggs in the bark, and the white grubs which hatch from the eggs burrow into the wood. Eventually the leaders and terminal twigs turn brown and die. Small trees may be killed by this pest.

Control: A methoxychlor spray applied in April, when the beetles are feeding, will control this insect.

CELASTRUS SCANDENS (BITTERSWEET)

Diseases

Leaf Spots (*Phyllosticta celastri, Ramularia celastri,* and *Marssonina thomasiana*). The first-mentioned has been reported from West Virginia, the second is of general occurrence, and the third has been reported from Maryland and New York.

Control: Pick off and discard spotted leaves. Heavy infections can be prevented by copper sprays.

Powdery Mildews (*Microsphaera alni* and *Phyllactinia corylea*). These fungi attack leaves, covering them with a white, moldy growth which causes the death of the leaves.

Control: Valuable ornamental specimens may be sprayed with wettable sulfur, Benlate, or Karathane.

Other Diseases. This host is occasionally affected by crown gall, caused by the bacterium *Agrobacterium tumefaciens,* and stem canker, caused by the fungi *Glomerella cingulata,* and *Physalospora obtusa.*

Insects

Euonymus Scale (*Unaspis euonymi*). This most harmful pest of bittersweet also infests *Pachysandra* and *Euonymus.* The female scales are dark brown and shaped like oystershells. The males are smaller and narrower, pure white, and are very prominent on the leaves and stems (Fig. 130). Oystershell and

San Jose scales also occasionally infest bittersweet.

Control: Heavy infestations of scales can be brought under control by applying a "superior" type dormant oil spray plus ethion before the new growth starts in spring, and following this with several applications of Cygon, malathion, Meta-Systox R, or Sevin at 2-week intervals starting in mid-May.

Aphids (*Aphis fabae* and *A. spiraecola*). The bean and spirea aphids occasionally infest bittersweet.

Control: Spray with Meta-Systox R or malathion when aphids first appear.

Two-Marked Treehopper (*Enchenopa binotata*). A small, bird-like insect occasionally infests bittersweet.

Control: A malathion spray applied in mid-May will control this pest.

CELOSIA (COCKSCOMB)

Diseases

Leaf Spots (*Cercospora celosiae, Phyllosticta* sp., and *Alternaria* sp.). Leaf spotting by three species of fungi may occur during wet seasons.

Control: Pick off and destroy badly spotted leaves. Zineb sprays will also provide control.

Other Diseases. Among other diseases reported on this host are damping-off of seedlings caused by *Pellicularia filamentosa,* charcoal rot by *Macrophomina phaseoli,* and curly top by the beet curly top virus.

Pests

Two-Spotted Mite (*Tetranychus urticae*). During hot, dry weather this plant is seriously infested by the red spider mite and other mites.

Control: See *Althaea.*

Other Pests. The Southern root-knot nema

Meloidogyne incognita occurs on cockscomb in the Middle West and South.

CELTIS (HACKBERRY)

Diseases

Leaf Spots (*Cercosporella celtidis, Cylindrosporium defoliatum, Phleospora celtidis, Phyllosticta celtidis,* and *Septogloeum celtidis*). Many fungi cause leaf spots on hackberry in rainy seasons.

Control: Leaf spots are rarely serious enough to warrant control, but a copper or dithiocarbamate fungicide would probably be effective.

Witches' Broom. The cause of this disease, which appears as bunched or close clusters of twigs throughout the tree, is not clearly understood. An *Eriophyes* mite and the powdery mildew fungus, *Sphaerotheca phytophylla,* are almost consistently associated with the trouble and are believed to be responsible for the deformation of the buds that results in the bunching of the twigs. Recently Japanese scientists have shown that many witches' broom diseases are associated with the presence of mycoplasma-like organisms similar to those thought to cause aster yellows.

Control: No effective control measures are known. Spray with dormant strength lime sulfur before growth starts in spring, followed by several applications at 2-week intervals of Kelthane starting in mid-May.

Powdery Mildew (*Uncinula parvula* and *U. polychaeta*). Both sides of the leaves are attacked, the mildew being visible either as a thin layer over the entire surface or in irregular patches. The small black fruiting bodies, ascocarps, develop mostly on the side opposite the mildew.

Control: Spray valuable specimens with Karathane when mildew begins to become prevalent.

Ganoderma Rot (*Ganoderma lucidum*). This fungus is capable of attacking living trees, cuasing extensive decay of the roots and trunk bases. See *Acer.*

Insects and Related Pests

Hackberry Nipple-Gall Maker (*Pachypsylla celtidismamma*). Small round galls opening on the lower leaf surfaces and resembling nipples are caused by a small jumping louse or psyllid. Another species of psyllid, *Pachypsylla celtidisvesicula,* produces blister galls.

Control: Spray with Cygon, Diazinon, or Sevin when the leaves are one-quarter grown.

Mourning-Cloak Butterfly (*Nymphalis antiopa*). The caterpillars of this butterfly are about 2 inches long at maturity and have reddish spots. They feed in groups on leaves of branch tips.

The puss caterpillar *Megalopyge opercularis* also infests this host occasionally.

Control: Spray with Sevin when the caterpillars are young.

Scales. Several species of scales including camphor, cottony maple, oystershell, Putnam, and San Jose occasionally infest this host.

Control: Malathion or Sevin sprays when the young are crawling about in spring will provide control. Where infestations are heavy, a dormant oil or lime sulfur spray before leaves emerge in spring should also be applied.

CENTAUREA (CORNFLOWER)

Diseases

Downy Mildew (*Bremia lactucae*). This fungus usually causes the development of pale greenish or reddish irregular spots on the upper sides of the leaves, while the undersides may be covered with a soft moldy growth. The leaves collapse and the attacked parts die. Young plants are especially susceptible.

The downy mildew fungus *Plasmopara halstedii* has been reported from Iowa.

Control: Remove and destroy badly infected plants. Space plants widely apart and provide full light and aeration. An occasional application of Bordeaux mixture or some other copper fungicide will also help to curb downy mildews.

Stem Rots (*Phytophthora cactorum, Sclerotinia sclerotiorum,* and *Pellicularia filamentosa*). *Centaurea* is unusually susceptible to these soil-borne fungi.

Control: Use clean soil, or pasteurize old soil as suggested in Chapter 4.

Wilt (*Fusarium oxysporum* var. *callistephi*). The fungus responsible for aster wilt also affects this host.

Control: See *Callistephus.*

Rusts (*Puccinia cyani* and *P. irrequisita*). The leaves and stems may be completely covered with brown pustules of these parasites.

Control: Wettable sulfur or ferbam sprays will control the rust disease.

Aster Yellows. The California strain of the aster yellows also occurs on this host.

Control: Spray with malathion to control the insect vectors.

Insects

Aphids (*Brachycaudus helichrysi*). This pest, also known as the leaf curl plum aphid, occasionally infests *Centaurea.* Another species of aphid attacks the roots of cornflowers, causing the plants to weaken and finally to die. These aphids, shown in Fig. 77, are snow white in color.

Control: Drench the soil in the vicinity of infested plants with Diazinon or with a dilute solution of malathion prepared from the emulsifiable concentrate.

Other Insects. Cornflowers may also be attacked by the stalk borer *Papaipema nebris*

and the aster leafhopper *Macrosteles fascifrons.*

Control: Methoxychlor sprays are effective in controlling the former, and Diazinon, Meta-Systox R, or Sevin sprays will control the latter.

CEPHALANTHUS (BUTTONBUSH)

Diseases

Leaf Spots (*Ascochyta cephalanthi, Coniothyrium cephalanthi, Phyllosticta cephalanthi, Ramularia cephalanthi,* and *Septoria cephalanthi*). Many fungi cause leaf spots on this host. A leaf blight caused by *Cercospora perniciosa* occurs in Texas.

Control: Valuable ornamental species can be protected in rainy seasons with an occasional application of a copper fungicide.

Powdery Mildews (*Microsphaera alni* and *Phyllactinia corylea*). These fungi also cause mildew on many other hosts.

Control: Spray with wettable sulfur or Karathane when the mildew appears.

Rusts (*Puccinia seymouriana* and *Uredo cephalanthi*). The former rust occurs on this host from New England to Florida and the central states; the latter in Florida.

Control: Control measures are rarely used.

Insects

San Jose Scale (*Quadraspidiotus perniciosus*). This scale is the only insect pest recorded on buttonbush.

Control: Spray valuable ornamental specimens with a dormant strength miscible oil or lime sulfur. Then spray in mid-May and June with malathion, Meta-Systox R, or Sevin.

CERCIDIPHYLLUM (KATSURA-TREE)

The only diseases recorded on *Cercidiphyllum* are cankers caused by a species of *Phom-*

opsis and a species of *Dothiorella,* and a root rot caused by *Armillaria mellea.*

Control: Pruning cankered branches below the infected area should keep the canker diseases under control. The root rot disease cannot be controlled.

CERCIS (REDBUD)

Diseases

Dieback (*Botryosphaeria dothidea*). This, the most destructive disease of redbud, also affects many other trees and shrubs. On redbud the cankers begin as small sunken areas and increase slowly in size. The bark in the center of the canker blackens and cracks along the edges. The wood beneath the cankered area becomes discolored. When the canker girdles the stem, the leaves above wilt and die. The causal fungus is easily recovered from discolored wood by standard tissue culture techniques in the laboratory. The causal fungus was formerly known as *Botryosphaeria ribis.*

Control: Prune and destroy branches showing cankers. Surgical excision of cankered tissue on the main stem is occasionally successful if all bark and wood is removed. Paint all wounds promptly with a wound dressing containing 200 ppm Benlate fungicide. Periodic applications of a copper fungicide during the growing season may help to prevent new infections.

Leaf Spots (*Mycosphaerella cercidicola, Cercosporella chionea,* and *Phyllosticta cercidicola*). The leaf spot diseases are prevalent in rainy season.

Control: Valuable specimens can be protected by periodic applications of copper or dithiocarbamate fungicides in late spring and early summer.

Other Diseases. Among other fungus diseases of redbud are wilt caused by *Verticillium albo-atrum,* and root rots by *Clitocybe tabescens, Ganoderma curtisii,* and *Phymatotrichum omnivorum.*

In Mississippi, branch dieback attributed to automobile exhaust fumes has been noted.

Insects

Two-Marked Treehopper (*Enchenopa binotata*). The leaves and stems of redbud are occasionally punctured by a dusky-brown insect $^3/_{10}$ inch long. A hornlike projection from the upper part of its body makes the insect resemble, in outline, a bird at rest. Locust, sycamore, hickory, and willow are also infested by this tree-hopper.

Control: Spray the leaves and stems with Diazinon, Meta-Systox R, or Sevin when the insects are young.

Control: Spray the leaves and stems with malathion when the insects are young.

Caterpillars. The larval stage of the California tent caterpillar, *Malacosoma californicum,* and the grape leaf folder, *Desmia funeralis,* occasionally infest redbuds.

Control: Spray with methoxychlor or Sevin when the young caterpillars begin to chew the leaves.

Scales. Eleven species of scales infest the twigs and branches of redbud.

Control: Dormant lime sulfur or oil sprays usually are sufficient to control scales. Severely infested trees should also be sprayed in May and June with malathion or Sevin.

Other Insects. The Rhabdopterus beetle *Rhabdopterus deceptor,* the redbud leaf roller *Fascista cercerisella,* the two-marked treehopper *Enchenopa binotata,* and the greenhouse whitefly *Trialeurodes vaporariorum* all attack redbud.

Control: Sevin sprays will control these pests.

CEREUS—see CACTACEAE

CHAENOMELES (FLOWERING QUINCE)

Bacterial and Fungus Diseases

Crown Gall (*Agrobacterium tumefaciens*).

This disease occasionally affects this host.

Control: See *Rosa.*

Fire Blight (*Erwinia amylovora*). Flowering quince, like other rosaceous hosts, is subject to this disease.

Control: Destroy nearby neglected and unwanted pear and apple trees. Spray with an antibiotic at mid-bloom stage.

Brown Rot (*Monilinia fructicola* and *M. laxa*). These fungi are usually more destructive on fruit trees than on the ornamental varieties. They cause a leaf blight and a blossom and twig blight of flowering quince.

Control: Periodic applications of captan or Benlate sprays during the early growing season are effective.

Rust (*Gymnosporangium clavipes*). This bright orange-colored rust is more commonly found on fruiting trees than on the flowering varieties. It attacks the fruit as well as the leaves and young twigs. It also attacks apples and hawthorns. The alternate host is the common redcedar, *Juniperus virginiana.* Though very destructive to the common quince, it does little damage to the cedar.

Another rust, G. *libocedri,* also attacks flowering quince leaves.

Control: Spray periodically with ferbam or wettable sulfur during the growing season.

Leaf Spots (*Fabraea maculata* and *Cercospora cydoniae*). These leaf spots can become quite troublesome and cause premature defoliation in rainy seasons.

Control: Spray with Benlate or zineb early in the growing season.

Other Diseases. Among other diseases occasionally found on flowering quince are: twig blight caused by *Botryosphaeria dothidea,* cankers caused by *Nectria cinnabarina, Phoma* sp. and *Physalospora obtusa,* and root-knot nema *Meloidogyne* sp.

Control: Controls are given under flowering cherry.

Insects

Cotton Aphid (*Aphis gossypii*). The young leaves and upper ends of tender branches may be heavily infested with these aphids.

Control: See *Gladiolus.*

CHAMAECYPARIS (WHITECEDAR)

Diseases

Blight (*Phomopsis juniperovora*). The leaves of whitecedar may be attacked by this fungus. See *Juniperus.*

Witches' Broom (*Gymnosporangium ellisii).* This fungus enters the leaves of whitecedar and travels down into the living bark of the twigs. The presence of the fungus stimulates the formation of a large number of buds which develop to form characteristic witches' brooms, shown in Figs. 19 and 20. Eventually the branch with its broom dies. During the early spring (in April) brown telial horns grow out from infected branches; they are about ¼ inch long and threadlike. Spores from these horns are carried in the wind to the bayberry, *Myrica,* which in turn becomes infected; a light orange-colored rust appears on the leaves and does considerable damage. The rust occasionally affects sweet-fern, *Comptonia.* When the seedlings of whitecedar are attacked, the trees become dwarfed; trees 15 to 20 years old, if they live, may not be over a foot or two high. When young trees are infected at the growing point, the main trunk is prevented from developing normally and the tree is stunted. The fungus is deep-seated; sometimes it is even found in the pith region. Heavily broomed trees may die.

Control: No effective control has been proposed other than separating the two hosts. The fungus acts slowly, and thus removal of the brooms prevents the spread of the parasite to the barberry, which otherwise endangers the evergreens.

Spindle Burl Gall (*Gymnosporangium biseptatum*). This rust fungus is more or less local in its infection, probably first infecting the leaves and then penetrating into the young branches. It stimulates an excessive growth of wood into long burls, which may be several inches in diameter. The branches which bear these burls eventually die. When infection occurs at the base of a young tree, the burl may continue to grow with the tree without doing particular damage. Burls a foot across have been seen at the bases of trees of about the same diameter. Occasionally two species of rust attack the trees at the same point, and a combination of burl and witches' broom results. The alternate host of the rust which causes the latter abnormality is the common *Amelanchier* or serviceberry. Ornamental cedars grown individually are rarely infected.

Another species of rust, *Gymnosporangium fraternum,* attacks the leaves of *Chamaecyparis.* It is of little consequence on this host but does some damage to chokeberry, *Aronia,* its alternate host.

Root Rot (*Phytophthora lateralis*). This highly destructive disease affects native *Chamaecyparis* in the Pacific Northwest. It is especially serious on Port Orford cedar or Lawson cypress, *C. lawsoniana.* The fungus infects leaves, stems, and trunk in addition to the roots. Another species, *P. cinnamomi,* causes root rot of Lawson cypress seedlings in Louisiana.

Control: No satisfactory controls have been developed.

Insects

Among the pests which attack whitecedar are the larvae of the imperial moth *Eacles imperialis,* the bagworm *Thyridopteryx ephemeraeformis,* and the juniper scale *Carulaspis juniperi.* Details on control are to be found under more popular hosts.

CHEIRANTHUS CHEIRI (WALLFLOWER)

Bacterial and Fungus Diseases

Bacterial Wilt (*Xanthomonas campestris*). This bacterium, common on other members of the cabbage family, causes the inflorescence to become stunted and the leaves to turn yellow, wilt, and fall from the lower part of the stem. The water-conducting vessels of the stems are discolored brown, or blackish.

Control: Rogue out and destroy diseased plants. Treat seeds with hot water to eliminate any seed-borne bacteria. Plant in clean or steam pasteurized soil.

Club Root (*Plasmodiophora brassicae*). This disease affects many species of the cabbage family. It is readily distinguished from crown gall by the failure of the root system to develop.

Control: It is advisable to rotate the plantings, for the organism enters the soil from these decayed abnormal growths. Avoid planting where cabbage, turnips, and related varieties have been grown previously (especially if they have shown the club root disease) unless the soils are first pasteurized or well limed.

The club root organism in commercial fields of cabbage and related crops has been controlled with PCNB (Terraclor) and sodium methyl dithiocarbamate (Vapam). These materials should also be effective in controlling *Plasmodiophora brassicae* in wallflower plantings.

White Rust (*Albugo candida*). The leaves, inflorescence, and stems are subject to attack by this parasiste. It breaks out in glistening white pustules which discharge milk-white powdery spores. Sections of the pustules show that the spores, like the aeciospores of the true rust, are borne in chains.

Control: Remove and destroy infected parts. Sprays are impractical.

Gray Mold (*Botrytis cinerea*). Characteristic brown spots covered with gray mold develop at the base of the branches. Disease weakens the branches so that they break off. The main branches also may be attacked and killed, after which the plant wilts and dies.

Control: Space the plants farther apart and do not keep them too moist. If many plants become diseased, spray with captan or zineb.

Insects

Lily Aphid (*Neomyzus circumflexus*). This yellow-and-black species also attacks many other plants.

Control: Spray with malathion or Sevin.

Diamondback Moth (*Plutella xylostella*). Cabbage, turnips and other vegetables of the cabbage family, should not be planted close to greenhouses and other locations where wall-flowers are grown, since this moth is always present on such vegetable plants, and is apt to deposit its eggs on the wallflowers.

Control: Spray with Sevin when the larvae are small.

Beetles (*Entomoscelis americana* and *Phyllotreta ramosa*). The former, known as the red turnip beetle, is bright red with black patches on the head and three black lines on its wing covers. The latter, named the western striped flea beetle, is shiny black with a conspicuous, irregular, yellow-white band down each wing cover.

Control: Spray with Sevin if these pests become troublesome.

CHELONE (TURTLE-HEAD)

Diseases

A leaf spot caused by the fungus *Septoria mariae-wilsonii* occurs in the East and Middle West. Two species of powdery mildew fungi, *Erysiphe cichoracearum* and *E. polygoni*, are found on this host in the same areas. A rust, *Puccinia andropogonis* var. *penstemonis*, oc-

curs in the East. The alternate stage of the rust is found on *Andropogon.*

Control: Control measures are rarely applied on these perennial herbs. Wettable sulfur sprays will control serious outbreaks of any of the diseases listed.

CHIONANTHUS (FRINGE-TREE)

Diseases

Leaf Spots—Four species of fungi *Cercospora chionanthi, Phyllosticta chionanthi, Septoria chionanthi,* and *S. eleospora*—are known to cause leaf spotting on this host.

Control: Spray with a copper fungicide or with one of the dithiocarbamates.

Powdery Mildew (*Phyllactinia corylea*). The leaves of fringe-tree are occasionally affected by this disease.

Control: Where mildew is severe, spray with Karathane, wettable sulfur, or Benlate.

Other Diseases. Fringe-tree is occasionally subject to several canker diseases caused by *Botryosphaeria pyriospora, Phomopsis diatrypea,* and *Valsa chionanthi.*

Insects

Scales. The rose scale *Aulacaspis rosae* and the white peach scale infest *Chionanthus.*

Control: A dormant oil spray applied in early spring will control these pests. Malathion or Sevin applied in mid-May and again in mid-June will control the crawler stage.

CHIONODOXA (GLORY-OF-THE-SNOW)

The only serious pest of this host is the stem and bulb nema *Ditylenchus dipsaci.* See *Narcissus.*

CHLOROPHYTUM

The cabbage looper, *Trichoplusia ni,* feeds on several species of greenhouse ornamentals. *Chlorophytum* is one of the favorite hosts of a similar looper, which may destroy many leaves in one night. The caterpillars are light green with rather inconspicuous white stripes along the body; they are about 1¼ inches long and taper toward the head.

Control: Spray with Sevin when the loopers are young. Rotenone sprays or dusts also kill the young caterpillars.

CHRYSANTHEMUM MAXIMUM (SHASTA DAISY)

Diseases

Leaf Spots (*Cercospora chrysanthemi* and *Septoria leucanthemi*). The former causes a leaf spot on this host in Oklahoma; the latter on Shasta daisy on the Pacific Coast.

Control: Remove and destroy infected leaves. Severe outbreaks can be prevented by spraying with copper or dithiocarbamate sprays.

Stem Rots (*Pellicularia filamentosa, Sclerotinia sclerotiorum, Fusarium roseum,* and *F. solani*). These fungi occasionally infect this host via the roots or lower stems.

Control: Soil-borne fungi are controlled by the heat or chemical treatments described in Chapter 4.

Crown Gall (*Agrobacterium tumefaciens*). Occasionally in garden plantings one finds large swellings on the crown and nearby roots. The bacteria also attack *Chrysanthemum morifolium* and *C. frutescens.*

Control: Rogue out and destroy infected plants.

Insects

Four-Lined Plant Bug (*Poecilocapsus lineatus*). This yellow-green bug with four black stripes on its wings attacks Shasta daisy, besides many other garden plants. The infested foliage has a spotted appearance. The leaves turn brown and die.

Control: Spray with Sevin when the bugs begin to feed.

Other Insects. Among the insects that feed on Shasta daisy are the larvae of the checkerspot butterfly, *Euphydryas chalcedona,* and the chrysanthemum leaf miner, *Phytomyza syngenesiae.*

Control: Malathion or Sevin sprays applied when the pests are first observed provide effective control.

CHRYSANTHEMUM MORIFOLIUM (CHRYSANTHEMUM)

Bacterial Diseases

Bacterial Blight (*Erwinia chrysanthemi*). This is a relatively new bacterial disease of chrysanthemums. The most pronounced symptom is a rot of the upper part of the stem, resulting in wilt and collapse of the distal portion. Cuttings infected with this bacterium may show a brown to black decay at their bases. Occasionally the only symptom of the disease is a marginal leaf scorch.

Control: Soil in which diseased plants grew should be pasteurized with heat before reuse. In tests at Cornell University, cuttings dipped for 4 hours in solutions of antibiotics such as chloromycetin, streptomycin, Aureomycin, and Terramycin, before being placed into the rooting medium, were disease-free.

Fasciation (*Corynebacterium fascians*). This bacterium causes symptoms on chrysanthemums similar to fasciation of sweet peas. The stems are shortened and thickened near the crown and develop aborted and misshapen leaves. The plants are dwarfed and form an abnormal number of buds. Plants are affected early and the disease develops as the plant matures.

Control: Soil pasteurization or renewal is advised for eradication of the organism.

Good cultural conditions should be maintained.

Crown Gall (*Agrobacterium tumefaciens*). See *Dahlia*.

Bacterial Leaf Spot (*Pseudomonas cichorii*). Spots produced by this bacterium are dark brown to black, slightly sunken, and have concentric zonations.

Control: Spray weekly during rainy spells with either a copper bactericide or Agrimycin.

Fungus Diseases

Wilt (*Verticillium albo-atrum*). Wilt is one of the most destructive fungus diseases of chrysanthemums and many other woody and herbaceous plants. On chrysanthemums the first symptom is a conspicuous yellowing and browning of the leaves, which die from the base of the plant upwards. Infected plants are stunted and often fail to produce flowers. The fungus is soil-borne and enters the plant through the roots, later invading the vessels of the stem and cutting off the water supply. It is essentially a disease of greenhouse chrysanthemums, but hardy garden varieties are often attacked.

Another wilt of chrysanthemums is caused by *Fusarium oxysporum* var. *tracheiphilum*.

Control: Soil in which plants have become diseased, if it is to be used again, must be pasteurized with heat or with some effective chemical such as chloropicrin. Commercial growers can achieve almost complete control by using the so-called indexing of cuttings method recommended by the late Dr. A. W. Dimock of Cornell, and then growing the cuttings in pasteurized soil in raised benches, or in concrete-bottom ground beds.

Rust (*Puccinia chrysanthemi*). The rust pustules start as blister-like swellings, which break open and discharge masses of brown, powdery spores. Severely infected plants are much weakened and fail to bloom properly. The rust may be carried on stock and thus introduced into greenhouses. The disease is severe on garden chrysanthemums only in the cooler regions of the United States.

Control: Remove infected leaves as soon as possible. Set new plants farther apart and provide better ventilation. Water the soil in the pots directly without wetting the plants. Spray with wettable sulfur, ferbam, or zineb where severe infections are likely to occur.

Leaf Spot (*Septoria chrysanthemi* and *S. chrysanthemella*). These spots are at first yellowish, then become dark brown and black, increasing from 1/8 to 1 inch or more in diameter. Serious infection may result in premature withering of the leaves; the dead leaves hang to the stem for some time. The lower leaves are infected first. The leaf nema disease is often mistaken for this *Septoria* spot disease. With a hand lens, white masses of spores may be seen on the minute specks which are numerous in the diseased area. The spores are long and slender, and marked by cross-walls.

Several other fungi cause leaf spots on this host. Most prevalent are *Alternaria chrysanthemi*, *Cercospora chrysanthemi*, *Phyllosticta chrysanthemi*, and *Cylindrosporium chrysanthemi*. The latter produces dark brown spots with yellowish margins. These increase in size so as to involve the whole leaf, which dies and hangs down on the stem like one infected with *Septoria*.

Control: For greenhouse culture and for small garden plantings, hand picking and destroying the infected leaves is a good practice. Avoid wetting the leaves while watering greenhouse plants. Outdoors, early infection may occur through splashing of soil onto the lower leaves. Mulching with peat moss or some other appropriate material will prevent such infection. Weekly applications of Phaltan, maneb, captan, or zineb sprays also provide good control.

Powdery Mildew (*Erysiphe cichoracearum*). The leaves become covered with a whitish, ash-gray powdery growth. The spores require a very moist atmosphere in which to germinate and spread the infection (they do not germinate well in water).

Control: Spray with Benlate, Karathane, or wettable sulfur. Some commercial growers paint the steam pipes with a mixture of sulfur and lime.

Gray Mold (*Botrytis cinerea*). This mold attacks flowers in moist greenhouses, causing the development of brown water-soaked spots. Infected parts become covered with a grayish-brown, powdery mass of spores. These are scattered from plant to plant by syringing, and by air currents. This disease may be confused with the ray blight disease discussed below.

Control: Provide better ventilation, space plants for free circulation of air, and avoid syringing. Mist-spray buds and blooms with captan. For outdoor chrysanthemums, spray as directed below for the control of ray blight.

Ray Blight (*Mycosphaerella ligulicola*). Originally discovered in North Carolina more than 60 years ago, when the causal fungus was known as *Ascochyta chrysanthemi*, this disease has recently appeared in commercial greenhouses on Long Island, New York. The ray flowers are attacked, so that the blooms are deformed and one-sided. Early infection may cause blasting of the buds.

Control: Commercial growers alternate with weekly sprayings of ferbam and zineb when the plants are small. After the buds have formed, the amount of fungicide is decreased and is applied as a fine mist to protect the buds and opening flowers. Maneb can be substituted for the ferbam or zineb in the late applications. Recent tests have revealed that Benlate is very effective as a foliar spray when applied at label rates.

Ray Speck (*Stemphylium* spp. and *Alternaria* spp.). These fungi cause brown or white necrotic specks surrounded by colored halos on the fully expanded ray florets when humidity and temperatures are high.

Control: The fungicides recommended for ray blight will control ray speck.

Stem Rots (*Fusarium* sp. and *Pellicularia filamentosa*). A basal decay may result from infection by these fungi.

Control: Use clean soil, or pasteurize old soil as described in Chapter 4.

Pythium Wilt (*Pythium aphanidermatum*). The Iceberg varieties of chrysanthemum are especially susceptible to this wilt disease in southern Florida.

Control: Soil drenches with Dexon on Truban provide excellent control.

Virus Diseases

Chrysanthemums are subject to a large number of virus diseases. Most of our information on these is available through the brilliant researches of the late Dr. Philip Brierley and his colleagues of the United States Department of Agriculture. A brief presentation follows of the more important viruses of chrysanthemums.

Aspermy (Tomato aspermy virus). Distortion of flowers and abnormal coloration result from this virus. The virus is probably of East Asiatic origin inasmuch as it is constantly recovered from chrysanthemums imported from Asia. The infectious principle is transmitted in nature by several species of aphids, including *Acyrthosiphon solani*, *Macrosiphoniella sanborni*, and *Myzus persicae*.

Control: Thorough rouging of infected chrysanthemum stock plants at flowering time, care in propagating new "sports" (which frequently are aspermy-infected material), and controlling aphids with Sevin or malathion early in the season are suggested control practices. This virus was eliminated from "Nightingale" chrysanthemums by grafting scions 4 to 8 mm. long from the tips of branches onto healthy "Good News" chrysanthemums. Potted chrysanthemums infected with aspermy were cured by placing the plants in an incubator at 97°F. for 3 to 4 weeks. Cuttings taken from such plants produced healthy plants.

Flower Distortion (Chrysanthemum flower distortion virus). Ray florets are short, narrow, and incurved when this virus is present. Sometimes a number of rays are suppressed, and in other cases they are short and flat. The causal virus is transmissible by grafting but not by the usual mechanical methods.

Mosaic (Many viruses). Drs. P. Brierley and F. F. Smith of the United States Department of Agriculture were able to distinguish eight mosaic and two rosette viruses of chrysanthemum on the basis of reactions by chrysanthemum varieties, petunia, and cineraria, and of transmissibility by sap and the aphid, *Myzus persicae.* Their work is too technical to present in a book of this type.

Virus (Tomato spotted wilt). Ring and line patterns, pale areas, mottling, and necrotic spots occur in infected plants. This virus has been reported from the states of California and Washington.
Control: Virus diseases are difficult to control. Plants known to be infected should never be used for propagation inasmuch as cuttings taken from such plants will harbor the virus. Heat treatments of infected material have not proved commercially practicable. Because aphids and leafhoppers commonly spread viruses, these pests should be kept under control with malathion sprays.

Yellow Strapleaf (*Aspergillus wentii*). This disease has recently appeared in large commercial plantings of chrysanthemums in Florida. Affected plants have narrow, pale yellow leaves with axillary buds that are yellow and slightly swollen.
Control: Lifting young plants showing strapleaf and resetting them in the same location is about 60 per cent effective. Older affected plants do not respond to this treatment.

Other Diseases

Aster Yellows. This disease, caused by a mycoplasma-like organism, is characterized by the production of green-colored flowers instead of the normal color for the variety. Sometimes the upper branches of a flowering stem are thin, yellowish, and more upright than usual. Affected plants die within a few months of becoming diseased.
Control: Remove infected plants. Spray with malathion to control sucking insects.

Stunt (viroid). Plants, leaves, and flowers are reduced in size; bronze, pink, and red flowers are bleached to lighter shades; and the flowers appear earlier when affected by the stunt viroid. Symptoms may appear 6 to 8 months after the plants are infected.

Experimentally the stunt viroid has been transmitted to many species of plants which exhibit no symptoms.

The chlorotic mottle disease is also caused by a viroid.

Insects and Other Pests

Aphids. The following kinds of aphids infest chrysanthemums: chrysanthemum, foxglove, green peach, leaf-curl plum, melon, myrtle, and thistle. One of the most common, the chrysanthemum aphid *Macrosiphoniella sanborni,* is large, dark chocolate-brown. It clusters on tender terminal shoots and on the underside of the leaves resulting in stunting, leaf-curling, and sometimes the death of the entire plant.
Control: All species of aphids are easily controlled with malathion or Meta-Systox R sprays. The newest control for the green peach and chrysanthemum aphids is Pirimor.

Beetles. Among the various kinds of beetles which feed on this host are the following: Asiatic garden, blister, Fuller rose, goldsmith, rose chafer, and spotted cucumber.
Control: Spray with Sevin.

Stalk Borer (*Papaipema nebris*). This rather dark striped caterpillar also attacks leaves and stems of bluegrass and other plants in the vicinity. The borer migrates to the chrysanthemums at flowering time and does considerable damage.

The European corn borer, *Ostrinia nubilalis,* also attacks this host. It is flesh-colored with rows of small, round, dark spots.

Control: Cut and destroy weeds in the vicinity. Spray with a mixture of Sevin and Kelthane when the plants are 8 to 10 inches tall. Repeat every 10 days until the flowers open.

Bugs. Many kinds of bugs attack chrysanthemums. Among the most common are the four-lined plant, harlequin, lygus, and the tarnished plant. The last, *Lygus lineolaris,* attacks stems just below the bud, causing wilt.

Control: Malathion or methoxychlor sprays applied as necessary will control most bugs.

Caterpillars. Yellow woollybear and zebra caterpillars chew the leaves of this host.

Control: Spray with *Bacillus thuringiensis* or Sevin when the caterpillars are small.

Checkerspot Butterfly. See *Buddleja.*

Chrysanthemum Gall Midge (*Diarthronomyia chrysanthemi*). This midge is primarily a pest of greenhouse chrysanthemums and is little known on garden plants. The fly lays eggs in masses on the surface of new foliage; this foliage is covered with hairs which protect the eggs. The eggs hatch in 3 or 4 days, and the larvae soon enter the leaf, where they stimulate the formation of small, pimple-like galls, familiar to all growers of these plants. The infested foliage is much distorted and unsuitable for the market. The damage is illustrated in Fig. 117.

Control: Diazinon or methoxychlor sprays are effective against the gall midge.

Chrysanthemum Leaf Miner (*Phytomyza syngenesiae*). The leaf miner feeds on the inner tissues of the leaf just under the epidermis, making irregular tunnels especially near the margins.

Control: Spray with Diazinon to kill the insects just beneath the epidermis. Repeat 2 weeks later if necessary.

Greenhouse Leaf Tier (*Udea rubigalis*). These caterpillars feed on the more tender tissues of the underside of the leaves, avoiding the veins.

Control: Hand-picking is useful if the plants are not too numerous; otherwise they can be sprayed with Sevin.

Chrysanthemum Lace Bug (*Corythucha marmorata*). The adult stage of this pest has lace-like wings. Both the young and adult stages suck out leaf juices, causing bleaching of the leaves and injury to the stems. Aster and scabiosa are also attacked.

Control: Spray with malathion, Diazinon, or Sevin, directing the material mainly to the lower leaf surfaces.

Mealybugs. Among the mealybugs which infest chrysanthemums are the citrus, ground, greenhouse, and the Mexican. The last, known scientifically as *Phenacoccus gossypii,* is primarily a pest of greenhouse chrysanthemums.

Control: Ants, which are largely responsible for the spread of these insects, can be eradicated by dusting or spraying the soil surface lightly with Diazinon or Dursban. Sprays may also be applied directly to the mealybug-infested plants. Malathion sprays are also effective.

Thrips. Three species of thrips, the banded greenhouse, the chrysanthemum, and the greenhouse, attack chrysanthemums. They cause flecking or silvering of the leaves of greenhouse-grown plants.

Control: Spray with Sevin.

Variegated Cutworm (*Peridroma saucia*). Cutworms sometimes feed on the foliage of outdoor chrysanthemums.

Control: See *Asparagus.*

Whitefly. See *Fuchsia.*

Fig. 117. Effect of the chrysanthemum gall midge *Diarthronomyia chrysanthemi*. The midges are visible on the detached leaf in the upper left corner.

Mites. Three species of mites infest chrysanthemums: broad, cyclamen, and two-spotted. Broad and cyclamen mites are discussed under *Cyclamen.* The two-spotted mite, *Tetranychus urticae,* causes distorted foliage and shriveled, discolored blooms.

Control: Spray with Cygon, Meta-Systox R, or Kelthane from time to time as needed.

Eastern Subterranean Termite (*Reticulitermes flavipes*). Like other garden plants, the roots of chrysanthemums are sometimes attacked by this termite. These are more frequently pests of greenhouse plants, where they find their way to potted plants through the wooden bench legs. They also make their galleries along the wooden benches. Termites feed on the woody tissues of the roots and stems, destroying many plants. They enter the pots through the drainage holes. They evidently find their way to roots of garden plants from infested buildings or tree stumps.

Control: For greenhouse plants, use Diazinon in the soil or on the cinders on which potted chrysanthemums are set.

Foliar Nema (*Aphelenchoides ritzemabosi*). This nema has long been known to be a pest of greenhouse chrysanthemums, but only in recent years have they become very injurious to hardy chrysanthemums grown outdoors. When the stems are wet, the worms swim up through the film of water and enter the stomata of the leaves. The first symptom of infecton is a yellowish-brown spotting of the leaves. The spots are more or less bounded by the larger veins; they enlarge and run together so that the entire leaf is involved (Fig. 118). The leaves die, become brittle, and fall. The symptoms may be con-

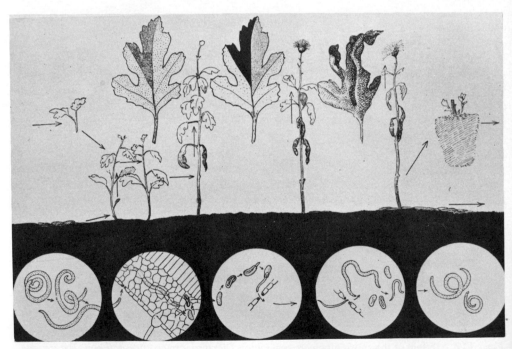

Fig. 118. Life cycle of the foliar nema of chrysanthemum (*Aphelenchoides ritzema-bosi*). The arrows indicate the progress of this nema through the season. It overwinters in infested leaves in the soil or in leaves of young plants. In late spring and early summer it moves up the stems during rainy weather to infest successive layers of leaves. The circular inserts below show the mode of entry and exit via the stomata (breathing pores) of the leaves. (After Voss)

fused with the leaf spot disease caused by the fungus *Septoria,* but the spots caused by eel-worms are brownish and not black. The worms also infest the ray flowers and prevent proper development of them. Seriously infested plants die without developing much good foliage or blooms.

Several precautions must be observed in controlling these pests on garden chrysanthemums. First, propagate only by taking cuttings from the tops of long, vigorous shoots. Do not propagate by dividing an old clump. Avoid replanting chrysanthemums in the same area year after year. As soon as the soil has warmed, mulch the surface with peat moss or some other material. This helps to prevent infection of the lower leaves by nemas that may have survived in old, infested leaves. Commercial growers also spray outdoor plants with parathion, 3 times at 2- to 3-week intervals, from July to early September, but this material is not recommended for amateur growers. Diazinon sprays are suggested for non-professional growers. Commercial growers of greenhouse mums can apply ½ pound of technical demeton per 1000 square feet of bench area. The demeton (Systox) should be diluted in enough water to apply at least 1 pint of the solution per square foot. After treatment, water the area thoroughly.

The root-knot nemas *Meloidogyne incognita* and *M. hapla* infest the roots of chrysanthemums. See under Nemas in Chapter 3.

Japanese Weevil. See *Ligustrum.*

Combination Spray for Chrysanthemums

The following combination spray will control all the more prevalent fungus diseases and insect pests of outdoor chrysanthemums:

Sevin, 50% wettable powder	2 Tablespoonfuls
Malathion, 25% W P	4 Tablespoonfuls
Zineb, 65% W P	1 Tablespoonful
Kelthane, 35% W P	1½ teaspoonfuls
Water	1 gallon

Mix the four ingredients dry, then add enough water to make a very thin paste. Pour this mixture into the spray tank, preferably through a fine screen or cheesecloth, add water, and stir.

CHRYSPOSIS (GOLDEN ASTER)

Diseases

Leaf Spots (*Cercospora macroguttata* and *Ramularia chrysopsidis*). Occasionally leaves of golden aster are spotted by two species of fungi.

Control: Pick off and destroy spotted leaves as they appear.

Rusts (*Coleosporium solidaginis, Puccinia grindeliae,* and *P. stipae*). Of the three rusts which affect this host, the first listed is most common. It also occurs on perennial asters and goldenrod and its alternate host on pines.

Control: Control measures are rarely adopted. Wettable sulfur sprays will prevent infections.

Powdery Mildew (*Erysiphe cichoracearum*). This mildew is common on this host. Wettable sulfur, Benlate, or Karathane sprays will control it.

CIBOTIUM—see FILICES

CIMICIFUGA (BUGBANE)

Diseases

Leaf spots caused by the fungi *Ascochyta actaeae* and *Ectostroma afflatum,* a rust disease by *Puccinia rubigo-vera,* and a smut by *Urocystis carcinodes* are the only diseases reported on this host. The southern root-knot nema *Meloidogyne incognita* may also affect bugbane.

CINERARIA

Fungus Diseases

Blight (*Botrytis cinerea*). Young plants grown under high humidity and low light intensity are subject to blighting by this fungus.

Control: Space plants adequately, improve ventilation, and spray with captan.

Downy Mildew (*Plasmopara halstedii*). Pale green spots develop on the upper epidermis of the leaves, and a felt-like, whitish mold appears on the undersides of the leaves, corresponding to the spots on the top. Wherever the leaves are attacked by this fungus, they shrink and die. It is especially destructive to young plants.

Control: Remove and destroy all infected parts. Keep the plants as dry as possible. Space the plants so that they will be well lighted. Spray with Bordeaux mixture or some other copper fungicide if the disease is very prevalent.

Powdery Mildew. (*Erysiphe cichoracearum*). This mildew attacks leaves, stems, and flower buds, covering them with a whitish, powdery growth. It dwarfs and stunts the parts attacked. It does not develop vigorously in greenhouses at low temperatures, around 45°F.

Control: Spray with Karathane or Benlate when mildew first appears. Repeat when necessary.

Stem Rots (*Fusarium* sp., *Phytophthora cinnamomi,* and *Sclerotinia sclerotiorum*). Three soil-harbored fungi cause root and stem decay of cineraria.

Control: Use clean soil, or steam-pasteurize old soil with heat, or treat it with a mixture of Dexon and Terraclor.

Other Diseases. A root rot caused by *Pythium ultimum,* a leaf spot by *Alternaria senecionis,* and wilt by *Verticillium alboatrum* occur occasionally.

Virus. The tomato spotted wilt virus affects cineraria.

Control: Rogue out and destroy affected plants. Spray with malathion to control insects that spread the virus.

Aster Yellows. This disease affects cineraria.

Control: Same as for spotted wilt.

Insects and Other Pests

Aphids. The leaves of cineraria are very susceptible to four species of aphids—the green peach, leaf-curl plum, melon, and the potato aphid.

Control: Meta-Systox R, malathion, or Sevin sprays are very effective against aphids. Fumigation with nicotine is also effective.

Variegated Cutworm (*Peridroma saucia*). Cutworms not only cut off young plants near the soil, but feed on the leaves and flower buds. All stages of the insects may be present at one time in the greenhouse. The larvae feed at night and are thus not usually discovered until some damage has been done.

Control: Apply Diazinon or Dipterex to the soil surface or spray the leaves with Sevin.

Cabbage Looper. See *Calendula.*

Greenhouse Leaf Tier. See *Antirrhinum.*

Mealybugs. See *Chrysanthemum.*

Two-spotted Mite. See *Calluna.*

Leaf Miner. See *Chrysanthemum.*

White Fly. See *Fuchsia.*

CIRSIUM (PLUMED THISTLE)

Diseases

Leaf Spots (*Cercospora* spp., *Phyllosticta cirsii,* and *Septoria cirsii*). At least two species of *Cercospora,* a species of *Phyllosticta,* and one of *Septoria,* cause leaf spotting of this host.

Control: Leaf spots rarely become serious enough to warrant control measures.

Rusts (*Puccinia cirsii* and *Uromyces junci*). Two rust fungi occasionally infest *Cirsium.* A species of the white rust fungus, *Albugo tragopogonis,* has also been recorded on this host.

Control: As with leaf spots, control measures are rarely practiced.

Root Rot (*Pellicularia filamentosa*). This disease has been reported from New Jersey.

Control: See under more favored hosts.

Insects

Aphids (*Capitophorus elaegni, Aphis fabae, A. gossypii,* and *Brachycaudus cardui*). Four species of aphids occur on thistles.

Control: Spray valuable ornamental specimens with malathion.

Bugs (*Poecilocapsus lineatus* and *Leptoglossus phyllopus*). The four-lined plant bug and the leaf-footed bug attack this host. The former is of general distribution; the latter occurs in the Southeast and as far west as Arizona.

Control: These pests do not cause enough damage on *Circium* to warrant control measures.

Caterpillars. The larvae of the painted beauty and painted lady butterflies, the celery leaf tier, and the oblique-banded leaf roller also chew the leaves of *Circium.*

Control: Spray with Sevin when the young caterpillars begin to feed.

CISSUS (GRAPE IVY, KANGAROO VINE)

Diseases

Leaf Spots. Three fungi—*Cercospora viticola, C. arboreae,* and *Phyllosticta cissicola* —cause leaf spots on *Cissus* in Texas and Louisiana.

Control: Leaf spots are not serious enough to warrant control measures.

Other Diseases. Rust caused by *Aecidium mexicanum,* smut by *Mycosyrinx cissi,* root rot by *Phymatotrichum omnivorum,* and a powdery mildew also occur on *Cissus.*

Control: Same as for leaf spots.

Insect

Mealybug (*Pseudococcus longispinus*). The long-tailed mealybug often infests *Cissus.*

Control: Spray the leaves, especially their lower surfaces, and stems with malathion.

Repeat every 10 days until the infestation is cleaned up.

CITRUS (ORANGE, LEMON, GRAPEFRUIT, ETC.)

Members of the citrus family, particularly those grown for fruit in the South, Southwest, and Pacific Coast, are subject to at least 50 fungus, bacterial, and virus diseases, and to nearly as many insect and related pests. A detailed discussion of these is beyond the scope of this book. Such information is readily available to commercial growers of citrus from their State Agricultural Experiment Stations.[15] The principal troubles likely to be encountered in growing members of the *Citrus* family as ornamentals in greenhouses and in homes in the cooler parts of the country are either due to unfavorable growing conditions or to insects and related pests.

Leaf Yellowing. Citrus leaves turn yellow and drop prematurely from many causes. Plants that have been kept in the same container for several years without being shifted may become potbound. Excessive amounts of chemical plant foods, overwatering, and lack of sufficient sunlight are additional causes for leaf yellowing. Sometimes lack of plant food, particularly the nitrogen and iron constituents, may be responsible. In addition, scales and mites, discussed below, may play a part in the leaf yellowing complex. Where lack of iron is involved, spraying the foliage or mixing into the soil a small amount of iron chelate will cure the condition.

Insects and Related Pests

Scales. At least 17 species of scales infest citrus. Only two or three kinds, however, oc-

---

[15] An excellent publication on diseases is *Color Handbook of Citrus Diseases* by L. J. Klotz and H. S. Fawcett, published by the University of California Press.

cur on trees grown indoors in the cooler parts of the country. These appear as more or less circular, brown, or yellowish flat bodies closely appressed to the leaf and stem surfaces. These are the adult stages which have lost their ability to move. The young crawling stages are much smaller and barely visible without a hand lens. In addition to the direct damage caused by scales, these pests secrete a sticky substance which covers citrus leaves and on which a black, sooty mold fungus grows.

Control: Malathion and Sevin sprays are very effective in combating the young stages of scales. Malathion sprays have an unpleasant odor and hence are best applied on plants brought outdoors on a mild day. An improved malathion, known as Cythion, is less malodorous. If only a few plants are being grown, the adult scale can be lifted off the leaves and stems with the tips of finger-nails or a soft-bristle toothbrush.

Mealybugs. Four species of mealybugs—citrus, citrophilus, grape, and long-tailed—also infest citrus. These insects are related to scales and are also controlled with malathion sprays. Commercial growers of citrus under glass also use certain water-miscible oil sprays to control these insects.

Aphids. Six species of aphids have been reported on members of the *Citrus* family. Only one or two species, however, infest plants grown indoors. Meta-Systox R or malathion sprays provide effective control of aphids.

Whiteflies, Thrips. These are two other insects that occasionally become troublesome on greenhouse-grown citrus. The former is controlled by synthetic pyrethroid sprays, the latter with Cygon or Diazinon.

Ants (*Iridomyrmex humilis*). The Argentine and other species of ants also make successful culture of citrus indoors difficult. They do not feed on citrus but help to spread scales, mealybugs, and aphids in order to assure themselves a steady supply of so-called "honeydew."

Control: Dust the soil and base of citrus plants with 2 per cent Diazinon powder.

Mites. Several species of mites infest citrus leaves. These usually suck juices from the lower leaf surfaces, causing a yellowish mottling of the upper surfaces.

Control: Mites are effectively controlled with Kelthane.

CLADRASTIS (YELLOW-WOOD)

Few diseases and no insect pests have been recorded on this host. A powdery mildew caused by *Phyllactinia corylea,* canker by *Botryosphaeria dothidea,* wilt by *Verticillium albo-atrum,* and a decay of the butt and roots of living trees by *Polyporus spraguei,* and a virus disease caused by the bean yellow mosaic virus occur occasionally.

CLARKIA

Diseases

Damping-off (*Pythium debaryanum* and *Pellicularia filamentosa*). Seedlings rot at the soil line as a result of invasion by these two soil-inhibiting fungi.

Control: Use steam-pasteurized soil or grow seedlings in sifted sphagnum moss. Where only *Pellicularia filamentosa* is involved, treat the soil with PCNB (Terraclor).

Stem Canker (*Botrytis cinerea*). A serious stem canker and blight may be caused by this gray mold fungus.

Control: Space plants adequately, improve ventilation in the greenhouse, and spray with captan or zineb if necessary.

Stem Rots (*Fusarium* sp. and *Phytophthora cactorum*). Occasionally the lower stems and roots may be invaded by these fungi.

Control: Use steam-pasteurized soil.

Rusts (*Puccinia oenotherae* and *Puccinias-trum pustulatum*). The former rust occurs in the western states; the latter has been reported from the state of Alaska.

Control: Severe outbreaks can be prevented with wettable sulfur sprays.

Aster Yellows. The aster yellows organism occurs on this host in California.

Control: Remove and destroy infected plants.

Insect

Leafhopper (*Macrosteles fascifrons*). The aster leafhopper transmits the aster yellows organism.

Control: See *Callistephus.*

CLEMATIS

Diseases

Leaf Spot and Stem Rot (*Ascochyta cle-matidina*). In the field this disease attacks the stems near the soil, but in the greenhouse both leaves and stems become infected. Small water-soaked spots, which become buff-colored with reddish margins, develop on the leaves. The fungus extends down into the stems, girdling them and causing the upper parts to die. Individual shoots may wilt suddenly and die from this disease. Infection may occur from spores shed from fruiting bodies developed on the stumps of old stems. Another leaf spot, caused by *Cylindrospor-ium clematidis*, causes the loss of a few lower leaves. More or less irregular reddish-brown spots occur on the leaves. Other leaf spots are caused by *Cercospora rubigo, C. squali-dula, Glomerella cingulata, Phyllosticta cle-matidis, Ramularia clematidis,* and *Septoria clematidis.*

Control: Pick off and destroy diseased leaves and infected stems. Spray with a copper or dithiocarbamate fungicide several times at 2-week intervals early in the growing season.

Other Diseases. *Clematis* is occasionally subject to several other diseases. Among these are: powdery mildew caused by *Ery-siphe polygoni;* smut by *Urocystis carci-nodes;* leaf blight by *Phleospora adjusta;* crown gall by the bacterium *Agrobacterium tumefaciens;* and three rusts by the fungi *Puc-cinia recondita* var. *agropyri, P. pulsatillae,* and *P. stromatica.*

Insects and Other Pests

Black Blister Beetle (*Epicauta pennsyl-vanica*). The flowers and leaves of *Clematis* may be devoured by this pest.

Control: Spray with Sevin.

Clematis Borer (*Alcathoe caudata*). The fleshy roots and crown of *Clematis* are attacked by a ²/₃-inch-long, dull white larva. The adult is a clear-winged moth. Infested vines are stunted and lack vigor.

Control: Dig out the larvae and cut out and put infested portions in the trash can. Methoxychlor sprays applied several times at 2-week intervals around the base of the plant and soil during the growing season may be helpful.

Other Pests. Several species of mites, two of whiteflies, and two scales also infest this host. Malathion sprays will control the insects, and Kelthane will control the mites.

Root-Knot Nemas (*Meloidogyne incognita* and *M. hapla*). The root-knot nemas are capable of killing the entire vine.

Control: See under Nemas in Chapter 3.

Japanese Weevil. See *Ligustrum.*

CLEOME (SPIDER-FLOWER)

Diseases

Leaf Spots (*Cercospora cleomis, C. con-spicua,* and *Heterosporium hybridum*). The leaves of *Cleome* may be spotted by one of three fungi during rainy seasons.

Control: Pick off and destroy spotted leaves. Other control measures are usually unnecessary.

Rust (*Puccinia aristidae*). This rust occurs in the Middle West and Southwest. Its alternate stage is found on grasses.

Control: Controls are rarely adopted.

CLERODENDRUM (GLORYBOWER)

Diseases

Leaf Spot (*Cercospora* sp. and *Septoria phlytaenioides*). Two species of fungi affect this host.

Control: Periodic applications of captan or ferbam will provide control.

Viruses. The cucumber mosaic virus has been reported on *C. fragrans* and an unknown virus which produces zonate ringspots on the leaves has been reported from Florida.

Control: Take cuttings only from healthy plants and rogue out and destroy diseased plants.

Insects

Among the insects that infest *Clerodendrum* are the green shield scale *Pulvinaria psidi,* the brown soft scale *Coccus hesperidum,* and the mealybug *Planococcus citri.*

Control: Malathion sprays will control these pests.

Other Pest. The southern root-knot nema, *Meloidogyne incognita,* is occasionally present on *Clerodendrum.* Controls are given in Chapter 4.

COBAEA

A leaf blight is caused by the fungus *Septoria oligocarpa.* The leaves become bronzed and faded; the plants curl, dry out, and cease flowering. No control measures have been suggested.

COCCOLOBA (SEA-GRAPE)

This widely used plant for southern Florida seaside locations is subject to black mildew caused by several species of *Lembosia,* and to the fungus *Verticicladium effusum.* Its most serious pest is the sea-grape borer *Hexeris enhydris.* Other insects that attack it are three species of aphids, 17 kinds of scales, and the woolly whitefly.

CODIAEUM (CROTON)

Diseases

Anthracnose (*Glomerella cingulata*). Large, yellowish-gray spots develop, particularly on the upper sides of the leaves. The fungus penetrates deeply. As the disease progresses the spots turn whitish and dry out. Salmon-colored spore pustules develop on the spots. This disease is most important in the greenhouse.

Control: Avoid syringing plants, which scatters the spores from diseased to healthy plants. Severe outbreaks can be prevented with copper or dithiocarbamate sprays, but these leave a highly undesirable residue on the foliage. An ammoniacal copper carbonate spray leaves a less unsightly residue but is not as effective in controlling the disease.

Other Diseases. Other diseases that occasionally occur on croton are thread blight caused by *Pellicularia koleroga,* leaf spot by *Phyllosticta codiaei,* and a root rot by *Phymatotrichum omnivorum.*

Insects

Scales. Eight species of scale insects—black, chaff, Florida wax, glover, green shield, hemispherical, lesser snow, and purple—have been recorded on this host.

Control: Repeated applications of malathion or Sevin sprays will control these pests.

Mealybugs. Two species of mealybugs—the citrus and the long-tailed—infest crotons in the greenhouse.

Control: Same as for scales.

Greenhouse Thrips (*Heliothrips haemorrhoidalis*). Occasionally greenhouse plants of the thinner-leaved variety are badly injured by the larvae of this species of thrips. One characteristic of the larvae is the large drop of colored excreta which they carry around and finally deposit; these give the plants a finely dotted appearance. On croton the feeding of these insects is irregular and not confined to any particular spots like that of nasturtium thrips.

Control: Use malathion or Cygon to control this pest.

COLCHICUM (AUTUMN-CROCUS)

Diseases

Leaf Smut (*Urocystis colchici*). This disease appears as abnormal black swellings or streaks on the leaves and corms of autumn-crocus. Flowers and stems may also be smutted. The disease also has been recorded on Solomon's-seal and false Solomon's-seal.

Control: Remove and destroy infected plants.

Other Diseases. A leaf spot and tip blight caused by the fungus *Botrytis elliptica* has been reported from the state of Washington.

COLEUS

Diseases

Damping-off (*Pythium* spp. and *Pellicularia filamentosa*). Several species of *Pythium* and the fungus formerly known as *Rhizoctonia solani* cause damping-off of seedlings and rot of cuttings. In the latter case the base of the stems becomes blackened and water-soaked.

Control: Destroy diseased plants. Start seeds and cuttings in stem-pasteurized soil.

Leaf Spots (*Alternaria* sp., *Phyllosticta* sp., and *Botrytis cinerea*). These three species of fungi have been reported as the cause for leaf spotting of coleus. The last , reported from Alaska, also causes a stem rot.

Control: Pick off and destroy spotted leaves.

Insects and Other Animal Pests

Mealybugs. Coleus is extremely susceptible to two species of mealybugs, the citrus and the long-tailed. The latter produces white cottony masses in the leaf axils which amateur gardeners frequently and mistakenly believe is a fungus.

Control: Spray with malathion whenever mealybugs appear.

Greenhouse Orthezia (*Orthezia insignis*). This is a dark-green or ochre scale insect with a white waxy secretion which extends backward in a long plate.

Control: Same as for mealybugs.

Other Pests. Among the other pests of greenhouse *Coleus* are mites and whiteflies. The former cause puckering and leaf-distortion. The young stages of the latter appear as small pearl-gray bodies adhering to the lower leaf surfaces. The adults appear as hordes of tiny whiteflies that are very active when the leaves are disturbed.

Control: For mites use a good miticide and for white flies use malathion or Sevin to control the nymphal stage. The synthetic pyrethroid Resmethrin will also control whiteflies.

Nemas (*Meloidogyne incognita* and *Aphelenchoides olesistus*). The former, the southern root-knot nema, causes swellings or galls on the roots. The latter, the fern leaf nema, causes brown areas in the leaves.

Control: Root-knot nemas are controlled by steaming the soil or treating it with chemicals (see Chapter 3). Leaf nemas can be controlled by treating plants in hot water.

Other Pests

Broom-Rape (*Orobanche racemosa*). The roots of foliage plants in greenhouses may be heavily infected by this parasitic flowering plant, which has no well-developed leaves or green color. It sends delicate spiral filaments into the roots of the host, which contain stored food. A flask-shaped swelling is developed at the point of contact. Secondary filaments invade the water-conducting cells of the host. The infection may cause the death of a large percentage of the planting, especially if root nemas are present.

Control: Remove all soil from the greenhouse benches and wash the benches with copper sulfate solution. Pasteurize the soil with steam before re-using it as described in Chapter 4.

COLLINSIA

This host is subject to a few relatively unimportant fungus diseases and to no insects. The smut *Entyloma collinsiae* and the rusts *Aecidium insulum* and *Puccinia collinsiae* have been reported as causing slight leaf spotting in the West. A leaf spot caused by *Septoria collinsiae* has been reported from Illinois and a root rot by *Pythium mamillatum* from California.

COLOCASIA (ELEPHANTS-EAR)

Diseases

Soft Rots (*Erwinia carotovora* var. *aroideae*). These bacteria cause a soft rot of this host in Florida.

Control: Set plants in clean, uninfested soil. Avoid wounding plants. Infested soils should be pasteurized with steam.

Other Diseases. A black rot caused by a species of *Diplodia* and a powdery gray rot by *Fusarium solani* are other fungus diseases recorded for this host.

Southern Root-Knot Nema (*Meloidogyne incognita*). This nema occasionally infests the roots of *Colocasia* in the Deep South.

Control: See *Nemas* in Chapter 3.

COMPTONIA (SWEET-FERN)

Rust (*Cronartium comptoniae*). The parasite, which has the pine as its alternate host, develops on the under sides of the leaves of sweet-fern, and causes long, thin, brown, thread-like horns to extend out from the surface. These contain large numbers of the spores which can live over winter and when they germinate can infect the pine. The disease is of no importance on sweet-fern.

One other rust, rarely found unless the alternate host, southern whitecedar, grows in the vicinity, is *Gymnosporangium ellisii*. On sweet-fern this causes a curling or ram's-horn effect on the leaves, which bear many aecial cups filled with bright golden-orange spores. No control is necessary.

CONVALLARIA (LILY-OF-THE-VALLEY)

Fungus Diseases

Stem Rot (*Botrytis paeoniae*). This disease appears in early summer in the garden or propagating beds on plants 2 or 3 years old. It is characterized by arrested growth and, under very humid conditions, by the decay of the inflorescence. In the greenhouse, peduncles and blossoms are attacked as the buds open. Small round yellowish or grayish specks first appear on stalks and leaves, and later develop into dark brown sunken spots. Decayed spots appear on the stalks near the attachment of the leaves, and from them the disease spreads upward into the leaves and downward into the lower parts of the stem. The pulpy tissues of the stem are entirely destroyed so that the plant breaks over and the upper parts die. The same thing happens to infected flower stalks. The underground parts are not attacked. New growths are stunted by the lack of stored nourishment. The fungus develops most rapidly in humid greenhouses with poor aeration. It may spread over a cluster of flowers even after the plants have been marketed if they have been kept moist under paper overnight. The black sclerotia which usually live through the winter are formed on the lower part of the stem.

Control: Since this fungus also attacks peonies, *Convallaria* should not be grown near them; avoid working on this host after handling diseased peonies. Do not handle *Convallaria* while the plants are wet, for this spreads the fungus to clean plants. Avoid excessive dosages of high nitrogenous fertilizers. Space the plants well apart. Remove and destroy all decayed foliage in the fall. Destroy all diseased plants as soon as possible. Reduce moisture in the greenhouse and provide more air. Replace infested soil with fresh soil or steam-pasteurize the beds before replanting. For propagating, avoid the use of pips taken from diseased plants.

Anthracnose (*Gloeosporium convallariae*). Circular or oval brown spots with purplish-red margins, up to more than 1/2 inch or more in diameter, may develop on the leaves. The diseased tissues drop out and expose the water-conducting vessels. Lesions occur also on leaf and flower stalks. The foliage dies prematurely. Young plants are dwarfed because of poorly developed root systems.

Control: Remove and destroy all diseased foliage in the fall. Avoid propagating from infected plantings. Change the location of the plantings. Spray repeatedly with a copper fungicide, beginning as soon as the young shoots appear. Avoid propagating with pips taken from diseased plantings.

Leaf Spots (*Kabatiella microsticta* and *Phyllosticta* sp.). The former causes brown spots bordered by purple-brown margins; the latter causes more or less circular, small, brown spots.

Control: If the stem rot disease is controlled, leaf spots will not be serious.

Other Diseases. A leaf blotch caused by *Ascochyta majalis,* whose perfect stage is *Mycosphaerella convallaria,* and a crown rot by *Pellicularia rolfsii* are two other fungus diseases which occur occasionally.

Physiological Disease

If conditions are abnormally moist, especially where the soil is a heavy clay, plants may fail to develop properly in propagation. Blossoms open imperfectly or not at all; they soon become grayish-brown and dry up.

Control: Avoid an excess of nitrogenous fertilizer and provide good storage conditions for the pips.

Insects and Other Animal Pests

Lily-of-the-Valley Weevil (*Hormorus undulatus*). A peculiar notching of the leaves results from feeding by this weevil.

Control: Because the leaves are chewed well after flowering time, control measures are not attempted.

Nemas (*Meloidogyne incognita* and *Pratylenchus pratensis*). These nemas are occasionally present in the roots of pips imported from abroad. They may account for some failures of forced pips.

Japanese Weevil. See *Ligustrum.*

CONVOLVULUS (CALIFORNIA-ROSE)

The white rust *Albugo ipomoeae-panduratae,* the rusts *Coleosporium ipomoeae* and *Puccinia convolvuli,* and several leaf spots including *Phyllosticta batatas, Septogloeum convolvuli,* and *Septoria calystegiae* have been reported on *Convolvulus japonicus,* the California-rose.

Control: Copper-containing sprays will control the leaf-spotting fungi and sulfur sprays will control the rusts.

CORDYLINE—see DRACAENA

COREOPSIS (TICKSEED)

Fungus Diseases

Leaf Spots (*Cercospora coreopsidis, Phyllosticta coreopsidis,* and *Septoria coreopsidis*). Three species of fungi cause leaf spotting of this host.

Control: Pick off and destroy infected leaves.

Rust (*Coleosporium inconspicuum*). In the southern and western states this disease forms golden-yellow pustules on the leaves. It is a common disease but not destructive. Long-leaf and Virginia pines are also susceptible.

Other Diseases. A blight caused by *Botrytis cinerea* in Alaska, root and stem rot by *Pellicularia filamentosa* and *P. rolfsii,* and wilt by *Verticillium albo-atrum* are other fungus parasites of *Coreopsis.* Drooping of flowers and necrosis of the pedicel tissues are believed to be the result of the injection of a toxin into the pedicels by an unidentified species of leafhopper.

Virus. *Coreopsis* is subject to the beet curly top virus.

Control: Rogue out and destroy infected plants. Spray with Diazinon, Meta-Systox R, or Sevin to control the insect vectors.

Insects

Potato Aphid (*Macrosiphum euphorbiae*). This is one of the larger plant lice and is common also on a number of other ornamental plants. It is easily controlled with malathion, Meta-Systox R, or Sevin sprays.

Four-Lined Plant Bug (*Poecilocapsus lineatus*). This insect is yellowish-green, marked with four stripes down the wings. It causes serious damage to *Coreopsis* and other garden plants in certain areas. See *Chrysanthemum.*

Spotted Cucumber Beetle (*Diabrotica undecimpunctata howardi*). Six black spots mark each wing cover of this beetle. It eats small holes in the petals and leaves.

Control: Hand picking and dropping the beetles into a can of kerosene and water is one way to control these insects. Spraying with Sevin is effective when applied at beetle feeding time.

CORNUS (DOGWOOD)

Fungus Diseases

Crown Canker (*Phytophthora cactorum*). An unthrifty appearance is the first general symptom of this disease. The leaves are smaller and lighter green than normal, and turn prematurely red in late summer. At times, especially during dry spells, they may curl and shrivel. Later, twigs and even large branches die. At first the diseased parts occur principally on one side of the tree, but within a year or two they may appear over the entire tree. The most significant symptom and the cause for the weak top growth is the slowly developing canker on the lower trunk, at or near the soil level, or on the main roots. Although the canker is not readly discernible in the early stages, it can be located by careful examination. Cutting into it will reveal that the inner bark, cambium, and sapwood are discolored. Later, the cankered area becomes sunken, and the bark dies and falls away, leaving the wood exposed. When the canker extends completely around the trunk base or the root collar, the tree dies.

Control: Crown canker cannot be controlled after the fungus has invaded most of the trunk base or root collar. Control is possible if the infection is confined to a relatively small area at the trunk base. After the cankered area is outlined, a strip of healthy bark approximately 1 inch wide should be removed all around the edge of the canker. The bark removal should be deep enough to uncover the cambium. Within the area thus left bare, all discolored bark and sapwood should be carefully cut out with a gouge. The edge of the wound should be painted with orange shellac and the area between with any good tree paint. Success with this procedure will depend on early detection of the infection and thorough and complete surgical treatment.

Because the disease has been found only on transplanted trees, and because the fungus appears to enter the host plants more readily through wounds, some observers have suggested that infection occurs primarily through unavoidable injuries inflicted during transplanting. Another avenue of entrance suggested, especially on long-established trees, is wounds made by lawn machinery and cultivating tools. Consequently, all wounds should be painted immediately with shellac and then a good tree paint, after they have been properly shaped. The possibility of injury to valuable lawn specimens can be decreased by providing some protection around the trunk base, such as a No-Trim Tree Guard.

Areas where dogwoods have died from *Phytophthora* infections, should not be replanted with dogwoods for several years unless the soil is fumigated. Where losses have occurred in nurseries, drench the soil with Dexon or Terrazole to kill any of the fungus still present in the soil. The chemical treatments will not cure already infected trees.

Dieback (*Botryosphaeria dothidea*). Dieback of dogwood branches, particularly the pink-flowering kinds, is frequently caused by this species of *Botryosphaeria*. The dieback is often erroneously attributed to dogwood borers by some arborists.

Control: See *Cercis.*

Flower and Leaf Blight (*Botrytis cinerea*). In rainy seasons this fungus causes fading of the white flower bracts and rots the leaves onto which the bracts drop (Fig. 119).

Control: Spray the tree with Benlate, cap-tan, Mertect 160, or zineb early in the flowering period.

Leaf Spots (*Ascochyta cornicola, Cercospora cornicola, Colletotrichum gloeosporioides, Elsinoë corni* (Fig. 120), *E. floridae, Phyllosticta globifera, Ramularia gracilipes, Septoria cornicola,* and *S. floridae*). Many species of fungi cause leaf spots on this host.

Control: A number of fungicides are effective in combating leaf spots. Among these are Fore, maneb, Benlate, or zineb. Applications should be made once a month starting in April when the flower buds are in the cup stage and continuing until the flower buds for the following year are formed in late summer.

Powdery Mildews (*Microsphaera alni* and *Phyllactinia corylea*). Powdery mildews may attack dogwood, entirely covering the leaves with a thin white coating of the fungus.

Control: Spray with Benlate or Karathane.

Twig Blights (*Myxosporium everhartii, Cryptostictis* sp., and *Sphaeropsis* sp.). Cankering and blighting of dogwood twigs may be caused by three species of fungi.

Control: Prune and destroy infected twigs. Fertilize and water to increase vigor of the tree.

Other Diseases. Other diseases of dogwood include root rots caused by *Armillaria mellea* in the North, its counterpart *Clitocybe tabescens* in the South, and *Phymatotrichum omnivorum.* The Pacific dogwood (*Cornus Nuttallii*) is subject to canker caused by *Nectria galligena,* and collar rot by *Phytophthora cactorum.*

Insects

Borers. At least seven kinds of borers attack dogwoods. The most serious are the flat-headed borer, *Chrysobothris femorata,* and the dogwood borer, *Synanthedon scitula.*

Control: In the latitude of New York, paint or spray the trunks and branches with methoxylchlor 3 times at 20-day intervals starting in mid-May. Endosulfan (Thiodan) spray in

Fig. 119. *Botrytis* infection of flowering dogwood leaves. (Oxford University Press)

early June and again 2 weeks later also gives good control. In some states this material can only be used by arborists or nurseries under permit.

Dogwood Club-Gall Midge (*Mycodiplosis clavula*). Club-shaped galls or swellings, ½ to inch long, on twigs of flowering dogwood are caused by a reddish-brown midge which attacks the twigs in late May. Small orange larvae develop in the galls, which drop to the ground in early fall.

Control: Pruning and destroying twigs with the club-galls during the summer will provide control. Spraying weekly 6 to 7 times with Sevin starting in late May will also control this pest.

Leaf Miner (*Xenochalepus dorsalis*). The flat, yellowish-white larvae, up to ¼ inch long, occasionally attack dogwood leaves, making blister-like mines on the under sides. Adult beetles skeletonize the leaves by feeding on the under sides. Spray with malathion when adult beetles are feeding on the leaves, or before larvae enter the leaves.

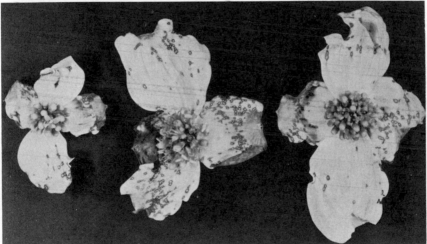

Fig. 120. Leaf and flower spot of flowering dogwood (also known as "spot anthracnose") caused by *Elisnoë corni*.

Scales. Six species of scales may infest dogwood: dogwood, cottony maple (Fig. 121), European fruit lecanium, obscure, oystershell, and San Jose.

Control: Spray with a lime sulfur or miscible oil, dormant strength, in late fall or early spring. Follow with malathion or Sevin in mid-May and again in June.

Other Insects. Among other insects which occasionally infest dogwood are the melon aphid, pitted ambrosia beetle, red-humped caterpillar, giant hornet, leafhoppers, locust leaf miner, leaf roller, mulberry whitefly, and the dogwood sawfly. The control for most of these pests is discussed under more favored hosts.

Fig. 121. Cottony maple scale, *Pulvinaria innumerabilis,* on dogwood leaves. (Oxford University Press)

CORYDALIS

A downy mildew caused by *Peronospora corydalis,* two rusts by *Puccinia aristidae* and *P. brandegei,* and a leaf spot, by *Septoria corydalis* are among the fungus diseases of this host. The mildew may kill plants grown in extreme shade and moisture. The southern root-knot nema *Meloidogyne incognita* infests the roots of *Corydalis* in Florida.

CORYLUS (HAZELNUT, FILBERT)

Bacterial and Fungus Diseases

Blight (*Xanthomonas corylina*). In the Pacific Northwest severe losses may be caused by this organism, which blights leaves and branches in April. The disease is similar to walnut blight caused by X. *juglandis.*

Control: Four weekly applications of a copper fungicide, starting at the early pre-bloom stage, will prevent this disease. Streptomycin sprays are also effective.

Other Bacterial Diseases. This host is subject to crown gall caused by *Agrobacterium tumefaciens* and leaf spot by *Pseudo-*

monas colurnae. The latter produces circular to angular, brown, necrotic spots on the leaves of Turkish hazlenut.

Twig Blight (*Apioporthe anomala*). While this disease is not important in ornamental plantings, it damages plants of commercial value. The cankers girdle the stems and the parts above die.

Control: Prune off affected parts and destroy them.

Leaf Spots (*Cylindrosporium vermiformis, Gloeosporium coryli, Septogloeum profusum,* and *S. corylina*). Four fungi may cause leaf spotting of this host.

Control: Valuable ornamental plants can be protected by periodic applications of copper fungicides, as for the blight disease.

Other Diseases. A leaf curl caused by *Taphrina coryli* and two powdery mildews by *Phyllactinia corylea* and *Microsphaera alni* are other fungus diseases which affect this host. The powdery mildews are important diseases of this host in the Northwest.

Control: A dormant lime sulfur spray will control leaf curl and Karathane sprays will control mildews.

Insects

Japanese Leafhopper (*Orientus ishidae*). *Corylus* may be infested by a ¹/₅-inch-long, dark gray leafhopper with milky wings and brown veins. The nymphs are brown with white spots. Leaves are scorched.

Control: See *Aesculus.*

Caterpillars. Three kinds of caterpillars chew the leaves of *Corylus:* California tent, yellow-necked, and filbertworm. The oblique-banded leaf roller also rolls the leaves together.

Control: Sevin sprays applied when the larvae are young will control these pests.

Scales. The European fruit lecanium and oystershell scales also infest this host.

Control: Spray with lime sulfur or miscible oil, dormant strength, before growth starts in early spring, or with malathion or Sevin when the young scales are crawling about in late spring.

COSMOS

Diseases

Bacterial Wilt (*Pseudomonas solanacearum*). A sudden wilting and collapse of the plants characterize this disease. Wilted plants may seem to recover during the night, but they usually shrivel and become dry within a few days, and the plants finally die, with many leaves still attached.

Control: See *Dahlia.*

Canker (*Diaporthe stewartii*) At blooming time stems and branches are attacked at the nodes. The lesions are first dark-brown and later ash-gray. As these spots encircle the stem, the part above wilts, collapses, breaks off, and dies.

Control: Remove and destroy infected plants as soon as noticed. In the fall gather and destroy all aboveground infected parts.

Leaf Spots (*Cercospora* sp. and *Septoria* sp.). Occasionally the leaves of cosmos are spotted by these fungi.

Control: Remove and destroy spotted leaves.

Powdery Mildew (*Erysiphe cichoracearum*). This disease is occasionally found on the leaves and smaller branches in late autumn.

Control: If necessary spray with Benlate or Karathane.

Root and Stem Rots (*Macrophomina phaseoli, Pellicularia filamentosa, P. rolfsii,* and *Phymatotrichum omnivorum*). In the southern states one or another of these fungi has been found to cause considerable damage in gardens, especially where plantings have been overwatered.

Control: Soil-borne fungi are difficult to control without resorting to the special treatments described in Chapter 4.

Viruses. Cosmos is subject to two widespread viruses: tomato spotted wilt and beet curly top.

Control: Remove and destroy affected plants. Control insect vectors with Meta-Systox R, malathion, or Sevin sprays.

Aster Yellows. This mycoplasma-caused disease also affects cosmos.

Control: The same as for virus diseases.

Insects and Related Pests

Aphids (*Aphis fabae* and *Macrosiphum euphorbiae*). These species suck the juices from leaves and stems. The western aster root aphid, *Brachycaudus middletonii,* clusters around the roots of this and several other hosts.

Control: Leaf-infesting aphids are easily controlled with malathion, Meta-Systox R, or Sevin sprays; the root-infesting kinds by wetting the soil around the base of infested plants with a dilute solution of Diazinon or malathion.

Beetles. The Japanese beetle, *Popillia japonica,* feeds on the leaves and flowers of cosmos, one of its favorite hosts. The Asiatic garden beetle, *Maladera castanea,* feeds at night and is usually not discovered unless one digs around the base of the plant where it hides in the daytime.

The spotted cucumber beetle, *Diabrotica undecimpunctata howardi,* occasionally feeds on cosmos leaves.

Control: Several insecticides are available for controlling these beetles. For best control the insecticide must be applied often enough when the beetles are about. This is especially true where Japanese beetles are involved. Sevin, Diazinon, or methoxychlor are effective. In small plantings, hand picking and dropping the beetles into a jar containing kerosene and water is practical.

Aster Leafhopper (*Macrosteles fascifrons*). This pest attacks a wide variety of other plants and is also capable of transmitting the yellows disease.

Control: See *Callistephus.*

Bugs. The four-lined plant bug and the tarnished plant bug attack cosmos. These are discussed in other parts of this book.

European Corn Borer (*Ostrinia nubilalis*). See *Dahlia.*

Termites. See *Chrysanthemum morifolium.*

Two-Spotted Mite (*Tetranychus urticae*). This mite affects greenhouse- and garden-grown cosmos, producing a grayish mealy color of the leaves.

Control: See *Althaea.*

COTINUS (SMOKE-TREE)

Diseases

Rusts (*Puccinia andropogonis* var. *onobrychidis* and *Pileolaria cotini-coggyriae*). Two rust fungi are reported on this tree. The latter, found in Georgia several years ago, produces conspicuous spots with hypertrophied centers surrounded by dead tissue.

Control: These diseases are not serious enough to warrant control measures.

Leaf Spots. (*Cercospora rhoina, Pezizella oenotherae, Septoria rhoina,* and a species of *Gloeosporium* cause leaf spotting of *Cotinus.*

Control: Valuable specimens can be protected with a copper fungicide.

Scab (*Venturia inaequalis*). See *Malus.*

Wilt (*Verticillium albo-atrum*). Smoketree is quite susceptible to this wilt. Sapwood discoloration appears as dark- or reddish-brown streaks or flecks.

Control: See *Acer.*

Insects

Oblique-Banded Leaf Roller (*Choristoneura rosaceana*). The leaves may be mined and rolled in June by pale yellow larvae. The adult moth is reddish-brown and has a wingspread of 1 inch, with the front wings crossed by three distinct bands of dark brown. Other trees subject to this pest are ash, birch, dogwood, hawthorn, horse-chestnut, linden, maple, oak and poplar.

Control: Spray early in June with Sevin.

San Jose Scale (*Quadraspidiotus perniciosus*). This scale occasionally infests smoketree. Malathion or Sevin sprays will control the crawler stage.

COTONEASTER

Diseases

Leaf Spots (*Fabraea maculata, Phyllosticta cotoneastri,* and *P. cydoniae*). The first-named fungus also causes leaf spots on hawthorn, mountain-ash, and serviceberry. *Phyllosticta cotoneastri* produces reddish-brown spots bordered by darker zones, outside of which is a zone of Indian red.

Control: Spray with a copper fungicide or with zineb.

Canker (*Physalospora obtusa*). This fungus also causes cankers on birch, bittersweet, and catalpa.

Control: Prune and destroy infected branches.

Fire Blight (*Erwinia amylovora*). This disease occasionally affects cotoneaster but not so frequently as hawthorn and mountain-ash. The following species are said to be resistant to fire blight: *Cotoneaster adpressa, C. microphylla, C. dielsiana* var. *elegans, C. francheti,* and *C. simonsi.*

Control: See *Crataegus.*

Insects and Other Pests

Hawthorn Lace Bug (*Corythucha cydoniae*). Symptoms are much the same as on *Crataegus* and *Amelanchier* attacked by these sucking insects—a gray, lacy spotting of the upper leaf surfaces, and a brown specking of the lower surfaces by the excrement of the insects.

Control: Spray in late May with Diazinon, malathion, or Sevin directing the spray to the lower leaf surfaces where the lace bugs feed.

Scales. Four species of scales attack cotoneaster: greedy, olive parlatoria, oystershell, and San Jose.

Control: Spray with dormant strength lime sulfur in early spring, and with malathion or Sevin in mid-May and in mid-June.

Cotoneaster Webworm (*Cremona cotoneaster*). The larvae skeletonize the leaves and spin ugly webs all over the plant.

Control: Spray with Sevin when the larvae are young.

Sinuate Pear Tree Borer (*Agrilus sinuatus*). Slender, very flat, ⅓-inch-long, purplish-bronze beetles feed on the leaves of pear, hawthorn, and mountain-ash in addition to this host.

Control: Spray with Sevin when the beetles emerge in May or June, depending on the locality.

Pear Leaf Blister Mite (*Eriophyes pyri*). Reddish or brownish blisters up to one-eighth inch in diameter appear on the under sides of the leaves. The surface of the spots is somewhat raised or thickened. The mites, which live over winter in the bud scales, travel to the leaves as soon as they unfold, and enter them through the under sides. Other hosts for this mite are mountain-ash, pear and serviceberry. The leaves of pear turn black.

Control: Spray with dormant strength lime sulfur in early spring just before growth starts and then with Kelthane or chlorobenzilate as the leaves emerge. Repeat in 10 days.

CRASSULA (See also under ROCHEA)

Diseases

Few diseases have been recorded on this host. Anthracnose caused by a species of *Gloeosporium* has been reported from New Jersey, a leaf spot by a species of *Phomopsis* from Connecticut, and a root rot by a species of *Pythium* in New York and New Jersey.

Insects and Other Pests

Mealybugs. See *Rochea.*
Cyclamen Mite. See *Rochea.*

CRATAEGUS (HAWTHORN)

Bacterial and Fungus Diseases

Fire Blight (*Erwinia amylovora*). The fire blight organism is responsible for one of the most destructive diseases of ornamental hawthorn, causing a blight of young twigs and limbs. These dying branches, which appear as if burned, are very conspicuous during the summer and detract greatly from the beauty of the trees as ornamentals. The bacteria live over in the cankers and ooze out during warm spring rains. Bees and other insects carry the organisms from tree to tree while gathering honey from the blossoms; this causes a blossom blight.

Control: Prune out infected branches, cutting well below the blighted region. Spraying

Fig. 122. Leaf blight of *Crataegus* caused by *Fabraea theumenii.*

with the antibiotic Agri-strep, as directed on the container, gives excellent control of the blossom flight phase of this disease. *Crataegus mollis* should not be sprayed with the antibiotic. A zineb spray at mid-blossom time also provides control. Avoid heavy fertilization because this practice makes the tree more susceptible to fire blight.

Leaf Blight (*Diplocarpon theumenii*). This fungus affects several ornamental varieties of hawthorn rather frequently, especially English hawthorn, *C. oxyacantha,* and Paul's scarlet thorn, *C. oxyacantha* var. *paulii.* The first symptoms of this disease are the small, angular, reddish-spots on the upper side of the leaf in spring and early summer. They increase in size and run together. See Fig. 122. Much defoliation is due to this fungus. Under the microscope the spores are very characteristic, looking rather like minute insects; each consists of two or three large cells with appendages that suggest insect legs.

Control: Since this fungus winters on the fallen leaves, the first precaution is to rake these up and destroy them. Spray the trees in early spring, while they are still dormant, with concentrated lime sulfur, 1 part in 8 parts of water. As soon as the leaves begin to unfurl spray with zineb and repeat in 2 weeks. The antibiotic Acti-dione applied 3 times at 10-day intervals starting in mid-July will also control leaf blight. Recent research suggests that Benlate sprays, applied when the flower buds are opening and again when spots develop on the leaves, will control this disease.

Rusts. At least nine rust fungi attack hawthorns. Of these the orange rust *Gymnospor-*

angium clavipes and *G. globosum* are the most common on ornamental species. The former, shown in Fig. 123, attacks both the leaves and the fruits of hawthorn, causing severe defoliation and deformation of the fruit. The twigs are also attacked and deformed, developing abnormal, antler-like branches. The fungus breaks out in little cup-like structures called cluster-cups, from which quantities of bright orange spores are shed. These spores are borne by the wind to nearby redcedars and infect their leaves and young twigs. The fungus is perennial in the cedars but annual in the hawthorns (see under *Juniperus*). *Gymnosporangium globosum* produces on the leaves spots which vary from light gray to brown. The cluster-cups are long, slender, tube-like. This fungus also attacks apple trees; it seldom does much damage to hawthorn. Another stage of the fungus lives for two or three years on the redcedar before killing the small branches which it attacks (see under *Juniperus*).

Another rust, *Gymnosporangium confusum,* was reported as attacking *Crataegus oxyacantha* in California in 1967. This was the first case in the United States. The alternate host is *Juniperus sabina.*

Control: If practicable, eliminate susceptible junipers within one mile of hawthorns. If not practicable, spray the hawthorns with Daconil 2787, Plantvax, ferbam, or a mixture of ferbam and wettable sulfur four to five times at 7- to 10-day intervals when orange masses appear on junipers. Rusts can also be controlled by spraying the alternate hosts, junipers, with cycloheximide (Actidione). The Washington thorn (*C. phaenopyrum*) and the Cockspur thorn (*C. crus-galli*) are resistant to rusts.

Fig. 123. Gall on *Crataegus* fruit and leaf caused by *Gymnosporangium clavipes*. (Illinois Natural History Survey)

Leaf Spots. A large number of fungi are known to cause leaf spots on hawthorns. Among the more common ones are: *Cercospora confluens, C. apiifoliae, Cercosporella mirabilis, Cylindrosporium brevispina, C. crataegi, Gloeosporium crataegi, Hendersonia crataegicola, Septoria crataegi,* and *Monilinia johnsonii.* The last also causes spots on the fruits, as does the scab fungus *Venturia inaequalis.*

Control: Zineb or Benlate sprays will control most of the fungi listed.

Powdery Mildews (*Phyllactinia corylea* and *Podosphaera oxyacanthae*). Two mildew fungi attack this host.

Control: Spray with Benlate or Karathane.

Scab (*Venturia inaequalis*). See *Malus.*

Insects and Other Pests

Aphids. Many species of aphids infest hawthorn: apple, apple grain, hawthorn, rosy apple, woolly apple, and woolly hawthorn.

Control: Spray with malathion or Diazinon before the pests become numerous.

Borers. Four borers infest hawthorns: flatheaded apple tree, roundheaded apple tree, pear, and the shot-hole.

Control: Maintain trees in good vigor by feeding when necessary and watering during dry spells. Paint or spray the trunk and branches with methoxychlor at periodic intervals during the growing season. State entomologists will supply the proper dates for each locality.

Western Tent Caterpillar (*Malacosoma californicum*). Tawny or brown caterpillars with a dorsal row of blue spots feed primarily on hawthorns as well as wild cherry and alder, making tents at the same time as the fall webworm. The moths are smaller and somewhat lighter than the eastern tent caterpillar adults.

Other caterpillars that may feed on hawthorns include the eastern tent, the forest tent, the red-humped, the variable oak leaf, and the walnut caterpillar. The caterpillar stages of the gypsy moth and the western tussock moth also occur on this host.

Control: Spray with *Bacillus thuringiensis,* Dylox, methoxychlor, or Sevin when the caterpillars begin to chew the leaves.

Apple Leaf Blotch Miner (*Phyllonorycter crataegella*). This leaf miner can be very destructive in hawthorn nurseries and ornamental plantings near New York City. The principal damage is done during May or June. The first symptom is a small channel in the leaf, which widens to a blisterlike area light brown in color. The miner begins work at one edge of the leaf near the stalk and continues on that side toward the point of the leaf. The inner parts of the leaf are usually completely consumed, only the epidermis and veins remaining. Only the leaves that are unfolding are attacked. Much defoliation follows the work of these insects. The same species attacks many fruit trees, including apple, cherry, plum, quince, and sweet-scented crabapple.

Control: Spray in early May and repeat twice at 2-week intervals with malathion or Sevin.

Lace Bugs (*Corythucha cydoniae, C. arcuata*). Lace bugs are not common on hawthorn, but occasionally appear to be rather serious. They feed on the under sides of the leaves, depositing small, brown, sticky spots of excreta. Once the infestation is started, the insects breed during summer and become rather numerous.

Control: Spray with Diazinon, malathion, or Sevin.

Leaf Miner (*Phyllonorycter crataegella*). Blotches are produced on the leaves of *Crataegus* by this pest.

Control: Spray with malathion or Sevin in early June and repeat 2 weeks later.

Apple and Thorn Skeletonizer (*Anthophila pariana*). This pest feeds on leaves of apple, pear, and hawthorn in the northeastern United States. The adult moth is dark gray to reddish-brown with a ¹/₂-inch wing expanse. The full grown larva is ¹/₂ inch long, with a yellowish-green body and a pale brown head.

Control: Spray with Sevin when the larvae begin to feed.

Planthopper (*Anormensis septentrionalis*). These sucking insects often attack wild grape vines and feed on the tender shoots. They are also found on *Crataegus* at times. The insects are a beautiful pale bluish-green, covered with white powder. The powder and other whitish excretions also cover the young on the limbs and branches. The insects are nearly ¹/₂ inch long, very thin vertically.

Control: See *Prunus serrulata.*

Scales. The following kinds of scales infest hawthorn: barnacle, cottony maple, European fruit lecanium, Florida wax, lecanium, Putnam, scurfy, soft, and San Jose.

Control: Spray with lime sulfur or miscible oil, dormant strength, just before plant growth begins in spring. Follow in mid-May and in June with malathion or Sevin sprays to control the crawler stages.

Two-Spotted Mite (*Tetranychus urticae*). During the summer months, especially in dry weather, these mites often become sufficiently numerous to injure foliage. The symptoms are the same as those of other plants attacked by them.

Control: If the hawthorn is given a dormant clean-up spray in spring with commercial lime sulfur, the eggs of the mites are killed. If not, spray with chlorbenzilate, Kelthane, Meta-Systox R, or Tedion in early June and repeat in a few weeks, if necessary.

CRINUM

Crinum is subject to much the same diseases and insect pests as those found on *Amaryllis.* These plants have a tendency to turn a dark brownish-red in streaks and spots wherever they are attacked by fungi or insects; this makes it difficult to determine by superficial examination the particular cause of the disease. For the leaf scorch disease caused by *Stagonospora curtisii,* see under *Amaryllis.* A leaf spot caused by fungus *Cercospora pancratii* occurs on this host in the Deep South and an unidentified mosaic virus has been reported from California.

CROCUS

Bacterial and Fungus Diseases

Scab (*Pseudomonas marginata*). This bacterial disease is important on gladiolus. Occasionally it occurs on imported crocus stocks.

Control: See *Gladiolus.*

Dry Rot (*Stromatinia gladioli*). This fungus produces lesions on the corms and decay of the leaf sheath, much as it does with *Gladiolus.*

Control: See *Gladiolus.*

Other Diseases. A corm rot caused by the fungus *Fusarium oxysporum,* a blue mold rot by a species of *Penicillium,* and mosaic by the iris mosaic virus, also occur.

Pests

Green Peach Aphid (*Myzus persicae*). Crocus is one of the many hosts for this aphid.

Control: Spray with malathion or Meta-Systox R.

Bulb Mite (*Rhizoglyphus echinopus*).

Control: See *Tulipa.*

Tulip Bulb Aphid. See *Iris.*

CROTALARIA

Powdery Mildews (*Microsphaera diffusa* and *Oidium erysiphoides* var. *crotalariae*). These two mildew fungi have been reported on *C. retusa,* the only member of this genus grown for ornament. A wilt and root rot caused by a species of *Fusarium* has been reported from Georgia and Texas. The two-spotted mite, *Tetranychus urticae,* occasionally infests the leaves. Spraying with a good miticide will control it. Crotalarias grown as cover crops are subject to many diseases and insect pests. *C. spectabilis,* however, is one of the few plants that is immune to the southern root-knot nema, *Meloidogyne incognita.*

CRYOPHYTUM (ICE-PLANT)

Ice-plant is subject to the southern root-knot nema, *Meloidogyne incognita;* the yucca mealybug, *Puto yuccae;* and the lesser snow scale, *Pinnaspis strachani.*

Control: The nema can be controlled by measures described in Chapter 3; the mealybug and scale by means of malathion sprays.

CRYPTOMERIA

Leaf Blight (*Phomopsis* sp.). The leaves and twigs of this host may be browned and blighted by this fungus during rainy seasons. This disease should not be confused with wind-burn or winter-drying which appears in late winter on trees planted in wind-swept areas.

Control: Pruning out affected leaves and twigs is usually sufficient. Copper fungicides can be used on valuable specimens. Dormant oil sprays, which may cause serious damage, should never be used on this host.

Leaf Spots (*Pestalotia cryptomeriae* and *P. funerea*). Two fungi are associated with spotting of the leaves of this host. Infection probably follows winter injury or some other agent.

Control: Same as for leaf blight.

CUPHEA

Among the relatively few fungus diseases of this host are a blight caused by *Botrytis cinerea,* a leaf spot by *Septoria maculifera,* a powdery mildew by *Erysiphe polygoni,* and a root rot by *Pellicularia filamentosa.* The southern root-knot nema, *Meloidogyne incognita,* also infests the roots of *Cuphea.*

CUPRESSUS (CYPRESS)[16]

Diseases

Canker (*Coryneum cardinale*). The causal fungus attacks the living bark and cambium, progressively killing the tissues until the branch or trunk is completely girdled at the point of attack.

Cypresses, particularly the Monterey cypress, junipers, and oriental arbor-vitae, are all subject to this disease. The perfect stage of this fungus is said to be a species of *Leptosphaeria.*

Control: Because the fungus spores are spread by wind-splashed rain, by pruning tools, and perhaps by insects and birds, control is difficult. Remove and destroy severely infected trees. Drastically prune mildly infected ones and spray periodically with a copper fungicide, starting at the beginning of the rainy period.

Cytospora Canker (*Cytospora cenisia* var. *littoralis*). Smooth reddish-brown cankers, from which resin flows, develop on young branches. Diseased bark on older branches becomes cracked and distorted, with a more abundant flow of resin. The columnar form of Italian cypress, *C. sempervirens,* along the California coast is most subject to this disease. Occasionally it also affects the horizontal form of Italian cypress and the smooth cypress.

Control: Prune and discard dead or dying branches. Trees with cankers on the trunks should be removed and destroyed.

Other Diseases. Cypresses are subject to several other diseases: needle blight caused by *Cercospora thujina, C. sequoiae,* crown gall by the bacterium *Agrobacterium tumefaciens,* monochaetia canker by *Monochaetia unicornis,* and twig blight caused by *Phomopsis juniperovora,* discussed under *Juniperus.*

---

[16] Certain species of *Chamaecyparis* and *Taxodium* are also called "Cypress."

Insects

Cypress Aphid (*Siphonatrophia cupressi*). This large, green aphid infests blue and Monterey cypress.

Control: Spray with malathion or Sevin when the young begin to feed.

Cypress Mealybug (*Pseudococcus ryani*). Primarily a pest of Monterey cypress in California, this species also infests arborvitae, redwood, and other species of cypress.

Control: Same as for cypress aphid.

Caterpillars. The caterpillars of the following moths feed on this host: tip moth, *Argyresthia cupressella;* webber, *Epinotia subviridis;* imperial, *Eacles imperialis;* and white-marked tussock moth, *Hemerocampa leucostigma.*

Control: Spray with *Bacillus thuringiensis,* Imidan, Sevin, Dylox, or methoxychlor when the caterpillars are small.

Bark Scale (*Ehrhornia cupressi*). This pink scale covered with loose white wax infests Monterey cypress primarily. It occasionally attacks Guadalupe and Arizona cypress and incense-cedar. Leaves of heavily infested trees turn yellow then red or brown.

Control: Malathion sprays applied to the trunk and branches are said to be effective in combating this scale.

Other Scales. Several other scales, including the cottony-cushion and the juniper, occasionally infest cypresses. These are controlled with malathion or Sevin sprays.

CYCAS (SAGO-PALM)

Diseases

Relatively few diseases affect this host. A leaf spot caused by the fungus *Ascochyta cycadina* has been reported from Missouri and Texas; and an endophytic alga, *Anabaena cycadeae,* inhabits coralloid roots. In Florida, a blight of unknown cause starts with pale green areas on pinnae of young leaves, followed by leaf curling, branch dieback, and finally death of the entire plant. Several fungi, including *Gloeosporium* and *Phoma,* are associated with blight. Eradication of blighted plants is the only control measure known.

Insects

Greenhouse-grown *Cycas* are subject to a number of very troublesome insect pests.

Scales Ten species of scales—black, California red, chaff, Florida red, green shield, hemispherical, oleander, pineapple, purple, and soft—infest *Cycas.*

Control: Spraying the foliage at 10-day intervals with malathion or Sevin is effective against the young crawler stage of these pests.

Mealybug (*Pseudococcus longispinus*). This close relative of scales also becomes very troublesome on *Cycas* in greenhouses.

Control: Spray with malathion.

Dracaena Thrips (*Heliothrips dracaenae*). This pest, dusky yellow, with netted head, thorax, and wings, also infests dracaena, rubber tree, Kentia palm, and century plant in California.

Control: Malathion sprays are effective against thrips.

CYCLAMEN

Bacterial and Fungus Diseases

Tuber Rot (*Erwinia carotovora*). The causal bacterium enters the cyclamen tuber via wounds and causes a soft, wet decay.

Control: Avoid wounding of tubers. Plant them in steam-pasteurized soil.

Blight (*Botrytis cinerea*). Buds and leaves may be rotted and flower petals spotted by this fungus. Another fungus, *Glomerella cingulata,* causes a leaf and bud blight.

Control: Avoid overcrowding of plants. Pick off and destroy spotted leaves as soon as noticed. Mist-spray periodically with Benlate.

Stunt (*Ramularia cyclaminicola*). Plants are stunted with the flowers remaining below the small, sometimes yellow, leaf blades. Reddish-brown necrotic areas may be seen when infected tubers are sliced open. The fungus is systemic, invading the shoots and roots.

Control: Discard diseased plants. Start seed from healthy plants in new or pasteurized soil.

Other Diseases. Root rot caused by *Thielaviopsis basicola* and wilt by a species of *Fusarium* have been reported from Connecticut.

Insects and Other Pests

Black Vine Weevil (*Otiorhynchus sulcatus*). The grubs of this weevil feed on the roots of cyclamen; the plant is dwarfed or stunted and usually wilts and dies.

Control: Prevent weevils from entering the propagating houses. Avoid using infested soil unless it is first steam-pasteurized.

Aphids (*Neomyzus circumflexus* and *Aphis gossypii*). These two common aphids, particularly the former, can become quite prevalent on cyclamens.

Control: Spray the plants with rotenone or pyrethrum at blooming time. At other seasons malathion is preferable.

Thrips (*Heliothrips haemorrhoidalis*). The common greenhouse thrips sometimes attack cyclamens, causing the leaves to turn a reddish color and the surface to become more or less rough from the deposition of small black specks. They also cause a white flecking of the blossoms.

Control: Spray with Cygon or malathion, directing the material to the lower leaf surfaces.

Cyclamen Mite (*Steneotarsonemus pallidus*). This mite is one of the smallest that attack ornamental plants. The mites are often found on the corms of cyclamens in storage

and are thus transported by trade. All parts of the plant are subject to attack, but especially the young parts, which when infested do not usually form normal buds. If the buds open, the blooms are distorted and usually fall early. The blooming period of infested plants is very short. Infested leaves of more mature plants become deformed, curling from the outside and becoming wrinkled into pockets and depressions.

Control: For commercial growers of cyclamen, it is suggested that as soon as plants are potted in 3-inch or larger pots, 3 applications of Kelthane at 10- to 14-day intervals be made.

Broad Mite (*Polyphagotarsonemus latus*). This mite has the same coloring as the cyclamen mite, but is broader and smaller and moves much faster.

Control: Same as for cyclamen mite.

Nemas. The De Man's meadow nema, *Pratylenchus pratensis;* the southern root-knot nema, *Meloidogyne incognita;* and a leaf-infesting kind, *Aphelenchoides* sp., occur on this host. Control of these pests is discussed in Chapter 3.

CYNOGLOSSUM (HOUND'S-TONGUE)

Diseases

Leaf Spots (*Cercospora cynoglossi, Phyllosticta decidua,* and *Ramularia lappulae*). Three leaf spotting fungi attack this host.

Control: Pick off and destroy the first-spotted leaves. Other controls are usually unnecessary.

Other Diseases. A downy mildew caused by *Peronospora cynoglossi,* and stem decays by two soil-inhabiting fungi, *Pellicularia rolfsii* and *Sclerotinia sclerotiorum,* are other diseases occasionally reported on varieties of *Cynoglossum* grown as ornamentals. The southern root-knot nema, *Meloidogyne incognita,* also occurs on members of this genus.

CYTISUS (BROOM)

Diseases

Leaf Spot, Blight (*Ceratophorum seto-sum*). This fungus has been reported as causing heavy damage to *C. hybridus,* and *C. scoparius.* It kills the plants within 2 weeks after infection. Small irregular spots first appear on the leaf blades, enlarge rapidly, and cause a blotch or blight. Brown spots also appear on the stems.

Control: Destroy all diseased material and spray all plants with a copper fungicide several times at weekly intervals.

Other Diseases. Several other fungi, among them species of *Gloeosporium, Nectria, Phomopsis,* and *Physalospora* are associated with dead and dying branches of this host.

Control: Prune and destroy infected branches.

Pests

The De Man's meadow nema, *Pratylenchus pratensis,* has also been reported on *Cytisus.*

DAHLIA

Bacterial Diseases

Crown Gall (*Agrobacterium tumefaciens*). Large tumors of abnormal tissue develop at the base of the plant and on the roots. Infected plants become stunted and the shoots spindling.

Control: Roots and crown of plants with tumors should be destroyed as soon as they are discovered. Dipping roots at planting time in a streptomycin solution will destroy any bacteria present on the surface. Changing the location of the planting will also help curb the disease.

Bacterial Wilt (*Pseudomonas solanacearum*). Infected plants usually droop and wilt rather suddenly. The conducting system will be found plugged with yellowish masses of bacteria, which ooze out when the stems are cut. The wet soft rot of the stems near the soil is characteristic and distinguishes this wilt from that caused by the *Verticillium* and the *Fusarium* wilt funti mentioned below.

Control: Destroy all wilted plants; be sure that no infected parts are thrown into the compost pile. This bacterium, like the wilt fungi, winters in the soil. Heavily infested soil must be pasteurized with steam. The best way to avoid this disease is to practice rotation, as the farmer does to avoid soil-borne diseases.

Bacteriosis (*Erwinia carotovora* var. *carotovora*). This disease, first discovered on dahlias grown at the New York Botanical Garden, appears as a browning and softening of the stem. The layers of pith that line the hollow stem are moist and blackish with the rot, which extends into the bark. If one uses a compound microscope, great masses of the large bacteria can be seen swimming about. The rot gives off a foul odor. This disease also affects the tubers.

Control: Special methods for the control of this disease have not as yet been found.

Fungus Diseases

Botrytis Blight (*Botrytis cinerea*). In the garden during dull, cloudy weather, and in propagating houses, especially in greenhouses where ventilation is not adequate, the young shoots and the flower buds may become infected with the gray mold, which causes a fading and browning of petals and the destruction and death of other infected parts. In moist weather the buds may be attacked by a soft rot and all infected parts may become covered with the grayish, powdery mold. The spores of this mold are carried by the wind and by insects to other plants.

Control: As far as practicable remove all old flowers and infected leaves. Spray with

Benlate, Fore, or zineb. Avoid throwing the debris from dahlia plantings onto the compost pile.

Powdery Mildews (*Erysiphe polygoni* and *E. cichoracearum*). Powdery mildew is not usually a very destructive disease. In propagating plots of the nursery, where plants are crowded, the fungus may become more serious. During September and October the lower leaves may become covered with a white ash-gray mold. Badly infected leaves become distorted and fall. The fungus is entirely superficial except for the haustoria or sucking organs, which penetrate the epidermal cells (Fig. 13).

Control: Same as for chrysanthemum.

Wilt (*Verticillium albo-atrum* and *Fusarium* sp.). These soil fungi enter the roots, in which their presence is made evident by brown or black streaks along the conductive tissue. The plants wilt and die because of lack of water, which is cut off by the blocking or destruction of the water-conducting vessels, or because their living tissues are injured by toxins produced by the fungus. The *Verticillium* fungus is not usually found far up in the stems and leaves, at least not until after the plants have been killed.

Control: Since these wilt fungi may attack roots in storage, discolored or decayed parts should be cut away before planting. Use only healthy tubers for propagation. Pull up and destroy wilted plants to prevent accumulation of the fungus in the soil, where it will live through the winter. Rotate plantings. If badly infested soil is to be used again for dahlias, it may require pasteurization with steam or treatment with some appropriate chemical. Do not throw the old dahlia stems into the compost pile.

Stem Rot (*Sclerotinia sclerotiorum*). Plants growing in heavy wet soil infested with this fungus usually wilt and die suddenly; the symptoms develop more rapidly than in the *Verticillium* wilt. The stem rot fungus attacks the main stem and branches near the base of the plant. A white mold may completely encircle the stem. The black sclerotia, propagating bodies of the fungus, develop inside the stem, where they are often present in considerable numbers. These bodies carry the parasite through winter and other unfavorable periods. The same fungus may attack young plants in propagating houses, where it causes them to wilt and rot. Infected stems have a water-soaked appearance.

Many other fungi may cause stem rot of *Dahlia*. Among the most common are *Pythium debaryanum, P. oedochilum, P. ultimum, Pellicularia filamentosa,* and *P. rolfsii.*

Control: Heavy soil should be lightened with a mixture of perlite, vermiculite, or cinders and good drainage should be provided. Plants should not be crowded. If possible, the plantings should be rotated each year. Soils heavily infested with these fungi should be pasteurized with steam or treated with the appropriate chemicals as described in Chapter 4.

Smut (*Entyloma dahliae*). The leaves are marked, especially in humid weather, by more or less circular spots, at first yellowish-green, later becoming brownish. The infected parts dry out and turn brown. The primary spores of the fungus are formed within the tissue of the leaves and germinate there, sending to the outside projections which form the secondary spores; these spread the disease. Dead tissue falls out leaving a "shothole" appearance.

Control: Control measures have not been developed.

Virus Diseases

Mosaic (Dahlia mosaic virus and cucumber mosaic virus). Several virus diseases affect dahlias; among the most serious is mosaic, shown in Fig. 21. The leaves become mottled and develop pale green bands along the mid-ribs and larger secondary veins. This is referred to as "clearing of the veins"; it is not always manifest. The leaves are dwarfed and show a general mosaic or pale yellow spotting. Plants developed from roots which carry the virus seldom reach full height. Some varieties are more tolerant to mosaic and show few to no outward symptoms.

Control: Since the virus is systemic and spreads to all parts of the plant, the roots of infected plants should not be used for propagation. Ruthless roguing of infected plants will often prevent the spread of the disease to healthy plants. Since the virus is carried from plant to plant by the green peach aphid, *Myzus persicae,* thorough control of this insect,

up to the time the plants are killed by the first frost, will help to prevent spread of mosaic.

In addition to mosaic, stunting of dahlias may be due to injury from excessive feeding of aphids or from the effects of leafhoppers, European corn borer, thrips, or other insects, or red spider mite. This type of stunting does not persist from year to year when the roots from stunted plants are used for propagation. Stunt caused by a virus is shown in Fig. 23.

Virus (Tomato spotted wilt virus). This virus disease, also known as ring spot, appears as a characteristic ring pattern on the leaves (see Fig. 124). Plants infected during the sum-

Fig. 124. Ringspot of dahlia caused by the tomato spotted wilt virus.

mer near flowering time may not show any symptoms until the following year, when early mosaic and stunting will be manifested.

Control: Spray with malathion or Meta-Systox R to control the vector insects. Roots from dahlia plants affected by a virus should not be used in propagation. Dahlias grown from seed are free from virus until infected by aphids.

Dr. F. O. Holmes was able to eliminate the tomato spotted wilt virus from severely infected plants by rooting small stem tip cuttings. The virus evidently does not move readily towards the growing tips but lags behind stem development. Cuttings rooted from infected plants remained healthy when grown at a distance from infected older plants.

Insects and Other Animal Pests

Aphids. Three species of aphids infest dahlias; bean, green peach, and leaf-curl plum.

Control: Spray with Meta-Systox R or malathion as soon as the aphids appear.

There are also several species of root aphids which may attack dahlias below the surface of the ground. They are carried about by ants. Frequent tilling of the ground kills off the aphids. Wetting the soil around the base of each plant with a dilute solution of Diazinon or malathion is also helpful.

European Corn Borer (*Ostrinia nubilalis*). The borers are at first flesh-colored, later smoky and reddish along the back. Each abdominal segment is marked with four dark spots which carry stout spines. There are two broods each season in the vicinity of New York; one in late May and the other in August and September. The latter infestation is the more serious in Connecticut and New York. Beginning in August or about the first of September each moth lays about 15 or 20 eggs on the flowering tips. After hatching (in about a week) the young larvae feed on the tender bud ends, flower parts, and leaves, causing them to become distorted and turn brown. The affected tips usually die completely, after which the borers move down through the stem, causing a wilting of all parts above the lowest region of invasion. This borer infests a large number of crop plants as well as many species of ornamental plants.

Control: For good control, dahlias should be sprayed every week during the summer months with a mixture of Sevin and Kelthane. Sanitation is very important. Stalks of corn, dahlia and weeds susceptible to this borer should be cleaned up and destroyed in late fall, or certainly before mid-April, to destroy overwintering borers.

Stalk Borer (*Papaipema nebris*) and **Burdock Borer** (*P. cataphracta*). Since these insects are not very numerous, individual borers may be killed by inserting a wire in each puncture. The destruction of weeds and other kinds of plants liable to infestation in the vicinity of the dahlia planting is helpful against these pests as against many others.

Control: In areas where the pests are especially troublesome, spray with a methoxychlor-Kelthane mixture in late June and repeat twice at 10-day intervals.

Leafhopper (*Empoascus fabae*). These insects cause a discoloration of the leaf, which appears first along one margin and spreads toward the mid-vein. The affected area is at first pale yellowish; later it becomes brown and brittle. The infested plants often become quite stunted unless the leafhoppers are controlled. The insects are small, slender, pale green, about 1/8 inch long. They feed on many species of plants in the vegetable garden as well as in the flower garden. The rose leafhopper, *Edwardsiana rosa,* also attacks dahlias.

Control: Spray with malathion or Meta-Systox R when the plants are 8 to 10 inches tall and repeat every 10 days until flowers appear.

Bugs (*Lygus lineolaris* and *Poecilocapsus*

lineatus). The tarnished plant bug and the four-lined plant bug attack dahlias as well as many other plants.

Control: Same as for leafhoppers.

Thrips (*Heliothrips haemorrhoidalis, Frankliniella tritici,* and *Thrips tabaci*). Three species of thrips are apt to infest the flowers; they rasp the surface and feed on the exuding juice. The under surfaces of petals turn whitish and wither.

Control: Same as for leafhoppers.

Giant Hornet (*Vespa crabro germana*). This pest attacks dahlias occasionally. It gnaws the bark from the stem at the base, sometimes completely girdling the plant.

Control: See *Buxus.*

Mulberry Whitefly (*Tetraleurodes mori*). The larval stage of this whitefly is elliptical, 1/35 inch long, jet-black edged with a white fringe of waxy filaments. It adheres closely to the lower surfaces of the leaves. The adult is a small, very active whitefly.

Control: Spray the lower leaf surfaces with malathion to control the nymphal stage, or with Resmethrin to control the adults and nymphs.

Two-Spotted Mite (*Tetranychus urticae*). This mite feeds on the undersides of leaves, where it sucks the juice from the cells; the leaves turn pale and become spotted on the upper sides. The eggs and the mites themselves are usually covered with a delicate web.

Control: See *Althaea.*

Cyclamen Mite (*Steneotarsonemus pallidus*). This mite has been found on greenhouse-grown dahlias. Its effects are shown in Fig. 125. See *Cyclamen* for control.

Fig. 125. Injury to dahlia by the cyclamen mite *(Steneotarsonemus pallidus).*

Nemas (*Meloidogyne incognita* and *M. hapla*). Two root-knot nemas occur on the roots of dahlias when plants are grown in infested soil.

Control: See Chapter 3.

Potato Rot Nema (*Ditylenchus destructor*). This nema was recently found on dahlia tubers in Oregon. Diagnosis for this pest is difficult because of the lack of aboveground symptoms and of any striking root symptoms. All tuberous roots having a cortex with unusual transverse and longitudinal cracking, sloughing, or flaking of the surface, or rotted areas, should be examined for the presence of this pest.

Control: No control is known, although hot water treatment of tubers may be effective.

DAPHNE
Diseases

Leaf Spots (*Gloeosporium mezerei* and *Marssonina daphnes*). Both these fungi produce small, thick, brown spots which appear on both sides of the leaves. Infected leaves turn yellowish, wilt, and die. Twigs are also attacked.

Control: Pick off and destroy infected leaves and branches. Spray with a copper or dithiocarbamate fungicide.

Crown Rot (*Pellicularia rolfsii, P. filamentosa,* and *Sclerotium delphinii*). These fungi have been reported as causing crown and stem rot of *Daphne*, especially of plants grown in rather shady places. Characteristic mycelium or sclerotia may be found at the base of the plant and on the ground nearby. A species of *Phytophthora* also has been reported as the cause of a stem rot.

Control: Use clean soil or steam-pasteurize old soil.

Twig Blight (*Botrytis* sp.). A blighting of twigs by this fungus has been recorded from the Northeast and the Pacific Northwest.

Control: Cut off and destroy infected parts.

Canker (*Nectria cinnabarina*). Rough cankers covered with many small, reddish fruiting bodies occur on infected twigs.

Control: Same as for twig blight.

Viruses (Cucumber mosaic virus and alfalfa mosaic virus). In the Pacific Northwest many plantings of *Daphne odora* with mottled leaves were found to harbor one of these viruses.

Control: Remove and destroy infected plants. Control the insect vectors with malathion sprays.

Insects

Several species of aphids, the citrus mealybug, and three species of scales—gray citrus, greedy, and yellow—infest *Daphne*.

Control: Spray with malathion whenever the pests appear.

DELPHINIUM (LARKSPUR)[17]

Bacterial Diseases

Black Leaf Spot (*Pseudomonas delphinii*). This bacterial disease causes irregular, shining, tar-like spots (Fig. 126), especially on the upper surfaces of the leaves; on the opposite side of the leaf the spots are browner. The petioles, stems, and flower parts also may be attacked. The lower leaves are the first to show the symptoms. The disease spreads in cool wet weather. *Aconitum napellus* is also susceptible.

Control: Remove and destroy affected leaves as soon as noticed. Cut and discard old stems in the fall. Streptomycin sprays may be helpful.

Soft Crown Rot (*Erwinia carotovora*). This disease occurs during periods of very hot and sultry weather. The causal organism is common in the soil at all times, but only

---

[17] Commercial growers distinguish between annual species, which they call "larkspur," and perennial species, to which they apply the name "delphinium." Botanically, all these plants are species of the genus *Delphinium*.

Fig. 126. Black leaf spot of delphinium *(Pseudomonas delphinii).*

under certain conditions does it enter the crowns and roots and cause their decay; it invades the host through wounds. Infection results in a rapid wilting of the whole plant, and finally death. The decay is characterized by a strong, offensive odor.

Control: Control this disease by dipping infected crowns, from which rotted parts have been cut out, for several minutes in streptomycin solution.

Black Leg (*Erwinia carotovora* var. *atroseptica*). As a result of early infection by this bacterium, the tops of *Delphinium ajacis* and other species are stunted or killed back nearly to the ground; they may later, however, produce healthy branches. The roots and lower leaves may be perfectly healthy at the time. The dying tops give off a foul odor. Black discoloration and softening of the stem may extend down nearly to the ground. If one splits open a stem, mucilaginous masses of bacteria ooze out from the torn tissues. This disease can be readily distinguished from black leaf spot by the strong odor of the blighted plants and the irregularity of the blackened regions. See Fig. 5.

Another species of bacterium that causes symptoms similar to black leg is *Erwinia chrysanthemi.*

Control: Avoid overwatering of the soil, which favors development of these diseases. Spraying with a streptomycin solution may be helpful.

Crown Gall (*Agrobacterium tumefaciens*). This disease occurs occasionally on delphinium. Control measures are described under more susceptible hosts.

Fungus Diseases

Diplodina Crown Rot (*Diplodina delphinii*). This fungus disease of *Delphinium* is primarily a crown rot. The fungus also causes cankers and necrotic lesions on the stems and leaf stalks. It fruits abundantly, the pycnidia being arranged in zones on the affected areas;

they may also be found commonly on necrotic lesions at the base of the leaf stalks. The fungus has been shown to cause a tarry black leaf spot when the spores are sprayed on the leaves. There is some basis for the belief that leaf spots commonly attributed to the bacterium *Pseudomonas delphinii* may often be due to this fungus. The crown rot becomes noticeable usually after the plants have been grown for two or more seasons. Infected plants often fail to survive the winter, or, in the spring, a few uninvaded buds may become shoots which sooner or later become rotted at the base. The disease seems to be favored by excessive moisture and is more destructive on very succulent tissues.

Control: Controls have not been developed for this disease.

Pythium Crown Rot (*Pythium ultimum*). This fungus occasionally attacks *D. ajacis, D. consolida, D. cardinale,* and hybrid delphiniums under both greenhouse and field conditions. The disease is sometimes important in the culture of these delphiniums. It causes a rot of the roots and basal parts, and the plants later wilt. *D. ajacis* turns brown. The disease appears to be favored by cool, moist conditions.

Control: Treat seed flats as described under the formaldehyde treatment in Chapter 4. Drenching infested soil with Dexon or Truban is also effective.

Crown Rot (*Sclerotium delphinii*). The causal fungus enters the plants through the roots and crown and cuts off the water supply, so that the most striking symptoms may be the sudden wilting and death of the plants. The lower leaves may become yellowed in the early stages of the disease. Badly infected plants can be easily pulled up which shows that most of the root system and part of the crown have been destroyed. In mild cases of infection new shoots may develop from buds that have not been killed. The appearance of hard yellow-brown or buff-colored sclerotia

scattered through the soil in the vicinity of diseased plants, as shown in Fig. 10, is usually sufficient to indicate the presence of the fungus in a delphinium planting. These bodies first appear as white masses of mycelial threads or as red puffs on the stalks. Later their heads become tan-colored or reddish-brown. These structures live through the winter or other unfavorable conditions. As they become more or less buried in the soil, they become a corky color or a reddish-brown. The disease is spread through a planting by distribution of the sclerotia on tools and other cultivating instruments or by water in rainy weather.

In the southern states a similar disease is caused by *Pellicularia rolfsii*. The two organisms are apparently identical except for the size of the sclerotia, *Sclerotium delphinii* producing much larger ones (see Fig. 65).

Control: This fungus attacks a large number of garden plants and may therefore be widely distributed in the soil. Delphiniums should not be planted where it is known to have been present, unless the soil is first replaced with clean soil, steam-pasteurized, or treated with one of the chemicals mentioned in Chapter 4. Drenching the soil with Terraclor (1 pound in 100 gallons of water) will also provide control.

Botrytis Basal Rot (*Botrytis cinerea*). *D. consolida* is subject to a brown basal rot when grown in greenhouses. Plants wilt and fall over with a soft rot much like that described for the *Pythium* crown rot. The weft of gray mold, which forms many spores, develops on the basal tissue.

Control: Spraying with captan or zineb sometimes helps. Young seedlings should be transplanted before they become too crowded.

Stem Canker (*Fusarium oxysporum* var. *delphinii*). This disease appears as light brown, water-soaked areas on stems. The canker usually begins as one or more small brown spots, which gradually enlarge and in time may involve a considerable portion of the stem. Eventually the fungus may reach the crown and roots and invade the vascular tissues, causing the death of the plant. Other characteristic symptoms are the numerous salmon-colored pads of sporebearing hyphae called "sporodochia" on the cankered areas and the abundant white floccose mycelium within the affected stems.

Plants affected with *Fusarium* begin to show a yellowing of the leaves which progresses from the base of the stem upwards, and in advanced stages the inflorescence droops and the leaves curl upward.

Other fungi that also cause cankers on the stems are a species of *Phoma* and one of *Volutella.*

Control: Remove affected stems as soon as they are detected. New plantings should be set out in steam-pasteurized or chemically treated soil as described in Chapter 4.

Damping-off (*Pellicularia filamentosa, Pythium debaryanum,* and *Botrytis cinerea*). Seedlings are subject to damping-off by these fungi.

Control: Sow seeds in sifted sphagnum moss, or treat soil in flats with formaldehyde as described in Chapter 4. Where *Pellicularia* is the primary cause, drench the soil with Dexon or PCNB (Terraclor). In flats infected with *Botrytis,* spray with a copper fungicide.

Smut (*Urocystis sorosporioides*). Swellings on the leaves and petioles are caused by this fungus.

Control: Remove and destroy affected parts.

Powdery Mildew (*Erysiphe cichoracearum, E. polygoni,* and *Sphaerotheca humuli* var. *fuliginea*). This disease is serious in cool, moist seasons. The white, powdery masses that characterize the disease are composed of the mycelium and summer spores of the fungus. These spores are blown by the wind to other plants and spread the infection.

Gray powdery blotches are formed on the leaves. In severe cases the young leaves and tender growing tips become curled and stunted. The ascocarps are formed late in the season and live through the winter. The delphiniums vary greatly in their resistance to mildew. *Delphinium cheilanthum, D. formosum, D. maackianum,* and *D. tiroliense* have been reported very susceptible, while *D. ajacis, D. consolida, D. grandiflorum,* and *D. tatsienense* have been found very resistant. The resistance of hybrid delphiniums to mildew varies from extreme susceptibility to a high degree of immunity.

Control: Space plants far apart to provide circulation of air. Avoid planting where the soil is too wet or where aeration is poor. Late in the season when mildew is apt to be serious, spray with Benlate or Karathane.

Diaporthe Blight (*Diaporthe arctii*). This is a disease of infrequent occurrence. It has been reported especially on the annual larkspur, *D. ajacis.* The lower leaves of plants that have reached the flowering stage become dry and brown and remain attached to the stem. Brown lesions are found near the base of the stem. These may completely girdle the stem and cause the withering and dying of the entire foliage. The pycnidia or fruiting bodies of the fungus are within the stems, petals, and leaf blades of the uppermost leaves. The crowns and roots are enveloped in a cottony mass of mycelium during rainy periods. Toward the close of the growing season pycnidia appear on the capsules and affect their development. The diseased capsules are a means by which the blight is transmitted. The fungus has a pycnidial stage of the *Phomopsis* type. The ascocarps live on the dead parts during the summer and spring months.

Control: Remove and destroy infected plants.

Leaf Spots (*Ascochyta aquilegiae, Cercospora delphinii, Ovularia delphinii, Phyllosticta* sp., and *Ramularia delphinii*). At least five fungi cause leaf spotting of delphinium.

Control: Spray with copper or dithiocarbamate fungicides.

Rusts (*Puccinia delphinii* and *P. recondita*). Two rust fungi occur on delphinium, the former in California and the latter from Nebraska to the West Coast.

Control: Control measures are rarely practiced for these rusts.

Virus Diseases

Delphiniums are subject to more virus diseases than most herbaceous ornamentals. The following are some of the more prevalent ones.

Ringspot (Delphinium ringspot virus). Faint chlorotic rings appear on the leaves, following the primary veins. Irregular chlorotic spots or rings with yellow bands appear on mature leaves.

Calico (Alfalfa mosaic virus). The basal and middle leaves have amber-orange or lemon-yellow areas, but the younger leaves are a normal green.

Curly Top (Beet curly top virus). This virus affects many crop plants, especially sugar beets, in the Southwest and on the Pacific Coast.

Mosaic (Cucumber mosaic virus). This virus affects a large number of other species of food and ornamental plants.

Stunt. This disease is believed to be caused by a combination of the calico and delphinium ringspot viruses.

Control: Remove and destroy virus-infected plants. Spray with malathion or Sevin to control sucking insects.

Other Disease

Aster Yellows (Mycoplasma-like organism). In the western United States aster yellows is common. The flowers, though fully formed, are green like the leaves, and the inflorescence has the characteristic "bunchy" appearance (Fig. 127).

Control: Same as for virus diseases.

Insects and Other Animal Pests

Aphids. Three species of aphids infest delphiniums. A common species, *Brachycaudus rociadae,* causes the leaves to cup downward. The other species are the green peach, the crescent-marked lily, and the brown ambrosia, which infest a wide variety of other plants.

Control: Spray with malathion.

Dingy Cutworm (*Feltia subgothica*). Plants recently transplanted to the garden are often cut off by this species. Certain other species climb the plants and feed on the foliage and inflorescence. They feed mostly at night and bury themselves during the day in the soil near the plants.

Control: Spray plants with Sevin.

Borers (*Papaipema cataphracta* and *P. nebris*). The burdock and common stalk borers are especially attracted to delphinium. Infested stalks are weakened, wilt, and fall over.

Control: Collect and destroy the aboveground parts of delphiniums and nearby weeds in the fall. Spray with a methoxychlor-Kelthane mixture in early summer to control the borers before they enter the stems. Where this practice is not followed, kill the borers with a flexible wire or by sticking pins through the stalk in several places.

Larkspur Leaf Miner (*Phytomyza delphinivora*). Several larvae of this species may be found feeding together in a single mine. Large areas of leaf-blades become discolored and collapsed as though blighted (Fig. 128). The larvae pupate just outside the leaves near a mine in brown seedlike cases, which are often attached to the leaf.

Fig. 127. Greens of delphinium caused by the aster yellows organism.

Control: Pick off and destroy all infested leaves. Spray with Diazinon or malathion in plantings where this pest is prevalent.

Beetles. The Asiatic garden beetle and the Japanese beetle occasionally infest delphinium.

Control: See *Callistephus.*

Sowbugs (*Armadillidum vulgare* and *Porcellio laevis*). While these pests usually feed on manure and decaying vegetable material, they frequently injure the stems and roots of plants and occasionally feed on the foliage.

Fig. 128.   Injury caused by the larkspur leaf miner *Phytomyza delphinivora.*

Armadillidum vulgare rolls itself into a ball when disturbed; *Porcellio laevis* seeks a hiding place.

Control: Treat infested areas with a 5 per cent Sevin dust or with 1 oz. of 50 per cent wettable methoxychlor powder in 2 gallons of water.

Slugs (*Limax maximus*). Slugs are snails with shells. (See Fig. 90.) They usually feed at night on the leaves, flowers, and stems, causing ragged holes. They leave an iridescent slime on parts over which they have been crawling.

Control: Baits containing metaldehyde, or applications of Zectran or Slug-geta, applied as directed by the manufacturer will give control. These should not be used near food plants.

Ground Mealybug (*Rhizoecus falcifer*). This species infests the roots of many ornamental plants, including annual larkspur.

Control: Pour a dilute mixture of malathion, prepared from the emulsifiable concentrate, around the base of infested plants.

Cyclamen Mite (*Steneotarsonemus pallidus*). This mite causes serious injury to delphiniums in garden and commercial plantings, causing the so-called "blacks." The leaves are badly deformed, deeply cut, more or less thickened and brittle, curled or twisted (see Fig. 37). The flower buds also are much deformed and distorted. Dark brown or blackish spots appear in streaks or blotches on the stems, petioles, and other infested parts. The more indefinite spotting, the stunting and deforming of the vegetative and flowering parts easily distinguishes this disease from the black spot disease caused by bacteria. The mites are very minute, visible only with a good magnifying glass. They are usually found in the shoot buds and unexpanded leaves, where they are well protected, and are rarely seen crawling about on exposed leaflets. They are about $1/100$ inch in length. The eggs, which are considerably smaller, are transparent, smooth, and shining. It requires about 2 weeks for the life cycle of the insect to be completed. The adult mites live through the winter in the crown of the plant, which is buried about $1/2$ inch in the soil. The mites crawl from plant to plant where the leaves intermingle; if the plants are spaced so that the foliage does not touch, the infestation will not spread, unless the mites are carried on the hands or tools of the gardener, in which case clean plants are infected during pruning and cultivating operations. Insects also are thought to transport the mites.

Control: Spray with Kelthane or Dimite starting when the plants are young and repeat several times at weekly or 10-day intervals.

Broad Mite (*Polyphagotarsonemus latus*). Since this mite is unable to live through the winter outdoors in northern regions, it is more common in greenhouses than outdoors. It is less injurious than the cyclamen mite. The leaves of infested plants have a glassy or shining appearance on the undersides, and are curled downward rather than upward. The growing points also are subject to attack and injury; there is no other stunting or distortion of the plant parts, however. The eggs of the broad mite are nearly round, somewhat flattened, and whitish, while those of the cyclamen mite are oblong and transparent.

Control: Spray with Kelthane or Dimite.

Two-Spotted Mite (*Tetranychus urticae*). This widely prevalent species also infests del-

phiniums, particularly during hot, dry weather. The leaves show the familiar whitish mottling on the upper surfaces as though they have been etched with a fine instrument. The leaves of badly infested plants may turn brown and dry out.

Control: See *Althaea.*

Nemas (*Meloidogyne incognita, M. hapla,* and *Aphelenchoides ritzema-bosi*). Two root-knot nemas and one leaf nema also infest this host.

Control: See nemas, Chapter 3.

DEUTZIA

Diseases

Leaf Spots (*Cercospora deutziae* and *Phyllosticta deutziae*). Two fungi are recorded in a few states as the cause of leaf spots on *Deutzia.*

Control: No control measures are necessary.

Insects and Other Animal Pests

Aphids. The bean, melon, and currant aphids infest this host. The latter, known scientifically as *Cryptomyzus ribis,* also attacks currants and the snowball bush.

Control: Spray with Meta-Systox R, malathion, or Sevin when aphids are seen and before they cause leaf-curl.

Leaf Miner (*Gracillaria syringella*). Tan blotches in the leaves are caused by faint yellow larvae, $1/4$ inch long.

Control: Spray with Diazinon or malathion when the first small blotches appear in late spring.

Southern Root-Knot Nema (*Meloidogyne incognita*). Damage caused by this nema may be severe in some southern states.

Control: See Chapter 3.

Japanese Weevil. See *Liqustrum.*

DIANTHERA (WATER-WILLOW)

In the southern states this host is affected in nature by a leaf spot caused by the fungus *Cercospora diantherae,* a black mildew by *Dimerosporium langloisii,* black knot by *Dothideovalsa diantherae,* and a rust by *Puccinia lateripes.*

DIANTHUS BARBATUS
(SWEET WILLIAM)

This species is subject to attack by many of the same parasites and pests that affect the carnation, *D. caryophyllus.* They are discussed below under that host.

Two fungi that frequently attack sweet william are *Puccinia arenariae* and *Fusarium oxysporum* var. *barbati.* The former causes a rust, which also occurs on *D. chinensis.* The latter causes a highly destructive wilt. Early symptoms are yellowing of the new growth, with the leaves pointing downward, and stunting of the plants.

Control: Rust can be prevented by periodic applications of wettable sulfur, Daconil 2787, or ferbam. The *Fusarium* disease can be controlled by using clean or steam-pasteurized soil, or by drenching infested soil with Benlate or PCNB (Terraclor).

DIANTHUS CARYOPHYLLUS
(CARNATION)

Bacterial Diseases

Bacterial Wilt (*Pseudomonas caryophylli*). This bacterium first causes the leaves to turn grayish-green, then yellow, and finally to die. Yellow streaks of frayed tissue in the vascular region may extend a foot or more up the stem.

Another wilt disease is caused by a strain of *Erwinia chrysanthemi.* It produces a rapid wilting and stunting in some plants, or "crook-neck" side shoots, and twisting, curling, stunting of lower leaves in other plants.

Control: Avoid taking cuttings from plants having even the first signs of wilt. Do not transplant healthy plants to pots where this disease has been evident. Destroy wilted plants; they should not be thrown into the compost pile. Dip cuttings in potassium permanganate solution before inserting them in the propagating bench. Take cuttings from plants grown in the greenhouse the year round.

Bacterial Spot (*Pseudomonas woodsii*). These very characteristic spots can be easily recognized by their elongated shape, their light gray color, and the surrounding border; they later become brown. General or widespread infection soon kills the plants. With a hand lens one can see whitish granules; these are little masses of the bacteria which have oozed out of the stomata. Millions of bacteria are developed in each spot.

Control: The organisms are carried by syringing or by rain to the leaves, which they enter through the stomata. In greenhouses the disease can be checked by adequate ventilation and by keeping the foliage as dry as possible. Sulfur sprays may also help.

Fasciation (*Corynebacterium fascians*). Leaves are distorted and growth is stunted when infected by this bacterium. The disease is more striking on *Lathyrus.*

Control: See *Lathyrus.*

Pimple (*Xanthomonas oryzae* var. *dianthi*). This bacterium was found by Colorado Experiment Station workers to cause pimple-like spots, 1 mm. in diameter, on leaves and stems. Severely infected leaves shrivel and die. Control measures have not yet been developed.

Crown Gall (*Agrobacterium tumefaciens*). This disease, described in greater detail in other parts of this book, also affects carnations.

Fungus Diseases

Several fungi cause diseases of carnations, variously referred to as wilt, root rots, stem rots, blights, and damping-off. Three or four different species of fungi have often been isolated from one diseased plant, and scientists have disagreed on the particular fungus primarily responsible for the disease. Some of the diseases develop in fields and are carried to the greenhouse when cuttings are made; there they continue to cause damage in the propagating beds and later in greenhouse plantings.

Wilt (*Phialophora cinerescens*). This fungus causes the plant to wilt by invading the water-conducting vessels, and so cutting off the water supply to stems and leaves, and by developing toxins harmful to the living tissues of the host. It attacks plants of all ages, entering through wounds, and through small root tips and root hairs. The infected tissues become brown, the brown color passing gradually into the green without a distinct boundary. The stems are more or less solid.

Control: See below under Control of Wilts.

Fusarium Wilt (*Fusarium oxysporum* var. *dianthi*). This fungus causes abnormal growth and stunting of the young shoots. The leaves become yellowish and the stems are softened so as to be easily crushed. The brown striping or zonation is sharply bounded, and the diseased tissue may be easily distinguished from the healthy. The fungus may gain entrance through the wounds made at the time the cuttings are set. Another species, *Fusarium roseum* var. *cerealis* "Culmorum," is said to cause a wilting of the shoots and a more general rotting of all parts of the stem.

Control of Wilts. Since all the fungi involved in these diseases are more or less soil-borne, the first point in control is to avoid contaminated soil. If propagating beds have become contaminated, the sand or soil must be replaced or pasteurized with steam. Avoid wounding field plants during weeding and cultivation. Take cuttings only from greenhouse-grown plants, if possible. Spray carnation stock plants weekly with captan. Benlate is effective as a soil drench applied as directed by the manufacturer.

Stem Rot (*Pellicularia filamentosa*). Plants wilt suddenly as a result of fungus decay of the stems just below the soil surface. In cutting benches, the fungus causes a soft, wet rot which starts at the point of callus formation. It may cause a serious collar-rot. It is said to be favored by excessive moisture in the soil and by high temperature. In outdoor plantings the disease is more prevalent in warm, rainy seasons.

Control: PCNB (Terraclor) can be used as a soil drench for stem rot control on living carnation plants. Mix 1 to 1½ pounds of 75 per cent wettable Terraclor powder in 100 gallons of water and apply to 1000 square feet of bench area. Plants showing disease symptoms should be removed before treatment, and the areas from which these plants were removed and an area 2 feet beyond the infested area should be drenched with the mixture.

Leaf Spot (*Septoria dianthi*). The leaf spots are more or less circular, light brown with a purplish-brown border. They are scattered over the leaves and stems, especially the lower leaves. Eventually the ends of the leaves die for lack of nutrients and water, which are cut off from below by the enlargement of the spots. The small black pinpoint-like specks on the spots are the fruiting bodies of the fungus and develop spores. These spores are spread by syringing and by rains.

Control: The disease is best controlled in the greenhouse by keeping the foliage as dry as possible and, when necessary, spraying occasionally with ferbam, Bordeaux mixture, or Fore.

Flower Spot (*Botrytis cinerea*). Brown spots on the flower petals or rotting of the flowers may be caused by this fungus. Rot shows first on outer petals on the outside of the bud. It is most prevalent in cool greenhouses.

Control: Best control is obtained by using heat and ventilation to keep the humidity low.

Greasy Blotch (*Zygophiala jamaicensis*). The fungus responsible for greasy blotches on carnation leaves was originally described on banana leaves in Jamaica. It has recently been reported on carnation leaves in southern Pennsylvania. The disease is severe only during periods of high humidity.

Control: Spray with captan or zineb. The disease is most prevalent under conditions of high humidity and in poorly ventilated or leaky greenhouses. It is more prevalent on second-year plantings because of denseness of foliage.

Rust (*Uromyces dianthi*). Rust is a very common disease of greenhouse carnations, world-wide in distribution. Chocolate-brown, powdery spore masses, varying in length from $1/16$ to $1/4$ inch, break out on both sides of the leaves, stems, and flower buds. Infected plants often become stunted and their leaves curl up. Only one stage, the so-called "red rust" or uredospore stage, is known on carnations in America.

Control: Well-ventilated greenhouses kept at a temperature between 50° and 58°F. do not favor the development of rust. Avoid splashing spores from one plant to another by syringing; if syringing is necessary, it should be done on a bright, sunny day. Use surface watering where possible. Where wetting of foliage is unavoidable, spray weekly with zineb or captan. The foliage must be covered completely with this material for best results. Take cuttings from rust-free plants. Plantvax, a systemic fungicide, has recently been found to control rust.

A fungus parasite, *Darluca filum*, attacks this rust, but is not an important factor in its control.

Bud Rot (*Fusarium poae*). This disease may be recognized by the rotting of the buds before the blooms open. If petals emerge at all, they are distorted and unsalable. The fungus is carried from plant to plant by a mite which also infests various grass species and causes "silver-top" of June grass.

Control: Destroy all rotting buds. Control weeds in and around the greenhouse. Spray with a good miticide. Diazinon sprays may also be helpful.

Branch Rot (*Alternaria dianthi*). This blight or rot occurs at the leaf bases and around the nodes, which are girdled. The fungus very frequently attacks the lower leaves and branches, especially if the plants are crowded. The spots are first ash-gray, but become dark brown or black from the presence of vast numbers of spores attached in chains. Each spore is composed of many cells, any one of which may germinate and spread the disease.

Control: Since this fungus is spread from plant to plant by spores in much the same way as rust is spread, surface watering should be practiced rather than careless syringing. Spray the plants weekly with zineb or captan, being sure to coat the foliage thoroughly with the fungicide. Treatment must begin before the disease has become established. Destruction of infected branches is practicable only in small greenhouses. Growing carnations under glass the year round will practically eliminate the disease.

Anther Smut (*Ustilago violacea*). The variety Noroton White is particularly susceptible to this fungus. Various other species of the pink family (Caryophyllaceae) are also subject to attack by this smut. See *Lychnis.*

Storage Rot (*Botrytis cinerea*). Cut carnation flowers stored for varying periods are subject to attack by this fungus, which causes a water-soaked flecking of the outer petals. A stem rot of stored cuttings is also caused by this fungus. Sprays and dips with captan or zineb will control the cutting rot. No effective control has been developed for the flower flecking.

Wilt (*Armillaria mellea*). Carnations in a California greenhouse wilted and died when infected by the shoestring root rot fungus.

Control: Steam-pasteurize infested soil.

Virus Diseases

Carnations are subject to many virus diseases, the most common ones being streak, mosaic, mottle, and ringspot. Brierley and Smith of the United States Department of Agriculture have determined the percentage of these viruses in 151 carnation varieties from eight states as follows: streak, 11; mosaic, 3; mottle, 92; and ringspot, 1. Only mottle proved transmissable by root contact, and only it and ringspot by the cutting knife. The following are the principal symptoms of these viruses.[18]

Streak (Carnation streak virus). Yellow or red spots and streaks occur parallel to the leaf veins. The lower leaves may turn yellow and die.

Mosaic (Carnation mosaic virus). Light green mottling and irregular to elongate blotches occur on the leaves. Conspicuous breaking of flower color also occurs. The green peach aphid, *Myzus persicae*, transmits this virus in nature.

Mottle (Carnation mottle virus). This virus is very common in commercial carnation varieties, in which it produces either faint leaf mottling or no symptoms at all. It causes breaking of flower color in "Perpetual Giant" seedlings.

Ringspot (Carnation ringspot virus). Irreg-

[18] For a more detailed discussion, see "Carnation Viruses in the United States," by Brierley and Smith, in *Phytopathology* 47:714–721 (December, 1957).

ular gray or yellow spots appear on the leaves. The leaf margins are wavy. The green peach aphid also transmits this virus in nature.

Control: Virus diseases in carnations are less prevalent than formerly. One reason is that many commercial growers keep their carnations indoors the year round, and also use so-called "mother blocks" as the sources of cuttings. These practices have been adopted primarily to control *Alternaria* branch rot, bacterial wilt, and *Fusarium* wilt; but they also have helped to curb virus diseases.

These viruses can be destroyed by subjecting infected plants of most varieties to dry heat at 38°C. for two months. Less heat-tolerant carnations, such as Littlefields and Viking, survive better if the heat is dropped to 30°C. for about 5 days near the middle of the run and then returned to 38°C.

Insects and Other Pests

Variegated Cutworm (*Peridroma saucia*). This cutworm feeds on a number of greenhouse and garden plants. The eggs, 50 or more, are laid on the stems or on the undersides of leaves by adult moths. The full-grown caterpillar is about 2 inches long. It climbs the stems of carnations and feeds on the buds, often cutting off the stem just below. Young plants are often cut off at the surface of the ground. The worm is most prevalent in fields during June and July.

Control: See *Asparagus*.

Green Peach Aphid (*Myzus persicae*). This aphid, which spreads several carnation viruses, can easily be controlled with malathion or Sevin sprays.

Cabbage Looper (*Trichoplusia ni*). See *Calendula*.

Other Caterpillars. The oblique-banded leaf roller and the greenhouse leaf tier also infest carnations. These are easily controlled by early applications of *Bacillus thuringiensis* or Sevin.

Onion Thrips (*Thrips tabaci*). Onion thrips do some damage to carnations in greenhouses and in the fields.

Control: Spray with Cygon.

Two-Spotted Mite (*Tetranychus urticae*). Leaves turn pale and have a dusty coating and fine webs, and the plant is stunted when heavily infested with these tiny pests.

Control: In the greenhouse this pest is best controlled with miticide aerosols. On outdoor plants, chlorobenzilate, Kelthane, Meta-Systox R, or Tedion sprays are effective.

Southern Root-Knot Nema (*Meloidogyne incognita*). This nema occasionally infests the roots of carnations.

Control: See Chapter 3.

Sow Bugs. See *Lathyrus.*

DICENTRA (BLEEDING-HEART)

Bleeding-heart, *Dicentra spectabilis,* is subject to a stem rot caused by *Pellicularia rolfsii,* a storage rot and wilt by *Sclerotinia sclerotiorum,* and a wilt by a species of *Fusarium.*

Control: The causal fungi are all soilborne. Hence use clean soil or treat infested soil with steam or an appropriate chemical before re-use.

Squirrel-corn, *Dicentra canadensis,* is affected by a downy mildew caused by *Peronospora dicentrae* and a rust by *Cerotelium dicentrae.* The alternate stage of the latter occurs on wood-nettle.

Control: Neither disease is important enough to warrant control measures.

DICKSONIA (TREE-FERN)—see FILICES

DIDISCUS—see TRACHYMENE

DIEFFENBACHIA

Diseases

Bacterial Leaf Spot (*Xanthomonas dieffenbachiae*). The spots are at first minute, yellow, or yellowish-orange with translucent centers. Under moist air conditions large mounds of bacterial ooze appear on the lower surfaces of the spots. As this dries, it becomes a waxy, silvery-white layer which covers the spots. Later the ooze may appear on the upper surfaces. The spots enlarge up to 1/2 inch in diameter and run together. Under drier conditions the spots do not enlarge but turn reddish-brown, giving the leaves a speckled appearance. They are somewhat limited in size by the larger veins. If they are sufficiently numerous, the result is a general yellowing, wilting, and death of the infected parts of the leaves, which turn brown and become thick and tough. The author was the first to discover this disease many years ago.

Control: Space the plants farther apart. Avoid syringing under moist conditions, and lower the temperature.

Brown Leaf Spot (*Leptosphaeria* sp.). In Florida, this disease causes extensive damage to several species of *Dieffenbachia.* Infected leaves may have 50 or more lesions with diameters less than 1 mm. to a few circular spots of greater size. The centers of the spots are yellowish brown with an outer halo of dark orange-yellow.

Control: This leaf spot can be controlled by periodic sprays of maneb.

Leaf Spot (*Cephalosporium dieffenbachiae*). Quite unlike the foregoing leaf spot is that caused by this fungus. Very small reddish-brown lesions appear in the young leaves. When the leaves are unrolled the spots may be 1/4 inch or more in diameter, with a dark border. As the lesions run together, a yellowing and death of the entire leaf may sometimes occur. Infection commonly occurs through wounds caused by mealybugs, which feed under the leaf sheaths.

Control: Avoid promiscuous syringing; space the plants; keep temperatures and humidity down as far as practical; control mealybugs by killing off ants and by timely spraying with malathion.

Anthracnose (*Glomerella cincta*). Another leaf spotting fungus has been recorded on this host in New Jersey.

Control: Same as for leaf spot.

Stem and Leaf Rot (*Erwinia chrysanthemi*). This disease appears as brownish, watersoaked, sunken, soft areas on the stems, and irregular, brownish, soft spots on the leaves.

Control: Infected canes to be used for propagation should be dipped in Agrimycin or in hot water.

Root and Stem Rots (*Phytophthora palmivora* and *Pythium* sp.). The roots and lower stems may rot from invasion by these so-called water molds.

Control: In California control of these fungi has been obtained by dipping 2-foot-long sections of hardened canes in hot water at 125°F. for 30 minutes. The canes are then cooled and placed in steamed sphagnum moss until roots and buds start. Soft canes or soft leafy shoots will not withstand the hot-water treatment.

DIERVILLA (BUSH-HONEYSUCKLE)

Diseases

Leaf Spots (*Cercospora weigeliae, Phyllosticta diervillae, Septoria diervillae, Ramularia diervillae,* and *R. umbrina*). Five fungi are known to cause leaf spots of bush-honeysuckle.

Control: Where severe infections are likely to occur, spray with a copper or a dithiocarbamate fungicide several times at 10-day intervals in late spring.

Powdery Mildew (*Microsphaera alni*).

Where this fungus is prevalent, spray with Benlate, Karathane, or wettable sulfur.

Insects and Other Animal Pests

Scale (*Lecanium* sp.). This insect does considerable damage to this host by infesting twigs and main stems.

Control: Spray the plants while dormant in early spring with lime sulfur or a "superior" type miscible soil, and in May and June with Diazinon, malathion, or Sevin.

Southern Root-Knot Nema (*Meloidogyne incognita*). See Chapter 3 for control measures.

DIGITALIS (FOXGLOVE)

Fungus Diseases

Anthracnose (*Colletotrichum fuscum*). This disease appears on the leaves as light or purplish-brown, circular or somewhat angular spots, at first very small, later reaching 1/8 inch in diameter. The spots are indefinitely bordered, with purplish margins. Numerous small, black, fruiting bodies of the fungus may be seen at the center of the spots. Infected seedlings damp off.

Leaf Spot (*Ramularia variabilis*). This fungus attacks the lower leaves more frequently than the upper and causes the formation of irregular spots up to 1/4 inch in diameter. The spots are snuff-brown in color with a reddish border. Heavy infection results in the shriveling and death of the entire leaf. The development of conidia (spores) of the fungus in tufts which emerge through the stomata gives a white moldy appearance to the leaves. Another leaf spot caused by *Phyllosticta digitalis* also occurs in some areas.

Control: Spray with a copper or dithiocarbamate fungicide.

Root and Stem Rots (*Fusarium* sp., *Pellicularia filamentosa, P. rolfsii,* and *Sclerotinia sclerotiorum*). Four soil-inhabiting fungi are known to cause root and stem decay of this host.

Control: Treat soil with heat or chemicals as described in Chapter 4.

Wilt (*Verticillium albo-atrum*). This fungus occurs occasionally on foxglove.

Control: Same as for root rot above.

Virus Diseases

Mosaic (Tobacco mosaic virus). This virus disease occasionally affects foxglove. Fulton in Wisconsin reported that in some fields as many as 50 per cent of the *Digitalis lanata* plants were affected by this virus.

Curly Top (Beet curly top virus). This virus causes leaf curl, the development of many rootlets, and stunting of the plants. It is transmitted by the beet leafhopper *Circulifer tenellus.*

Control: Rogue and destroy affected plants. Spray with malathion, Meta-Systox R, or Sevin to control the insect vector.

Insects and Other Pests

Aphids (*Acyrthosiphon solani* and *Neomyzus circumflexus*). The foxglove and crescent-marked lily aphid infest this host.

Control: Spray with malathion, Meta-Systox R, or Sevin.

Beetles. The Asiatic garden and Japanese beetles and the rose chafer feed on foxglove leaves and flowers.

Control: Spray with methoxychlor or Sevin when the beetles are about.

Mealybug (*Pseudococcus fragilis*). Foxglove is one of the many kinds of plants infested by this mealybug.

Control: Spray with malathion or Sevin as soon as the white insects are seen.

Stem and Bulb Nema (*Ditylenchus dipsaci*). While this nema is not serious on fox-

glove, it has been reported to cause the development of angular leaf spots. Under very moist conditions the worms may enter the stomata and cause leaf spots similar to those that result from infestation by the leaf nema, *Aphelenchoides ritzema-bosi.*

Control: Pick off and destroy infested leaves.

DIMORPHOTHECA (CAPE-MARIGOLD)

Diseases

Blight (*Botrytis cinerea*). This widely prevalent fungus occasionally causes leaf blight of this host under conditions of high humidity.

Control: Spray with captan or zineb at periodic intervals.

Downy Mildew (*Plasmopara halstedii*). This mildew attacks many other ornamentals in addition to cape-marigold. White, downy mycelium develops on the surface of the leaves.

Control: Spray with zineb or a copper fungicide during the summer.

Rust (*Puccinia flaveriae*). This fungus has also been reported on *Calendula.*

Control: Spray with wettable sulfur or ferbam.

Wilt (*Verticillium albo-atrum* and *Fusarium* sp.). Both greenhouse and outdoor plants have been reported susceptible to these fungi.

Control: Use steam-pasteurized soil.

Root Rot (*Macrophomina phaseoli, Pythium ultimum,* and *Pellicularia filamentosa*). These fungi occasionally affect cape-marigold.

Control: Same as for wilt.

Aster Yellows. This disease also occurs on cape-marigold.

Control: Remove and destroy affected plants. Control the insect vectors with Sevin combined with Kelthane.

Insects

Leafhopper (*Macrosteles fascifrons*). The aster leafhopper spreads the aster yellows organism.

Control: See *Callistephus.*

DIOSPYROS (PERSIMMON)

Persimmons in the wild and those grown for their fruits are subject to a great number of diseases and pests. Those grown as ornamentals, however, are relatively free of problems. Wilt caused by the fungus *Cephalosporium diospyri* is perhaps the most destructive disease of this host. Originally discovered in Tennessee in 1933, it now occurs from the Carolinas to Florida and west to Texas. Oriental persimmons appear to be resistant to this disease.

Other diseases of lesser importance on this host include dieback, caused by *Botryosphaeria dothidea,* twig blight by *Physalospora* spp., and root rot by *Phymatotrichum omnivorum.*

Among the many insects that infest persimmon are three species of borers—flatheaded appletree, persimmon, and redheaded ash,—three kinds of caterpillars—hickory horned devil, redhumped, and variable oakleaf,—twenty-five species of scales, and the greenhouse thrips, citrus whitefly and several kinds of beetles.

DODECATHEON (SHOOTING-STAR)

This host, occasionally grown in perennial borders, is relatively free of diseases and pests. The rust fungus, *Puccinia ortonii,* and the leaf spot disease caused by *Phyllosticta dodecathei* are the most frequently reported diseases.

DORONICUM (LEOPARD'S-BANE)

Few diseases and pests affect this host. A powdery mildew caused by *Erysiphe cichoracearum* has been recorded from California. The crescent-marked lily aphid, *Neomyzus circumflexus,* a black and yellow species, and the sawfly, *Amestastegia pallipes* (described under *Viola*), occasionally infest leopard's-bane.

The fern nema, *Aphelenchoides olesistus,* produces spots which are first transparent, then brown to black. They are limited by the veins as in the leaves of ferns (Figs. 34 and 114). Heavy infestations result in the death of the plants.

The southern root-knot nema, *Meloidogyne incognita,* also infests this host.

Control: See Chapter 3.

DRABA (WHITLOW-GRASS)

Species planted in rock gardens may be subject to infection by several fungus parasites. Among them are the downy mildew fungus, *Peronospora parasitica;* the white rust, *Albugo candida;* and the true rust, *Puccinia drabae.* These diseases are rarely serious enough to warrant control measures.

DRACAENA[19]

Diseases

Leaf Spot (*Phyllosticta maculicola*). Plants of any age may show irregular, small, brown spots with yellowish margins. The black fruiting bodies (pycnidia) develop long coils of spores, which may be spread from plant to plant during syringing of greenhouse-grown plants. Other fungi which cause leaf

---

[19] Plants classified under the genera *Dracaena* and *Cordyline* are closely related and subject to much the same diseases. The two genera are not separately treated in this book.

spots are *Glomerella cincta, Phyllosticta dracaenae,* and *Lophodermium dracaenae.*

Control: Cut off and destroy infected leaves. Avoid wetting the foliage.

Stem Rot (*Aspergillus niger* var. *floridanus*). This disease has caused heavy losses of *D. sanderiana* cuttings in some Florida nurseries.

Control: Control measures have not been developed.

Fusarium Leaf Spot (*Fusarium moniliforme*). Circular or slightly raised, reddish brown lesions surrounded by a yellow halo are characteristic of this disease, first reported from Florida.

Control: Weekly applications of Daconil 2787, preferably before potting, provide excellent control.

Tip Blight (*Physalospora dracaenae*). The diseased areas become shrunken and straw-colored. The disease begins on the lower leaves, which may be killed while the center leaves are dead only at the tips. Another species, *P. rhodina,* has been reported on this host from Maryland.

Control: Same as for leaf spot.

Root Rot (*Pellicularia filamentosa*). This is not common but has been reported on *Cordyline terminalis.* Another root rot is caused by a species of *Phytophthora.*

Control: Drenching the soil with a mixture of Dexon and PCNB (Terraclor) will control these fungi.

Insects

Dracaena Thrips (*Heliothrips dracaenae*). This species feeds on the leaves of rubber plant, kentia palm, sago-palm, and century plant.

Control: Spray with Cygon.

Mealybug (*Pseudococcus longispinus*). This pest occasionally infests dracaenas.

Control: Same as for thrips.

DURANTA REPENS
(GOLDEN DEWDROP)

In the southern states, especially in Florida, a stem rot caused by *Pellicularia rolfsii* occasionally becomes serious in garden plantings. A black leaf spot caused by *Phyllachora fusicarpa* also has been reported from Florida. Several species of aphids, including *Aphis gossypii* and *Myzus persicae,* may become troublesome on this host. Malathion, Meta-Systox R, or Sevin sprays will control the insect pests.

ECHEVERIA

Diseases

Rust (*Puccinia echeveriae*). This rust has been reported from California on *Echeveria caespitosa* and *E. farinosa.*

Control: Remove and destroy infected plant parts.

Leaf Spot (*Stemphylium bolicki*). See *Sedum.*

Insects and Related Pests

Black Vine Weevil (*Otiorhyncus sulcatus*). Serious injury may result from the feeding of the thick, short larvae on the roots. The leaves wilt and die from lack of water.

Control: See *Taxus.*

Southern Root-Knot Nema (*Meloidogyne incognita*). For control refer to Chapter 3.

ECHINACEA
(PURPLE CONEFLOWER)

The varieties grown in borders and in wild gardens are subject to two leaf spots caused by the fungi *Cercospora rudbeckiae* and *Septoria lepachydis* and to an unidentified mosaic virus.

ECHINOPS (GLOBE THISTLE)

Diseases

Crown Rot (*Pellicularia rolfsii*). This soil-inhabiting fungus occasionally infects the roots and crown of globe thistle.
Control: Use steam-pasteurized soil.

Insects

Green Peach Aphid (*Myzus persicae*). This aphid makes the leaves of this host turn downward.
Control: Spray the leaves with malathion or Meta-Systox R before they are curled tightly enough to protect the aphids.
Four-lined Plant Bug (*Poecilocapsus lineatus*). This bug makes small, round, tan spots in the leaves of this and many other hosts.
Control: Spray with Sevin when the bugs begin to feed.

ECHIUM (VIPER'S BUGLOSS)

Aside from a leaf spot caused by *Cercospora echii* and a root rot by a species of *Rosellinia*, this plant is relatively free from pests.

ELAEAGNUS (RUSSIAN-OLIVE)

Diseases

Leaf Spots (*Cercospora carii, C. elaeagni, Phyllosticta argyrea, Septoria argyrea*, and *S. elaeagni*). Five species of fungi cause leaf spots on this host.
Control: These fungi are rarely severe enough to warrant the use of protective fungicides.
Cankers (*Botryodiplodia theobromae, Nectria cinnabarina, Fusicoccum elaeagni, Fusarium sp.,* and *Phytophthora cactorum*). Cankers on the branches and trunk of Rus-

sian-olive may be caused by any of these fungi.
Control: No control measures have been developed.
Rusts (*Puccinia caricis-shepherdiae* and *P. coronata* var. *elaeagni*). The alternate host of the former is *Carex*, and of the latter, *Calamagrostis*.
Control: These rusts are rarely serious enough to require control measures.
Wilt (*Verticillium albo-atrum*). This disease was first found on Russian-olive in a nursery planting in New Mexico in 1958.
Control: See under more favored hosts.
Other Diseases. Russian-olive is occasionally affected by crown gall caused by *Agrobacterium tumefaciens*, hairy root by *A. rhizogenes*, and canker by *Phomopsis elaegni*.

Insects

Oleaster-Thistle Aphid (*Capitophorus elaeagni*). This pale yellow and green aphid also known as the Russian-olive aphid, lives on thistle during the summer and overwinters on Russian-olive.
Control: Control measures are unnecessary.
Scales (*Parlatoria oleae* and *Lepidosaphes beckii*). The olive and the purple scale as well as 17 other species of scales have been recorded on Russian-olive.
Control: Spray with malathion or Sevin in late May and again in late June to control the crawler stage of scales.

ENKIANTHUS

Cottony-Cushion Scale (*Icerya purchasi*). This scale occasionally infests *Enkianthus*.
Control: Spray with malathion.

EPIGAEA REPENS (TRAILING ARBUTUS)

Relatively few diseases and no insects affect this lovely member of the Ericaceae. Two leaf spot fungi, *Cercospora epigaeae* and *Pyllosticta epigaeae*, a powdery mildew, *Microsphaera alni* var. *vaccinii*, and a wilt caused by *Phytophthora cinnamomi* are known. The last was isolated by the author from wilted plants some years ago.

EPIPHYLLUM—see CACTACEAE

ERANTHEMUM

Greenhouse eranthemums are subject to oedema, especially if too heavily watered or in very humid greenhouses. The general appearance of the disease is shown in Fig. 11. The intumescences, which are rust-colored spots, are composed of quite elongated cells of the tissues of the leaf. They occur mostly on the upper surface, to which they give a sandy appearance. On these overgrowths one often finds the fruiting bodies of a *Phyllosticta*-like fungus. This physiological disease is easily mistaken for the work of the red spider mite, and gardeners often spray the plants with a miticide because of this error. The disease can be controlled by avoiding overwatering, especially in damp weather, also by providing additional ventilation.

ERICA (HEATH)

Diseases

Wilt (*Phytophthora cinnamomi*). Leaves infected with *Phytophthora* become grayish, and the tops of the plants wilt. The plants finally die as a result of infection at the base.

Control: Treat the soil with steam as described in Chapter 4, or drench the soil with Dexon.

Powdery Mildew (*Erysiphe polygoni*). Whitish or grayish mats of the fungus develop on the leaves and tender shoots. The leaves may turn brown and fall. Badly infected plants may be killed.

Control: Spray with Benlate or Karathane.

Rust (*Uredo ericae*). This rust occurs on *Erica hyemalis* in California.

Cultural Diseases. Plants may become sickly and stunted through lack of adequate nutrition or through incorrect acidity of the soil (which should be rather acid).

Control: Avoid the use of lime either in hard water or by direct application.

Insects

Scales (*Hemiberlesia rapax*, *Aspidiotus nerii* and *Lepidosaphes ulmi*). The greedy, oleander, and oystershell scales infest heaths.

Control: Spray with malathion or Sevin when the young scales are crawling about in late spring and early summer.

ERIGERON (FLEABANE)

Diseases

Downy Mildews (*Basidiophora entospora* and *Plasmopara halstedii*). These two downy mildew fungi occasionally infect *Erigeron*.

Control: Remove and destroy infected leaves as they appear.

Leaf Spots (*Cercospora cana*, *Cercosporella colubrina*, and *Septoria erigerontis*). Three leaf spotting fungi have been reported. These occur only during very rainy seasons.

Control: Valuable ornamental species of *Erigeron* can be protected with copper or dithiocarbamate sprays.

Powdery Mildews (*Erysiphe cichoracearum*, *Sphaerotheca humuli*, and *Phyllactinia corylea*).

Control: Spray valuable specimens with Benlate or Karathane when mildew appears.

Rusts (*Puccinia cyperi*, *P. dioicae* [*extensicola*] var. *erigerontis*, *P. grindeliae*, and *Coleosporium solidaginis*). Four true rusts are known to occur on this host.

Control: Control practices are rarely attempted for rusts on fleabanes.

Aster Yellows. This disease has been reported from many eastern and midwestern states.

Control: Destroy affected plants.

Insects

Aphids. (*Aphis armoraciae,* western aster root aphid, and *Brachycaudus helichrysi,* leaf-curl plum aphid). The former infests the roots and the latter the leaves of this host.

Control: Drench the soil around plants infested with the western aster root aphid with a dilute solution of malathion of Diazinon. Spray the leaves infested with the leaf-curl plum aphid with malathion, Sevin, or Meta-Systox R.

ERODIUM (HERONSBILL)

Few diseases affect members of this genus that are grown in rock gardens. A leaf spot caused by the bacterium *Pseudomonas erodii,* a stem and crown rot by two species of fungi, *Pellicularia filamentosa* and *P. rolfsii,* and curly top caused by the beet curly top virus are found on this host.

ERYNGIUM (ERYNGO)

A smut caused by the fungus *Entyloma eryngii,* two leaf spots by *Cylindrosporium eryngii* and *Septoria eryngicola,* and a stem rot by *Macrophomina phaseoli* have been recorded on this host.

ERYTHRINA (CORAL-TREE)

Three fungus diseases have been reported on *Erythrina:* thread blight caused by *Pellicularia koleroga,* wilt by *Verticillium alboatrum,* and root rot by *Phymatotrichum om-*

nivorum. The southern root-knot nema, *Meloidogyne incognita,* also infests the roots of this host.

ERYTHRONIUM

Diseases

Leaf Blights (*Ciborinia gracilis* and *C. erythronii*). These fungi cause minute lesions which give the leaves a speckled appearance. This is followed by general yellowing, drying, and collapsing of the leaves. Sclerotia develop on the dead leaves and give rise to ascocarps in the spring. Spores from these fruiting bodies reinfect new leaves as they develop. A species of *Botrytis* may also cause leaf blight in rainy springs.

Control: Pick off and destroy badly spotted or blighted leaves when noticed.

Black Spot (*Asteroma tenerrimum* var. *erythronii*). This fungus causes small black spots on the leaves of this host in the western United States.

Control: Control measures are unnecessary.

Rust (*Uromyces heterodermus*). This disease occurs on *Erythronium,* in the Mountain and Pacific Coast States.

Control: Same as for black spot.

Leaf Smuts (*Urocystis erythronii* and *Ustilago heufleri*). Large dusty pustules form on the leaves, followed by cracking and dying of the leaves.

Control: Pick off and destroy smutted leaves as soon as they are noticed.

Other Diseases. Californian species of *Erythronium* planted in gardens in the eastern states seem to have a physiological trouble like the dwarfing and distortion caused by nemas and parasitic fungi.

Insect

Green Peach Aphid (*Myzus persicae*). This aphid occasionally infests this host.

Control: Spray with Meta-Systox R, malathion, or Sevin.

ESCHSCHOLTZIA (CALIFORNIA-POPPY)

Bacterial, Fungus, and Virus Diseases

Bacterial Blight (*Xanthomonas papavericola*). Minute, water-soaked black spots surrounded by a colorless ring appear on this host and other kinds of poppies.

Control: Gather and destroy severely infected plants. Remove spotted leaves of mildly infected ones.

Leaf-Mold (*Heterosporium eschscholtziae*). This disease may cause death of seedlings, or lesions on leaves, stems, roots, flower, and fruit of California-poppy on the West Coast.

Control: Set plants in clean soil or soil that has not grown this species during the 2 previous years. The fungus may be seed-borne; seed should therefore be soaked for 30 minutes in hot water at 125°F.

Powdery Mildew (*Erysiphe polygoni*). This common disease occurs on this host in California.

Control: Severe outbreaks in commercial fields may be controlled with wettable sulfur or Karathane sprays.

Other Diseases. Occasionally the following fungus diseases are found on California-poppy: smut caused by *Entyloma eschscholtziae*, wilt by *Verticillium albo-atrum*, and collar rot by a species of *Alternaria*.

Aster Yellows (Mycoplasma-like organism). This disease occurs on this host in the eastern United States. The California strain has been found on the West Coast.

Control: Lift out and destroy affected plants.

EUCALYPTUS

Diseases

Leaf-Spots (*Hendersonia* spp., *Monochaetia monochaeta*, *Mycosphorella moelleriana*, and *Phyllosticta extensa*). Several species of fungi cause leaf spots of Eucalyptus. They are rarely serious enough to justify control measures.

Crown Gall. The bacterium *Agrobacterium tumefaciens*, and many wood decaying fungi, also occur on this host.

Other Fungus Diseases. Among other diseases of this host are dieback and twig blight caused by *Botryosphaeria dothidea*, root rot by *Armillaria mellea* in California, root rot by *Clitocybe tabescens* in Florida, and *Phymatotrichum omnivorum* in Texas.

Physiological Disease

Oedema. Several species of Eucalyptus grown in greenhouses as ornamentals are subject to a physiological disease which is manifested by intumescences or blister-like galls on the leaves. Sections of these galls show several layers of cells formed one above the other. These growths usually crack open and become rust-colored. The disease is difficult to diagnose because it looks so much like the work of a blister-mite or a rust fungus. It is not caused by a parasite, but results from the accumulation of too much water through poor ventilation of the greenhouse or through over-watering of the plants.

Insects and Related Pests

Cowpea Aphid (*Aphis craccivora*). This black aphid with white legs infests Eucalyptus in addition to many other plants.

Control: Heavy infestations can easily be controlled with malathion or Meta-Systox R.

Borers Two borers, the California prionus *Prionus californicus* and the Pacific flatheaded *Chrysobothris mali*, infest Eucalyptus.

Control: Valuable specimens may be protected by spraying with methoxychlor before the newly hatched borers enter the bark. State entomologists will suggest spraying dates and perhaps other control measures.

Caterpillars. The omnivorous looper, the orange tortrix, and the California oakworm chew the leaves of Eucalyptus.

Control: Spray with Sevin.

Scales. Seven kinds of scales—black, California red, Florida red, greedy, oleander, purple, and San Jose—may attack this host.

Control: Valuable specimens may be sprayed with malathion, Meta-Systox R, or Sevin to control the young crawler stage.

Mealybug (*Pseudococcus longispinus*). This common species also attacks a great variety of plants outdoors in the warmer parts of the country, and in the greenhouse and homes in colder parts.

Control: Spray with malathion or Sevin when mealybugs appear.

Mites. The avocado red, the platani, and the southern red mite infest Eucalyptus.

Control: Valuable specimens should be sprayed with Aramite, Dimite, or Kethane.

EUCHARIS (AMAZON-LILY)

Only two fungus diseases have been recorded thus far on this host in the United States—blight caused by *Botryis cinerea* in Florida and leaf scorch by *Stagonospora curtisii* in California.

EUGENIA

Diseases

Leaf Spots (*Asterinella puiggarii* and *Colletotrichum gloeosporioides*). Two fungi have been reported to cause leaf spot on *Eugenia* in the southern United States. A leaf spot caused by *Pezizella oenotherae* was reported from New York State, presumably on greenhouse-grown plants.

Insects

Citrophilus Mealybug (*Pseudococcus fragilis*). This pest infests *Eugenia* grown in greenhouses.

Control: Spray with malathion or Sevin.

Scales (*Icerya purchasi* and *Chrysomphalus aonidum*). The former, known as the cottony-cushion scale, is common in greenhouses where acacia and oleanders are grown. It moves from these hosts to *Eugenia*, where it infests the topmost leaves. The latter, known as Florida red scale, attacks *Eugenia* and many other plants outdoors in the Deep South.

Control: Malathion or Sevin sprays will control these pests. Repeat every 10 days until the infestation is cleaned up.

EUONYMUS

Diseases

Anthracnose (*Gloeosporium frigidum* and *G. griseum*). Brown lesions on the leaves, in which tiny fungus fruiting bodies may be seen with a hand lens, are characteristic of this disease.

Control: Severe outbreaks in the warmer parts of the country may be prevented with periodic applications of dithiocarbamate or copper sprays.

Crown Gall (*Agrobacterium tumefaciens*). Euonymus may be severely infected by the crown gall bacterium. Both the roots and stems bear good-sized galls (Fig. 129).

Control: Destroy heavily infected plants. If only a few galls are present, cut off and destroy the stems on which they occur. Dip pruning shears in 70 per cent denatured alcohol from time to time.

Leaf Spots (*Cercospora destructiva, C. euonymi, Exosporium concentricum, Phyllosticta euonymi, P. pallens, Septoria euonymi, S. atropurpurei, S. euonymella, Ramularia euonymi,* and *Marssonina thomasiana*). Ten fungi are capable of causing leaf spots on this host.

Control: Severe outbreaks in rainy seasons may be prevented by occasional applications of copper or dithiocarbamate sprays.

Powdery Mildews (*Oidium euonymijaponici* and *Microsphaera alni*). The former, eu-

Fig. 129. Crown gall of euonymus caused by the bacterium *Agrobacterium tumefaciens.*

onymus mildew, is very prevalent and destructive in the southern states and the Pacific Coast.

Control: Spray with Acti-dione PM, Karathane, or Benlate when the mildew appears. Repeat in 10 days. Do not apply these materials when the temperatures are above 85°F.

Dieback (*Sclerotinia* (*Whetzelinia*) *sclerotiorum*). A severe dieback of four-year old *Euonymus alatus* occurred in Rhode Island in 1974 and 1975. Symptoms included premature reddening of the leaves, followed by wilting and browning, and then dieback of large branches. Sclerotia were present in the vicinity of cankers on the affected branches, and beneath the dead bark of basal cankers.

Control: Remove and destroy affected branches. Spraying with Benlate just as the buds open and again 4 to 5 days later provide good protection.

Phomopsis Dieback (*Phomopsis* sp.). The author has found that dieback of *Euonymus vegetus* was also caused by this fungus.

Control: Prune back and destroy affected branches.

Insects

Aphids. Three species of aphids infest euonymus: bean, green peach, and ivy.
Control: Spray with malathion or Sevin.

Thrips (*Heliothrips haemorrhoidalis*). Occasionally the so-called greenhouse thrips infest this host.

Control: Spray with malathion or Cygon.

Scales. Many species of scales infest euonymus—California red, chaff, cottony maple, dictyospermum, euonymus, Florida red, Florida wax, and greedy. Of these, the most common and destructive is the euonymus scale, *Unaspis euonymi* (Fig. 130). The males of this species are narrow and white, and they cluster in great numbers on the leaves and stems. The females are rather dark brown and shaped somewhat like the oystershell scale. A dwarf species of euonymus grown in rock gardens is so susceptible as to be killed unless protected. Bittersweet, *Celastrus scandens,* and pachysandra, *Pachysandra terminalis,* are also susceptible to euonymus scale. Other ground covers such as

Fig. 130. Euonymus scale (males).

English ivy, *Hedera helix,* growing near infested euonymus or pachysandra, may also be attacked.

Control: Heavy infestations can be cleaned up only by applying both dormant and summer sprays. In late March or early April spray with "superior"-type dormant oil plus ethion. The summer spray should be applied from June 5 to June 15, depending on the locality and season. The dosage is two teaspoons of 50 per cent malathion liquid or 4 tablespoons of 25 per cent malathion wettable powder per gallon of water. Cygon, Meta-Systox R, or Sevin may be substituted for the malathion.

EUPATORIUM (MISTFLOWER)

Disease

Very few diseases occur on the cultivated species of *Eupatorium.* Powdery mildew caused by *Erysiphe cichoracearum* is of general occurrence in the eastern and central states.

Insects

Aphids (*Dactynotus ambrosiae* and *Brachycaudus helichrysi*). The former, a large red species with long legs, also infests golden-glow. The latter, known as the leaf-curl plum aphid, varies from pale green to dark green and reddish brown.

Control: Spray with malathion, Meta-Systox R, or Sevin.

Chrysanthemum Leaf Miner (*Phytomyza syngenesiae*). The chrysanthemum leaf miner also infests this host, producing irregular, light-colored mines extending over the leaf surface just under the epidermis.

Control: Spray with Diazinon or malathion as soon as the first leaf miners appear on the leaves.

Barnacle Scale (*Ceroplastes cirripediformis*). Female barnacle scales are reddish-brown covered with white wax shading to gray or light brown.

Control: Spray with malathion or Sevin when the young scales are crawling about.

EUPHORBIA LACTEA

Stem Rot (*Coniothyrium euphorbiae*). This is a rather serious disease in greenhouses where the fungus has become established. The rotted areas are dark-colored and soft. A

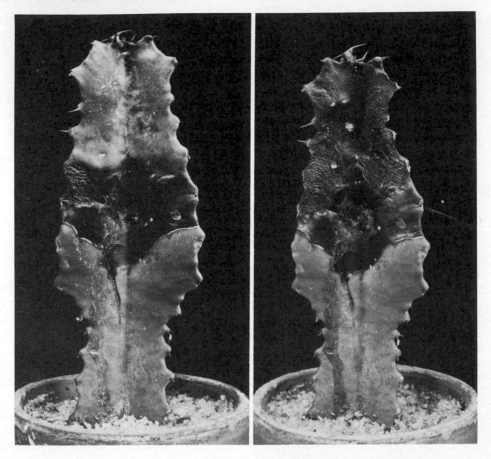

Fig. 131. Stem rot of *Euphorbia lactea* caused by *Coniothyrium euphorbiae*. The photograph on the right was taken one week later than that on the left.

branch once attacked is usually killed (see Fig. 131). While the rot resembles a decay caused by bacteria, there is no foul odor; bacteria are present but are not the cause of the disease. The small black fruiting bodies (pycnidia) of the fungus send out long tendrils, each of which contains over a million spores. These spores, when splashed about in the greenhouses by syringing and watering, cause the disease to spread to other plants, especially those that have been slightly wounded. Cuttings placed in soil that contains spores soon die from this rot. *Euphorbia cooperi* is very susceptible, as are other varieties.

Control: Avoid splashing water from plant to plant in syringing. Take cuttings from disease-free plants to propagate in some other house.

EUPHORBIA PULCHERRIMA (POINSETTIA)

Bacterial and Fungus Diseases

Bacterial Canker (*Corynebacterium poinsettiae*). This bacterial disease, first discovered in the United States by the author in New Jersey in 1941 and more recently in Florida by Dr. D. B. Creager, appears as longitudinal, water-soaked streaks on the green stems, and as spots or blotches on the leaves. Severe infections can result in loss of leaves and death of the entire plant.

Control: Take cuttings only from healthy stock plants. Avoid syringing of greenhouse plants. Use a clean rooting medium.

Crown Gall (*Agrobacterium tumefaciens*). Occasionally bacterial galls develop at the bases of poinsettia plants.

Control: Remove and destroy affected plants. Use steam-pasteurized rooting media. Avoid wounding plants.

Gray Mold (*Botrytis cinerea*). This disease is especially serious on double varieties. In greenhouses that are kept rather cold and moist, the inflorescence is attacked by the gray mold, which causes a blasting and browning of the flower clusters and colored bracts. The mold appears in a grayish, powdery mass on the old dead parts.

Control: Spraying with a soluble copper fungicide helps to control the mold without injuring the foliage. It is more advisable, however, to prevent the mold from appearing. Raise the temperature of the house as high as practicable for good culture, and provide better ventilation.

Leaf Spot (*Xanthomonas poinsettiaecola*). This disease appears as circular to angular, chocolate-brown to rust-colored spots, 1 to 2 mm. in diameter. Infected leaves turn yellow and drop prematurely.

Control: In Florida weekly applications of tribasic copper sulfate, 4 pounds per 100 gallons of water, controlled this disease.

Root Rot (*Phymatotrichum omnivorum*). This disease has been reported from the southern states. Methods of control are difficult because of the widespread occurrence of the causal fungus.

Stem and Root Rots (*Erwinia carotovora, Pellicularia filamentosa, Pythium ultimum,* and *Thielaviopsis basicola*). These organisms account for most of the stem and root rots on greenhouse-propagated and greenhouse-grown plants. At times one or more of these cause exceptionally heavy losses in the cutting bench and after rooted cuttings are potted.

Control: Use a light, well-drained soil for potting, one which cannot become waterlogged. Do not place the pots or pans on a soil bed, but place them on a layer of coarse gravel in the bed or benches, or on bare benches. Steam-pasteurize soil to be used for potting or panning, as described in Chapter 4. Practice strict sanitation. Workers should wash hands with soap and water before working with poinsettias. The ends of the watering hose should be kept off the walks and the tools to be used in poinsettia soil should be disinfested or thoroughly scrubbed with soap and water. Use chemical treatments where an effective one is available and where facilities for steam-pasteurization are not available. PCNB (Terraclor) is effective where *Pellicularia filamentosa* (*Rhizoctonia*) is involved. A mixture of Dexon and Terraclor can be used when both *Pellicularia filamentosa* and *Pythium ultimum* are causing stem and root rot. Thiabendazole (Mertect) is effective in controlling root rot caused by *Thielaviopsis basicola*.

Rust (*Uromyces euphorbiae* [*proeminens*] var. *poinsettiae*). This rust has been reported from several southern states.

Control: Remove and destroy infected leaves.

Scab (*Sphaceloma poinsettiae*). Circular pale buff spots on the leaf veins and leaf margins and cankers on the stems (Fig. 132) are characteristic of this disease.

Control: This disease rarely becomes severe enough to warrant control measures.

Physiological Disease

Chlorosis. Yellowing of poinsettia has been reported on plants grown in soil defi-

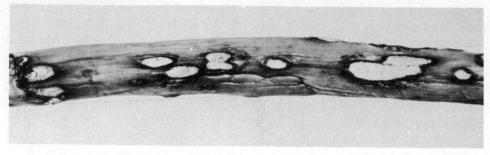

Fig. 132. Scab disease on poinsettia stem caused by the fungus *Sphaceloma poinsettiae.*

cient in certain elements necessary for the production of chlorophyll.

Control: Use a complete fertilizer.

Insects and Related Pests

Root Aphid (*Pemphigus* sp.). When large plants are potted during September and October, they are apt to become infested with root aphids. The aphids are a pale yellowish-green and surrounded by a cottony covering. They infest roots which are easily accessible, especially those just outside the earth ball. Where plants are grown in benches, the aphids infest only the roots exposed through cracks.

Control: Dust the soil ball and the inside of the pot with Diazinon. This treatment will also control ants.

Mealybugs (*Planococcus citri* and *Pseudococcus longispinus*). These pests infest the undersides of leaves and leaf axils.

Control: Remove mealybugs with a toothpick from the axils of leaves of individual plants, and wash them from the undersides of the leaves with a fine spray or water from a hose. This procedure, of course, will be satisfactory only where a few plants are infested.

Two-Spotted Mite (*Tetranychus urticae*). This species occasionally infests greenhouse-grown poinsettias.

Control: See *Althaea.*

Scales. Three species of scales—cottony-cushion, oleander, and soft—infest this host.

Control: Commercial growers use a Sulfo-tepp aerosol bomb.

EUSTOMA (TEXAS BLUEBELL)

Diseases

Stem Blight (*Sclerophoma eustomonis*). The cortical tissue becomes rotted, and in it flat, lens-shaped pycnidia are formed, embedded in a thick fungus layer. The spores of the fungus are spread by the mealybug. *Pseudococcus maritimus.* Certain narrow-leaved strains of this bluebell are reported to be highly resistant to stem blight. A species of *Alternaria* has also been associated with stem blight of this host.

Control: Ornamental specimens can be protected with copper sprays during the growing season. Malathion, applied in early spring, will control the mealybug.

Root Rot (*Fusarium solani*). This fungus causes a crown rot and damping-off.

Control: Use clean soil. Rotate plantings.

Leaf Spots (*Cercospora eustomae, C. nepheloides,* and *Phyllosticta* sp.). In Texas these three species are responsible for leaf spotting.

Control: Pick off and destroy spotted leaves.

FAGUS (BEECH)

Fungus Diseases

Leaf Spots (*Gloeosporium fagi* and *Phyllosticta faginea*). Leaf spots develop late in the growing season.

Control: Control can be achieved by spraying with copper or dithiocarbamate fungicides.

Powdery Mildew (*Microsphaera alni* and *Phyllactinia corylea*). Two species of powdery mildew fungi occasionally develop on beech leaves in late summer.

Control: Karathane, Benlate, or wettable sulfur sprays will control powdery mildews.

Bleeding Canker (*Phytophthora cactorum*). Oozing of a watery, light brown, or thick reddish-brown liquid from the bark of beech, elm, oak, and other shade trees is the principal external symptom. On dogwood the disease appears as a canker near the trunk base.

Control: No effective preventive measures are yet known. Severely infected specimens should be cut down and destroyed to prevent spreading to nearby trees. Avoid bark wounds near the base of the tree. Mildly affected trees have been known to recover.

Leaf Mottle (cause unknown). Small translucent spots surrounded by yellowish-green to white areas appear on the young unfurling leaves. These spots turn brown and dry, and by the first of June the mottling is very prominent, especially between the veins near the midrib and along the outer edge of the leaf. Within a few weeks the brown areas increase in number until the entire leaf presents a scorched appearance. A considerable part or, in some instances, all of the leaves then drop prematurely. Where complete defoliation occurs, new leaves begin to develop in July. The second set of leaves in such cases appears quite normal and drops from the trees at the normal time in the fall.

Control: Until more is known about the cause, the only recommendation that can be made is to provide adequate fertilization. The bark of particularly valuable specimens that are completely defoliated might well be protected from the midsummer sun with burlap or some other material until the second set of leaves has developed sufficiently to provide the necessary shade.

Beech Bark Disease (*Nectria coccinea* var. *faginata* and *Cryptococcus fagisuga*). This disease is caused by the combined attack of the woolly beech scale and a *Nectria* fungus. Infestations of the scale on the bark always precede those of the fungus. During August and September, countless numbers of minute, yellow, crawling larvae appear over the bark. By late autumn they settle down and secrete a white fluffy material over their bodies. This substance is very conspicuous, and the trunks and branches appear as though coated with snow. Through the feeding punctures of the insect, the *Nectria* fungus then penetrates the bark and soon kills it. The insects soon die because of the disappearance of their source of food.

Control: Because infestations of the woolly beech scale must precede fungus penetration, the eradication of the insect pest will prevent the start of the disease. Malathion sprays applied to the trunk and branches of valuable ornamental trees growing in the infested areas in early August and in September should control the young scales. A dormant lime sulfur spray applied to the trunk and branches will control overwintering adult scales. Oil sprays are also effective but are not reliably safe on beech trees.

Cankers (*Asterosporium hoffmanni, Cytospora* sp., *Phytophthora cactorum, Strumella coryneoidea, Nectria galligena,* and *N. cinnabarina*). Canker and branch dieback of beech may be caused by any one of the six fungi listed.

Control: Prune and destroy infected branches.

Insects

Aphids (*Prociphilus imbricator* and *Phyllaphis fagi*). The former, known as the beech blight aphid, is a blue insect covered with a white cottony substance. It punctures the bark and extracts the juices. The latter, called woolly beech aphid, is a cottony-covered insect, the cast skins of which adhere to the lower leaf surface.

Control: Spray with malathion or Meta-Systox R when the pests first appear in late May and repeat 2 weeks later if necessary.

Brown Wood Borer (*Parandra brunnea*). Winding galleries in the wood, made by the white-bodied, black-headed borers 1¼ inches long, and tiny holes in the bark, made by emerging shiny, brown beetles ¾ inch long, are typical signs of brown wood borer infestation. The eggs are deposited in bark crevices or in decayed wood.

Control: Infestations can be prevented to a large extent by avoiding mechanical injuries to bark and wood and by treating open wounds.

Beech Scale (*Cryptococcus fagisuga*). White masses on the bark of the trunk and lower branches, composed of tiny circular scales, ¹/₄₀ inch in diameter, are the common signs of beech scale infestation. The eggs are deposited on the bark in late June and early July, and the young crawling stage appears in August and September. The pest overwinters as a partly grown adult scale. Beech scale is primarily a pest of forest trees and is mentioned here only because of its association with the beech bark disease.

Control: See beech bark disease, above.

Two-Lined Chestnut Borer (*Agrilus bilineatus*). Trunks and branches of trees defoliated by the leaf mottle disease or those weakened by other causes are subject to attacks by the two-lined chestnut borer. Cankers of varying sizes appear on the sides of the branches exposed to the sun's rays. A dark red liquid exudes from a small puncture in the center of such cankers. The formation of several cankers along a branch reduces the sap flow and weakens the distal portions of the infested branch.

Control: Keep trees in good vigor by feeding and watering when necessary.

Scales. In addition to the scale mentioned above, beech trees are subject to the following scales: black, cottony-cushion, European fruit lecanium, oystershell, Putnam, and San Jose.

Control: Spray with malathion or Sevin when the young scales are crawling about and with dormant lime sulfur in early spring.

Caterpillars. Many caterpillars chew the leaves of beech, including the eastern tent, hemlock looper, saddled prominent, walnut, and the yellow-necked. The larval stage of the following moths also infest the leaves of this host: gypsy, imperial, io, leopard, luna, and the rusty tussock.

Control: Valuable ornamental specimens can be protected from any of these pests with *Bacillus thuringiensis,* methoxychlor, or Sevin sprays. These are most effective if applied when the caterpillars are small.

FATSIA JAPONICA

This plant is extremely susceptible to spider mites. Kelthane sprays will control these pests. Three species of scales—Florida red, green shield, and pyriform—also infest *Fatsia*. Malathion or Sevin sprays will control the crawler stage of scales.

FELICIA (BLUE DAISY)

Powdery Mildew (*Erysiphe cichoracearum*). This mildew, which is common on many species of the composite family, has been reported as attacking *Felicia* severely in some greenhouses. Infected leaves become dry, die prematurely, and fall. Numbers of the reddish-brown fruiting bodies (perithecia) develop on the older spots.

Control: Spray with Benlate, wettable sulfur, or Karathane.

FICUS ELASTICA (RUBBER-PLANT)

Diseases

Anthracnose (*Glomerella cingulata*). This disease may appear as a tip-burn, the ends of the leaves turning at first yellowish, then tan, and finally dark-brown. The scorching may extend completely around the leaf, working in from the margins until the entire leaf is destroyed. See Fig. 3. This fungus disease, shown in Fig. 133, must be clearly distinguished from the scorch and tip-burn due to unfavorable growing conditions, and from the leaf spots caused by other fungi (described below). It resembles the scorching of plants brought into apartments, where the hot, dry air, a result of steam heat and little ventilation, frequently leads to leaf-fall of varieties of *Ficus* used as house plants. Anthracnose develops pale rose-colored pustules, sometimes in zones, but usually more or less scattered along the veins. This is the asexual stage; vast quantities of spores are developed in the pustules and are easily washed away by syringing and so carried to other leaves and plants. The perfect or ascocarpic stage also develops on the leaves. The ascocarps are blackish, pear-shaped bodies within which spore sacs, each containing eight spores, are developed in considerable numbers (see Fig. 50). It has been found by experiment that slight wounds by insects, breaking of leaves, or collection of water on the leaves for considerable periods favors infection. It may be that the fungus can penetrate directly through the cuticle and epidermis. *Ficus lyrata* appears to be rather susceptible to this disease.

Control: Avoid syringing the leaves so frequently that water stays on the leaves for a considerable time. Pick off and destroy infected leaves.

Fig. 133. Anthracnose of *Ficus.*

Twig Blight and Canker (*Fusarium lateritium*). Lesions on the stems bear pink, corky bodies containing one to several septate spores. The perfect stage of this fungus is *Gibberella baccata.*

Control: Prune affected branches.

Gray Mold (*Botrytis cinerea*). In Florida this disease appears as brown leaf spots with concentric rings. The growing tips develop necrotic lesions between the leaf sheath and the newly emerging leaf.

Control: Remove infected plant parts and spray with Botran or zineb.

Leaf Spots (*Alternaria* sp., *Leptostromella elastica, Mycosphaerella bolleana, Phyllosticta roberti,* and *Phyllachora ficuum*). Five species of fungi are capable of causing leaf spots. Most of these occur in the southern states.

Control: Pick off and destroy badly spotted leaves. Fungicidal sprays are rarely used on this host. The leaf spots rarely develop on plants grown in homes because the atmosphere is much too dry to favor their spreading.

Crown Gall (*Agrobacterium tumefaciens*). This bacterial disease is found occasionally on rubber-plant.

Control: Discard infected plants.

Physiological Diseases

Leaf Scorch and Leaf Fall. This disease is often caused by faulty cultural methods and unfavorable conditions in the greenhouse. The soil in pots may become water-logged through the stopping-up of drainage; or, because of excessive drainage, it may be too dry; either of which results in balling of the root system. Excessive dryness of the air, as in steam-heated apartments, and too much exposure to direct sunlight often lead to scorching and leaf-fall. Many other varieties of plants suffer similarly when brought into apartments from the florist's shop or greenhouse. Such plants should be somewhat hardened before leaving the greenhouse.

Oedema. This trouble appears as roughened corky swellings on the petioles and on the lower leaf surfaces after exposure of the plants to excessive soil moisture with poor lighting and low temperatures.

Leaf Spot. In Florida, a leaf spot of *Ficus elastica* var. "Decora" was attributed to a lack of potassium in the soil. The addition of a nutrient solution high in potassium greatly diminished the leaf spotting.

Insects and Other Animal Pests

Mealybug (*Pseudococcus longispinus*). These insects collect in great numbers on the bases of the leaves and on the undersides of the leaf-blades; they shed much honeydew, upon which sooty mold is apt to grow and cause still further damage by cutting off the light.

Control: Spray with malathion.

Scales. Twenty-one species of scales may infest this host.

Control: Malathion or Sevin sprays applied when the young scales are crawling about are very effective. Repeat the application 10 days after the first.

Thrips. Three kinds of thrips affect rubber-plants: banded greenhouse, dracaena, and the greenhouse.

Control: Spray with Cygon or malathion when the thrips are seen.

Nemas (*Meloidogyne incognita* and *M. fici*). The former, known as the root-knot nema, infests the roots of many other plants. The latter, known as the fig nema, was found for the first time in the United States on nursery-grown *Ficus elastica* in 1954 at San Bernardino, California. The foliar nema *Aphelenchoides besseyi* was first reported to cause a leaf disease of field grown *Ficus elastica* var. "Decora" in Florida in 1966.

Control: See under Nemas, Chapter 3.

FILICES (FERNS)

Fungus Diseases

Anthracnose (*Glomerella nephrolepis*). The Boston-fern. *Nephrolepis exaltata* var. *bostonensis,* is subject to attack by this blight mold at the soft growing tips of the fronds. The ends turn brown and shrivel, marring the beauty of the plants.

Control: Regulate the temperature, moisture, and air in the greenhouse. Keep the foliage dry. Remove and destroy all diseased leaves.

Tip Blight (*Phyllosticta pteridis*). Among the various causes of tip-burn of ferns is this blight, which causes a loss of the green color of the leaves and later ash-gray spots with purple-brown margins. The fruiting bodies (pycnidia) of the fungus appear as black pimple-like spots.

Control: Spray with a diluted (1-1-50) Bordeaux mixture. Avoid wetting the foliage when watering the soil.

Leaf Spot (*Alternaria polypodii*). The brown, circular, or oblong spots are usually concentrically zonate. Infection is most common along the margin of the fronds. The chains of brown, many-celled spores are borne superficially in loose tufts and are readily scattered from plant to plant by syringing or by air currents.

Other fungi causing leaf spots on various species of ferns are: *Catacauma flabellum, Cryptomycina pteridis, Septoria asplenii, Mycosphaerella* sp., *Gloeosporium osmundae, Cercospora phyllitidis,* and *C. camptosori.*

Control: Same as for anthracnose.

Leaf Blister (*Taphrina filicina*). Definite yellow regions on both sides of the leaflets characterize this disease of the Christmas-fern, *Polystichum acrostichoides.* Spore sacs of the fungus are borne in layers near the surface of the leaf without being included in definite fruiting bodies. The same fungus also attacks the sensitive-fern, *Onoclea sensibilis,* and the wood-fern, *Dryopteris spinulosa.*

Other leaf blister fungi occur as follows: *Taphrina cystopteridis* on bladder-fern, *Cystopteris; T. faulliana* and *T. polystichi* on Christmas-fern, *Polystichum acrostichoides; T. struthiopteridis* on ostrich-fern, *Pteretis nodulosa; T. hiratsukae* on sensitive-fern, *Onoclea sensibilis;* and *T. californica, T. lutescens, T. fusca,* and *T. gracilis* on wood-fern *Dryopteris* sp.

Control: No control measures have been developed for leaf blister fungi on ferns.

Sooty Mold (*Fumago vagans*). A number of species of ferns grown in greenhouses or outdoors in the southern states may become covered with spores and mycelium of the black molds, which ordinarily grow on the honeydew secreted by scales and other sucking insects. See Fig. 134.

Fig. 134. Sooty mold *(Fumago sp.)* on *Osmunda cinnamomea.*

Control: Spray repeatedly with nicotine sulfate and soap to control the scales and other sucking insects. Ced-O-Flora sprays are also effective. Malathion sprays or aerosols may cause injury to Boston- and maidenhair-ferns. They should be used with great caution on all species of ferns.

Rusts A large number of rust fungi affect woodland ferns under natural conditions. Most of them have alternate hosts, one of the most common being firs. These diseases, however, are unimportant in the growing of ornamental ferns, and hence are not discussed in this book.

Damping-off (*Pythium* spp.). Those who propagate ferns by sowing spores are familiar with the destruction of the prothalli by damping-off, caused by two or three different species of fungi. The prothalli become soft, dark-colored, and collapse. A damping-off of the prothalli of some ferns is caused by the fungus *Completoria complens.*

Control: Sow spores in steam-pasteurized soil or on sifted sphagnum moss. The latter treatment is preferred by the author because steam-pasteurized soil is frequently overrun by the fungus *Pyronema confluens,* which prevents fern spore germination or chokes out the young plants. Wetting the soil with Dexon solution before sowing the spores is also helpful in combating damping-off.

Leaf Blotch (*Cylindrocladium pteridis*). This fungus first causes a leaf spot on *Polystichum adiantiforme.* Then reddish-brown areas are formed which coalesce to involve large areas. The fungus also affects the Boston-fern.

Control: Pick off and destroy infected fronds.

Insects and Other Animal Pests

Nemas (*Aphelenchoides fragariae*). Many species of greenhouse ferns are subject to attack by these little eelworms. The disease is easily recognized on certain ferns by the red-dish-brown or blackish bands which extend from the midribs to the borders, the spots being limited by the parallel side veins. This feature is illustrated in Fig. 34. In other kinds of ferns the spots are more or less irregular. In the bird's-nest fern, *Asplenium nidus,* the bases of the leaves first become infested, the brown discoloration extending upward until more than half of the leaf becomes involved (Fig. 40). When all the leaves in a cluster are attacked in this way, the plant usually dies. Some of the leaves may escape, and the plant may live for many months although heavily infested. By teasing out small fragments of the brown areas in water and examining them under the microscope, one readily sees the little worms moving about. They are colorless, round worms with rather sharply pointed ends (see Fig. 89).

Control: Remove and destroy infested leaves. Destroy badly infested plants. Do not throw them on compost heaps, since the worms live a long time in such debris and infest other plants grown in soil that includes material from such compost piles. Bird's-nest ferns and similar species can be freed of nemas by immersing them in hot water at a temperature of 110°F. for 10 to 15 minutes.

Fern Aphid (*Idiopterus nephrolepidis*). This small, pitch-black aphid with whitish legs and conspicuous, black, clouded areas in the wings is common on ferns in greenhouses and homes.

Control: Spray with a weaker than normal strength malathion solution (½ teaspoon per quart of water). Some ferns, such as Boston, maidenhair, and Pteris, are sensitive to malathion and other organic phosphate sprays. Ced-O-Flora sprays are also helpful.

Thrips (*Heliothrips haemorrhoidalis* and *Thrips tabaci*). In addition to the greenhouse thrips, a second species, the onion thrips, infests ferns heavily. These insects cause a brownish appearance of the fronds of *Pteris cretica.*

Control: Same as for aphids.

Scales. Seven species of scales infest ferns: fern, Florida wax, green shield, hemispherical, oleander, brown soft, and tea. Of these the brown soft scale, *Coccus hesperidum,* is perhaps the most destructive. It is reddish-brown and flat. The oleander scale, *Aspidiotus nerii,* a yellow and flat species, is also common on ferns.

Control: Malathion sprays are extremely effective against the crawler stages of all scales. Unfortunately a few kinds of ferns are sensitive to this and other organic phosphate sprays. Commercial growers and others handling a wide variety of ferns should test the malathion sprays on a few plants before using them extensively. Repeated applications of nicotine sulfate and soap also will clean up scale infestations. Since ants frequently carry young scales around, these pests should be controlled by dusting the soil surface lightly with Diazinon or Dursban.

Mealybugs. The citrus and long-tailed mealybugs also infest ferns. Controls suggested for scales will eliminate these pests.

Florida Fern Caterpillar (*Callopistria floridensis*). This caterpillar is about 2 inches in length, and varies in color from dark green to velvety black. It feeds on the fronds in greenhouses.

Control: Scatter poison bait on the soil or treat the soil surface with 2 per cent Diazinon dust.

Black Vine Weevil (*Otiorhynchus sulcatus*). The larvae feed on the rhizomes (underground stems) just below the soil level, as well as on the leaves.

Control: See *Taxus.*

Greenhouse Whitefly (*Trialeurodes vaporariorum*). These sucking insects occasionally infest leaves of ferns. Another species, *Aleyrodes nephrolepidis,* occurs on various kinds of ferns in California homes and greenhouses.

Control: See *Fuchsia.*

Fern Moth (*Euplexia benesimilis*). The green caterpillars of this moth feed on fern fronds in greenhouses and homes. The adult moth is medium-sized and is a rich, velvety maroon, mottled with gray.

Control: Spray or dust with pyrethrum or rotenone.

Other pests that also feed on ferns include armyworms; crickets; grasshoppers; Japanese beetles; the orange tortrix, *Argyrotaenia citrana;* and the yellow woolly-bear, *Diacrisia virginica.*

Control: The control for these pests is discussed under more favored hosts.

Fern Snail (*Deroceras laeve*). This naked snail is from 1/2 to 3/4 inch in length and dark gray in color. During the day it hides in the soil at the base of the plant or under pots and at night it feeds on the undersides of the leaves. It feeds on the parenchyma tissue without destroying the tissues on the upper sides. On maidenhair fern the feeding runs in strips parallel to the veins. This snail does not leave a trail of slimy mucus.

Control: Dust the soil in the vicinity of the plants with 15 per cent metaldehyde powder. Repeat in 2 weeks. Mesurol and Zectran will also control snails.

Surinam Cockroach (*Pycnoscelus surinamensis*). This species feeds at night on the leaves of bird's-nest and other ferns in greenhouses and at times causes extensive damage. The insects also feed on other plants including roses and Easter lilies. During the day they hide in crevices, beneath stones and greenhouse benches or in any dark area.

Control: Treat the infested area with Baygon, Diazinon, or Dylox.

FITTONIA

Diseases

Stem and Root Rots (*Pellicularia filamentosa* and *Pythium* sp.). The roots and stems of this host are decayed by these two species of fungi.

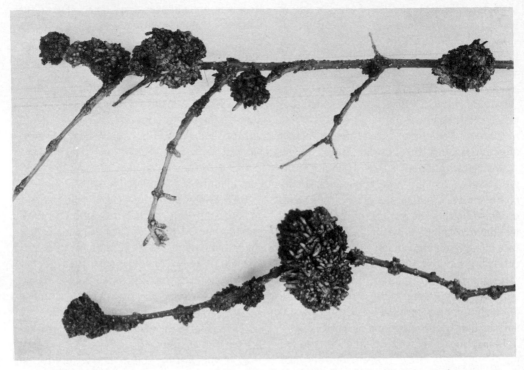

Fig. 135. Galls on *Forsythia* caused by the bacterium *Agrobacterium tumefaciens*.

Control: Use steam-pasteurized soil for starting new plants. Infected plants can sometimes be cured by immersing them in hot water at 124°F. for 30 minutes. Such plants should be hardened off before treatment. Unhardened plants should be immersed in 120°F. water. After the plants are cooled, they should be divided, or cuttings should be made and then planted or rooted in a mixture of perlite (Perl-lome) and peat. Soils infested with the two fungi should be treated with a mixture of Dexon and PCNB (Terraclor).

FORSYTHIA

Diseases

Crown Gall (*Agrobacterium tumefaciens*). Nodular abnormal growths (Fig. 135) along the stems are typical of the crown gall disease. When the galls are present in considerable numbers, the canes die back, and the bushes are unsightly after the leaves have fallen.

Control: Cut off and discard all canes and branches that bear galls.

Leaf Spots (*Alternaria* sp., *Phyllosticta discincola*, *P. forsythiae*, and *P. terminalis*). The leaves of forsythia may be spotted by these four fungi.

Control: Pick off and destroy spotted leaves. Copper or dithiocarbamate sprays will prevent leaf spots, but they are rarely used on this host.

Dieback (*Sclerotinia sclerotiorum*). This fungus first invades blossoms and flower stalks, then grows into the twigs and kills them for some distance. The black sclerotia develop either on the surface or inside the infected twigs.

Control: Prune and destroy dead twigs and stems.

Insects and Other Animal Pests

Four-Lined Plant Bug (*Poecilocapsus lineatus*). This insect makes characteristic tan circles in the leaves.
Control: Spray with Sevin when the bugs begin to feed.
Japanese Weevil (*Pseudocneorhinus bifasciatus*).
Control: See *Ligustrum*.
Other Pests. The northern root-knot nema, *Meloidogyne hapla*, and spider mites also infest forsythias.

FRANKLINIA[20] (FRANKLIN-TREE)

Diseases

Leaf Spot (*Phyllosticta gordoniae*). Spots on the leaves of this host occasionally occur in rainy seasons.
Control: Valuable specimens can be sprayed with copper or dithiocarbamate fungicides.
Black Mildew (*Meliola cryptocarpa*). In the Deep South leaves of Franklin-tree may be covered by this black fungus.
Control: Measures are rarely adopted to control this fungus.
Wilt and Dieback (*Phytophthora* spp.). Rutgers University plant pathologists recently found that container-grown Franklin-trees are rather subject to this disease. Affected trees wilt suddenly followed by defoliation and death. Cankers develop along the stem or near the soil line.
Control: Monthly application of Banrot is said to provide control.

Insects

Scales. The red bay scale, *Chrysomphalus*

[20] The Franklin-tree, *Franklinia alatamaha*, was formerly called *Gordonia alatamaha*.

perseae, infests *Franklinia* and many other species of trees particularly in the more southerly parts of the country. The author has found an undescribed species of scale on this host.
Control: Spray with Diazinon, malathion, or Sevin in mid-May to control the crawler stage. Repeat in 2 to 3 weeks.

FRAXINUS (ASH)

Diseases

Rust (*Puccinia sparganioides*). The leaves of green and red ash are conspicuously distorted and the twigs are swollen by this fungus. The spores of the fungus, yellow powder in minute cups, appear over the swollen areas. The spores produced on ash are incapable of reinfecting ash, but infect the so-called "marsh and cord" grasses.
Control: The disease is rarely destructive enough to warrant special control measures. Sulfur sprays can be used where the disease is serious on valuable specimens.
Leaf Spots (*Gloeosporium aridum*). This fungus causes leaf spot and leaf scorch in rainy springs. Large areas of the leaf, especially along the edges, turn brown. Premature leaf-fall may result.

Other leaf spotting fungi on ash are *Cercospora fraxinites, C. lumbricoides, C. texensis, Cylindrosporium fraxini, Mycosphaerella effigurata, Phyllosticta fraxinicola, Septoria besseyi, S. leucostoma,* and *S. submaculata*.
Control: Gather and destroy fallen leaves. This practice is usually sufficient to keep leaf spot diseases at a minimum. Where the disease was severe the previous year and spring conditions remain wet, spray with captan or zineb 2 or 3 times at 10-day intervals beginning when the buds start to open.
Cankers (*Cytospora annularis, Diplodia infuscans, Dothiorella fraxinicola, Nectria cinnabarina, N. coccinea,* and *Sphaeropsis* sp.). At least six fungi cause branch and trunk cankers on ash.

Control: Prune out infected branches. Maintain trees in good condition by proper feeding, watering, and spraying.

Dieback (cause unknown). In the northeastern United States, white ash has been affected by a branch dieback and, since 1940, occasional death of the tree. The primary cause of this disease has not been clearly established, although a ringspot-like virus has been associated with it by Dr. Craig Hibben of the Brooklyn Botanic Garden. The virus was transmitted both by grafting and by nemas.

Control: No controls have been developed.

Witches' Broom (mycoplasma-like organism). More recently Dr. Hibben was successful in transmitting the mycoplasma-like organism from declining white ash trees by means of the parasitic flowering plant known as dodder (*Cuscuta*).

Control: No control is known.

Insects and Related Pests

Ash Borer (*Podesesia syringae fraxini*). This borer attacks ash and mountain-ash in the Prairie States. It burrows into the tree trunk at or just below the soil line.

Control: Cut out and destroy severely infested trees. Methoxychlor spray applied around the trunk when the adult moths are depositing eggs may be helpful.

Lilac Borer (*Podesesia syringae syringae*). Rough knot-like swellings on the trunk and limbs and the breaking of small branches at the point of injury are indications of the presence of the lilac borer, a brown-headed, white-bodied larva ³/₄ inch long. The adult female appearing in early fall is a moth with clear wings having a spread of 1¹/₂ inches, the front pair of which is deep brown. The larvae pass the winter underneath the bark.

Control: Spray the trunk and main branches with methoxychlor in early May and repeat twice at 2-week intervals.

Carpenter Worm (*Prionoxystus robiniae*). Large scars along the trunk, especially in crotches, and irregularly circular galleries about ¹/₂ inch in diameter, principally in the heartwood, are produced by a 3-inch, pinkish-white caterpillar, the carpenter worm. The adult moth, with wingspread of nearly 3 inches, deposits eggs in crevices or rough spots on the bark during June and early July. A period of 3 years is necessary to complete the life cycle.

Control: Spray or paint bark of trunk and main branches with methoxychlor in late June and repeat twice at 2-week intervals. Inject commercial borer paste such as Bortox into burrows and seal openings.

Other Borers. Many other borers infest ash. Among the more common are brown wood, California prionus, flatheaded apple tree, and the Pacific flatheaded borer. State entomologists will supply spraying dates and other information necessary to control these pests.

Brown-Headed Ash Sawfly (*Tomostethus multicinctus*). Trees may be completely defoliated in May or early June by yellow sawfly larvae. The adult is a bee-like insect that lays eggs in the outer leaf margins. Winter is passed in the pupal stage in the ground.

Control: Spray with Diazinon about the middle of May.

Fall Webworm (*Hyphantria cunea*). In fall webworm infestations, the leaves are chewed in August and September and the branches are covered with webs or nests, which enclose skeletonized leaves and pale-yellow or green caterpillars 1 inch long. The adult moth has white- to brown-spotted wings with a spread of 1¹/₂ inches.

Control: Cut out or remove nests, or spray the tree throughly with *Bacillus thuringiensis,* Diazinon, Dylox, or Sevin when the webs are first visible.

Lilac Leaf Miner (*Gracillaria syringella*). Light yellow, ¹/₄-inch larvae first mine the

Fig. 136. Flower-gall of ash caused by the mite *Aceria fraxinivorus.*

leaves of ash, deutzia, privet, and lilac and then roll and skeletonize the leaves. Small moths emerge from overwintering cocoons in the soil in May to deposit eggs on the underside of the leaves. A second brood emerges in July.

Control: Spray with Diazinon or malathion before larvae curl the leaves. Repeat in mid-July.

Ash Flower-Gall (*Aceria fraxinivorus*). This disease is caused by small mites which attack the staminate flowers of the white ash. The flowers develop abnormally and form very irregular galls up to ½ inch in diameter (Fig. 136). These galls dry out, forming clusters which are conspicuous on the trees during the winter.

Control: Kelthane spray applied after the buds swell and before the new growth emerges in spring will provide control.

Oystershell Scale (*Lepidosaphes ulmi*). Masses of brown bodies shaped like an oystershell and about ¹/₁₀ inch long, covering twigs and branches, are characteristic of this insect. The pests overwinter in the egg stage under the scales. The young crawling stage appears in late May.

Control: Spray in late spring, before the buds open, with 1 part concentrated lime sulfur in 10 parts of water, or with dormant oil plus ethion according to the directions of the manufacturer. Malathion or Sevin sprays applied when the young are crawling about in May and June also give control.

Scurfy Scale (*Chionaspis furfura*). A grayish scurfy covering on the bark indicates the presence of this pest. The scale covering the adult female is pear-shaped, gray, and about ¹/₁₀ inch long. The pest overwinters as purple eggs under the female scale.

Control: Spray in late spring, before the leaf buds open, with dormant oil plus ethion, or in mid-May and again in early June with malathion or Sevin.

Japanese Weevil. See *Ligustrum*.
Linden Looper. See *Tilia*.

FREESIA

Diseases

Bacterial Scab (*Pseudomonas marginata*). Bacteria similar to those that cause scab of gladiolus have been isolated from reddish or dark-brown spots on the husks. The disease has been reported from Long Island, New York, and Washington (state).

Control: See *Gladiolus*.

Iris Leaf Spot (*Didymellina macrospora*). On freesia leaves, spots resembling those on the more common host, iris, are produced. The imperfect stage of this fungus is known as *Heterosporium iridis*.

Control: See *Iris*.

Wilt (*Fusarium oxysporum* var. *lilii.*). The first symptoms of this disease are a yellowing and wilting of the leaves, which collapse and die. The dead foliage is light yellowish or white. The disease attacks the tops, main roots, and rootlets, which may have the pink coloration characteristic of these fungi. Yellowish-brown spots develop on the surface of the corms, which later undergo a dry, crumbly rot. The roots may remain firm even when infected. The dark brown discoloration which first appears at the center of the corm spreads through the water-conducting vessels of the stem.

Control: See bulb rot, under *Lilium*.

Dry Rot (*Stromatinia gladioli*). See *Gladiolus*.

Mosaic (Iris mosaic virus). The same mosaic that affects iris is occasionally found on this host.

Control: Remove and destroy affected plants.

Insects and Other Animal Pests

Lily Aphid (*Neomyzus circumflexus*). Greenhouse-grown freesias may be attacked by the crescent-marked lily aphid.

Control: Spray with malathion.

Bulb Mite (*Rhizoglyphus echinopus*). This mite may infest freesia corms, causing a soft, mushy decay.

Control: See *Tulipa*.

Thrips. See *Gladiolus*.

Southern Root-Knot Nema (*Meloidogyne incognita*). This nema is occasionally reported as serious in freesia plantings in California.

Control: See Nemas, Chapter 3.

Tulip Bulb Aphid. See *Iris*.

FRITILLARIA

A leaf spot caused by the fungus *Phyllosticta fritillariae*, a rust by *Uromyces miurae*, and an undetermined mosaic virus are the only diseases reported on this host.

The lily weevil also attacks *Fritillaria*. See *Lilium*.

FUCHSIA

Diseases

Blight (*Botrytis cinerea*). Leaves are blighted and then covered with a gray mold when plants are overcrowded or grown under conditions of high humidity and poor ventilation.

Control: Cut off and put infected parts into the trash can.

Rootlet Rot (*Pythium rostratum* and *P. ultimum*). The finer roots are killed by these two species of *Pythium*.

Control: Use well-drained, fresh soil, or steam-pasteurized old, infested soil. Soil drenched with Dexon will also control these fungi.

Rusts (*Pucciniastrum epilobii* and *Uredo fuchsiae*). The former has been reported from the West Coast and the latter from Ohio.

Control: Pick off and destroy infected leaves.

Wilt (*Verticillium* sp.). In California this fungus is rather prevalent in outdoor fuchsias.

Control: Take cuttings only from healthy plants. Use steam-pasteurized soils to grow young plants.

Other Fungus Diseases. A dieback caused by a species of *Phomopsis,* a leaf spot by *Septoria* sp., and a root rot by *Phytophthora parasitica* are among the other fungus diseases reported on *Fuchsia.*

Virus (Tomato spotted wilt virus). This virus occurs occasionally on outdoor plantings of fuchsia in California.

Control: Remove and destroy infested plants. Do not plant fuchsias near other plants susceptible to spotted wilt.

Insects and Other Animal Pests

Aphids. Three species of aphids attack this host: crescent-marked lily, ornate, and potato aphids.

Control: Spray with malathion or Meta-Systox R.

Beetles. The Fuller rose, the strawberry flea, and Japanese beetles chew the leaves of fuchsias.

Control: Spray weekly with malathion or Sevin, starting when the beetles begin to feed.

Mealybugs. The citrus and long-tailed mealybugs infest greenhouse-grown fuchsias.

Control: Spray with malathion.

Mites. Four species of mites attack this host: privet, broad, cyclamen, and two-spotted.

Control: Use a miticide such as Aramite, chlorobenzilate, or Kelthane when the pests are first observed and repeat within 10 days.

Scales. Three scales are known to infest fuchsias: black, California red, and greedy.

Control: Same as for mealybugs.

Greenhouse Thrips (*Heliothrips haemorrhoidalis*). The greenhouse thrips make a "pepper-and-salt" pattern on the leaves.

Control: Spray with malathion as soon as the thrips are first observed and repeat, if necessary, within 10 days.

Greenhouse Whitefly (*Trialeurodes vaporariorum*). The greenhouse whitefly can become one of the most serious pests of greenhouse-grown fuchsias. The nymphs are pearly white and closely attached to the lower leaf surfaces. The adults are pure white, small flies that dart away swiftly when the leaves are disturbed.

Control: Both the adult and nymphal stages can be controlled by spraying with 1 teaspoon of a 10 per cent synthetic pyrethroid, Resmethrin, per gallon of water. Three applications at 2-week intervals are necessary. This chemical is available in aerosol cans under the name Pratt White Fly Spray.

Other Insect. In California the iris whitefly, *Aleyrodes spiraeoides,* infests fuchsias in addition to its favorite host, iris.

Southern Root-Knot Nema (*Meloidogyne incognita*). This nema can become quite destructive to the roots of greenhouse-grown fuchsias.

Control: See Nemas, Chapter 3.

FUNKIA—see HOSTA

FURCRAEA

Many of the diseases and insect pests found on *Agave* also attack *Furcraea.* Occasionally, if the plants have not received sufficient amount of water or have been grown at too low a temperature, large white spots with purple-brown borders develop on the leaves. Each spot develops on both sides of the leaf so that all the green tissue collapses and only the fibrous part remains. The only remedy required is to supply sufficient moisture and heat. See Fig. 27. A somewhat similar effect has been seen when lilies grown at high temperature in greenhouses are sprayed with nicotine sulfate. The spots due to spray injury are soon evident on both sides of the leaf.

Southern Root-Knot Nema (*Meloidogyne incognita*). The roots of *Furcraea gigantea* were found to be infested by this nema in Maryland.

GAILLARDIA

Diseases

Leaf Spot (*Septoria gaillardiae*). In the Middle West and South, the leaves may be spotted by this fungus.

Control: Spray with a copper or dithiocarbamate fungicide if the disease becomes prevalent.

Powdery Mildews (*Erysiphe cichoracearum* and *Sphaerotheca humuli* var. *fuliginea*). Two species of mildew fungi attack this host forming a white, moldy coating over the leaves.

Control: Where serious, mildews can be controlled with Benlate or Karathane sprays.

Rust (*Uredo gaillardiae*). This rust has been reported from California.

Control: Pick off and destroy infected leaves.

Smut (*Entyloma polysporum*). Light-colored spots in the leaves are caused by this fungus.

Control: As a rule, no control measures are necessary.

Virus. The tomato spotted wilt virus occurs on gaillardia in California.

Control: Spray with malathion to control the insect vectors.

Aster Yellows. This disease also affects gaillardia.

Control: The same as for the tomato spotted wilt virus.

Insects

Leafhopper (*Macrosteles fascifrons*). The adult insects, grayish in color and up to 1/8 inch in length, spread the aster yellows mycoplasma.

Control: See *Callistephus.*

Four-Lined Plant Bug (*Poecilocapsus lineatus*). In early summer this rather large leaf-bug becomes a pest on *Gaillardia.*

Control: Spray with Diazinon, Meta-Systox R, or Sevin.

Thrips. The flower and onion thrips occasionally infest this host.

Control: Spray with Cygon or malathion.

Other Pests. The Asiatic garden beetle, *Maladera castanea,* and the Japanese beetle, *Popillia japonica,* also infest *Gaillardia.* Spraying with Sevin, methoxychlor or Diazinon at the time the beetles are feeding will provide control.

The stalk borer, *Papaipema nebris,* is occasionally troublesome. See *Dahlia.*

Gaillardias are among the hosts injured by wire worms, or click beetles (*Elateridae*).

GALANTHUS (SNOWDROP)

Diseases

Gray Mold (*Botrytis galanthina*). The sclerotial stage of this fungus, *Sclerotinia galanthina,* has been found on bulbs imported from abroad.

Control: Before planting, remove the outer scales which contain the small black sclerotia.

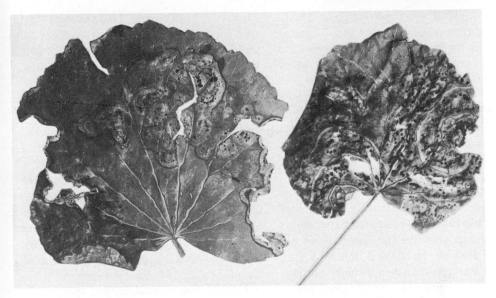

Fig. 137. Spots on *Galax* leaves caused by the fungus *Pezizella oenotherae.*

Insects and Other Pests

Narcissus Bulb Fly (*Merodon equestris*). The larvae of this fly occasionally infest *Galanthus* bulbs.

Control: See *Narcissus.*

Stem and Bulb Nema (*Ditylenchus dipsaci*).

Control: See *Narcissus.*

GALAX

Leaf Spots. A spot caused by *Phyllosticta galactis* is apt to develop seriously on leaves and plants kept in cold storage. In North Carolina, plants in the wild show the destructive effect of the fungus *Pezizella oenotherae*, which causes large irregular spots with light gray centers and darker brown borders. The amber-colored fruiting bodies of the parasite develop on the gray centers (Fig. 137). Later, as the leaves die, rather large, flat, closed pycnidia are formed. Another leaf spot is caused by *Laestadia galactina* and a black spot by *Clypeolella leemingii.*

Control: These diseases rarely become destructive enough to necessitate control practices.

GARDENIA JASMINOIDES (GARDENIA)

Algal, Bacterial, and Fungus Diseases

Canker (*Diaporthe gardeniae*). Conspicuous symptoms are the wilting, yellowing, shriveling, and falling of the leaves of infected plants, and frequently the falling of flower buds before they have opened. The cankers girdle the stems. Even partial girdling results in stunting of the plants. Oblong cankers develop on branches and stems not in contact with the soil. The woody cylinder is sometimes exposed at the point of infection, or the bark is rough and corrugated. Cankers on the crowns become overgrown with corky tissue extending longitudinally in both directions from the point of infection, increasing the diameter to twice the normal size or more. These overgrowths are confined to parts in contact with the soil where moisture is available. The imperfect stage, *Phomopsis gardeniae,* develops its black fruiting bodies on the lesions; two kinds of spores are formed, one small and roundish, the other long and thread-like.

Control: The author was the first to show that the fungus frequently enters the host through leaf joints at the base of cuttings set in the rooting bed. The freshly cut leaf bases afford an excellent point of entrance. The rooting medium, sand and peat, should be steam-pasteurized. Dipping the stems in ferbam solution before imbedding the cuttings might help to reduce infections. Experiments have shown also that the fungus gains entrance through mechanical injuries; care should therefore be taken to make cuttings with a sharp knife and to avoid ragged edges. Injuries due to careless cultural practices should be avoided.

Leaf Spots. The leaves of gardenias may be spotted by several fungi and an alga. A species of *Pellicularia* (*Rhizoctonia*) first spots the lower leaves. Upward spread of the spotting occurs only when the plants are kept very wet or are overcrowded. The midribs and petioles of the leaves are sometimes attacked, which causes the death of the leaves. The spots vary in size up to 1/4 inch in diameter; they are more or less circular and marked by zones (Fig. 138). The variety "Pride of Daisy Hill" seems to be most susceptible to this disease, but other varieties have been shown not to be immune. Other fungi which cause leaf spots are *Mycosphaerella gardeniae, Pestalotia langloisii,* and a species of *Phyllosticta.* The alga *Cephaleuros virscens* causes spotting of gardenias in the Gulf States.

Control: The *Pellicularia* leaf spot can be controlled by picking off and destroying infected leaves, by providing sufficient space between plants, and by not wetting the leaves during watering. The other leaf spots are

Fig. 138. Spots on gardenia leaves caused by the fungus *Pellicularia* sp. (*Rhizoctonia*).

Fig. 139. Effect on gardenia leaves of infection by the bacterium *Pseudomonas gardeniae:* more-or-less circular spots with light water-soaked margins.

rarely serious enough to warrant control measures.

Bacterial Leaf Spots (*Pseudomonas gardeniae* and *Xanthomonas maculifolliigardeniae*). The first bacterium listed produces large, circular spots on leaves of eastern plants (Fig. 139). The first case of this disease was discovered by the author in 1938. The second bacterium causes smaller, more angular spots, principally in greenhouses in the western United States.

Control: Avoid wetting the foliage, space plants widely, and aerate the houses.

Bud Rot (*Botrytis cinerea*). This fungus rots the buds of greenhouse-grown plants in the eastern United States, and those of outdoor plants in California.

Control: Pick off and destroy infected buds.

Powdery Mildew (*Erysiphe polygoni*). This disease occurs on gardenias in Texas.

Control: Severe cases can be treated with sprays containing Karathane, Benlate, or wettable sulfur.

Physiological Diseases

Chlorosis. This important disease of gardenias is due to cultural conditions. The plants prefer a light, open, slightly acid soil; heavy clay is unfavorable. Excessive lime restricts the root action by killing the tips. Plants with chlorosis due to a deficiency of iron (Fig. 140) do not necessarily lose their leaves, but lack of iron retards the growth, particularly of young plants.

Control: Chlorosis due to a deficiency or unavailability of iron can be cured by applying to the soil so-called iron chelates in water solution. The rate is 0.2 gram for each plant in a 4-inch pot, or 14 ounces for each 100 square feet of bench space. The yellow leaves should begin to "green up" within 2 weeks after the application. If the leaves remain green, no additional applications are necessary.

Bud Drop (Nonparasitic). Flower buds turn yellow and drop off, usually just before they open, because the atmosphere in the home is too dry, too warm, and there is insufficient light.

Control: In winter, place the gardenia in a cool, well-lighted room. Increasing the hu-

Fig. 140. Gardenia leaves showing chlorosis due to an iron deficiency. (Geigy Co.)

midity around the plant will also help to reduce the amount of bud drop.

Dieback. Loss of leaves and dying back of branches of greenhouse-grown gardenias has been attributed to root smothering resulting from overwatering.

Insects and Other Animal Pests

Mealybugs. The citrus and the longtailed mealybugs frequently infest the leaves of gardenias. These white pests may be mistaken for fungi by amateur gardeners.

Control: Spray with malathion or Cygon from time to time as the mealybugs appear.

Scales. The Florida wax, green shield, and soft scales attack this host.

Control: Same as for mealybugs.

Thrips. The banded greenhouse and the flower thrips cause speckling of gardenia leaves.

Control: See mealybugs.

Other Insects. Occasionally gardenias are attacked by the Fuller rose beetle, the greenhouse orthezia, and the citrus whitefly. The sooty mold fungus grows on the honeydew secreted by the last. Occasionally mites may infest the leaves. These are controlled with a miticide.

Southern Root-Knot Nema (*Meloidogyne incognita*). This nema is particularly severe on greenhouse-grown gardenias in the northeastern United States. Affected plants do not grow to normal height and the leaves may be mottled.

Control: See Nemas in Chapter 3.

GARRYA

Leaf Spots. Three fungi cause leaf spots of *Garrya elliptica* in California and Texas: *Cercospora garryae*, *Dothichiza garryae*, and *Phyllosticta garryae*. Root rot caused by *Phymatotrichum omnivorum* is recorded from Texas.

GAULTHERIA (WINTERGREEN)

The principal diseases of this host are leaf spots caused by the following fungi: *Cercospora gaultheriae*, *Discosia maculicola*, *Mycosphaerella gaultheriae*, *Phyllosticta gaultheriae*, *Pestalotia gibbosa*, *Schizothyrium gaultheriae*, and *Venturia gaultheriae*. Other diseases include black mildew caused by *Meliola nidulans*, red leaf gall by *Synchytrium vaccinii*, and powdery mildew by *Microsphaera alni*.

Control: These diseases rarely occur on plants used for ornament. Picking off and placing infected leaves in the trash can, usually suffices as a control measure.

GELSEMIUM (YELLOW JESSAMINE)

The foliage of *G. sempervirens* is occasionally spotted by *Phyllosticta gelsemii* and *Asterina stomatophora*. Twigs may be cankered by *Nectria rubicarpa, Physalospora obtusa,* and *P. rhodina.*

GENISTA (BROOM)

Diseases

A dieback caused by a species of *Diplodia,* a powdery mildew by *Erysiphe polygoni,* and a rust by *Uromyces genistaetinctoriae* are the only fungus diseases recorded on this host.

Insects

The bean aphid *Aphis fabae,* the greedy and oleander scales, and the genista caterpillar, *Tholeria reversalis,* attack broom. The last is orange-green with black and white markings. It webs the foliage and may completely defoliate plants.

Control: Malathion sprays will control all these pests.

GENTIANA (GENTIAN)

Fungus Diseases

Blight (*Botrytis cinerea*). Very light brown spots or blotches with darker borders are the first symptoms of this disease. Cankers may also form on the stem.

Control: Remove and destroy infected parts.

Leaf Spots (*Cercospora gentianae* and *Mycosphaerella andrewsii*). Two fungi are capable of causing leaf spots on this host. The fungus *Asteromella andrewsii,* also commonly reported on gentian, is believed to be the conidial stage of the *Mycosphaerella.*

Control: Valuable plantings in wild gardens can be protected with occasional applications of copper or dithiocarbamate sprays.

Root Rot (*Fusarium solani*). This soil-infesting fungus has been reported from Maryland.

Control: Use clean soil or treat infested soil with heat as described in Chapter 4.

Rusts (*Puccinia gentianae* and *Uromyces eugentianae*). Two species of rust fungi occur on this host. The former first appears as yellow spots which turn dark brown when the rust pustules break open. The disease progresses from the basal leaves toward the top.

Control: Destroy infected plants.

GERANIUM[21] (CRANESBILL)

Bacterial and Fungus Diseases

Bacterial Leaf Spots (*Pseudomonas erodii* and *Xanthomonas pelargonii*). Two species of bacteria may affect plants grown in borders and rock gardens.

Control: Pick off and destroy spotted leaves.

Leaf Spots (*Botrytis cinerea, Cercospora geranii, Dilophosphora geranii, Pestalozziella subsessilis, Phyllosticta geranii, Ramularia geranii, Septoria expansa, Venturia glomerata,* and *V. circinans*). Only a few of the nine fungi listed ever appear on cultivated species of cranesbill.

Control: Remove and destroy spotted leaves as they appear.

Rusts (*Puccinia leveillei, P. polygoniamphibii,* and *Uromcyces geranii*). Three species of rust are common on wild forms. Occasionally they may appear on cultivated kinds.

Control: Remove and destroy infected leaves.

Other Diseases. A downy mildew caused by *Plasmopara geranii,* two powdery mildews by *Erysiphe polygoni* and *Sphaerotheca humuli,* and a leaf gall by *Synchytrium geranii* may occur on *Geranium.*

---

[21] For the greenhouse or florists' geranium, see under *Pelargonium.*

Virus Disease

Mosaic (Cucumber mosaic virus). This virus was reported on *Geranium* from Florida.

Control: Remove and destroy infected plants.

Insect

Four-Lined Plant Bug (*Poecilocapsus lineatus*). Cranesbill is a favored host of this bug.

Control: See *Aconitum*.

GERBERA (TRANSVAAL DAISY)

Diseases

Blight (*Botrytis cinerea*). This disease, also referred to as gray mold, has been recorded on *Gerbera,* from New York and Florida.

Control: Remove and destroy infected parts.

Leaf Spot (*Gloeosporium* sp.). A fungus that causes leaf spot and stem rot has been reported from New York.

Control: Same as for blight.

Powdery Mildew (*Erysiphe cichoracearum*). This fungus has been reported on *Gerbera* in California and Oklahoma and probably exists elsewhere in this country.

Control: Spray with Benlate or Karathane if the disease becomes prevalent.

Ray Speck (*Alternaria dauci* var. *solani*). A severe speckling of ray florets has been reported from two Florida nurseries. The specks are brown, at first circular, and later becoming elongate up to 1.5 mm. in length.

Control: No control measures are known.

Root Rot (*Phytophthora cryptogea*). See *Callistephus.*

Insects and Other Pests

Mites (*Polyphagotarsonemus latus* and *Steneotarsonemus pallidus*). Greenhouse-grown *Gerbera* are quite subject to the broad mite and the cyclamen mite.

Control: Spray with Dimite, chlorobenzilate, or Kelthane.

Southern Root-Knot Nema (*Meloidogyne incognita*). This nema is occasionally serious on *Gerbera.*

Control: Use clean or steam-pasteurized soil. Infested plants can be freed of the pests with hot water. Immerse bare-root plants in water heated to 118°F. for 20 minutes.

GINKGO

Ginkgo, also known as maidenhair-tree, is unusually resistant to fungus and insect attack. A fungitoxic substance, α-hexenal, is believed to be responsible for its resistance to fungus diseases. Leaf spots have been attributed to three fungi: *Glomerella cingulata, Phyllosticta ginkgo,* and *Epicoccum purpurascens.* The damage by these fungi is negligible. In 1966 the author isolated a bacterium from another leaf spot (Fig. 141) but was unable to prove definitely that it was responsible for the spotting. In Czechoslovakia a similar disease is attributed to a virus.

Several wood decay fungi, including *Polyporus hirsutus, P. lacteus, P. tulipiferus, P. versicolor,* and *Fomes meliae,* have also been reported, but these are of rare occurrence.

Insects and Other Pests

Few insects attack the tree. Among those occasionally found are the omnivorous looper *Sabulodes caberata,* the grape mealybug *Pseudococcus maritimus,* the white-marked tussock moth *Hemerocampa leucostigma,* and the fruit tree leaf roller *Archips argyrospilus.*

The southern root-knot nema *Meloidogyne incognita* has been reported on Ginkgo in Mississippi.

Fig. 141. Leaf spot of *Ginkgo biloba,* the cause of which is unknown.

GLADIOLUS

Bacterial Diseases

Bacterial Blight (*Xanthomonas gummisudans*). This disease is especially serious in wet weather or on plants grown in poorly drained soils. The infected areas are first evident as irregular water-soaked spots, which later dry out and turn brown. The whole leaf may finally become involved and die. On the infected parts a slimy exudate may accumulate in which particles of soil become glued together. These symptoms are similar to those of scab under certain conditions.

Control: Treat corms as for the scab disease discussed below.

Scab (*Pseudomonas marginata*). This disease, also known as neck rot and stem rot, is common on gladiolus and on tigridia. Pale yellow, water-soaked circular lesions appear on the corms. These eventually turn brown or nearly black, become sunken with raised brittle margins that are scab-like, and exude a gummy substance. Early symptoms on the leaves are reddish raised specks near their bases. As the disease progresses, the neck or fleshy basal parts rot so that the leaves fall over like that of an iris plant affected by bacterial soft rot.

Control: Discard corms that show disease symptoms. Plant healthy corms in a new area. The bulb mite *Rhizoglyphus echinopus* is associated with the severity of scab.

Soft Rot (*Erwinia carotovora*). A soft rot of gladiolus corms was reported from Michigan.

Control: Remove and destroy all rotted corms.

Fungus Diseases

Corm Rots (*Penicillium gladioli* and *Rhizopus arrhizus*). The Penicillium storage rot of corms is introduced only through mechanical injury. The decay is corky, with sunken lesions; these are reddish brown, and at low temperatures become covered with the green mold of the fungus. The infection usually originates where the husks are attached to the corms. This causes a series of infection rings which eventually carry the disease upward and downward. Numerous light-brown minute sclerotia about the size of bulb mites serve to carry the fungus bodies through unfavorable conditions. They retain their vitality for several months, being surrounded by layers of thick-walled cells.

Control: In handling the corms care should be taken to avoid wounding. They should be stored in a cool, dry cellar with the temperature ranging from 35 to 45°F. to prevent initial infection. Prompt curing and drying of corms is urgent. Freshly harvested corms should be cured at about 85°F. for 10 or 15 days. Dipping the corms in Benlate (2 tablespoonfuls per gallon of warm water, 80 to 85°F.) for 15 to 30 minutes will also provide some control of Penicillium corm rots. The corms should be dried after treatment.

Hard Rot (*Septoria gladioli*). The symptoms of hard and dry rot are much the same. To distinguish the two diseases it is often necessary to cultivate the fungus found in the lesions and examine the fruiting bodies microscopically. Doubtless both species may be present in a corm at the same time. The little black, pear-shaped fruiting bodies of the *Septoria* of hard rot contain long, colorless, septate spores, while the sclerotia of dry rot are solid, hard structures. Both rots develop in storage and mummify the corms. Hard rot is not so deeply seated as is dry rot, but the scabs or lesions which result from both diseases are much deeper than the scabs of the bacterial disease. The *Septoria* causes circular leaf spots, varying from brown to purplish-brown, especially on seedlings and plants that have been developed from cormels, less commonly on plants developed

from old corms. The lower part of the corm is usually most severely attacked.

Control: Discard all badly infected corms and, if possible, plant clean corms in clean fields. It may be possible to kill the fungus in corms that are not badly infected by dipping them in a suspension made by mixing 2 ounces of Tersan 75 per gallon of water. Dry the corms before storing them. For leaf spot of seedlings or first-year plants, spray with a copper fungicide.

The *Rhizopus* rot, a relatively new disease, causes a light brown decay of freshly harvested corms that have been heat-cured at 85 to 95 degrees F. and then stored under humid conditions.

Control: Improve drying and curing practices.

Dry Rot (*Stromatinia gladioli*). This disease can be distinguished from hard rot and scab in the later stages of infection by the presence of many small, hard, black sclerotia which develop on the leaf bases and the husks of the corms. The spots on the corms are usually more or less circular and sunken, but have no shining or gummy surface like those of scab. The brown or black lesions or scabs that appear on the corms may run together and destroy the whole corm, especially in moist storage rooms. The infected corms finally become mummified and black. Corms that appear normal when first dug may develop dry rot in storage rooms that are too moist; this is less apt to happen to well-cured corms. The husks or leaf bases of infected plants are snuff-colored and brittle. This brown discoloration is often a good symptom of the disease. In the fields, leaves from infected corms turn yellow and decay at the base (Fig. 142). Roots do not develop well on new corms. This disease is not serious during dry seasons. It is interesting that this ascomycete provided the first demonstration that the minute conidia (spermatia) bring about fertilization in sexual reproduction. The fruiting bodies that develop after fertilization are

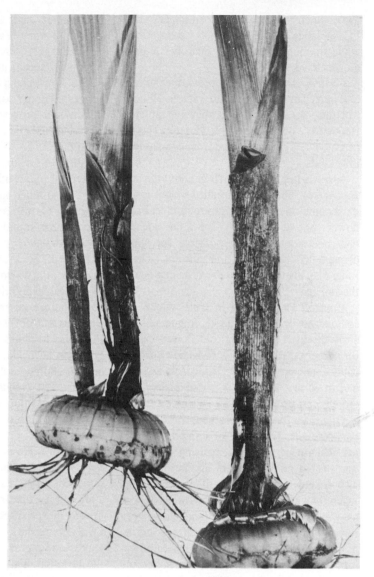

Fig. 142. Gladiolus stem decay caused by the dry rot fungus *Stromatinia gladioli*. (Union Carbide)

light brown, disc-shaped structures on short stalks. By cutting through the discs and examining them with a microscope one may see hundreds of spore sacs, the asci, each containing eight spores. This stage is often called the "perfect" or sexual stage. This fungus also attacks crocus and freesia.

Control: Use a new planting area each year, or steam-pasteurize soil. In Florida, Botran-treated soil provides control.

Stemphylium Leaf Blight (*Stemphylium* sp.). One of the newest diseases of gladiolus, particularly of Florida-grown plants, causes small, round, translucent, pale yellow spots on the leaves. The centers of the spots are reddish-brown; hence the name "redspot" given to it by commercial growers. The blight was first observed in Florida plants around 1940, and it caused serious damage to gladioli in New Jersey and New York in 1946 and

1947. Such varieties as "Stoplight" and "Casablanca" are extremely susceptible, while the popular variety "Picardy" is only moderately so.

Control: Dithane D-14 plus zinc sulfate and lime, Dithane Z-78, and Parzate all control this disease provided they are applied frequently. Very susceptible varieties should be grown at a good distance from less susceptible kinds.

Botrytis Dry Rot (*Botrytis gladiolorum* and *B. cinerea*). The first-mentioned fungus is the most common cause of corm rot and leaf and flower spot of gladiolus. The other species may occasionally be responsible for some damage to the leaves and flowers. These fungi may also rot the stems at or just below the soil line.

Control: Plant corms in areas where the soil and air drainage is good. Rogue and destroy diseased plants and old flower-spikes. Spray periodically with a fungicide such as captan, nabam, or zineb. Dig corms as early and in as dry weather as possible. Dry and store corms properly.

Fusarium Dry Rot (*Fusarium oxysporum* var. *gladioli*). This is the most important storage disease of gladiolus, causing an annual loss of 1½ million dollars in Florida alone. The fungus may be present on the corms when they are dug; the infected areas appear as water-soaked spots. Rot develops very rapidly in storage, especially if the corms have not been thoroughly dried and cured before being stored. The lesions on the corms vary in color from very light brown to tan. The spots are sunken and wrinkled in concentric rings. A similar zonation sometimes accompanies the corm rot caused by *Penicillium gladioli*.

Control: Commercial growers should make every effort to maintain healthy corm stocks. Because cormels are far more tolerant to heat treatments than corms, the fungus can be controlled in infected stock as follows: presoak cormels overnight in water. Then soak them in hot water containing 5 per cent alcohol for 30 minutes at a temperature of 128°F.

Recent tests have revealed that infections by the *Fusarium* dry rot fungus can be reduced by soaking the corms in Benlate as suggested under corm rots, above.

Amateur growers should discard any infected corms and plant clean corms in a new location.

Wilt (*Fusarium orthoceras* var. *gladioli*). Leaves of plants affected by this disease during the summer turn yellow and the stems collapse. Corms from mildly infected plants may appear sound when dug, but develop a rot in storage.

Control: Soak cleaned corms for 15 to 30 minutes in a warm dip (80 to 85°F.) of Benlate, 2 tablespoonfuls per gallon water. Dry corms before storing.

Smut (*Urocystis gladiolicola*). This disease was founded in 1942 on gladiolus seedlings in California, where it caused a blistering, shredding, and necrosis of stem and leaf tissues. The fungus is frequently found on the scales of imported gladiolus corms.

Control: Control measures have not been developed.

Leaf and Flower Spot (*Curvularia trifolii* var. *gladioli*). This serious disease ruined hundreds of acres of gladioli in Florida in 1947 and has continued to be a limiting factor in cut-flower production since that time. Oval, tan to dark-brown spots appear on the leaves and stems. Florets fail to open when the stems are heavily infected.

Control: Weekly applications of Dyrene, Fore, or zineb sprays provide protection under average conditions. Under ideal conditions for fungus development in Florida, sprays may have to be applied as often as every 3 to 5 days to protect the flower spikes.

Virus Diseases

A number of viruses are known to affect gladioli. Among these are tobacco ringspot

Fig. 143. Gladiolus flower infected with the cucumber mosaic virus. (U.S. Department of Agriculture)

and cucumber mosaic. The latter is illustrated in Fig. 143.

Separation of these viruses on the basis of symptoms is difficult for any but virus experts. Plants suspected of harboring a virus should be submitted to a plant virologist of the United States Department of Agriculture or to the local state plant pathologist for a correct diagnosis. Most of the viruses of gladiolus are transmitted by aphids or leafhoppers. Tobacco ringspot can be transmitted on tools during the harvesting of flowers and corms.

Control: Since the viruses are carried over from one season to the next in the corms, plants known to be affected should be discarded completely. Controlling the leafhoppers and aphids with malathion or other suitable sprays should help to reduce the prevalence of the viruses.

An aluminum foil mulch on the soil is effective in repelling aphids and also controls weeds. Losses from cucumber mosaic virus can be reduced by planting gladiolus early in the growing season. The disease is most serious in late plantings.

Petal Protrusion. A disorder characterized by the development of cone-shaped protrusions on the back side of the petals is said to be caused by a virus which is transmitted via corms and cormels. Controls have not been developed.

Other Diseases

Aster Yellows. This disease, caused by a mycoplasma-like organism, also occurs on gladioli.

Control: Rogue out diseased plants and spray with malathion or Meta-Systox R to control sucking insect vectors.

Insects and Other Animal Pests

Aphids (*Aphis gossypii*). This is one of the commonest of the plant lice that attack gladioli in the hot months of summer. There are two kinds of females: (a) The wingless aphid varies from pale yellow to very dark green and produces young aphids; this is the form that is seen on the gladiolus plant. (b) The winged female is more slender and the greater part of the head and thorax are dark-colored. These are seldom seen on plants, but their former presence is indicated by the jet-black, shining oval eggs that they have deposited. This insect should be controlled, especially since it is the carrier of the mosaic virus.

The potato aphid, *Macrosiphum euphorbiae,* also infests the leaves of gladioli.

Control: Spray with Sevin, Meta-Systox R, or malathion as soon as aphids appear on the leaves. Repeat the application in 2 weeks, if necessary.

Thrips. Four species of thrips infest gladioli: gladiolus, banded greenhouse, greenhouse, and western flower. The gladiolus thrips, *Taeniothrips simplex,* is most prevalent and troublesome. These insects feed by rasping the tender epidermal layers of leaves, flowers, and corms. This causes a flow of plant juices, which the insects later suck into their bodies. Infested surfaces are of an unnatural glistening whitish-gray color, because the cells in drying out become filled with air and so reflect the light. The young thrips are light yellow in color and move about irregularly when disturbed. They feed under the leaf sheaths and appear mostly in cloudy weather, seldom in bright sunlight. The older thrips, about $1/16$ inch long, are black with lighter markings on the wings. The wings have layers of hairs which are arranged like the parts of a feather. Each female insect lays about 200 eggs in slits on the surface of a plant. Brown spots on the dead tissue show where the eggs were laid. Young thrips are found under the sheaths; they may surround the stems in great numbers. Infested flowers are discolored and spotted; they dry up and shrivel as though burned (Fig. 144). Infested spikes often fail to bloom. The foliage of infested plants has many whitish spots that make the surface appear light. Later the leaves turn brown and dry out.

Infested corms are often sticky from the sap that oozes out as a result of injury by thrips. They are darker in color than normal corms and their surface tends to become rough. Badly infested corms develop such weak root systems, that the plant forms small flowers and leaves, if any.

From 2 to 4 weeks are required for the thrips to reach maturity, so there may be as many as five or six generations maturing during the summer. In northern areas the thrips hibernate on the corms in storage, but in warmer climates they may winter in corms or parts left in the ground through oversight.

Control: Spray with Diazinon, Cygon, methoxychlor, or Sevin during the early part of the growing season. These materials should be used before flowers are formed because they may damage the delicate petals. Soaking corms for 3 hours just before planting in $1^{1}/4$ tablespoons of Lysol in a gallon of

Fig. 144. Work of gladiolus thrips *(Taeniothrips simplex): (left)* infested buds; *(right)* flowers that will not open.

water will also help to control thrips. Storage of corms at 40°–45°F. is also effective.

Grape Mealybug (*Pseudococcus maritimus*). These insects feed in depressions at the base of the corm. If the corms are stored at 60°F. or above, the insects multiply on them and cause them to shrink to such an extent that they may not grow, or, if they do, will produce sickly plants.

Control: The corm dip described under the control of gladiolus thrips will also control this pest on stored corms. An older treatment which is still effective is to dip the corms from 2 to 3 hours in a bath prepared by dissolving a pound of laundry soap in 25 gallons of water heated to 100°F. to which 4 ounces of nicotine sulfate are added just before dipping the corms. A few commercial growers of gladiolus still use the nicotine-soap dip.

Tulip Bulb Aphid (*Dysaphis tulipae*). This pest is more common on gladiolus grown in light, sandy soil, especially where weeds have previously grown or are still growing along the edges of the planting. The aphids pass the winter on the corms and also feed on them, establishing new colonies early in the season. They are not particularly active during late summer. Infested corms develop stunted and deformed plants if they develop at all, and any shoots that are formed usually wither and die.

Control: Dust corms with Sevin powder before storage. Spray plants during the growing season with Diazinon or malathion.

Tarnished Plant Bug (*Lygus lineolaris*). These sucking insects feed on the flower buds, causing them to blast or to develop abnormally and making them unsalable. The nymphs or young insects are greenish in color. The adults are mottled, yellowish, or reddish-brown, ¼ inch in length and half as wide, with flat, oval bodies.

Control: Since these insects live on common weeds and certain ornamental plants and hibernate on weeds in hedgerows and other places, destruction of such weeds near gladiolus plantings is necessary. Spray with Cygon or Sevin just as the flower buds begin to develop and for good control repeat just before the buds open.

White Grubs (*Phyllophaga, Popillia*, etc.). Such insects are troublesome only when the corms are planted in grounds previously sodded, where the grubs of June beetles, Japanese beetles, or Asiatic brown beetles are present.

Control: See lawn grubs, under *Gramineae*.

Wireworms (*Elateridae*). These are the larvae of the interesting little click beetles that are able to "right" themselves suddenly after they have been placed on their backs. The larvae feed on the corms and roots, especially in low-grade muck land. They bore holes in the neck or the base of the leaves and flower stalks. They are reddish-brown, long and narrow with a hard, many-jointed body shell. As a result of a late attack by these larvae, the shoots turn yellow and become deformed and stunted.

Control: Avoid planting gladiolus corms in heavy soil. Treating the soil with Diazinon will control wireworms.

European Corn Borer (*Ostrinia nubilalis*). This pest feeds on gladioli occasionally. See *Dahlia*.

Two-Spotted Mite (*Tetranychus urticae*). This mite occasionally infests this host and may become very prevalent after repeated use of chlorinated hydrocarbon insecticides.

Control: See *Althaea*.

Bulb Mite (*Rhizoglyphus echinopus*). This mite is associated with several soil-borne diseases, particularly *Fusarium* dry rot, *Stromatinia* dry rot, and bacterial scab. See *Tulipa* for additional details.

Root-Knot Nemas (*Meloidogyne incognita* and *M. hapla*). These nemas cause heavy losses in commercial plantings of gladiolus in some parts of the country.

Control: See Nemas in Chapter 3.

GLEDITSIA (HONEY LOCUST)

Fungus and Virus Diseases

Leaf Spot (*Linospora gleditsiae*). This is rather a serious blight in the southern states. Numerous black fruiting bodies (acervuli) of the fungus develop on the lower side of the leaves. The ascocarpic stage develops throughout the summer and lives through the winter. In the Middle West other leaf spots are caused by *Cercospora condensata* and *C. olivacea*.

Control: Gathering and discarding of all fallen leaves should provide practical control.

Cankers. Five fungi—*Thyronectria austro-americana, T. denigrata, Cytospora gleditschiae, Dothiorella* sp., and *Kaskaskia gleditsiae*—are known to cause stem cankers of honey locust. The author found that the first-named fungus killed a number of honey lo-

Fig. 145. The honey locust *(Gleditsia triacanthos)* at the left in the United Nations Gardens died as a result of infection by the fungus *Thyronectria austro-americana.*

custs at the United Nations gardens in New York several years ago (Fig. 145).

The last named fungus causes extensive areas of necrosis, cracking, and peeling of the trunk bark along with a brown discoloration of the sapwood.

Control: Effective control measures have not been developed.

Witches' Brooms. Honey locust and black locust are subject to this condition. The disease, though common on the sprouts, rarely occurs on the large trees. It is characterized by production in late summer of dense clusters or bunches of twigs from an enlarged axis. The bunched portions ordinarily die during the following winter. The disease was long considered as being virus-induced but recent evidence educed by Japanese and

American scientists indicates that a myco-plasma-like organism is the cause of many witches' broom diseases.

Control: Infected trees appear to recover naturally. No definite control measures are known.

Powdery Mildew (*Microsphaera alni*). This mildew fungus is widespread on honey locusts.

Control: Control measures are never used for this disease on this host.

Rust (*Ravenelia opaca*). One rust disease is known to occur on honey locust.

Control: No control measures are necessary.

Wood Decay. Like most trees, honey locusts are subject to wood-decaying fungi. Among the more prevalent ones are a species of *Fomes*, *Daedalea ambigua*, *D. elegans*, *Ganoderma curtisii*, *G. lucidum*, and *Xylaria mali*. *G. lucidum* occurs on living trees, which suggests that it is a vigorous parasite, as it is on species of *Acer*.

Control: No effective controls are known. Avoid mechanical injuries around the base of the tree, provide good growing conditions, and feed and water the tree to maintain good vigor.

Insects and Related Pests

Honey Locust Borer (*Agrilus difficilis*). A flat-headed borer burrows beneath the bark of honey locust and eventually may girdle the tree. Large quantities of gum exude from the bark near the infested nodes. The adult beetles, which emerge in June, are elongate, 1/2 inch long, black with a metallic luster.

Control: No really effective controls are known, although it is likely that methoxychlor sprays applied to the trunks during the egg-laying period in mid-June and early July might prove effective.

Pod Gall Midge (*Dasineura gleditschiae*). This midge causes globular galls 1/8 inch in diameter at the growing tips (Fig. 146). The pest seems to prefer some of the newer thornless varieties such as Moraine and Shademaster to the ordinary honey locust. The adult midge appears in April when the leaves begin to emerge. It deposits eggs singly or in clusters among the young leaflets. The larvae hatch within a few days and begin to feed on the inner surface of the leaflets.

Control: No effective control is available at present.

Honey Locust Plant Bug (*Diaphnocoris chlorionis*). Discoloration of leaves and stunting of new growth is caused by this widely distributed pest. Complete defoliation may occur during heavy infestations. Adults are $3/16$ inch long and pale green. Both adults and nymphs are difficult to detect because their color blends with foliage and growing tips on which they feed. Yellow-leaved strains such as "Sunburst" are more susceptible to this bug than are green-leaved ones like "Shademaster."

Control: Spray susceptible varieties with Sevin a week or 10 days after buds burst.

Webworm (*Homadaula anisocentra*). This pest is more common on the silk tree, *Albizia julibrissin*, but in some parts of the country it is a serious pest of honey locust.

Control: Spraying with Sevin will control this pest, but 3 to 5 applications are necessary to provide season-long protection. A single soil application of either phorate (Thimet) or Di-Syston or injection of Bidrin into the trunk base will also provide control. These materials, however, are extremely toxic and should be handled only by a professional arborist or nurseryman who has been issued a use permit.

Spider Mite (*Eotetranychus multidigituli*). This mite causes yellow stippling of the leaves which drop prematurely. Defoliated trees usually leaf out again in late summer but are considerably weakened.

Control: Spray with Kelthane, Meta-Systox R, or Tedion early in July and repeat every 2 weeks as needed.

Fig. 146. Pod gall of honey locust caused by the insect *Dasineura gleditschiae*. Uninfested leaves are seen on the lower left side.

Bagworm. See *Thuja*.
Cottony Maple Scale. See *Acer*.
San Jose Scale. See *Prunus*.
Spring and Fall Cankerworms. See *Ulmus*.

GLOXINIA—see SINNINGIA

GODETIA

Diseases

Downy Mildew (*Peronospora arthuri*). This mildew occurs on *Godetia* in California.
Control: Measures are rarely adopted to control this disease.

Root Rots (*Pythium ultimum, Phytophthora cryptogea,* and *Pellicularia filamentosa*). Three soil-infesting fungi may cause root rot or damping-off of this host.
Control: See Chapter 4.

Rusts (*Puccinia oenotherae, P. pulverulenta,* and *Pucciniastrum epilobii*). Three rust diseases have been reported on *Godetia*.
Control: Remove and destroy infected plants.

Aster Yellows. This disease occurs on *Godetia* on the West Coast.
Control: Remove and discard infected plants.

Animal Pests

Southern Root-Knot Nema (*Meloidogyne incognita*). This nema occasionally infests the roots of *Godetia*.
Control: See under Nemas, Chapter 3.

GOMPHRENA (GLOBE-AMARANTH)

Few diseases occur on this host. A leaf spot caused by the fungus *Cercospora gomphrenae* occurs in the southern United States. *Gomphrena globosa* is subject to several virus diseases. It is used by plant virologists an

index plant for detecting hydrangea and tomato ringspot viruses.

GORDONIA—see FRANKLINIA

GRAMINEAE (GRASSES)[22]

Fungus Diseases

Brown Patch (*Pellicularia filamentosa*). Early in the morning, turf affected by this disease shows large brown or blackened areas which suggest sunscald; the grass may be covered with a light weft of moldy growth. The leaves in these patches are more or less water-soaked and blackened, and finally collapse and usually die. The roots and the growing points of the shoots are not usually killed. This fungus often kills the roots of such plants as potatoes and tomatoes, but less frequently those of grasses; it prefers the tops of grasses. The disease occurs more frequently in lawns surrounded by trees, which reduce the circulation of air. Brown patch occurs on the following grasses: bent, blue (Kentucky and Merion), rye, Bermuda, fescue, centipede, brome, carpet, and Zoysia.
Control: If too much nitrogenous fertilizer is used during the summer, the grass is apt to be very tender and soft. When high humidity occurs in warm weather, this disease is apt to develop rather rapidly. Acid soils also are said to favor the disease. Many materials sold in garden supply stores will control this disease. Among the more commonly available ones are Dyrene, Fore, Tersan LSR, and thiabendazole.

Dollar Spot (*Sclerotinia homeocarpa*). The irregular circular patches may be slightly pinkish in color because of the fungus spores, which develop in very large quantities. The leaves rot, becoming soft and slimy. The fungus can live in the soil at low temperatures and develops on the grass at temperatures

[22] Only lawn grass diseases and pests are described.

close to freezing; in this respect it is much like *Fusarium nivale.* Dollar spot is most apt to occur during mild, wet weather towards the close of the growing season. The spots sometimes run together, forming irregular patches at first brown. When the grass is dead it seems bleached and straw-colored. Without making cultures of the fungi that are present it is impossible to distinguish with certainty this disease from ordinary brown patch. Brown patch is caused by a species of basidiomycete (*Pellicularia*), as noted above; dollar spot is caused by an ascomycete. The mycelium produces sclerotia from which develop the funnel-shaped ascocarps.

The following grasses are susceptible to dollar spot: bent, blue, Bermuda, zoysia, fescue, St. Augustine, centipede, and bahia.

Control: Among the many chemicals available for dollar spot control are Acti-dione-Thiram, Dyrene, Fore, or Tersan 1991. Some of these are more effective on one kind of grass than another. Follow the manufacturers' directions carefully.

Powdery Mildew (*Erysiphe graminis*). Powdery mildew appears as dirty spots or blotches on the leaf sheaths, varying in color from light gray to brownish. It is caused by a fungus closely related to those that cause powdery mildew of wheat, barley, and other cereals. It is especially apt to develop in wet weather and on lawns not properly drained. The infection is spread by the numerous white spores formed on infected leaves.

Control: Sprays containing Acti-dione-Thiram, Karathane, or Tersan 1991 will control powdery mildew.

Downy Mildew (*Sclerophthora* sp.). In 1969, St. Augustine grass in Florida and Texas was found to be affected by this disease.

Control: The disease does not appear to be serious enough to warrant control measures.

Red Thread (*Corticium fuciforme*). Pinkish patches from 3 to 15 inches in diameter develop during rainy weather. The grass in the patches is pink and dead and contains coral-red masses of mycelium. These become gelatinous in wet weather. Short coral-red horns develop near the tips of the grass leaves. The disease is more common on the fescues. The fungus grows best from 60° to 70°F., this means that it is favored by very hot weather, since the temperature of the soil and grass is much below that of the air.

Control: Spray with Caddy, Cadminate, Dyrene, or with Terson LSR in late May, June, August, and September at 10- to 14-day intervals.

Snow Mold (*Calonectria nivalis*). Several different fungi are responsible for the snow mold disease. One most frequently mentioned is *Fusarium nivale,* the conidial stage of the *Calonectria.* In Pennsylvania, snow mold of colonial bent has been found to be due to a basidiomycete, *Typhula itoana,* and in the Yukon to *T. idahoensis.* Dead areas appear in the turf after the snow has melted. The mycelium that covers these dead areas has a pinkish cast when exposed to the sun. At times an excessive development of mycelium causes a bunching together of the grass leaves throughout the affected areas; when this happens the grass underneath is usually killed outright. Other patches are a dirty gray. The snow mold organisms attack the leaves first and recovery may follow, but under certain conditions, the roots and stems may be attacked and killed later. If snow falls before the ground is frozen, the damage is serious. The spores are transported by water.

Control: Apply Daconil, Dyrene, Fore, or Tersan SP diluted according to the manufacturers' directions. Best results are obtained when these materials are applied in early winter before the first snow is forecast. A second application should be made in late winter when the grass is free of snow. Phosphate fertilizers are said to decrease the damage caused by *Typhula.*

Fig. 147. Spots on Merion bluegrass are caused by the fungus *Helminthosporium vagans*. (Nassau County Co-op Association)

Melting Out (*Helminthosporium vagans*). Kentucky bluegrass is particularly susceptible to this disease; the infection may be sufficiently extensive to cause a foot rot. It is sometimes referred to as a spot blotch if the spots are bluish-black with gray or straw-colored centers. The eye spot appearance shows in the advanced stages of the spotting (Fig. 147). If the leaves are infected when the blades are folded together, two symmetrical spots later appear opposite each other. The infection may spread into the sheath which encircles the shoot, and may kill it and thus become a foot rot. See Fig. 148 for the development cycle of this fungus. The fungus is said to be seed-borne.

Control: Among the chemicals available for controlling melting out are Dyrene, Fore, Tersan LSR, Acti-dione-Thiram, or zineb. During cool, moist springs these should be applied at frequent intervals.

Helminthosporium Blights (*Helminthosporium cynodontis, H. dictyoides, H. erythrospilum, H. giganteum, H. siccans,* and *H. sorokinianum*). Fescues, bents, and blue grasses are subject to several species of fungi closely related to the melting out fungus.

Control: Use the same materials recommended for melting out, above.

Fairy Ring (*Marasmius oreades* and others). Fairy rings of mushroom fruiting bodies are a familiar sight to everyone who frequents grasslands. A mycelium starts in one spot and spreads in all directions. Various species of mushrooms may grow in this way; that named above is the commonest. Some species kill the grass through toxic action. At certain times of the year the fruiting bodies, mushrooms, are developed near the outer borders of the year's growth of mycelium. The grass within the ring may appear to be healthy but later on may collapse and die. Fairy rings are more conspicuous on unfertilized lawns, and their presence can be masked somewhat by adequate fertilization.

Control: Chemicals are seldom helpful in controlling this disease. The fruiting bodies should be broken off as they appear. It is possible to control the fungus by fumigating the soil with methyl bromide but this practice is rarely followed by home gardeners.

Copper Spot (*Gloeocercospora sorghi*). Bent grasses are subject to this disease, which appears as coppery-colored spots in the turf.

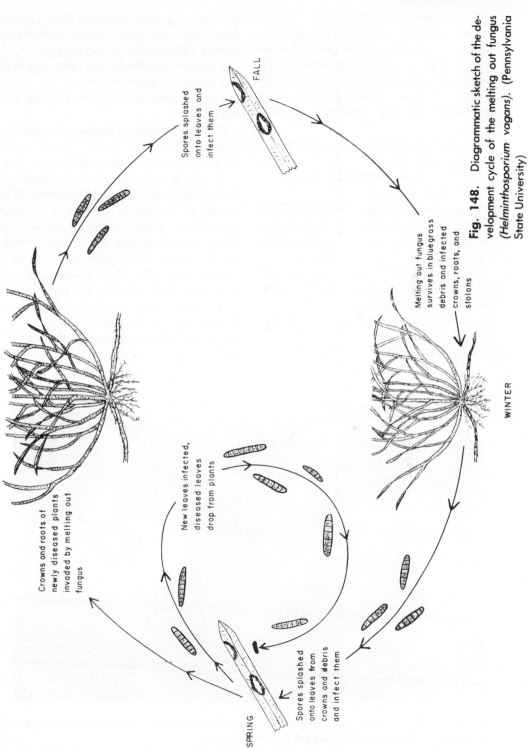

Fig. 148. Diagrammatic sketch of the development cycle of the melting out fungus (*Helminthosporium vagans*). (Pennsylvania State University)

FALL

Spores splashed onto leaves and infect them

Melting out fungus survives in bluegrass debris and infected crowns, roots, and stolons

WINTER

SUMMER

Crowns and roots of newly diseased plants invaded by melting out fungus

New leaves infected, diseased leaves drop from plants

SPRING

Spores splashed onto leaves from crowns and debris and infect them

Control: Same as for dollar spot.

Rust (*Puccinia graminis* var. *agrostis*). Merion bluegrass, a special strain of Kentucky bluegrass, is very susceptible to this disease, which appears as small, reddish spots on the leaves. The alternate host for this fungus is wild barberry, *Berberis vulgaris.*

Control: Acti-dione-Thiram, Daconil, Dyrene, Fore, Tersan LSR, or zineb, applied 2 or 3 times at 10-day intervals starting in late July will control this rust.

Other Rusts. *Puccinia coronata* affects ryegrass, *P. stenotaphri* occurs on St. Augustine grass in Florida, and *P. zoysiae* affects species of Zoysia in many southern states.

Gray Leaf Spot (*Piricularia grisea*). This highly destructive disease attacks St. Augustine grass in the South in summer, particularly during periods of heavy rainfall and high humidity. Lesions first appear as minute brown dots on the leaves, which later enlarge to form oval, then elongated dots. Lesions containing spores have depressed, blue-gray centers with irregular, brown margins.

Cercospora fusimaculans also causes a leaf spot of St. Augustine grass.

Control: Treat with Dyrene, Fore, or Tersan LSR.

Fusarium Blight (*Fusarium roseum* var. *cerealis* "Culmorum" and *F. tricinctum*). In the past several years many Merion and Kentucky bluegrass lawns in the northeastern United States turned brown in midsummer as a result of this disease. Symptoms resemble those caused by the fungi associated with the fading out and melting out diseases. Small, tan or straw colored spots appear in early summer (Fig. 149). These enlarge and coalesce until large areas of the lawn are involved. The disease is active only during the warmest part of the summer, and the first area to be infected is usually the warmest one. The disease does not occur in shaded

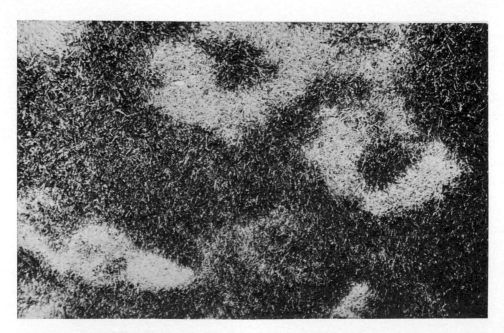

Fig. 149. Browned areas in a lawn may be caused by the fungus *Fusarium roseum* f. *cerealis* "Culmorum." (Nassau County Co-op Association)

areas. Frequent sprinkling of the lawn aggravates the condition. This *Fusarium* differs from the snow mold fungus mentioned earlier as the conidial stage of *Calonectria nivalis*.

Control: Tersan 1991, 50% W P, 6 oz. in 10 gallons of water per 1000 sq. ft. applied at earliest appearance of the disease and repeated at 10 to 14 day intervals during the warm season will provide control. Water sufficiently to wet the soil to a depth of 1 inch below any mat or thatch present immediately after applying the fungicide.

Pythium Blight (*Pythium aphanidermatum* and *P. ultimum*). This disease, also referred to as grease spot and cottony blight, occurs on bentgrasses, bluegrasses, ryegrass, Bermudagrasses, fescues and Zoysia.

Control: Spray with Tersan SP, Dexon, Fore, or Koban at 7-to-14 day intervals from July to September.

Stripe Smut (*Ustilago striiformis*). Long narrow striations develop on the leaves of bluegrasses, especially Merion bluegrass, and bentgrasses.

Control: Benlate or Fungo 50 will provide control. The fungicide should be drenched into the turf in November and again in early March.

Ophiobolus Patch (*Ophiobolus graminis*). This disease first appears as small light brown spots of turf which enlarge rapidly to two feet or more. Both shoots and roots are attacked, resulting in complete killing of the grass plants. The disease occurs mainly in the western part of the state of Washington.

Control: The use of ammonium sulfate or mono-ammonium phosphate fertilizers will control this disease.

Other Related Diseases

Slime Molds (*Physarum cinereum*). A slimy growth of varying colors covers small areas of lawn grasses during very wet, cloudy weather. The mold is not a grass parasite and is more unsightly than harmful.

Control: Remove the mold mechanically by mowing, raking, or washing.

Algae (green scum). These plants are apt to grow in bare spots of lawns that are situated in poorly drained areas or that are shaded excessively. Scraping the surface to break up the green patches and applying hydrated lime at the rate of 2 to 5 pounds for each 100 square feet of turf will largely eliminate the algae. Spraying with Fore will also provide control.

Nemas. More than 20 species of eelsworms are known to attack grasses. Some of these can be controlled by drenching the turf with 1 pint of Nemagon or Fumazone in 10 to 15 gallons of water per 1000 sq. ft. The turf should be watered immediately after application to insure penetration of the nemacide into soil and prevent toxic effects. Follow the manufacturer's directions carefully.

Virus Disease

Mosaic (Brome mosaic virus). Mosaic symptoms, including chlorotic-mottling and striping of leaves of Kentucky bluegrass, were found to be caused by this virus. Similar symptoms are produced in St. Augustinegrass by the sugar cane mosaic virus. This virus is widespread in southern Florida and also occurs in Louisiana.

Insects and Other Animal Pests

Bluegrass Aphid (*Schizaphis graminum*). This aphid, also known as the greenbug, may become troublesome on turf grasses, although it is primarily a pest of cereal grasses.

Control: A Diazinon or malathion spray will provide control.

Bluegrass Billbug (*Sphenophorus parvulus*). This widely distributed species produces damage to lawns (Fig. 150) similar to that of soil inhabiting grubs. Although the adults do some damage by feeding and oviposition,

Fig. 150. Lawn severely damaged by bluegrass billbugs. (Gertrude Catlin)

most of the damage is caused through feeding by the larvae (Fig. 151).

Control: Apply Diazinon or Sevin to newly mowed lawn between June 20 and July 10 at the rate of 1 pound in 50 gallons of water per 1000 square feet.

Ants. Many species of ants infest lawns. The most common are the argentine, cornfield, and pavement ants. These pests make mounds of earth in the lawn, especially during dry spells. They may cause some of the grass to dry out by loosening the soil around the roots.

Control: Dust the lawn lightly with Diazinon or Dursban.

Green June Beetle (*Cotinis nitida*). These large green beetles with brown-yellow margins are about 1 inch long and half as wide. The adults feed on the foliage of peach trees and other plants. The grubs feed on grass

roots in lawns and golf courses as well as on other vegetation in the soil. The dirty white grubs have the interesting habit of crawling along on their backs. They are present as far north as New York City but are much more common farther south.

Control: See lawn grubs below.

Lawn Grubs (Japanese beetle, *Popillia japonica;* oriental beetle, *Anomala orientalis;* Asiatic garden beetle, *Maladera castanea;* rose chafer, *Macrodactylus subspinosus;* May beetle, *Ochrosidia villosa* and *Phyllophaga* sp.). The white grubs of these beetles are common enemies of the sod in lawns, golf courses, and parks. They can be readily distinguished by the distribution of the hairs on their ends. The adult Japanese beetle lays two or three eggs a day in shallow burrows in the lawn. The eggs soon hatch and begin feeding on the young grass roots. See Fig. 69.

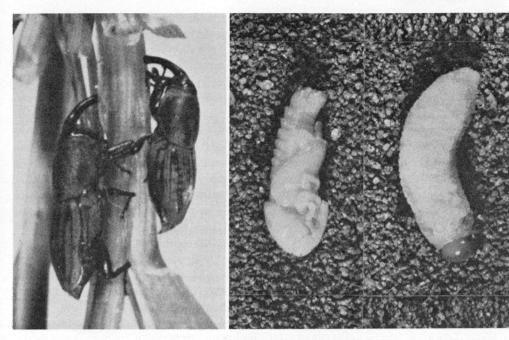

Fig. 151. Adult billbugs at left and larval stage at right. (Gertrude Catlin)

Control: Dasanit, Diazinon, Dursban or Dylox will control grubs. An annual treatment during August is necessary. Water the area well immediately after applying the insecticide.

The Japanese beetle grubs are probably more generally prevalent over the eastern United States than any of the other pests mentioned above. Hence most of the grub-proofing of lawns is directed primarily against this pest. One material which is effective only against the grubs of Japanese beetle is the so-called "milky-disease" spore powder. Sold under the name Doom, it contains bacterial spores capable of infecting and killing the grubs. This material does not work immediately, but takes at least 2 years to reduce the infestation. Two to 8 pounds of spore powder per acre should be spread on low-value lawn areas, parks, and golf course roughs. Only one treatment is necessary. The bacteria released from the spore dust are washed into the soil, where they come in contact with the Japanese beetle grubs. They infect the grubs and multiply inside them by the millions. When the grubs die from the infection, millions of additional bacteria are released into the soil to infect other grubs. The process is a slow one, and gardeners cannot expect any appreciable reduction in the treated areas for several years. "Milky disease" spore powder should not be used on areas treated with insecticides. It is most useful on large, marginal, low value areas.

Chinch Bugs (*Blissus leucopterus leucopterus*). The chinch bug and its close relative the hairy chinch bug, *Blissus leucopterus hirtus*, are frequently the cause of much damage to lawns in the eastern United States, especially in the vicinity of New York and Long Island. Patches of the sod turn light grayish brown in color and die out as though attacked by brown patch or dollar spot fungi. Sod killed by the larvae of the Japanese beetle presents much the same appearance, except that it is loose and can be rolled up easily. When chinch bugs are the cause of the damage, they can be found by spreading the dying grass with the hands so as to expose the crowns and top roots. Numerous small, bright, orange-colored insects barely visible to the naked eye, as well as the larger brown insects with white markings on their backs, can be seen scurrying in all directions. They cannot fly, but develop rudimentary wings which assist them in springing over long distances. The wings of the older insects are fairly well developed, appearing whitish on their backs. These chinch bugs are sucking insects which remove the juice from the crowns and bases of stems and leaves. They feed by thrusting their beaks into the plant. The proboscis is four-jointed and contains four delicate stylets. When the insects are numerous, the grass may be killed. There are usually two broods a year, one in June and another in early August, the later being the more destructive. Damage by chinch bugs is usually associated with hot, dry weather, but the bug may destroy lawns in wet weather, provided conditions are unsuitable for fungus parasites which destroy the young bugs.

Control: The insects winter in rubbish, hedgerows, and lawns where old grass is allowed to accumulate. If these places are cleaned up, many of the insects will be destroyed. Protection of the lawn can be obtained by applying any one of the following materials on each 5000 square feet of lawn area: Sevin—1 qt. flowable, or 2 lbs. 50 per cent wettable, or 10 lbs. 10 per cent granular; or, Aspon—2 pints 4E emulsion; or Diazinon —1 to 2 pints 25 emulsion, or 1½ lbs. 25 per cent wettable, or 20 lbs. 5 per cent granular. Dursban controls chinch bugs on St. Augustinegrass in the South as well as on lawn grasses in the North.

Other insecticides that will control chinch bugs include Baygon, and Dylox. Where chinch bugs are numerous and where suscep-tible grasses such as bents are being grown, treatments are suggested for each brood. These will vary with the locality but usually range from June 1 to 15 for the first, and August 1 to 15 for the second brood.

Bluegrass Webworms (*Crambus teterrellus*). Webworms are the larvae of moths or millers, called "close-wing moths" because they fold their wings close to their bodies while resting. The eggs are cream-colored and bead-like; they are dropped by the female moths while on the wing and hatch in 10 days. The worms feed on the grass leaves. They form protective silken webs, where they spend their larval life. Close to the soil surface they construct little tunnels covered with dirt, lined with silk, and reinforced with their excrement and bits of grass; in these they live quite safely as they cut off the blades of grass. At maturity the larvae, ³/₄ inch long, spin silken cocoons beneath the soil surface and spend from 10 days to 2 weeks in the pupal stage. The pupa is a narrowly oval, reddish-brown, helpless object. Infested turf looks ragged and patchy and may be entirely killed.

Control: In the North, sod webworm can be controlled by spraying the lawn with Akton, Baygon, Diazinon, Dursban, Dylox, or Sevin in June and repeating once a month until fall. Evening treatments are best. Do not water in treatments after application.

On St. Augustinegrass in Florida, Akton, applied when the insects first appear, gives good control.

Variegated Cutworm (*Peridroma saucia*). These worms produce one or two generations a year. The eggs are laid on the grass in the middle or late summer, and the worms feed until partly matured during the late summer and early autumn. They hibernate in soil cavities until March or April, and feed intensely.

Control: Same as for bluegrass webworms.

Blind Mole (*Scalopus aquaticus*). Though

these animals destroy many grubs and the pupae of many insects, the unsightly ridges that they cause are undesirable in the garden and lawn. The breaking of the sod and the consequent drying of the roots damage the grass.

Control: Setting spiked traps will destroy the animals, but this requires experience.

Grub-proofing lawns as suggested above under lawn grubs will force moles to seek food elsewhere.

Other Pests. Among the other pests which infest lawn grasses are armyworms, mole crickets, earwigs, earthworms, cicada-killer wasps, and wireworms. Most of these can be controlled with Diazinon or Dursban applied in mid-April and again in mid-May. The clover mite, *Bryobia praetiosa,* may infest turf grasses and fruit trees, and then move indoors to become a household pest in late winter and spring. Spray the grass near the house with Kelthane. The *Hyperodes* weevil, a recently discovered pest, feeds on grasses, particularly annual bluegrass, *Poa annua,* on golf courses in the Northeast. Diazinon or Dursban applied in mid-April and again in mid-May will control this pest.

Another turfgrass pest, *Ataenius spretulus,* is causing considerable damage on golf courses in Connecticut, New Jersey, Ohio, and on Long Island, New York. Control measures have not been developed.

Nemas. In recent years failures in lawns have been found to be due to parasitic nemas on roots of lawn grasses. Diagnosing for nemas on these hosts requires the services of a nematologist. Great improvement in turf grasses results from treating soils with materials such as Nemagon or Mobilawn before making a new lawn.

GYMNOCLADUS
(KENTUCKY COFFEE TREE)

Diseases

Leaf Spots (*Cercospora gymnocladi, Phyllosticta gymnocladi,* and *Marssonina* sp.).

Three species of fungi cause leaf spots on this host.

Control: Special control measures are rarely required, but periodic application of copper or dithiocarbamate fungicides will protect valuable specimens.

Other Diseases. A root rot caused by the fungus *Phymatotrichum omnivorum* and a wood rot by *Polyporus pulchellus* are the only other fungus diseases known on *Gymnocladus.*

Insect

Scale (*Parlatoria oleae*). This is the only insect known to infest *Gymnocladus.*

Control: This pest is not serious enough to warrant control measures.

GYPSOPHILA (BABY'S-BREATH)

Diseases

Crown Gall (*Erwinia herbicola*). Soft nodular galls up to one inch in diameter develop in the region of the union on grafted plants. The abnormal tissue may extend completely around the stem or root and cause the death of the plant. The galls are very soft and fall apart easily.

Control: Unlike the common crown gall organism, *Agrobacterium tumefaciens,* this organism does not attack a great number of hosts. Avoid propagation from plants that bear galls. Dipping the roots for 2 minutes in a streptomycin solution will kill the bacteria, on the surface. Knives used in making the grafts should be dipped in Physan.

Blight (*Botrytis cinerea*). Ash-gray spots develop on bud scales and stems and may cause the plant to die down several nodes from the top.

Control: Spray with captan or zineb.

Damping-off (*Pythium debaryanum* and *Pellicularia filamentosa*). These fungi cause damping-off and stem rot of this host.

Control: Use clean soil, or treat soil as described in Chapter 4.

Aster Yellows. This disease affects *Gypsophila* as well as asters.

Control: Gather and destroy infected plants.

Fasciation (*Corynebacterium fascians*). See *Lathyrus*.

Insects

Leafhopper (*Macrosteles fascifrons*). In addition to sucking out leaf juices from plants, this leafhopper spreads the aster yellows disease.

Control: See *Callistephus*.

HALESIA (SILVER-BELL)

The only diseases reported on *Halesia* are a fungus leaf spot caused by *Cercospora halesiae* and a wood rot by *Polyporus halesiae*.

HAMAMELIS (WITCH-HAZEL)

Diseases

Leaf Spots (*Gonatobotryum maculicola, Monochaetia monochaeta, Mycosphaerella* sp., *Phyllosticta hamamelidis,* and *Ramularia hamamelidis*). Five species of fungi cause leaf spotting of witch-hazel. These are rarely serious on cultivated specimens.

Control: Valuable ornamental specimens can be protected with copper or dithiocarbamate sprays.

Powdery Mildew (*Podosphaera biuncinata*). This mildew is rather uncommon on witch-hazel.

Control: Spray with Benlate, Karathane, or wettable sulfur.

Insects

Saddled Prominent Caterpillar (*Heterocampa guttivitta*). This caterpillar is green to brown or yellow, with a reddish-brown sad-dle-spot in the middle of the back. It feeds on beech, maple, apple, and other trees and shrubs in addition to this host.

Control: Spray valuable specimens with Sevin.

Witch-hazel Leaf Gall Aphid (*Hormaphis hamamelidis*). The galls, about ½ inch long, are green below with reddish tips, formed on the upper sides of the leaves. The aphids that cause them migrate in late May or early June to the leaves of birch trees; the injury is more serious to birch than to witch-hazel. The aphids resemble the nymphs of whitefly. They return to witch-hazel in the fall, where the female lays its eggs, and in this stage they live through the winter.

Control: Spray the birch with Diazinon, Cygon or malathion. This prevents migration of the insects to witch-hazel. A dormant oil spray applied to the witch-hazel before the buds open in spring will also control these pests.

Spiny Witch-hazel Gall (*Hamamelistes spinosus*). The galls are coarsely spined, resembling the fruit. They are about ¾ inch long, greenish and tinged with red. The aphid that causes the galls migrates to the leaves of birch, where it causes a corrugation or puckering of the leaves and does considerable damage.

Control: Spray plants while dormant with lime sulfur or miscible oil.

HAWORTHIA

This host is subject to the same diseases and pests as *Aloe*.

HEBE [23]

Diseases

Wilt (*Fusarium oxysporum* var. *hebae*). This disease, first noted in California in 1957

---

[23] *Hebe* is closely related to *Veronica*. Hence it is subject to many of the same diseases and pests.

on *Hebe buxifolia,* starts as a progressive chlorosis followed by browning of the leaves from the base of the stem upward.

Control: No control measures have been developed.

Leaf Spot (*Septoria exotica*). Numerous small circular spots are formed on the leaves by this fungus.

Control: Pick off and destroy the first leaves that are spotted.

HEDERA HELIX (ENGLISH IVY)

Diseases

Bacterial Leaf Spot and Stem Canker (*Xanthomonas hederae*). The leaf spots are at first light green and water-soaked; later they turn brown or black; their margins are more or less reddish (Fig. 152). The leaf stalks also become black and shriveled. A black decay extends from the tips of the twigs downward into the old wood, and definite cankers may

Fig. 152. Bacterial leaf spot of *Hedera.*

girdle the stem. The organism may enter the plant either through wounds or stomata and water-pores. Under warm, moist conditions a bacterial ooze is present on the stems. Doubtless several of the leaf spots described below may follow this bacterial disease.

Control: Avoid high temperatures, moist conditions, and unnecessary syringing; water the plants from below.

Leaf Spots (*Amerosporium trichellum, Glomerella cingulata, Phyllosticta concentrica,* and *Ramularia hedericola*). At least four species of fungi are capable of causing leaf spots on English ivy. The first-mentioned may also infect the stem, causing girdling, collapse, and death of the distal portions.

Control: Infected leaves should be picked off and destroyed and the remaining foliage sprayed with a copper fungicide.

Other Diseases. Occasionally English ivy is subject to powdery mildew caused by *Erysiphe cichoracearum,* root rots by *Pellicularia filamentosa* and a species of *Phytophthora,* and scab by *Sphaceloma hederae.* The sooty mold fungus may develop on English ivy growing beneath certain trees. This mold lives on the secretions of aphids and scales which fall from the trees above.

Insects and Related Pests

Aphids. Three species of aphids are common on this host: bean, green peach, and ivy. The last, *Aphis hederae,* is dark, purplish-green, brown, or black, and clusters on the growing tips.

Control: Spray with malathion as soon as the pests appear.

Caterpillars. Four caterpillars feed on the English ivy leaves: cabbage looper, omnivorous looper, eight-spotted forester, and the puss caterpillar. The latter, *Megalopyge opercularis,* is capable of inflicting a painful sting to persons.

Control: Spray with Sevin when the larvae are young.

Mealybugs. Three kinds of mealybugs infest this host: citrus, grape, and Mexican.

Control: Spray with malathion.

Scales. Many species of scales attack English ivy both indoors and outdoors. Among the most common are: dictyospermum, Florida red, greedy, oleander, olive parlatoria, peach, pineapple, and soft scale.

Control: The crawler stage of scales are readily controlled with malathion or Sevin.

Two-Spotted Mite (*Tetranychus urticae*). This pest is especially serious on ivy grown indoors in sunny windows. The leaves turn grayish and have a mealy coating on the lower surfaces.

Control: Spray with chlorobenzilate, Kelthane, or Tedion.

Other Pest

Dodder (*Cuscuta approximata* var. *urceolata*). This parasitic flowering plant frequently infests English ivy, chrysanthemums, and other outdoor plants. The yellow strands of this plant must be cut out, including some of the ivy or other hosts, before the dodder forms seeds in the fall. Spraying infested areas with Dacthal in spring will prevent germination of any dodder seeds that may be in the soil.

HELENIUM (SNEEZEWEED)

Diseases

Leaf Spots (*Cercospora helenii* and *Septoria helenii*). Brown spots on the leaves may be caused by these fungi.

Control: Sprays are rarely necessary. Pick off and discard spotted leaves.

Rusts (*Puccinia conspicua* and *P. dioicae* [*extensicola*] var. *solidaginis*). Two species of rusts occur on *Helenium* in the Middle West and Southwest.

Control: Pick off and destroy infected leaves.

Smut (*Entyloma compositarum* and *E. polysporum*). Light yellow spots in which spores are embedded appear on the leaves.

Control: Same as for rust.

Other Diseases. Powdery mildew caused by the fungus *Erysiphe cichoracearum* and aster yellows by a mycoplasma-like organism are other diseases reported on this host.

Insect

Helenium Snout Beetle (*Baris confinis*). This very small snout beetle infests the young growing tips in May and June, occasionally even later in the season.

Control: Valuable specimens should be sprayed from time to time with a Sevin-Kelthane mixture.

HELIANTHEMUM (SUN-ROSE)

Late in the season *Phyllosticta nelsoni* may infect the leaves and cause development of minute white circular spots with purple margins. The pycnidia appear on the upper sides of the spots. Another fungus of the same genus may develop on dying leaves and flower parts; it is a secondary parasite.

Two other fungi may also cause leaf spots of this host: *Cylindrosporium eminens* and *Septoria chaemaecisti*.

Control: If leaf spots occur on valuable rock garden specimens, spray with a copper or dithiocarbamate fungicide.

HELIANTHUS (SUNFLOWER)

Bacterial Diseases

Bacterial Leaf Spot (*Pseudomonas helianthi*). This disease has been observed in Florida. The spots are at first very small and water-soaked but as they increase in size become dark brown with green borders. Finally they run together and cause the death of large areas of the leaves. No control has been suggested.

Crown Gall (*Agrobacterium tumefaciens*). Occasionally plants in natural borders are attacked by this organism. Crown gall is not usually a serious disease of sunflowers.

Bacterial Wilt. A highly destructive disease of solanaceous plants caused by *Pseudomonas solanacearum*. It has been reported on sunflowers in Florida.

Fungus Diseases

Leaf Spots (*Alternaria zinniae, Ascochyta compositarum, Cercospora helianthi, C. pachypus, Colletotrichum helianthi, Phyllosticta helianthi*, and *Septoria helianthi*). Seven species of fungi cause leaf spots on sunflower.

Control: Control measures are rarely adopted except where this plant is grown commercially for its fruit.

Powdery Mildew (*Erysiphe cichoracearum*). This species, which attacks *H. annuus,* has been shown to exist in two forms, distinct in their sexual reactions and the development of their ascocarp stage. If the latter stage is absent, the parasite must winter on the protected buds of perennial species.

Control: Spray with Benlate, Karathane, or wettable sulfur.

Rust (*Puccinia helianthi*). Rust from wild sunflowers may seriously attack the cultivated species, especially varieties of *Helianthus annuus.* The rust exists in several different biologic races. Numerous brown pustules, in which the repeating spores are formed, develop on the undersides of the leaves. Rusted leaves dry up and fall.

Other species of rust fungi which are found on *Helianthus* are: *Puccinia massalis, Uromyces junci, U. silphii,* and *Coleosporium helianthi.*

Control: Remove infected leaves and destroy them. Valuable ornamental specimens might be protected with periodic applications of wettable sulfur sprays.

Wilt (*Plasmopara halstedii*). The roots of seedlings and young plants are invaded through their root-hairs as the zoospores germinate in the moisture of the soil. The mycelial threads enter the roots and move upward into the stems and leaves, causing an early wilt and the death of the plant. Older plants that become infected may not die, but have mosaic-like patterns of light yellowish mottling mixed with the natural green of the leaf. Spore-bearing branches project through the stomata on the undersides of the leaves. Whether the parasite invades the embryo of the seed is a question, but it is well known that the disease may be carried over by the seeds. The fungus also lives in the soil in the oospore stage.

Another wilt disease is caused by the fungus *Verticillium albo-atrum,* which also produces a leaf-mottling before the wilting and death of the plant. This fungus may be carried in seed.

Control: Rotate the plantings. The use of steam-pasteurized soil will prevent the initiation of the disease.

Stem Rot (*Sclerotinia sclerotiorum*). This is a very serious disease of sunflowers. The plants may be infected when they are several feet high. Young seedlings are not usually infected. A thick, whitish felting develops on the stems. The host tissues beneath become discolored. Numerous sclerotia are formed on the inside of the stem. In wet weather the stems wilt and collapse at the point of attack.

Control: Destroy all infected plants. Avoid planting sunflowers in the same plot for at least 2 years. Avoid close planting and moist situations.

Insects

Aphids. Many species of aphids infest sunflowers. The most common ones include the dogwood, hop, leaf-curl plum, melon, and potato aphids.

Control: All are easily controlled with malathion sprays.

Bugs. Six kinds of bugs infest this host: four-lined plant, harlequin, pumpkin, Say stink, southern green stink, and tarnished plant bugs.

Control: Sevin, pyrethrum, or rotenone sprays will control these pests.

Beetles. The following beetles infest sunflowers: carrot, pale-striped flea, potato flea, and western cucumber.

Control: Same as for bugs.

Yellow Woollybear (*Diacrisia virginica*). These caterpillars feed in great numbers on the heads, flower parts, and young seeds.

Control: Spray with Sevin. Destroy nearby thistles, which serve as a source of infestation.

Other Insects. Sunflowers are also infested by the larval stage of the painted lady butterfly, the corn earworm, and the oblique-banded leaf roller. These are controlled with the material recommended for the yellow woollybear.

The sunflower maggot, *Strauzia longipennis;* citrophilus mealybug, *Pseudococcus fragilis;* and the cottony-cushion scale, *Icerya purchasi,* are other insects which attack this host.

HELICHRYSUM BRACTEATUM (STRAWFLOWER)

Few diseases affect strawflower. Wilt caused by *Verticillium albo-atrum* occasionally causes severe damage to this host in California. Stem rot caused by a species of *Fusarium* and root-knot by the nema *Meloidogyne incognita* have been reported from Florida. The aster yellows disease occurs in the eastern and central United States, and in California.

The only insect reported on this host is the aster leafhopper, *Macrosteles fascifrons,* which sucks out the sap from plants, in addition to spreading aster yellows.

HELIOTROPIUM (HELIOTROPE)

Diseases

Heliotrope is subject to relatively few fungus diseases. Among the more commonly reported ones are a shoot blight caused by *Botrytis cinerea,* a leaf spot by *Cercospora heliotropii,* a rust by *Puccinia aristidae,* and wilt by *Verticillium albo-atrum.*

Insects and Other Animal Pests

Aphids. Several species of aphids infest this host, the most common being the green peach and the crescent-marked lily.

Control: Sevin or malathion sprays are very effective in combating these pests.

Mealybugs. Two species, the citrus and the citrophilus, infest heliotrope. A close relative of mealybugs, the greenhouse orthezia, *Orthezia insignis,* also feeds on this host.

Control: Spray with malathion.

Two-Spotted Mite (*Tetranychus urticae*). The two-spotted mite may appear on greenhouse-grown plants. Dark spots develop on the leaves and young shoots, and the leaves may dry up and die.

Control: See *Althaea.*

Eastern Subterranean Termite (*Reticulitermes flavipes*). Termites are known to eat out stems of heliotrope when wooden benches are connected directly with the soil. In modern greenhouses with concrete benches, however, termites are not a problem.

Greenhouse Whitefly (*Trialeurodes vaporariorum*). Heliotrope leaves turn yellow when infested by this pest. Both greenhouse-grown and outdoor plants are susceptible.

Control: See *Fuchsia.*

Southern Root-Knot Nema (*Meloidogyne incognita*). The roots of greenhouse-grown heliotropes are frequently infested with this nema.

Control: See Chapter 3.

HELLEBORUS NIGER (CHRISTMAS-ROSE)

Fungus Diseases

Black Spot (*Coniothyrium hellebori*). Rather large, irregular black spots develop on both sides of the leaves, often running together and having a concentric zonation. Many leaves turn yellow prematurely and die. The plants are weakened and fail to mature the normal number of leaves. Garden plants are seriously attacked in the spring, having black, canker-like spots on leaves, stems, and flower stalks. The stems shrivel at the point of attack and fall over, the leaves and unopened flower buds wilt. The petals of the flowers also may be black-spotted. This is one of the two most serious diseases of this host in the United States.

Control: Cut off and destroy all diseased leaves. Spray the remainder with captan several times at 2-week intervals. Use only sound plants for propagating.

Blight (*Botrytis cinerea* and *Gloeosporium* sp.). These fungi blight the plants and also cause a spotting of the flowers.

Control: Remove and destroy severely infected plants or infected flowers.

Crown Rot (*Sclerotium delphinii*). This disease is also a serious disease of Christmas-rose. The author has seen extensive plantings wiped out by the causal fungus.

Control: Use clean or steam-pasteurized soil as described in Chapter 4.

HEMEROCALLIS (DAYLILY)

Diseases

Leaf Spot (*Cercospora hemerocallis*). Black spots on the leaves may be caused by this fungus.

Control: Gather and destroy spotted leaves as they appear.

Russet Spot (cause unknown). Greenish-yellow spots on the leaves which gradually enlarge and turn orange-brown are common on the leaves of *H. fulva rosea* and varieties derived from it. The flowers on affected plants are fairly satisfactory despite the leaf russeting. Plants grown in partial shade seem to be more free of the trouble.

Insects and Other Animal Pests

Flower Thrips (*Frankliniella tritici*). *Hemerocallis multiflora, H. citrina,* and *H. thunbergi* may be severely injured by this species of thrips. Thrips feed on the flower buds and the tips of the branches so that the entire flower cluster may die without developing. Lateral branches and flower buds may be killed before they develop. The scapes have corky lesions which extend over several inches.

Control: Cygon, Diazinon, or Meta-Systox R sprays applied when growth begins in spring and repeated 2 or 3 times at 10-day intervals provide good control.

Other Pests. Among other pests which occasionally affect daylilies are the imported long-horned weevil, Japanese beetle, grasshoppers, mites, slugs, and wasps. These are discussed on more favored hosts in other parts of this book.

Southern Root-Knot Nema (*Meloidogyne incognita*). Occasionally the roots of daylilies may be infested by this nema.

HEPATICA (LIVERLEAF)

Diseases

Rust (*Tranzschelia pruni-spinosae*). This systemic rust, which also attacks species of anemone, often becomes established in *Hepatica* plants. It is perennial in them, causing the early development of great numbers of very crowded leaves. Many aecidial pustules break out on the undersides of the leaves.

Control: See *Anemone.*

Other Diseases. A downy mildew caused by *Plasmopara pygmaea,* leaf spot by *Septoria hepaticae,* and leaf and stem smut by *Urocystis anemones* are other fungus diseases that affect *Hepatica.*

Control: Remove and destroy infected parts.

HESPERIS (ROCKET)

Diseases

Hesperis is subject to some of the same diseases that affect other members of the Cruciferae. Among these are club root caused by *Plasmodiophora brassicae,* downy mildew by *Peronospora parasitica,* and white rust by *Albugo candida.* A mosaic disease, probably caused by the turnip mosaic virus, has been recorded in Oregon. See under *Matthiola.*

HEUCHERA

Diseases

Leaf Spots (*Cercospora heucherae, Phyllosticta excavata, Ramularia mitellae,* and *Septoria heucherae*). Four species of fungi may cause leaf spots of this host.

Control: Pick off and destroy spotted leaves. In rainy seasons an occasional spraying with a copper or dithiocarbamate fungicide will prevent serious epidemics of leaf spot.

Powdery Mildew (*Erysiphe cichoracearum, Sphaerotheca humuli* var. *fuliginea,* and *Phyllactinia corylea*). Three powdery mildew fungi occur on this host in the western United States.

Control: Valuable ornamental specimens can be protected with sprays containing Benlate, wettable sulfur, or Karathane.

Stem Rot (*Sclerotinia sclerotiorum*). *Heuchera* is among the many hosts subject to a stem rot caused by this fungus. Under moist conditions a white mycelium appears on the infected part. White sclerotia, which later turn black, develop in the pith cavity of the stem. See *Antirrhinum.*

Leaf and Stem Smut (*Urocystis lithophragmae*). This disease has been recorded from Utah. Control measures have not been developed.

Insects and Other Animal Pests

Strawberry Root Weevil (*Otiorhyncus ovatus*). Many plants in a bed may be destroyed by the grubs which feed on the roots and crowns in the spring. The crowns turn black and die. These white grubs are about ½ inch long and rather plump; the head is light brown; they have no legs; the body is usually somewhat curved. They move only slowly when exposed. The adults are blackish snout-beetles about ¼ inch long.

Control: See *Taxus.*

Foliar Nema (*Aphelenchoides ritzemabosi*). This nema, which is so destructive to garden chrysanthemums and other border plants, may also attack *Heuchera.* See *Chrysanthemum morifolium.*

Other Pests. Occasionally mealybugs infest this host. Malathion sprays will control them. The four-lined plant bug also infests *Heuchera.* Spraying with Sevin is recommended.

HIBISCUS (ARBORESCENT FORMS, ROSE-OF-SHARON, COTTON-ROSE, AND CHINESE HIBISCUS)

Diseases

Leaf Spots (*Alternaria tenuis, Cercospora hibisci, Colletotrichum gloeosporioides, C. hibisci,* and *Phyllosticta hibiscina*). The five fungi listed cause leaf spots primarily on *Hibiscus* grown in the South.

Control: Remove and destroy spotted leaves.

Bacterial Leaf Spot (*Pseudomonas syringae*). The bacterium that causes blight of lilacs is capable of causing a leaf spot on this host.

Control: Remove and destroy affected parts.

Blights (*Pellicularia filamentosa, P. koleroga,* and *P. rolfsii*). Three soil-inhabiting fungi attack this host. *P. koleroga* infects the leaves, whereas the other two attack the stems.

Control: Soil-inhabiting fungi are difficult to control. See Chapter 4.

Canker (*Nectria cinnabarina*). Branches and sometimes the entire plant may die as a result of infection by this fungus. Bright reddish-orange fruiting bodies appear in the diseased bark.

Control: Prune infected branches to sound wood. Where the main stem is invaded, the plant may be beyond help.

Rust (*Kuehneola malvicola*). This rust is common on *Hibiscus* in the Gulf States.

Control: Valuable specimens can be protected by occasional applications of wettable sulfur or Karathane.

Other Diseases. A blighting of flowers and leaves caused by *Botrytis cinerea* and a flower blight by *Choanephora infundibulifera* occur occasionally in the southern parts of the country, and a chlorotic leafspot caused by a virus.

Control: Control measures for these diseases are rarely adopted.

Physiological Diseases

Strapleaf (nutrient deficiency). In some acid Florida soils the leaves of some *Hibiscus* turn dark green, assume a straplike shape, and have deformed flowers. The addition of molybdenum in molybdic acid or sodium molybdate corrects this condition.

Bud Drop. In Florida, *Hibiscus* may drop its buds or fail to flower for a number of reasons. Too much or too little water, over-dosing with chemical fertilizers, and heavy infes-

tations of thrips are among the most common causes.

Insects and Related Pests

Aphids (*Aphis craccivora* and *A. gossypii*). The former species is black with white legs. It clusters at the tips of rose-of-Sharon branches. The latter is usually dark green but may vary from pale yellow to nearly black. It occasionally causes curling of the leaves.

Control: Spray with Sevin or malathion.

Japanese Beetle (*Popillia japonica*). The flowers of any *Hibiscus* are especially attractive to the adult beetles.

Control: See *Aesculus.*

Boll Weevil (*Anthonomus grandis thurberiae*). While the larvae feed only on cotton, the weevils feed on *Hibiscus* also. Spraying with Sevin prevents early damage to leaves.

Mining Scale (*Howardia biclavis*). This insect bores into the epidermis of the leaves and twigs. Reddish-brown spots appear on infested leaves. The white scales are not evident unless the epidermis is ruptured.

Control: Spray with malathion or Sevin.

Foliar Nema (*Aphelenchoides fragariae*). This nema was found capable of infecting *Hibiscus rosa-sinensis* leaves in Florida.

Control: Controls on this host have not yet been developed.

Japanese Weevil. See *Ligustrum.*

Whitefly. See *Fuchsia.*

HIBISCUS PALUSTRIS (ROSE-MALLOW)

Fungus and Bacterial Diseases

Leaf Spots (*Ascochyta abelmoschi, Cercospora kellermanii, Phyllosticta hibiscina,* and *Septoria* sp.). Four fungi cause leaf spots on rose-mallows. Another, *Colletotrichum hibisci,* causes a dieback of the top in addition to a leaf spot.

Control: Pick and destroy infected parts.

Other Diseases. A rust caused by the fungus *Puccinia schedonnardi* and galls by the bacterium *Agrobacterium tumefaciens* are the other diseases reported on this host.

Insects

Cotton Aphid (*Aphis gossypii*). Rose-mallows are frequently infested with this species.

Control: Spray with Meta-Systox R or malathion.

Scales. Six species of scales infest this host: California red, green shield, lesser snow, mining, pineapple, and San Jose.

Control: Spray with malathion or Sevin to control the crawler stage.

Other Pests. Rose-mallows may be attacked by Japanese beetles, the corn earworm, the larva of the abutilon moth, and the greenhouse whitefly. The controls for these pests are discussed under more favored hosts in other parts of this book.

HIPPEASTRUM—see AMARYLLIS

HOLODISCUS (ROCK-SPIREA)

Diseases

Canker (*Nectria cinnabarina*). Cankers on the twigs turn coral-pink when the fruiting bodies appear on the surface.

Control: Prune and destroy cankered twigs.

Leaf Spots (*Cylindrosporium ariaefolium, Rhapalidium cercosporelloidis,* and *Septogloeum schizonoti*). Three species of fungi cause leaf spots of this host in the western United States.

Control: Valuable ornamental specimens can be protected with copper or dithiocarbamate sprays.

Powdery Mildews (*Podosphaera oxyacanthae* and *Phyllactinia corylea*). Two powdery mildew fungi also occur in the western part of the country.

Control: Spray valuable plants with Benlate, wettable sulfur, or Karathane.

Witches' Brooms. Plants affected by this disease have very short and stout internodes of the stems. The plants do not blossom and many buds develop at the nodes into short, lateral branches or wiry shoots, which form the witches' broom. The leaves are small and become bronze-red in the summer. The disease has been transferred by bud grafting and by *Aphis spiraecola.* It is known in the northwestern United States. The cause of this disease may be a mycoplasma-like organism or a virus.

Control: Remove and destroy infected plants.

HOSTA (PLANTAIN-LILY)

Diseases

Leaf Spots (*Colletotrichum omnivorum, Alternaria* sp., and *Phyllosticta* sp.). The first of these fungi causes large, white or grayish spots with brown borders, which disfigure the leaves and stems. The others form smaller spots and may be troublesome in very rainy seasons.

Control: Spray with a copper or dithiocarbamate fungicide.

Crown Rot (*Botrytis cinerea, Pellicularia rolfsii,* and *Sclerotium delphinii*). *Botrytis* has been reported from the states of New Jersey and Alaska as the cause of a decay of the crowns. The others are common soil-inhabiting organisms that affect many kinds of plants. See *Delphinium* for details on control.

HOUSTONIA

Diseases

Downy Mildew (*Peronospora calotheca* and *P. seymourii*). These two fungi occur more frequently on wild than cultivated plants. Hence no controls are necessary.

Leaf Spots (*Cercospora houstoniae* and *Septoria* sp.). Spots on the leaves may be caused by these fungi in very rainy seasons.

Control: Pick off and destroy spotted leaves.

Rusts (*Puccinia lateritia, Uromyces houstoniatus,* and *U. peckianus*). In nature three species of rust fungi are common. The alternate hosts for *Uromyces* are grasses.

Control: Control measures are rarely required on cultivated forms of *Houstonia.*

HOYA (WAX-PLANT)

Insects

Only two insects have been reported on Wax-plant, the oleander aphid and the citrus mealybug. These can be controlled with nicotine sulfate-soap sprays.

HYACINTHUS (HYACINTH)

Bacterial Diseases

Yellow Rot (*Xanthomonas hyacinthi*). Yellowish water-soaked stripes begin near the tip of the leaf and extend downward; these stripes turn brown and die. Infected flower stalks also have a water-soaked appearance and become brown and shriveled. Cross-sections of infected leaves, flower stalks, and bulbs show masses of yellowish slime oozing from the vascular tissues and from pockets which contain vast numbers of bacteria. Decay begins first in the pockets or rotted areas of the bulbs and within a few days affects the entire bulb. The disease progresses from the leaves into the bulb or vice versa. It is said that this bacterium does not live in the ground through the winter; if this is true, soil pasteurization is unnecessary for replanting. The disease-producing organisms are spread by splashing of rain, by wind, or by cultivation. The spread is generally circular or in the direction in which the wind is blowing. Leaves and flowerstalks can easily

be pulled out of diseased bulbs, like those of irises affected with the soft rot organism.

Control: Destroy all plants affected by this rot. Do not plant infected bulbs. In Holland, where this disease is serious, stringent measures are taken to keep it under control.

Soft Rot (*Erwinia carotovora*). The failure of bulbs to produce flowers is a common symptom of this disease. Such bulbs are said to be "blind." Blossoms fall off before completely unfolding, or are formed irregularly and fall off later. The stalk rots at the base and collapses. Infected bulbs undergo a white, viscous, foul-smelling soft rot. Many varieties of hyacinths are subject to this rot.

Control: Care should be taken to store the bulbs in a dry, well ventilated room. Separate the bulbs so that they are not in contact with each other. Avoid excessive watering, especially about the bulbs, and freezing the bulbs. Avoid also excessively high temperatures in forcing; only well-rooted plants should be forced.

Fungus Diseases

Black Slime (*Sclerotinia bulborum*). The leaves become yellowish and the plants are retarded; later they wither and are easily detached from the bulbs. The bulbs are discolored inside; they are more or less disintegrated and penetrated by the white mycelium of the fungus. Between the scales and the outer part of the bulb long, flat sclerotia are found, at first white, later black; they are about 1/2 inch broad. The fungus lives over winter by means of these sclerotia, which remain in the soil. The same fungus is said to affect a number of related species of plants. The mycelium also grows in strings, which penetrate the ground and may infect sound plants.

Control: Special care should be taken to pasteurize the soil where the disease has been present. Dusting PCNB (Terraclor) over bulbs in furrows before covering is said to provide some control.

Root Rot (*Fusarium* sp.). This is a disease of *H. orientalis*. Plants are dwarfed and develop poor blossoms. Most of the roots decay and the basal plate of the bulb is destroyed.

Control: Discard infected bulbs. Dip the remainder in a suspension of Benlate, 1 ounce of the 50 per cent wettable powder in 3 gallons of water. Soils in which the plants have become diseased must be steam-pasteurized or bulbs planted in another locality.

Gray Mold (*Botrytis hyacinthi*). The leaves are discolored at the outer ends; they become shrunken, rotted, and covered with a layer of gray mold. In cold, wet weather the blossoms become rotted. Black sclerotia about the size of a pinhead later develop on parts that previously showed the gray mold. This disease was first found in the Pacific Northwest in 1949, in commercial fields of *H. orientalis*. Other outbreaks were recorded in 1956 and 1957. It may become an important disease of this host in the future.

Control: Avoid working in fields during wet weather or when the plants are wet with rain or dew. Collect all diseased blossoms and destroy them. Spray repeatedly with a fungicide such as Benlate, Botran, or zineb.

Rust (*Uromyces muscari* var. *hyacinthi*). This fungus occasionally attacks hyacinth leaves, bursting out in masses of dark brown teliospores.

Control: Thus far the disease has not proved to be serious enough to warrant control measures.

Virus Disease

Mosaic (Ornithogalum mosaic virus). Leaves show blue-green mottling, streaking, and blotching, often accompanied by reduction and withering of flowers. The virus has been transferred from hyacinth to *Ornithogalum thyrsoides* by the potato aphid, *Macrosiphum euphorbiae*. Bulb plants belonging to the genera *Lachenalia* and *Galtonia* are also susceptible to this disease.

Control: Same as for mosaic of *Iris*.

Insects and Other Animal Pests

Aphids. (*Myzus persicae, Acyrthosiphon solani*, and *Aphis fabae*). These species frequently attack hyacinth leaves and act as carriers of virus diseases.

Control: Meta-Systox R, malathion, or Sevin sprays applied from time to time as needed will provide control.

Bulb Mite (*Rhizoglyphus echinopus*). Little brown spots develop on the bulbs of hyacinths. The mites make their way into the tissues of the bulb scales, multiplying very rapidly. As a result of their feeding, the bulb becomes a dry powdery mass. The surfaces of the bulb scales become rather hard and brown. Other animal and fungus parasites enter the bulb scales as a result of mite injury. The mites work best at a rather high humidity and high storage temperatures.

Control: See *Tulipa*.

Lesser Bulb Fly (*Eumerus tuberculatus*). This pest occasionally attacks hyacinth bulbs. It is most common, however, in narcissus bulbs and at times in iris rhizomes. See *Narcissus* for details on control.

Yellow Woollybear (*Diacrisia virginica*) occasionally attacks hyacinths but ordinarily need not be considered a serious pest. If necessary, spray the plants with Sevin. Handpicking will probably suffice. See *Canna*.

White Grubs (*Phyllophaga* sp.) and **Japanese Beetle Grubs** (*Popillia japonica*) may feed on hyacinth bulbs and destroy the roots. The adult beetles will also feed on the foliage at times. Cutworms may also attack young hyacinth plants.

Control: Where grubs are known to exist, the best control procedure is to grub-proof the soil, as described under Gramineae.

Stem and Bulb Nema (*Ditylenchus dipsaci*). Many leaves are deformed, bent, and yellowish; they later turn brown. The formation of blossoms is much reduced. Individual scales of the bulbs turn brown and become rotted. Cross-sections of the bulbs show a dark ring. The infested parts of bulb scales or leaves often become swollen or distorted. The nemas migrate from infested leaves into the bulbs and then by the decay of the bulbs are dispersed and spread in the soil, where they spend the winter. They also migrate through the soil to sound bulbs. This nema affects a number of other garden plants, such as phlox, amaryllis, and tulip.

Control: Quarantine regulations now prevent the shipping of infested bulbs. Soil in which infested plants have been grown must be pasteurized with heat or treated with any of the excellent nemacides on the market. Infested bulbs can be dipped for 3 hours in hot water at 110°F. to which one part of formalin to 200 parts of water has been added.

HYDRANGEA

Bacterial and Fungus Diseases

Bacterial Wilt (*Pseudomonas solanacearum*). Blighting of the inflorescence and young leaves of arborescent hydrangeas has been reported as extremely serious after heavy rains and hot weather. It has been noted that wilting and root rot are sufficient to destroy many plants. No control has been suggested.

Bud Blight (*Botrytis cinerea*). This disease may occur on dense flower clusters of outdoor plants during wet seasons, or on the buds of greenhouse plants subjected to the dark treatment.

Control: Spray field-grown plants with Botran when symptoms first appear and then every 10-days in wet seasons. Plants in storage should be sprayed with Botran or Benlate.

Leaf Spots (*Ascochyta hydrangeae, Cercospora arborescentis, Corynespora cassicola, Phyllosticta hydrangeae,* and *Septoria hydrangeae*). Five species of fungi may cause leaf spotting of hydrangeas.

Control: Spray periodically with zineb.

Powdery Mildew (*Erysiphe polygoni*). The undersides of the infected leaves, especially, become covered with a light-gray mold which turns brownish in spots or patches. The upper surface of infected leaves may remain green or turn purplish-brown in color. The buds of certain varieties may be badly deformed. The tender stem ends and flower stalks may also be mildewed. The leaves die prematurely, and the blooms become stunted and spotted or develop abnormally and die.

Control: Spray the leaves when they show the first signs of mildew with Karathane or Benlate. Repeat in 2 weeks, if necessary.

Rust (*Pucciniastrum hydrangeae*). Certain ornamental varieties in greenhouses and borders are subject to attack by this parasite. The leaves may be spotted with large numbers of yellowish rusty-brown pustules, especially on the undersides. Such leaves tend to dry up and become brittle.

Control: The disease is spread via spores which are carried by the wind or by watering or syringing in greenhouses. Spraying with a ferbam-sulfur mixture should be helpful. Since the alternate host of this parasite is hemlock, one might think that destroying hemlock would eliminate the rust; but this is not true. Evidently the rust can winter on old plant parts, and thus get along very well from year to year without the hemlock.

Virus Diseases

Hydrangeas are known to be subject to several ringspot viruses. One known as hydrangea ringspot is thought to be the cause of so-called "running-out" of the florists hydrangea, *Hydrangea macrophylla*. This virus is capable of causing a change in the normal flower to leafy structures, a condition known as phyllody. It can be transmitted by means of knives used in cuttings. Dipping the knives in Physan 20 will prevent the virus from spreading.

The tobacco ringspot virus has been found on naturally infected hydrangeas in Florida.

The tomato ringspot virus also occurs on this host.

Control: Use only healthy plants for propagation. Destroy infected plants, inasmuch as they cannot be cured, and any cuttings taken from them will harbor the virus.

Physiological Diseases

Sunscald. If the temperature reaches 102°F. in the shade, it will be found that the top leaves especially of rapidly growing plants may be burned by the sun. Plants appear as if frosted or injured by sprays.

Control: Temporary shading of the plants with lattice-work or cheesecloth prevents such injury.

Chlorosis. Yellowish discoloration of the leaves of hydrangeas is not uncommon where the soil is more or less alkaline; these plants require slightly acid soil. An application of ammonium sulfate to acidify the soil is recommended. Avoid excessive use of lime, which makes the iron in the soil unavailable. A new way to cure chlorosis is to use iron chelates either as foliage sprays or through the soil. These are sold under such trade names as Sequestrene of Iron, Versenol, and Perma Green Iron 135.

Insects and Related Pests

Aphids. The crescent-marked lily and the melon aphid infest hydrangea. Malathion, Meta-Systox, or Sevin sprays are effective in combating these pests.

Four-Lined Plant Bug (*Poecilocapsis lineatus*). See *Aconitum.*

Leaf Tier (*Exartema ferriferanum*). This small green caterpillar ties the terminal leaves over the buds.

Control: Spray with Sevin before the caterpillar encloses itself in the leaves.

Rose Chafer (*Macrodactylus subspinosus*). This insect has been reported as occasionally attacking hydrangeas in gardens.

Control: See *Rosa.*

Oystershell Scale (*Lepidosaphes ulmi*). This scale is known to attack hardy hydrangeas. It usually appears on the upper ends of the stems.

Control: Spray hardy hydrangeas while dormant with lime sulfur, or when in leaf in early June with malathion or Sevin.

Two-Spotted Mite (*Tetranychus urticae*). Symptoms like those of sunscald, described above, have been found to be sometimes due to attacks of the two-spotted mite. The leaves are burned especially about the margins.

Control: See *Althaea.*

Nemas (*Meloidogyne incognita, M. hapla,* and *Ditylenchus dipsaci*). Occasionally hydrangeas may be infested with the southern root-knot nema, the northern root-knot nema, or the stem nema. Controls are described in Chapter 3.

HYDRASTIS (GOLDENSEAL)

Fungus Diseases

Blight (*Alternaria panax*). This fungus causes a leaf spot and blight of goldenseal. Another fungus, a species of *Botrytis,* causes circular leaf spots with brown centers and darker brown borders. All parts of the plant, even the underground stem, are affected; the leaves are blighted and the leaf stalks rotted at the base. Blossoms and seed heads are often destroyed. Seedlings are at times very susceptible. The very small sclerotia which carry the fungus through the winter are imbedded in the diseased petioles.

Control: Neither copper fungicides nor sulfur has proved effective in combating these fungi. Zineb might be more effective. Avoid crowding plants in the seed bed.

Stem Rots (*Pellicularia filamentosa* and *Phytophthora cactorum*). These fungi occasionally cause stem decay of this host.

Control: Set plants in clean soil well apart from soil which has had diseased plants.

Wilt and Root Rot (*Fusarium* sp.). Occasionally goldenseal may be affected by this fungus.

Control: Discard diseased plants and replace infested soil with clean soil.

HYMENOCALLIS (SPIDER-LILY)

Diseases

Leaf Spot (*Cercospora pancratii*). This disease occurs in the Deep South.

Control: Pick off and destroy infected leaves.

Leaf Scorch (*Stagonospora curtisii*). See *Amaryllis.*

Insects

Three insects attack spider-lily: the Spanish moth caterpillar, *Xanthopastis timais;* the lesser snow scale, *Pinnaspis strachani;* and the banded greenhouse thrips, *Hercinothrips femoralis.* All can be controlled with malathion sprays.

HYPERICUM (ST. JOHN'S-WORT)

Leaf spots caused by *Cercospora hyperici, Cladosporium hyperici,* and *Septoria hyperici* mar the foliage but need not cause much concern. Black knots on stems caused by *Gibberidea heliopsidis,* a powdery mildew of leaves by *Erysiphe cichoracearum,* a rust by *Uromyces triquetrus,* and a root rot by the fungus *Rosellinia (Dermatophora) necatrix,* are other fungus diseases that occasionally appear on this host.

The southern root-knot nema *Meloidogyne incognita* occurs on St. John's-wort in the southern part of the country.

IBERIS (CANDYTUFT)

Diseases

Club Root (*Plasmodiophora brassicae*). This organism, which lives in the soil, attacks roots and causes much deformation and stunting of the root system.

Control: Soil that harbors the organism must be pasteurized if ornamentals of the mustard family are to be planted in it. Acid soils favor its growth; liming discourages its growth. Inasmuch as the chemical PCNB (Terraclor) has given good control of the same organism on cabbage, it might be worth trying in soils growing infected candytuft.

Damping-off (*Pellicularia filamentosa*). This fungus causes stems to curl and plants to collapse.

Control: Use clean soil, steam-pasteurize infested soil, or treat it with PCNB (Terraclor) or with Benlate.

Other Diseases. A downy mildew caused by *Peronospora parasitica,* a powdery mildew by *Erysiphe polygoni,* and a white rust by *Albugo candida* are other fungus diseases of candytuft.

Insects and Other Animal Pests

Oystershell Scale (*Lepidosaphes ulmi*). This scale occasionally infests the hardy candytuft, *Iberis sempervirens.*

Control: Spray with malathion or Sevin in May and June to control the crawler stage.

Diamondback Moth. See *Cheiranthus.*

Southern Root-Knot Nema (*Meloidogyne incognita*).

Control: See Chapter 3.

ILEX (HOLLY)

Diseases

Tar Spot (*Phacidium curtisii*). Yellow spots appear on the leaves of American and English hollies in May. These turn reddish-brown and finally black by fall.

Control: Gather and destroy badly spotted leaves. Spray with a copper fungicide several times at 2-week intervals starting in late spring. Such sprays may cause slight injury if the season is cool.

Leaf Spots (*Cercospora ilicis, C. pulvinula, Englerulaster orbicularis, Gloeosporium aquifolii, Macrophoma phacidiella, Microthyriella cuticulosa, Phyllosticta concomitans, P. terminalis, Rhytisma ilicinicolum, R. velatum,* and *Septoria ilicifolia*). Many fungi cause brown spots of the leaves.

Control: Infected leaves should be picked off and destroyed and the vigor of the trees improved by incorporating oak-leaf mold or cottonseed meal into the soil. In addition, water should be provided during dry spells. Applications of Bordeaux mixture or any other copper spray in late summer and in early fall will largely prevent the formation of the spots. More lasting results are obtained, however, by improving the soil conditions. Copper fungicides may cause some injury, especially to leaves that have been punctured by the holly leaf miner. They also leave an unsightly residue which persists for some time. Ferbam or Fore sprays should be used where copper sprays are likely to cause injury.

Canker (*Diaporthe eres, Nectria coccinea, Physalospora ilicis, Phomopsis crustosa, Diplodia* sp., and *Gloeosporium* sp.) Sunken areas on the twigs and stems may be caused by these fungi.

Control: Prune diseased branches and spray with copper fungicide several times in late spring.

Bacterial Blight (*Corynebacterium ilicis*). This disease was first found in a holly orchard on Nantucket Island in 1957. Leaves and shoots of the primary growth appear scorched in June and July in that latitude. Diseased shoots wilt, droop, and dry but persist. The infection progresses into the woody shoots of the previous year's growth, where the leaves turn black.

Control: Copper fungicides will probably control this disease. Excessive use of nitrogenous fertilizers and cultivation of soil beneath the trees increase the trees' susceptibility to bacterial blight.

Twig Dieback (*Phytophthora ilicis*). Black stem cankers and black spots on the leaves are caused by this fungus in the Pacific Northwest. The disease was earlier thought to be caused by the fungi *Boydia insculpta* and *Phomopsis crustosa*.

Control: Although control measures have not been worked out, it is highly probable that Bordeaux mixture or any good copper fungicide will be effective. Applications should be started in the autumn at the onset of the cool, rainy weather.

Spot Anthracnose (*Elsinoë ilicis*). Tiny black spots or a large leaf-distorting spot may appear on the leaves of Chinese holly, *Ilex cornuta*, in the South.

Control: Spray periodically with a copper fungicide.

Leaf Rot, Drop (*Pellicularia filamentosa*). As a result of invasion by the *Rhizoctonia* stage of the causal fungus, the leaves of American holly cuttings may decay and drop about two weeks after the cuttings are inserted into the rooting medium. The disease first appears as a cobwebby coating, a combination of the fungus threads and grains of sand adhering to the undersides of the leaves that touch the sand.

Control: Insert cuttings in clean, fresh sand or in pasteurized old sand. Do not use cuttings taken from holly branches that touch the ground.

Powdery Mildews (*Microsphaera alni* and *Phyllactinia corylea*). In the South, holly leaves may be affected by these mildew fungi.

Control: Where the disease becomes prevalent, spray with Benlate, Karathane, or wettable sulfur.

Other Diseases. The inflorescences of American hollies are blighted by a species of *Botrytis*, a red leaf spot is caused by a species of *Sclerophoma*, and several species of nemas cause root-knot.

Nonparasitic Diseases

Spine Spot. Small, gray spots with purple halos are caused by the puncturing of the leaves by the spines of adjacent holly leaves. A careful examination with a hand lens will reveal tiny, circular holes or an irregular tear at the center of each spot.

Spine spot is often confused with slits made by the holly leaf miner. The latter have neither a gray center nor a purple halo.

Leaf Scorch. A browning or scorching of the leaves, common on holly in late winter or early spring, is of nonparasitic origin. Occasionally it is caused by the presence of water or ice on the leaves at the time the sun is shining brightly. This causes a scalding, followed by invasion by secondary organisms and finally by scorching.

Hollies planted in wind-swept areas are also more susceptible to so-called winterdrying. The leaves in late winter or early spring lose water faster than it can be replaced through the roots. As a result the leaf edges wilt and turn brown. In exposed situations, newly transplanted holly should be protected with some sort of windbreak or sprayed with an antidesiccant such as Wilt-Pruf NCF.

Insects

Holly Leaf Miner (*Phytomyza ilicis*). Yellow or brown serpentine mines or blotches in leaves are produced by the leaf miner, a small yellowish-white maggot, 1/6 inch long, that feeds between the leaf surfaces. The adult is a small black fly that emerges about May 1 and makes slits in the lower leaf surfaces, where it deposits eggs.

Another species, the native leaf miner, *P. ilicicola,* produces very slender mines and may occur on the same tree.

Control: Meta-Systox R, Dylox, or Diazinon sprays applied when the pests are first observed in mid-May and again in early July provide effective control.

Bud Moth (*Rhopobota naevana ilicifoliana*). Holly in the Pacific Northwest is subject to this pest, the larval stage of which feeds on the buds and terminal growth inside a web.

Control: Spray with methoxychlor or Sevin between the opening of the leaf bud and the time of blossoming.

Scales. Eleven species of scale insects attack hollies: black, California red, greedy, holly, lecanium, oleander, oystershell, peach, pit-making, soft, and tea.

Control: Most of these scales can be controlled with malathion or Sevin sprays applied when the young are crawling about in spring, the application being repeated several times at 10-day intervals.

Beetles. The black blister beetle, the Japanese beetle, and the potato flea beetle occasionally infest hollies.

Control: Spray with a Sevin-Kelthane mixture when the beetles first appear.

Whitefly. The citrus and mulberry whiteflies also occur on this host. Malathion and Cygon sprays are very effective against the nymphal stages of these pests. Sprays containing the synthetic pyrethroid, Resmethrin, are also very effective.

Berry Midge (*Asphondylia ilicicola*). The larvae of this pest infest holly berries and prevent them from turning red in the fall.

Control: Where only a few trees are involved, hand picking and destruction of infested berries should keep this pest under control. Diazinon spray applied in early June will control the midge where many trees are being grown.

Southern Red Mite (*Oligonichus ilicis*). This mite has become a serious pest of holly.

Control: Apply a dormant oil spray in March or April just before new growth starts, then spray with Meta-Systox R or Kelthane[24] about mid-May and repeat in 10 days.

Japanese Weevil. See *Ligustrum.*

ILEX VERTICILLATA (WINTERBERRY)

Diseases

Tar Spots (*Rhytisma concavum* and *R. prini*). Black spots on the leaves of winterberry are caused by two species of *Rhytisma.*

Control: Valuable ornamental specimens should be sprayed with ferbam.

Leaf Spots (*Phyllosticta haynaldi* and *Physalospora ilicis*). Small, brown spots may be caused by these fungi.

Control: Same as for tar spot.

Powdery Mildew (*Microsphaera alni*). This mildew disease has been recorded in Wisconsin.

Control: This disease can be controlled with Benlate, wettable sulfur, or Karathane sprays.

IMPATIENS BALSAMINA (GARDEN BALSAM)

Diseases

Bacterial Wilt (*Pseudomonas solanacearum*). In Wisconsin wilting of garden balsam has been attributed to the germ which also affects many solanaceous plants.

Control: Remove and destroy affected plants. Before replanting, steam-pasteurize soil in which diseased plants appeared.

Damping-off (*Pythium ultimum* and *Pellicularia filamentosa*). Young balsam plants are fairly subject to damping-off.

Control: Use clean soil or sow seed in moist, sifted sphagnum moss.

Leaf Spots (*Cercospora fukushiana*, *Septoria noli-tangeris*, *Phyllosticta* sp., and *Stemphyllium botryosum*). Small, more or less circular, brown spots may be caused by one of the fungi listed.

Control: Pick off and destroy infected leaves.

Other Diseases. A stem rot caused by *Pellicularia rolfsii* and a wilt by *Verticillium albo-atrum* are two additional fungus parasites of garden balsam.

Control: Use clean soil or treat infested soil with heat or a chemical (see Chapter 4).

Insects and Other Animal Pests

Balsam Aphid (*Macrosiphum impatientis*). This species can sometimes become very prevalent on this host.

Control: Spray with malathion, Meta-Systox R, or Sevin.

Spotted Cucumber Beetle (*Diabrotica undecimpunctata howardi*). The body of this beetle is black, the wing-cases are yellowish-green, each marked by six large spots. It feeds on the blossoms, eating holes in them and in the petioles.

Control: Spray with Diazinon, methoxychlor, rotenone, or Sevin.

Tarnished Plant Bug (*Lygus linearis*). The new shoots of garden balsam turn black when attacked by this bug.

Control: Same as for spotted cucumber beetle.

Cyclamen Mite. See *Cyclamen.*

Southern Root-Knot Nema (*Meloidogyne incognita*). In the southern states and in northern greenhouse plantings, this nema can be very injurious.

The root lesion nema, *Pratylenchus penetrans,* invades the roots and causes severe stunting of the above ground parts.

Control: See Chapter 3.

INULA

Diseases

Powdery Mildew (*Erysiphe cichoracearum*). This is the most serious disease of

[24] Kelthane may injure Chinese holly, *Ilex cornuta.*

Inula. It appears as a white coating over the leaves in late summer.

Control: Spray with Benlate or Karathane as soon as the mildew appears.

Other Diseases. A leaf spot caused by a species of *Ramularia* and a rust by *Puccinia hieracii* are two other fungus diseases that afflict *Inula.*

IPOMOEA (MORNING-GLORY)

Diseases

Canker (*Vermicularia ipomoearum*). Sunken, brown areas on the stems may be caused by this fungus.

Control: Destroy infected vines.

Leaf Spots (*Alternaria* sp., *Cercospora alabamensis, C. ipomoeae,* and *C. viridula*). Morning-glory leaves may be spotted by one of the four fungi listed.

Control: Pick off and destroy spotted leaves. In late fall, gather and destroy all aboveground parts.

Rusts (*Puccinia crassipes* and *Coleosporium ipomoeae*). Two rusts occur on *Ipomoea* in the South. The latter has its alternate stage on pines.

Control: Same as for leaf spots.

White Rust (*Albugo ipomoeae-panduratae*). In the southern states this disease has been reported as serious locally; it is not important farther north.

Insects

Cotton Aphid (*Aphis gossypii*). This aphid frequently infests morning-glory.

Control: Spray with Sevin or malathion.

Beetles. Six kinds of beetles—Asiatic garden, argus tortoise, golden tortoise, mottled tortoise, spotted cucumber, and sweet potato flea beetle—infest morning glories.

Control: Spray with a Sevin-Kelthane mixture if the beetles are numerous.

Yellow Woollybear (*Diacrisia virginica*).

Morning-glories are one of the many garden hosts attacked by this repulsive insect.

Control: Spraying the plants thoroughly with Diazinon or Sevin gives good control.

Morning-Glory Leaf Cutter (*Loxostege obliteralis*). This is another leaf eating insect on morning-glory which can be controlled by spraying the plants with Diazinon or Sevin.

Corn Earworm (*Heliothis zea*). This insect destroys the foliage of morning-glory and a number of other garden plants. It is controlled by spraying the plants with Sevin.

Morning-Glory Leaf Miner (*Bedellia somnulentella*). The eggs laid on the leaves hatch into small larvae, which enter the leaf tissues and make mines, at first serpentine, later running together to form blotch mines. Many blotches may cause the death of the leaves.

Control: While effective methods have not been suggested, spraying the plants with malathion after the eggs have hatched, or even after the larvae have entered the leaves, should control this pest.

Four-Lined Plant Bug (*Poecilocapsus lineatus*). Morning-glory is one of the hosts of this insect, which attacks many other species of flowering plants in the garden.

Control: Sevin or rotenone sprays are recommended.

Other Pests. Among the other insects that infest morning-glories occasionally are the garden fleahopper, the sweet potato weevil, the greenhouse whitefly, and two kinds of scales—the lesser snow and the soft. These are discussed on more favored hosts in other parts of this book.

IRESINE (BLOOD-LEAF)

A root rot caused by two species of fungi, *Helicobasidium purpureum* and *Pellicularia filamentosa,* and an inflorescence smut by *Thecaphora iresine* are the only fungus diseases known on this host in the United States.

The southern root-knot nema, *Meloidogyne incognita*, has been reported on bloodleaf in the South.

IRIS

While the diseases and pests that attack the common German iris may be somewhat different from those of Japanese iris and bulbous iris, the diseases and pests of the three groups are here treated together. If any trouble is of particular significance to one group, this is mentioned.

Bacterial Diseases

Bacterial Soft Rot (*Erwinia carotovora*). The foul-smelling soft rot of the rhizomes is probably the most serious disease of German iris. The bacteria may gain entrance into the plant through wounds in the young leaves made by the young larvae of the iris borer, shown in Fig. 41. Once in the soft tissue of the leaf, the bacteria multiply rather rapidly, destroying these tissues and causing a water-soaked appearance around the original hole made by the borer. They also destroy the leaves as they make their way towards the rhizome. Water-soaked streaks spreading out on the leaves are fairly conspicuous as symptoms of infection. The infection is certain to reach the rhizome unless prevented by the cutting of infected leaves. The first symptom will be the falling over of healthy leaves because of rot and collapse at the base. Such leaves are easily separated from the rotting rhizomes. The foul odor also provides a good means of diagnosis. This disease may appear immediately or soon after transplanting or after the weeding out of new irises, or it may appear after clumps have been established. It is not at all connected with crowded conditions, as are certain other diseases of irises mentioned below.

Control: Elimination of the iris borer is one of the first essentials of control of soft rot. The moths mature in August and September. They deposit their eggs on old iris leaves and rubbish in plantings. Where a winter covering of old leaves is essential to prevent frost injury, it may be necessary to delay the raking of leaves until early spring, when all such debris should be destroyed.

If the destruction of old leaves and other rubbish has been delayed until the young iris leaves have reached a height of 6 or 8 inches, spray the young plants with Cygon or malathion and repeat the application at two-week intervals. Other insecticides which will also control the young borers while they are still accessible are rotenone and pyrethrum. These must also be applied at closely spaced intervals to provide effective control.

When the rot is seen on the leaves, the descent of the bacteria may be prevented by cutting off the leaves well below the water-soaked areas. This should be done with shears dipped in 70 per cent denatured alcohol to disinfest them. If the rhizomes are rotted the plants should be dug up carefully and destroyed. Always disinfest the trowel or spade used in the digging.

The recent discovery that certain antibiotics effectively control many bacterial diseases of plants suggests the possibility that such materials as streptomycin might also give good control of iris soft rot when used as a dip. Do not plant rhizomes too deeply. When only partially buried, many bacteria on or near the surface of the rhizomes are killed by the sun's rays.

Bacterial Leaf Spot (*Xanthomonas tardicrescens*). Translucent spots of irregular shape which appear dark green in reflected light are the early symptoms. The spots may coalesce to involve the whole leaf when rainy weather continues for an extended period. This disease is often mistaken for that caused by the fungus *Didymellina macrospora* discussed below.

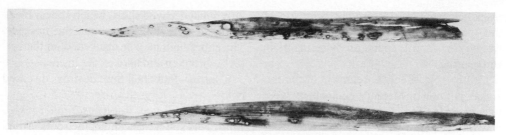

Fig. 153. Iris leaf spot caused by the fungus *Didymellina macrospora.*

Control: Remove and destroy spotted leaves early in the growing season. Remove and destroy the tops in the fall.

Fungus Diseases

Blossom Blight (*Botrytis cinerea* and *Glomerella cingulata*). In rainy seasons the blossoms may be spotted and blighted by two species of fungi.

Control: Pick off and destroy spotted flowers and leaves as soon as noticed. Reduce humidity by controlling heat and ventilation in the greenhouse and avoid splashing water. If these measures do not control the disease, try spraying with Benlate.

Leaf Spot (*Didymellina macrospora*). This fungus causes characteristic irregular eyespots (Fig. 153) which vary in size and run together; they have grayish centers with dark brown borders. The disease is usually more or less confined to the upper half of the leaf. Minute brown spots with water-soaked margins are the first symptoms, which may be mistaken for those of bacterial leaf spot. The disease is more serious after blooming. The premature death of the leaves weakens the rhizomes so that the plants die after a few years. The fungus does not infect the rhizomes or roots. This disease affects bulbous iris especially. The asexual stage of the causal organism is referred to as *Heterosporium iridis.*

Many other fungi cause leaf spotting of iris. Among them are *Alternaria iridicola, Ascochyta iridis, Mycosphaerella* sp., and *Phyllosticta iridis.*

Control: Spray periodically with freshly prepared Bordeaux mixture, 4-6-50, containing a wetting and sticking agent, or with one pound of zineb in 100 gallons of water. Maneb, Phaltan, and Fore sprays also provide good control. Raking and destroying old iris leaves in the fall or early spring will also help materially to prevent this disease.

Rust (*Puccinia iridis*). Rusty-red, powdery pustules break out on both sides of the leaves, causing considerable damage to many varieties, especially wild iris. The red rust spores spread the disease from leaf to leaf. The black or dark-brown spores, formed later, carry the parasite through the winter to infect the alternate host, which is as yet unkown. The red spores may live over winter on leaves that are not badly frozen. There are four special forms of this rust: *australis, californica, floridanum,* and *septentrionalis.* Another rust fungus of iris, *P. sessilis,* has *Phalaris* as its alternate host.

Control: Destroy all fallen leaves in the fall or winter, or before growth starts in the spring. Should rusts become important in ornamental plantings, the use of ferbam sprays will help to control them.

Rhizome Rot (*Botryotinia convoluta*). Rotting rhizomes on which many shining black sclerotia develop are characteristic of this disease. The fungus develops in cool, wet weather and is found on dying plants in early spring.

Control: No effective treatment of the rhizomes is known. Mercury compounds were recommended for many years, but their use is now banned.

Crown Rot (*Pellicularia rolfsii*). The leaf and flower stalk bases of crowded plants are invaded by this fungus, which later extends into the rhizome and causes a more or less dry rot. Though the tops of the leaves may turn brown, the fungus itself is confined to parts near the ground. The rot develops rather rapidly and extensively. The mycelium of the parasite soon spreads out on the crown and the rhizome to form at first whitish, then tan-colored, and finally brown or black sclerotia, about the size of mustard seeds.

Control: Remove both plants and soil from the diseased area and 6 inches beyond. When these are being removed, care should be taken not to scatter any soil beyond the infested area. PCNB (Terraclor) applied to infested soil, as directed by the manufacturer, will also reduce the prevalence of the disease.

Black Rot (*Sclerotinia sclerotiorum*). Plants affected by this disease either fail to emerge, or emerge, turn yellow, wilt, and die. The bulbs and shoots below ground are covered with grayish mold. Black, spherical sclerotia develop on old, decayed parts.

Control: Discard all diseased bulbs. Practice a 3- or 4-year rotation. Try treating infested soil with PCNB at rates recommended by the manufacturer.

Ink Spot (*Mystrosporium adustum*). The bulbous iris is subject to a bulb disease which causes ink-black stains on the outer skin of the scales. They are at first very small but later enlarge to patches which involve the whole area of the scale. The fungus then penetrates inward and attacks the bulb. At first only small decayed spots, which appear black in the center, develop around the margins. The entire bulb may be blackened on the surface, shrunken and hard on the inside.

Control: Pick out and destroy diseased bulbs.

Fusarium Basal Rot (*Fusarium oxysporum*). This soil fungus enters the roots of bulbous iris and then penetrates the base of the plant and the scales of the bulb.

Control: Dip infected planting stock as soon as cleaned for 15 to 30 minutes in Benlate, 2 tablespoonfuls per gallon of warm water (80-85°F.), then dry rapidly.

Blue Mold (*Penicillium* sp.). All types of bulbous irises are subject to the rot caused by blue mold, particularly by some species not as yet identified. Tulip bulbs also are subject to a similar attack by the same mold. Bulbs in storage are the most subject to attack. The fungus gains entrance into the bulb as a result of moist conditions and through wounds.

Control: Dip bulbs as suggested above for fusarium basal rot.

Virus Diseases

Mosaic (Iris mosaic virus). Both German and bulbous irises are subject to the mosaic disease, which causes a yellow striping or mottling of the leaves (Fig. 154) and flowers. The potato and peach aphids transmit this virus.

This disease is not particularly serious on the German iris, though the plants are stunted and the flowers are much smaller. It is much more serious on bulbous iris. The bud sheath of bulbous iris is marked by bluish-green blotches on a pale-green background, less commonly by yellowish streaks.

Control: Since the virus is carried over in bulbs and rhizomes, the most practical control is to discard all infected plants. Control of the virus carriers, the aphids, with malathion would, of course, help to prevent the

Fig. 154. Mosaic virus disease of *Iris dichotoma*. (U.S. Department of Agriculture)

spread of the disease in commercial plant-ings.

The tobacco ringspot virus has also been recovered from naturally infected German iris.

Insects and Other Animal Pests

Aphids. Three species of aphids infest iris leaves: crescent-marked lily, lily, and melon.

Control: Spray with Sevin or malathion.

Tulip Bulb Aphid (*Dysaphis tulipae*). This aphid infests bulbous and rhizomatous iris in storage.

Control: Before storing, dust the bulbs or rhizomes with Sevin powder. Aphids that la-ter appear on the foliage can be controlled with malathion sprays.

Lesser Bulb Fly (*Eumerus tuberculatus*). Larvae of this insect infest the bulbs of Japa-nese iris.

Control: See *Narcissus*.

Iris Borer (*Macronoctua onusta*). Iris growers find the iris borer perhaps their most destructive insect pest, not only on account of the damage it does directly, but also be-cause it may introduce the bacterium *Erwinia carotovora* which causes the foul-smelling soft rot. The borer pupates in the soil or in the old rhizomes, and emerges in August or September as a gray moth about 1¼ inches across the wings. The eggs are laid in small clusters on old iris leaves or other debris, and winter there.

In the spring, when the iris leaves are 5 or 6 inches high, the eggs hatch and the young caterpillars enter the leaves a few inches above the ground. The irregular tunnels which they make as they feed can be seen in the leaves. The full grown borers (Fig. 41) are about 1¼ inches long, whitish with black heads. Hundreds of them may be found in a small planting, and they may be very destruc-tive to some kinds of iris, such as *Iris tecto-*

rum; the delta irises seem to be especially susceptible, though bacterial rot may not be introduced by the borer.

In certain seasons, hatching of eggs may be delayed so that the larvae enter the flower buds and cause these to turn brown with a watery rot. The borers then penetrate the flower stalks, still carrying the rot bacteria, so that eventually the stalks also collapse with a wet, foul-smelling rot.

Control: Since the insects winter as eggs on old leaves and on debris left on the beds as a protection, such material should be raked up and destroyed. Recent research has revealed that this pest can be controlled by thorough spraying with one part of 47.5 per cent Thimet diluted in 200 to 400 parts of water.

Other materials that will control borers are listed under bacterial soft rot, above.

Florida Red Scale (*Chrysomphalus aonidum*). This scale frequently occurs on irises grown in greenhouses, especially where species of citrus are also grown. Affected plants are very much disfigured with conspicuous chlorotic spots about the insects, converging into large yellow areas (Fig. 155).

Control: Spray with malathion or Sevin to control the crawler stage.

Iris Thrips (*Iridothrips iridis*). Japanese iris is especially susceptible to thrips. The adults may be seen crawling about between the folds of the leaf bases, sometimes even appearing on the outer surface. The young are at first white and so can be distinguished from the yellow gladiolus thrips. Iris thrips rasp the surface of the inner folds of leaves, making them susceptible to further injury by fungi. The thrips feed from May to November, causing a russeting and soot-like blackening of the foliage and much stunting of growth. The tops usually die out and turn brown and in older clumps almost all of the roots die. The adult lives over winter in close contact with the leaf buds, being protected by the bases of the old leaves.

Control: Thrips can be controlled with periodic application of Cygon or malathion sprays. The sprays should be directed down into the leaf bases, for many of the insects feed between the folds of the leaves. Where thrips are abundant, the treatment should be made every 5 to 7 days until the infestation is cleaned up.

Gladiolus thrips, tobacco thrips, and rose thrips attack iris at times. These species are also controlled by Cygon or malathion sprays. Thrips and mites carried over on bulbs can be controlled by treating with Sevin dust as suggested above for the tulip bulb aphid.

Verbena Bud Moth (*Endothenia hebes-*

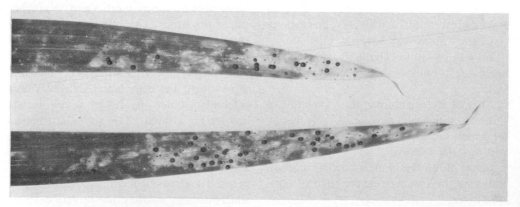

Fig. 155. Iris leaves infested with the Florida red scale, *Chrysomphalus aonidum.*

ana). Small green caterpillars attack the seed pod and feed on its contents. A few days after the eggs hatch, the larvae feed on the outside of the plant. At this stage they are very conspicuous. Later they also enter the pod, leaving only a slight scale or depression at the point of entrance. Just before pupating, the larvae make a hole to the outside and pupate when halfway out, the brown case projecting from the black-ringed hole. There are at least four generations during a season. The insect winters as a larva or cocoon on leaves or in seeds. They have been found to do much damage, especially where breeding of irises is carried on.

Control: Spray with Sevin. The first application should be made soon after the pods have developed, the second about 8 or 10 days later, and, if necessary, a third application 20 days after the first one.

Iris Weevil (*Mononychus vulpeculus*). This is another insect that attacks iris seeds. It tunnels through the seeds, eating out the embryo and reducing each seed to only a thin ring. At the end of a tunnel which sometimes extends through a whole row of seeds, the small dark weevil may be found with its flat, disc-shaped body fitting snugly into the last seed it has mutilated. The limited extent of its injury to cultivated plants has not warranted a study of control methods, but, as the adult weevils are flying as early as May, applications of a methoxychlor spray early in the season should kill the insect before its eggs are laid and the larvae bore into the pod.

Zebra Caterpillar (*Ceramica picta*). This caterpillar also is a nuisance in iris plantings because of its habit of feeding on the leaves and flower stalks and also on the valuable seed pods.

Control: Spraying with Sevin or *Bacillus thuringiensis* will control the young larvae.

Bulb Mite (*Rhizoglyphus echinopus*). This mite may infest bulbous iris in the field and in storage in the Pacific Northwest.

Control: Discard rotting or soft bulbs containing mites. Soak the remainder for 1 hour in hot water held at 111 degrees F.

Stem and Bulb Nema (*Ditylenchus dipsaci*). In the Pacific Northwest this nema first attacks the stem and sheath, then enters the bulb. The parasites do not enter the parts above the soil level. Discoloration and streaking at the base of the stem are made visible by scraping off the outer coating.

Control: A 3-hour dip in a 1:200 formalin solution at 100°F. will provide control. Additional details on harvesting and aftercare of bulbs are obtainable from state and federal plant pathologists.

Grubs. In the eastern states the grubs of Japanese beetle and other turf-destroying insects feed on the rhizomes and roots of iris. Soil treatment with Diazinon will control these pests.

De Man's Meadow Nema (*Pratylenchus pratensis*). This species causes root lesions. Infested plants become dwarfed and die out.

Control: Steam-pasteurize infested soil, or treat with a nemacide mentioned in Chapter 3.

Southern Root-Knot Nema (*Meloidogyne incognita*). This nema was recently found on the roots of rhizomatous iris.

JASMINUM (JASMINE)

Jasmine is subject to several diseases including crown gall caused by the bacterium *Agrobacterium tumefaciens;* a blossom blight by a species of *Phoma;* a leaf spot by *Colletotrichum gloeosporioides,* and a root rot caused by *Clitocybe tabescens.* In Florida the alga *Cephaleuros virescens* caused a leaf spot; root-knot is produced by the nema *Meloidogyne incognita.*

Insects

Scales. Twelve species of scales infest jasmine: barnacle, black, California red, camphor, chaff, Florida red (Fig. 155), green shield, mining, purple, olive, parlatoria, and soft scale.

Control: Valuable specimens should be sprayed with malathion or Sevin to control the crawler stages of these pests.

Citrus Whitefly (*Dialeurodes citri*). This pest infests jasmine in Florida.

Control: Sprays containing synthetic pyrethroids are very effective against adult whiteflies. Malathion or Cygon sprays will control the nymphal stage of this pest.

JUGLANS (BUTTERNUT, JAPANESE WALNUT, AND WALNUT)

Fungus and Bacterial Diseases

Brown Leaf Spot (*Gnomonia leptostyla*). Both butternut and walnut may be badly spotted by this fungus. The leaflets are attacked early in the summer and are marked by irregular dark brown or blackish spots, somewhat similar to those caused on elm leaves by a closely related fungus. Much defoliation may result.

Marssonina juglandis forms irregularly circular brown spots in early summer. *Ascochyta juglandis, Cercospora juglandis, Phleospora multimaculans, Marssonina californica,* and *Cylindrosporium juglandis,* also occasionally spot leaves.

Control: Because the leaves harbor the causal fungi, all fallen leaves should be gathered and destroyed to eliminate this important source of inoculum. Black walnuts and butternuts of ornamental value should be sprayed periodically with Cyprex, maneb, or zineb. The first application should be made when the buds start to open; the second about 10 days later; and the third when the leaves are full grown.

Yellow Leaf Blotch (*Microstroma juglandis*). This fungus causes a yellow blotching on the upper sides of the leaves. The snow-white coating of fungus growth on the under-sides is composed of enormous numbers of spores, which spread the disease. It also causes the witches' broom disease of shagbark hickory.

Control: Same as for brown leaf spot.

Canker (*Nectria galligena*). Scattered, often numerous, rough, sunken, or flattened cankers with a number of prominent ridges of callus wood arranged more or less concentrically on the trunks or branches are characteristic symptoms. When the canker completely girdles the stem, the distal portion dies.

In California a bark canker on *Juglans regia* is caused by the fungus *Phomopsis juglandina.*

Control: All badly diseased trees should be felled. The cankered tissues of valuable trees should be cut out and destroyed, and the wounds covered with a good tree paint.

Dieback (*Melanconium juglandis*). A slow dieback of branches of butternut and Japanese walnut is characteristic of this disease. The bark on affected branches changes from the normal greenish-brown to reddish-brown and finally to gray.

Control: Severely affected trees should be removed and destroyed. Where the disease is still confined to the upper ends of the branches, pruning to sound wood will help to check further spread. In addition, fertilization, watering, sanitation, and insect and leaf-disease control measures should be adopted to help the tree regain its vigor.

Trunk Decay. The trunks of black walnut and butternut often show a white or a brown decay of the heartwood. The former is caused by the so-called "false tinder" fungus, *Fomes igniarius,* which forms hard gray, hoof-shaped fruiting bodies, up to 8 inches in width, along the trunk in the vicinity of the decay. The latter is caused by the fungus *Polyporus sulphureus,* which forms soft, fleshy, shelf-like fruiting structures which are orange-red above the brilliant yellow below. The fruiting bodies become hard, brittle, and dirty-white as they age. These fungi usually enter the trunk through bark injuries and dead branch stubs.

Control: Once these decays become extensive, little can be done to eradicate them. Cleaning out the badly decayed portions and applying a wound dressing are suggested. Initial infections can be kept at a minimum by maintaining the vigor of the trees and by protecting the wounds as soon as they are formed.

Bacterial Blight (*Xanthomonas juglandis*). This disease first appears as small, irregularly shaped black spots on the leaves and petioles. Young fruits may be spotted and killed; nearly ripe ones may have large black spots.

Control: Cut out and destroy badly infected shoots. Spray with streptomycin, 50 ppm plus a spreader-sticker, as flower buds open, at full bloom and at petal fall.

Bark Canker (*Erwinia nigrifluens*). This bacterial disease, first found in California in 1955 on Persian walnut, appears as irregular, large, shallow, dark-brown necrotic areas in the trunk and scaffold branches. The cankers enlarge in summer and are inactive in winter.

A phloem canker of *Juglans regia* in California is attributed to the bacterium *Erwinia rubrifaciens.*

Control: Control measures have not been developed for these diseases.

Other Diseases. A leaf spot and blasting of the nutlets of *Juglans mandchurica* in California is attributed to the bacterium *Pseudomonas syringae,* which also attacks lilacs; blackline, a disorder characterized by formation at the graft union of a narrow, dark-brown, corky layer of nonconducting tissue that results in girdling, is suspected of being caused by a virus, and *Juglans regia* in California is affected by crown gall caused by *Agrobacterium tumefaciens.*

Walnut Bunch Disease (Mycoplasmalike organism). This disease, formerly called witches' broom and walnut brooming, was first thought to be caused by a virus. It is characterized primarily by the appearance of brooms or sucker growths on main stems and branches, tufting of terminals, profuse development of branchlets from axillary buds, leaf dwarfing, and, at times, death of the entire tree. These symptoms vary from mild to severe and are particularly pronounced on Japanese walnut. Butternut, Persian walnut, and eastern black walnut are also susceptible but to a lesser degree.

Control: Walnut bunch can be transmitted by grafting. An insect vector has not been associated with the disease and hence no control measures have been developed.

Insects and Related Pests

Walnut Aphid (*Chromaphis juglandicola*). This pale yellow species is common on the undersides of English walnut leaves on the West Coast. It secretes large quantities of honeydew or aphid honey.

The giant bark aphid, *Longistigma caryae,* occasionally infests butternut and walnut.

Control: Spray with Meta-Systox R, Sevin, or malathion.

Walnut Caterpillar (*Datana integerrima*). Trees are defoliated by this caterpillar, which is covered with long, white hairs and which grows to 2 inches in length. The adult female moth has a wingspread of 1½ inches. Its dark buff wings are crossed by four brown lines. Eggs are deposited in masses on the lower sides of the leaves in July. Winter is passed in the pupal stage in the soil.

Other Caterpillars. The following caterpillars also attack walnut: hickory horned devil, orange tortrix, omnivorous looper, redhumped, and yellow-necked.

Control: Spray with *Bacillus thuringiensis* or Sevin when the larvae are small.

Walnut Lace Bug (*Corythuca juglandis*). This pest is occasionally abundant on park trees, causing a bad spotting of the foliage.

Control: Spray early infestations with Diazinon, malathion or Sevin.

Walnut Scale (*Quadraspidiotus juglansre-giae*). Part or all of a tree may be severely weakened by masses of round brown scales, 1/8 inch in diameter. The adult female is frequently encircled by young scales. The pest winters on the bark.

Other Scales. Nut trees are also susceptible to many other scales including black, California red, calico, cottony-cushion, greedy, oystershell, Putnam, scurfy, and white peach.

Control: Spray with lime sulfur when the trees are dormant, or with malathion, Meta-Systox R, or Sevin in late spring and again in early summer.

Mites. The following species of mites infest *Juglans:* European red, platani, southern red, and walnut blister. The last-mentioned, known scientifically as *Aceria erinea,* causes yellow or brown feltlike galls on the undersides of leaves.

Control: Spray twigs and bark with Diazinon, chlorobenzilate, or Kelthane before new growth begins in spring. A second application should be made to the newly formed leaves in late spring.

JUNIPERUS VIRGINIANA (REDCEDAR)

Fungus Diseases

Twig Blight (*Phomopsis juniperovora*). The tips of branches affected by this disease first turn brown; this is followed by progressive dying back until an entire branch or even the entire tree is killed. Although primarily a disease of seedlings and nursery stock, twig blight may appear on 8- to 10-foot trees in ornamental plantings, and on larger native redcedars in some parts of the country. The disease becomes progressively less serious, however, as the trees become older, and little damage occurs on trees over 5 years old. While the disease is most common on redcedar and its horticultural varieties, twig blight has been found on more than a dozen other groups, among which are other species of

Juniperus, arbor-vitae, cypresses, retinosporas, and whitecedar.

The following cultivars, all of *Chamaecyparis pisifera,* are reported to be resistant: *filifera aureovariegata, plumosa aurea, plumososa argentea, plumosa lutescens,* and *squarrosa sulfurea.*

Control: Where practicable, prune out and destroy infected branch tips. Spray with Benlate plus a spreader-sticker once in fall and 3 or 4 times at 2-week intervals in spring starting when warm weather begins.

Cedar-Apple Rust (*Gymnosporangium juniperi-virginianae*). Where apples and redcedars grow together promiscuously, the redcedars may become covered with hundreds of galls an inch or more in diameter. The infection occurs on the leaves, which are stimulated by the fungus to develop the galls. The second spring after infection the galls form numerous long, yellow, tongue-like outgrowths, especially during warm, rainy weather (Fig. 16). The spores from these projections germinate to produce other small spores, which are spread by the wind. These spores infect the leaves of apples, which may become so seriously diseased as to fall prematurely. The leaves of certain flowering crabs are often badly infected. The damage to the redcedars is not serious, unless several hundred galls are formed on a single tree. The ends of the branches that bear the galls usually die. A similar rust is caused by *G. globosum* (Fig. 156). The galls fruit at least 2 years in succession. The alternate hosts of this parasite are hawthorn and apple. See under *Crataegus.* Another rust, *G. clavipes,* is not very destructive to redcedar. Young branches may be killed, but if they live through the first year's infection they usually recover. An infected trunk is shown in Fig. 157. The fungus may persist in it for many years without serious damage. Trunk infections are superficial, although they may extend for some distance around the bole (see under *Crataegus*).

Fig. 156. Telial horns of *Gymnosporangium globosum* on twig of redcedar.

Fig. 157. *Gymnosporangium clavipes* on redcedar in Arlington Cemetery, Virginia.

The common juniper, *J. communis,* is badly injured by the rust fungus *G. clavariaeforme.* It attacks the trunks or large branches and causes long, rough cankers, which may be so extensive as to cause the drying out and killing of living bark and cambium. It also causes witches' broom of *J. communis* in the Rocky Mountain area. The alternate hosts of this fungus are *Amelanchier, Aronia, Cydonia,* and *Pyrus.* See under *Amelanchier.*

Control: On apple, hawthorn, and other rosaceous hosts, as many as six applications, at 10-day intervals, of a wettable sulfur or a mixture of wettable sulfur and ferbam may be needed for good control of cedarapple rust. The initial application should be made just before an expected rainy spell and as soon as the leaves emerge in the spring. On junipers, a single application of 100 parts of cycloheximide in 1 million parts of water, when the galls have formed, will prevent spore formation and thus prevent infections on nearby apples and crabapples. This concentration is prepared by dissolving one 380-milligram Actispray tablet is each gallon of water.

Root Rot (*Phytophthora cinnamomi*). Although junipers are considered to be resistant to this fungus, two trees in an Oregon nursery were found to be infected with it in 1957.

Control: See *Rhododendron.*

Nonparasitic Diseases

Hybrid junipers are among evergreens that may be seriously injured and even killed by coatings of ice which last for several days.

Individual branches or whole trees may die from the after effects.

Insects and Related Pests

Rocky Mountain Juniper Aphid (*Cinara sabinae*). Twig growth may be checked and the entire tree weakened by heavy infestations of the Rocky Mountain aphid, a reddish-brown insect ⅛ inch long. The so-called honeydew that it secretes is a good medium for the sooty mold fungus, which may completely coat the leaves and further weaken the tree.

Control: A dormant oil spray in April or a spray containing Cygon or Diazinon applied in May will control this pest.

Bagworm (*Thyridopteryx ephemeraeformis*). Redcedars are among the most susceptible of ornamentals to the attacks of bagworms. The feeding of these insects is apt to be overlooked because of the protecting bags made of green leaves. See Figs. 71 and 84.

Control: See *Abies*.

Juniper Midge (*Contarinia juniperina*). Blisters at the bases of the needles and death of leaf tips are produced by small yellow maggots, the adult stage of which is a small fly.

Control: Spray the leaves in mid- to late April with malathion. Cultivating the soil beneath infested trees will destroy the overwintering stage.

Juniper Mealy Bug (*Pseudococcus juniperi*). This dark red mealy bug infests junipers in the Middle West.

Control: Spray with Cygon, malathion or Sevin when the pests appear.

Juniper Scale (*Carulaspis juniperi*). The needles, particularly of the Pfitzer juniper, turn yellow as a result of sucking by tiny circular scales, which are at first snowwhite, then turn gray or black. The pest overwinters in the female adult stage.

Control: Spray with 1 part of concentrated lime sulfur solution in 10 parts of water, or a dormant oil plus ethion, before growth starts in spring, or 1 pound of 25 per cent wettable malathion powder in 25 gallons of water during warm weather in May. A second malathion spray should be applied about the middle of June for best results. Sevin or methoxychlor will also control the crawler stage.

Juniper Webworm (*Dichomeris marginella*). The twigs and needles are webbed together, and some turn brown and die when infested by the juniper webworm, a small, ½-inch-long, brown larva with longitudinal reddish-brown stripes. The adult female, a moth with a wingspread of ⅗ inch, appears in June and deposits eggs that hatch in 2 weeks. The winter is passed in the immature larval stage. This pest also attacks the creeping juniper, *J. horizontalis*.

Control: Spray with Diazinon, Dylox, or Sevin plus Kelthane, in late July and again in mid-August.

Redcedar Bark Beetle (*Phloeosinus dentatus*). The adult beetle is about 1/16 inch long. It lays its eggs in narrow excavations about 1 or 2 inches long. As the young grubs hatch, they bore out sidewise, making galleries of a characteristic pattern which resemble the markings made in elms by the elm bark beetle.

Control: The cedar bark beetle is more apt to attack trees recently transplanted or those that are suffering from lack of water. Spraying with methoxychlor will probably help.

Two-Spotted Mite (*Tetranychus urticae*). The leaves assume a gray or yellow cast when severely infested by tiny green, yellow, or red mites 1/50 inch long. Infested leaves and twigs are occasionally covered with fine silken webs. Winter is passed primarily in the egg stage.

Spruce Spider Mite (*Oligonychus ununguis*) is also a serious pest of juniper. Both species of mites infest the creeping juniper, *J. horizontalis*.

Control: To control both species of mites,

spray with 1 part concentrated lime sulfur in 10 parts of water or with "superior" type dormant oil before growth begins in spring, and with a good miticide such as chlorobenzilate, Dimite, Kelthane, or Tedion during the growing season.

KALANCHOË

Diseases

Crown Rot, Wilt (*Phytophthora cactorum*). The disease first appears at the base of the stems, causing black lesions. The rot extends upward into the flower stalks, which, with the leaves and flowers, soon wilt.

Control: Avoid too much watering. Use a light porous soil. Do not plant too deep, and avoid packing the soil too closely around the plants. Infested soil should be steam-pasteurized before re-use.

Stemphylium Leaf Spot (*Stemphylium floridanum* var. *Kalanchoë).* A severe spotting of the leaves of several species of *Kalanchoë* has been reported from Florida (Fig. 158).

Control: Measures to control this leaf spot have yet to be developed.

Powdery Mildew (*Sphaerotheca humuli* var. *fuliginea*). This disease appears as a grayish-white mealy growth on the leaves. The infected parts dry out and the leaves are killed.

Control: Benlate sprays applied every 2 weeks during spring and summer provide excellent control.

Other Disease. A virus disease, mosaic, occurs on *Kalanchoë* in Florida. Yellow-green streaks or blotches appear anywhere on new leaves.

Control: Control measures have not been developed.

Insects

Lesser Snow Scale (*Pinnaspis strachani*). The female lesser snow scale is pear-shaped, white, semitransparent, and sometimes speckled with brown. The male is white and elongate.

Control: Spray with Ced-O-Flora or with nicotine sulfate and soap mixture. Malathion spray should not be used on this host because it is occasionally phytotoxic.

Aphids and Mealybugs. These pests occasionally infest *Kalanchoë*. For control see lesser snow scale above.

KALMIA LATIFOLIA
(MOUNTAIN-LAUREL)

Diseases

Leaf Spot (*Mycosphaerella colorata*). This fungus, more frequently referred to by its conidial stage, *Phyllosticta kalmicola,* produces irregular or circular, light gray spots with a purplish-brown border, as shown in Fig. 159. They vary from the size of a pinhead to ½ inch in diameter. The black fruiting bodies (pycnidia) are usually present on these gray spots. Leaves on which many spots occur fall prematurely.

A number of other fungi such as *Cercospora kalmiae, C. sparsa, Venturia kalmiae, Septoria angustifolia,* and *S. kalmicola* cause leaf spots of mountain-laurel.

Control: Hand pick infected leaves, collect fallen ones and destroy them. Where the disease has been severe the previous year, spray with Benlate plus a spreader-sticker when the buds open and again 10 and 20 days later. An additional application may be necessary in September or October if wet weather prevails.

Blight (*Diaporthe kalmiae*). This disease may be mistaken for winter injury or sunscald. The spots, however, are more irregular and much larger, sometimes covering large parts of the leaf, especially along the margin. They are purple-brown and appear more or less zoned. The fungus may penetrate into the tip ends of the twigs and cause some

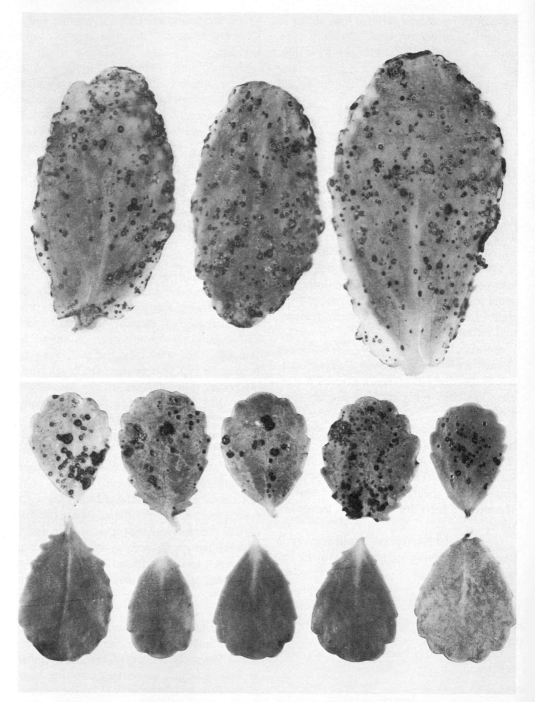

Fig. 158. *(Top row) Stemphylium* leaf spot on *Kalanchoë fedtschenkoi* "Marginata"; *(middle row)* on leaves of *K. fedtschenkoi*. The lowermost leaves are healthy. (E. K. Sobers, Florida Department of Agriculture)

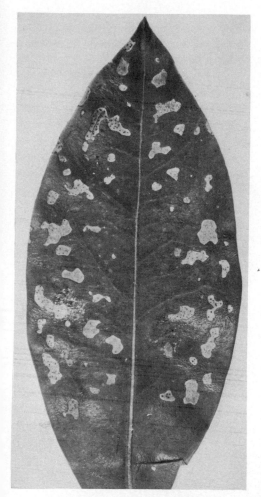

Fig. 159. Leaf spot of *Kalmia* caused by the fungus *Phyllosticta kalmicola (Mycosphaerella colorata)*. Notice the tiny black fruiting bodies in the diseased areas.

blighting. See Fig. 160. The conidial stage of this fungus is *Phomopsis kalmiae.*

Control: Same as for leaf spot.

Flower Blight (*Ovulinia azaleae*). This disease occasionally appears on mountain-laurel flowers although it is primarily a disease of azaleas. See azalea petal blight, under *Rhododendron.*

Chlorosis. This nonparasitic disease (Fig. 25) is usually caused by an iron deficiency. The leaves turn yellow while the veins remain green.

Control: See *Rhododendron.*

Insects

Mulberry Whitefly (*Tetraleurodes mori*). The mulberry whitefly, which is frequently abundant on a number of other shrubs, attacks *Kalmia* also (see Fig. 161). During the summer the undersides of the leaves may be thickly covered with the black nymphs; these are marked by whitish borders that consist of a waxy secretion. At this time they closely resemble scale insects.

Control: Sprays containing synthetic pyrethroids are effective against the adult stage of this pest. Malathion sprays will control the nymphal stage adhering to the lower leaf surfaces.

Other Pests. Mountain-laurel may also be infested by the rhododendron lace bug, and azalea stem borer, the rhododendron borer, and the black vine weevil. See *Rhododendron.*

KENTIA—see PALMACEAE

KERRIA

Diseases

Leaf and Twig Blight (*Higginsia kerriae*). This fungus, formerly referred to as *Coccomyces kerriae* or *Cylindrosporium kerriae*, causes round to angular, light to reddish-brown spots with darker borders on the leaves. When the spots are numerous the leaves turn yellow and die prematurely. Stem cankers also develop, causing dieback of the distal portions.

Control: Prune and destroy diseased stem tips and rake up and discard fallen leaves. Spray with ferbam four times at 10-day intervals starting when the leaves are ¼ inch long.

Fig. 160. Spots on *Kalmia* caused by the fungus *Diaporthe kalmiae*. With a hand lens one can see the small black pycnidia of the fungus in each spot.

Fig. 161. Mulberry whitefly *(Tetraleurodes mori)* on leaves of mountain-laurel. The leaf on the right is enlarged.

Twig Blight (*Phomopsis japonica*). Oval or long, irregular, tan-colored spots with slightly raised margins appear on the main stems. Clusters of tiny, black fruiting bodies of the causal fungus may be seen in these spots. The leaves above the heavily infected stems turn brown and die.

Control: Prune and destroy infected stems. Spray with ferbam as for leaf and twig blight, above.

Other Diseases. This host is also subject to a canker caused by *Nectria cinnabarina,* a leaf spot by a species of *Septoria,* and root rot by *Phymatotrichum omnivorum.*

Insects

Japanese Beetle (*Popilla japonica*). *Kerria* is a favorite host for this pest.

Control: See *Aesculus.*

KOELREUTERIA (GOLDENRAIN-TREE)

Diseases

Coral Spot Canker (*Nectria cinnabarina*). Small, depressed, dead areas in the bark near wounds or branch stubs are caused by this fungus. Tiny, coral-pink bodies are formed on the dead bark.

Control: Prune infected branches back to sound wood. Fertilize and water to maintain vigor.

Other Fungus Diseases. The only other fungus diseases reported as affecting *Koelreuteria* are a leaf spot caused by a species of *Cercospora,* wilt by *Verticillium albo-atrum,* and root rot by *Phymatotrichum omnivorum.*

Control: For wilt, see *Acer.* The other diseases are never destructive enough to warrant control measures.

Insects

Scales. Three species of scales, the lesser snow *Pinnaspis strachani,* mining *Howardia biclavis,* and white peach *Pseudaulacaspis pentagona* infest *Koelreuteria.* Dormant oil sprays applied in early spring will control these scales. Malathion or Sevin sprays applied in late May and in mid-June will control the crawler stage of the pests.

LABURNUM (GOLDEN-CHAIN)

Diseases

Leaf Spot (*Phyllosticta cytisii*). Leaves are subject to spotting when infected by this fungus. The spot, at first light-gray, later turning brown, has no definite margin. The black fruiting bodies (pycnidia) of this fungus dot the central part of the spot. Another fungus, *Cercospora laburni,* also causes leaf spots.

Control: In areas where these leaf spots are troublesome, apply a copper fungicide several times at 2-week intervals during rainy springs.

Twig Blight (*Fusarium lateritium*). Brown lesions on the twigs followed by blighting of the leaves above the affected area in very wet springs are characteristic of this disease. The sexual stage of this fungus is *Gibberella baccata. Sophora japonica* is also susceptible to twig blight.

Control: Prune and discard infected twigs and spray as for leaf spot.

Laburnum Vein Mosaic (*virus*). Conspicuous vein-banding of *Laburnum alpinum* in Maryland is said to be due to a virus. Although tobacco ringspot virus was isolated from infected plants, there was no evidence that it caused the disease.

Control: Remove and destroy infected plants.

Insects

Aphids (*Aphis craccivora*). The cowpea aphid, black with white legs, clusters at the tips of the branches. The bean aphid, *A. fabae,* also infests golden-chain.

Control: Spray with Meta-Systox R, malathion, or Sevin when the aphids appear in late spring.

Grape Mealybug (*Pseudococcus maritimus*). The grape mealybug occasionally infests golden-chain, both aboveground and belowground.

Control: Mealybugs infesting the branches and twigs can be controlled with malathion sprays. Those infesting the roots can be curbed by wetting the soil with Diazinon or malathion.

LAGENARIA (BOTTLE GOURD)

Diseases

Anthracnose (*Colletotrichum lagenarium*). The leaves are spotted and the fruits spotted and rotted by this fungus.

Control: Pick off and destroy the spotted leaves as soon as they appear.

Downy Mildew (*Pseudoperonospora cubensis*). This mildew is occasionally serious in the eastern and southern United States.

Control: Spray the vines with Bordeaux mixture or other copper fungicides if the disease is serious and if it is practical to spray.

Fruit Spots (*Phoma subvelata* and *Stemphylium* sp.). The fruits of this host may be spotted by two other fungi in addition to the *Colletotrichum* mentioned above.

Other Diseases. *Lagenaria* is also subject to bacterial spot caused by *Pseudomonas lachrymans,* thread blight by the fungus *Pellicularia koleroga,* powdery mildew by *Erysiphe cichoracearum,* and mosaic by the cucumber mosaic virus.

Insects

Squash Bug (*Anasa tristis*). The leaves of infested plants become crisp and blackened, and large portions of the vines die. The yellowish-brown eggs are laid in clusters on the undersides of the leaves. The grayish nymphs vary in length up to ½ inch. The brown or black adults hide under dead leaves and vines when disturbed.

Control: All rubbish offering winter protection to adult squash borers should be removed. Spray the plants with Sevin.

LAGERSTROEMIA (CRAPEMYRTLE)

Diseases

Powdery Mildew (*Erysiphe lagerstroemiae*). This mildew is most serious in the spring and fall months. The leaves and shoots are distorted and stunted. Inflorescences are also attacked, the flower buds failing to open. The shoots and leaves may be coated with white growth, the leaves tending to assume a reddish color beneath the mildew. The whole plant may sometimes be affected.

Two other species, *Phyllactinia corylea*

and *Uncinula australiana* occasionally infect this host.

Control: Acti-dione PM spray is very effective in controlling the powdery mildew on this host. Wettable sulfur, Benlate, and Karathane sprays also control it. A dormant lime sulfur spray just before buds open in the spring is recommended, in addition to the other sprays, where mildew is unusually prevalent.

Other Fungus Diseases. Black spot caused by a species of *Cercospora,* tip blight by *Phyllosticta lagerstroemia,* leaf spot by *Cercospora lythracearum* and *Pestalotia guepini,* and root rot by *Clitocybe tabescens* are other diseases of this host.

Insects

Crapemyrtle Aphid (*Tinocallis kahawaluokalani*). This species attacks only crapemyrtle. It exudes a great amount of honeydew, on which the sooty mold fungus, *Capnodium* sp., thrives.

Control: Spray with Meta-Systox R, malathion, or Sevin early in the growing season.

Florida Wax Scale (*Ceroplastes floridensis*). This reddish- or purplish-brown scale covered with a thick, white, waxy coating tinted with pink attacks a wide variety of trees and shrubs in the South.

Control: Spray with malathion or Sevin when the crawler stage is about.

LANTANA

Diseases

Lantanas are subject to the following fungus diseases: black mildew caused by *Meliola cookeana,* leaf spot by a species of *Alternaria,* rust by *Puccinia lantanae,* and wilt by a species of *Fusarium.* These rarely become destructive enough to warrant control measures.

Insects and Other Animal Pests

Latania Aphid (*Cerataphis lataniae*). The wingless form of this aphid is dark, disc-like, with a white fringe. It is frequently mistaken for a species of whitefly.

Control: Spray with malathion or Sevin.

Caterpillars. The orange tortrix caterpillar and the greenhouse leaf tier infest the leaves of lantana.

Control: Spray with *Bacillus thuringiensis* or Sevin when the larvae are young.

Mealybugs. Three kinds of mealybugs infest lantanas and become very troublesome: citrus, Mexican, and yucca.

Control: Spray with malathion.

Greenhouse Whitefly (*Trialeurodes vaporariorum*). The greenhouse whitefly can become almost as troublesome as mealybugs.

Control: See *Fuchsia.*

Mites. The broad mite and the cyclamen mite occasionally infest lantanas in the greenhouse.

Control: See *Cyclamen.*

Nemas. The southern root-knot nema *Meloidogyne incognita* and the leaf nema *Aphelenchoides* sp. also infest this host.

Control: See Chapter 3.

LARIX (LARCH)

Fungus Diseases

Cankers (*Trichoscyphella wilkommii, T. ellisiana, Aleurodiscus amorphus, Leucostoma kunzei,* and *Phomopsis* sp.). Several fungi cause cankers in larch. *T. wilkommii* was found in 1927 on trees imported from Great Britain. The disease was eradicated by strict sanitary measures. A resurvey in 1965 of the originally infested area in Massachusetts revealed that no infested trees were present.

Control: Canker diseases are difficult to control. Keeping trees in good vigor by feeding and watering when needed will help to reduce the severity of infection.

Leaf Cast (*Hypodermella laricis*). The needles of the American and Western larches and the spur shoots that bear them may be killed by this disease. Early symptoms are yellowing, followed by browning of the needles. Very small, elliptical, black fruiting bodies of the fungus appear on the dead leaves during the winter.

Several other fungi, including *Cladosporium* sp., *Lophodermium laricis, L. laricinum,* and *Meria laricis,* also cause leaf cast or leaf blights of larch. The leaf cast diseases are most common on ornamental larches in the western United States.

Control: Gather and destroy the needles in late fall or winter to eliminate the most important source of inoculum. This usually ensures satisfactory control. Spraying trees of ornamental value with dilute lime sulfur solution or with Bordeaux mixture or other copper fungicide may be advisable.

Needle Rusts. Three rust fungi attack larch needles. They develop principally on the needles nearest the branch tips. Affected needles turn yellow and have pale yellow fungus pustules on the lower surfaces.

The fungus *Melampsora paradoxa* occurs on American, European, Western, and Alpine larches. Its alternate hosts are several species of willows. Larches can be infected only by spores developing on willows, but the spores on willows can reinfect the willow.

The fungus *Melampsora medusae* attacks American larch and its alternate host, poplar. As with *M. paradoxa,* spores on larch cannot reinfect larch but must come from poplars.

Melampsoridium betulinum affects American larch and several species of birches. The spore stage on birch can infect birch as well as larch.

Control: Where larches are the more valuable specimens in an ornamental planting, the removal of the alternate host will prevent infection. Infected needles should be submitted to a rust specialist for determination of the exact species involved before attempts to eradicate the alternate hosts are made. Spraying trees of ornamental value with a dilute lime sulfur solution or with a copper fungicide may be advisable.

Wood Decay. Several species of fungi are constantly associated with the various types of wood decay of larch. Those most common in the eastern United States are *Fomes annosus, F. roseus, F. pini,* and *Polyporus schweinitzii.* They are found mainly on older, neglected trees.

Control: Little can be done to check wood decays by the time they are discovered. Maintaining valuable specimens in good vigor by periodic fertilization and by watering during dry spells will do much to prevent initial infections. Wounds on the trunks of such trees should be treated promptly.

Insects

Larch Casebearer (*Coleophora laricella*). In May and June larches infested with this caterpillar suffer from an extensive browning of the leaves. The leaves are mined by a small caterpillar, which uses pieces of the needles to form a small cigarshaped case, ¼ inch long. The blackheaded caterpillar eats a hole in the leaf either at the end or in the middle and feeds as a miner in both directions as far as it can without leaving the case. The miners winter in the cases, which are attached to the twigs. The moths emerge in late June and July.

Control: To kill the casebearers that have survived the winter, spray in early spring with dormant strength lime sulfur or with a miscible oil. If this is not done, spray with methoxychlor or Sevin as soon as the insects begin to feed in late spring.

Larch Sawfly (*Pristiphora erichsonii*). In sawfly infestations, the needles are chewed by ³/₄- to 1-inch-long, olive-green larvae covered with small brown spines. The adult is a wasp-like fly with a wingspread of ⁴/₅ inch.

Eggs are deposited in incisions on twigs in late May and June. The larvae overwinter in brown cocoons on the ground.

Control: Gather and destroy fallen needles beneath the tree. If necessary, spray with methoxychlor or Sevin in June or early July as soon as the insect begins to feed.

Woolly Larch Aphid (*Adelges strobilobius*). White woolly patches adhering to the needles are typical signs of this pest. The adult aphids are hidden beneath the woolly masses. The winged adults migrate to pines, and another generation returns to the larch the following season. Eggs are deposited at the bases of the needles in the spring. Young aphids overwinter in bark crevices.

Control: Spray with 1 part concentrated lime sulfur in 10 parts of water before growth starts in early spring, or with malathion, Meta-Systox R, or Sevin when the young are hatching in May.

Other Insects. The larvae of the gypsy moth, *Porthetria dispar,* and the whitemarked tussock moth, *Hemerocampa leucostigma,* chew larch leaves.

Control: Spray with *Bacillus thuringiensis* or Sevin when the pests begin to feed.

LATHYRUS ODORATUS (SWEET PEA)

Fungus Diseases

Anthracnose (*Glomerella cingulata*). The fungus that causes the bitter rot disease of apples is most destructive to garden sweet peas. Leaves, flowers, and shoots are at first marked with whitish spots; these spread extensively, so that the parts attacked finally wilt and dry up; the seed pods shrivel and lose their color. Heavy infection results in much loss of leaves. The wilting that follows the disease works downward from the tips of the younger shoots, which become whitish and sometimes break off. If they do not break off, the disease progresses downward and causes further damage. Old plant parts are not easily killed. With a hand lens many minute salmon-colored pustules bearing great quantities of spores can be seen on the diseased parts.

Control: Gather and destroy all infected plant parts after the flowering season. Choose only seed pods wich are plump and sound in appearance for planting. Since the disease attacks seed pods, many spores of the fungus become attached to the seeds. Seeds for planting should be selected from disease-free pods. An occasional application of zineb spray during the growing season also helps to control this disease.

Black Root Rot (*Thielaviopsis basicola*). This soil-borne organism, often mistakenly referred to the genus *Thielavia* (a well-known ascomycete) attacks the crown, seldom invading the stems more than a few inches above the ground. The roots are destroyed and the stubby ends are black. New roots are soon killed; rootlets may persist for some time. Infected plants are noticeably dwarfed, pale yellow, and sickly. The stems can be removed from the crown very easily, like stems of aconite and delphinium that have been attacked by the *Sclerotium* crown rot disease. Black root rot is most important in greenhouse but is known to attack commercial plantings in the open.

Other root rots of sweet peas are caused by the following fungi: *Aphanomyces euteiches, Fusarium* sp., *Phymatotrichum omnivorum, Phytophthora cactorum, Pellicularia filamentosa,* and *Pythium* sp.

Control: Since these organisms are soil-borne, the soil in greenhouses or gardens where they are present should be steam-pasteurized or treated with an appropriate chemical mentioned in Chapter 4. If such treatments are impractical, use new soil for greenhouse plantings or rotate the plantings outdoors. Preplanting applications of thiabendazole (Mertect), as recommended by the manufacturer, have been successful where

the *Thielaviopsis* fungus was responsible for the root rot, and Benlate soil drenches have been effective where the *Pellicularia* and *Fusarium* fungi caused root rot.

Downy Mildew (*Peronospora trifoliorum*). This mildew, which is very common on other members of the legume family in America, is known to attack garden sweet peas. Young plants are susceptible. Under moist conditions the leaves become covered with a grayish moldy growth. The thick-walled brown resting spores are developed within the moldy tissue.

Control: Since this is not a serious disease of this host, control measures have not been worked out.

Leaf Spots (*Colletotrichum pisi, Isariopsis griseola, Phyllosticta orobella,* and *Mycosphaerella pinodes*). At least four species of fungi cause leaf spots of sweet peas.

Control: Pick off and destroy spotted leaves as soon as they appear.

Powdery Mildew (*Microsphaera alni*). Mildew is occasionally serious on greenhouse sweet peas. The leaves shrivel and dry.

Control: In greenhouse culture, proper temperature and adequate ventilation help to curb this disease. Spraying with Benlate or with Karathane will also provide control.

White Mold (*Ramularia deusta* var. *odorati*). This mold, which may cover both sides of the leaves, may be mistaken for powdery mildew. Faint, dull-colored, irregular, elongated spots, which may be somewhat sunken, appear. The spots on the leaf margins, at first water-soaked in appearance, later have a reddish-brown discoloration that suggests the streak disease. Tufts of spore-bearing hyphae develop from the stomatal openings between epidermal cells.

Another strain of this fungus, *R. deusta* var. *latifolia,* affects the perennial sweet pea, *L. latifolius.*

Control: Spray with zineb as soon as white mold is noticed.

Bacterial Diseases

Fasciation (*Corynebacterium fascians*). The dense witches' broom, distortions, and fasciations develop at the base of the stem or from below the soil line. They are very short, extend not over 1 or 2 inches above the ground, and are not more than 3 inches in diameter. The upper parts of the stem, though dwarfed, are not otherwise abnormal. The same bacterium causes abnormal growths on carnations, chrysanthemums, and other ornamental plants. It is distinct from that which causes crown gall.

Control: Effective control measures have not been developed.

Streak (*Erwinia herbicola*). Garden sweet peas as well as those grown under glass have been reported subject to a bacterial disease which usually starts at flowering time. This organism causes purplish-brown streaks on the stems, beginning at the base and extending upwards. The petioles, flowers, flower stalks, and pods are also streaked. Small round spots appear on the leaves, running together gradually until the whole leaf is affected. Leaves may become dark brown or be entirely destroyed.

Control: The bacteria that cause this disease may be carried on the seed. Dipping the seed in a streptomycin solution may be helpful.

Other Bacterial Diseases. This host is subject to crown gall, caused by *Agrobacterium tumefaciens,* and leaf spot by *Pseudomonas pisi.*

Virus Diseases

Mosaic (Pea mosaic virus). This virus disease may appear on seedlings 3 or 4 weeks old. It causes a curling of the leaves and a dwarfing of plants. The leaves become yellow and finally mottled in a mosaic pattern. Such plants produce very few flowers. The blossoms have discolored streaks called "breaks."

Control: Infected plants should be destroyed as soon as mosaic is evident. Since the virus is carried by aphids, the plants should be sprayed with malathion. Because sweet peas are susceptible to most legume viruses, one should avoid planting them near bean and other leguminous plants.

Spotted Wilt (Tomato spotted wilt virus). Purplish spots on the stems and leaves develop after the leaves are mottled. Discolored or bleached spots may appear on the blossoms.

Control: Since this disease is carried by thrips, control of these pests with Cygon or malathion sprays may help to curb its spread. Tomato and dahlia plantings should be well isolated from sweet peas or other susceptible plants. All plants with spotted wilt should be destroyed.

Physiological Disease

Bud Drop. This disease is due entirely to faulty culture; it results in the production of soft, succulent growth and a lowered carbohydrate accumulation. A deficiency of phosphorus and potassium in the soil, coupled with a low-light intensity is believed to aggravate the condition.

Control: If possible, provide extra light in the greenhouse during cloudy weather. Avoid overwatering and overfeeding with high-nitrogenous fertilizers.

Insects and Other Animal Pests

Aphids. Three species of aphids attack sweet peas: the corn root, pea, and potato. The first infests the roots; the others attack the leaves and stems.

Control: For the corn root aphid, drench infested soil with a dilute malathion solution, prepared from the emulsifiable concentrate. Meta-Systox R, malathion, or Sevin sprays will control the leaf-infesting aphids.

Greenhouse Leaf Tier (*Udea rubigalis*). This pale-green caterpillar feeds on the undersides of the foliage, leaving the upper sides untouched. A single leaf may be rolled or several leaves may be tied together by a web.

Control: Spray with Sevin before the leaves are rolled or webbed together.

Corn Earworm (*Heliothis zea*). This larva feeds upon the buds and foliage of sweet pea.

Control: Spray with Sevin when the young larvae begin to feed.

Pea Moth (*Laspeyresia nigricana*). The larva attacks field and garden peas, and also feeds on sweet peas, spoiling the seeds. When the infested pod opens, the excrement (masses of pellets) and the silk of the caterpillar can be seen. The pods turn yellow and ripen prematurely. Unless sweet peas are grown in the vicinity of garden peas, little trouble will be encountered from this pest.

Other Insects. Sweet peas are occasionally infested by the four-lined and tarnished plant bugs, cutworms, the serpentine leaf miner, and the western and onion thrips. These are discussed on more favored hosts in other parts of this book.

Two-Spotted Mite (*Tetranychus urticae*). Sweet pea leaves turn yellow and have a mealy coating when infested by this mite.

Control: See *Althaea.*

Sowbugs (*Porcellio laevis* and *Armadillidium vulgare*). These are jointed animals with glossy, crusty shells (Fig. 76). They are about $1/2$ inch long, oval in shape, dark gray in color, brown below, with seven pairs of legs. These common greenhouse pests live in places where decay occurs and in flower pots. They feed on the roots and other tender portions of both sweet peas and carnations.

Control: All decaying materials should be removed and destroyed. Apply a 2 per cent Diazinon dust over the infested area. Ready-made sowbug baits are also available in horticultural supply stores.

Southern Root-Knot Nema (*Meloidogyne incognita*). The nemas cause the formation of oval or elongated galls all along the roots. These should not be mistaken for the root nodules commonly found on roots of the sweet pea family. Root tubercules due to beneficial bacteria are found nearer the tips of the roots. The plants are not killed by the nemas but grow slowly and are more or less stunted and yellowish. This disease is serious in garden plantings farther south where the worms live over winter in the soil. In the North it is largely confined to greenhouse plantings.

Another nema *Pratylenchus pratensis* is associated with blackening of the roots.

Control: See Chapter 3.

LAURUS NOBILIS (SWEET BAY)

Disease

Anthracnose (*Gloeosporium nobili*). This disease has been reported on sweet bay in New Jersey, but it is not of great importance. The author found this fungus on sweet bay leaves grown indoors in New York City in 1974.

Insects

Laurel Psyllid (*Trioza alacris*). An imported species from Europe, this pest occurs on sweet bay in California and some eastern states. It attacks the leaf edges causing them to curl and become unsightly. It also may cause premature defoliation. Eggs are deposited on the leaves and shoots. In California, canary laurel and laurel cherry may also be attacked.

Control: Spraying with Cygon or Diazinon before the leaves curl up is the most effective control measure.

Eye-Spotted Bud Moth (*Spilonota ocellana*). The larval stage of this moth, a small brown worm with a black head, occasionally infests sweet bay, although fruit trees are more favored hosts.

Control: Spray with Sevin when the worms begin to chew the foliage.

Scales. Nine species of scale insects infest this host: black, California red, cottony-cushion, dictyospermum, Florida red, glover, greedy, green shield, and soft.

Control: Valuable plants should be inspected carefully from time to time to detect any scale infestations. If any appear, malathion, Meta-Systox R, or Sevin sprays should be applied. If scales and other insects are properly controlled during late summer while the sweet bay is kept outdoors, few or no insects will develop on these plants when brought indoors for protection against freezing temperatures.

LAVANDULA (LAVENDER)

Diseases

Only two fungus diseases have been reported on *Lavandula,* a leaf spot caused by *Septoria lavandulae* and a root rot by *Armillaria mellea.* The former can be held in check by picking off and destroying infected leaves. The latter is soil-borne and can be controlled only by steaming the infested soil or replacing it with clean soil.

Insects and Other Animal Pests

Caterpillars. The orange tortrix and yellow woollybear chew the leaves of *Lavandula.*

Control: Spray with Sevin when the caterpillars begin to feed.

Four-Lined Plant Bug (*Poecilocapsus lineatus*).

Control: Same as for caterpillars.

Northern Root-Knot Nema (*Meloidogyne hapla*). This nema infests *Lavandula* in the northern United States.

Control: See Chapter 3.

LEDUM (LABRADOR-TEA)

Diseases

Anthracnose (*Elsinoë ledi*). The lesions on the leaves are grayish-white with reddish-brown borders surrounded by purplish margins. The capsules, calyx, leaf stalks, and branches also are subject to attack. It is not a serious disease.

Leaf Galls (*Exobasidium vaccinii, E. ledi,* and *Synchytrium vaccinii*). These fungi produce leaf galls and red leaf spots on many plants belonging to the Ericaceae. See *Rhododendron* (Azalea).

Rusts (*Chrysomyxa ledi* var. *ledi* and *C. ledicola*). The alternate stage of the former rust occurs on black, red, and Norway spruces. The alternate stage of the latter occurs on white, black, red, blue, Englemann, and Sitka spruces.

Control: Control practices are not usually used on *Ledum* because of the relative unimportance of the host.

Leaf Spot (*Cryptostictis arbuti*). This disease occurs on the West Coast but is rarely serious enough to warrant control measures.

LEPTOSYNE—see COREOPSIS

LEUCOTHOË

Fungus Diseases

Leaf Spots (*Cercospora kalmiae, C. leucothoës, Cryptostictis* sp., *Lophodermium orbiculare, Mycosphaerella* sp., *Pestalotia leucothoës, Phyllosticta terminalis,* and *Ramularia andromeda*). At least eight species of fungi cause leaf spots on this host.

Control: Pick off and destroy spotted leaves. Where the spots are extremely numerous each year, spray with ferbam 3 times at 2-week intervals starting when the leaves appear in early spring.

Other Diseases. A leaf gall caused by *Exobasidium vaccinii,* and black leaf spot by *Asterina diplodioides* also occur on *Leucothoë.* These fungi effect other members of the Ericaceae.

LIATRIS (GAYFEATHER)

Fungus Diseases

Leaf Spots (*Phyllosticta liatridis* and *Septoria liatridis*). Two fungi are known to cause brown spots on the leaves of this host.

Control: Pick off and destroy spotted leaves. Other control measures are usually unnecessary.

Rusts (*Coleosporium laciniariae* and *Puccinia liatridis*). The former has *Pinus rigida* and the latter has certain species of grasses as the alternate hosts.

Control: These rust diseases are not serious enough to warrant control measures.

Other Diseases. A stem rot caused by *Sclerotinia sclerotiorum* and wilt by *Verticillium albo-atrum* have also been recorded on this host.

Pest

Southern Root-Knot Nema (*Meloidogyne incognita*). *Liatris* may be infested by this nema which produces galls or knots on the roots.

Control: See Chapter 3.

LIBOCEDRUS (INCENSE-CEDAR)

Incense-cedar is susceptible to crown gall caused by *Agrobacterium tumefaciens,* leaf rust by *Gymnosporangium libocedri,* and the leafy mistletoe by *Phoradendron juniperinum.*

LIGUSTRUM (PRIVET)

Fungus and Bacterial Diseases

Anthracnose, Twig Blight (*Glomerella cingulata*). The symptoms associated with this disease include the drying out of leaves, which cling to the stem; the blighting of twigs; and the development of cankers at the bases of the main stems. The cankers are spotted with pinkish pustules (acervuli). The bark and wood of diseased portions become brown, and the bark on the cankers splits, exposing the wood. Death occurs when the cankers completely encircle the twigs or stems. The disease is widespread in the United States. The following varieties are said to be fairly resistant: Amur privet, *L. amurense;* Ibota privet, *L. ibota;* regal privet, *L. obtusifolium* var. *regelianum;* and California privet, *L. ovalifolium.* For climates in which winterkilling is not a factor, the California privet is preferable for planting.

Control: When the disease is found, prune and destroy all diseased branches. Then spray with ferbam at weekly intervals until no new infections are seen.

Leaf Spots (*Cercospora adusta, C. lingustri, C. lilacis,* and *Phyllosticta ovalifolii*). Four species of fungi cause spotting of privet leaves. These are prevalent only during very rainy seasons and in overcrowded, poorly aerated plantings.

Control: Fungicidal sprays are rarely recommended for privets. If they are necessary, use a copper or dithiocarbamate compound.

Galls (*Phomopsis* sp.). Nodular galls on the common privet are occasionally mistaken for galls produced by the bacterium, *Agrobacterium tumefaciens.* The galls develop rather rapidly and reach a diameter of 1½ inches within 5½ months. In the southern states the same fungus attacks *Jasminum nudiflorum,* causing similar galls.

Control: Although wounding enables the fungus to gain entrance, trimming does not lead to the formation of galls. Only wounds incurred at points lower down in such a way that the living tissues do not dry out lead to infection and gall formation.

Powdery Mildew (*Microsphaera alni*). This mildew develops mostly on the upper surfaces of the leaves and appears as whitish blotches. Minute black fruiting bodies of the fungus develop in these.

Control: Important plantings of privet can be protected from this disease with Benlate or Karathane sprays.

Root Rots (*Armillaria mellea, Clitocybe monadelpha, C. tabescens, Phymatotrichum omnivorum,* and *Rosellinia necatrix*). These soil-inhabiting fungi are extremely difficult to control. Remove and destroy infected plants and the soil immediately adjacent to them. Replace with healthy plants and new soil.

Virus Diseases

Variegation (Privet infectious variegation virus). Chlorotic or yellow spotting of privet leaves is thought to be caused by an undetermined virus. The disease can be transmitted by grafting and hence differs from the chlorotic or yellow leaves that arise from a genetic change.

Control: Rogue out infected plants and destroy them.

Insects and Other Animal Pests

Privet Aphid (*Myzus ligustri*). The leaves of privet may be tightly curled lengthwise by this aphid.

Control: Spray with Meta-Systox R, malathion, or Sevin early in the season when the leaves begin to curl.

Leaf Miners. Two species of miners, the lilac and the privet, mine and blotch the leaves of this host.

Control: Spray early in the season with malathion just as the first miners appear in the leaves.

Scales. The following scales infest privet: black, California red, camphor, Japanese, mining, olive parlatoria, San Jose, and white peach.

Control: Spray with either a dormant miscible oil or a commercial lime sulfur. The latter should not be used if fences or painted surfaces are nearby. During May and June spray with Diazinon, malathion, or Sevin to control the young crawler stage.

Privet Thrips (*Dendrothrips ornatus*). This pest can become so prevalent in some seasons as to give privet hedges a grayish, dusty appearance (see Fig. 162). The larvae are yellow and spindle-shaped; the adults are dark brown to black with a bright red band.

Control: Spray with a mixture of malathion and Sevin twice at 14-day intervals when the thrips are first seen.

Mealybugs. Two species of mealybugs, the citrophilus and the ground, infest privet. The former affects aboveground and the latter belowground parts.

Control: Spray with malathion or Meta-Systox R to control the citrophilus mealybug and treat the soil around infested privet with malathion, prepared from the emulsifiable concentrate, to control the ground mealybug.

Japanese Weevil (*Pseudocneorhinus bifasciatus*). The beetles are about ¼ inch in length, varying from light to dark brown, with striations on the wing covers. They feed heavily on California privet but also on leaves of azalea, Japanese barberry, chrysanthemum, clematis, deutzia, forsythia, geranium, hemlock, holly, lilac, lily-of-the-valley, mountain-laurel, rhododendron, rose, rose-of-Sharon, oak, weigela, and veronica. Privet hedges may be badly injured by the destruction of new tender shoots.

Control: Sevin sprays applied in late July and in mid-August will control this pest.

Mites. Three species of mites infest privet: citrus flat (*Brevipalpus lewisi*), privet (*B. obovatus*), and tuckerellid (*Tuckerella pavoniformis*).

Fig. 162. Injury to privet by the thrips *Dendrothrips ornatus,* on the right. Uninfested privet on the left. (Dr. J. C. Schread)

Control: Spray with chlorobenzilate or Kelthane.

Whitefly (*Dialeurodes citri*). The citrus whitefly is very common on privet in southern gardens.

Control: See *Fuchsia.*

Nema. The southern root-knot nema, *Meloidogyne incognita,* and a leaf nema, *Aphelenchoides* sp., affect privet.

Control: See Chapter 3.

LILIUM (LILY)

Bacterial and Fungus Diseases

Bacterial Soft Rot (*Erwinia carotovora*). A soft, wet decay of the bulbs may be caused by this organism.

Control: Discard all rotted bulbs. Plant bulbs in well-drained soil. Avoid wounding plants during the growing season. Dig bulbs carefully to avoid injury.

Gray Mold (*Botrytis elliptica*). Of all the diseases of lilies the gray mold is the most serious and widespread. While the symptoms vary considerably with the weather conditions and with parts of the plant attacked, one can always be sure of a correct diagnosis by placing the diseased parts for a few days under a bell jar, where moist conditions prevail. If the disease is caused by *Botrytis,* the characteristic gray mold develops in a short time. Infection of leaves causes characteristic circular or oval spots from yellowish to reddish-brown in color. In some spots the central part is light gray in color while the outer region is dark purple, shading into green, healthy tissue. The spots dry out in dry weather and the fungus stops spreading. In moist weather the spots run together so that the whole leaf may be blighted. Stems also are attacked and when the disease has progressed sufficiently the stems may break over at the point of infection. The fungus may attack the buds or opened flowers and cause them to develop abnormally and turn brown. If young plants are attacked, the growing point is usually killed and the plants will have a later growth during the summer. The bud rot develops very rapidly, especially in moist, warm weather.

Some authorities believe that *B. elliptica* causes the initial spotting of the foliage and that *B. cinerea* blotches the flowers and completes the destruction of the foliage.

The sclerotia which serve to carry the fungus through unfavorable conditions seldom develop on the bulb. They appear more frequently on parts of flowers that have fallen to the ground during the summer. The gray mold develops from these sclerotia in the spring and scatters spores which carry the infection to young plants. Spores germinate most rapidly at about 60°F. and in a saturated atmosphere. The disease therefore spreads rapidly among lilies grown in low situations and in places where nights are cool and dew is plentiful. Under such conditions the disease may become serious. The fungus may spread so rapidly as to destroy the leaves, which lose their color and hang down on the plant, and the stems may become covered with the gray mold and eventually break over in different places.

Control: As a rule the fungus does not penetrate bulb scales to any extent. Bulbs from infected plants can be used for propagation provided they are dusted with sulfur and planted in a new location with a dry southern exposure.

Gather and destroy all leaves of infected plants as soon as they are seen. If plants are disbudded by growers to induce the formation of larger flowers, the old buds should be destroyed and not left in the field. If a second crop is to be planted in the same soil in the greenhouse, all debris of the first crop should be removed and destroyed. Force plants only once in the same soil. Keep the humidity of the house low by heating it in the spring if necessary. Avoid watering the foliage, for this often increases the humidity sufficiently for spore germination. Spray outdoor plants with Bordeaux mixture or Fore containing a good spreader-sticker every 10 days, being careful to coat the under as well as the upper sides of the leaves. In the greenhouse, mist-spray buds and blooms with zineb, 4 ounces in 50 gallons of water, to prevent spotting of flowers in storage. Provide adequate light and air in the greenhouse. Botran or Benlate sprays are also effective.

Foot Rot (*Phytophthora cactorum*). Stems are attacked by this fungus just below the surface of the soil. Infected parts become much shrunken; the plants wither, topple over, and die. If the attack occurs when the bulb is sprouting, only the tip of the young shoot suffers. The stump, with its rosette of leaves, remains attached to the bulb, which is uninjured.

Another species of *Phytophthora, P. parasitica,* occurs in several eastern states. This species affects the upper part of the plant, including the flowers and the stem.

Control: Dig up and destroy all affected plants. Plant in well-drained soil. Avoid wounding crowns when weeding and cultivating, and wash mud and dirt out of the young crowns as the lilies emerge. Protect new growth by spraying with Bordeaux mixture or some other copper fungicide plus a spreader-sticker. In commercial fields, a degree of control is possible by planting lilies on ridges. Drenching the soil with Dexon or Terrazole will kill the *Phytophthora* fungus present in the soil.

Soft Bulb Rot (*Rhizopus stolonifer* and *Rhizopus* sp.). A species related to that which causes "leak" of strawberries and other fruits during shipment and marketing causes a very destructive storage and transit bulb rot of lilies. The bulbs become soft and have an acrid odor. The spots on the scales are at first water-soaked and then turn dark. The soil and packing material stick together and adhere to the bulb because of the soft, rotted condition of the bulbs. The bulbs may become covered with a thick mat of mycelial growth. The fungus enters only through wounds in the bulb scales. The mycelium penetrates down the scales to the basal plate and from there enters other scales. In warm conditions the bulbs are destroyed within 2 days.

Control: Avoid wounding bulbs in digging and packing. Keep the temperature as low as possible during shipment.

Blue Mold Bulb Rot (*Penicillium cyclopium* and *P. corymbiferum*). These fungi cause a dry, punky rot. They work slowly in cold storage, requiring several weeks for destruction of the bulb. They are recognized by the characteristic blue-green color when the spores develop in masses on the rotting bulb scales.

Control: Avoid wounding the bulbs in digging and packing, and keep the temperature down in transit and in storage. This disease can be held in check by mixing 5½ ounces of calcium hypochlorite powder in each 50 pounds of packing soil.

Recent tests have revealed that soaking Easter lily bulbs for 15 to 30 minutes in warm water (80 to 85° F.) containing 2 tablespoonsfuls of Benlate per gallon of water will check blue mold bulb rot. The bulbs should be dried after treatment.

Bulb Rot (*Fusarium oxysporum* var. *lilii*). This fungus rot develops in storage or in transit. It is confined to the base of the scales, which become detached from the basal portion of the bulb. The basal leaves of plants that grow from infected bulbs become yellow or purple and die prematurely. Flowering stems are seldom produced, and if they develop, are usually stunted and inferior. Diseased bulbs, when not destroyed outright, tend to split and become smaller. Wounding of bulbs greatly facilitates infection, but the fungus may enter uninjured bulbs also.

Control: The Benlate soak as suggested above for blue mold bulb rot should also control bulb rot.

Brown Scale (*Colletotrichum lilii*). This disease, sometimes serious on Easter lily, is also known as "brown bulb" and "black bulb." The soil-borne fungus infects the outer scales of the bulbs. Small brown spots also appear on some of the inner scales.

Control: Avoid excessive watering, especially about the bulbs. Avoid freezing of the bulbs. Dipping the bulbs in Benlate (1 oz. in 3 gallons water) may provide some control.

Stem Canker (*Pellicularia filamentosa*). Cankers form at the stem bases and roots are decayed by this fungus.

Control: As soon as lily bulbs are potted, drench the soil with a mixture of Dexon and Terraclor (1 oz. of 70 per cent Dexon and 1 oz. of 70 per cent Terraclor in 25 gallons of water).

Rust (*Uromyces holwayi*). Dusty circular pustules develop mostly on the undersides of the leaves. The entire life cycle of this fungus develops on the lily. Another species, *Puccinia sporoboli*, occurs on *Lilium hollandicum*.

Control: Pick and destroy infected leaves. Ferbam-sulfur sprays will provide control in areas where these rusts are prevalent.

Wilt (*Pellicularia rolfsii* and *Sclerotium delphinii*). These soil-inhabiting fungi attack a wide variety of plants in addition to lilies.

Control: See Chapter 4.

Virus Diseases

Mosaic (Lily symptomless virus and cucumber mosaic virus). The former is widespread on lilies, except on *Lilium hansoni*. Cucumber mosaic virus produces a masked infection or chlorotic mottling unless it is mixed with the lily symptomless virus, in which case it causes a necrotic-fleck disease.

Control: Bulbs from diseased plants should not be used for propagation, since the virus is carried in them from year to year. The melon aphid, which carried the virus from plant to plant, can be controlled to a certain extent by spraying the plants frequently with malathion. Complete extermination of them, however, is extremely difficult, especially in field plantings, and unless they are all destroyed, the spread of the disease is not appreciably reduced by spraying. In commercial plantings frequent inspection to discover infected plants must be made and plants showing mosaic should be rogued out. Commercial growers are advised to check with their state plant pathologists for the names of varieties which can be grown together.

Rosette (Lily rosette virus). This is a serious disease in Florida and Bermuda where Easter lilies are grown commercially. Diseased plants have a flat, rosette appearance, the leaves being pale green or yellowish without mottling or streaking (Fig. 163). The younger leaves are curled downward and twisted. The whole plant is stunted.

Control: Same as for mosaic.

Other Viruses. The tobacco ringspot virus occurs in Easter lily. The hybrid lily "L.T.A. Havermeyer" is susceptible to the mottle virus complex but not to the *L. henryi* virus. The latter lily grows with amazing vigor despite the virus infection. It is therefore suitable for planting alone or in locations where susceptible lilies or tulips are not present, or in locations where only lilies that "can live with virus" are grown.

Physiological Diseases

Noninfectious Chlorosis. Two types of noninfectious leaf yellowing which result in severe stunting of the plants and a poor root system have been observed. One type occurs in plants grown in pots, in which the leaves are generally yellow except near the veins. This type can be cured by applications of iron sulfate or iron chelates.

Frost Injury. Light frosts may result in "puffy leaf," and the plants are stunted by the death of the growing point. Mulching is a

Fig. 163. Rosette virus on lily. (U.S. Department of Agriculture)

protection for young shoots and is helpful to prevent frost injury in the spring.

Leaf Scorch. Rapid forcing and wet soil were formerly suggested as a cause of brown tip. The tip ends and leaves turn yellowish, then brown, and blight about ½ inch or so back from the end. Recent research has revealed that manganese and aluminum salts will cause leaf scorch if they are present in large quantities. The addition of lime to the soil sharply reduces leaf scorch.

Bud Blast. The buds of Easter lilies in greenhouse may "blast" or dry up and fail to open. The condition is associated with a shortage of water at the top of the plant. Any root injury or a cold soil will contribute to the trouble. At times the buds will blast if the lilies are subjected to high temperatures during cloudy weather or if they are shaded to excess.

Insects and Other Animal Pests

Aphids. Five species of aphids infest this host: crescent-marked lily, green peach, foxglove, melon, and purple-spotted lily.

Control: Spray with malathion, or Sevin whenever aphids appear.

Fuller Rose Beetle (*Pantomorus cervinus*). This grayish-brown weevil, with a short, broad snout and a white diagonal stripe across each wing-cover, attacks lilies and a wide variety of other plants. It is a night feeder, eating ragged areas from the margins of the leaves.

Control: Spray susceptible plants with Sevin.

Lily Weevil (*Agasphaerops nigra*). This weevil attacks lilies in commercial plantings in the Pacific Northwest, as well as wild lilies and fritillarias. Damage is done by the grub stage which feeds on the stem below ground.

Control: No effective control measure is available.

Other Weevils. Several weevils, including the black vine (*Otiorhynchus sulcatus*), strawberry (*O. ovatus*), and rugose strawberry (*Brachyrhinus rugostriatus*), occasionally attack lilies in commercial fields and home gardens.

Control: See *Taxus.*

Stalk Borer (*Papaipema nebris*). The common stalk borer that attacks asters, hollyhock, phlox, and other garden plants may be found feeding on stalks of lily. The larvae are about 1 inch long.

Control: To save valuable plants it may be worth while to slit the stalks open and destroy the larvae feeding in the pith. Nearby burdock, ragweed, and other plants on which eggs are laid should be destroyed. Spraying with methoxychlor may be helpful.

Thrips (*Taeniothrips simplex* and *Liothrips vaneeckei*). While thrips are not generally troublesome in lily culture, they may congregate occasionally in considerable numbers between the bulb scales of certain species. The infested scales turn light brown and dry out, and bulb decay may follow through secondary infections of fungi. Plants grown from infested bulbs are stunted.

Control: Soaking the bulbs in Tedion as suggested for bulb mite, below, should control this pest.

Bulb Mite (*Rhizoglyphus echinopus*). Marked injury to lily bulbs results from infestation by mites, which is made easy by the loose structure of the bulbs. The mites feed around the basal plate of the bulb and destroy the roots. Later they infest the scales, and burrow into the stems. Leaves and stems developed from infested bulbs suddenly become yellow and the basal parts of the stem are corroded. Death of infested plants is not infrequent. Various bacterial and fungus rots enter the bulbs through wounds made by the mites.

Control: Bulbs for plantings should be carefully selected and infested bulbs discarded. Bulbs should be grown in properly drained soil and crop rotation should be practiced. They should be stored at 35°F., since this prevents feeding by the mites during storage. Soaking mite-infested bulbs for 24 hours in a solution containing 2 ounces of 25 per cent wettable Tedion in 12 gallons of water will also provide control.

Bulb and Leaf Nema (*Aphelenchoides fragariae*). This nema causes dieback of field grown Easter lilies in the Pacific Northwest. The normal green color in the leaves becomes blotched with yellow, fading into a brownish-yellow, and finally to a dark brown. The nemas live over in the bulbs to initiate new infections. Nema-infested bulbs forced in the greenhouse may produce "blind" buds, which fail to produce flowers.

Control: Commercial stocks of bulbs should be soaked for 1 hour in a hot water-formalin bath. One part of commercial formaldehyde solution (38 to 40 per cent) in 200 parts of water heated to 111°F. is the standard treatment.

Root Lesion Nemas (*Pratylenchus pratensis* and *P. penetrans*). These nemas cause premature yellowing of Easter Lily foliage in the Pacific Northwest in the fall. Infested plants may be severely stunted and numerous dead spots or lesions are present on the roots.

Control: Pruning away all roots from infested bulbs and rotation of plantings are suggested. Heavily infested soils should be treated with an effective fumigant before lilies are replanted in them. State plant pathologists can suggest the proper fumigant for each locality where these nemas are prevalent. The chemicals Mobilawn (formerly known as VC-13) and Nemagon have proved very effective in some areas.

Surinam Cockroach. See *Filices.*

LIMONIUM[25] (SEA-LAVENDER)

Diseases

Leaf Spots (*Alternaria* sp., *Cercospora insulana, Fusicladium staticis, Phyllosticta* sp., and *P. staticis*). Five species of fungi are capable of causing leaf spots on this host.

Control: Pick off and destroy spotted leaves when they first appear.

Other Diseases. A rust caused by the fungus *Uromyces limonii,* aster yellows by a mycoplasma-like organism, crown rot by *Pellicularia filamentosa* and *P. rolfsii,* mosaic by the turnip mosaic virus, and root-knot by the nema *Meloidogyne incognita* are other afflictions of *Limonium.*

LINARIA (TOADFLAX)

Diseases

The upper portions of this plant are subject to several fungus diseases, including anthracnose caused by *Colletotrichum vermicularioides,* downy mildew by *Peronospora linariae,* and two leaf spots by *Alternaria* sp. and *Septoria linariae.* These are rarely serious enough to warrant control measures.

The following soil-infesting fungi cause root or stem rot: *Phymatotrichum omnivorum, Pellicularia filamentosa, P. rolfsii, Sclerotinia sclerotiorum,* and *Thielaviopsis basicola.* The control of soil-borne fungi is discussed in Chapter 4.

Pests

Nemas (*Ditylenchus dipsaci* and *Meloidogyne incognita*). The former infests leaves and stems of *Linaria,* the latter causes knots or galls on the roots. See Chapter 3 for control measures.

[25]This genus was formerly known as *Statice.*

LINUM GRANDIFLORUM (FLOWERING FLAX)

Flowering flax is subject to damping-off caused by the fungus *Pellicularia filamentosa,* a stem rot by *Sclerotinia sclerotiorum,* and root-knot by the nema *Meloidogyne incognita.*

LIPPIA—see ALOYSIA

LIQUIDAMBAR (SWEETGUM)

Diseases

Bleeding Necrosis (*Botryosphaeria dothidea*). Sweetgums affected by this disease may be killed in a relatively short time. The profuse bleeding on the bark of the trunk and branches appears as though oil had been poured on the tree. Beneath the bleeding area, the inner bark and sapwood are brown and dead. The author found the first cases of this disease in New Jersey in 1941.

Control: No control is known. Removal and destruction of diseased trees is suggested.

Leaf Spots. Six fungi—*Actinopelte dryina, Cercospora liquidambaris, C. tuberculans, Exosporium liquidambaris, Leptothyriella liquidambaris,* and *Septoria liquidambaris*— may occasionally spot the leaves of this host.

Control: Leaf spots are rarely serious enough to warrant control measures.

Other Diseases. Several other important diseases of sweetgum have been reported in recent years. For most the causal agent is still unknown. One, leader dieback, is caused by the fungus *Diplodia theobromae.* It was found capable of causing dieback of the leader branch under certain predisposing environmental conditions.

The disease known as sweetgum blight has caused death of many trees in Maryland and adjacent states. At this writing no causal organism has been associated constantly with the disease.

Insects

Sweetgum Webworm (*Salebria afflictella*). The leaves are tied and matted together by small larvae.

Control: Spray with Sevin before the leaves are matted together.

Caterpillars. The leaves of sweetgum are occasionally chewed by the caterpillars listed below, as well as by those of several species of moths including the luna, *Actias luna*, polyphemus, *Antheraea polyphemus*, and promethea, *Callosamia promethea*.

Control: Spray with *Bacillus thuringiensis* or Sevin when caterpillars begin to feed.

Cottony-Cushion Scale (*Icerya purchasi*). This insect, which is more destructive to silver maples, has been known to infest sweetgum branches and leaves. See Figs. 79 and 99, and under *Acacia* for control.

Sweetgum Scale. (*Aspidiotus liquidambaris*). This scale is occasionally found on sweetgums in the eastern United States.

Control: Spray with a "superior" type miscible oil in spring before growth begins and with malathion or Sevin in early June.

Walnut Scale (*Quadraspidiotus juglansregiae*). The insect winters in the adult stage, the eggs being laid in the spring. Feeding of the young begins early in June. In severe infestations twigs, limbs, and trunks may become encrusted.

Control: See *Aesculus*.

Bagworm. See *Thuja*.

Fall Webworm. See *Fraxinus*.

Forest Tent Caterpillar. See *Acer*.

LIRIODENDRON (TULIPTREE)

Fungus Diseases

Cankers. At least six species of fungi—*Botryosphaeria dothidea*, *Cephalosporium* sp., *Fusarium solani*, *Myxosporium* sp., *Nectria magnoliae*, and *Nectria* sp.—cause cankers in tuliptree. The first mentioned is perhaps the most destructive.

Control: Prune and cart away infected branches. Valuable trees should be sprayed with a copper fungicide, and fed and watered to increase their vigor.

Leaf Spots. At least six species of fungi—*Cylindrosporium cercosporioides*, *Gloeosporium liriodendri*, *Mycosphaerella llriodendri*, *M. tulipiferae*, *Phyllosticta liriodendri*, and *Ramularia liriodendri*—cause leaf spots of tuliptree.

Control: Leaf spots rarely become sufficiently destructive to warrant control measures other than gathering and destroying infected leaves. The use of copper sprays may be justified on valuable trees.

Powdery Mildews (*Phyllactinia corylea* and *Erysiphe polygoni*). Two species of fungi produce a white coating over the leaves of this host.

Control: Where particularly valuable small trees are affected, spray with Karathane or Benlate.

Root and Stem Rot (*Cylindrocladium scoparium*). This disease has been associated with decline of large tuliptrees in Georgia and North Carolina.

Control: Control measures have not been developed.

Wilt (*Verticillium albo-atrum*). This disease has been found in Connecticut and Illinois.

Control: See *Acer*.

Sapstreak (*Ceratocystis coerulescens*). Sapstreak occasionally occurs on tuliptree.

Control: See *Acer*.

Physiological Disease

Leaf Yellowing. Starting in midsummer, during dry, hot periods, many tuliptree leaves turn yellow and drop prematurely. The yellowing is due to climatic conditions and not to any destructive organism. The leaves of recently transplanted trees exhibit yellowing more frequently than those of well-established trees. Very often, small, angular, brownish specks appear on the leaves between the leaf veins as a preliminary stage of yellowing and defoliation.

Insects

Tuliptree Aphid (*Macrosiphum liriodendri*). This small green aphid secretes copious quantities of honeydew. Hence leaves of other plants growing beneath the tree are coated with honeydew, which is then overrun by the sooty mold fungus.

Control: Late spring and early summer applications of Meta-Systox R, malathion, or Sevin will control this aphid.

Tuliptree Scale (*Toumeyella liriodendri*). Trees may be killed by heavy infestations of oval, turtle-shaped, often wrinkled, brown scales, 1/3 inch in diameter. The lower branches, which are usually the first to die, may be completely covered with scales. Like the tuliptree aphid, this scale insect secretes much honeydew. The secretion drops on leaves and is soon covered by sooty, black mold. Tuliptree scales overwinter as partly grown young. They grow rapidly until they mature in August. Young scales are produced in late August, at which time the old females dry up and fall from the tree.

Control: Spray the trees with a dormant miscible oil on a relatively warm day in late March or early April before the buds open. Or spray with Meta-Systox R, or Sevin in late August or early September when the young are crawling about, and repeat the spray 2 weeks later.

Other Scale Insects. In addition to the very common and destructive tuliptree scale, this host is also subject to oystershell and willow scale.

Tuliptree Spot Gall (*Thecodiplosis liriodendri*). A gallfly produces purplish spots about 1/8 inch in diameter on the leaves (Fig. 164). These are frequently mistaken for fungus leaf spots.

Control: The damage is more unsightly than detrimental to the tree. Hence sprays are rarely used to control this pest.

Sassafras Weevil (*Odontopus calceatus*). See *Sassafras*.

LOBELIA

Fungus Diseases

Leaf Spots (*Cercospora lobeliae, C. lobeliicola, Phyllosticta bridgesii,* and *Septoria lobeliae*). Four fungi cause leaf spotting of this host.

Control: Pick off and destroy spotted leaves as soon as they appear.

Other Fungus Diseases. Lobelias are occasionally affected by gray mold caused by *Botrytis cinerea*, damping-off by *Pythium debaryanum*, root rots by *Phymatotrichum omnivorum* and *Pellicularia filamentosa*, rust by *Puccinia lobeliae*, and smut by *Entyloma lobeliae*.

Virus Diseases

The beet curly top virus and the tomato spotted wilt virus have been recorded on this host in Texas.

Insects and Other Animal Pests

Negro Bug (*Corimelaena pulicaria*). This small black bug, about 1/10 inch in length, which occasionally does a great deal of damage to celery, also feeds sometimes on lobelias. The nymphs vary from reddish to black. By sucking the sap they cause leaves to wilt and die.

Control: Since the bugs feed on any type of weed or grass around the garden, clean culture is required. Malathion sprays will also control them.

Red-Banded Leaf Roller (*Argyrotaenia velutinana*). Leaves are rolled and tied to-

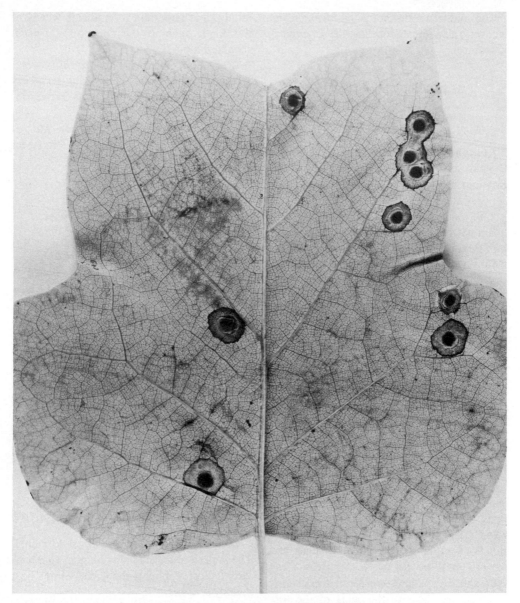

Fig. 164. Tuliptree spot gall on *Liriodendron* caused by the gallfly *Thecodiplosis liriodendri.*

gether and thus a hiding place is made in which the caterpillar feeds.

Control: Spray early before the leaves are rolled with Diazinon or Imidan.

Wireworms (Elateridae). Wireworms have been reported to do considerable damage to lobelias. Soils heavily infested with these pests should be treated with Diazinon.

The southern root-knot nema *Meloidogyne incognita* also infests lobelias. See Chapter 3 for control.

LOBULARIA MARITIMA[26]
(SWEET ALYSSUM)

Diseases

Damping-off (*Pythium ultimum*). Sweet alyssum seedlings frequently damp-off when grown in heavy soils, or when overcrowded or overwatered.

Control: Improve growing conditions. Use steam-pasteurized soil or treat infested soil with Dexon.

Downy Mildew (*Peronospora parasitica*). Occasionally this mildew appears on this host.

Control: Where mildew is a problem, spray with a copper fungicide.

Wilt (*Pellicularia filamentosa*). During wet weather the stems may be attacked by the imperfect stage of this fungus, *Rhizoctonia solani*. A cobwebby mycelium may develop, and the parts above the infection wilt and die. The lower leaves of infected plants rot, shrink, and shrivel.

Control: Drench soil with 1 tablespoon of PCNB (Terraclor) per gallon of water.

White Rust (*Albugo candida*). Pale yellow regions appear on the leaves on the undersides of which smooth, white pustules develop. These break open and discharge clouds of white spores. Infected stems and flowers may be seriously deformed. The spores in the pustules are formed in chains, much as are those in the aecia of the true rusts. The oospores remain alive in dead and decayed tissue.

Control: Remove and destroy diseased plants and all debris. Since the same fungus infects many other members of the mustard

family, it is important to eradicate weeds of this kind, such as the common *Caspella,* shepherd's-purse.

Club Root (*Plasmodiophora brassicae*). This disease, so common on many members of the mustard family, also affects *Lobularia.*

Control: See *Cheiranthus.*

Aster Yellows. The leafhopper *Macrosteles fascifrons* spreads this disease to sweet alyssum and many other plants.

Control: See *Callistephus.*

Insects and Other Animal Pests

Caterpillars. The imported cabbageworm *Pieris rapae,* and the diamondback caterpillar, *Plutella xylostella,* feed on the foliage of sweet alyssum in greenhouses. Damage may be serious.

Control: Sanitation is important. Clean up and destroy rubbish in the vicinity. Where the diamondback caterpillar is serious, handpicking and destruction of the cocoons is helpful. Sevin or *Bacillus thuringiensis* sprays will give good control.

Nema. The southern root-knot nema *Meloidogyne incognita* also infests this host. For control see Chapter 3.

LONICERA (HONEYSUCKLE)

Fungus and Bacterial Diseases

Leaf Blight (*Herpobasidium deformans*). The imperfect stage of this fungus, *Glomerularia lonicerae,* blights the leaves of this host in rainy seasons.

Control: Severe outbreaks on valuable plantings can be prevented by an occasional application of a copper fungicide or Fore.

Leaf Spots (*Cercospora antipus, C. lonicerae, C. varia, Guignardia lonicerae, Kabatia lonicerae, Lasiobotrys affinis, Leptothyrium periclymeni, Marssonina lonicerae,* and *Septoria sambucina*). At least nine species of fungi cause leaf spots of honeysuckle.

[26] This was formerly known as *Alyssum maritimum.*

Control: Most leaf spots are not destructive enough to warrant control measures.

Powdery Mildews (*Microsphaera alni* and *Erysiphe polygoni*). The former fungus is rather widespread in the United States on honeysuckle; the latter occurs in the western part of the country.

Control: Control measures are rarely applied for mildews on this host. When necessary, use Acti-dione PM, Benlate, or Karathane.

Other Diseases. Honeysuckle is also subject to thread blight caused by *Pellicularia koleroga,* twig blight by *Phoma mariae,* and rust by *Puccinia festucae.* Two bacterial diseases also occur: crown gall caused by *Agrobacterium tumefaciens* and hairy root by *A. rhizogenes.*

Insects

Woolly Honeysuckle Aphid (*Prociphilus xylostei*). This yellow woolly aphid with a black head and thorax causes leaf curling.

Control: Spray with Meta-Systox R, malathion or Sevin before the leaves are curled.

Leaf Rollers. Three kinds of leaf rollers infest honeysuckle: oblique-banded, red-banded, and the European honeysuckle. These caterpillars feed inside the rolled up leaves.

Control: Spray early with Meta-Systox R, malathion, or Sevin before the caterpillars are inside the rolled leaves.

Honeysuckle Sawfly (*Zaraea inflata*). The caterpillars are one inch long when full grown; yellow and black-spotted with orange bands.

Control: Spray with Diazinon or Sevin.

Four-Lined Plant Bug (*Poecilocapsus lineatus*). The orange-colored or reddish nymphs are marked by black dots on the body and later with yellow stripes on each side of the wing-pad. The mature insects are yellowish-green with four black stripes down the wing covers. They usually feed on the topmost leaves and cause an irregular bronze or brown spotting.

Control: Spray with Sevin.

Planthopper (*Anormensis septentrionalis*). The young insects are enveloped within a cottony fungus-like mass. They are very pale green, about ¼ inch long, with an upturned tail covered with a hairy growth.

Control: See *Prunus serrulata.*

Greenhouse Whitefly (*Trialeurodes vaporariorum*). This pest infests bush honeysuckles and causes the characteristic blackening of the leaves.

Control: See *Fuchsia.*

Other Insects. Honeysuckle may be infested by the flea beetle, omnivorous looper caterpillar, long-tailed mealybug, fall webworm, and three species of scales—greedy, oystershell, and San Jose.

LUNARIA (HONESTY)

Diseases

Lunaria, grown for its ornamental flowers and seed pods, is susceptible to a black, leaf-and-pod spot caused by *Alternaria oleracea,* leaf spot by *Helminthosporium lunariae,* stem canker by *Leptothyrium lunariae,* and club root by *Plasmodiophora brassicae.* Most of these are not serious enough to warrant control measures. Club root can be controlled by treating the soil with Terraclor prior to planting.

LUPINUS (LUPINE)

Fungus Diseases

Leaf Blight (*Hadrotrichum globiferum*). Lupines grown in the western United States are subject to this leaf blight. Control measures are rarely adopted for this disease.

Other blights of this host are caused by *Botrytis cinerea, Pellicularia rolfsii,* and a species of *Ascochyta.*

Leaf Spots. Fourteen species of fungi—
Alternaria sp., *Cercospora longispora, C. lupini, C. lupinicola, Cylindrosporium lupini, Mycosphaerella pinodes, Ovularia lupinicola, Phoma lupini, Phyllosticta ferax, P. lupini, Ramularia lupini, Septogloeum lupini, Septoria lupinicola,* and *Stictochorella lupini—*
cause leaf spots on *Lupinus.*

Control: Leaf spots are rarely destructive enough to require control measures other than picking off and destroying spotted leaves.

Crown Rot (*Pellicularia filamentosa*). The Texas bluebonnet, *L. subcarnosus,* is subject to this fungus, which is soil-borne.

Control: Disinfest seed before planting, and use steam-pasteurized soil. Infested soil can also be treated with PCNB (Terraclor) or Dexon.

Powdery Mildews (*Erysiphe polygoni* and *Microsphaera diffusa*). These fungi are rather prevalent on ornamental lupines. The latter is serious on greenhouse-grown plants.

Control: Spray with Benlate or Karathane.

Rusts (*Puccinia andropogonis* var. *onobrychidis, Uromyces lupini,* and *U. occidentalis*). Three species of rust occur on lupines. Control measures are rarely adopted for these.

Virus Diseases

The tomato spotted wilt virus and an unidentified ringspot virus have been reported on lupines.

Insects

Lupine Aphid (*Macrosiphum albifrons*). This species, green and covered with white wax, may be quite troublesome.

Control: Spray with Meta-Systox R, Sevin, or malathion.

Four-Lined Plant Bug (*Poecilocapsus lineatus*). This sucking insect also is apt to do much damage to lupines. It spends the winter in the egg stage on a number of species of shrubs, and feeds on them during the summer; from them it may move to herbaceous plants. The young insects are bright red-orange with yellow stripes on each wing-pad.

Control: Spray with Sevin.

LYCHNIS (PINKS)
Diseases

Anther Smut (*Ustilago violacea*). Seedlings or young plants are attacked by this fungus, which finally penetrates the growing stamens and develops smut spores in the anthers. In pistillate flowers the rudimentary stamens are stimulated to develop to full size and the anthers become smutted.

Control: Since the infection is systemic, the plants never bear normal flowers and should be destroyed.

Leaf Spots (*Alternaria dianthi, Leptothyrium lychnidis, Phyllosticta lychnidis,* and *Septoria lychnidis*). Four species of fungi cause leaf spots of this host. The first mentioned also affects the greenhouse carnation, *Dianthus caryophyllus.*

Control: Pick off and destroy spotted leaves or other diseased parts. Spray with Bordeaux mixture or a ready-made copper fungicide if the leaf spotting is extensive.

Root Rots (*Pellicularia filamentosa, Phymatotrichum omnivorum,* and *Corticium galatinum*). Three soil-inhabiting fungi cause root rot of *Lychnis.* The last also causes a white root rot of apple trees and several woody shrubs.

Control: See Chapter 4.

Rusts (*Puccinia arenariae, Uromyces suksdorfi,* and *U. verruculosus*). Of the three rusts on this host the last is most prevalent.

Control: Pick and destroy rusted plants. Other controls are usually unnecessary.

Virus. A ringspot virus was found in *Lychnis divaricata* in California in 1959. The virus differs from most of the other known ringspot viruses.

Control: Control measures have not been developed.

LYCIUM HALIMIFOLIUM (MATRIMONY-VINE)

Diseases

Leaf Spots (*Alternaria* sp., *Cerospora lycii*, and *Phyllosticta lycii*). In rainy seasons three species of fungi may cause spotting of the leaves.
Control: Pick off and destroy spotted leaves.

Powdery Mildews (*Erysiphe polygoni, Microsphaera diffusa,* and *Sphaerotheca pannosa*). Powdery mildew fungi are among the most common parasites of matrimony-vine.
Control: Spray with Benlate or Karathane as soon as white powdery areas appear on the leaves. Repeat in 10 days if the mildew reappears.

Rusts (*Puccinia globosipes* and *P. tumidipes*). These rusts are rarely serious enough to warrant control measures.

Insects and Related Pests

Aphids. Several species of aphids, particularly the crescent-marked lily, infest matrimony-vine.
Control: Spray with Sevin or malathion.

Potato Tuberworm (*Phthorimaea operculella*). Although this borer is primarily a pest of potato tubers, it occasionally infests the stems and leaves of *Lycium.*
Control: Pick and destroy infested parts.

Leaf Blister Gall (*Eriophyes eucricotes*). This mite is the most prevalent pest of matrimony-vine. It produces flat greenish blister-like galls, 1/8 to 1/4 inch across, with sunken centers. The galls greatly mar the foliage.
Control: Spray the vines when dormant with misicible oil at the strength recommended by the manufacturer. Then spray with Kelthane or chlorobenzilate just as the leaves begin to emerge from the buds, and repeat in 10 days.

MACLURA (OSAGE-ORANGE)

Diseases

Leaf Spots. Leaves are occasionally spotted by 3 species of fungi: *Cercospora maclurae, Ovularia maclurae,* and *Phyllosticta maclurae.*
Control: Leaf spots are rarely serious enough to warrant control measures.

Other Diseases. Osage-orange is susceptible to a leaf blight caused by *Sporodesmium maclurae* and rust by *Physopella fici.*

Research workers at Rutgers University found that the wood of osage-orange contained about 1 per cent of the chemical, 2,-3,4,5-tetrahydroxystilbene, which was toxic to a number of fungi. This may explain why this host is remarkably resistant to decay-producing fungi.

Scales. Five species of scale insects—cottony cushion, cottony maple, European fruit lecanium, Putnam, and San Jose—infest osage-orange.

The citrus mealybug and the citrus whitefly also attack this tree.
Control: Malathion, Meta-Systox R, or Sevin sprays will control the scales. The synthetic pyrethroid, Resmethrin, will control whitefly.

MAGNOLIA

Fungus Diseases

Black Mildews (*Irene araliae, Meliola amphitrichia, M. magnoliae,* and *Trichodothis comata*). A black, mildewy growth covers the leaves of magnolias in the Deep South.
Control: Deciduous magnolias may be sprayed with Acti-dione PM; others with wettable sulfur.

Leaf Blight (*Pellicularia koleroga*). The leaves of *Magnolia grandiflora* may be blighted by this fungus, which also affects apple, citrus, dogwood, Japanese persimmon, pecan, quince, and many shrubs in the South.

Control: Valuable specimens can be protected with two or three applications of copper fungicides or Difolatan.

Leaf Spots (*Alternaria tenuis, Cladosporium fasciculatum, Mycosphaerella milleri, Colletotrichum* sp., *Coniothyrium olivaceum, Epicoccum nigrum, Exophoma magnoliae, Glomerella cingulata, Hendersonia magnoliae, Micropeltis alabamensis, Phyllosticta cookei, P. glauca, P. magnoliae, Septoria magnoliae,* and *S. niphostoma*). These fifteen species of fungi cause leaf spots on magnolia.

Control: Fungus leaf spots on valuable specimens can be controlled by periodic applications, early in the growing season, of copper or dithiocarbamate fungicides.

Dieback (*Phomopsis* sp.). Cankers with longitudinal cracks in the bark are formed on the larger limbs and trunks. The wood is discolored a blue-gray. The bark is dark brown over the affected areas. Apparently healthy branches also may be discolored. No suggestion for control has been made.

Nectria Canker (*Nectria magnoliae*). This fungus produces symptoms similar to those of *N. galligena,* but infects only magnolia and tuliptrees.

Control: Prune and destroy cankered branches. Keep trees in good vigor by watering, spraying, and feeding when necessary.

Leaf Scab (*Elsinoë magnoliae*). In the deep South *Magnolia grandiflora* leaves may be spotted by this fungus.

Control: The disease is not serious enough to warrant control measures.

Wood Decay. A heart-rot, associated with the fungi *Fomes geotropus* and *F. fasciatus,* has been reported on magnolia. Affected trees show sparse foliage and dieback of the branches. In early stages the rot is grayish-black, with conspicuous black zone lines near the advancing edge of the decayed area. The mature rot is brown. The causal fungi gain entrance through wounds.

Control: No control measures are effective once the rot has become extensive. Avoid trunk wounds and maintain good vigor by fertilization and watering.

Other Diseases

Algal Spot (*Cephaleuros virescens*). Leaves and twigs infested by this alga have velvety, reddish-brown patches. Control measures are usually unnecessary.

Wilt caused by *Verticillium albo-atrum,* angular leaf spot by *Mycosphaerella milleri,* and leaf scab by *Sphaceloma magnoliae* are among other diseases of magnolia.

Insects

Magnolia Scale (*Neolecanium cornuparvum*). Underdeveloped leaves and generally weak trees may result from heavy infestations of the magnolia scale, a brown, varnish-like hemispherical scale, $1/2$ inch in diameter, with a white, waxy covering (Fig. 165). The young scales appear in August and overwinter in that stage.

Control: A dormant oil-ethion spray in early spring just before new growth emerges will control the adult, overwintering scales. The crawler stage of both this and the tuliptree scale, unlike most scales, appear in late summer. Hence the use of Sevin or a mixture of malathion and methoxychlor sprays for the crawler stage should be delayed until late August or early September.

Tuliptree Scale (*Toumeyella liriodendri*) also infests magnolia and linden at times.

Control: Same as for magnolia scale.

Other Pests. The following scales also occur on magnolias: black, chaff, cottony-cushion, European fruit lecanium, Florida wax, glover, greedy, oleander, purple, and soft.

Control: Spray the young, crawler stages of these scales in May and June with malathion or Sevin.

Fig. 165. Magnolia scale *(Neolecanium cornuparvum)*. (Dr. J. C. Schread)

The Comstock mealybug, the omnivorous looper caterpillar, and the citrus whitefly also infest this host. Malathion sprays, applied when the pests appear, give good control.

A species of Eriophyid mite infests *Magnolia grandiflora* in the South. Kelthane or Tedion sprays will control this pest.

Sassafras Weevil *(Odontopus calceatus)*. See *Sassafras*.

MAHONIA (OREGON-GRAPE)

Fungus Diseases

Rust *(Puccinia graminis)*. Oregon-grape, like barberry, is an alternate host of the wheat rust fungus. *Mahonia aquifolium* and *M. bealei* are among the most resistant species of *Mahonia* to this rust. However, crosses of *M. aquifolium* and *Berberis vulgaris*, producing *Mahoberberis neubertii*, are very susceptible. The planting of susceptible kinds is prohibited in certain wheat-producing areas. A list of varieties which may be shipped interstate under permit is available from the United States Department of Agriculture's Bureau of Entomology and Plant Quarantine, Washington, D.C.

Other Rusts. The following species of rust fungi also occur on *Mahonia*: *Cumminisella mirabilissima, C. texana, C. wootoniana, Puccinia koeleriae,* and *P. oxalidis*. The first-mentioned is usually not very conspicuous, but in a wet growing season causes leaf blight. These rusts are rarely serious enough to require control measures.

Leaf Spots (*Phyllosticta berberidis, P. japonica, P. mahoniaecola* and *P. mahoniana*). Brown spots in which tiny, black fruiting bodies are visible with a hand lens are characteristic of these fungi.

Control: Pick off and destroy spotted leaves.

Physiological Disease

Leaf Scorch. The leaves of *Mahonia* grown in wind-swept spots in the cooler parts of the country are severely damaged during late winter and early spring. Provide a windbreak for such plants or spray them on a mild day in late fall with Wilt-Pruf NCF.

Insects

Barberry Aphid (*Liosomaphis berberidis*). This aphid, more common on barberry, attacks Oregon-grape in California.

Control: Spray with Meta-Systox R, malathion, or Sevin.

Other Insects. The greedy scale and the inconspicuous whitefly also attack this host. Malathion sprays are recommended.

MALUS (FLOWERING CRAB-APPLE)

Bacterial and Fungus Diseases

Blight (*Erwinia amylovora*). This disease will not be serious on the flowering crab if commercial orchards of pears and apples are not nearby. Several varieties of hawthorn are far more susceptible to this bacterial disease which causes blighting of the ends of branches.

Control: See *Crataegus.*

Rusts (*Gymnosporangium juniperi-virginianae*). When common redcedar with cedar-apple galls is transplanted from the wild to a garden, a number of brown or orange spots,

bearing the pycnidial stage of the rust, may later be very conspicuous on the leaves of flowering crab-apples nearby. Much defoliation may follow heavy infection.

Control: If practicable, eliminate any red-cedars (*Juniperus*) within a mile radius, or spray with Fore as directed by the manufacturer, or with 1/2 pound of ferbam and 3 pounds of elemental sulfur per 100 gallons of water. Four to five application at 7- to 10-day intervals are needed, starting when the orange fungus masses appear on junipers. For most effective results, the sprays should be applied before rainy periods.

Plantvax sprays are also effective in combating rusts. In the New England states, Thylate sprays will control rusts, scab and several other crab-apple diseases.

Scab (*Venturia inaequalis*). Olive drab spots 1/4 inch in diameter appear on the leaves and smaller spots on the fruits. Leaves drop prematurely and the fruits are disfigured. The imperfect stage of the fungus, *Fusicladium dendriticum,* overwinters on the twigs.

Control: Spray with captan, dodine, Fore, or Polyram, 4 or 5 times at 10-day intervals starting when the leaves are half-grown.

Canker (*Physalospora obtusa* and *Phoma mali*). Two species of fungi cause cankers on the trunks of crab-apples. They often gain entrance through wounds made by lawn mowers and other maintenance equipment.

Control: Avoid wounding trees. Increase the tree's vigor by feeding and watering.

Insects and Related Pests

Most insects that infest the leaves and twigs, such as aphids, alder lace bug, leafhoppers, and several kinds of caterpillars, are easily controlled with malathion, if applied when the young are feeding. Oystershell, San Jose, and Putnam scales can be controlled with a dormant oil spray, or with malathion or Sevin when the young scales are crawling

Fig. 166. Female periodical cicadas lay their eggs in young, growing twigs and branches. (Union Carbide)

about in late spring. Malathion can be safely combined in the ferbam-sulfur spray recommended for rust control.

Periodical Cicada (*Magicicada septendecim*). This pest (Fig. 166), also known as the 17-year locust, damages branches of crab-apple, apple, and many other fruit trees by making deep slits in the bark during the egg-laying period. Such branches are easily broken during windy weather.

Control: A spray containing 1 ounce of Sevin in 5 gallons of water gives excellent control if applied in July at the time the cicadas are in the trees.

European Red Mite (*Panonychus ulmi*). This species also infests the leaves of black locust, elm, mountain-ash, and rose, in addition to many kinds of fruit and nut trees.

Control: A "superior" type, dormant oil applied in early spring just before new growth begins will give good control. When infestations are particularly heavy, applications of chlorobenzilate, Kelthane, or Tedion in late May and again 2 weeks later, may be necessary.

MALVA (MALLOW)

Diseases

Leaf Spot, Stem Canker (*Colletotrichum malvarum*). The pustules which develop on the leaves or stems are at first yellowish-brown and covered with stiff, brown bristles. The same parasite attacks greenhouse althaeas with very destructive effects. It infects all green parts of the plant.

Control: See anthracnose, under *Althaea*.

Other Diseases. Ornamental mallows may also be affected by powdery mildew caused by *Erysiphe cichoracearum,* and rusts by *Puccinia heterospora* and *P. malvacearum.*

Two viruses, beet curly top and tomato spotted wilt, occur on *Malva* in California.

Control: Remove and destroy affected plants.

MANGIFERA INDICA (MANGO)

Diseases

Anthracnose (*Glomerella cingulata*). This is perhaps the most prevalent disease of mango in the South. Leaves are spotted, flowers and twigs blighted, and fruits rotted by this fungus.

Control: Spray valuable specimens periodically with a copper or dithiocarbamate fungicide.

Powdery Mildew (*Oidium mangiferae*). Flower panicles and foliage may be injured when infected by this powdery mildew fungus.

Control: Spray Karathane or Benlate when mildew appears.

Other Fungus Diseases. In Florida mango is subject to twig blight caused by a species of *Phomopsis;* leaf spots by *Pestalotia mangiferae, Phyllosticta mortoni,* and *Septoria* sp.; scab by *Elsinoë mangiferae;* and sooty mold by species of *Capnodium.*

Insects

Scales. Twenty six species of scale insects infest mango.

Control: Spray with malathion or Sevin.

Other Insects. The long-tailed mealybug and green house thrips also infest mango.

Control: Same as for scales.

MATTHIOLA (STOCK)

Bacterial and Fungus Diseases

Bacterial Rot (*Xanthomonas incanae*). This disease occurs on plants of all ages. Seedlings affected have dark green water-soaked lines in the main stem. Later they turn dark brown and crack open, and the plant dies. When infected stems of older plants are cut across, yellow liquid containing millions of bacteria oozes out.

Control: Since the bacteria are seed-borne, it is necessary to treat the seed before planting. Commercial growers soak stock seed in hot water at 130°F. for 10 minutes.

Damping-off (*Pythium debaryanum* and *Pellicularia filamentosa*). Roots and basal parts of older plants as well as younger plants in greenhouses turn black and eventually die. On older plants the first symptoms are yellowing of the lower leaves; later the plant wilts because of stem girdling at the soil line.

Other soil-inhabiting fungi, such as *Phytophthora megasperma* and *Sclerotinia sclerotiorum,* may attack seedlings or cause foot or root rot of older plants.

Control: Disinfest all seeds, seed flats, and soil with either heat or an appropriate chemical. A mixture of Dexon and PCNB (Terraclor) applied to the soil will control the two fungi, causing damping-off.

Downy Mildew (*Peronospora parasitica*). This fungus, also referred to occasionally as *P. matthiolae,* may be troublesome on greenhouse stocks. The leaves wilt and the plants become blighted. The leaves develop pale green spots on the upper sides; on the opposite sides of these the downy mold growth develops. The tender stems and flower parts are also attacked, stunted, and dwarfed.

Control: Avoid crowding the plants. Remove infected parts and destroy them. Maintain as dry a condition in the propagating house as possible. Do not sow seeds too close together, and steam-pasteurize seedbed soil.

Gray Mold (*Botrytis cinerea*). Young plants in seed beds may die from damping-off caused by this fungus or may decay completely. Flowers of mature plants may become covered with a dense growth of gray mold which sheds great quantities of light grayish spores. The fungus is thus spread through the air and in the soil. Seeds may also carry spores on their outer coats.

Control: Surface-sterilize seeds with Arasan and spray seedlings with captan or zineb.

Leaf Spot (*Alternaria raphani*). On the lower leaves this parasite causes pale grayish-green depressed dry spots up to 1/2 inch in diameter. The spots may become blackish with concentric zones covered with large quantities of the brown, many-celled spores.

Control: Remove infected leaves as soon as detected. This is not a common disease, but when it is present spraying plants with a copper fungicide may be necessary.

Club Root (*Plasmodiophora brassicae*). Many cruciferous plants are subject to infection by this so-called "slime mold." The feeding roots are entirely destroyed and the main roots develop abnormally and form what look like very irregular crown galls. Infected plants usually die without developing an inflorescence.

Control: Avoid planting in unpasteurized soil where the disease has occurred. Practice clean cultivation; destroy cruciferous weeds in the garden. Lime the soil heavily before setting plants out.

Because PCNB (Terraclor) has given excellent control of the same "slime mold" in cabbage plantings, it is worth trying in soils which have produced diseased stocks.

Fusarium Wilt (*Fusarium oxysporum* var. *matthioli*). Premature leaf drop, stunting, and vascular discoloration are common symptoms of this disease on older plants. Seedlings infected by this fungus have conspicuous vein clearing of the leaves, stunting, and wilting.

Control: Use hot-water treated seed, and set plants in uninfested soil.

Verticillium Wilt (*Verticillium albo-atrum*). This disease is prevalent on garden stock in the cut-flower producing regions of California. The lower leaves turn yellow and wilt. Plants infected early in their development are severely stunted. Vascular tissues are frequently discolored.

Control: Avoid planting stock or other susceptible plants in wilt-infested soil. Fumigating infested soil with chloropicrin is said to eradicate this soil-borne fungus.

White Rust (*Albugo candida*). Snow-white pustules containing chains of colorless spores usually develop on the undersides of the leaves, which become pale yellowish and later brown in color where attacked.

Control: Remove and destroy all diseased plants or plant parts and destroy all debris at the end of the season. In outdoor planting, practice clean cultivation, especially destroying all cruciferous weeds nearby. Spray with a copper fungicide if the disease threatens to be serious.

Virus Diseases

The following virus diseases occur on this host: curly top caused by the beet curly top virus, mosaic by the turnip mosaic virus, flower-breaking by the cauliflower mosaic virus, and spotted wilt by the tomato spotted wilt virus.

Control: Rogue out and destroy all plants showing virus symptoms. Spray with malathion or Sevin to control aphids and leafhoppers.

Insects

Diamondback Moth (*Plutella xylostella*). The small greenish caterpillars, up to ½ inch long, first begin to feed on the underside of the leaf, leaving the upper surface intact. Later, bits of the upper surface may fall out, so that shot-hole develops. Sometimes the larvae act as leaf miners. They also feed on leaves and shoots under the webs. These insects feed in gardens during the summer, but migrate to greenhouses in cool weather.

Control: Hand-picking the cocoons is helpful in serious infestations. Destroy all rubbish near the greenhouse, where the adults live through the winter. Several sprays have been effective in combating this pest. Among these are Sevin and *Bacillus thuringiensis*. Because there are from two to six generations a year, it may be necessary to spray susceptible plants rather frequently.

Flea Beetles. Three species of flea beetles infest stocks: striped, western black, and western striped. These beetles, which are about ¹/₁₀ inch long, eat round holes in the leaves, sometimes completely destroying the plants.

Control: Spray with Sevin.

Garden Springtails (*Bourletiella hortensis*). These minute insects cause very small dead spots to develop and the lower leaves to wither. They are occasionally troublesome on seedlings in greenhouses.

Control: Dust the soil surface in early morning or evening with malathion or Diazinon powder.

MECONOPSIS

Downy Mildew (*Peronospora arborescens*). Leaves, buds, calyx, capsules, and seed coats are all invaded by this fungus. On the upper sides of the leaves yellowish or light brown blotches occur, which later turn very dark in color. On the opposite sides of the leaves the spots may be covered with a light gray coating of mold.

Control: Since the fungus lives through the winter in the soil and on plant parts that have become more or less buried by debris, all parts of infected plants should be gathered and carted away. Use only seeds from uninfected plants.

MELIA (CHINA-BERRY)

Diseases

Leaf Spots (*Cercospora leucosticta, C. meliae, C. subsessilis, Phyllosticta azedarachis,* and *P. meliae*). *Melia azedarach* in the southern states is subject to leaf spots caused by five species of fungi.

Control: Leaf spots are rarely serious enough to warrant use of copper fungicides.

Other Fungus Diseases. China-berry is also subject to limb blight caused by *Pellicularia koleroga,* canker by *Nectria coccinea,* and powdery mildew by *Phyllactinia corylea.* These diseases are rarely serious enough to warrant control measures.

Insects and Related Pests

Scales. Three species of scale insects infest China-berry: California red, greedy, and lesser snow.

Control: Malathion or Sevin sprays will control the crawler stage of these pests.

Pacific Spider Mite (*Tetranychus pacificus*). The Pacific spider mite causes leaf yellowing of this host on the Pacific Coast.

Control: Valuable specimens can be protected with Kelthane, Tedion, chlorobenzilate, or Meta-Systox R sprays.

Citrus Whitefly (*Dialeurodes citri*). China-berry is a preferred host of the citrus whitefly. This pest develops in great numbers on *Melia.*

Control: See *Fuchsia.*

MENTZELIA (BLAZING-STAR)

Diseases

A root and stem rot caused by *Pellicularia filamentosa,* two leaf spots by *Phyllosticta mentzeliae* and *Septoria mentzeliae,* and two rusts by *Puccinia aristidae* and *Uredo floridana* are diseases recorded on this host. They are rarely serious enough to require control measures.

MERTENSIA (BLUEBELLS)

Diseases

Among the fungus diseases reported on *Mertensia* are downy mildew caused by a species of *Peronospora,* powdery mildew by *Erysiphe cichoracearum,* leaf spot by *Septoria poseyi,* stem rot by *Sclerotinia sclerotiorum,* smut by *Entyloma serotinum,* and rusts by *Puccinia mertensiae* and *Puccinia recondita* (*rubigo-vera*) var. *apocrypta.* None of these diseases is serious enough to warrant control measures.

MESEMBRYANTHEMUM— see CRYOPHYTUM

MESPILUS (MEDLAR)

Medlar is susceptible to the bacterial disease fire blight caused by *Erwinia amylovora,* leaf spot by *Fabraea maculata,* and rust by *Gymnosporangium clavipes.* Controls for these are given under more favored hosts.

MEZEREUM—see DAPHNE

MIRABILIS (FOUR-O'CLOCK)

Four-o'clock is subject to five fungus diseases: leaf spot caused by *Cercospora mirabilis*, root rot by *Phymatotrichum omnivorum*, rusts by *Aecidium mirabilis* and *Puccinia aristidae*, and white rust by *Albugo platensis*.

Other problems on this host are the beet curly top virus and the southern root-knot nema, *Meloidogyne incognita*. These are rarely important enough on cultivated *Mirabilis* to require control practices.

MITCHELLA (PARTRIDGE-BERRY)

In nature and occasionally in culture the fungus *Meliola mitchellae* produces unsightly black spots on the leaves. No control is usually necessary. In Maryland the fungus *Pellicularia rolfsii* has been reported as causing stem rot.

MOLUCELLA (BELLS OF IRELAND)

Crown Rot (*Myrothecium* sp.). This disease appears as a necrosis of the stems near the soil line. Affected plants wilt rapidly and die. It has caused heavy losses to commercially grown Bells of Ireland in Texas. No control measures have been developed.

MONARDA (HORSEMINT)

Diseases

Leaf Spots (*Cercospora* sp., *Phyllosticta decidua, P. monardae, Ramularia brevipes,* and *R. variata*), Five species of fungi cause leaf spots of this host. None is important enough to warrant control measures.

Rusts (*Puccinia angustata* and *P. menthae*). These rusts are relatively unimportant on horsemint.

Other Diseases. This host is also subject to crown rot caused by *Pellicularia rolfsii*,

leaf gall by *Synchytrium holwayi,* and an undetermined mosaic virus.

Insects

Stalk Borer (*Papaipema nebris*). See *Delphinium.*

MORUS (MULBERRY)

Diseases

Bacterial Blight (*Pseudomonas mori*). Water-soaked spots appear on leaves and shoots; they later become sunken and black. The leaves are distorted and the shoots have black stripes. The leaves at the twig tips wilt and dry up.

Control: Some control is obtainable on young trees by pruning dead shoots in autumn and spraying with a copper fungicide the following spring. Streptomycin sprays may also be effective.

Leaf Spots (*Cercospora moricola, C. missouriensis,* and *Cercosporella mori*). The leaves of mulberry are spotted by these fungi in very rainy seasons.

Control: The *Cercosporella* fungus can cause defoliation of older trees. Valuable specimens should be sprayed with a copper fungicide if leaf spots are serious.

Popcorn Disease (*Ciboria carunculoides*). This disease, known only in the southern states, is largely confined to the carpels of the fruit. It causes them to swell and remain greenish, and interferes with ripening.

Control: The disease is of little importance. It does not lessen the value of the tree as an ornamental.

False Mildew (*Mycosphaerella mori*). The foliage of mulberries grown in the southern states may suffer severely from attacks of this mildew. It appears in July as whitish, indefinite patches on the undersides of the leaves. Yellowish areas then develop on the upper sides. The fungus threads that will produce spores emerge from the stomata on the undersides and spread out so as to form a white, cobweb-like coating; the general appearance is that of a powdery mildew. The asexual spores are colorless, each composed of several cells. The infected leaves fall to the ground and the overwintering or ascocarpic stage matures in the spring on these leaves.

Control: Gather and destroy all fallen leaves in autumn. Spray with a copper fungicide as soon as the mold appears in July.

Cankers At least six species of fungi may cause cankers on twigs and branches and dieback of twigs: *Cytospora* sp., *Dothiorella* sp., *D. mori, Gibberella baccata,* var. *moricola, Nectria* sp., and *Stemphyllium* sp. These can be distinguished only by microscopic or laboratory tests.

Control: Prune and destroy dead branches. Keep trees in good vigor by watering and fertilizing.

Powdery Mildews (*Phyllactinia corylea* and *Uncinula geniculata*). The lower leaf surface is covered by a white, powdery coating of these fungi.

Control: Valuable specimens can be protected by occasionally spraying with Benlate, Karathane, or wettable sulfur.

Insects and Related Pests

Citrus Flatid Planthopper (*Metcalfa pruinosa*). This very active insect, also called "Mealyflata," is ¼ inch long with purple-brown wings and is covered with white woolly matter.

Control: Spray with pyrethrum or rotenone or a combination of the two.

Cerambycid Borer (*Dorcaschema wildii*). In the South this borer mines large areas of cambium and tunnels into the wood of mulberry trees. Branches or even entire trees are girdled and killed.

Control: Spray trunks and branches of val-uable trees with methoxychlor twice at monthly intervals starting in mid-May.

Scales. The following scales infest mulberry: California red, cottony maple, Florida wax, greedy, olive parlatoria, peach, San Jose, and soft.

Control: Spray with malathion or Sevin to control the crawler stage of these pests.

Other Pests. The Comstock mealybug and the mulberry whitefly also infest this host. Malathion or Sevin sprays are effective. In dry seasons the two-spotted mite (*Tetranychus urticae*) may be abundant and injurious. Leaves are mottled and yellow.

Control: Valuable specimens should be sprayed with chlorobenzilate, Kelthane, Meta-Systox R, or Tedion after the fruits are gone.

MUSA (BANANA)

Plants of the cultivated banana, *Musa paradisiaca* var. *sapientum,* are subject to a number of serious bacterial and fungus diseases, as well as many insects. Such plants grown in northern greenhouses for display and educational purposes are subject to mealybugs, whiteflies, and scales. These can be controlled with malathion sprays.

In Florida the dwarf banana, *M. nana,* is subject to anthracnose caused by the fungus *Gloeosporium musarum,* leaf blight by the bacterium *Pseudomonas solanacearum,* and the southern root-knot nema, *Meloidogyne incognita.* The burrowing nema, *Radopholus similis,* occurs in Louisiana on the roots of ornamental banana trees.

MUSCARI (GRAPE-HYACINTH)

This host is unusually free from insect pests and fungus diseases. The smut fungus *Ustilago vaillantii* infects the flowers, and a species of *Sclerotium* attacks the bulbs. The northern root-knot nema, *Meloidogyne hapla,* and the stem and bulb nema *Ditylenchus dipsaci* also infest grape-hyacinth.

MYOSOTIS (FORGET-ME-NOT)

Diseases

Blight (*Botrytis cinerea*). The flowers of greenhouse and outdoor-grown *Myosotis* may be blighted by this fungus under conditions of high humidity, overcrowding, and low light intensity.

Control: Pick off and destroy blighted flowers.

Downy Mildew (*Peronospora myosotidis*). The lower sides of the leaves usually have a downy growth, on which are produced large quantities of spores. Pale spots appear on the upper surfaces of the leaves corresponding with the mold below.

Control: Valuable plantings can be protected from this disease with Bordeaux mixture or any ready made copper fungicide.

Wilt (*Sclerotinia sclerotiorum*). Plants wilt, turn brown, and assume a scalded appearance. The causal fungus enters the plant at the soil level.

Another soil-inhabiting fugus, *Sclerotium delphinii,* may also attack this host.

Control: Remove and discard infected plants together with the soil immediately adjacent to them. Steam-pasteurize infested soil before using it again.

Rust (*Puccinia eatoniae* var. *myosotidis*). This rust is never serious enough to require control measures.

Aster Yellows. This disease may affect *Myosotis.*

Control: Control measures are rarely necessary.

Insects

Aphids (*Myzus persicae* and *Brachycaudus helichrysi*). The peach and the leaf-curl plum aphid frequently infest forget-me-not.

Control: Spray with malathion, Meta-Systox R, or Sevin.

Potato Flea Beetle (*Epitrix cucumeris*). This small, black, quickly moving beetle makes tiny pinholes in the leaves.

Control: Sevin sprays control this pest.

Other Insects. This host is also subject to the larval stages of the painted beauty butterfly and the celery leaf tier. Sevin sprays will control these pests.

MYRICA CERIFERA (WAX-MYRTLE)

Diseases

Black Mildew (*Irene calostroma* and *Irenina manca*). A black mildew coating of the leaves of this host occurs in the Deep South.

Control: This disease is never serious enough to require control measures.

Leaf Spots (*Phyllosticta myricae* and *Septoria myricae*). Wax-myrtle in the East and South may be spotted by these fungi.

Control: Pick and destroy spotted leaves.

Rust (*Gymnosporangium ellisii*). Bright orange pustules break out in large numbers on the leaves, especially on the undersides. The alternate host of the fungus is southern whitecedar, *Chamaecyparis,* and where this plant grows naturally or is planted as an ornamental, the rust on *Myrica* may be serious. Unless both hosts are present, however, the rust does not occur. The same fungus causes a "ram's horn" effect on leaves of sweetfern, *Comptonia.*

Control: Control measures are rarely adopted for this disease.

MYRICA GALE (SWEET GALE)

Sweet gale is subject to a twig blight caused by a species of *Diplodia,* two leaf spots by *Ramularia moniliodes* and *Septoria myricata,* and rusts by *Cronartium comptoniae* and *Gymnosporangium ellisii.*

MYRICA PENNSYLVANICA (BAYBERRY)

Diseases

Yellows (Bayberry yellows virus). Yellowing of the leaves and stunting of plants and few to no fruits are the principal symptoms. This does not resemble any of the other yellows virus diseases.

Control: Rogue out and destroy infected plants.

Bayberry is also subject to two leaf spotting fungi, *Mycosphaerella myricae* and *Phyllosticta myricae,* and a rust fungus, *Gymnosporangium ellisii.*

Insect

Red-Humped Caterpillar (*Schizura concinna*). This yellowish-brown caterpillar with a bright-red head and a red hump on its back, feeds on this host as well as many other ornamental trees and shrubs.

Control: Spray with Sevin or *Bacillus thuringiensis.*

MYRTUS (MYRTLE)

Diseases

A leaf spot caused by *Pestalotia decolorata* and a stem rot caused by *Pellicularia rolfsii* are the only fungus diseases reported on this host.

Insects

Aphid (*Neomyzus circumflexus*). The crescent-marked lily aphid infests this host.

Control: Spray with Meta-Systox R, Sevin, or malathion.

Scales. Seven species of scale insects infest myrtle: black, barnacle, greedy, green shield, oystershell, rose, and soft.

Control: Spray with malathion or Sevin when the young scales are crawling about.

Citrus Mealybug (*Planococcus citri*). This mealybug occasionally infests myrtle.

Control: Malathion sprays will control this pest.

NANDINA

Few fungus diseases affect this host. Most common are a red leaf spot caused by *Cercospora nandinae,* anthracnose by *Glomerella cingulata,* and root rot by *Phymatotrichum omnivorum.* The northern root-knot nema, *Meloidogyne hapla,* also has been reported on *Nandina.*

NARCISSUS

Fungus Diseases

Blue Mold Rot (*Penicillium* sp.). Bulbs in storage may be affected by a rot caused by blue mold; this follows mechanical injury or damage by mites, and develops under moist conditions. A white mycelium penetrates the bulb scales; it later becomes hard and dry.

Control: Dip bulbs in Benlate as suggested under *Gladiolus* corm rots. Dry bulbs rapidly after treatment.

Crown Rot (*Pellicularia rolfsii* and *Sclerotium delphinii*). In regions where *Pellicularia rolfsii* is present in the soil, the surface of the bulb may be covered with layers of coarse, white mold. The small reddish-brown sclerotia may be also found mingled with the mold. The sclerotia of *S. delphinii* are considerably larger than those of *P. rolfsii* (Fig. 65).

Control: Carefully remove infected plants, including all underground parts, and steam-pasteurize the soil. Avoid planting narcissus in an infected region until an interval of 2 or 3 years has elapsed. Infected bulbs can be soaked in hot water-formalin solution.

Dry Scale Rot (*Sclerotinia narcissi*). This disease is caused by a fungus which is closely related to that which causes a dry rot of gladiolus, *Stromatinia gladioli.* The fungus, with its sclerotia, may be found on dead scales several layers deep. It has been found to follow serious infestation by nemas, and it develops most noticeably in heavy soil, especially if the bulbs are planted wet after a hotwater treatment.

Control: Treat bulbs in a hot water-formalin mixture. Dry rapidly before planting.

Basal Rot (*Fusarium oxysporum* var. *narcissi*). Decay begins at the roots or at the bases of the scales and spreads upward through the inside, especially through the center; it may extend out in all directions. It is most serious on the "trumpet" type of narcissus. Certain varieties are said to be somewhat resistant. The final result is a dwarfing of the plants and an abnormal development of the blossoms.

Control: While it is difficult to determine by an early inspection whether or not a bulb is infected, any bulbs that have a few shriveled or discolored roots and diseased pockets should be discarded. In valuable bulbs evidence of decay should be sought by stripping off the dry, outer scales. Early stages of infection can be eliminated by chemical treatment, such as soaking the bulbs for 15 to 30 minutes in Benlate, 2 tablespoonfuls per gallon of warm water (80-85°F.).

Fire (*Sclerotinia polyblastis*). In humid weather this fungus causes a spotting and rotting of flowers which later spreads to the foliage and destroys it rapidly. It does not cause a bulb rot. The earliest symptoms of the disease on leaves are dark reddish-brown spots very distinct from the green tissue of the leaf. The spots are somewhat elongated parallel to the veins. They may be covered with spores clustered together on stalks. In warm wet weather infection spreads rapidly through a field, killing the foliage very suddenly. The resting stage of the fungus consists of large sclerotia which may be ½ inch in diameter; they develop on dead leaves which have fallen in moist places.

Control: Rake and discard old foliage. Spray with ferbam or zineb in spring to protect newly developing leaves and flowers. In rainy springs, sprays should be applied 2 or 3 times weekly until flowers appear. Pick off and destroy leaves that show fungus lesions; do not throw them on the ground near the narcissus beds.

Leaf Spot (*Didymellina macrospora*). After the blooming season this fungus, which causes a spotting of iris, freesia, and certain other garden plants, may attack narcissus. The leaves develop large spots or blotches, which finally cause them to wither and die. As a result, the bulbs are not sufficiently nourished and fail to ripen thoroughly.

Control: Remove and destroy plants with diseased foliage. Spray early in the growing season with a copper fungicide or with Fore, to which a spreader-sticker has been added.

Scorch (*Stagonospora curtisii*). On the west coast of America this disease has frequently proved rather serious, often killing plants before they have reached maturity. The affected spots are brownish; there is usually a yellowing of the surrounding tissues. The fungus may be found at the tops of the bulb-scales; the leaves are apt to become infected as they emerge from the bulb. The same fungus attacks *Amaryllis* and *Crinum*, on which it causes a red spotting; no such discoloration appears on narcissus. The disease is not uncommon also in the eastern United States.

Control: See *Amaryllis*.

Smolder (*Sclerotinia narcissicola*). This fungus causes a decay of stored narcissus bulbs and a rot of foliage and flowers in cold wet seasons.

Control: Remove and destroy affected plants and soil immediately adjacent. During rainy springs spray every 2 weeks with a copper fungicide.

Root Rot (*Cylindrocarpon radicicola*). A disease which causes a yellowing of the leaves and stunting and withering of the plants is ascribed to this fungus. The roots have yellowish or brown discolored stripes and decayed regions. The bulbs remain sound. Some think that this or a similar rot is caused by nemas.

Control: The disease is said to be more serious in soil long given over to narcissus cultivation. If it is necessary to continue planting in the same region, the soil should be steam-pasteurized or treated with one of the fumigants mentioned in Chapter 4.

White Mold (*Ramularia vallisumbrosae*). This fungus causes a rapid decay of leaves and flower stalks in the Pacific Northwest. The first spots or lesions develop near the tips of the leaves. The pale green circular areas bear powdery white or buff spores. Outside the spore-bearing regions is a zone of green, darker than the normal tissue. Outside this appears a zone of yellow. Toward the end of the season, as soon as the leaves wither, minute black resting sclerotia develop in great numbers. These live through unfavorable conditions and seasons. In dry weather they are not formed, nor do the whitish spores which characterize the spots develop.

Control: Since the fungus is not carried in the bulb, it is necessary to rake up and destroy all old foliage which may harbor the resting stage of the fungus. During the season plants can be sprayed with a copper fungicide. The disease is especially serious where the humidity is high, when the plants are little cultivated, and on plants weakened from other causes.

Virus Diseases

Yellow Stripe (Narcissus yellow stripe virus). Strong yellow streaks and mottling and roughening of the leaves are characteristic of this disease. Roughening and streaking of the flowers also occur.

Control: Rogue out diseased plants early in the growing season. Six species of aphids are known to act as vectors. Hence Sevin or malathion sprays should be applied from time to time.

Mosaic (Narcissus mosaic virus). This virus disease, also known as mild mosaic, has no striking symptoms when the plants first emerge. Toward flowering time, the leaves exhibit blue-green mottling. Flowers are not streaked.

Control: Affected plants should be rouged from foundation or "mother block" stocks.

Flower Streak (Virus). Flowers of the variety King Alfred are strongly streaked when infected by this virus. Infected bulbs, therefore, are unfit for forcing.

Control: Roguing of commercial and foundation stocks at flowering time is suggested.

White Streak (Narcissus silver leaf virus). This disease, once called "Zilverblad" by the Dutch, is often present with another virus which causes chocolate-colored spots and purple tips on the leaves. White-streak virus alone, or with other viruses, causes a general decline of plants in late season. The complex is not too clearly understood.

Control: Commercial growers should rouge out all diseased plants. The symptoms appear about 2 weeks before harvest. Hence speed is essential.

Insects and Other Animal Pests

Tulip Bulb Aphid (*Dysaphis tulipae*). This aphid is destructive to bulbs in storage and feeds on the leaves and other parts above the ground during the spring.

Control: If aphids are present before planting, dip bulbs in Diazinon, 1 lb. in 50 gallons of water. Spraying growing plants with Diazinon or malathion is effective.

Bulb Mite (*Rhizoglyphus echinopus*). Plants grown from infested bulbs have a sickly appearance. The leaves are stunted and the flowers are deformed or do not develop at all. The mites are small and whitish in color. They develop in large numbers and feed on the bulb scales. They are from $1/50$ to $1/25$ of an inch long and scarcely visible without a lens.

Control: Soak bulbs for 24 hours in a solution containing 2 ounces of 25 per cent wettable Tedion in 12 gallons of water.

Bulb Scale Mite (*Steneotarsonemus laticeps*). This mite sometimes attacks the bulb scales of narcissus seriously.

Control: Destroy all soft mushy bulbs at digging time or at planting time. Store bulbs at a low temperature, around 35°F. preferably. Hot-water dips or methyl bromide fumigation also provide control of these mites.

Bulb Fly (*Merodon equestris*) and **Lesser Bulb Fly** (*Eumerus tuberculatus*). Soft bulbs which fail to grow and have brown scars on their outer scales may be infested with the whitish or yellowish-white larvae of bulb flies. The adult insects of *M. equestris* look like small bumblebees. The female lays eggs on leaves and necks of the bulbs; the young grubs enter the scales and bore into the bulbs, opening the way for rots caused by fungi and bacteria. The grubs are from 1/2 to 3/4 inch long. See Fig. 107. The adults of the lesser bulb fly, *Eumerus tuberculatus,* are blackish-green and about 1/3 inch long. The grubs are yellowish and about 1/2 inch long.

Control: Apply 2 ounces (10 level tablespoonfuls) of Proxol 80 SP in 10 gallons of water as a drench per 100 feet of row. Direct stream to base of plants at beginning of adult fly activity (early May to June). Repeat treatment annually.

Millipedes (*Orthomorpha gracilis*). These pests feed on the undersides of the bulbs causing great damage.

Control: Apply Diazinon, Dursban, or Sevin to the soil surface prior to planting.

Stem and Bulb Nema (*Ditylenchus dipsaci*). This is called the "ring disease" because when an infested bulb is cut across, the attacked scales appear in dark-colored circles in contrast to the normal white pulp of the uninfested scales. The yellowish pockets in the scales contain many nemas. Badly infested bulbs usually do not grow in the spring, or, if they develop, they fail to form flowers. Infested leaves have small swellings

of yellowish tissue which can be felt by pulling the leaves through the fingers. The shoots may be more or less abnormal and twisted.

Control: Inspect plants in the spring. Infested leaves have small yellowish spots which are more conspicuous in the shade. Remove individual plants in such a way as to include the bulb and some of the surrounding soil. Destroy all weeds and other plants that harbor the same nema. Avoid wet, rich soil with a high content of humus. Infested bulbs can be freed of eelworms by applying the hot-water treatment as given below.

Root Lesion Nema (*Pratylenchus* sp.). This nema causes premature death of the leaves, starting from the older ones and progressing upward to the younger ones. Infested plants have few roots, which are short and stubby. Such roots have necrotic lesions or dead spots, which are frequently reddish, turning dark brown to black.

Control: This nema is very susceptible to drying out. Hence few nemas are able to survive on bulbs held in storage. Most infestations occur from infested soil. Soils should be fumigated with Nemagon or some other suitable fumigant before planting.

Hot-Water Treatment for the Control of Mites, Nemas, and Bulb Flies

Bulbs that are dug early should cure from 3 to 5 weeks before being treated, while those dug later in the season should be treated within 2 or 3 weeks. If these precautions are not followed, the bulbs may be seriously injured by the treatment and the quality of flowers reduced. The bulbs should be packed loosely in wire baskets or in sacks with open meshes, such as onion sacks. Adequate equipment includes some means for keeping the water in circulation, such as propellers in the tank, and at a temperature of 110 to 111 degrees F. for 3 hours depending on the size of the bulbs. Before treating another lot of bulbs in the same water, raise the temperature 20 to 30 degrees to kill any fungus spores then cool the water again to treatment temperature. If the bulbs are likely to be infected by *Fusarium, Trichoderma,* or other fungi, one should add Formalin at the rate of 1 pint to 25 gallons of water. Bulbs should be planted soon after treatment; otherwise they must be thoroughly dried. Provision should be made for preventing contamination of the treated stock if infested stock is handled in the meantime.

Commercial growers of narcissus in the major bulb-producing states should consult their state plant pathologists and entomologists for additional details on hot-water treatments.

NELUMBO (LOTUS)

Fungus Diseases

Alternaria Leaf Spot (*Alternaria nelumbii*). Small reddish-brown spots appear, usually bordered with light green. They increase in size. The leaves curl up and die from the margin inward.

Another leaf spot that occasionally appears on this host is caused by *Cercospora nelumbonis.*

Control: Although no controls have been developed, it is likely that applications of copper or dithiocarbamate sprays will control these leaf spots.

Insects

Aphids (*Rhopalosiphum nymphaeae* and *Aphis gossypii*). The waterlily and cotton aphids infest *Nelumbo.* Leaves are disfigured and decayed and flowers are discolored. The former species may cause much damage to Japanese cherry trees growing near waterlily ponds. It passes the winter in many kinds of fruit trees.

Control: Spray with Meta-Systox R, Sevin, or malathion.

Japanese Beetle (*Popillia japonica*). During July and August the adult beetles may be very destructive. They feed on the leaves and flowers.

Control: See *Aesculus.*

NEPETA (CATNIP)

Diseases

Leaf Spots (*Ascochyta nepetae, Cercospora nepetae, Phyllosticta decidua,* and *Septoria nepetae*). Four fungi cause leaf spotting of catnip.

A bacterium, *Pseudomonas tabaci,* causes a leaf spot of this host in Wisconsin.

Control: Leaf spots on catnip are not serious enough to warrant control practices.

Other Diseases. Stem rot caused by the fungus *Pellicularia rolfsii,* root rot by *P. filamentosa,* and a mosaic virus are the only other diseases thus far recorded on catnip.

NERIUM (OLEANDER)

Diseases

Bacterial Gall (*Pseudomonas savastanoi* var. *nerii*). Wart-like growths on all aboveground parts, including the flowers, are caused by this bacterium. See Fig. 167. Canker-like lesions are also formed on young shoots. It is possible that infestation by scale insects or mealybugs opens the way for infection by the bacteria.

Control: Cut off and destroy infected parts, carefully disinfecting the shears after each pruning by dipping them in 70 per cent denatured alcohol. Propagate only from healthy plants.

Sphaeropsis Gall (*Sphaeropsis tumefaciens*). Oleander in southern Florida is very subject to galling, brooming and branch dieback.

Control: Controls have not been developed but pruning affected branches to sound wood may help to keep the disease in check.

Fig. 167. Bacterial galls on oleander caused by the bacterium *Pseudomonas savastanoi* var. *nerii*.

Leaf Spots (*Cercospora neriella, C. repens, Gloeosporium* sp., *Macrosporium nerii, Phyllosticta nerii*, and *Septoria oleandrina*). At least five species of fungi cause leaf spots on oleander.

Control: Pick off and destroy spotted leaves as soon as they appear.

Other Diseases. *Sphaceloma oleandri* causes spot anthracnose in Florida; *Capnodium elongatum* causes sooty mold in the

Gulf States; *Clitocybe tabescens* causes a root rot in Florida.

Insects

Aphids. Three species of aphids infest oleander: bean, green peach, and oleander.

Control: Spray with Meta-Systox R, Sevin, or malathion, and repeat within two weeks if additional aphids appear.

Oleander Scale (*Aspidiotus nerii*). In colder climates this insect is rather common on oleander grown in greenhouses. The scale is circular in form, pale yellow, and up to $^1/_{10}$ inch in diameter. In the southern states and in subtropical countries it is a serious pest of oleander and other shrubs grown in gardens. The insects crowd together on the stems or leaves, occasionally completely covering them.

Control: Spray repeatedly with malathion or Sevin when the young insects are moving about on the leaves. Inspect plants brought into the greenhouses to be sure they are free from scales.

Cottony-Cushion Scale (*Icerya purchasi*). In some greenhouses this scale is more serious than the oleander scale. The mature insects are $^1/_4$ inch long. The female is often marked by ridges and by a white cottony substance within which are found large numbers of eggs (see Figs. 79 and 99).

Control: Same as for oleander scale.

Hemispherical Scale (*Saissetia hemisphaerica*). This scale also infests oleander in the greenhouse. The mature scale is highly convex, smooth, and brown. The female lays over 500 eggs. The young feed along the veins and are active for a month or more.

Other scales which may infest oleander are black, Florida red, Florida wax, lesser snow, olive parlatoria, peach, and soft.

Control: Same as for oleander scale.

Mealybugs (*Pseudococcus longispinus* and *Planococcus citri*). Oleander, like many other greenhouse plants, is subject to mealybugs. The control of these pests is the same as for scales.

Subterranean Termite (*Reticulitermes flaviceps*). This pest occasionally infests oleander. Control measures are discussed under *Chrysanthemum*.

NICOTIANA (FLOWERING TOBACCO)

Diseases

Species and hybrids of tobacco grown as ornamentals in borders are subject to many of the same diseases that affect smoking and chewing tobaccos. Among the more common fungus diseases of flowering tobacco are downy mildew caused by *Peronospora tabacina*, leaf spot by *Alternaria longipes*, powdery mildew by a species of *Oidium*, and root rot by *Phymatotrichum omnivorum*. These are rarely serious enough to warrant control measures.

Viruses

Three virus diseases occur on this host in nature: curly top, caused by the beet curly top virus; mosaic, by tobacco mosaic virus; and ringspot, by the tobacco ringspot virus. This host is also susceptible to a wide range of other viruses that affect commercial tobaccos.

Control: Rogue out diseased plants as soon as discovered.

Insects and Other Animal Pests

Beetles. Three kinds of beetles infest flowering tobacco: Colorado potato, potato flea, and tobacco flea.

Control: When these pests become abundant, spray with Sevin.

Other Insects. Cutworms and hornworms also infest this host. The former are controlled by dusting or wetting the soil with Diazinon, Dylox, Proxol, or Sevin just before setting the plants out in spring. The latter can be destroyed by spraying plants with Sevin.

Southern Root-Knot Nema (*Meloidogyne incognita*). This pest attacks the roots of this host in ornamental plantings. For control, see Chapter 3.

NUPHAR—see NYMPHAEA

NYMPHAEA (WATERLILY)

Diseases

Leaf Spots (*Alternaria* sp., *Cercospora exotica, C. nymphaeacea, Helicoceras nymphaearum, Helicosporium nymphaearum, Mycosphaerella pontederiae, Ovularia nymphaearum, Phyllosticta fatiscens., P. nymphaeacea,* and *P. nymphaeicola*). Many fungi cause leaf spots on waterlily.

Control: Pick and destroy leaves that show spots. Captan sprays also control leaf spots.

Other Diseases. A white smut caused by the fungus *Entyloma nymphaeae* and a leaf and stem rot by a species of *Pythium* are the other fungus diseases known on this host.

Insects

Waterlily Aphid (*Rhopalosiphum nymphaeae*). This aphid is one of the most destructive pests of waterlilies. It attacks both foliage and flowers of a number of aquatic plants. It spends the autumn, winter, and spring on peach or plum trees, and turns to waterlilies as soon as they put out their leaves.

The corn leaf aphid, *R. maidis,* also infests waterlily occasionally.

Control: Spray the plants, as soon as the aphids are detected, with a strong pyrethrum solution. Malathion and Sevin sprays are also effective. Avoid using rotenone where fish are present. Nicotine sulfate and soap solutions are apt to disfigure the flowers.

False Leaf Mining Midge (*Cricotopus or-*

natus). New leaves that are attacked turn brown very rapidly and rot. The miners feed in serpentine channels which open the way for bacterial rot. When many larvae are present, the leaf is soon destroyed. The mature insect is a small fly.

Control: Effective controls have not been developed.

Waterlily Leaf Cutter (*Synclita obliteralis*). This beautiful brown-marked moth lays its yellowish-brown eggs during the summer months near the edge of the leaf or on the lower surface. The grubs are cream-colored with a dark line along the back, the head very small and light brown. They feed for a short time as miners. They then make themselves a protecting case by cutting out lens-shaped pieces of leaves and fastening them together with silk. This elastic case, open at both ends, admits air to the grubs but keeps water out. The grub feeds in much the same way as the bagworm, pushing out its head and a few segments of the body. As the larva grows, it makes larger cases. When full-grown it may be 1 inch long. Attacked leaves become very ragged and much rotted. This insect feeds also on other water plants, such as *Potamogeton, Hydrocharis,* and *Sagittaria.*

Control: If fish are numerous in the pond, no other control is necessary, for they feed on the larvae. Flooding or submerging the plants by hand washes off the protecting cases and makes the larvae more accessible to the fish. If fish are absent, the water should be lowered and the leaves dusted with equal parts of pyrethrum powder and tobacco dust. The dusting should be repeated in 20 minutes. The first dusting drives the larvae out of their cases and the second kills them. This treatment should never be used where fish are present.

Waterlily Leaf Beetle (*Pyrrhalta nymphaeae*). These dark brown beetles, about ¼ inch long and half as wide, feed on the leaves and flowers of waterlilies, causing damage similar to that made by rose weevils. They feed on both sides of leaves that are not submerged.

Control: Effective controls have not been developed.

NYMPHOIDES (FLOATING-HEART)

This aquatic host is subject to a rust caused by the fungus *Puccinia scirpi* and a leaf smut by *Burrillia decipiens,* neither of which is of great importance.

NYSSA (TUPELO)

Diseases

Canker. Five species of fungi—*Botryosphaeria dothidea, Fusarium solani, Nectria galligena, Strumella coryneoidea, and Septobasidium curtisii*—produce stem cankers or dieback on tupelo.

Control: Prune and destroy infected branches. Keep trees in good vigor by watering and fertilizing when necessary.

Leaf Spots (*Mycosphaerella nyssaecola*). Irregular purplish blotches, which later enlarge to an inch or more in width, are commonly scattered over the upper surfaces of the leaves of young tupelo trees in the southeastern states. Minute black fruiting bodies of the fungus are visible in the infected areas.

Two other fungi, *Cercospora nyssae* and *Pirostoma nyssae,* also cause leaf spots.

Control: Copper fungicides are suggested as preventive sprays. Raking and destroying infected leaves in the fall should also help to reduce infections.

Rust (*Aplospora nyssae*). This rust fungus occasionally infects tupelos from Maine to Texas.

Control: Control practices are not warranted.

Insects

Tupelo Leaf Miner (*Antispila nysaefoliella*). Leaves are first mined by the larval stage. When mature, the larvae cut oval section out of the leaves and fall to the ground with severed pieces.

Control: Spray with malathion in May when the adult moths emerge. Repeat within 10 days.

Tupelo Scale (*Phenacaspis nyssae*). This scale is nearly triangular in shape, flat, and snow white.

Control: A dormant oil spray in early spring will provide control.

Other Pests. Two other pests have been reported on tupelo: the azalea sphinx moth and San Jose scale. Malathion or Sevin sprays will control the larval stage of the former and the crawler stage of the latter.

OENOTHERA (EVENING PRIMROSE)

Diseases

Leaf Spots (*Alternaria tenuis, Cercospora oenotherae, C. oenotherae-sinuatae, Pezizella oenotherae, Pestalotia oenotherae, and Septoria oenotherae*). At least six pieces of fungi cause leaf spots of this host.

Control: Pick and destroy spotted leaves as soon as they appear.

Rust (*Puccinia dioicae* [*estensicola*] var. *oenotherae*). The orange-colored clustercup stage occurs on this host, while the overwintering teliospore stage develops later on a sedge, *Carex.*

Other rusts recorded on this host are *Aecidium anograe, Puccinia aristidae, P. oenotherae, and Uromyces plumbarius.*

Control: Rusts are seldom serious enough to warrant control measures.

Other Diseases. A downy mildew caused by the fungus *Peronospora arthuri* and powdery mildew by *Erysiphe polygoni* also occur on evening primrose. Neither is important enough to require control practices.

Insect

Aphid (*Aphis oenotherae*). This small, robust, dark green species is common in the East and attacks wild and cultivated species of the evening primrose in California.

Control: Spray with Meta-Systox R, Sevin, or malathion.

OPUNTIA (PRICKLY-PEAR)

Diseases

Anthracnose (*Mycosphaerella opuntiae*). This disease is prevalent in the southern states. Once the fungus enters the host, it spreads very rapidly throughout the segment affected, causing a rather moist light brown rot, illustrated in Fig. 168. Many light pink pustules, containing the spores of the fungus, break out on the surface. The sharply curved (lunate) spores are characteristic. These spores belong to the imperfect stage of the fungus, known as *Gloeosporium cactorum*.

Control: No serious attempt has been made to develop control measures for rots of ornamental cacti. Clearly the cutting out and destruction of diseased segments as soon as rot appears should be the first step. No dis-

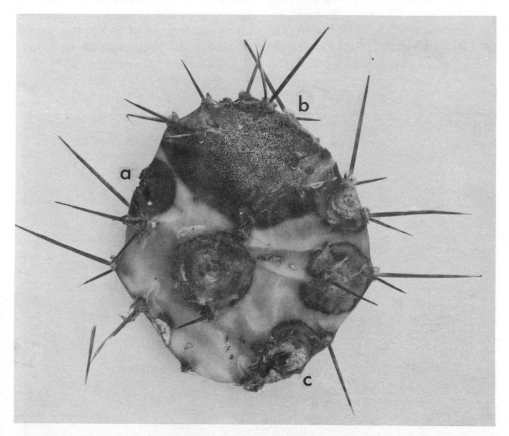

Fig. 168. Anthracnose of *Opuntia* caused by *Mycosphaerella opuntiae*. The small dark area at the left *(a)* is an early stage; above it and to the right *(b)* a similar spot has greatly enlarged and is covered with small spore-pustules. The other (zonate) spots *(c)* are caused by *Leptodermella opuntiae*.

eased segments should be used for propagation. Since many of the rot-causing fungi can live in soil and in portions of old plants, soil in which rot has appeared must be removed and benches disinfested. It is advisable to move cacti from positions in gardens in which rot has been evident. In nurseries in which many cacti are propagated, spraying with Bordeaux mixture may be advisable.

Charcoal Spot (*Stevensea wrightii*). This disease is a very common and destructive disease of *Opuntia* in Florida and Texas, but is uncommon in the northern states. Small spots ¼ inch or more in diameter first appear, each surrounded by a ring of young fruiting structures. The spots gradually enlarge but maintain their individuality. The fungus is rather deeply seated, sending its sucking organs into the central cells as well as into the epidermis. The substomatal cavities are filled with a mass of fungus tissue from which ascocarpic fruiting bodies arise. This fungus is closely related to certain species of *Elsinoë*, which cause anthracnose of roses, goldenrod, citrus trees, and other ornamentals. The fruiting bodies are superficial.

Control: Remove and destroy severly infected specimens.

Dry Rot (*Phyllosticta concava*). Greenhouse opuntias are sometimes attacked by a dry-rot which is common on wild plants in Bermuda and in southern states. The disease, shown in Fig. 169, begins as small black circular spots, which increase slowly until they reach a diameter of an inch or two. Further advance of the fungus into the host is pre-

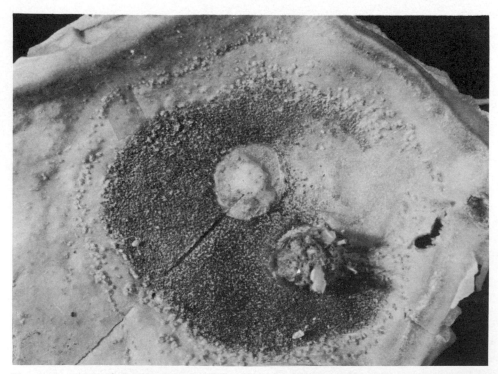

Fig. 169. Spot of *Opuntia* greatly enlarged. The dark area is due to *Phyllosticta concava;* the light bodies around the dark area are the fruiting bodies of *Leptodermella opuntiae*.

vented by the formation of a layer of callus. The diseased area becomes sunken by the collapse of the cells. Many minute black fungus fruiting bodies dot the surface of diseased spots. The spores are very small. Other spots similar in appearance bear the ascocarpic fruiting bodies of *Mycosphaerella*. Another fungus often associated with the dry rot appears as a number of light pink, raised fruiting bodies suggestive of the fungus that causes anthracnose. These usually develop deep in the tissues of the infected segment. This fungus, *Leptodermella opuntiae*, is easily distinguished from *Mycosphaerella* by the more deeply seated fruiting bodies and the longer spores.

Control: See anthracnose, above.

Fusarium Rot (*Fusarium oxysporum* var. *aurantiacum*). The young segments become dark gray or black; the diseased area is dry and brittle, sharply delimited. Older lesions are markedly decayed, brown-blotched, and irregular. Bases of segments are most frequently attacked.

Control: Remove all diseased young plants from the propagating beds and destroy them. Spray the beds with Bordeaux mixture. Avoid syringing, which is apt to spread spores from plant to plant. Space cuttings widely enough to provide dry conditions. Since spores are often found on fruits and seeds of diseased plants, the seeds should be disinfested if used for propagation.

Soft Rot. (*Gnomoniella opuntiae*). This fungus causes a soft wet rot that turns the invaded segment a faded grayish-black. For control see under anthracnose.

Other Rots. Many other fungi cause rot of opuntia: *Aspergillus alliaceus, Colletotrichum dematium, Diplodia opuntiae,* and *Phoma* sp. The bacterium *Erwinia carotovora* causes a soft, wet rot of this host. In California, *Opuntia ficus-indica* is subject to the shoe-string root rot fungus *Armillaria mellea.*

Sunscald (*Hendersonia opuntiae*). This is said to be the most serious and common fungus trouble of the "Texas pear." The segments turn a reddish-brown color and finally die. The spots first formed are distinctly zoned. The center of the diseased area is grayish-brown and cracked. Another fruiting body, which contains the asci of *Leptosphaeria opuntiae,* is sometimes found with *Hendersonia* and may be mistaken for it.

Insects

Cactus Fruit Gall Midge (*Asphondylia opuntiae*). This small gray midge with white larvae is often present in great numbers on the green and ripening fruit of *Opuntia.* Brown pupal skins protrude fom the exit holes. Control measures are never adopted for the pest.

Other Diseases and Pests. See *Cactaceae.*

ORCHIDACEAE (ORCHIDS)[27]

Bacterial Diseases

Bacterial Soft Rot (*Erwinia carotovora*). This disease attacks some of the most valuable orchids and destroys them. Amber-colored spots develop on the leaf blades. These turn brown and spread very rapidly so that the entire leaf is involved and becomes chestnut-brown. If the infection occurs on the lower ends of the leaf, the upper part become yellowish from lack of food. The rot may involve the entire plant and so destroy it.

Control: Since infection is presumed to take place only through wounds, wounding the plants should be avoided. When diseased leaves are removed, the cut surface should be

[27]For an excellent presentation on the control of insects and diseases of orchids, see *The Orchids,* edited by C. L. Withner and published by The Ronald Press Company, New York, 1959.

treated with Physan 20. Streptomycin dips may also be effective.

Brown Rot (*Phytomonas cattleyae*). On *Phalaenopsis* this disease starts as a soft, water-soaked lesion which eventually becomes brown or black. On *Cattleya* species it is limited to the older leaves, appearing as sunken black spots which are clearly delimited.

Control: Dipping plants in a Natriphene solution is said to provide control.

Fungus Diseases

American Anthracnose (*Glomerella cincta*). The disease usually starts at the tips of the leaves and spreads toward the bases. The diseased regions are dark-colored and decayed. The line of advance is well marked. Many spore pustules develop on decaying leaves and stems, so that is difficult to control the disease.

Control: Cut off and destroy infected leaves and spray with ammoniacal copper carbonate or Bordeaux mixture. Avoid as much syringing as possible. Do not propagate from badly infected plants. Since this disease is serious, prevention is very desirable.

Anthracnose (*Physalospora cattleyae* and *Gloeosporium* spp.). Several species of fungi have been described as causing anthracnose of many kinds of orchids. Much of the trouble comes in with plants introduced from the tropics Now that quarantine is usual, the diseased and dead leaves are removed before being passed. Even so, many plants with the disease reach the greenhouse. It is well to grow plants first in isolated houses.

The spots vary from yellowish to light brown, and become soft, more or less circular, and somewhat sunken. They may occur on leaves or tubers. There is a tendency for the spore-bearing pustules to be arranged in concentric rings. Rose-colored or reddish-yellow masses of spores ooze out from these pustules. When the disease is severe, the leaves and even the tubers may be killed.

Control: The same as for the American Anthracnose. It is especially necessary to avoid sprinkling with water and using too much nitrogenous fertilizer. Plants should be kept in light, well-aired houses.

Black Rot (*Phytophthora cactorum*). This fungus attacks the leaves, pseudobulbs, rhizomes, and flower buds of species of *Cattleya, Vanda,* and *Grammatophyllum* in Florida. Affected areas on the leaves are purplish-brown or black (Fig. 170). When the pseudobulb is infected, the distal portion withers and dies.

Control: Discard badly infected plants. Prune infected leaves or pseudobulbs. Disinfest knives used in dividing plants by dipping in Physan 20 solution. Dip infected plants in Natriphene solution as directed by the manufacturer. If the rot continues, repeat the treatment in 1 week.

Leaf Blight (*Phythium ultimum*). The symptoms of this disease are similar to those produced by *Phytophthora cactorum.* This fungus will also cause damping-off of seedlings in community pots. Only laboratory isolation tests can enable one to separate the two causal agents.

Control: Same as for black rot.

Leaf Spots (*Cercospora epipactidis, C. massalonga, C. peristeriae, Chaetodiplodia* sp., *Diplodia laeliocattleyae, Leptothyrium* sp., *Phyllosticta* spp., *Selenophoma* sp., and *Volutella albido-pila*). At least nine species of fungi cause leaf spots on orchids.

Control: If leaf spots are prevalent, spray with a copper fungicide to prevent further spread.

Basal Rot (*Pellicularia rolfsii*). This soil-borne organism invades the root collar and extends into the leaves, which wilt, become discolored, and dry out, usually breaking off at the base. The base of the stem is usually covered with a felt of fungus growth, which produces the small round sclerotia. These are at first white, then yellowish, finally dark brown in color. It is said that these propagat-

Fig. 170. Leaf blight of *Cattleya* caused by *Phytophthora cactorum.*

ing bodies live as long as 4 years. The disease may be very severe in greenhouses where high humidity and high temperature prevail.

Control: Remove the sclerotia and as much of the felty mycelium as possible without injury to the plant, and immerse the plants in 1 per cent solution of copper sulfate (blue vitriol). Pasteurize the pots and soil or fiber by dipping them in hot water at 140°F. for 15 minutes.

Root Rot (*Pellicularia filamentosa*). Another root rot disease of orchids results from a brown mycelium which develops on the leaves and roots of potted plants. The fungus probably comes into the greenhouse with soil that has previously been planted with potatoes or other crops on which it is prevalent.

Control: Effective controls have not been developed. Dipping the base of the plant in Natriphene, as suggested for black rot, might be effective.

Petal Blight (*Sclerotinia fuckeliana*). Small spots, sometimes bordered by delicate rings of pink, spread over the petals. They may become enlarged and sometimes destroy the petals, which soon fall. The gray mold, *Botrytis cinerea,* develops on the spots under humid conditions, and diseased blooms are the source of the spread of the disease in greenhouses.

Control: Cut and destroy diseased flowers as soon as they appear.

Rust (*Uredo behnickiana*). Orange-yellow patches appear on the lower leaf surfaces. The upper surfaces show yellow-green chlorotic areas directly above the patches. This rust occurs on species of *Cattleya, Epidendrum, Laelia, Oncidium,* and *Schomburgkia.* In Florida it is particularly serious on *Phaius grandiflorus.*

Control: Destroy all severely infected plants. Isolate mildly infected ones from other susceptible species. Spray with wettable sulfur when the plants are not in flower.

Other Rusts. Among other rusts known to attack orchids are *Uredo guacae* and *U. nigropuncta.* The former attacks *Epidendrum tampense* most frequently.

Wilt (*Fusarium oxysporum* var. *cattleyae*). This fungus causes a leaf wilt and leaf abscission, and death of pseudobulbs and rhizomes of cattleya orchids. It also infests the osmunda fibre in which the orchids are grown.

Control: Effective controls have not been developed.

Virus Diseases

Cattleya Flower Break (Orchid strain of tobacco mosaic virus). Abnormal color patterns and malformation of the flower result from infection by this virus. The green peach aphid, *Myzus persicae,* spreads it.

Control: Discard infected plants and control aphids with malathion sprays.

Mosaic (Cymbidium mosaic virus). In cattleyas and related orchids, this virus causes a leaf necrosis expressed by rings, streaks, and irregular, sunken areas of brown to black necrotic tissue, mostly in the older foliage. In *Cymbidium,* the most striking symptom is a mottling of the leaves, while brown, necrotic areas also develop on the older leaves of many plants.

Control: Cymbidium mosaic virus and some other orchid viruses can be transmitted via contaminated cutting tools. Dipping knives, pruning shears and other implements in Physan 20 or a solution of trisodium-orthophosphate will kill any sap-transmissible viruses.

Infected plants should be discarded and others sprayed with malathion to control sucking insects which also transmit virus diseases.

Other Viruses. Other important viruses that affect orchids are cattleya mosaic virus and Odontoglossum ringspot virus.

Insects and Other Animal Pests

Aphids (*Cerataphis orchidearum* and *Neomyzus circumflexus*). The orchid and crescent-marked lily aphids infest orchids.

Control: Spray with malathion or Sevin.

Orchid Weevil (*Diorymerellus laevimargo*). Wherever orchids are grown, this weevil usually becomes known to the grower. The adult is about ⅛ inch long, shining, black, and smooth. The larva is a white, legless grub about 1/16 inch long when fullgrown. It feeds on the new roots, hollowing out the inside and causing the tips to turn black. The adult beetles feed to some extent on the roots, but they cause much injury to young, tender leaves, to the sheaths surrounding the flower buds, and to bulbs. They also feed on the petals before the flowers open; they make irregular holes through which fungi and bacteria enter to cause blossom decay.

Control: Spray plant with methoxychlor.

Orchid Bulb Borer (*Metamasius graphipterus*). The blackish adults are slightly over ½ inch in length, with large pale yellowish blotches on the wing covers. They feed on the leaves and other parts of the plant. The larvae feed inside the bulb, and so open the way to fungus rots.

Control: Spray with methoxychlor.

Orchid Fly (*Eurytoma orchidearum*). This insect was introduced from the tropics. It is a small black wasp-like fly, $1/8$ inch long. Its eggs are deposited at the bases of the pseudo-bulbs, or sometimes on young leaves and rhizomes. The eggs hatch within a week or two; the maggots feed at first in separate galleries. After the flies have emerged, the buds turn brown or black and no flower appears.

Control: Reject all suspected plants or isolate them and make frequent inspections, cutting out and destroying the whole shoot rather than merely the infested part. Good control has been obtained by cutting out and discarding the swollen areas on the pseudobulbs, and by spraying with methoxychlor to kill the flies.

Orchid Mealybug (*Pseudococcus micro-circulans*). This species is found on orchids in California and Florida.

Control: Spray with Cygon, Diazinon, Meta-Systox R, or malathion.

Cattleya Midge (*Parrallelodiplosis cattle-yae*). The yellowish maggots, $1/8$ inch in length, feed in the tip ends of young roots of various kinds of orchids, causing them to form unsightly nut-like galls.

Control: Cut off and destroy the galls. Repot the plants and spray with methoxychlor when the midges come out.

Cattleya Weevil (*Cholus cattleyae*). The adult weevils are somewhat less than $1/2$ inch in length, and have white marks on the back. They injure the pseudobulbs by feeding on the surface and they will also puncture the leaves. The larvae feed on the leaves and develop on stems and pseudobulbs. This opens the way for decay and results in the failure of plants to bear flowers.

Control: Spray with methoxychlor.

Dendrobium Borer (*Xyleborus morige-*

rus). Minute brown beetles bore into the pseudobulbs and deposit many eggs in brood galleries. The larvae in feeding make rather long galleries. Badly infested bulbs wither and die.

Control: Cut out and destroy infested bulbs as soon as they are detected. Spray plants with methoxychlor.

Orchid Plant Bug (*Tenthecoris bicolor*). The mature insects vary from orange to bright red, with a black design down the back. The wing covers are steel blue. Irregular white spots on the undersides of leaves are a result of the feeding of both adults and young.

Control: Spray with methoxychlor.

Scales. The following species of scale insects infest orchids: black, Boisduval's (Fig. 171), chaff, cyanophyllum, Florida red, hemispherical, latania, oleander, oystershell, purple, tea, and tessellated.

Control: Malathion and Sevin are effective against scales, particularly the crawler stage.

Thrips. Several species of thrips by their rasping and sucking cause a browning or blotching of the leaves and a blasting of the buds. The symptoms are the familiar light gray discolorations and silvery appearance of the leaves and flower surfaces and finally a brown discoloration. *Cattleya* especially may be severely injured by the minute yellowish nymphs of *Chaetanaphorthrips orchidii*. The greenhouse thrips, *Heliothrips haemorrhoidalis* and *Hercinothrips femoralis,* are not uncommon on orchids.

Control: Commercial growers of orchids resort to Sulfotepp, which is dangerous to handle. Cygon and malathion sprays also control thrips.

Mite Blotch. Apparently a blotch on *Coelogyne* is due to an unidentified species of mite. The casts with appendages fore and aft may be found rather deeply sunken in the tissues of the leaf, which has been corroded and has turned black in characteristic patterns. The injury is shown in Fig. 172.

Fig. 171. Scale *(Diaspis boisduvali)* on orchid.

Fig. 172. Mite blotch on leaf of *Coelogyne dayana.*

Control: Spray twice with Kelthane or Dimite at 2- to 3-week intervals before the plants flower.

Slugs. These mollusks feed on bud and blossoms, the surfaces of leaves, and the tender stems of orchids.

Control: For commercial orchid ranges, apply a 15 per cent metaldehyde dust 3 times at 10-day intervals to surfaces over which slugs crawl. Or spray with ½ pint of metaldehyde emulsifiable concentrate in 10 gallons of water for each 100-square-yard area. A res-

pirator should be worn when making the applications. Zectran or Mesurol, used as directed by the manufacturer, also control slugs.

Nemas. The fern nema, *Aphelenchoides olesistus,* which commonly infests ferns in greenhouses, also attacks orchid leaves. It forms brown or blackish spots bounded by the larger veins, like those on infested fern leaves. Infested leaves finally die. The phlox stem nema, *Ditylenchus dipsaci,* also enters the base of the lower leaves and pseudobulbs of orchids, causing some deformation; the leaves may become brittle and snap off easily. Several species of nemas have been found associated with the roots of orchids. Two or three species may cause some damage. See under *Filices* and *Phlox*.

The DeMan's meadow nema, *Pratylenchus pratensis*, has been reported as a parasite of orchid roots.

ORNITHOGALUM (STAR-OF-BETHLEHEM)

Diseases

Two leaf spots caused by the fungi *Didymellina ornithogali* and *Septoria ornithogali* occasionally mar the foliage of this host. In California, the fungus *Pellicularia rolfsii* causes a stem rot.

Mosaic (Ornithogalum mosaic virus). Young leaves or *Ornithogalum thyrsoides* are finely mottled with light and dark green and more conspicuously mottled with gray or yellow as they mature. This virus is spread by several species of aphids.

Control: Destroy infected plants and spray with Meta-Systox R, Sevin, or malathion to control aphids.

OSMANTHUS (SWEET-OLIVE)

Osmanthus fragrans is subject to three fungus diseases: black mildew or black spot caused by *Asterina* sp., leaf spot by *Gloeosporium oleae*, and root rot by *Armillaria mellea*.

It is also subject to twelve species of scale insects: acuminate, brown soft, camellia, black thread, chaff, dictyospermum, Florida red, latania, parlatorialike, red bay, white peach, and oleander.

Osmanthus ilicifolius is susceptible to two leaf spots: *Phyllosticta oleae* and *P. sinuosa*.

OSMUNDA—see FILICES

OSTRYA (HOP-HORNBEAM)

Diseases

Hop-hornbeam is susceptible to cankers caused by *Aleurodiscus* spp., *Nectria* sp., and *Strumella coryneoidea;* to leaf spots by *Cylindrosporium dearnessi, Gloeosporium robergei,* and *Septoria ostryae;* to powdery mildews by *Microsphaera alni, Phyllactinia corylea,* and *Uncinula macrospora;* to root rots by *Armillaria mellea* and *Clitocybe tabescens;* to a leaf blister by *Taphrina virginica;* and to a rust caused by *Melampsoridium carpini.*

Control: The controls for most of these diseases are discussed under more seriously affected hosts.

Insects

Among the insects that attack hop-hornbeam are the birch lace bug, the melon aphid, pitted ambrosia beetle, two-lined chestnut borer, and two species of scales, cottony-cushion and latania. Controls for these pests are given under more seriously affected hosts.

OXALIS

Fungus Diseases

Leaf Spots (*Cercospora oxalidiphila, Phyllosticta guttulatae, P. oxalidis, Ramularia oxalidis,* and *Septoria acetosella*). The leaf spots of this host are not important enough to require control measures.

Rust (*Puccinia sorghi*). The importance of this rust on *Oxalis* is that its alternate host is corn, on which it often causes a destructive rust. On *Oxalis* the rust first appears as neat, yellowish dots near the margins of the leaves; later pale orange pustules break out on the leaf. They do little damage, however.

Red Rust (*Puccinia oxalidis*). In Florida this rust has been known to cause 100 per cent loss of ornamental plants, killing all the foliage within two weeks. The alternate stage occurs on *Mahonia.* A control has not yet been worked out.

Other Diseases. Oxalis is also subject to a root rot caused by the fungus *Thielaviopsis basicola,* a seed smut by the fungus *Ustilago oxalidis,* and curly top by the beet curly top virus.

OXYDENDRUM (SORREL-TREE)

Diseases

Leaf Spots (*Cercospora oxydendri* and *Mycosphaerella caroliniana*). Two fungi occasionally spot the leaves of sorrel-tree. The latter produces reddish or purple blotches with dry brown centers in midsummer.

Control: Spray with a copper fungicide, starting when the leaves are fully expanded and repeating in 2 weeks.

Twig Blight (*Sphaerulina polyspora*). This fungus occasionally causes blighting of leaves at the tips of the branches. Trees injured by fire or in poor vigor appear to be most subject to this disease.

Control: Pruning infected twigs is usually sufficient to keep the disease under control. Feed and water when necessary to keep trees in good vigor.

PACHISTIMA

A leaf spot caused by the fungus *Sporonema oxyocci* has been reported from Virginia. No control measures are necessary.

PACHYSANDRA
(JAPANESE PACHYSANDRA)

Diseases

Leaf Blight (*Volutella pachysandrae*). While leaf spots due to species of *Phyllosticta* and *Gleosporium* occasionally mar the foliage, much more damage may result from attacks by the *Volutella.* The leaves first have brown blotches and finally more or less of a blight. Stem cankers also are numerous (Fig. 173). Many spore masses cause the spread of the disease, which is especially rapid among

Fig. 173. Leaf blight and stem canker of pachysandra caused by the fungus *Volutella pachysandrae.*

plants that have been weakened by the attacks of scale insects or by winter injury. The sexual stage of this fungus is *Pseudonectria pachysandricola.*

Control: Lift out and destroy severely diseased plants. Then spray with a copper fungicide, ferbam, or Fore three times at weekly intervals beginning when new growth starts. Control scale (see below), and mulch with material that does not hold moisture.

Insects and Other Animal Pests

Pachysandra Leaf Tier (*Archips purpurana*). The leaves are tied together and chewed by a pale, olive-green larva which has two prominent black spots near the end of its body and which is 3/4 inch long at maturity. The adult moths, light brown, bell-shaped, and approximately 1/2 inch long, appear in early July. They deposit eggs in clusters along the veins of the upper leaf surfaces. The larva hatches in late July and early August, ties two leaves together, and feeds in concealment until fall. It passes the winter as a partially grown larva and resumes feeding the following spring.

Control: Spray with Sevin or Imidan in late July and early August to control the young larvae before they tie leaves together and thus becomes less susceptible to sprays.

Scale (*Unaspis euonymi*). The scale insect that attacks *Euonymus* and *Celastrus* attacks *Pachysandra* also. The females are brown and shaped like the oystershell scale. The undersides of the leaves may appear whitish from the large number of male insects, which are white and ridged down the center of the back. The oystershell and San Jose scales also attack this host.

Control: See *Celastrus.*

Mites. Several species of mites, particularly the two-spotted mite, attack *Pachysandra* when the plants are overcrowded.

Control: Spray with Aramite, chlorobenzilate, or Kelthane.

Northern Root-Knot Nema (*Meloidogyne hapla*). The roots of *Pachysandra* are frequently invaded by this nema. Controls are rarely adopted, because the nema does not seriously impair growth of this host.

PAEONIA (PEONY)

Fungus Diseases

Botrytis Blight (*Botrytis paeoniae*). The most common disease of garden peonies is that caused by the gray mold. The characteristic symptoms appear on young leaf bases in the spring when the shoots are about 1 foot long. The leafy shoots wilt rather suddenly and fall over. When they are pulled out or cut off below the ground, a brown or blackish rot is seen at the base of the leaves and stem. Just above the ground level the stalk will usually be found to be covered with a gray mold which sheds large numbers of spores. These are carried by the wind and by insects to young leaves and flower buds and cause a leaf blight and bud rot. Small buds that are attacked turn black and wither without much further development. Leaf blight usually occurs somewhat after the blooming season. Flowers that have recently opened are also attacked. All infected parts turn brown and later develop a covering of gray mold. On the leaves, large irregular brown areas spread widely. The sclerotia of this fungus develop along the base of the rotting stalks. They carry the fungus through the winter and other unfavorable periods.

Control: Measures for control should begin in the early fall, at which time old leaves and stalks should be cut down below the soil level. This debris should be destroyed, not thrown into the compost pile. If mulching is necessary to prevent freezing, it should be removed in early spring and the ground allowed to dry out. Peonies should not be planted so that water is apt to cover the bases of the plants; nor should the soil be heaped

up about the leaf bases so that they are prevented from drying out. Heavy clay soil
should be lightened by the addition of sand.
If manure is used as fertilizer, it should not
be allowed to come in contact with new
growth. Spray the plants with Benlate when
young tips break through the ground. Follow
2 weeks later with another application. If leaf
blight and bud blast develop later, a third application may be necessary. It is important to
remove the young infected shoots in the
spring as soon as they begin to wilt.

Downy Mildew Blight (*Phytophthora cactorum*). This disease is similar in appearance
to that caused by the *Botrytis*, except that it
forms no characteristic mold and is never
seen covering the bases of infected shoots or
infected leaves or buds. The entire shoot may
turn black and die. Cankers appear along the
stems and cause them to fall over. The *Botrytis* mold seldom invades the crown, but *Phytophthora* often does and causes a wet rot to
develop there, often destroying the entire
plant. The author found that the variety
"Avalanche" is particularly susceptible to
Phytophthora.

Control: Because infections occur in the
roots and lower portions of the stems, fungicidal sprays are of no value. Confirmed cases
should be lifted out together with adjacent
soil and thrown into the trash can. Such material should never be placed in the compost
pile. Planting healthy clumps in a new spot
where the soil is well drained usually prevents further trouble.

Leaf Spots (*Alternaria* sp., *Cercospora
paeoniae*, C. *variicolor*, *Cryptostictis paeoniae*, *Pezizella oenotherae*, *Phyllosticta* spp.,
and *Septoria paeoniae*). Many fungi cause
spots of varying sizes and colors on this host.

Control: Thorough sanitation, including
the removal of all leaves and stalks in the fall,
is the first step in combating leaf spots of
peony. Zineb or captan sprays applied several times during the early growing season
will also provide some control.

Red Spot, Measles (*Cladosporium paeoniae*). Small circular discolored spots first appear on the leaves. A number of spots may
run together so that the leaves appear irregularly blotched. The under surface becomes
light brown, the upper, dark purple. On
young stems the spots appear merely as reddish-brown streaks. All parts of the plant
may become spotted.

Control: Same as for leaf spots.

Root Rots (*Armillaria mellea, Fusarium*
sp., *Phymatotrichum omnivorum, Pellicularia filamentosa*, P. *rolfsii*). These soil-inhabiting fungi cause root rot and decay at the
base of the plant.

Control: Use clean soil, or treat soil with
heat or chemicals as described in Chapter 4.

Stem Rot (*Sclerotinia sclerotiorum*). This
fungus, which causes a stem rot of many garden plants, occasionally attacks peonies,
causing the shoots to wilt suddenly and the
stem to rot. The large black sclerotia of the
fungus develop inside the stems. A gray mold
stage is evident.

Control: Same as for downy mildew blight.

Wilt (*Verticillium albo-atrum*). Occasionally the foliage and shoots of plants wilt during the blooming season even though the
basal parts of the shoots appear to be perfectly sound. Cross sections show that the
water-conducting vessels have turned brown
and microscopic examination shows them to
be plugged with fungi. This parasite is soil-
borne and overwinters in crown and roots.

Control: Diseased plants should be removed and destroyed and the soil pasteurized
with steam or replaced with fresh soil before
replanting. Avoid propagating from infected
clumps.

Virus Diseases

Ringspot (Peony ringspot virus). Circular
areas consisting of concentric bands of alter-
nating dark and light green develop on the

leaves. At times small necrotic spots also form. Plants are not dwarfed by this virus.

Control: Infected plants should be lifted and destroyed to prevent spread to nearby healthy specimens. Most peony growers rarely worry about this disease.

Leaf Curl (unidentified virus). Affected plants are dwarfed to half their normal height, the flower stalks are crooked and the leaves curled. The plants are even more dwarfed, with thin, weak shoots and no flowers the second season of infection. This virus is graft-transmissible.

Le Moine Disease (cause unknown). Dwarfed plants, with spindling shoots which fail to bloom, are a common sight in peony plantings. The roots of such plants are found to be elongated and irregularly swollen with very few long feeding roots. The feeding roots do not extend deeply into the soil and the fleshy roots are short and irregularly swollen.

Control: Diseased plants should be destroyed, although there are reports that infected plants recover after some years.

Crown Elongation (cause unknown). This disease is distinct from Le Moine disease. It causes elongated crowns to be more numerous than usual; the shoots are slender and weak. The foliage is dwarfed by both these diseases. Some have claimed that both diseases are easily distinguished from root-knot caused by nemas, others have suspected that they are forms of the latter. Whether or not this is true, it would probably be well to change the planting if these diseases are evident.

Physiological Diseases

Bud Blast. Failure of buds to open after they have reached the size of a small pea is often blamed on the *Botrytis* fungus. Actually no organism is involved and hence sprays will do no good. The author, working with a colleague, Dr. O. W. Davidson, at Rut-gers University many years ago, found that bud blast was associated with a lack of potassium in the plant, dry spells, low temperatures during early spring, and root infection by the nema *Meloidogyne incognita*. Other observers report that bud blast also may be caused by too-deep planting, infertile soil, and excessive shade.

Oedema. This disease is associated with excessive atmospheric and soil moisture. Numerous small brown or purple spots develop on all parts of the plant above the ground. It is not a serious disease. Practical methods of preventing development of these blister-like growths are not known.

Insects and Other Animal Pests

Ants (Formicidae). Peonies may harbor large numbers of ants at the time the sugary solution is secreted by the buds. There is little evidence that these pests spread the *Botrytis* blight spores, despite the statements in many gardening publications.

Control: Dust the base of the plants and the surrounding soil lightly with Diazinon or Dursban.

Japanese Beetle (*Popillia japonica*). The blooms of the late-flowering peony are apt to become badly infested with Japanese beetles. The leaves are also subject to attack, but the beetles will usually leave them to feed on the blooms of other plants in the vicinity.

Control: See *Aesculus.*

Rose Chafer (*Macrodactylus subspinosus*). This beetle does its greatest damage during the 6 weeks beginning in late May and June. It is not usually so destrictive to peony blooms as to roses.

Control: See *Rosa.*

Rose Leaf Beetle (*Nodonota puncticollis*). This small, shining-green to blue beetle also infests the leaves and flowers of peony.

Control: Same as for Japanese beetle.

Scales. Three species of scales may attack garden peonies, usually in late summer after the flowering season: oystershell, peony, and San Jose.

Control: Since these pests are found on the stalks and leaf bases well below the surface of the ground, care should be taken, in trimming the old leaves and stems in the fall, to cut them as near the ground as possible without injury to the plant. If scales reappear the following year despite sanitation, spray with malathion or Sevin in late May and in mid-June.

Flower Thrips (*Frankliniella tritici*). These minute insects sometimes attack the blooms and suck the juice from the petals, causing brown spots on the light-colored varieties and red spots on the dark varieties.

Control: Spray with Sevin just before the blooms open. Supplement by destroying infested blooms and rubbish.

Fall Webworm (*Hyphantria cunea*). This caterpillar sometimes forms nests among the foliage during the late summer and early autumn.

Control: See *Fraxinus.*

Southern Root-Knot Nema (*Meloidogyne incognita*). Small galls ⅛ inch or more in diameter develop on the finer roots. This disease is more common in the southern United States but is frequently serious along the Eastern Seaboard. Cross sections of the gall show brown spots which contain large numbers of nemas. The lower ends of these roots usually die, and the plants are weak, spindling, and stunted, and fail to bloom. The northern root-knot nema, *M. hapla,* is also commonly found in the northern parts of the country.

Control: Dipping nema-infested roots in hot water at 120°F. for 30 minutes has been suggested as a control measure. The author treated hundred of infested peony roots in this manner some years ago, and to his regret every plant died. Untreated controls of the same varieties lived, though still infested with nemas.

PAEONIA SUFFRUTICOSA (TREE PEONY)

Diseases

Stem Wilt (*Leptosphaeria coniothyrium*). The imperfect stage of this fungus, *Coniothyrium fuckelii,* causes the flowering stems of tree peonies to wilt and die quickly. The wilt is caused by cankers which girdle the stems at the base, cutting off the water supply. Young buds, just ready to open, have a water-soaked appearance, then become brown. The petals dry out and become brittle. Such buds hang on the plant a long time.

Control: Satisfactory methods of control have not as yet been developed, but the spread of the disease has been checked by digging up and destroying the infected plants.

Other Diseases and Pests. Tree peonies are subject to some of the other diseases and pests of herbaceous peonies.

PALMACEAE (PALMS)

Diseases

Lethal Yellowing (Mycoplasma-like organism). This highly fatal disease, first observed in Jamaica nearly a century ago, is presently responsible for the death of thousands of coconut palms (*Cocos nucifera*) in southern Florida. First observed in the Key West area in 1955, it has now spread as far north as Palm Beach county.

An early symptom is the appearance of dead tips of the inflorences when they emerge from the spathes. Leaf yellowing of the lower fronds follows.

Another symptom is "shelling," that is, premature dropping of coconuts, regardless of size.

The disease progresses until the bud becomes necrotic, and the tree dies.

In Florida lethal yellowing has also resulted in death of *Veitchia Arikuryroba, Washingtonia,* and *Pritchardia* palms.

Control: No practical control is presently available, although cessation of symptom development and resumption of normal growth has been obtained by injecting affected coconut palm trees with tetracycline antibiotics.

Seed nuts of resistant palms have been imported from Jamaica to be used as replacements. "Malayan Dwarf" coconut palm is one of the more resistant kinds presently available. Actually it is not a true dwarf because it will reach a height of 40 to 60 feet in Florida. It begins to flower and produce nuts when four or five years old.

Butt Rot (*Ganoderma sulcatum*). This is one of the most serious fungus diseases of palms in Florida. The spores of the fungus enter through wounds at the base of the tree made by lawn mowers or other instruments. The lower leaves die and new leaves are stunted. Typical fruiting bodies of the fungus appear at the base of the infected tree near the soil line.

Control: Control measures have not been developed. Affected trees should be removed and destroyed. Clean or steam-pasteurized soil should replace soil in the vicinity of the diseased tree.

Bacterial Wilt (*Xanthomonas* sp.). A wilt and trunk rot of coconut and Cuban royal palm is caused by this bacterium. At first the lower leaves turn gray and wilt. This is followed by gummosis of the trunk, discoloration of the vascular tissues, and finally collapse of the crown.

Control: No control measures are known.

False Smut, Leaf Scab (*Graphiola phoenicis*). Palms belonging to the genera *Arecastrum, Arenga, Howea, Phoenix, Roystonea,* and *Washingtonia* suffer from a parasite that causes a yellow spotting of the leaves and the formation of numerous small black scabs or warts. The outer part of these fruiting bodies is dark, hard, and horny. From the inner parts protrude many long, flexuous, sterile hyphae. Within the inner membrane of the structure, powdery yellow or light brown masses of spores arise. The exact place of this unique fungus in the system of classification is not known. Severely infected leaves soon die.

In an experimental planting of date palms in Texas, the variety Kustawy from Iraq developed only light infections from this fungus. In Texas this disease is most troublesome in areas with consistently high humidities.

Control: Cut out and destroy infected leaves or leaf parts at the first sign of the disease, and spray with a copper fungicide. On greenhouse palms, control insects with insecticides rather than by syringing, a practice that helps to spread false smut.

Leaf Blights (*Pestalotia palmarum* and *P. palmicola*). The first of these fungi infects *Cocos romazoffiana* (*plumosus*) and other palms in the axils of the leaves and where leaflets are attached to the leaf stalk. The fungus penetrates into the deeper tissues, causing a brown discoloration. Gray-brown spots develop on the leaf blades and run together to form large blotches. Brown septate spores with characteristic appendages develop in black masses on the upper parts of the leaves.

Blight, caused by *P. palmicola*, is reported to be very destructive in Florida to *Phoenix, Cocos,* and *Washingtonia*. The blight begins at the tips and works toward the leaf stalk, killing the tissues, which turn brown.

Control: Copper fungicides will probably control these diseases.

Still another serious leaf blight of *Washingtonia* is caused by the fungus *Cylindrocladium macrosporium*. Numerous small dark brown spots with light-colored margins disfigure the leaves.

Along the Pacific coast in southern California the fungus *Penicillium vermoeseni* causes three diseases which result in a great loss of ornamental palms; leaf base rot of *Phoenix,* bud rot of *Washingtonia,* and trunk canker of *Cocos romanzoffiana.* Among the effects are a successive decay of the leaf bases from the oldest to the youngest of the tightly folded bud leaves, and the weakening and breaking of the trunk.

Leaf Spot (*Exosporium palmivorum*). This leaf spot is especially serious in greenhouses where insufficient light is provided. The spots are small, round, yellowish, and transparent. They often run together to form large irregular gray-brown blotches, which may result in death of the leaf. The spores are long, club-shaped, many-celled, and brown. They are formed on tufts of short basal cells.

Control: Same as for false smut.

Stem and Root Rots. Species of several genera of fungi, among them *Pythium, Fusarium, Phymatotrichum,* and *Armillaria,* have been reported as causing root disease of palms in Florida and several western states.

The *Pythium* root rot is accompanied by yellowing and wilting of the leaves one after another, until the bud falls from the top of the plant. *Fusarium* has been associated with stem and root rot of the royal palm, *Roystonea. Armillaria mellea* has been thought to cause root rot of the date palm, *Phoenix,* in California.

In certain palm houses numerous fruiting bodies of *Xylaria schweinitzii* have been found growing from roots of *Howea* and other palms. Since another species of *Xylaria* is known to cause root rot of apple, poor condition of some greenhouse palms possibly may be due to this fungus. No control has been suggested. As a precautionary measure, however, all black, club-shaped fruiting bodies about 2 inches long should be removed.

In Florida, a stem rot of *Chamaedorea seifrizii* is caused by *Gliocladium vermoeseni.*

Bud Rot and Wilt (*Phytophthora* spp.). Wilting and bud rot of the coconut palm have been at various times referred to different species of *Phytophthora,* such as *P. palmi-* *vora, P. arecae, P. faveri.* When this disease occurs in ornamental plantings, it is controlled by cutting out the crown of the infected plant.

Black Scorch and Heart Rot (*Ceratocystis paradoxa*). This disease may be destructive to date palms of plantations and ornamental gardens in California. It is found in all structures of the plant except the roots and stems. Lesions are dark brown or black, hard, carbonaceous, having the appearance of a black scorch. The fungus gains entrance even in the absence of wounds. The disease is most serious as a terminal bud rot.

Control: All infected fronds, leaf bases, and flower parts should be pruned out and destroyed, and the cuts disinfested. Copper sprays give promise of control.

Insects

Palm Aphid (*Cerataphis variabilis*). In its wingless form this aphid is often mistaken for a whitefly because it is dark and disc-like with a white fringe. The green peach aphid, *Myzus persicae,* also infests palms.

Control: Spray with Sevin or malathion when the aphids appear.

Palm Leaf Skeletonizer (*Homaledra sabalella*). In Florida, this is a major pest, feeding on the leaves of many species of palms under a protective web of silk. Leaves are blotched, then shrivel and die.

Control: Cut out and destroy infested fronds or spray with Sevin.

Mealybugs. Four species of mealybugs infest palms: citrus, ground, long-tailed, and palm.

Control: All but the ground mealybug can be controlled with malathion or Sevin sprays. The ground mealybug can be destroyed by drenching the soil around the roots it infests with Diazinon or malathion solution.

Scales. Palms are extremely susceptible to many species of scale insects. At least 23 species have been recorded on this host.

Control: Palm scales control in northern greenhouses begins with repeated syringing of the plants. If climatic conditions allow, spray the plants forcibly with water from the hose. The second step is to control ants, which are very active in spreading the young insects. A light dusting of Diazinon around the bases of the palms will go a long way toward controlling ants. Then a direct attack on the scales themselves can be made with malathion or Sevin sprays. These are primarily effective against the crawler stages of scales and hence must be applied 2 or 3 times at 2-week intervals to control the young scales, since they hatch out over a long period.

Thrips (*Heliothrips haemorrhoidalis, H. dracaenae,* and *Hercinothrips femoralis*). Although these species have been reported on palms, they are not considered serious pests. They are not troublesome where scale insects and mealybugs are controlled.

Black Vine Weevil (*Otiorhynchus sulcatus*). Greenhouse palms are among the hosts occasionally attacked by the larvae of this weevil. See *Taxus.*

Mites. Three species of mites—Banksgrass, privet, and tumid spider—infest palms.

Control: Aramite, chlorobenzilate, or Kelthane sprays will control these pests.

PANDANUS (SCREW-PINE)

Diseases

Leaf Blotch (*Melanconium pandani*). This disease is illustrated in Fig. 4. Large leaf spots up to 2 inches wide and 3 or 4 inches long may develop from the leaf margin inward. Black fruiting pustules develop in a light gray zone along the inner margin of the spot. Similar spots may develop along the leaf blade at any point.

Control: Prune off infected leaves and spray with a copper fungicide. Badly infected plants should be destroyed.

Insects

The pests that attack screw-pines are the long-tailed mealybug (*Pseudococcus longispinus*), and 13 species of scales.

Control: Spray with malathion whenever the pests appear.

PAPAVER (POPPY)

Diseases

Bacterial Blight (*Xanthomonas papavericola*). Water-soaked spots, which later turn black, appear on leaves, stems, and flower parts, as well as on the seed pods. The other organs affected turn brown and much defoliation occurs. Plants are killed when the stems become girdled.

Control: Old plants and plant parts in beds that harbor this organism should be destroyed. If the same plot must be used again, the soil should be steam-pasteurized, otherwise rotation of crops should be practiced. Collect seed only from healthy plants.

Downy Mildew (*Peronospora arborescens*). This disease often appears as a seedling blight in gardens. On older plants pale spots appear on both sides of the leaves. These spots are usually covered by a white or grayish mold, but occasionally are pale violet. Stems become much distorted and blossoms fail to develop. As the base of the stem becomes infected, the plant collapses. The parasite is said to be carried in the seeds.

Control: Spray with a copper fungicide. Several applications may be necessary for control. At the earliest opportunity in the spring, destroy infected plants. Collect seeds only from disease-free plants. Avoid planting in damp situations.

Leaf Spots (*Cercospora papaveri, Cercosporella* sp., and *Septoria* sp.). Three species of fungi have been reported as the cause of leaf spots of this host.

Control: Pick off and destroy spotted leaves as soon as they appear.

Other Fungus Diseases. Poppies are occasionally affected by blight caused by *Botrytis cinerea,* powdery mildew by *Erysiphe polygoni,* root rot by *Pellicularia filamentosa,* smut by *Entyloma fuscum,* and wilt by *Verticillium albo-atrum.* The controls of these diseases are discussed under more favored hosts.

Virus Diseases

Two virus diseases occur on *Papaver:* curly top caused by the curly top virus and spotted wilt caused by the tomato spotted wilt virus.

Control: Destroy infected plants and spray with malathion or Meta-Systox R to control the insects which spread these viruses.

Insects and Other Animal Pests

Aphids. The bean, green peach, and melon aphids frequently infest this host. The first mentioned, a black species, is most common.

Control: Spray with Meta-Systox R, Sevin, or malathion.

Other Insects. The rose chafer, the four-lined and tarnished plant bugs, the aster leafhopper, and the grape mealybug are other insects which infest poppy. Malathion, Diazinon, or Sevin sprays applied at the time these insects appear will provide control.

Northern Root-Knot Nema (*Meloidogyne hapla*). This nema infests poppies in the northern United States.

Control: See Chapter 3.

PARTHENOCISSUS (BOSTON IVY AND VIRGINIA CREEPER)[28]

Fungus Diseases

Canker (*Coniothyrium fuckelii*). Cankers on the stems of Virginia creeper are caused by this fungus.

[28]Boston ivy, *P. tricuspidata,* and Virginia creeper, *P. quinquefolia,* were formerly in the genus *Ampelopsis.*

Control: Prune below infected areas and if practicable, spray with Bordeaux mixture or any other copper fungicide.

Downy Mildew (*Plasmopara viticola*). Greenish-yellow blotches appear on the upper surfaces of Virginia creeper leaves, which later turn brown. On the lower surfaces are light brown spots covered with white mold. Heavily infected leaves may fall in large numbers. The same fungus causes even more serious damage to cultivated grapes.

Control: Spray with a copper fungicide.

Leaf Spots (*Cercospora ampelopsidis, C. psedericola, Guignardia bidwelli* var. *parthenocissi, Phleospora ampelopsidis,* and *Sphaeropsis hedericola*). Many leaf spotting fungi occur on Boston ivy and Virginia creeper in rainy seasons.

Control: As a rule application of sprays is not practicable where these plants are growing on walls. If feasible, pick off and destroy the first spotted leaves. Copper and dithiocarbamate fungicides are effective in preventing infections by these fungi.

Powdery Mildew (*Uncinula necator*). This fungus, also common on grapes, frequently infests Virginia creeper late in the growing season.

Control: Valuable plantings can be protected by spraying with Benlate, Karathane, or wettable sulfur.

Wilt (*Cladosporium herbarum*). Wilting and leaf spotting of Boston ivy on buildings of Rutgers University was investigated many years ago by several plant pathologists including the author. The damage extended down the branches to the main trunk. Diseased parts soon dried out and died.

Control: Prune out all diseased branches. Spray with a copper fungicide to prevent new infections.

Other Diseases. *Parthenocissus* is also affected by anthracnose caused by *Elsinoë parthenocissi,* thread blight by *Pellicularia koleroga,* and root rot by *Phymatotrichum omnivorum.*

Insects and Related Pests

Beetles. Three beetles chew the leaves of *Parthenocissus:* Japanese beetle, grape flea beetle, and rose chafer.

Control: Spray with methoxychlor.

Eight-Spotted Forester (*Alypia octomaculata*). The bluish-white caterpillar of this moth feeds on grape, Virginia creeper, and Boston ivy, frequently causing complete defoliation. The moth is black, with a wingspread of 1½ inches with two yellow spots in each fore wing and two white spots on each hind wing, making a total of eight.

Control: If practicable pick off larvae by hand, or spray with *Bacillus thuringiensis* or Imidan when the larvae begin to feed. Do not use Sevin on Virginia creeper and Boston ivy because it will defoliate the vines.

Leaf Hoppers. Three kinds of leaf hoppers infest Virginia creeper: grape, three-banded, and the Virginia creeper. The leaves are stippled as a result of their feeding.

Control: Spray thoroughly with Cygon or Diazinon.

Scales. Among the species of scale insects known to infest *Parthenocissus* are: calico, cottony-cushion, cottony maple, olive, parlatoria, oystershell, peach, and San Jose.

Control: Spray with a dormant oil just before buds open in spring, or with malathion or Sevin in June.

Other Pests. *Parthenocissus* may also be infested by the rusty plum aphid. *Hysteroneura setariae;* yellow woollybear, *Diacrisia virginica;* and the caterpillar of the achemon sphinx moth, *Eumorpha achemon.*

Boston ivy and Virginia creeper may be infested by mites. These can be controlled by spraying with Kelthane.

PASSIFLORA (PASSION-FLOWER)

Diseases

Leaf Spots (*Alternaria passiflorae, Colletotrichum gloeosporioides, Cercospora biformis, C. fuscovirens, C. regalis, C. truncatella, Gloeosporium* sp., and *Phyllosticta* sp.). Passion-flower is subject to many leaf spotting fungi in the Deep South.

Control: Control measures are rarely adopted. Severe outbreaks of leaf spots can be prevented by spraying occasionally with a copper fungicide.

Other Diseases. *Passiflora* is also subject to a blight caused by *Pellicularia rolfsii* in Florida, collar rot by a species of *Sclerotinia,* a virus disease caused by the cucumber mosaic virus in California, and a root rot by the fungus *Phymatotrichum omnivorum* in Texas.

Insects

Caterpillars. The omnivorous looper and the larva of the greenhouse leaf tier chew the leaves of this host.

Control: Spray with *Bacillus thuringiensis* or Imidan when the larvae begin to feed.

Mealybugs. The citrus and grape mealybugs suck the juices of *Passiflora.*

Control: Spray with malathion.

Scales. Nine species of scales infest passion-flower: barnacle, California red, greedy, green shield, latania, lesser snow, purple, proteus, and pustule.

Control: Same as for mealybugs.

Other Pests. An unidentified species of mites has been found on this host by the author.

Control: Spray with Kelthane.

PAULOWNIA (EMPRESS-TREE)

Diseases

Leaf Spots (*Ascochyta paulowniae* and *Phyllosticta paulowniae*). Two species of fungi cause leaf spots on this host in very rainy seasons.

Control: Gather and destroy fallen leaves. Preventive sprays containing copper or dithiocarbamate fungicides can be used on extremely valuable specimens in rainy seasons.

Mildew (*Phyllactinia guttata* and *Uncinula clintonii*). Two species of powdery mildew fungi occasionally infect *Paulownia* leaves.

Control: Benlate or Karathane sprays will control these fungi.

Wood Decay (*Polyporus spraguei* and *P. versicolor*). These fungi are constantly associated with a wood decay of this host.

Control: As with the other wood decaying fungi, control is difficult. Avoiding wounds near the trunk base and keeping the tree in good vigor by feeding and watering when necessary are suggested.

Twig Canker (*Phomopsis imperialis*). Occasionally twigs and small branches are affected by this disease.

Control: Prune and destroy infected branches.

PELARGONIUM (GERANIUM)

Bacterial Diseases

Bacterial Leaf Spot (*Xanthomonas pelargonii*). This disease is most serious in greenhouses where young plants are overcrowded and forced too rapidly, particularly during warm, humid weather. Spotting is evident also on the leaves of garden geraniums in warm, wet weather, especially if the plants are too close together in beds. The spots are at first as large as a pinhead, circular or irregular, brown, and sunken (see Fig. 30). Many spots may occur on one leaf, especially among the older lower leaves. The spots often run together and kill a large portion of the leaf, which then drops off. The disease is favored by high temperatures. The same organism is capable of causing a black rot of the stems (see Fig. 174).

The bacterium *Pseudomonas erodii* also causes a leaf spot of geraniums.

Control: Pick off and discard all leaves on which infection is visible. Space plants farther apart on benches. Avoid syringing,

Fig. 174. Bacterial stem rot of geranium, caused by *Xanthomonas pelargonii*.

which may splash germ-laden water from one plant to another. Regulate the ventilation so as to reduce humidity. Since the bacteria can live in the soil of the propagating bed, one should avoid splashing bits of infested soil onto healthy plants. If necessary spray with a copper fungicide.

Other Bacterial Diseases. Geraniums are also subject to crown gall caused by *Agrobacterium tumefaciens,* and fasciation by *Corynebacterium fascians.* The control of these diseases is discussed under more favored hosts.

Fungus Diseases

Alternaria Leaf Spot (*Alternaria tenuis*). Geraniums growing in southern California during the winter are frequently affected by this disease. Spots vary from 1 to 10 mm. in diameter; the larger ones are at times dark brown with concentric rings. They are sometimes mistaken for those produced by *Xanthomonas pelargonii*. The fungus is more common on the lower leaves.

Control: Remove and destroy spotted leaves. Commercial plantings should be sprayed with a copper fungicide.

Black Leg (*Fusarium* sp.). The stems of geraniums affected by this fungus are coal-black, somewhat resembling those caused by *Pythium splendens,* described below.

Control: Drenching the soil with Benlate, as directed by the manufacturer, should control this disease.

Black Stem Rot (*Pythium splendens*). This disease is most serious on cuttings of young plants, but has been known to attack full-grown plants, causing them to drop their leaves, become stunted, and eventually die. The rot of cuttings starts at the base and progresses upward until the leaves wilt and die. The blackening of the stem of older plants progresses toward the tip; the lower parts become shrunken and defoliated (see Fig. 175).

Control: Take cuttings from healthy plants only. Root them in clean rooting-medium and plant the rooted cuttings in steam-pasteurized soil. Use Dexon soil drench to prevent reinfestation of pasteurized soil.

Botrytis Leaf Spot, Blossom Blight (*Botrytis cinerea*). This disease is most common in cool moist greenhouses where plants are syringed frequently. The brown water-soaked areas later dry out, and a grayish-brown mass of fungus spores becomes evident. Blossoms also are attacked; the petals are discolored, and the flowers wilt and fall. *Botrytis cinerea* also produces a brown decay of cuttings.

Fig. 175. Stem rot of geranium, caused by artificial inoculation with the fungus *Pythium splendens.*

Control: Spray with Benlate, Botran, captan, or zineb. Regulate the ventilation of the greenhouse and raise the temperature so as to reduce the relative humidity. Recent tests have shown that Termil is very effective in controlling this disease in geraniums.

Leaf Spots (*Ascochyta* sp., *Cercospora brunkii,* and *Pleosphaerulina* sp.). Several other fungus leaf spots occasionally appear on geraniums.

Control: Same as for *Botrytis* leaf spot.

Fig. 176. *Pelargonium* rust on florists' geranium. (H. H. Lyon, Cornell University)

Root Rots (*Sclerotinia sclerotiorum* and *Thielaviopsis basicola*). These fungi are capable of causing severe damage to geraniums once they infest the soil used for growing this crop.

Control: Steam-pasteurize infested soil or use new soil. PCNB (Terraclor) soil drenches will control *Sclerotinia* and thiabendazole (Mertect) will control *Thielaviopsis.*

Rust (*Puccinia pelargonii-zonalis*). Brown, powdery, spore pustules develop on leaves, petioles, and stems of geraniums (Fig. 176). The leaves eventually turn yellow, dry and drop prematurely. The disease has recently been found in California and New York. It may become a serious disease of geraniums.

Control: Maneb, Polyram, or zineb sprays applied every 10 days to the lower and upper leaf surfaces will control rust.

Virus Diseases

A number of virus diseases affect the greenhouse geranium. Among the most common are crinkle or leaf curl caused by the *Pelargonium* leaf curl virus (Fig. 177), curly top by the beet curly top virus, mosaic by the cucumber mosaic virus, and spotted wilt by the tomato spotted wilt virus.

Control: Destroy plants known to harbor any of these viruses. Because virus symptoms may be masked at times, commercial growers should watch stock plants carefully over an extended period to be sure that the plants are healthy.

Physiological Disease

Oedema, Dropsy. The disease develops in greenhouses; it appears first as water-soaked plants, which later become rust-colored and corky. Corky ridges develop also on the petals. The disease can be controlled by proper cultural practices. It is more severe in late winter and in cloudy weather when plants are over-watered. Light should be admitted and ventilation regulated to lower the moisture in the air. Under good conditions the plants recover.

Spindly Growth. Insufficient light, excessive feeding and watering, and overcrowding result in spindly growth and poor to no flowering.

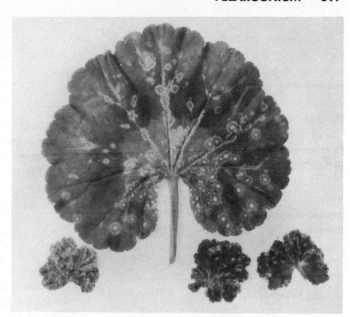

Fig. 177. Geranium crinkle disease, caused by the *Pelargonium* leaf curl virus.

Insects and Other Animal Pests

Aphids (*Arcythosiphon pelargonii* and *Myzus persicae*). The geranium and green peach aphids frequently infest this host.

Control: Spray with malathion or Sevin.

Caterpillars. The cabbage looper, the fall cankerworm, the omnivorous looper, the orange tortrix, the oblique-banded leaf roller, and the greenhouse leaf tier are among the many caterpillars that feed on the leaves of *Pelargonium.*

Control: Spray with *Bacillus thuringiensis* or Sevin when the young caterpillars first appear.

Geranium Plume Moth (*Platyptilia pica*). The caterpillar stage of this moth feeds on the flower beds of geranium. When fully grown this yellow-green or "port-wine" red caterpillar is ½ inch in length.

Control: Spray with Sevin when the caterpillars begin to feed and repeat in 10 days.

Mealybugs. The citrus and Mexican mealybugs may infest geraniums at times.

Control: Spray with malathion when mealybugs appear.

Four-Lined Plant Bug (*Poecilocapsus lineatus*). See *Aconitum.*

Mites. The broad and cyclamen mites may infest greenhouse-grown geraniums. Infested leaves are curled, distorted, or scorched.

Control: Spray with Dimite or Kelthane.

Scales. Two species of scales may infest geraniums: cottony-cushion and lesser snow.

Control: Same as for mealybugs.

Slugs. The greenhouse and the spotted garden slugs may chew the leaves of geraniums at night.

Control: Dust the soil, over which the slugs travel, with 15 per cent metaldehyde dust, or with Zectran, or Slug-geta.

Black Vine Weevil (*Otiorhynchus sulcatus*). The black snout-beetle is about ½ inch long; its wings are flecked with yellow scales. It lays its eggs in old strawberry beds and in lawns and other grassy places. The larvae feed on the roots and invade the crown. They attack geraniums in greenhouses during the winter, and are common on strawberries in gardens, also on cyclamen, gloxinia, primula, and other ornamentals.

Control: See *Taxus.*

Greenhouse Whitefly. (*Trialeurodes vaporariorum*). The undersides of geranium leaves are often completely covered with the nymphs and adult flies of this insect. By sucking the sap they cause leaves to turn yellow and fall. They secrete honeydew, which is then attacked by the black mold fungus, *Fumago vagans,* which disfigures the foliage.

Control: See *Fuschsia.*

Eastern Subterranean Termite (*Reticulitermes flavipes*). These pests do not always confine their activities to the wood of houses and tree stumps. They also at times attack geraniums, chrysanthemums, and other plants. They enter through the drainage holes in the pots and tunnel through the stems, causing the plants to turn yellow and die.

Control: Apply a 2 per cent Diazinon dust to areas over which the termites travel.

Southern Root-Knot Nema and **Northern Root-Knot Nema** (*Meloidogyne incognita* and *M. hapla*). Geraniums infested with these nemas should be destroyed. Soil in which they grew should be steam-pasteurized or treated with one of the chemicals mentioned in Chapter 3 before reuse.

Japanese Weevil. See *Ligustrum.*

PENSTEMON

Fungus Diseases

Leaf Spots (*Ascochyta penstemonis, Cercospora penstemonis, Cercosporella nivosa, Phyllosticta antirrhini,* and *Septoria penstemonis*). Five species of fungi cause leaf spotting of this host.

Control: Pick off and destroy leaves when the spots first appear.

Rusts (*Puccinia andropogonis* var. *penstemonis, P. penstemonis, P. confraga,* and *P. palmeri*). Four rusts occur on *Penstemon.* They are rarely serious enough to warrant control measures.

Other Diseases. This host is occasionally affected by root rot caused by *Pellicularia filamentosa* and *Phymatotrichum omnivorum,* and powdery mildew by *Erysiphe cichoracearum.*

Insects

Two species of aphids, the foxglove and the crescent-marked lily, the Fuller rose beetle, and the larva of the checker spot butterfly infest this host.

Control: Spray with Meta-Systox R, Sevin, or malathion when the insects begin to feed.

PEPEROMIA

Peperomias grown in greenhouses and homes are subject to a ringspot virus disease. Affected plants are stunted; the leaves are distorted and marked by chlorotic or brown necrotic rings (Fig. 178). This disease can be transmitted by grafting but no insect vector is known.

A crown rot caused by the fungus *Phytophthora nicotiane* var. *parasitica* also occurs on peperomia.

A nonparasitic trouble known as "corky scab" is also common on this host. Copper-colored scab-like swellings develop on the lower leaf surfaces. They are thought to be similar to oedema on *Pelargonium.*

PERSEA (AVOCADO)

Diseases

Anthracnose (*Colletotrichum gloeosporioides*). Greenhouse plants in the northern states and garden plants in the southern are subject to attack by this fungus. It causes a general wilting of the ends of branches and the development of cankers on the stem and spots on the leaves and flowers.

Control: If necessary, spray with Bordeaux mixture or some other copper fungicide.

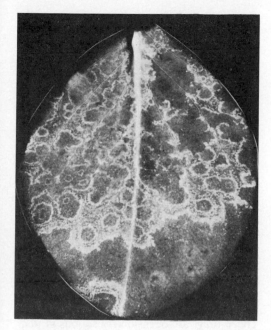

Fig. 178. Ringspot of *Peperomia*, caused by a virus.

Root Rot (*Phytophthora cinnamomi*). Root Rot, also known as "decline," is the most destructive disease of avocado in California. The causal fungus is soil-borne and seed-borne.

Control: Treat seed in hot water at 120° to 125°F. for 30 minutes to eliminate seed-borne infections. The avocado variety Duke is said to be rather resistant to attack by the causal fungus.

Scab (*Sphaceloma perseae*). This is a serious disease of avocado in Florida and Texas.

Control: Copper sprays will control this disease.

Other Diseases. Other important diseases of avocado are canker caused by *Botryosphaeria dothidea*, root rot by *Armillaria mellea* and wilt by *Verticillium albo-atrum*.

Physiological Disease

Oedema. In greenhouses where the temperature and humidity are excessively high, small wart-like or gall-like abnormal growths break out on the upper surfaces of the leaves. These growths crack open and later turn rust-colored, causing the disease to resemble the effects of a rust fungus.

Control: Reduction of moisture and temperature in the greenhouses will result in recovery.

Insects

There are also a great number of insect and related pest on this host. Information on the control of diseases and pests of plants grown for their fruits is available at agricultural experiment stations in states where avocados are grown.

Other Problems. Because of the ease of germinating seeds, many avocado consumers plant seeds and raise young plants in homes. Such plants do well for the first year or so and then succumb either from spider mites or unfavorable growing conditions.

PETUNIA

Diseases

Bacterial Wilt (*Pseudomonas solanacearum*). This disease, more common on other members of the Solanaceae, causes a rapid wilting and death of infected plants.

Control: No effective control is known.

Crown Rot (*Phytophthora parasitica*). Petunias grown in greenhouses and in home gardens near Denver, Colorado, are subject to this disease. A black discoloration and dry rot of the crown and lateral branches occur near the ground line. Wilting and death of the affected plants follow.

Control: Soil treatments with Dexon, Mylone, or Terrazole, are said to provide control.

Stem Rots (*Pellicularia filamentosa*, *Sclerotinia sclerotiorium,* and *Fusarium* sp.).

Three soil-inhabiting fungi cause decay of roots and stems of petunias.

Control: Use steam-pasteurized soil.

Virus Diseases. *Petunia hybrida* is susceptible to many virus diseases. Among the more common ones are curly top caused by the beet curly top virus, mosaic by the cucumber and tobacco mosaic viruses, ringspot by the tobacco ringspot virus, and spotted wilt by the tomato spotted wilt virus.

These viruses are spread in nature by sucking insects. Some, like ringspot, can be transmitted via seeds. Others, such as cucumber and tobacco mosaic, can be transmitted by persons using infected smoking or chewing tobacco.

Control: Destroy infected plants. Wash hands thoroughly with soap and water before handling petunias.

Aster Yellows. This disease has also been reported on petunias.

Control: Remove diseased plants. Control sucking insects with malathion or Sevin sprays.

Insects and Related Pests

Beetles. Among the beetles known to feed on petunias are the Asiatic garden, Colorado potato, potato flea, and spotted cucumber.

Control: Spray with Sevin if these pests become prevalent.

Bugs. The garden fleahopper and the tarnished plant bug occasionally attack the leaves of this host.

Control: Spray with Sevin.

Caterpillars. Yellow woollybear, tobacco and tomato hornworms, and the larva of the white-lined sphinx also chew the leaves of petunias.

Control: Spray with *Bacillus thuringiensis* or Sevin as soon as the caterpillars begin to feed.

Greenhouse Orthezia (*Orthezia insignis*). This scale insect may be recognized by the whitish or waxy marginal fringe on its body; a long, white, fluted egg-sac may be present.

Control: Spray with malathion or Sevin.

Southern Root-Knot Nema (*Meloidogyne incognita*). This nema also infests petunias. For control see Chapter 3.

PHILADELPHUS (MOCK-ORANGE)

Diseases

Canker (*Nectria cinnabarina*). Rough cankers first appear on the stems, followed by dieback of the distal portions. Small, round, reddish fruit bodies appear in the cankered areas.

Control: Prune and destroy affected branches.

Leaf Spots (*Ascochyta philadelphi, Ramularia philadelphi,* and *Septoria philadelphi*). These fungi are occasionally serious in very rainy seasons.

Control: Pick off and destroy the spotted leaves as soon as they appear. Copper or dithiocarbamate sprays may be used to prevent leaf spots in areas where these are very prevalent.

Other Fungus Diseases. Mock-orange is subject to sooty blotch caused by *Sarcinella heterospora,* powdery mildews by *Phyllactinia corylea* and *P. guttata,* and rust by *Gymnosporangium speciosum.*

Insects and Other Animal Pests

Two species of aphids, the bean and the green peach, infest this host. An undetermined species of leaf miner also attacks mock-orange.

Control: Spray with Meta-Systox R, Sevin, or malathion.

Nemas. The morthern root-knot nema (*Meloidogyne hapla*) and Cobb's meadow nema (*Pratylenchus penetrans*) infest the roots of mock-orange.

Control: See Chapter 3.

PHELLODENDRON (CORK TREE)

Cork trees are unusually free of pests. The only insects recorded on this host are two species of scales, lesser snow and pustule. Malathion or Sevin sprays will control the crawler stage of these pests.

PHILODENDRON

Diseases

A leaf spot caused by the fungus *Colletotrichum philodendri,* a stem rot by an undetermined species of bacterium, and a stem and root rot by the fungi *Pellicularia filamentosa* and *P. rolfsii* are the only parasitic diseases recorded on this host.

Commercial growers can control the bacterial stem rot on *Philodendron pertusum* and that caused by *Pellicularia filamentosa* on *Philodendron cordatum* by soaking propagating canes in hot water at 120°F. for 30 minutes. The treated canes should be cooled and placed in steamed sphagnum moss until roots or buds appear. They should then be cut into sections of one or two buds and planted in clean soil.

One strain of the bacterium *Erwinia chrysanthemi* causes irregular, water-soaked areas on leaves and collapse of petioles in some Florida nurseries. The disease can be controlled by spraying with Agrimycin.

Physiological Diseases

Philodendrons as a group can tolerate the unfavorable environment of most apartments and homes better than most house plants. Nevertheless they frequently contract several troubles that are mistaken for parasitic diseases.

Yellowing of the lower leaves, failure of the new leaves to attain normal size, and browning and death of the growing tips are usually due to insufficient light. Although these plants do not require direct sun, they need a great deal of indirect light. Another cause for these troubles is an excessively dry atmosphere. Philodendrons are tropical plants that thrive under high humidity.

Among other causes for poor growth of this host are overwatering, improper soil drainage, an excess or lack of plant food, and a pot-bound condition of the roots.

PHLOX

Diseases

Leaf Spots (*Ascochyta phlogis* var. *phlogina, Cercospora omphakodes, C. phlogina, Macrophoma cylindrospora, Phyllosticta* sp., *Ramularia* sp., *Septoria divaricata,* and *Stemphylium botryosum*). Many fungi cause left spots of phlox. *Septoria divaricata* is among the most common and destructive. It attacks the lower leaves primarily, producing dark brown, circular spots up to ¼ inch in diameter, the centers of which are light gray, almost white. Infected leaves dry up and die prematurely. This symptom must not be confused with the leaf blight discussed below under Physiological Disease.

Control: Remove and destroy infected plant parts in the fall of the year. Dusting with a fine grade of sulfur not only controls the fungus disease, but also helps to control red spider mites. Bordeaux mixture (2-2-50) is very satisfactory, but is not advisable if discoloration of the leaves is an important factor.

Powdery Mildews (*Erysiphe cichoracearum* and *Sphaerotheca humili*). Late in the growing season, these fungi produce a white coating on the leaves. They do not cause any permanent damage.

Control: Benlate, Karathane, or Acti-dione sprays applied as soon as the mildew appears will provide control.

Rusts (*Puccinia douglasii* and *Uromyces acuminatus* var. *polemonii*). The former rust affects *Phlox subulata* primarily. Neither rust is important enough to warrant control measures.

Crown Rots (*Pellicularia rolfsii, Sclerotium delphinii,* and *Thielaviopsis basicola*). These soil-inhabiting fungi can cause serious losses of phlox seedlings.

Control: Use steam-pasteurized soil as described in Chapter 4.

Other Diseases. Phlox is subject to many other diseases. Among these are crown gall caused by the bacterium *Agrobacterium tumefaciens,* stem blight by the fungus *Pyrenochaeta phlogina,* and wilt by *Verticillium albo-atrum.* Aster yellows and several virus diseases also affect this host.

Physiological Disease

Leaf Blight. The author was first to investigate a disease of this host characterized by dying of the lower leaves from the base progressively upward until the entire shoot is killed. No organisms or viruses are associated with this blight. The disease is most severe on old clumps and is entirely absent on seedlings or newly rooted cuttings. After several years of research the author concluded that the old stems, from which new shoots arise in spring are unable to supply enough water to prevent dying of the lower leaves. The trouble somewhat resembles the blossom end rot of tomato fruits which occurs when the rapidly growing leaf tips draw water from the fruits during dry spells. The only place in North America where this leaf blight is not found is in Victoria Park, Niagara Falls, Canada, where the constant mist from the falls reduces transpiration sufficiently to prevent blighting of the lower leaves.

Insects and Other Animal Pests

Beetles. Five kinds of beetles attack phlox: Asiatic garden, black blister, golden tortoise, June, and potato flea.

Control: Spray with Sevin or Diazinon.

Phlox Plant Bug (*Lopidea davisi*). This sucking insect feeds in all its stages on the leaves of perennial phlox, attacking the upper sides of the more tender leaves and developing buds. Whitish or light green spots on the leaves follow infestation. The adult bugs are about 1/4 inch long, greenish-yellow with four black stripes down the back. The young are orange or bright red.

The four-lined plant bug also attacks phlox, causing brown circular spots on the leaves.

Control: Remove and destroy infested tops in the fall. Spray as for beetles during the growing season as soon as the bugs appear.

Other Insects. Phlox is also attacked by the corn earworm, the aster leafhopper (which spreads the aster yellow disease), black and soft scales, and wireworms. The controls for these pests are discussed under more favored hosts.

Two-Spotted Mite (*Tetranychus urticae*). This mite is perhaps the most common pest of perennial phlox. It sucks the juices from the leaves, causing them to be stippled on the upper surfaces at first and completely yellow later. A hand lens will reveal all stages of this pest on the lower leaf surfaces.

Control: See *Althaea.*

Bulb and Stem Nema (*Ditylenchus dipsaci*). The nema that causes this disease enters the plants through the stomata of the young shoots, working upward as the stems develop, and causing the leaves to take all sorts of abnormal forms. Swelling of the tissues may occur in advance of the actual infestation. The nema enters the stem also at the base where rootlets have burst through. The leaves may be thread-like, spindling, or of normal size but wrinkled or curled (Fig. 179). The stem may be swollen near the tops. Many basal buds are stimulated to develop by the presence of nemas. The stems may be bent sidewise at an angle. At first the stems and leaves are deep green in color. The

Fig. 179. Effects of infestation of phlox by the nema *Ditylenchus dipsaci.*

plants, however, are much stunted and usually fail to bloom; they die prematurely. Certain varieties of phlox are very susceptible, while others escape infestation. This nema, which is more common on ferns, chrysanthemums, and other plants, causes individual leaf blotches; the stem nema, however, is more systemic. It feeds in the intercellular spaces of the cortex and other parenchyma tissues. The nemas are spread by their own activity in the soil or are carried by water, or garden tools, and on the feet of animals. Seeds also may become infested, the worms being carried under the seed coats.

Control: Infested plants should be dug up and destroyed immediately, or dipped in boiling water or some chemical compound. Change the location of phlox plantings, unless the soil can be properly pasteurized with heat. Take cuttings only from sound plants. (Some of the shoots that appear in the early spring are, however, free from the nema. Root cuttings also are free from infestation.) Induce strong growth with fertilizers, especially highly nitrogenous ones. Use resistant varieties if possible. Avoid planting other susceptible species of ornamentals in places where infested phlox has been recently grown, unless the soil has been throughly pasteurized.

Stalk Borer. See *Lilium.*

PHOENIX—see PALMACEAE

PHOTINIA

Diseases

Leaf Spots (*Entomosporium maculatum* and *Septoria photiniae*). The former fungus, more frequently referred to by its perfect stage, *Fabraea maculata,* affects several other members of the Rosaceae. It occurs on

Photinia arbutifolia in California and on *P. glabra* and *P. serrulata* in Louisiana.

Control: Periodic applications of copper or a dithiocarbamate fungicide will control leaf spots.

Powdery Mildews (*Podosphaera leucotricha* and *Sphaerotheca pannosa*). Severe outbreaks of these mildew fungi have been reported from the western states.

Control: Spray with Karathane, Acti-dione PM, or Benlate.

Twig Blight (*Erwinia amylovora*). Leaves stems, and fruits are blighted by this bacterium. See fire blight under *Crataegus*.

Insects

Toyon Lace Bug (*Corythucha incurvata*). *Photina arbutifolia* in California and Arizona is seriously damaged by this lace bug. Infested leaves lose their color, and brown flecks are formed on the lower surfaces. The pests secrete an abundance of honeydew.

Control: Spray with Diazinon, malathion, or Sevin as soon as the insects appear. Direct the spray to the lower leaf surfaces.

Caterpillars. The larval stage of the California tent caterpillar, the omnivorous looper, and the western tussock moth also attack *P. arbutifolia* on the West Coast.

Control: Spray with *Bacillus thuringiensis* or Sevin.

Scales. Five species of scales infest *Photinia:* black, European fruit lecanium, Italian pear, oystershell, and San Jose.

Control: Spray with malathion or Sevin to control the crawler stages of these pests.

Other Pests. *Photinia arbutifolia* may be infested by thrips—greenhouse and Toyon—and four species of whiteflies: crown, inconspicuous, iridescent, and pruinose. Malathion or Sevin sprays will control the immature stages of these insects.

PHYSALIS ALKEKENGI (CHINESE LANTERN-PLANT)

A bacterial wilt, caused by *Pseudomonas solanacearum*, a fungus wilt by a species of *Verticillium* a leaf spot by a species of *Phyllosticta*, white smut by *Entyloma australe*, and a mosaic virus are the only diseases reported on this host. Controls for these are given under more favored hosts.

Several species of tortoise beetles, the imported long-horned weevil, and the striped cucumber beetle attack Chinese lantern-plant. The cucumber beetle not only devours the foliage but also transmits mosaic virus. Malathion or Sevin sprays will control these pests.

PHYSOSTEGIA

Diseases

Crown Rot (*Pellicularia rolfsii, Sclerotinia sclerotiorum,* and *Sclerotium delphinii*). Three soil-inhabiting fungi cause plants to wilt suddenly after they invade the roots or stem bases.

Control: See Chapter 4.

Other Diseases. A leaf spot caused by *Septoria physostegiae* and a rust by *Puccinia physostegiae* are the other fungus diseases of this host. They are rarely serious enough to warrant control measures.

PICEA (SPRUCE)

Diseases

Canker [*Cytospora* (Valsa[29]) *kunzei* var. *piceae*]. This is the most prevalent and destructive disease of Norway spruce and Colorado blue spruce. The most striking symptoms are the browning and death of the branches, usually starting with those nearest

[29] *Valsa* is the perfect or sexual stage of this fungus.

the ground and slowly progressing upward. Occasionally branches high in the tree are attacked, even though the lower ones are healthy.

The needles may drop immediately from infected branches or may persist for nearly a year, eventually leaving dry, brittle twigs that contrast sharply with unaffected branches. White patches of pitch or resin may appear along the bark of the dead or dying branches. Cankers occur in the vicinity of these exudations. They are not readily discernible, but can be found by cutting back the bark in the area that separates diseased from healthy tissues. In the cankered area, tiny, black, pin-point fruiting bodies of the causal fungus are a positive sign of the disease (Fig. 180).

Many other trees weakened by adverse growing conditions such as drought, winter injury, insects, fire, and mechanical injuries are subject to different species of *Cytospora*. The following are the most common, in addition to *C. kunzei* var. *piceae* mentioned above and *C. chrysosperma* discussed in other parts of this book: *C. acerina* on Japanese maple; *C. ambiens* on American elm; *C. annularis* on black and red ash; *C. corni* on dogwood; *C. leucostoma* on Norway spruce; *C. microspora* on American mountain-ash; *C. mollissima* on Chinese chestnut; *C. pinastri* on balsam fir; *C. rubescens* on American and European mountain-ash; and an undetermined species on walnut and white mulberry.

Control: Infected branches cannot be saved. They should be cut off a few inches

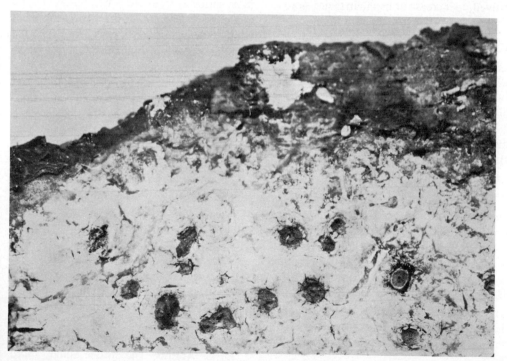

Fig. 180. Fruiting bodies of the canker fungus *Cytospora (Valsa) kunzei* var. *piceae* on spruce branch.

below the dead or infected parts, or at the point of attachment to the main stem. Because of the danger of spreading spores to uninfected branches, pruning should never be undertaken while the branches are wet. Inasmuch as the available evidence indicates that the fungi enter the branches only through wounds, bark injuries by lawn mowers and other tools should be avoided. Some plant pathologists believe, however, that there is no way of preventing infections. Others report that spraying the lower branches and the trunk 3 or 4 times in the spring with a copper fungicide will help to prevent further spread. The applications should be spaced at 2- to 3-week intervals starting about mid-April. The disease appears to be most prevalent on trees in poor vigor. Consequently, trees should be fertilized at least every few years, watered during dry spells, and the soil improved, to increase or maintain their vigor.

Needle Casts (*Lophodermium filiforme, L. piceae,* and *Rhizosphaera kalkhoffii*). The lower branches of red, black, and Sitka spruces may be defoliated by one of these fungi. The leaves are spotted, and turn yellow before they drop.

Control: Spray valuable ornamental specimens with Bordeaux mixture, Benlate, or Bravo in June and July.

Rusts (*Chrysomyxa ledi* var. *cassandrae, C. empetri, C. ledicola, C. chiogenis, C. piperiana, C. roanenis,* and *C. weirii*). Several species of rust fungi occur on spruce needles. Each requires an alternate host to complete its life cycle. On the spruce, the fungi appear as whitish blisters on the lower leaf surfaces. Affected needles turn yellow and may drop prematurely. The names of the alternate hosts for each of the fungi listed can be obtained from state or federal plant pathologists.

Control: Removal of the alternate hosts in the vicinity of valuable spruces is suggested. Protective sprays containing sulfur or ferbam are rarely justified.

Wood Decay. Spruces are subject to a number of wood decays caused by various fungi. Among those most commonly associated with various types of decay are *Trametes pini, Polyporus schweinitzii, P. sulphureus,* and *Fomes pinicola.*

Control: Little can be done once these decays become extensive. Avoidance of wounds and fertilization to increase vigor are suggested preventive measures.

Insects and Other Animal Pests

Spruce Gall Aphid (*Adelges abietis*). Elongated, many-celled, cone-shaped galls less than 1 inch long (Fig. 181), result from feeding and irritation by this pest. Trees are weakened and distorted when large numbers of these galls are formed. Norway spruce is most seriously infested; white, black, and red spruces are less so. In the spring the adult wingless females deposit eggs near where the galls later develop. Immature females hibernate in the budscales.

Control: Spray the tips of twigs and bases of buds with a 60- or 70-second "superior" oil in April when the trees are still dormant, or with Sevin, or Meta-Systox R in May.

Cooley Spruce Gall Aphid (*Adelges cooleyi*). Galls ranging from 1/2 to 2 1/2 inches in length on the terminal shoots of blue, Englemann, and Sitka spruces and Douglas-fir are produced by feeding and irritation by an aphid closely related to that which infests the Norway spruce. The adult female overwinters on the bark near the twig terminals and deposits eggs in that vicinity in the spring.

Control: Because Douglas-fir is an alternate host for this pest, avoid planting that species near spruces. Spray with Sevin in spring just before new growth emerges.

Other Aphids. The spruce aphid, *Elatobodium abietinum,* and the pine leaf chermid, *Pineus pinifoliae,* also infest spruce leaves. The balsam twig aphid, discussed under *Abies,* at times attacks this host. Meta-Sys-

Fig. 181. Galls produced by the spruce gall aphid. (T. H. Everett)

tox R, Sevin, or malathion sprays are very effective against these species.

Spruce Budworm (*Choristoneura fumiferana*). One of the most destructive pests of forest and ornamental evergreens, this pest attacks spruce and balsam firs in forest plantations and also infests ornamental spruce, balsam fir, Douglas-fir, pine, larch, and hemlock. The opening buds and needles are chewed by the caterpillar, which is dark, reddish-brown with a yellow stripe along the side. The adult female moths, dull gray, marked with brown bands and spots, emerge in late June and early July.

Western Spruce Budworm (*Choristoneura occidentalis*). This pest defoliates various conifers in Western North America.

Jack Pine Budworm (*C. pinus*). This budworm causes considerable damage to jack pine and to a lesser extent to red and white pine in the Lake States.

Control: Forest areas can be protected with airplane applications of Sevimol. Ornamental spruces, pines, firs, hemlocks and larches can be sprayed with Sevin just as the buds burst in spring.

Spruce Bud Scale (*Physokermes piceae*). Globular red scales, about 1/8 inch in diameter, may occasionally infest the twigs of Norway spruce. The young crawl about in late July, and the winter is passed in the partly grown adult stage.

Control: Before growth starts in spring, spray most spruces with a "superior" type dormant oil. For blue spruce, which is sensitive to this type of spray, use malathion or Cygon in late June.

Spruce Needle Miner (*Taniva albolineana*). The light greenish larvae web the leaves together and mine the inner tissues. They enter through small holes at the base of the leaves, and as they feed inside, the leaves turn brown. The adult is a small grayish moth.

Another species, the spruce leaf miner (*Recurvaria piceaella*), also mines the leaves of spruce.

Control: Spray with malathion in mid-May and again in mid-June.

Pine Needle Scale (*Phenacaspis pini-foliae*). Although this pest infests pines primarily, it will attack spruces, especially those that are in poor vigor.

Control: Spray with lime sulfur or with dormant oil-ethion, in spring just before growth starts.

Spruce Epizeuxis (*Epizeuxis aemula*). Or-

namental spruces in the Northeast may be attacked by small brown larvae with black tubercles which web needles together and fill them with excrement.

Control: Spray with Sevin when the larvae begin to feed in late summer.

Sawflies (*Pikonema alaskensis* and *Diprion hercyniae*). The former, known as the yellow-headed sawfly, may sometimes defoliate trees completely. Ordinarily, however, infestation results merely in a ragged appearance. The latter, the European spruce sawfly, feeds on the old foliage, and consequently the trees are not killed although the growth may be stunted. The larvae overwinter in cocoons on the ground where they are subject to attack by mice.

Control: Spray the trees with Sevin as soon as the caterpillars are noticed.

White Pine Weevil (*Pissodes strobi*). Oriental spruce and occasionally other kinds may suffer from attacks of this beetle, which feeds on the terminal shoots and causes a heavy flow of sap. The larvae cause much injury by boring within the terminal shoots, tunneling downward and inward, as shown in Fig. 182. Their work is manifested in July by the brown dying ends of the "leaders." The leader is usually killed and the tree stunted. The work of the weevil is easily distinguished from that of the pine shoot moth by the greater length of the shoots killed and by the holes in the bark from which the beetles have emerged (Fig. 182).

Control: This pest is not easy to control. Cut off and destroy all infested shoots as soon as they are noticed in early summer. Make the cuts well below the points where grubs are present. Protect growing shoots by spraying in early spring, when the buds are swelling, with methoxychlor or Meta-Systox R. To replace the leader branch, tie the next lower lateral to a stick and then tie the stick to the main stem. Cut away all other laterals in the immediate vicinity of the one tied to the stick.

Spruce Spider Mite (*Oligonychus unun-*

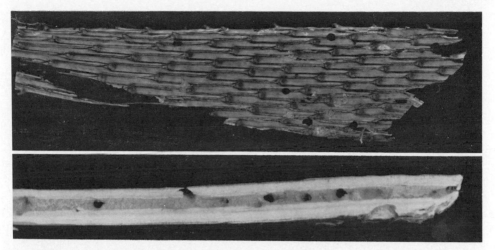

Fig. 182. Work of the white pine weevil *(Pissodes strobi)* in a spruce branch. On the top may be seen the small holes through which the adults emerged; on the bottom is a twig split to show their work inside.

guis). Yellow, sickly needles, many of which are covered with a fine silken webbing, indicate a severe infestation of the spider mite, a tiny pest only 1/64 inch long (Fig. 183). The young are pale green; the adult female is greenish-black. Winter is passed in the egg stage on the twigs and the needles. In addition to spruces, arborvitae, junipers, and hemlock are also attacked.

Control: Spray with lime sulfur or with "superior" type dormant oil in early spring just before new growth emerges. Or spray in mid-May with chlorobenzilate, Kelthane, Meta-Systox R, or Tedion to kill the young mites of the first generation. Repeat in September, if necessary. Blue spruces should not be sprayed with dormant oils.

Bagworm. See *Abies.*

PIERIS

Diseases

Leaf Spots (*Alternaria tenuis, Phyllosticta andromedae*, and *P. maxima*). During rainy seasons these fungi will cause leaf spots of *Pieris japonica* and *P. floribunda.*

Control: Periodic applications of ferbam sprays during the growing season, starting when the leaves are half grown, will control leaf spots.

Dieback (*Phytophthora* sp.). A species of *Phytophthora* causes dieback of this host. The fungus enters the roots from the soil, causing root decay and eventually death of the entire plant.

Control: No effective control is known.

Insects and Related Pests

Lace Bug (*Stephanitis takeyai*). This sucking insect (Fig. 184) causes leaves of *Pieris japonica* to be mottled gray or yellow. It is most prevalent in the northeastern United States and was probably introduced from Japan about the middle 1940's.

Control: Spray several times at two-week intervals with Meta-Systox R or Sevin starting in mid-May. The spray should be directed to the lower leaf surfaces.

Florida Wax Scale (*Ceratoplastes floridensis*). This reddish or purple-brown scale, covered with a thick, white, waxy coating

Fig. 183. Adult and egg stage of the spruce spider mite *Oligonychus ununguis* on spruce leaves, greatly enlarged. (Dr. J. C. Schread)

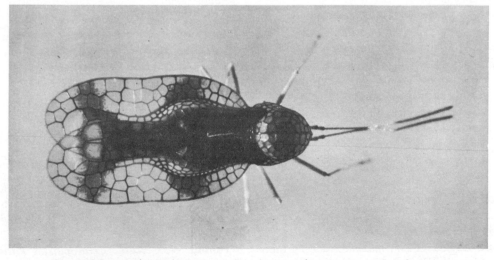

Fig. 184. Andromeda lace bug *(Stephanitis takeyai).* (Dr. J. C. Schread)

tinted with pink, may infest *Pieris* in the South.

Other scales that infest *Pieris* are the cottony maple, latania, and nigra.

Control: Spray valuable specimens with malathion or Sevin to control the crawler stage.

Two-Spotted Mite (*Tetranychus urticae*). This sucking pest also causes *Pieris* leaves to turn yellow.

Control: See *Althaea.*

Nemas (*Pratylenchus* sp. and *Tylenchorhynchus* sp.). Several species of nemas infest the roots of *Pieris*.

Control: See controls for nemas in Chapter 3.

PILEA (ALUMINUM-PLANT)

A leaf spot caused by the fungus *Septoria pileae* and root rot by a species of *Pellicularia* have been reported on *Pilea*. Other pests include the lesser snow scale *Pinnaspis strachani,* and root-knot nema *Meloidogyne* sp. Control measures are rarely used for these pests.

PINUS (PINE)

Fungus Diseases

Late Damping-off and Root Rot (*Pythium debaryanum, Fusarium discolor, Pellicularia filamentosa,* and *Phomopsis juniperovora*). In nurseries, coniferous seedlings too old to be susceptible to ordinary damping-off of very young seedlings are subject to a root rot and a top damping-off by these four fungi. Seedlings of *Pinus banksiana* and *P. resinosa* are especially susceptible.

Control: Disinfest seeds and then plant them in steam-pasteurized soil. Under some conditions PCNB (Terraclor) soil drenches give good control of some damping-off fungi and can be substituted for steaming.

Dieback, Tip Blight (*Diplodia pinea*).

Seedlings of young trees from 3 to 5 years old in nurseries may be seriously attacked by this fungus, which was formerly known as *Sphaeropsis ellisii.* It causes a rot which extends upward from the collar below the surface of the soil. The disease may be recognized by the deep red color of the bark and by the black streaks which occur in the wood. The scales of young cones also may be attacked. *P. strobus* and *P. resinosa* are especially susceptible as seedlings to the root and collar rot, while *P. nigra* and *P. virginiana* are susceptible to dieback. The fungus also causes a dieback of the branches of older trees. The new growth of such branches is stunted, the needles turn brown, and the terminal buds exude an excessive amount of resin. With a hand lens the minute black fruiting bodies (pycnidia) may be seen at the base of the diseased needles, especially in the leaf sheath. They are also found on the twigs, which may be killed back for some distance. Cankers may be formed at the nodes.

Control: No cure is possible for plants that are infected at the base. The use of steam-pasteurized soil is suggested for avoiding root and stem base infections.

Control is possible for the tip blight phase of the disease on older trees. As soon as the blight is noticed, the infected needles, twigs, and cones should be pruned to sound tissues and destroyed. Pruning should be done when the branches are dry, because there is less danger of spreading the spores by contact with the operator and with tools. Where infection has been particularly severe, preventive fungicides are also recommended. Benlate, or a copper fungicide should be applied very early in spring starting when the buds open and continuing twice at weekly intervals until the needles break through the needle sheaths. In rainy springs, a fourth application, about 10 days after the third, may be necessary. As a supplementary treatment, fertilization of the trees in fall or early spring is suggested.

Stem Blister Rust (*Cronartium quercuum*). This is a gall-forming stem blister rust. *Pinus sylvestris, P. rigida, P. banksiana,* and *P. virginiana* are all very susceptible to it. A very characteristic distortion or kink of the trunk is formed 3 or 4 feet from the ground. The rust may cause the growth of a deep canker instead of galls. Since the rust may appear at the base of a tree near the ground, it may be inconspicuous, even though the infected area may be a foot across. More or less spherical galls, 1 to 2 inches in diameter, appear on the branches; eventually the parts above the galls are killed. These galls may be so numerous on jack pines as to kill the trees. They should not be mistaken for galls caused by insects. The infection of trunks of small trees of scrub pine results in very striking sperical galls which entirely encircle the trunks. Galls 5 or 6 inches in diameter are not unusual.

The rust has species of oak as alternate host. Numerous long horns of brownish or dark brown spores are formed on the infected oak leaves. The basidiospores, developed on these horns, reinfect pines in the spring. No practical control for this rust has been suggested.

Comandra Blister Rust (*Cronartium comandrae*). This rust is widespread on at least 14 species of hard pines in the United States and has recently become severe on lodgepole pine. Spindle-shaped swellings are formed on branches and trunks of young trees, but on older trunks they may be constricted. Trunk cankers seldom exceed 3½ feet in length.

Control: Control measures have not been developed for this rust.

Cankers. A large number of canker diseases occur on all pines. These are more common on trees in forests than in ornamental plantings.

The fungus *Tympanis pinastri* attacks red pines and, to a lesser extent, white pine. It produces elongated stem cankers with or without definite margins, and with depressed centers that become roughened and open after 2 or 3 years. Each canker centers at a node, indicating that the fungus enters the branch at the base of the lateral branch. Trees in weakened condition are most susceptible.

Other cankers on pines are associated with the fungi *Dasyscypha pini, Atropellis pinicola, A. tingens, Caliciopsis pinea, Fusarium lateritium* var. *pini, Scleroderris lagerbergii, Sphaeropsis* sp., *Phomopsis* sp., and *Cytospora* (*Valsa*) *kunzei*.

Control: Removal of dead and weak branches, avoidance of bark injuries, and fertilization to increase the vigor of the trees are suggested. Surgical treatment of cankers should be attempted only on valuable specimens.

Cenangium Twig Blight (*Cenangium abietis*). The twigs of exotic species of pine and of white pine may be killed by this fungus. Early symptoms are the dying of terminal buds and reddening of the needles. Infection rarely spreads beyond the current season's growth.

Control: Affected twigs should be pruned to sound wood and destroyed. Because twig blight is usually severe only on weakened trees, fertilization and watering are suggested for valuable pines.

Leaf Casts (*Bifusella linearis, B. striiformis, Cytospora pinastri, Elytroderma deformans, Hypoderma desmazierii, H. hedgecockii, H. pedatum, H. pini, Hypodermella* spp., *Lophodermium nitens, L. pinastri,* and *Systremma acicola*). Many species of fungi cause leaf yellowing and, at times, premature defoliation of pines primarily in nurseries and in forest plantings.

Control: Leaf cast diseases rarely cause sufficient damage to large trees to warrant preventive practices. They can be controlled on small trees and on nursery stock by applying Bordeaux mixture, 4-4-50, or any other copper spray, when the needles are half grown and again about 2 weeks later. Because such sprays do not readily adhere to pine foliage, casein soap or some other material should be added as a spreading agent. Zineb sprays also provide good control.

Needle Blight (*Dothistroma pini*). This fungus causes slightly swollen, dark spots or bands on 1-year-old Austrian pine needles in late summer. The distal portion of the swollen needle turns light brown and dies. Severely affected trees show sparse foliage as a result of the premature dropping of needles.

Control: Bordeaux mixture or any copper fungicide applied first in late April or early May and for a second time 3 weeks later will control this disease. Benlate will also control needle blight.

Needle Rust (*Coleosporium asterum*). Needle rusts may be more or less serious. This rust is most common on pitch pine (*Pinus rigida*) in the eastern states, but two or three other species are susceptible. The blisters break out as pustules which open to discharge the bright orange-colored aeciospores of the rust. Infestation may be serious enough to cause defoliation. The pustules are from $1/16$ to $1/8$ inch high. The peridium or bounding layer remains visible after the spores have been discharged. The spores from these pustules infect either aster or goldenrod, on which plants the fungus forms golden or rust-colored pustules during summer. The rust is often able to winter on the crown leaves of goldenrods and asters, so that the rust can perpetuate itself on these hosts; but the rust on pine must first infect goldenrod or aster before it can be carried to the pine again. It is not perennial in the pine as is the blister rust.

Control: The destruction of wild asters and goldenrods near valuable pines, and spraying the pines with sulfur early in the season will provide control.

Scrub Pine Needle Rust (*Coleosporium pinicola*). *Pinus virginiana* and occasionally other species are seriously infected with this rust, which breaks out in the spring with reddish pustules on the needles. The pustules, up to $1/2$ inch long, fade and become inconspicuous later on. Defoliation may occur. This is a short-cycle rust, having no alternate host stage; the spores that develop in the pustules germinate there and shed secondary spores (basidiospores) which in spring reinfect the pines in the vicinity.

It is not a serious rust on ornamental pines except on *P. virginiana*. No control measures have been suggested.

Little Leaf (*Phytophthora cinnamomi*). This highly destructive disease occurs on shortleaf and loblolly pines in forest plantings of the southeastern United States. The disease is most easily recognized in its advanced stages when the crown is sparse and ragged in appearance, and the branches, lacking the mass of normal foliage, often assume an ascending habit. Leaves are only half their normal length. Trees die prematurely.

Control: Ornamental pines in home plantings appear to escape this disease even in areas where the causal fungus is known to be present in the soil.

White-Pine Blister Rust (*Cronartium ribicola*). This most serious disease in white pine forests is not known to be of consequence in ornamental plants because the quarantine regulations against growing currants, which are the alternate hosts, prevent the appearance of the rust in serious form, if at all. The rust attacks the living bark and cambium of white pine, first breaking out in blisters which exude a sweetish secretion, later forming larger, bright-orange-colored pustules. The latter are filled with the spores that carry the fungus to its alternate host, where it develops during the summer a red rust stage and later a winter stage. Spores from the currants again infect healthy pines. The disease spreads rapidly up and down the tree, soon killing the branches and the main trunk if it is attacked.

Control: In forest plantings, eradicate the

alternate hosts such as the European black currant (*Ribes nigrum*) within a one-mile radius, and all wild currants within 900 feet. To eliminate cankers on pine, prune off cankered lateral branches or excise stem cankers by removing bark at least 4 inches above and below, and 2 inches on either side of discolored bark. Paint wounds with orange shellac followed by tree paint. *Pinus peuce*, one of the five-needle pines, is said to be resistant to blister rust.

Wood Decay. Because pine wood contains a high percentage of resins, wood decays are not so frequent as in hardwoods and in some other evergreens. Some of the fungi commonly associated with wood decay are *Stereum sanguinolentum, Fomes pini, F. officinalis, F. roseus, Polyporus circinatus,* and *P. schweinitzii.* The first mentioned is commonly associated with improperly treated pruning wounds.

Control: No control is feasible where extensive decay occurs. Wounds should be avoided and the trees should be kept in good vigor.

Physiological Diseases

White Pine Blight. A needle blight of white pine, *Pinus strobus,* which appears as a browning of entire needles or tips of needles of the current season's growth has been prevalent throughout the northeastern United States for the last 25 years. The primary cause of the trouble is unknown. Some experts have attributed it to a deficiency or an excess of soil moisture, others to a nutrient deficiency and to fungi, and still others to a virus. The disease is not always fatal. Some trees recover without special treatment.

Stunt. Stunting and death of 5- to 40-year-old red pines, *Pinus resinosa,* may be due to poor soil damage. To avoid injury, select a well-drained planting site at the start.

Air Pollutants. Several chemicals, including sulfur dioxide and ozone, produce a tip burn or speckling of the leaves of several species of pines in areas where these materials are released into the atmosphere.

Salt. White pines planted within 50 feet of heavily used highways may be severely injured or killed by the salt used to melt snow and ice. Trees growing close to salt water may also suffer. Spraying trees in such locations with an anti-desiccant such as Foli-Guard, Vapor Guard, or Wilt-Pruf NCF on a mild day in December and again in February, will reduce injury.

Insects and Other Animal Pests

Pine Bark Aphid (*Pineus strobi*). Though commonly called the white pine bark louse, this aphid occasionally attacks balsam fir also. The insects usually work on the undersides of the limbs and on the trunk from the ground up. They may be recognized by the white, cottony material (Fig. 185) that collects in patches wherever they are present. In the eastern states white pine may be seriously injured. The winter is passed in the egg stage, the eggs being protected by the cottony covering. The eggs hatch in spring, and soon the young insects may be seen crawling about on the trunk and branches. Several generations are developed each summer.

Control: Apply a "superior" type dormant oil spray in early spring, and spray toward the end of April with either Cygon or Diazinon. Respray with either of these in mid-May and again in early July if some aphids appear.

Pine Leaf Chermid (*Pineus pinifoliae*). This insect infests species of pines and spruces. It winters over on pine, and then moves over in spring to spruces, on which it causes terminal galls. In summer the aphids move to white pine, on which they give birth to nymphs. These then suck out the sap from the new shoots, causing either the development of undersized leaves or the death of the new shoots.

Control: Spray the white pines with malathion or Meta-Systox R just after the first galls open on the spruces in June.

Fig. 185. Pine bark aphid on eastern white pine *(Pinus strobus).* (Oxford University Press)

White Pine Aphid (*Cinara strobi*). These aphids feed on the smooth bark of the twigs and smaller branches of young trees and cause a winter injury which results from drying out of the twigs. Sometimes several hundred aphids are clustered together. Sooty mold often develops on the honeydew.

Control: Same as for pine bark aphid.

European Pine Shoot Moth (*Rhyacionia buoliana*). This is a very serious pest of mugho pines and red pines in ornamental plantings. Austrian, Scots, and Japanese black pines also may be badly damaged. The caterpillars, by attacking the tip ends of young shoots, cause them to turn over and become deformed and killed or the lateral buds to be blasted. The caterpillars can be found working in the tip ends in May or the early part of June. Their presence is usually indicated by quantities of resin. The moths that are the adult stage of this caterpillar emerge about June 15 and lay their eggs in August on the new buds.

Control: For small plantings and low trees, hand-picking of infested shoots and buds is probably the most satisfactory method. An early spring (mid-April) spraying with Cygon, Diazinon, Dylox, or Sevin followed by a late June spraying, give good control. In states where its use is permitted, carbofuran, applied to the soil in granular form in late May or mid-June, will control this pest. Carbofuran sprays applied at the peak of moth flight are also effective.

Nantucket Pine Moth (*Rhyacionia frustrana*). This species attacks two- and three-needled pines in the eastern United States.

Control: Spray in mid-June with Cygon, Meta-Systox R, or Sevin.

Sawflies (*Diprion similis*). The caterpillars of the introduced pine sawflies are about 1 inch long and have a black head and greenish-yellow bodies with a double brown stripe down the middle of the back. They feed on the leaves of various species of pine during May and June and again during September. Four other species of sawflies attack pines: the balsam-fir, *Neodiprion abietis;* the red-headed, *N. lecontei;* the European pine. *N. sertifer;* and the jack-pine sawfly, *N. pratti banksianae.* In severe infestations the tree may be entirely defoliated.

Control: As soon as an infestation is observed, spray the trees with either methoxychlor or Sevin. The red-headed sawfly, *Neodiprion lecontei,* has broods through the season and hence may require spray applications in June, July, and August. The European pine sawfly, *N. sertifer,* in forest plantings has been controlled by airplane spraying of a virus suspension capable of infecting the larvae.

Pine Webworm (*Tetralopa robustella*). Masses of brown frass at the ends of terminal twigs result from infestations of the webworm, a yellowish-brown larva with a black stripe on each side of the body, which is $4/5$ inch long.

Control: Spray with Dylox, methoxychlor, or Sevin in mid-June when the larvae are young and before the needles are webbed. A second application in early August may be necessary.

Pine False Webworm (*Acantholyda erythrocephala*). The larvae of this pest are about $3/4$ inch long, greenish to yellowish-brown. They feed on the leaves and tie the masses of excreta and leaf-pieces together into loose balls. The damage is illustrated in Fig. 186.

Control: Same as for pine webworm.

Pine Needle Scale (*Phenacaspis pinifoliae*). Pine needles may appear nearly white (Fig. 187) when heavily infested with this scale, an elongated insect $1/10$ inch long, white with a yellow spot at one end. The pest overwinters in the egg stage under female scales. The eggs hatch in May. The black pine needle scale, *Aspidiotus californicus,* occasionally infests some species of pine.

Control: Spray with dormant oil in April, or with Cygon or Meta-Systox R in mid-May and again in mid-August.

Pine Needle Miner (*Exoteleia pinifoliella*). Ornamental pine needles turn yellow and dry up as a result of mining by a $1/5$-inch-long brown larva.

Control: Spray with methoxychlor or Supracide 2E in mid-June. A second application in summer when the yellow-brown moths are flying about is suggested where this pest is particularly prevalent.

Pine Spittlebug (*Aphrophora parallela*). This insect is perhaps most common on Scots pine, but white pine also is rather seriously attacked at times. It causes injury to smaller twigs by drawing the sap from them. It forms a foamy matter about itself which gives the

Fig. 186. Work of the pine false webworm *(Acantholyda erythrocephala)* in a branch of pitch pine *(Pinus rigida)*; infested branch at the left.

Fig. 187. Pine needle scale on white pine. (Oxford University Press)

branches a whitish appearance. The adult insect is sometimes ½ inch long, grayish-brown in color, and resembles small frogs. Another species, the Saratoga spittlebug, *A. saratogensis,* seriously damages jack and red pines.

Control: Spray with malathion, methoxychlor, or Sevin in mid-May and again in mid-July, directing the spray forcefully so as to hit the little masses of spittle that cover the insect.

Pine Tortoise Scale (*Toumeyella numismaticum*). This cherry-red or reddish-brown scale, about ¹/₈ inch long, attacks jack pine in reforested areas, at times destroying 50 per cent of the trees. It is closely related to *T. pini*, which occurs on Scots and mugo pines in some eastern states.

Control: A dormant lime sulfur spray will kill this scale. The crawler stage may be killed in mid-June with Diazinon, malathion, or Sevin.

Red Pine Scale (*Matsucoccus resinosae*). This species now infests red pines in the area of southeastern New York and southwestern Connecticut. The current season's growth on infested trees consists of yellowed needles, which turn brick-red; later the tree dies. The young and adult stages, very difficult to detect, are yellow to brown in color and are hidden in the bark or inside the needle clusters.

Control: Severely infested trees should be cut down and destroyed. Spray less severely-infested ones with Cygon early in June and repeat in early September.

Pales Weevil (*Hylobius pales*). The bark of young white, red, and Scots pines may be chewed by a night-feeding reddish-brown to black weevil ¹/₃ inch long. Young trees may be girdled completely.

Control: Spray the bark of seedlings and other conifers and the twigs of large conifers with methoxychlor in April.

Pine Root Collar Weevil (*Hylobius radicis*). Austrian, mugho, red, and Scots pines on Long Island and in southeastern New York may be severely damaged by this borer. The symptoms on infested trees are sickly and dead foliage, and masses of pitch around the base of the trunk 3 or 4 inches below the soil surface.

Control: No effective control is known.

White Pine Shoot Borer (*Eucosma gloriola*). The whitish caterpillars are about ¹/₂ inch long. They burrow down the centers of the lateral shoots, causing them to wilt and to die back several inches. The insect spends the winter in the soil, and appears as a moth in spring.

Control: Cut off and destroy infested branches as soon as they are discovered. This, of course, is practical only for young trees.

White Pine Tube Moth (*Argyrotaenia pinatubana*). Greenish yellow larvae make tubes by tying the needles together side by side and squarely eating off the free end. White pines in the east and lodgepole and whitebark pines in the Rocky Mountain region are susceptible.

Control: Spray with Diazinon or Imidan in early May and again in mid-July.

White Pine Weevil (*Pissodes strobi*). This weevil is a very common pest of white pine in estates and lawns where trees are planted as ornamentals. It is also injurious in forests of white pine. The larvae feed on the inner bark and the sapwood of the leading branches and terminal shoots of the main trunk. The leader is girdled and killed, and the branches that grow out to replace the leader are more or less distorted. The beetles begin to emerge in July, leaving characteristic holes in the bark. They are about ¹/₄ inch long, reddish-brown and somewhat white-mottled. The larvae are pale yellowish grubs about ¹/₃ inch long. This insect also attacks spruce, as shown in Fig. 182.

Control: Cut out and destroy all infested branches in early June so as to kill the insects before they emerge as beetles. Spray valuable trees with a mixture of methoxychlor and Kelthane in early May and repeat in 2 weeks. The methoxychlor kills the adults, which deposit eggs in the bark in May, and also kills the young larvae which hatch out of the eggs. The Kelthane helps to keep down mites which may become numerous if methoxychlor alone is used. Recent research has revealed that Meta-Systox R can be substituted for the methoxychlor-Kelthane mixture. Where the central leader is destroyed, a new leader may be encouraged to develop by tying the next lower lateral shoot in an erect position with a small stick and a soft rope. Pruning the dead leader branch at a 45 degree angle, rather than straight across, will encourage the development of a new leader.

Zimmerman Pine Moth (*Dioryctria zimmermani*). The bark of twigs and branches on many species of pines is invaded by white to reddish yellow or green $3/4$-inch larvae. The adult moth is reddish gray in color and has a wingspread of 1 to $1^1/2$ inches. Branch tips turn brown, and the entire tops of trees may break off as a result of boring by the larvae.

Control: Dylox or Thiodan spray applied just before the larvae emerge from hibernation in spring and another applied in early August will provide control.

Bark Beetles (Scolytidae). Trees in weakened or dying condition are subject to infestation by bark beetle larvae, small worms that mine the bark and engrave the sapwood. Tiny "shot-holes" on the bark surface where beetles emerge, varying from $1/20$ to $1/3$ inch in size (depending on the species) are present.

Control: No effective control measure is known. Trees should be kept in vigorous condition by feeding and watering. Severely infested trees should be cut down and destroyed, or, if left standing, should be debarked.

PIQUERIA

Young plants in propagating beds are subject to a basal rot or damping-off due to *Pellicularia filamentosa*. The sand or soil in the propagating bed should be steam-pasteurized or treated with PCNB (Terraclor).

This host, sometimes called "Stevia," is also subject to aster yellows caused by a mycoplasma-like organism. Control measures are rarely practiced.

PITTOSPORUM

Diseases

Leaf Spots (*Alternaria tenuissima, Phyllosticta* sp., and *Cercospora pittospori*). The first causes small, dark-brown necrotic spots surrounded by chlorotic areas. The last causes angular spots, leaf yellowing, and premature leaf drop.

Control: Pick off and destroy spotted leaves. Severe outbreaks can be prevented by spraying with copper or dithiocarbamate fungicides.

Stem Rot (*Pellicularia rolfsii*). The stems and roots of this host in southern states may be rotted by this fungus.

Control: Control practices are justified only on young plants in nurseries. See Chapter 4 for details.

Other Diseases. This host is also subject to thread blight caused by *Pellicularia koleroga*, a foot rot by a species of *Diplodia*, and a root rot by *Phymatotrichum omnivorum*.

Three virus diseases—an undetermined species of mosaic, one which causes leaf variegation, and one which causes rough bark—have also been reported on *Pittosporum*.

Insects and Other Animal Pests

Scales. Seven species of scale insects—camellia, black, cottony-cushion, Florida wax, greedy, lesser snow, and soft—are known to attack *Pittosporum*.

Control: Spray valuable specimens with malathion or Sevin from time to time to control the crawler stages of these pests.

Other Pests. *Pittosporum* is subject to aphids and mealybugs. These are also controlled with malathion.

The southern root-knot nema, *Meloidogyne incognita,* attacks the roots of this host in the South. See Chapter 3 for control measures.

PLATANUS ACERIFOLIA
(LONDON PLANETREE)

Diseases

Cankerstain (*Ceratocystis fimbriata* var. *platani*). Thousands of London planetrees have been killed by this disease in the eastern United States in recent years. Shrunken cankers appear on trunks, large limbs, and occasionally on small limbs (Fig. 188). The can-

Fig. 188. Trunk of planetree showing infection by cankerstain fungus, *Ceratocystis fimbriata* var. *platani.* (U.S. Department of Agriculture)

kers frequently have longitudinal cracks and roughened bark. Bluish-black or brown discolorations appear on freshly exposed bark over the cankers. The callus tissue formed at the margin of a canker usually dies early. Dark-colored streaks extend from the cankers inward through the wood to the central pith, and frequently radiating web-shaped brown streaks extend from the pith outward through the sound wood in other regions (Fig. 189). The rays are mostly dark-colored. As the disease progresses, there is a gradual thinning of the leaves, which are smaller than usual. The disease seems to be limited to shade trees and is spread largely through pruning saws, wounds made by tree climbers, and injury due to ropes and other implements used by tree men. There is some evidence that as many as 5 species of Nitidulid beetles are capable of disseminating the causal fungus. The sycamore, *P. occidentalis,* is said by some to be resistant to this disease; others say it is mildly susceptible.

Control: Diseased trees should be removed and destroyed as soon as the diagnosis is confirmed. All injuries to sound trees should be avoided. Saws and other implements used in pruning planes should be thoroughly disinfested by washing in denatured alcohol or some other strong disinfestant after use on each tree in the more heavily infested zones. Because of the possibility of spreading the fungus by means of infested wound dressings, the addition to the dressing of some mild disinfestant such as Benlate or thiabendazole that are toxic to the fungus but harmless to the tree tissues is suggested. Where such a disinfestant is not used, in localities where the disease is prevalent it is best not to apply a dressing on fresh wounds. Until a few years ago plant pathologists believed that the disease could not be spread by way of contaminated saws if pruning was done in winter, from December 1 to February 15. But newly uncovered evidence suggests that this belief was only wishful thinking and that all

Fig. 189. Cross-section of plane tree trunk infected by *Ceratocystis fimbriata* f. *platani*. The discoloration shows the spread of the fungus through the wood.

pruning tools should be sterilized with 70 per cent denatured alcohol after use on each tree regardless of season.

Dieback, Botryosphaeria Canker (*Botryosphaeria dothidea*). This fungus, like *Verticillium albo-atrum*, and *Armillaria mellea*, is far more widespread than most professional arborists and nurserymen realize. It has long been known to cause cankers and dieback of redbud, but the author was among the first to show that its asexual stage, *Dothiorella*, caused a highly destructive disease of London planetrees in New York City (Fig. 190). By cross-inoculation tests he also proved that the same fungus can infect other important shade trees including sweetgum. The fungus also has been isolated from naturally infected sweetgums showing branch dieback and discolored wood. Among other trees known to be susceptible to this fungus are apple, avocado, Japanese persimmon, hickory, pecan, poplar, quince, tupelo, and willow.

The author, working with E. C. Rundlett,

then Arboriculturist for the New York City Department of Parks, was also the first to record that leaf fires beneath streetside trees made the trees more susceptible to infection by the conidial stage *Dothiorella gregaria*. He also pointed out that this is true of infections by the cankerstain fungus discussed earlier.

Control: No control is possible once the fungus has invaded the main trunk. When infections are limited to the branches, pruning well below the cankered area may remove all the infected material. Wounds and damage to the bark by fires should be avoided. The trees should be kept in good vigor by feeding, watering during dry spells, and spraying to control leaf-chewing and leaf-sucking insects.

Powdery Mildew (*Microsphaera alni*). London planetrees are especially susceptible to attacks of powdery mildew. Leaves and young twigs are covered with a whitish mold to such an extent that much of the foliage is destroyed. The weather seems to determine the seriousness of the attack; during some seasons no mildew appears, while in others

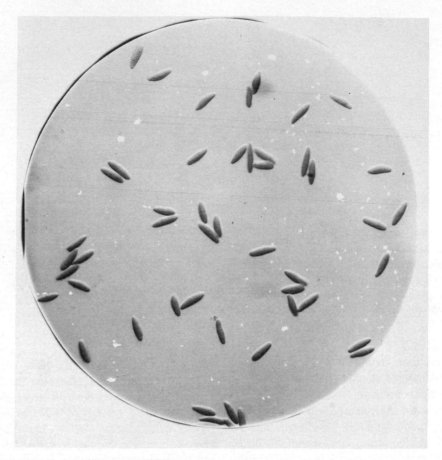

Fig. 190. Spores of the *Dothiorella* stage of the fungus *Botryosphaeria dothidea* from diseased planetrees as seen through a microscope.

the disease is serious, especially on young trees of a size for transplanting.

Control: In nursery plantings it is practical to spray trees with Karathane or Benlate for this disease. Individual specimens are rarely sprayed to control mildew.

Nonparasitic Disease

Dog Canker. Injury to trees planted along streets where it is customary to walk dogs is confined to the lower 2 feet of the trunk. Many trees up to 6 inches in diameter may be killed in this way. Placing a metal collar around trees visited by male dogs will help to eliminate cankers, but the dog's urine will still seep into the soil and root area to cause severe damage to the roots and premature death of the tree.

Insects

American Plum Borer (*Euzophera semifuneralis*). London planetrees, particularly streetside specimens whose bark has been damaged by leaf fires, are particularly susceptible to this pest. Damage to the inner bark and cambial regions by this larval stage, a dusky-white, pinkish, or dull brownish-green caterpillar, may be so extensive that the tree dies prematurely. Wild cherry, mountain-ash, and all kinds of fruit trees are also susceptible.

Control: Avoid damaging trees and keep them in good vigor by feeding and watering. Spray the main trunk with methoxychlor 3 times at 2-week intervals starting in mid-May.

Sycamore Lace Bug (*Corythucha ciliata*). London planetree is much more susceptible to this pest than sycamore. These bugs feed so extensively that the leaves are covered with light gray spots.

Control: Spray as soon as the eggs hatch on the leaves (about June 1 in the latitude of New York) with Diazinon, malathion, or Sevin. Some control is possible with a dormant spray applied just before growth begins in spring.

Other Insects. London planetrees may be attacked by other insects. These are discussed under *Platanus occidentalis.*

PLATANUS OCCIDENTALIS (SYCAMORE)

Diseases

Anthracnose (*Gnomonia platani*). The most serious fungus disease of sycamore is anthracnose. The first symptoms appear on the very young leaves as they unfold; they are apt to be overlooked or mistaken for frost injuries. At about the time that the leaves are becoming fully grown, light brown dead areas appear frequently along the veins. The spots may enlarge to include the whole leaf, which soon falls to the ground. The ends of the twigs to the length of 8 or 10 inches may also be killed, and either hang on the tree or fall to the ground with the dead leaves. Cankers may appear farther down on the young limbs (Fig. 191). They may develop also on rather

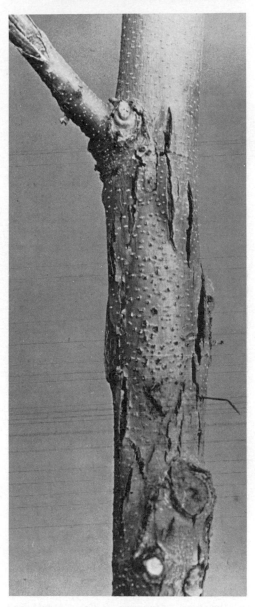

Fig. 191. Twig canker stage of sycamore anthracnose. Note fruiting bodies protruding from the bark. (Nassau County Co-op Extension Association)

large limbs, which are eventually killed, and unless pruned away are conspicuous even on large trees. Dead limb ends, several feet long, are not uncommon. Old leaves that are attacked show symptoms like the scorch frequently seen on maple trees along streets. The disease is spread rapidly by the spores developed on the leaves first infected.

The prevalence and severity of attack are governed mainly by weather conditions, frequent rains and cool temperatures favoring rapid spread. If the average temperature during the 2-week period following the emergence of the first leaves is below 55°F., the shoot blight stage of the disease will be very serious. If the average temperature is between 55 and 60°F., it will be less severe, and if it is over 60°F. no injury will occur.

Control: Control measures are rarely attempted on sycamores growing in open fields or in woodlands. They are justified, however, on particularly valuable specimens and on those used for shade and ornament.

All fallen leaves and twigs should be gathered and destroyed in autumn to destroy the overwintering mycelium, which produces spores for the following spring's infections. Infected spurs and dead twigs should be pruned whenever feasible and destroyed. To protect valuable specimens spray the leaves with maneb or zineb when the leaves unfurl, when the leaves reach full size, and again, 2 weeks later. Difolatan sprays also provide control.

Trees suffering from repeated attacks should be fertilized in the fall or the following spring to increase their vigor.

Other Diseases. Several diseases of minor importance include brown leaf spots caused by the fungi *Mycosphaerella platanifolia, Phyllosticta platani,* and *Septoria platanifolia.* These can be controlled by adopting the spray schedule suggested for the control of anthracnose.

In the South, a bark canker on sycamore is caused by the fungus *Botryodiplodia theobromae.*

Insects

Aphids (*Longistigma caryae*). The giant bark aphid, up to ¼ inch in length, frequently attacks the twigs of sycamore, and may gather in clusters on the undersides of the limbs. These insects are also called planetree aphids. They are the largest species of aphids known and exude great quantities of honeydew.

Another species, *Drepanosiphum platanoides,* infests maples in addition to sycamores throughout the country.

Control: Spray with Meta-Systox R, malathion, or Sevin.

Sycamore Plant Bug (*Plagiognathus albatus*). This bug in its adult stage, is ⅛ inch long, tan or brown in color, with dark eyes and brown spots on the wings. The young bugs are yellow-green, with conspicuous reddish-brown eyes. These pests suck out the plant juices on the upper sides of sycamore leaves, presumably leaving a poisonous material which results in yellowish or reddish spots. As the leaves grow, the injured areas drop out, leaving holes.

Control: Malathion sprays applied in early May and again 2 weeks later will control this insect.

Sycamore Tussock Moth (*Halisodota harrisii*). The caterpillar stage of this moth is yellow and has white to yellow hairs on its body. It occasionally becomes abundant on sycamores in the northeastern United States.

Four other species of tussock moths feed on the leaves of a wide variety of trees and shrubs. These are the pale tussock moth *Halisidota tessellaris;* the spotted *H. maculata;* the hickory *H. caryae;* and the Douglas-fir *Hemerocampa pseudotsugata.*

Control: Spray with Sevin or methoxychlor when the caterpillars are small.

Scales. Several species of scale insects, including black, cottony maple, grape, oystershell, sycamore, and terrapin, occasionally infest the sycamore and other species of *Platanus.*

Control: Malathion or Sevin sprays in late spring when the young scales are crawling about are effective. A dormant spray containing a "superior" type miscible oil should be applied in early spring where the infestations are unusually heavy.

Other Pests. *Platanus* species are infested by other pests including bagworms, borers, mites, whiteflies, root knot nema *Meloidogyne* sp., and several other species of parasitic nemas. These are discussed under more favored hosts.

PODOCARPUS

The only diseases recorded on this host are a root rot caused by the fungus *Clitocybe tabescens* and the burrowing nema *Rodopholus similis* in Florida. Nine species of scale insects have been recorded on *Podocarpus.*

PODOPHYLLUM (MAY-APPLE)

Diseases

Leaf Spots (*Cercospora podophylli, Glomerella cingulata, Pezizella oenotherae, Phyllosticta podophylli,* and *Septoria podophyllina*). Five species of fungi attack this host in nature. A few of them occasionally appear in shaded ornamental plantings of May-apple.

Control: Control measures are rarely used for leaf spots on this host.

Rust (*Puccinia podophylli*). A destructive rust of this host is very common on wild and cultivated *Podophyllum.* Large areas of the leaves turn yellowish in spots, and later brown. The leaves die because of the breaking out of the aecial stage of this rust, which superficially appears to be perennial. At least the rust appears on the new growth of early spring. The telial stage develops on the stems as well as on the leaves, breaking out in choc-olate-brown pustules. Complete eradication of the infected planting is necessary.

POINCIANA

Diseases

This tropical tree is subject to relatively few diseases. Perhaps the most destructive is dieback, caused by the fungus *Botryosphaeria dothidea.* Branches that show cankers should be pruned and destroyed.

Other diseases reported on this host are crown gall caused by the bacterium *Agrobacterium tumefaciens,* anthracnose by a fungus belonging to the genus *Gloeosporium,* a rust by the fungus *Ravenelia humphreyana,* and root rots by two fungi, *Clitocybe tabescens* and *Phymatotrichum omnivorum.*

Insect

Lesser Snow Scale (*Pinnaspis strachani*). The lesser snow scale frequently infests this host. The female is pear-shaped, white, semitransparent, sometimes speckled with brown. The male is narrow and white.

Control: Spray with malathion or Sevin to control the crawler stage.

POLEMONIUM

Diseases

Leaf Spots (*Cercospora omphakodes, Septoria polemonii,* and *S. polemoniicola*). Three leaf spot diseases are recorded on *Polemonium.*

Control: Control measures are rarely adopted. Pick and destroy spotted leaves.

Powdery Mildews (*Erysiphe cichoracearum* and *Sphaerotheca humuli*). In the western United States these mildews occur occasionally.

Control: As with leaf spots, control measures are rarely used.

Rusts (*Puccinia gulosa*, *P. polemonii*, and *Uromyces acuminatus* var. *polemonii*). Orange pustules on the leaves may be caused by any of these fungi.

Control: Destroy infected plants.

Wilt (*Verticillium albo-atum* and *Fusarium* sp.). These soil-inhabiting fungi have been reported to cause wilt of this host.

Control: As with most of the other diseases of this host, control measures are rarely warranted.

POLYGONUM AUBERTII (SILVER LACE-VINE)

The major problem on this host is Japanese beetle. Repeated applications of Sevin will control this pest.

Other species of *Polygonum* are important weeds in many parts of the country. They are subject to many diseases and insect pests.

POPULUS (POPLAR)

Diseases

Cytospora Canker (*Cytospora chrysosperma*). Carolina and silver-leaf poplars, particularly those low in vigor, are subject to this disease. Brown, sunken areas covered with numerous red pustules first appear on young twigs. The fungus moves down the stem and invades larger branches or even the trunk. The sexual stage of the causal fungus is known as *Valsa sordida*.

Control: Because cytospora canker is primarily a disease of weak trees, the most effective preventive is the maintenance of the trees in high vigor by fertilization, watering, and the control of insect and fungus parasites of the leaves. In addition, dead and dying branches should be removed and all unnecessary injuries avoided.

Poplar Canker (*Cryptodiaporthe populea*). The imperfect stage of the causal fungus is *Chondroplea populea*, previously known as *Dothichiza populea*. The disease appears as elongated, dark sunken cankers in the trunk, limbs, and twigs. The bark and cambium in the cankers are destroyed, and the sapwood is invaded and discolored. When the cankers completely girdle the trunks or branches, the distal portions die. Early in the growing season, the leaves may also be attacked by the fungus. Lombardy poplar, *P. nigra* var. *italica*, is by far the most susceptible species. Black and eastern cottonwoods and balsam, black and Norway poplars may also be affected.

Control: No effective control measures are known. Wounds of all sorts should be avoided. Pruning of diseased parts, as suggested for most canker diseases, does not appear to help control this disease; in fact, it often spreads it. Inasmuch as the leaves are attacked and the fungus enters the twigs through infected leaves, some investigators have recommended repeated applications of copper sprays to reduce leaf infections. As a rule, individual trees are not sufficiently valuable to justify four or more applications of a fungicide each year. Such a practice might be warranted, however, in nurseries where the disease threatens young stock. The only hope lies in the development of resistant varieties. The Japan poplar, *P. maximowiczii*, appears to show some resistance. Conflicting reports exist concerning the susceptibility of the Simon poplar, *P. simonii;* some persons assert that it is very resistant, others, that it is very susceptible.

Fusarium Canker (*Fusarium solani*). This disease occurs on *Populus deltoides* in the South, Middle West, and Canada.

Control: Control measures have not been developed.

Hypoxylon Canker (*Hypoxylon pruinatum*). Gray cankers of varying sizes appear along the trunk but never on the branches. The color changes to black as the outer bark falls away from the surface of the canker. Wefts of fungus tissue, resembling the chestnut blight fungus but different in color, are also visible beneath the peeled bark.

Control: This disease is so highly contagious and destructive that infected trees should be cut down and destroyed as soon as the diagnosis is confirmed. Injuries should be avoided as much as possible.

Septoria Canker (*Mycosphaerella populorum*). A leaf spot and stem canker of hybrid poplars and all species of native poplars is caused by this fungus. The asexual stage of this fungus is *Septoria musiva;* hence the common name for the disease. Fruit bodies of the *Septoria* stage are frequently found in the cankered areas.

Control: The most effective way of combating the canker stage of this disease is to use hybrid poplar clones that have proved to be naturally resistant. The leaf spot stage on ornamental poplars can probably be prevented by periodic applications of a copper fungicide.

Branch Gall (*Macrophoma tumefaciens*). Small globose galls up to $1\frac{1}{2}$ inches in diameter occasionally occur at the base of poplar twigs. Primarily the bark is hypertrophied, although some swelling of the woody tissues also occurs. Twigs and some branches may be killed, but the disease rarely becomes serious. Small, black, pinpoint fruiting bodies of the fungus are embedded in the bark of the gall, especially along the fissures.

Control: Pruning the galled branches and dead twigs to sound wood and destroying the removed wood are usually sufficient to hold the fungus in check.

Leaf Blister (*Taphrina aurea*). Brilliant yellow to brown blisters of varying sizes occasionally appear on poplar leaves after extended periods of cool, wet weather. Another species, *T. johansonii,* causes a deformity of the catkins.

Control: Spraying the trees in early spring with ferbam or ziram will control leaf blister. Such a practice is suggested only where particularly valuable specimens are involved.

Leaf Spots (*Ciborinia bifrons, C. confundens, Marssonina populi, Mycosphaerella populicola, Plagiostoma populi,* and *Phyllosticta alcides*). Many species of fungi, including *Mycosphaerella populorum* mentioned under the septoria canker disease, cause leaf spots of poplars. Of these, *Marssonina populi,* which produces brown spots with a darker brown margin and premature defoliation, is by far the most common. It also invades and kills the twigs.

Control: The first requisite in the control of leaf spot diseases is the gathering and destroying of all fallen leaves to remove an important source of inoculum. Poplars are rarely sprayed with fungicides, but Bordeaux or any other copper fungicide may be used early in the spring on valuable trees. Difolatan will also control leaf spots.

Leaf Rusts (*Melampsora medusae* and *M. abietis-canadensis*). Yellowish-orange pustules on the lower leaf surfaces are caused by these fungi. The alternate host of the former is larch, and that of the latter, hemlock.

Two other leaf rusts are caused by *Melampsora albertensis* and *M. occidentalis.*

Control: Leaf rusts rarely cause enough damage to necessitate special control measures.

Powdery Mildew (*Uncinula salicis*). This is a common superficial disease, appearing as a white mildew on both sides of the leaves; usually the damage is not serious.

Control: Spray with Karathane or Benlate if the specimens are valuable and the disease is serious.

Dieback (cause unknown). A dieback of the top and complete death of Lombardy poplar, cottonwood, and goat willow have been reported on trees in the vicinity of Washington, D. C., and in western Tennessee. On Lombardy poplar, the wood appears first water-soaked, then red, and finally brown. The tree dies when the entire cross-section of the trunk is stained brown. Although bacteria have been isolated from the margins of the discolored area, there is little evidence that they are the primary cause. There is a strong possibility that the water-soaked appearance and the subsequent staining actually result from extremely low winter temperatures and that the bacteria enter after the injury occurs.

Insects

Aphids (*Pemphigus populitransverus* and *Mordwilkoja vagabunda*). The former produces galls on the leaf petioles of certain poplars; the latter is responsible for convoluted galls at the tips of twigs.

Several other species of leaf-infesting aphids occur on this host.

Control: Valuable ornamental specimens can be sprayed with lime sulfur when the trees are dormant, or with Meta-Systox R, Sevin, or malathion just as the leaves unfurl in early spring.

Bronze Birch Borer (*Agrilus anxius*). Weakened trees are always more susceptible than vigorous trees to attack by the bronze birch borer. Branches are girdled and the upper parts of the tree die back as a result of feeding by the borer, a white, legless larva $3/4$ inch long. The adult beetle, which appears in June and feeds on the leaves for a short time, is $1/2$ inch long and bronze in color. The female deposits eggs in bark crevices in June.

Control: Spray the leaves, trunk, and branches with methoxychlor in early June, and repeat in 3 weeks. Remove and destroy severely infested parts. Water important trees during drought periods.

Poplar Borer (*Saperda calcarata*). Blackened and swollen scars on the limbs and trunk and sawdust at the base of the tree usually result from attack by the poplar borer, a white larva $1^{1}/4$ to $1^{1}/2$ inches long when full grown. The upper and lower parts of the larva's body have horny points. The adult female is a reddish brown beetle slightly over 1 inch in length, with black spots and yellow stripes.

Control: Remove and destroy badly infested trees. Spraying the trees with methoxychlor several times at 2-week intervals, starting in late July, may be justified for valuable trees.

Red-Humped Caterpillar (*Schizura concinna*). The leaves are chewed by clusters of red-humped caterpillars, yellow and black striped forms with red heads and red humps. The adult, a grayish-brown moth with a wingspread of $1^{1}/4$ inches, deposits masses of eggs on the lower leaf surfaces in July. Winter is passed in a cocoon on the ground.

Control: Spray with *Bacillus thuringiensis* or Sevin when the caterpillars are small.

Poplar Tent Maker (*Ichthyura inclusa*). The leaves are chewed and silken nests appear on twigs as a result of infestations of the tent maker, a black larva with pale yellow stripes, which attains a length of $1^{1}/4$ inches at maturity. The adult female is a moth with white-striped gray wings. The pupae overwinter in fallen leaves.

Control: Remove and destroy nests or spray with *Bacillus thuringiensis* or Sevin when the larvae are small.

Satin Moth (*Stilpnotia salicis*). The larval stage, black with conspicuous irregular white blotches, feeds on the leaves of poplar, willow and sometimes on oaks in late April or May. The adult, satin-white and with a wing expanse up to 2 inches, emerges in July.

Control: Spray with Sevin in early June and again in early August.

Scales. Many species of scale insects infest poplars. Among these are black, cottony maple, European fruit lecanium, greedy, lecanium, oystershell, San Jose, soft, terrapin, walnut, and willow.

Control: Valuable specimens infested with scales should be sprayed with lime sulfur or miscible oil in early spring just before growth starts, or with malathion or Sevin in mid-May and again in mid-June to control the crawler stage.

Imported Willow Leaf Beetle (*Plagiodera*

versicolora). Holes are chewed in the leaves by the willow leaf beetle, the metallic-blue adult form, ¹/₈ inch long; and the leaves are skeletonized by the black larvae, which are ¹/₄ inch long. The adult lives through the winter and deposits eggs on the lower leaf surface in the spring.

Control: Spray with methoxychlor or Sevin after the eggs hatch in late May or early June.

PORTULACA (PURSLANE)

Diseases

White Rust (*Albugo portulacae*). Swollen and badly formed branches and leaves bear white pustules of the fungus. Shoots tend to become more erect and spindling.

Control: See *Arabis.*

Other Diseases. This host is also subject to damping-off caused by the fungus *Pellicularia filamentosa* and to curly top by the beet curly top virus.

Insects and Other Animal Pests

White-Lined Sphinx Moth (*Hyles lineata*). The larval stage of this moth is green with a yellow head and horn and is about 3¹/₂ inches long at maturity. It feeds on a wide variety of other plants as well.

Control: Spray with Sevin when the young larvae begin to feed.

Southern Root-Knot Nema (*Meloidogyne incognita*). This eelworm occasionally infests the roots of *Portulaca.* For control, see Chapter 3.

POTENTILLA (CINQUEFOIL)

Diseases

In nature and in ornamental plantings this host is subject to a downy mildew caused by *Peronospora potentillae;* four leaf spots by *Marssonina potentillae, Fabraea dehnii,*

Phyllosticta anserinae, and *Ramularia arvensis;* two powdery mildews by *Erysiphe polygoni* and *Sphaerotheca humuli;* and a leaf rust by *Phragmidium andersonii.*

Insects

Two insects occur on this host, the rose aphid, *Macrosiphum rosae,* and the strawberry weevil, *Anthonomus signatus.*

PRIMULA (PRIMROSE)

Diseases

Bacterial Leaf Spot (*Pseudomonas primulae*). Irregular, circular spots surrounded by a yellowish halo characterize this disease. If one cuts through a spot with a sharp knife and examines the cut surface with a microscope, masses of bacteria can be seen oozing out. The spots are small and water-soaked at first with a yellowish center. They are from ¹/₈ to ¹/₄ inch in diameter. They may run together so as to kill large areas of the leaf. Many varieties of *Primula* have been proved susceptible, while others appear fairly resistant. Older leaves seem more susceptible.

Control: Avoid spreading bacteria from plant to plant by watering or syringing. Severe outbreaks can probably be curbed with copper fungicides or with Agrimycin.

Anthracnose (*Colletotrichum primulae*). Infected leaves in greenhouse culture become spotted and turn brown. The spore pustules are characterized by black, spiny hairs mixed with the spores and extending above the fruiting structure.

Control: Spray with zineb.

Leaf Spot (*Phyllosticta primulicola*). Spots appear on the leaves, grayish or brown with lighter-colored borders marked by numerous black fruiting bodies of the fungus. They often spread to become blotches on the leaves, which may later be destroyed.

Control: Spray with zineb or a copper fungicide if the disease appears in garden plantings.

Other Leaf Spotting Fungi. Primroses are subject to several other leaf spotting fungi: *Ascochyta primulae, Cercosporella primulae,* and *Ramularia primulae.* The last causes yellowish blotches on the leaves with ash-colored centers. It is often serious on varieties of *Primula* grown in rock gardens. These leaf spots are controlled with copper or dithiocarbamate fungicides.

Root Rot (*Pythium irregulare* and *Pellicularia filamentosa*). The former is particularly serious in commercial greenhouses on the West Coast, where it causes root rot of plants that are in full bloom as well as of seedlings.

Control: Avoid excessive watering and use clean soil for planting. The former fungus can be eliminated by drenching infested soil with Dexon; the latter, by drenching with Benlate. Follow the manufacturer's directions.

Rusts (*Puccinia aristidae* and *Uromyces apiosporus*). Two species of fungi produce yellow to orange rusty pustules on the leaves of primroses.

Control: Severe outbreaks can be prevented by spraying with zineb.

Other Diseases. Another crown rot and leaf blight which frequently appears in eastern greenhouses is caused by *Botrytis cinerea,* especially where plants are heavily watered and kept in rather cool houses. Often associated with this rot are many millipedes (*Orthomorpha gracilis*), which must be attracted to the plants by the rotting roots and crowns (see Fig. 88). In watering primulas, avoid wetting the leaves and crowns. Space the plants far enough apart to give them plenty of air.

Stem rots caused by a species of *Alternaria* and by *Sclerotinia sclerotiorum,* and a powdery mildew by *Erysiphe polygoni* are other fungus diseases of primrose.

Viruses. Two important virus diseases occur on *Primula:* mosaic caused by the cucumber mosaic virus, and spotted wilt by the tomato spotted wilt virus. Mosaic-infected plants have yellow and dark green mottling of the leaves, which should not be confused with the yellowish or whitish mottling of the leaves due to overmanuring or the excessive use of chemical fertilizer.

Control: Remove and destroy infected plants. Spray with malathion or Sevin to control insects such as aphids and leafhoppers, which are known to spread these viruses.

Aster Yellows. This disease also occurs on *Primula.*

Control: Same as for virus diseases.

Physiological Disease

Like many other plants grown under unfavorable conditions, too much moisture or a deficiency or excess of certain elements causes a mottling and bleaching of the leaves. Such diseases resemble the mosaic caused by viruses or the sumptoms of invasion by certain fungi. Some varieties of *Primula* are more susceptible to injury then others.

Chlorosis, or leaf yellowing, due to a lack or unavailability of iron can often be corrected by the application of ferrous sulfate or iron chelates to the soil.

Insects and Other Animal Pests

Aphids. Four species of aphids infest the leaves of *Primula:* cowpea, foxglove, green peach, and crescent-marked lily. The latter breeds on *Primula obconica* in greenhouses on the West Coast and transmits the mosaic virus.

Control: Spray with malathion, Meta-Systox R, or Sevin.

Corn Root Aphid (*Aphis maidiradicis*). This aphid, which feeds on the roots, has been reported as doing considerable damage to *Primula.* It causes the leaves to turn yellowish and the plants to develop very poorly.

Control: Soak the soil around the base of

infested plants with a weak solution of Diazinon or malathion.

Beetles. Four species of beetles may attack this host: fuller rose, potato flea, steel-blue flea, and strawberry flea.

Control: Spray with Sevin when the beetles appear.

Mealybugs. The long-tailed and the yucca mealybugs may infest *Primula.* Malathion sprays are effective against these pests.

Two-Spotted Mite (*Tetranychus urticae*). This mite causes the foliage of outdoor primroses to turn yellow in summer.

Control: Spray with chlorobenzilate, Kelthane, Meta-Systox R, or Tedion in June before the leaves turn yellow. Direct the spray to the lower leaf surfaces. Repeat in 10 days if necessary.

Slugs. (*Limax flavis, L. maximus*). Naked snails which eat holes in the foliage and leave a slimy trail are found on rock-garden primroses.

Control: Dust the soil where slugs are prevalent with 15 per cent metaldehyde powder. Zectran and Mesurol are also effective in combating slugs.

Black Vine Weevil (*Otiorhynchus sulcatus*). This black snout beetle, about $3/8$ inch long, attacks *Primula* as well as many other plants. The larvae feed on the roots, especially the smaller roots; they tunnel through the larger roots and finally invade the crown. They are often abundant in the greenhouse during the winter. The plants are weakened and many are killed.

Control: Infested greenhouse potting soil should be heat-treated to destroy the larvae. Sprays containing Sevin applied to the leaves will help to control the adult weevils.

Nemas (*Ditylenchus dipsaci* and *Meloidogyne incognita*). The bulb and stem nema and the southern root-knot nema occasionally infest *Primula.* See Chapter 3 for control measures.

PRUNUS AMYGDALUS (ALMOND)

A number of ornamental forms of almond exist. These are subject to many of the diseases and pests of other members of the genus *Prunus* discussed below.

PRUNUS BESSEYI
(WESTERN SAND-CHERRY)

Diseases

Blossom Blight and **Brown Rot** (*Monilinia fructicola*). Blossoms are blighted, and the leaves turn brown and die at the tips of twigs when affected by this disease. The dead portions are usually covered with masses of powdery, brown fungus spores. The edible fruit of this shrub, also known as Hansen's Bush Cherry, may also be infected.

Control: Prune and destroy infected twigs and branches. During wet springs, particularly if the disease was prevalent the previous year, spray with captan or Benlate just before the blossoms open and again 10 days later.

PRUNUS LAUROCERASUS
(CHERRY-LAUREL)

Diseases

Bacterial Leaf Spot (*Xanthomonas pruni*). See *Prunus serrulata.*

Leaf Spots (*Cercospora circumscissa, C. cladosporioides, Coccomyces lutescens, Phyllachora beaumontii, Phyllosticta laurocerasi,* and *Septoria ravenelii*). Many species of fungi cause leaf spots of this host. Some of the fungi listed above also affect the Catalina cherry, *P. lyonii,* and the holly-leaved cherry, *P. ilicifolia.*

Control: Valuable specimens may be protected with copper or dithiocarbamate sprays.

Twig Blight (*Monilinia fructicola*). The fungus discussed under *Prunus Besseyi* may cause a wilting of the twig tips on this host.

Control: Prune and discard diseased branch tips. Important plants can be protected by Benlate or captan sprays.

Other Diseases. A root rot caused by the fungus *Clitocybe tabescens* in Florida and a wilt by *Verticillium albo-atrum* in California are other diseases reported on this host.

Insect

Whitefly (*Dialeurodes citri*). The citrus whitefly infests this host in the southern United States.
Control: See *Fuchsia.*

PRUNUS MARITIMA (BEACH PLUM)

This host is extremely susceptible to a disease known as "plum pockets" caused by the fungus *Taphrina communis.* Fruits become enlarged, sometimes ten times the size of normal ones. Copper fungicides applied in spring before flower buds open will control this disease.

The plum curculio *Conotrachelus nenuphar,* the plum gouger *Coccotorus scutellaris,* and the plum rust mite *Aculus fockeui* also infest this host.

PRUNUS PERSICA (PEACH)

Varieties of peach grown for ornament are subject to all the diseases and insect pests that affect those grown for their fruits. The following are among the more common problems.

Disease

Leaf Curl (*Taphrina deformans*). When this fungus is involved, the leaves appear much thickened and individual leaves are puffed and folded with the edges curled inward. The affected leaves acquire red or purplish tints.
Control: Spray either with ziram or ferbam in late fall after the leaves drop or in the spring before buds open.

Insects

Green Peach Aphid (*Myzus persicae*). This insect has been found to be very injurious during the summer to a number of varieties of flowering peach and related ornamentals.
Control: Spray with malathion, Meta-Systox R, or Sevin when the insects first appear and repeat a week later if necessary.

Black Peach Aphid (*Brachycaudus persicae*). This aphid is common on commercial plantings of peaches.
Control: Same as for the green peach aphid.

Peach Tree Borer (*Sanninoidea exitiosa*). The grubs of the peach borer cause a great amount of damage to flowering peach as well as to related forms, frequently causing death of the trees. The damage is marked by profuse gummosis at the crown and on the main roots just below the surface of the soil. The trees fail to grow properly and the leaves turn yellowish. The frass or borings of the grubs becomes mixed with the gum. If one follows down the burrow with a chisel or a penknife, white flat grubs from $1/2$ to 1 inch long with brown heads may be found.
Control: The grubs must be removed from young trees by hand-grubbing; that is, the ground should be pulled back from the base of the tree and the grubs dug out with the aid of a grubbing chisel or other implement with a curved blade. The burrows should be followed down until the grubs are found. Young trees up to 3 years old should be examined twice a year. In trees over 3 years old the grubs can be controlled by the use of paradichlorobenzene (PDB). The soil should be dug away from the base of the tree to the depth of 3 inches and the cavity leveled off. For trees 3 years old, apply $1/2$ to $3/4$ ounce of the fumigant in a circle around the base of the tree.

For older trees use 1 to 1½ ounces. The soil is then replaced in the hole and mounded around the base. While paradichlorobenzene may be applied during the summer, it is safer to use it in late September or October. If it is applied earlier in the summer, the soil should be removed about 1 month or 6 weeks later. If it is allowed to remain too long in the soil during hot weather, injury is likely, especially to young trees.

Spraying or painting the trunk with methoxychlor in early July and repeating three times at 2-week intervals is a good preventive treatment. Dursban applications also provide control.

Lesser Peach Tree Borer (*Synanthedon pictipes*). This borer attacks growing tissue anywhere in the trunk from the ground to the main branches. The eggs are laid mainly in cracks of the trunk. Other species of *Prunus* also are attacked.

Control: The adult female of this borer begins to deposit eggs earlier than does the peach tree borer. Hence the methoxychlor applications should be started by mid-June. The insecticide should be applied to the main branches as well as to the main trunk.

White Peach Scale (*Pseudaulacaspis pentagona*). Where flowering peaches and close relatives are planted in parks near the Japanese cherry, the trees may be infested with same scale insect.

Control: Spray in mid-June with Diazinon, methoxychlor, or Sevin to control the crawler stage.

PRUNUS SERRULATA, P. YEDOENSIS, AND RELATED SPECIES (JAPANESE FLOWERING CHERRIES)

Bacterial and Fungus Diseases

Shot-hole (*Xanthomonas pruni*). The bacterium that attacks peaches and cherries in orchards is known to attack Japanese cherries also, causing a familiar "shot-hole" ap-

pearance. The infected tissue dries up and falls out, leaving a hole about 1/8 inch in diameter. Shot-holes in cherry leaves may be also due to the fungus *Coccomyces hiemalis*, discussed below, and to virus infection.

Control: Where the *Xanthomonas* bacterium causes serious damage to flowering cherries, spray with Cyprex, mentioned under leaf spot.

Leaf Spot (*Coccomyces hiemalis*). During rainy springs this disease is rather prevalent. The reddish spots on the leaves drop out, leaving circular holes in the leaves. Complete defoliation may follow the appearance of "shot-hole."

Control: Benlate, captan, Cyprex, or ferbam sprays will control this rather prevalent disease. The first application should be made when the flower petals fall followed by two more applications at 2-week intervals.

Black Knot (*Apiosporina morbosa*). Black, rough cylindrical shaped galls (Fig. 192) develop on the twigs of apricots, cherries, and plums. Neglected trees are especially subject to this disease.

Control: Prune knotted twigs and excise knots on large branches during the winter. Then spray with ferbam or zineb when the trees are dormant and at pink bud, full bloom stages, and 3 weeks later.

Powdery Mildew (*Podosphaera oxyacanthae*). The Japanese cherry is subject to the same powdery mildew that attacks the edible cherries. The leaves and twigs become coated with a mat of fungus growth, which causes dwarfing and death of these branches. The disease is uncommon.

Control: Acti-dione PM, Benlate, or Karathane sprays will control this disease.

Witches' Broom (*Taphrina cerasi*). *Prunus yedoensis* seems to be rather susceptible to this disease. Large branches will sometimes become deformed by development of many dwarfed, irregular branches to form a witches' broom (Fig. 18). The blossoms develop and the leaves come out on the brooms

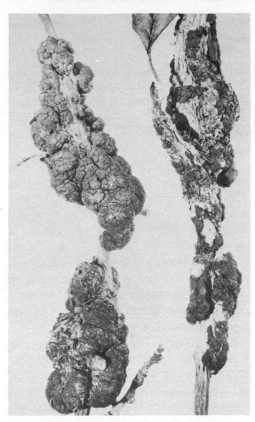

Fig. 192. Black knot of cherry caused by the fungus *Apiosporina morbosum*.

earlier than on the normal branches. Sometimes large numbers of very small brooms develop all over the tree, killing the end-branches and eventually the whole tree.

Control: Cut off and destroy the brooms. Spray with Ziram or ferbam in the fall or in early spring.

Virus Disease

Normal-appearing Japanese cherries of the varieties Kwanzan and Shiro-fugen have been found to carry a virus of the Little Cherry type. This fact is important only to cherry virus research workers who use flowering cherries for test plants.

Physiological Disease

Yellowing. Very often yellowing and premature defoliation of flowering cherry occur without previous spotting of the leaves. These symptoms are associated with excessively wet or dry soils or with low-temperature injuries to the crown and roots. As a rule, a second set of leaves is formed after the premature defoliation in the spring or early summer. The new leaves are normal to all appearances.

Insects and Other Animal Pests

Waterlily Aphid (*Rhopalosiphum nymphaeae*). Ornamental species of *Prunus* grown near waterlily ponds are seriously attacked by the waterlily aphid. The insects migrate to the trees in May and June and in autumn.

Control: Spray with malathion or Sevin when the insects appear on the leaves.

Asiatic Garden Beetle (*Maladera castanea*). The leaves are chewed during the night by a brown beetle 1/4 inch long. During the day, the insect hides just below the soil surface.

Control: Sevin sprays will keep this pest in check.

Planthoppers (*Metcalfa pruinosa* and *Anormensis septentrionalis*). These planthoppers injure shrubs and trees by sucking the juices of the more tender branches, which they cover with a woolly substance. One species is illustrated in Fig. 193.

Control: Apply sprays containing pyrethrum or rotenone, or a combination of the two, forcefully enough to wet the insects thoroughly.

Oriental Fruit Worm (*Graphiolitha molesta*). Wilting of the tips of twigs may be due to boring by the oriental fruit worm, a small pinkish-white larva about ½ inch long. The adult female is about ½ inch long and is gray

Fig. 193. Planthopper *(Anormensis septentrionalis)* on cherry branch.

americanum). Wild cherries are the natural hosts of the tent caterpillar (Figs. 194 and 195). Unless the plants are valued as ornamentals, they should be destroyed. When the caterpillar occurs on Japanese cherry, it can be controlled by spraying the tree with *Bacillus thuringiensis,* Dylox, methoxychlor, or Sevin as soon as the caterpillars appear in spring.

Other Pests. Flowering cherries may also be infested by Japanese beetle, peach tree borer, lesser peach borer, and many species of scales.

Root Nemas *(Pratylenchus penetrans).* Research at the New York State Experiment Station revealed that this nema attacks the roots of edible cherry trees. It is possible that the roots of Japanese flowering cherries are also susceptible to the same nema.

with chocolate-brown markings on the wings. Larvae overwinter in the soil.

Control: If only a few trees are involved, removal and destroying of wilted tips as they appear is usually sufficient. Large numbers of trees can be protected by periodic applications of methoxychlor sprays to which a mite killer such as Kelthane has been added, starting as soon as the leaves begin to emerge and repeating twice at 10- to 12-day intervals.

Pear-Slug *(Caliroa cerasi).* These so-called slugs, olive-green, semi-transparent, and slimy, are the larvae of a sawfly. They are about ½ inch long, swollen at the front, and shaped somewhat like a tadpole (Fig. 91). They occasionally infest *Prunus* and may completely skeletonize the leaves. There are two generations a year in the northern states and three in the southern.

Control: Spray with malathion when the slugs begin to feed.

Eastern Tent Caterpillar *(Malacosoma*

PRUNUS TRILOBA (FLOWERING ALMOND)

Diseases

Blossom Blight and Dieback *(Monilinia fructicola).* This disease, already mentioned under other species of *Prunus,* causes serious damage to flowering almond. Leaves turn brown and entire branches wilt.

Control: See *Prunus besseyi.*

Leaf Drop. Bordeaux mixture and some of the fixed copper fungicides will cause defoliation of flowering almond, peach, and some other members of the genus *Prunus.* Hence they are not recommended as treatment for these hosts.

Other Diseases. Flowering almond is susceptible to bacterial fire blight caused by *Erwinia amylovora,* bacterial leaf spot by *Xanthomonas pruni,* powdery mildew by the fungus *Podosphaera oxyacanthae,* root rot by fungus *Armillaria mellea* and mosaic by a virus.

Fig. 194 *(Inset).*   Egg masses of eastern tent caterpillar.
Fig. 195.   Eastern tent caterpillar *(Malacosoma americanum)* on wild cherry.

PSEUDOTSUGA TAXIFOLIA
(DOUGLAS-FIR)

Diseases

Cankers (*Cytospora* sp., *Dasyscypha ellisiana, D. pseudotsugae, Phacidiopycnis pseudotsugae,* and *Phomopsis lokoyae*). A number of fungi cause cankers on this host, most of them being prevalent in the Pacific Northwest.

Control: Control measures are rarely practiced except on important ornamental specimens.

Leaf Cast (*Rhabdocline pseudotsugae*). Yellow spots first appear near the needle tips in fall. The spots enlarge in spring, then turn reddish-brown, contrasting sharply with adjacent green tissues. With continued moist weather, the discoloration spreads until the entire needle turns brown. When many groups of needles are so affected, the trees have a brown, scorched aspect as viewed from a distance.

Two other fungi produce leaf cast of Douglas-fir: *Adelopus gaumanni* and *Rhabdogloeum hypophyllum.* The former produces symptoms closely resembling those of *Rhabdocline pseudotsugae,* and both may be present in the same tree.

Control: No control measures for large trees have been reported. Severe outbreaks in nurseries or on small trees can probably be prevented by spraying with copper fungicides at the time the spores are being discharged.

Other Diseases. Douglas-fir is susceptible to a leaf and twig blight caused by the fungus *Botrytis cinerea,* which is serious in wet springs; rust by the fungus *Melampsora albertensis* the alternate stage of which occurs on *Populus,* needle blight by *Rosellinia herpotrichioides,* and witches' broom by the mistletoe *Arceuthobium douglassii.*

The fungus *Dermea pseudotsugae* causes a dieback and death of young Douglas-firs in northern California. Controls have not been developed.

Insects

Aphids (*Adelges cooleyi* and *Essigella californica*). The former, the Cooley spruce gall aphid, is more common on *Picea;* the latter, the Monterey pine aphid, infests Monterey and ponderosa pines on the West Coast.

Control: The Cooley spruce gall aphid is controlled by a dormant oil spray applied in April when the trees are still dormant or with a Sevin spray in May. Nurserymen use either Endosulfan or Baygon sprays to control this pest. The Monterey pine aphid can be controlled with Sevin or malathion sprays in April and May.

Scales. Two scale insects, hemlock and pine needle, infest Douglas-fir. Malathion or Sevin sprays are very effective against the young crawler stage of these pests.

Other Insects. This host is also subject to the spruce budworm, the pine butterfly, the Zimmerman pine moth, and the strawberry root weevil. The controls for these pests are discussed under more favored hosts.

PSIDIUM GUAJAVA (GUAVA)

Diseases

In Florida this host is subject to a leaf and fruit spot caused by the fungus *Glomerella cingulata,* a thread blight by *Pellicularia koleroga,* a leaf spot by *Cercospora psidii,* and a root rot by *Clitocybe tabescens.*

Insects and Other Animal Pests

Scales. Nine species of scale insects infest guavas: barnacle, black, chaff, Florida red, Florida wax, greedy, green shield, hemispherical, and soft.

Control: Spray with malathion or Sevin to control the crawler stage of these pests.

Other Insects. Occasionally guava is attacked by the Mexican fruit fly, *Anastrepha ludens;* the long-tailed mealybug, *Pseudococ-*

cus longispinus, and the eastern subterranean termite, *Reticulitermes flaviceps.*

Southern Root-Knot Nema (*Meloidogyne incognita*). This nema infests guava roots in Florida. See Chapter 3 for control.

PTELEA (HOP-TREE)

Diseases

Leaf Spots (*Cercospora afflata, C. pteleae, Phleospora pteleae, Phyllosticta pteleicola,* and *Septoria pteleae*). These five species of fungi cause leaf spots on hop-tree.

Control: Pick off and destroy spotted leaves. Other control measures are rarely necessary.

Rust (*Puccinia windsoriae*). This fungus occasionally occurs on hop-tree. The alternate stage of the fungus is found on grasses. No controls are required.

Root Rot (*Phymatotrichum omnivorum*). Control measures have not been developed.

Fig. 196. Treehopper *(Enchenopa binotata)* egg masses on *Ptelea.*

Insects

Two-Marked Treehopper (*Enchenopa binotata*). These little sucking insects, ⅛ inch or slightly more in length, with a long, proboscis-like head portion, resemble miniature quail or partridges; they are dark brown in color with two white spots. When disturbed the insects jump very rapidly from place to place. They secrete honeydew. The egg-masses are covered by a snow-white frothy substance (shown in Fig. 196) like that secreted by spittle insects but much firmer in consistency. From a distance infested branches appear like those infested with woolly aphids or cottony-cushion scale.

Control: Spray with malathion or with a pyrethrum-rotenone compound.

White Peach Scale. See *Prunus persica.*

PYRACANTHA (FIRETHORN)

Diseases

Bacterial Fire Blight (*Erwinia amylovora*). This disease, although most common on apples and pears, also attacks firethorn. New shoots may wilt suddenly in late spring, turn black or brown, and die. The dead leaves hang downward on the affected twigs. *P. angustifolia* and *P. koidzumii* are quite susceptible, whereas *P. crenulata* is moderately susceptible.

Control: Plant resistant varieties or species such as *P. coccinea* var. *lalandii* or *P. fortuneana.* Prune out diseased branches of susceptible plants and spray with an antibiotic such as Agri-Strep when 25 per cent of the blossoms are open and at 5-to-10 day intervals during bloom.

Scab (*Fusicladium pyracanthae*). This disease closely resembles that known by the same name on apples, the name being derived from the scabby lesions produced on the fruits. The leaves are first covered with dark sooty areas. They soon turn yellow, then brown, and finally drop prematurely. Scabby lesions also often occur on the twigs. The Yunan firethorn, *Pyracantha crenato-sessata*, is said to be resistant to this disease.

Control: Spray with Benlate, ferbam or zineb starting when the buds break in spring and repeating twice at 10-day intervals.

Other Diseases. This host is also subject to twig blight caused by *Diplodia crataegi*, leaf blight by *Fabraea maculata*, canker by *Botryosphaeria dothidea*, and root rot by the fungi *Armillaria mellea* and *Phymatotrichum omnivorum*. Most of these are discussed under more favored hosts.

Insects

The insect pests of firethorn include the apple aphid, *Aphis pomi;* the hawthorn lace bug, *Corythucha cydoniae;* the greedy scale, *Hemiberlesia rapax;* the olive scale, *Parlatoria oleae;* and the calico scale, *Lecanium cerasorum.*

Control: Diazinon, malathion, or Sevin sprays will control these pests.

QUERCUS (OAK)

Fungus Diseases

Anthracnose (*Gnomonia quercina*). This fungus, whose asexual stage is *Gloeosporium quercinum*, is rather common in the northern states on white and red oaks, American elm, and black walnut. Rainy weather favors the disease, and may cause defoliation. Weak trees, if defoliated, frequently die. The spots on the leaves run together, causing the appearance of a leaf blotch or blight. The dead areas follow the veins or are bounded by the larger veins. These blotches are light brown. Infection may occur in midsummer.

Control: Three applications of maneb or zineb sprays will control this disease; the first when the leaves unfurl, the second when the leaves reach full size, and the third, 2 weeks later. Difolatan sprays also provide control.

Basal Canker (*Phaeobulgaria inquinans*). This fungus frequently develops in crevices of the sunken bark that overlies basal cankers. It enters through open wounds but then invades the surrounding bark and sapwood and eventually girdles and kills the tree. The mature fruit bodies are cup- or saucer-shaped and grow from short stems that extend into the bark. When moist, the fruiting bodies look and feel like rubber.

Control: Same as for the canker disease described below.

Canker (*Strumella coryneoidea*). Although primarily a disease of forest oaks, canker occasionally affects red and scarlet oaks in ornamental plantings. American beech, chestnut, red maple, tupelo, and pignut and shagbark hickories are also susceptible. Several types of cankers, depending on the age of the tree and the rate of growth of the causal fungus, are produced on the trunks. Smooth-surfaced, diffuse, slightly sunken cankers are common on young trees with a diameter of 3 to 4 inches. Cankers on older trees have a rough surface ridged with callus tissue. Open wounds may be present in the center of large cankers as a result of secondary decay and shedding of the bark.

Cankers on red oaks were found to be caused by the fungus *Fusarium solani*, those on *Quercus prinus* by a species of *Botryodiplodia*, and those on live oaks (*Quercus virginiana*) by *Endothia gyrosa*, *Hypoxylon atropunctatum*, *H. mediterranium*, *Fusarium* spp., and *Polyporus hispidus.*

Control: Prune dying and dead branches to eliminate an important possible source of inoculum. Remove small cankers on the trunk by surgical means, and fertilize and water the trees to improve their vigor.

Leaf Blister (*Taphrina coerulescens*). During cool, wet springs almost all species of oaks are subject to the leaf blister disease. Circular, raised areas ranging up to ½ inch in diameter are scattered over the upper leaf surfaces, causing a depression of the same size on the lower surfaces. The upper surface of the bulge is yellowish-white, and the lower, yellowish-brown. The leaves remain attached to the tree, and there is rarely any noticeable impairment of their functions.

Control: A single application at bud-swelling time in spring of any of the following fungicides, applied with a power sprayer so as to coat buds and twigs thoroughly, will give control: captan, Fore, maneb, or zineb. Dilute as directed by the manufacturer.

Leaf Spots (*Cylindrosporium microspilum, Dothiorella phomiformis, Gloeosporium septorioides, G. quercinum, G. umbrinellum, Leptothyrium dryinum, L. californicum, Marssonina martini, M. quercus, Microstroma album, Monochaetia monochaeta, Phyllosticta tumericola, P. livida, Septogloeum quercum, Septoria quercus,* and *S. quercicola*). Like most other trees, oaks are subject to a number of leaf spot diseases. These rarely cause much damage to the trees, inasmuch as they become numerous rather late in the growing season.

Control: Gathering and destroying all fallen leaves is usually sufficient to keep down most outbreaks in seasons of normal rainfall. Valuable oaks may be protected by several applications of copper or zineb sprays at 2-week intervals, starting in early spring when the leaves unfold.

Powdery Mildew. In the southern and western states *Sphaerotheca lanestris* is the most troublesome mildew-producer. It forms a white mealy growth on the undersides of the leaves; this later turns brown. The entire surface of the leaf, as well as the tip ends of the twigs, may be covered with the brown felt-like mycelium.

Other powdery mildew fungi affecting oaks include *Erysiphe trina, Microsphaera alni,* and *Phyllactinia corylea.*

Control: Leaf-infecting powdery mildew fungi can be controlled with Acti-dione PM, Benlate, or Karathane.

Rust (*Cronatrium quercuum*). The alternate hosts of this fungus are species of pine, such as *P. rigida* and *P. banksiana,* to which some damage is done by the development of gall-like growths. On oak leaves small yellowish spots first appear on the undersides; later brown, bristle-like horns of spores develop. Little damage is done to the oak; hence no control has been found necessary.

Twig Blights (*Coryneum kunzei, Diplodia longispora, Physalospora glandicola, P. obtusa, P. rhodina, Pseudovalsa longipes, Sphaeropsis quercina,* and *S. malorum*). Most of the fungi winter over in dead twigs and in cankers on larger branches. During rainy weather of the following spring, spores in large numbers ooze from the dead areas and are splashed onto young shoots and into bark injuries, where they germinate and cause new infections.

Control: During summer, prune infected twigs and branches to sound wood. As a rule, cutting to about 6 inches below the visibly infected area will ensure the removal of all fungus-infected tissue in the wood. In severely weakened trees, considerably more tissue must be removed, inasmuch as the fungus may penetrate down the branch for a distance of 2 or more feet.

Valuable trees should be fertilized and watered and their foliage covered with a combination spray containing methoxychlor and a copper fungicide to destroy leaf chewing insects and prevent infections by leaf spotting fungi.

Wilt (*Ceratocystis fagacearum*). This highly publicized disease of oaks in recent years is causing some concern to arborists, foresters, nurserymen, and tree owners in the Middle West. Affected trees have curled, drooping, brown leaves and at times a black or brown discoloration of the sapwood. Diseased trees usually die within a year of infection. The disease is spread by root grafts and by several insects and related pests, including fruit flies, Nitidulid beetles, the flatheaded borer, *Chrysobothris femorata,* and the mite *Garmania bulbicola.* This fungus has also been recovered from a species of bark beetle and from the two-lined chestnut borer. Recently two species of oak bark beetles, *Pseudopityophthorus minutissimus* and *P. pruinosa,* were also found capable of carrying the oak wilt fungus. Tools and climbing spurs used by lumberjacks, foresters, or arborists are other ways by which the fungus is spread. Squirrels are also believed to be vectors. Tree species belonging to the red oak group appear to be the most susceptible whereas the white oak is markedly resistant. In nature the fungus has been found on Chinese chestnuts and related genera, and it has been transmitted experimentally to a wide variety of trees, including apple.

Control: No effective control is known. For the present, eradication and destruction of infected specimens is being advocated.

Where diseased trees are not removed and destroyed, infection centers develop. Ammate applied to such trees results in the reduction of fungus inoculum available for spread via root grafts or root-inhabiting insects. Because the oak wilt fungus appears to be most infectious early in the growing season when the new spring wood vessels are developing, it is suggested that pruning operations in oaks be delayed until July or later.

Wood Decay. Oaks are subject to attacks by a number of fungi that cause decays beneath the bark, usually near the soil line. Two types of decay, known as white heart-rot and brown heart-rot, generally result. Fungi belonging to the genera *Stereum, Polyporus, Fomes,* and *Fistulina* are most commonly associated with these rots. The same tree may show infection by more than one of these fungi, although in most cases only one is involved. The fungus *Stereum gausapatum* has been isolated from most basal decays of oaks. In the early stages of decay, it forms white lines through the sound wood, producing a mottled effect when viewed longitudinally. These white lines or channels usually follow the spring wood vertically, but they branch frequently and at times penetrate the annual growth rings. Later much of the summer wood decays, and in the final stages all the wood becomes light-colored and brittle.

Control: Once wood decays have become extensive, little can be done to check their advance. Trees live for a long time, however, despite the presence of these decays. Except to eliminate a breeding place for vermin, cavity work is rarely done where extensive decay occurs.

Shoestring Root Rot (*Armillaria mellea*). Oaks are a favored host of this disease, which is discussed under *Rhododendron* (see Fig. 197).

Insects and Other Animal Pests

Galls[30]

There are hundreds of kinds of galls on oaks, and a special manual is needed to identify them. Galls are caused by many species of mites and insects which feed and grow completely protected inside the galls. The life cycles of gall insects and mites vary according to the species involved. The pests overwinter either on the trees or on the ground. The adults emerge in spring and travel to the leaves and twigs, in which they deposit eggs.

[30] An excellent treatment of galls is *Plant Galls and Gall Makers* by E. P. Felt, Hafner Publ. Co., New York, 1965.

Fig. 197. Mushroom stage of the shoestring root rot fungus *Armillaria mellea*.

The young which hatch from the eggs then mature in the galls which form around them. Most kinds of galls on oaks rarely affect the health of the trees. One of the most beautiful galls is the woolsower (Fig. 198) produced by the gall wasp *Callirhytis seminator*. It is found on white, chestnut, and basket oaks. Some, as the gouty gall (Fig. 199), the horned gall, and the oak/potato gall (Figs. 200, 201), may affect the health as well as the appearance of the tree by killing branches.

Control: Before growth starts in spring, spray the trees either with dormant strength lime sulfur or with a dormant miscible oil to destroy some of the pests overwintering on the branches. Valuable trees should also be given a methoxychlor-Kelthane spray in mid-May and again in mid-June. Heavily infested branches should be pruned and destroyed before the adults emerge.

Golden Oak Scale (*Asterolecanium variolosum*). Shallow pits are formed in the bark by these circular, greenish-gold scales, which

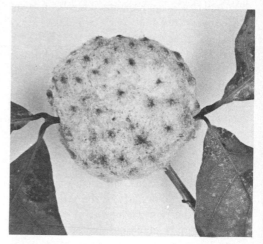

Fig. 198. Gall of the woolsower *Callirytis seminator* on white oak.

attain a diameter of only $1/16$ inch. Infested trees have a ragged, untidy appearance. Young trees may be killed outright, the lower branches dying first.

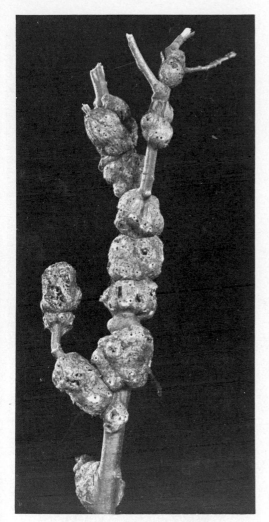

Fig. 199. Gouty oak gall.

Control: A "superior" type miscible oil spray applied in early spring will destroy most of the pests. Malathion plus methoxychlor, Diazinon, or Sevin sprays in July will control the crawler stage. A Cygon spray in August will kill the adult stage.

Lecanium Scale (*Lecanium corni* and *L. quercifex*). Branches and twigs infested with these pests are covered with brown, down-enveloped, hemispherical scales. The adults are ⅛ inch in diameter. The winter is passed in the partly grown stage. *L. quercitronis* in-

fests several species of oaks in the eastern states and live oak in California.

Control: Same as for **Golden Oak Scale**.

Oak Gall Scale (*Kermes pubescens*). Large, globular scale insects, about ⅛ inch in diameter, infest the twigs, leaf stalks, and midribs, and tend to gather on the young buds. They are illustrated in Fig. 202. A red and brown mottling characterizes the pest. The leaves become distorted and many of the twigs are killed, but the tree as a whole is not usually seriously injured.

Control: A dormant oil spray applied in March or early April is very effective. Malathion plus methaxychlor or Sevin sprays in late spring are effective against the crawler stage.

Obscure Scale (*Melanaspis obscura*). Tiny, circular, dark gray scales, ⅒ inch in diameter, may occasionally cover the bark of twigs and branches. The pest overwinters in the partly grown adult stage.

Control: Spray with dormant oil or winter-strength lime sulfur before growth starts in spring or with malathion or Sevin in late spring.

Purple Scale (*Lepidosaphes beckii*). The female of this species has an elongated, oyster-shaped, slightly curved, brown or purplish body. This species infests citrus trees primarily, but occurs also on many other species in California.

Control: Spray with malathion or Sevin when the young crawler stage is present.

Leaf-Eating Insects

There are so many species of insect larvae that feed on oak leaves that it is impossible to list them all. The following are some of the more important kinds:

Yellow-Necked Caterpillar (*Datana ministra*). The leaves are chewed by this caterpillar, a black-and-yellowish-white-striped larva 2 inches long. The adult female moth is cinnamon-brown with dark lines across the wings, which have a spread of 1½ inches. Eggs are

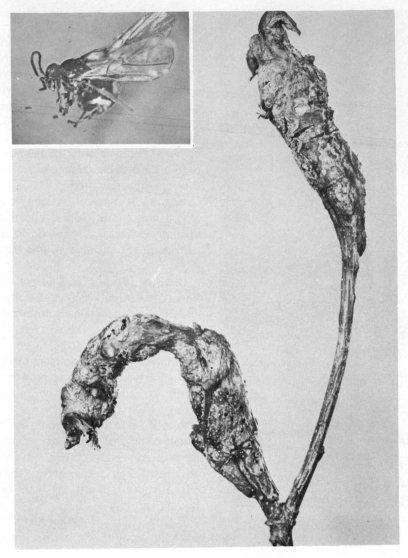

Fig. 200 *(Inset).* Adult of *Neuroterus batatus,* the cause of oak potato gall.

Fig. 201. Oak potato gall.

deposited in batches of 25 to 100 on the lower leaf surfaces. The insect hibernates in the pupal stage in the soil.

Control: Spray the leaves with methoxychlor or Sevin when the caterpillars are young.

Pin Oak Sawfly (*Caliroa lineata*). The lower surfaces of pin oak leaves are chewed by ³⁄₈- to ¹⁄₂-inch-long greenish larvae or slugs, which leave the upper epidermal layer of cells and a fine network of veins. Injured leaves turn a golden brown, and when the

Fig. 202. Scale *(Kermes pubescens)* on bur oak. The scale insects closely resemble the oak buds in the axils of the leaves and at the tips of twigs.

feeding by the larvae is extensive, the injury can be readily distinguished at a considerable distance. The adult stage is a small, shining-black, four-winged insect ¼ inch long.

Control: Spray the leaves with Sevin when the larvae begin to feed in early summer. Direct the spray primarily to the lower surfaces of the leaves. This pest appears to prefer the upper parts of the tree.

Saddleback Caterpillar *(Sibine stimulea).* This broad, spine-bearing, red caterpillar, with a large green patch in the middle of its back, attains an inch in length and occasionally chews the leaves of ornamental and streetside oaks. The adult is a small moth with a wingspread of 1½ inches. The upper wings are dark reddish-brown, the lower, a light grayish-brown.

Control: Same as for the yellow-necked caterpillar.

Oak Skeletonizer *(Bucculatrix ainsliella).*

The leaves of red, black, and white oaks may be skeletonized by a yellowish-green larva, ¼ inch long when fully grown. The adult, a moth with a wing expanse of ⁵⁄₁₆ inch, is creamy white, more or less obscured by dark brown scales.

Control: Spray with Diazinon, methoxychlor, or Sevin when the larvae begin to feed in early June and when the larvae of the second brood begin to feed in August.

Asiatic Oak Weevil *(Cyrtepistomus castaneus).* Severe damage to the leaves of oaks and chestnuts can be caused by a deep red or blackish weevil, ¼ inch long, with scattered green scales which have a metallic lustre. Its long antennae are characteristic of only one other species in this country, the long-horned weevil, *Calomycteris setarius.* Like the elm leaf beetle and the boxelder bug, they move into homes in the fall to hibernate.

Control: Methoxychlor sprays on foliage

at the time the weevils begin to feed provide good control.

Oak Leaf Tier (*Croesia albicomana*). Buds and leaves are chewed by the larval stage of this pest.

Control: Spray with Sevin no later than April 15, or before the buds begin to break.

Other Pests. Among other insects that chew oak leaves are the caterpillars of the io moth, *Automeris io;* the cecropia moth, *Platysamia cecropia;* the luna moth, *Actias luna;* the gypsy moth, *Porthetria dispar;* the American dagger moth, *Acronicta americana* (see Fig. 68); the oak leaf roller, *Argyrotoxa semipurpurana;* the Japanese weevil, *Pseudocneorhinus bifasciatus;* and the satin moth, *Stilpnotia salicis.*

Several species of cankerworms and leaf rollers also chew the leaves of oaks. All of these can be controlled by spraying with Diazinon or Sevin when the larvae begin to feed.

Borers and Leaf-Miners

Two-Lined Chestnut Borer (*Agrilus bilineatus*). Large branches are killed on some trees as a result of the formation of tortuous galleries underneath the bark by the two-lined chestnut borer, a white, flat-headed larva 1/2 inch long. The adult, a slender greenish-black beetle 3/8 inch long, appears in late June. The larvae pass the winter beneath the bark.

Control: Cut down and destroy all badly infested trees. Increase the vigor of the remaining trees by fertilizing and watering. Methoxychlor spray, applied to the bark of trunk and branches early in July will also help.

Flatheaded Borer (*Chrysbothris femorata*). Trees that are not growing vigorously are sometimes attacked by the apple tree borer. The eggs are deposited in crevices in the bark. The young grubs feed on the sapwood. They make flat galleries in the wood.

Control: Cut out and destroy dying trees.

Other Borers. Oaks may be invaded by other borers including the carpenter worm, *Prionoxystus robiniae,* discussed under *Robinia;* the leopard moth borer, *Zeuzera pyrina;* and the twig pruner, *Elaphidionoides villosus,* discussed under *Acer.*

Oak Blotch Leaf Miners (*Cameraria hamadryadella* and *C. cincinnatiella*). The former makes pale blotches on many kinds of oak leaves. One leaf miner larva is found in each blotch. The latter makes similar blotches on leaves of white oak, each blotch containing 10 or more larvae.

Control: Rake up and destroy fallen leaves because the insect overwinters in the mines of such leaves. Spray with malathion, Sevin, or Trithion in early June when the young miners hatch out of the eggs.

Sucking Pests

Oak Lace Bug (*Corythucha arcuata*). The leaves of many species of oaks, particularly the white oak, may turn whitish-gray when heavily infested with this lace bug.

Control: Spray with Diazinon, malathion, or Sevin when the young begin to feed in June.

Oak Mite (*Oligonychus bicolor*). Mottled yellow foliage results from the sucking of the leaf juices by the oak mite, a yellow, brown, or red, eight-legged pest. The pest usually overwinters in the egg stage.

Control: Spray with a dormant oil or lime sulfur during early spring or with either Kelthane, Meta-Systox R, or Tedion in mid-June and again 2 to 3 weeks later.

RANUNCULUS (BUTTERCUP)

Diseases

Leaf Spots (*Ascochyta infuscans, Cercospora ranunculi, Cylindrosporium ficariae, Di-*

dymaria didyma, Fabraea ranunculi, Ovularia decipiens, Ramularia aequivoca, Septocylindrium ranunculi, and Septoria spp.). Many fungi cause leaf spots of this host in nature. Few occur in cultivated plantings in wildflower gardens.

Control: Pick and destroy spotted leaves.

Mildews. The downy mildew fungus *Peronospora ficariae* and the powdery mildew fungi *Erysiphe polygoni* and *Sphaerotheca humuli* occasionally infect buttercups.

Control: The downy mildew is best controlled with copper sprays such as Bordeaux mixture. Powdery mildews are controlled with wettable sulfur or Karathane sprays.

Root Rot (*Pythium debaryanum*). In California the Persian buttercup, R. *asiaticus,* is attacked by this well-known fungus. It causes a general wilting, collapse, and death of the plants. Virtually all parts of the plant are affected, becoming dark brown, water-soaked, and limp. Infected leaf stalks are dark brown and have long diseased streaks extending from the base to the blade.

Among other soil-inhabiting fungi that attack *Ranunculus* are *Pellicularia rolfsii,* a species of *Sclerotinia,* and *Pythium ultimum.*

Control: Rogue out diseased plants. Select a new location for replanting or, if necessary to replant in the same area, use clean soil or treat infested soil as described in Chapter 4.

Rusts (*Puccinia andina,* P. *blyttiana,* P. *eatoniae* var. *ranunculi,* P. *recondita,* *Uromyces dactylidis,* and U. *jonesii*). At least six species of rust fungi affect buttercups.

Control: Destroy infected plants. Other control measures are rarely warranted.

Virus. The beet curly top virus is known to affect buttercups.

Control: Remove and destroy affected plants.

Aster Yellows. This disease also occurs in buttercups.

Control: Same as for curly top virus.

RESEDA (MIGNONETTE)

Diseases

Blight (*Cercospora resedae*). This disease develops very rapidly, frequently killing much of the foliage. Numerous small circular spots, pale-yellowish with reddish-brown borders, are caused by it. The spots run together, causing a reddish discoloration and a blight of the entire leaf. The lower leaves are the most seriously affected. The fungus that causes the disease spreads throughout the leaves, coming to the surface to develop large numbers of long club-shaped spores with thin cross-walls; the spores are carried by the wind and by rain-drops and spread the disease very rapidly to healthy plants.

Control: Spray with a copper fungicide or with wettable sulfur.

Other Fungus Diseases. This host is also susceptible to damping-off and root rot caused by *Pellicularia filamentosa,* and wilt by *Verticillum albo-atrum.*

Insects and Other Animal Pests

Caterpillars (*Pieris rapae* and *Trichoplusia ni*). The imported cabbageworm and the cabbage looper chew the leaves of mignonette.

Control: Spray with Sevin when the caterpillars begin to feed.

Potato Flea Beetle (*Epitrix cucumeris*). This pest makes tiny holes in the leaves.

Control: Same as for caterpillars.

Other Pests. Mignonette is also attacked by the corn earworm, the aster leafhopper, and the onion thrips. Controls for these pests are given under more favored hosts.

The two-spotted mite and the root-knot nema also infest mignonette.

RHAMNUS (BUCKTHORN)

Diseases

Leaf Spots (*Cercospora rhamni, C. aeruginosa,* and *Phyllosticta rhamni*). Three leaf spots are common on *Rhamnus* in the Middle West.

Control: Leaf spots rarely become serious enough to warrant control measures.

Rust (*Puccinia coronata*). One stage of this rust is found on the leaves of *Rhamnus.* It does little damage to this host but its presence near oat fields may cause considerable damage to that crop. In Iowa, R. *cathartica* is considered a pest for this reason and its eradication is recommended. In California, the rust *Puccinia mesnieriana* affects the coffeeberry, *Rhamnus californica.*

Other Diseases. A powdery mildew caused by *Microsphaera alni* has been reported from Wisconsin. A root rot caused by *Phymatotrichum omnivorum* and a virus disease by the cucumber mosaic virus also attack *Rhamnus.*

Insects

Aphids (*Aphis nasturtii* and A. *gossypii*). The buckthorn and cotton aphids infest buckthorn.

Control: Spray valuable specimens with Meta-Systox R, Sevin, or malathion.

Other Insects. The oriental moth, *Cnidocampa flavescens,* and two species of scales, black and San Jose, also infest *Rhamnus.*

Rhamnus californica on the West Coast is subject to the Pacific flat-headed borer, the California tent caterpillar, the western tussock moth, and four species of whitefly: glacial, greenhouse, inconspicuous, and iridescent.

RHODODENDRON (RHODODENDRON AND AZALEA)[31]

Fungus Diseases

Botrytis Blotch (*Botrytis cinerea*). Winter injury frequently leads to invasion by *Botrytis* as a secondary parasite. Under moist conditions slight injuries are aggravated by this gray mold, which continues to invade the healthy tissues of the leaves. The injury seldom calls for the application of a fungicide (See Fig 203.)

Bud and Twig Blight (*Briosia azaleae*). This fungus disease is destructive to azaleas. In certain plantings it has been known to kill 90 per cent of the flowers. The disease may be described as a bud blast rather than a bud rot. Terminal flower buds are infected mainly in July and August, after which leaf buds and twigs are attacked. Diseased twigs do not flower the following season. The diseased buds remain attached for 2 or 3 years. The fungus gains entrance through the axils of the bud scales and penetrates deeply into the bark and pith. The conducting vessels of the twigs become plugged so that conduction of water is prevented. The fungus develops its spore stage on long, thin outgrowths capped by slimy balls, each of which contains thousands of spores. These outgrowths appear like fine bristles growing from the bud-scales and bark of infected twigs. The spores are spread from plant to plant by insects (especially by bees during blossom time) and by the splashing of water.

Control: Prune and destroy infected branch tips. Spray with a copper fungicide once each month, starting when the blooms fade.

---

[31] Although growers commonly distinguish rhododendrons from azaleas, such a distinction seems impossible to maintain botanically. There are, for instance, well-known groups of evergreen azaleas and deciduous rhododendrons.

Fig. 203. Leaf blotches of rhododendron: *(left)* blotch caused by *Pestalotia macrotricha;* *(right)* two leaves attacked by *Botrytis cinerea.*

Gray Blight (*Pestalotia macrotricha*). The fungus that causes this disease usually follows winter-killing, sunscald, or other injury, as a secondary parasite. The spot is at first white in the middle with a dark brown margin; later it becomes a blotch (see Fig. 203). Small bodies the size of pin-points dot the surface; these are the fruiting bodies of the fungus.

Control: Plant rhododendrons where the blistering summer sun does not cause sunscald, and where the cold winds of winter do not freeze the leaves too severely.

Dieback, Botryosphaeria Canker (*Botryosphaeria dothidea*). Leaves are first attacked at the tips or around the margins. Spots are later formed that involve the entire leaf. Leaf stalks and twigs also become infected. The symptoms are much like those caused by *Phytophthora*, except that the surface of the parts infected with *Botryosphaeria* is much roughened by the protruding bodies of the fungus.

Control: Prune affected parts to sound tissue. Spray occasionally with a copper fungicide.

Crown Rot (*Phytophthora cryptogea*). Collected *Rhododendron maximum, R. catawbiense,* and R. *carolinianum* plants are susceptible to this disease. The fungus has been isolated from the main roots and basal portions of the stems, where it causes a brown discoloration of the wood. Infected branches wilt and die; severely infected plants become thin and leggy and eventually perish.

Control: Infected branches should be pruned out; severely infected plants should be removed from the planting, with the surrounding soil, and destroyed.

Phytophthora Dieback (*Phytophthora cactorum*). Terminal buds and leaves turn brown, roll up, and droop as though in a winter condition. The stem shrivels and a canker is formed which encircles the twig. All parts above the canker wilt and soon die.

Control: This fungus is the same as that which causes lilac twig blight; the two kinds of plants should be therefore widely separated. All diseased tips should be pruned out well below the infected parts. Bordeaux sprays applied as new leaves emerge and repeated two weeks later may help. Where losses have occurred in nurseries, drenching the soil with Dexon or Terrazole will kill the *Phytophthora* fungus present in the soil. Chemical treatments, however, will not cure already infected plants.

Damping-off (*Pellicularia filamentosa*). This fungus causes a stem rot at the soil level. It is common where young plants are crowded and over-watered. It occasionally kills larger plants.

Control: Plant seeds in milled sphagnum moss, or drench the soil before planting with PCNB (Terraclor) as recommended by the manufacturer.

Azalea Petal Blight (*Ovulinia azaleae*). This disease is largely confined to azaleas grown in the southern states along the coast from Maryland to Texas. Isolated cases have appeared elsewhere. Indian and kurume azaleas are especially susceptible. In the first stage, pale, circular spots about the size of a pinhead appear on the undersides of the petals. In favorable climatic conditions, the spots enlarge rapidly and run together, appearing white on colored flowers and brown on white flowers. The affected flowers become limp and are then covered with a delicate white bloom or a frost-like mat formed of spores of the fungus. These are easily carried away by wind and rain, also by bees and other insects, which spread the infection from flower to flower. After the flowers have been destroyed, the propagating bodies of the fungus, sclerotia, develop. When young they are soft and blue-gray; afterwards they become hard and black. These bodies are very common on old flowers that have fallen to the ground, and here they overwinter.

Control: The most important factor in control is prompt and persistent picking of the infected flowers. In some plantings it has been found advisable to remove all the blossoms, including the uninfected ones. In larger plantings where it is impossible to do this, spraying the soil surface with ferbam, before flowering, kills the ascospores which are formed in the fruiting structures. Protection of the flowers can be provided with Benlate sprays applied at 5-day intervals during bloom. The first application should be made when the flowers start to show color. This treatment should be effective for more than 1 year.

Azalea Gall (*Exobasidium vaccinii*). The leaves become thickened or fleshy either wholly or in part, and turn pale green or whitish. Sometimes a fleshy rosette of leaves appears at the tip end of the branch, or a gall which later becomes bladder-like as it decays and dries out (Fig. 60). The flower parts, especially the petals of evergreen species such as *R. maximum,* become greatly thickened so that the whole bloom is turned into a hard, fleshy, waxy, irregular gall (Fig. 61), the parts of which become covered with a whitish bloom. Even the seed pods become fleshy and gall-like. When found in nature, these fleshy galls are called "pinkster apples," and are eaten by those familiar with their qualities. Similar galls of a beautiful rose color develop sometimes on cranberries; they are called "rose apples." The fungus that causes these abnormalities is one of the simple basidiomycetes, which forms basidia superficially instead of in fleshy fruitbodies. Azalea gall is largely composed of abnormal leaf tissue.

Control: In greenhouses and garden plantings, where the disease is important, young galls can be hand-picked and destroyed. In larger plantings, just before the leaves unfurl, spray once with either ferbam or with zineb.

Leaf Spots (*Cercospora rhododendri, Colletotrichum* sp., *Coryneospora cassiicola, Cylindrocladium scoparium, Coryneum rhododendri, C. triseptatum, Cryptostictis mariae, Diplodina eurhododendri, Gloeosporium rhododendri, G. ferrugineum, Hendersonia concentrica, Laestadia rhodorae, Lophodermium melaleucum, L. rhododendri, Melasmia rhododendri, Monochaetia* sp., *Mycosphaerella* sp., *Phyllosticta maxima* and other species, *Physalospora rhododendri, Septoria rhododendri,* and *Venturia rhododendri*). A great many fungi cause leaf spots on azaleas and rhododendrons. These can be distinguished from one another only by a mycologist. Fortunately the control practices are the same for all.

Control: Benlate, ferbam, maneb, or zineb sprays applied immediately after flowering and repeated twice at 10- to 14-day intervals, will control most leaf spot fungi. Include a few drops of a spreader-sticker like DuPont's SS or Triton B 1956 to help the spray adhere more firmly to the leaves. Apply a generous mulch over the soil, use windbreaks, and control insects to keep foliage in sound condition and thus prevent the entrance of many leaf spot fungi, especially those that are weak parasites.

Leaf Scorch (*Septoria azaleae*). Dark reddish-brown spots develop on azalea leaves, which fall prematurely. The spots are at first yellowish-red with brown centers and purplish margins. The fruiting bodies in the center of the spots can be seen with a hand lens.

Control: Spraying with Bordeaux mixture, 2-2-50, or any readymade copper fungicide at two-week intervals from July 1 to August 15 will give adequate protection. Copper sprays may cause some injury to azaleas during periods of cool, wet weather.

Powdery Mildew (*Microsphaera alni*). This disease appears as a white, powdery coating of the leaves (See Fig. 204).

Control: Spray with Acti-dione PM, Benlate, Karathane or wettable sulfur.

Rust (*Pucciniastrum vaccinii*). Another disease common in nurseries and propagating houses is the rust on rhododendrons and azaleas. Quantities of seedlings, especially of *R. ponticum,* are sometimes destroyed. The disease may be known by the bright golden or brownish spores that break out from pustules on the under sides of the leaves. These repeating spores carry the parasite from plant to plant rather rapidly, but the fungus is able to complete its life cycle only by attacking the hemlock. Other fungi may follow rust as secondary parasites on *Rhododendron.* Infection of *Rhododendron ponticum* is often followed by the leaf spot caused by *Pestolotia macrotricha.*

Control: The rust is carried over winter on rhododendrons. Avoid planting azaleas and rhododendrons near hemlocks. Spray the ericaceous plants several times at 10-day intervals in July and August with 2 level tablespoons of ferbam and 2 of wettable sulfur per gallon of water.

Other Rusts. *Rhododendron* is susceptible to other rusts including *Chrysomyxa roanensis* and *C. piperiana.* In 1954 the rust *C. ledi* var. *rhododendri* was found for the first time in the United States in a commercial

Fig. 204.   Powdery mildew of rhododendron. (Pennsylvania State University)

nursery in western Washington. This rust is believed to have been introduced from Europe on imported plants; infected plants were distributed from the nursery before the disease was identified.

Shoot Blight (*Monilinia azaleae*). The spores of this fungus attack the leaves and young shoots when the plants are in full bloom early in June. Later the capsules also are attacked; the pseudosclerotia develop in them and fill their cavities with solid masses of thick-walled cells.

Control: No controls have been developed for this disease.

Shoestring Root Rot (*Armillaria mellea*). A wet decay of the cortex and bark accompanied by a distinct mushroom odor is the first symptom of the disease. Black strands of fungus tissue envelop the roots and enter the bark, and mushrooms also develop (Fig. 197). White fans of mycelium are usually present under the loosened bark immediately above the soil level. The entire plant eventually succumbs.

Control: Plants in good condition are seldom attacked. The crown of the plant should be exposed to the air, so that the bark is well dried. Severely infected plants rarely recover.

Wilt (*Phytophthora cinnamomi*). This is a seedling or nursery disease which affects plants up to 2 or 3 years old. The fungus is soil-borne; it enters the young roots and works its way up to the crown. The young leaves become yellowish and wilt. The fungus prefers cool situations and soil that is not sufficiently acid for good growth of the host; it is rare in soil adapted to good rhododendron growth. Overwatering of the plants causes death of the roots and thus affords entrance for the fungus. The fungus is more likely to attack plants recently transplanted, because of root injury in the operation.

Control: Temperature of the soil should be kept low by mulching, and the acidity of the soil should be increased by applying aluminum sulfate or sulfur. Heavily infested soil should be replaced with clean soil or be steam-pasteurized, or a soil drench of Dexon or Terrazole applied as directed by the manufacturer.

Other Diseases. In 1965 a serious disease of azaleas was found to be caused by *Pellicularia filamentosa* in a Florida nursery where nearly complete defoliation of 150,000 plants occurred. Periodic applications of thiram sprays helped the plants to recover.

Crown gall caused by the bacterium *Agrobacterium tumefaciens,* occasionally occurs on rhododendrons.

In South Carolina, branch dieback of azaleas, often attributed to cold and insect damage, is actually caused by a species of *Phomopsis. Phytophthora citricola* causes wilt and dieback of rhododendrons in Ohio.

A species of *Cylindrocladium* causes a stem canker.

Nonparasitic Problems

Chlorosis. Leaf yellowing or chlorosis of rhododendrons and azaleas is a common trouble when these plants are growing in alkaline soils or are planted near a cement wall. Under alkaline conditions, the plants are unable to absorb iron and thus become chlorotic.

Control: Treat the soil or spray the leaves with an iron chelate such as Sequestrene of Iron. Avoid using lime near ericaceous

plants, and do not plant them too close to cement or brick walls.

Salt Injury. Azaleas, like camellias are sensitive to excessive amounts of salts in the soil. See *Camellia.*

Winter Injury. When strong cold March winds follow warm days, many rhododendrons may be killed. The damage may not appear until 2 or 3 weeks later. The leaves become brown, especially at the edges and near the tips (see Fig. 205). This is due to a loss of water by the leaves at a time when the water in the soil is still frozen or unavailable for other reasons.

Wilt (black walnut Injury). If rhododendrons are planted near large black walnut trees, they may suddenly wilt and die. The greatest injury occurs along the roots of the walnuts and seems to be caused by toxins secreted by them. The author was among the first to study the effect of these trees on rhododendrons many years ago.

Control: Remove black walnut trees growing near rhododendrons.

Insects and Other Animal Pests

Rhododendron Aphid (*Macrosiphum rhododendri*). This pink and green species infests rhododendrons in Oregon.

Control: Spray with Meta-Systox R, malathion, or Sevin.

Azalea Stem Borer (*Oberea myops*). This borer enters into the tips of stems and bores out some of the twigs soon after blooming time. The borer is yellowish and about $1/2$ inch long. The adult stage is a beetle.

Control: Cut out and destroy infested stems. Spraying stems with methoxychlor in mid-May and again in mid-June will also control this pest.

Azalea Leaf Tier (*Archips argyrospilus*). This pest, also known as the fruit-tree leaf roller feeds on a wide variety of ornamental plants and fruit trees. The young worms are pale green with brown heads; the moths have

Fig. 205. Winter-drying of rhododendron leaves, an extremely common condition when rhododendrons are planted in wind-swept locations.

a wing expanse of ³/₄ inch and are brown with gold markings.

Control: Spray in mid-May and again two weeks later with Imidan or Sevin.

Black Vine and Strawberry Weevils (*Otiothyncus sulcatus* and *O. ovatus*). These weevils (Fig. 206) feed on the leaves at night, cutting holes along the margins (Fig. 207). They sometimes devour the whole leaf except the midribs and large veins. The grubs are root-feeders, often destroying so many roots of azaleas that they endanger the life of the plants, especially if the collars are bare and the stems are girdled as in Fig. 208.

Control: See *Taxus.*

Giant Hornet (*Vespa crabro germana*). This hornet gnaws away the bark, often girdling and killing the twigs. Other favored hosts are lilac and dogwood.

Fig. 206. Adult of black vine weevil.

Control: See *Buxus.*

Japanese Beetle (*Popillia japonica*) and **Asiatic Garden Beetle** (*Maladera castanea*) destroy the younger foliage and lay their eggs in the soil at the base of the plants. Their grubs feed on the roots and base of young stems.

Fig. 207. Black vine weevil injury to rhododendron leaves.

Fig. 208. Bark chewed from base of azalea by the black vine weevil.

Control: Spray the plants frequently with Diazinon, methoxychlor, or Sevin to control the adult stage.

Lace Bugs (*Stephanitis pyrioides* and *S. rhododendri*). The eggs are laid along the midribs and larger veins and live through winter. They hatch out in May and the young insects begin to feed on the under sides of the leaves, where their excreta appear as rather large brown, sticky spots. The upper side of the leaf is marked by numerous whitish specks like those due to leafhoppers and red spider mites on other plants. The lace bug is shown in Fig. 73.

Control: Spray the undersides of the leaves with either Meta-Systox R or Sevin as directed on the container, as soon as the eggs hatch in spring. Repeat in summer and fall if additional lace bugs appear.

Red-Banded Leafhopper (*Graphocephala coccinea*). The adult is beautifully striped or marked with pale blue and bright orange-red colors. It is about $5/16$ inch long. At mating time the insects may be found on the upper sides of the leaves. Control of lace bugs prevents injury by the leafhoppers.

Azalea Leaf Miner (*Gracilaria azaleella*). This pest, also known as leaf roller, first mines the leaves and then rolls them together. The larval stage is a yellow caterpillar

½ inch long. The adult is a small moth with a wingspread of ³/₈ inch. Eggs are laid on the leaves.

Control: Spray with Diazinon or malathion just as the larvae begin to mine the leaves.

Azalea Whitefly (*Pealius azaleae*). This pest is most common on evergreen azaleas. The pupal stage is greenish white, oval, and present in large numbers on the undersides of the leaves. The sooty mold fungus develops on the honeydew secreted by the immature stage.

This species also infests rhododendron, mountain-laurel, and andromeda.

Control: Spray with Diazinon or malathion in early June and repeat at least two more times at 10-day intervals.

Rhododendron Tip Midge (*Giardomyia rhododendri*). Newly developing leaves are rolled and their edges browned by small white maggots. New growth is stunted.

Control: Spray the growing tips with malathion or Sevin.

Mites. Four kinds of mites infest azaleas and rhododendrons: cyclamen, privet, southern red, and two-spotted.

Control: Spray with Aramite, Dimite or Kelthane. Repeat in 10 days if necessary.

Mealybugs. The citrophilus, the striped, and the *Taxus* mealybugs infest *Rhododendron.*

Control: Malathion sprays are very effective against these pests.

Pitted Ambrosia Beetle (*Corthylus punctatissimus*). Rhododendrons as well as many trees are attacked by this pest below ground. The grub is small and white, the adult beetle black, cylindrical, ⅛ inch long.

Control: Prune and destroy infested stems. Protect the base of the others with a methoxychlor spray about May 1 and again June 1.

Rhododendron Borer (*Synanthedon rhododendri*). The main stems of rhododendron, azalea, and mountain-laurel are bored (Fig. 209) by a ½-inch-long larva which leaves ugly scars and sometimes kills large

Fig. 209. Work of the rhododendron borer (*Synanthedon rhododendri*) on rhododendron.

branches. The adult, a clear-winged moth, emerges in mid-May and deposits eggs on the bark in June.

Control: Spray or paint the trunk and larger branches with methoxychlor 3 times at

20-day intervals starting when the adults begin to emerge.

Scales. The following scale insects infest azaleas and rhododendrons: azalea bark, oleander, peony, rhododendron, and soft azalea. The azalea bark scale appears white and cottony on the surface and dark red beneath. The peony scale appears like slight humps on the bark and is relatively inconspicuous. It is a serious pest in the South.

Control: The crawler stages of all scales are controlled with Cygon, malathion, or Sevin sprays. A dormant oil spray applied in early spring is also effective.

Thrips (*Thrips tabaci* and *Heliothrips haemorrhoidalis*). Thrips are often a serious pest of seedlings of *R. ponticum* and of greenhouse azaleas such as *R. indicum.* They feed on the undersides of the leaves, causing a glistening, whitish appearance. On the upper sides the effect is much like the work of the lace bug on larger plants, but the spots are larger and more irregularly blotched.

Control: Spray with malathion, Cygon, or Sevin at regular intervals, starting when the thrips are first seen.

Rhododendron Whitefly (*Dialeurodes chittendeni*). Yellowish mottling on the upper side of the leaves of rhododendrons, with a rolling of the margins, indicates infestation by this pest. The young insects are greenish, almost transparent, very flat, and oval in shape. They are often crowded closely together. Much honeydew is secreted; this furnishes nourishment for the black sooty mold, which may become so matted as to cut off the air and light from the growing leaves. The infestation occurs only on evergreen rhododendrons without hairs on scales on the under sides of the leaves.

Another whitefly, *Tetraleurodes mori,* also attacks this host.

Control: Spraying with Cygon or Diazinon will control whiteflies. The sprays whould be directed to the terminal clusters and the undersides of the leaves.

A recently developed synthetic pyrethroid, Resemethrin, is also very effective against whiteflies.

In the Pacific Northwest spraying with a 2 per cent white oil emulsion has also given good control. The material is effective against the egg and larval stages but must be used on cloudy days in order to avoid injury. Whiteflies frequently overwinter on evergreen varieties of rhododendrons.

Nemas. The following species of nemas have been found around unhealthy azaleas: *Tylenchorhynchus claytoni, Trichodorus christiei, Tylenchus* sp., and *Ditylenchus* sp. In Florida the leaf nema *Aphelenchoides fragariae* causes leaf lesions on azaleas.

Control: The control of nemas is described in Chapter 3.

Giant Hornet. See *Syringa.*

Japanese Weevil. See *Ligustrum.*

RHODOTYPOS (JETBEAD)

The only fungus diseases known to affect this host are anthracnose caused by a species of *Gloeosporium,* a leaf spot by *Ascochyta rhodotypi,* and a twig blight by *Nectria cinnabarina.*

Control: Pick off and destroy leaves affected by anthracnose and leaf spot. Prune and destroy twigs affected by *Nectria.*

RHUS (SUMAC)

Diseases

Cankers (*Cryptodiaporthe aculeans* and *Physalospora* sp.). Two species of fungi cause cankers on the stems and dieback of branches.

Control: Prune infected stems well below the cankered areas.

Fusarium Wilt (*Fusarium oxysporum* var. *rhois*). Leaves of staghorn sumac, *R. typhina,* wilt and hang down from the twigs when this fungus invades the plant through the roots. The wilt may be gradual, in which case dwarfing, yellowing, and premature reddening of the leaves may precede the death of the host. Another wilt caused by the fungus *Verticillium albo-atrum* occasionally affects sumac.

Control: No effective controls are known for either type of wilt.

Leaf Spot (*Pezizella oenotherae*). Several species of sumac, wild and ornamental, may have this rather common leaf spot. The gray centers of the spots show small but conspicuous spore-bearing structures varying from amber to black in color. The margins of the spots are usually purple-brown or nearly black. The spots are usually irregular, ¹/₂ inch in diameter; several of them coalesce to bring about a scorch or blight. This fungus is found on a large number of species of plants. It causes the most serious leaf spots, however, on *Shortia* and *Galax.* In ornamental sumac plants it will probably be of little consequence.

Control: Valuable ornamental specimens can be sprayed with Bordeaux mixture or any other copper fungicide.

Other Leaf Spots. Three other species of fungi cause leaf spots of sumac: *Phyllosticta* sp., *Phleospora irregularis,* and *Septoria rhoina.*

Powdery Mildew (*Sphaerotheca humuli*). The white coating of this fungus is common on the leaves during late summer and fall.

Control: Spray valuable ornamental specimens either with Benlate or with Karathane.

Rusts (*Pileolaria effusa* and *P. patzcuarensis*). Two rust fungi occur on Rhus in the West. Control measures for these are never practiced.

Insects and Related Pests

Among the pests of sumac are the sumac aphid, potato flea beetle, currant borer, sumac psyllid, a species of mite, and four species of scales: cottony maple, hemispherical, lesser snow, and San Jose.

Control: Spraying valuable ornamental specimens with malathion or Sevin will control most of these pests.

RIBES (FLOWERING CURRANT)

Fungus Diseases

The varieties of currants and gooseberries grown for their fruits are subject to a great number of diseases which are beyond the scope of this book. The diseases and pests discussed below include the more common ones found on the species grown for ornament.

Anthracnose (*Pseudopeziza ribis*). The golden currant, *R. odoratum,* and other ornamental species are subject to serious leaf spots which cause much premature defoliation. The lower leaves appear to become affected first. They turn yellow and gradually fall. The spots also occur on the leaf stalks and fruit. The canes may be infected but are not seriously injured. The spots are circular, brown or black.

Control: Collect and destroy the fallen leaves. Spray with Bordeaux mixture or with wettable sulfur at weekly intervals. Before the leaves develop in the spring, it is well to give the plants a dormant lime sulfur spray.

Dieback, Cane Blight (*Botryosphaeria dothidea*). The leaves of individual canes wilt and the canes become blighted to some distance from the tips.

Control: Cut out and destroy infected canes.

Leaf Spots (*Cercospora angulata, C. ribis, Cylindrosporum ribis,* and *Mycosphaerella ribis*). In very rainy seasons these fungi can cause some premature defoliation in addition to leaf spotting.

Control: Leaf spots can be controlled by spraying with a copper or a dithiocarbamate fungicide.

Rust (*Cronartium ribicola*). In regions where quarantine does not prevent the growing of currants, these plants may become seriously infected with a leaf-rust fungus which has its alternate stage on the white pine. On the white pine it causes the blister rust. On currants the under side of the leaves will be covered with dusty brown pustules. Older leaves are more susceptible. Where no white pines are present, this rust will not be found, for both hosts are necessary to carry the fungus through the winter.

Control: See *Pinus.*

Insects

Currant Aphid (*Cryptomyzus ribis*). Leaves are curled, crinkled, or humped up by this pinkish, yellowish, or dark green aphid. The curled areas turn red.

Control: Spray with Meta-Systox R, Sevin, or malathion early in the growing season before the leaves are curled.

Imported Currant Worm (*Nematus ribesii*). The caterpillars are dark green with black spots. The eggs are laid along the midribs on the lower sides of the leaves towards the end of May. The larvae eat small holes in the leaves. If infestation is heavy, almost all the leaves are eaten up.

Control: Spray ornamental *Ribes* with rotenone or Sevin when the caterpillars begin to feed.

Scales. Seven species of scale insects infest *Ribes:* cottony maple, European fruit lecanium, Forbes, oystershell, Putnam, San Jose, and walnut.

Control: Spray with lime sulfur or miscible oil when the plants are dormant. Malathion or Sevin sprays applied in mid-May and mid-June will control the young scales.

Currant Bud Mite (*Cecidophyopsis ribis*). This gall mite may be found by cutting open the swollen buds which appear in early spring. The buds do not open and the infested canes die or develop abnormally. When the infested buds die in May and June, the mites come out and attack buds on normally developed canes.

Control: Cut out and destroy all infested buds or shoots. Spray with wettable sulfur or Kelthane frequently during the spring.

RICHARDIA—see ZANTEDESCHIA

RICINUS (CASTOR-BEAN)

The dooryard castor-bean is said to be ordinarily immune to fungus diseases. It is believed that planting castor-beans in gardens acts as a repellent for insects. The diseases reported here occur largely on plants grown commercially, but may appear on plants grown for ornament. The seeds of this plant are poisonous.

Diseases

Bacterial Leaf Spot (*Xanthomonas ricini*). This disease occurs in commercial fields of castor-bean in the South. It also occurs throughout the castor-bean-producing areas of the southern Great Plains, but is not so destructive there. The causal organism is seed-borne and is spread in the field by wind-blown rain.

Control: Although no variety is completely immune, some like "Cimarron," are less seriously injured. The varieties "Anjou," "Baker 195," "Illinois 48-36," and "Western Oil Hybrid 9" also appear to be somewhat resistant.

Bacterial Wilt (*Pseudomonas solancearum*). The leaves of plants affected by this disease dry up, turn black, and fall from the blackened stalks and branches.

Control: Grow plants in clean soil. Treat seed before planting. See Disinfection of Seeds and Bulbs, Chapter 4.

Charcoal Rot (*Macrophomina phaseoli*). This fungus causes a blackening of the stem at or below ground level followed by early maturity and death of the plant. The sterile stage of this fungus is *Sclerotium bataticola*. Sclerotia are usually formed under the epidermis and in the pith.

Control: Keep plants in good vigor by feeding and watering. Control competing weeds.

Gray Mold Blight (*Botryotinia ricini*). This widespread cobwebby or woolly growth, from pale gray to olive-gray, develops on the inflorescence, stems, and leaves. The first infection is manifested by the appearance of small blackish spots from which drops of yellow liquid exude. The fungus threads which grow out from these spots spread the infection by developing spores of the imperfect stage, *Botrytis ricini*. The leaves become infected by the falling of small pieces of inflorescence from above.

Control: While spraying with Bordeaux mixture is helpful, it has been found commercially that the use of clean seed or seed obtained from regions free of the disease is the best prevention.

Other Diseases. Among other soil-inhabiting fungi known to infect this host are *Clitocybe tabescens*, *Pellicularia filamentosa*, *Phymatotrichum omnivorum*, *Pythium intermedium*, *Sclerotinia sclerotiorum*, and *Verticillium albo-atrum*.

Insects and Related Pests

Southern Armyworm (*Spodoptera eridania*). This species occurs from South Carolina to Florida. It is capable of causing defoliation and death of castor-bean.

Two-Spotted Mite (*Tetranychus urticae*). This pest is occasionally troublesome in southern gardens.

Control: See *Althaea*.

ROBINIA (BLACK LOCUST)

Diseases

Canker (*Aglaospora anomala*, *Nectria galligena*, and *Diaporthe oncostoma*). Cankers on twigs and death of the distal portions may be due to any one of three fungi.

Control: Prune and destroy infected twigs.

Damping-off (*Phytophthora parasitica*). In nurseries, serious damage to seedlings from 1 to 3 weeks old may be caused by this fungus. The young plants droop and their cotyledons curl. This is followed by wilting and the collapse of the entire seedling, which decays within a few days.

Control: Use clean soil or steam-pasteurize old soil for setting out seedlings.

Leaf Spots (*Cladosporium epiphyllum*, *Cylindrosporium solitarium*, *Gloeosporium revolutum*, *Phleospora robiniae*, and *Phyllosticta robiniae*). Many fungi cause leaf spots of *Robinia*.

Control: Control measures are seldom practiced.

Powdery Mildews (*Erysiphe polygoni*, *Microsphaera diffusa*, and *Phyllactinia corylea*). White coating of the leaves occurs only occasionally on black locust.

Control: These mildews are never serious enough to warrant control measures.

Wood Decay. Nearly all the older black locusts growing along roadsides and in groves in the eastern United States harbor one of several wood decay fungi. Nearly all these decays have followed infestations of the locust borer, *Megacyllene robiniae*.

The fungus *Fomes rimosus* causes a spongy, yellow rot of the heartwood. It infects the trunk through tunnels made by the locust borer or through dead older branches. After extensive decay of the woody tissues, the fungus grows toward the bark surface where it produces hard, woody, bracket- or hoof-shaped fruiting structures nearly 1 foot wide. The upper surface of the structure is brown or black and is cracked; the lower surface is reddish-brown.

The fungus *Polyporus robiniophilus* produces a soft, white rot of the heartwood. Like the *Fomes,* it infects the tree through locust borer tunnels and dead branches. The fruiting structures, which develop on dead bark, are at first white and firm, later brown and corky.

Control: Because wood decays of black locust become established mainly through locust borer tunnels, their prevention rests primarily on freedom from the insect pests. Effective control of the latter, however, cannot easily be attained, and for this reason heartwood decays will continue to be prevalent. Cavity treatments should never be attempted on black locusts.

Mycoplasma Disease

Witches' Broom. See *Gleditsia.*

Insects

Locust Borer (*Megacyllene robiniae*). The galleries formed by this borer may extend in all directions into the wood, which is discolored or blackened. The trees become badly disfigured. Young plantings may be entirely destroyed. The adult is a black beetle about ³/₄ inch long, spotted with bright yellow, transverse, zig-zag lines. The young grubs first bore into the inner bark and sapwood.

Control: Cut and destroy badly infested trees. Kill young borers in trunk and branches by inserting Bortox into the burrows and sealing the openings with chewing gum or putty. Spraying with methoxychlor in late August or early September gives effective control. Maintain trees in good vigor by proper watering, pruning, and feeding.

Carpenterworm (*Prionoxystus robiniae*). The borers vary from one to two inches in length. They are whitish or pink with brown heads and dark brown tubercles over the body. They make large holes in the limbs and trunks.

Control: Cut out the grubs from valuable trees, and dress the wounds. A nicotine paste may be injected into the burrows, the openings being closed with wax, putty, or chewing gum.

Locust Leaf Miner (*Xenochalepus dorsalis*). The beetles live through the winter and attack the young leaves in early May. They skeletonize the upper surfaces and lay their eggs on the under surfaces. The larvae enter the leaf and make irregular mines in the green tissue. A second generation of beetles emerges in September.

Control: Spray with Diazinon or Sevin early in July to kill the young larvae as they begin to mine the leaves.

Locust Twig Borer. (*Ecdytolopha insiticiana*). Elongated, gall-like swellings 1 to 3 inches long on the twigs are caused by the feeding and irritation of the pale yellow larvae of the locust twig borer. The adult female is a grayish-brown moth with a wing expanse of ³/₄ inch. The pest over-winters in the pupal stage among fallen leaves.

Control: Prune and destroy infested twigs in August, and gather and destroy fallen leaves in autumn.

Scales. Eight species of scale insects infest black locust: black, cottony-cushion, cottony maple, oystershell, Putnam, San Jose, soft, and walnut.

Control: Spray with malathion or Sevin when the young scales are crawling about in the spring. Repeat the application in about 2 weeks or so.

Other Pests

Dodder (*Cuscuta* sp.). This well-known flowering plant, which grows as a parasite on various plants, causes considerable damage to seedlings. It may also be a factor in transmission of certain virus diseases in border plantings.

Control: Dacthal spray applied to the soil in early spring will prevent germination of dodder seed.

ROCHEA

This native of South Africa, sometimes referred to as crassula, is subject to two pests, the citrus mealybug, *Planococcus citri,* and the cyclamen mite, *Steneotarsonemus pallidus.* Hot-water dips were formerly recommended for these pests, but the treatment was time-consuming and sometimes resulted in damage to the plants. Aramite, Dimite, or Kelthane sprays are recommended for mites, and malathion is suggested for mealybugs. The latter material occasionally damages certain succulents and should be tried on a few plants before being used on a large scale.

ROSA (ROSE)

Bacterial Diseases

Bacterial Leaf Spot (*Pseudomonas syringae*). A few varieties of roses are attacked by this bacterium, which is far more common on lilac and citrus. Dark brown, sunken spots appear on the leaf and flower stalks and calyx parts. Flower buds die without opening. This disease has been observed on a few species of roses in cold wet weather during the spring.

Control: Cut out and destroy infected parts.

Crown Gall (*Agrobacterium tumefaciens*). Though crown gall (Fig. 17) is not ordinarily very troublesome in rose gardens, whenever it is found infected plants should be destroyed. If the galls are above the ground, cut out the infected canes. Commercial rose nurserymen achieve control of this disease by cutting out the galls and dipping the roots and lower stems for 2 hours in a 500 parts per million streptomycin solution before planting.

Recent tests have shown that Bacticin is effective in controlling crown gall in almond, apricot, cherry, peach, pear, plum, and walnut. Bacticin may also work on roses. Follow the manufacturer's directions carefully.

Hairy Root (*Agrobacterium rhizogenes*). This disease occurs occasionally on roses. It causes much damage to bush roses in California. Infected plants should be destroyed.

Fungus Diseases

Rose Anthracnose (*Elsinoë rosarum*). This fungus attacks all parts of the plant above ground. On leaves the spots are more or less circular, $1/4$ inch in diameter. They are at first purplish-brown with a paler brown margin. The center of the spot turns gray at maturity and often falls out. Black spot is more uniformly black in color with an irregularly fringed margin. Anthracnose has not yet proved of great importance to rose growers.

Control: Control of black spot will keep this disease in check.

Black Mold (*Chalaropsis thielavioides*). The understocks of roses in grafting cases may be severely damaged by this fungus. It occurs primarily on American-grown *Rosa chinensis* var. *manetti* understocks. The fungus prevents the formation of callus so that the affected scions die. Newly infected grafts show first a white or grayish fungus growth which covers the cut surfaces of stock and scion. The mold takes on darker shades, from olive-green to dark brown and finally black. The parasite invades the cells of the cortex, wood, and pith of the rose stem. The cortex is particularly discolored, and the pith rays and pith also become discolored. Two kinds of spores are developed. The first, called "endoconidia," are formed internally in the end cells of conidiophores which are three or four cells in length, tapering rather gradually to a blunt end. The spores emerge one by one as they are formed and may adhere in chains. They are at first light-colored and later turn olive-green. The second type of spores, called "macroconidia," are borne in loose clusters. They are at first colorless, soon becoming olive-green and finally dark brown. This species is very similar to species of *Thielaviopsis* often found in connection with black root-rot of various plants.

Chalaropsis thielavioides may also cause damage to rose roots when the plants are kept in storage too long before planting, or when the plants are overwatered after planting.

Control: Use only uncontaminated stock for planting, or treat for 2 hours with one part of formaldehyde in 320 parts of water. Practice strict sanitation in the greenhouse and in storage bins.

Black Spot (*Diplocarpon rosae*). Several leaf spots of roses are caused by fungi, insects, and other agents. Black spot can be distinguished from other spots by the darker color and fringed borders of the spots, shown in Fig. 1. These occur on either side of the leaf. With a hand lens one can easily see very small black blister-like spore-producing bodies. Some roses lose their leaves very soon after infection; others hold them until the spots become as large as a dime. The fungus is said to produce ethylene gas, which causes the premature defoliation. Probably no rose variety is completely immune to black spot, but under ordinary garden conditions certain varieties are more susceptible than others. Leaves with black spot may be infected by the canker fungus *Leptosphaeria coniothyrium*, which ordinarily invades only the stems.

Control: While the powdery mildew fungus threads are almost entirely superficial, the threads (mycelium) of the black spot fungus are mostly under the protecting cuticle, so that fungicides cannot kill the fungus without destroying the leaf. For this reason it is necessary to have the young leaves protected at all times against the original invasion by the fungus. This can be done by spraying roses with any one of several fungicides at least once a week from the beginning of the growing season well into the fall. At The New York Botanical Garden the fungicide for black spot is applied at least 20 times each growing season. Given six or more hours without protection for the leaf, the fungus can gain entrance and its further progress cannot be halted without destroying the leaf. An ideal program for black spot control should begin with the gathering and destroying of all fallen leaves at the end of the growing season. The fungus overwinters in part in such leaves. Spores will be sent into the air from them the following spring.

Because the black spot fungus also survives in the canes, it is wise to prune these as drastically as possible without cutting too close to the grafted area. Research by U. S. Department of Agriculture rose scientists revealed that this practice alone greatly reduced black spot infections in the next growing season. The roses should also receive a dormant spray of lime sulfur, just about the time the leaves begin to emerge. This material may help to curb some fungi, but, more important, kills several kinds of overwintering pests. As soon as the growing season is well under way, periodic applications of sprays must be started. Details of what to use are discussed later in this section under "The control of fungus diseases of roses." Roses properly protected from black spot and pests are known to be less susceptible to winter injury than nonprotected ones.

Botrytis Blight (*Botrytis cinerea*). Certain hybrid tea roses are susceptible to this disease, which prevents the blooms from opening. The buds turn brown and decay (Fig. 210). Sometimes partially opened flowers are attacked, the individual petals turning brown and shriveling. The fungus is always present in rainy seasons when the old blooms are not gathered. Winter-killed canes also harbor the *Botrytis*.

Fig. 210. Botrytis blight *(Botrytis cinerea)* on rosebud; the diseased petals are easily lifted from the stem.

Control: Ferbam, a common ingredient of many rose sprays, is effective. Captan, maneb, Botran, or Benlate also control this fungus efficiently. Manure or leaf mulches used in the fall may keep the canes too wet and thus favor development of the fungus on the canes. Infection of rose buds and blooms is common during wet springs, particularly on white varieties. Susceptible kinds should be sprayed weekly during wet springs if good control is to be achieved. Picking off old faded blooms and placing them in the garbage can also help to reduce the amount of fungus inoculum.

Powdery Mildew (*Sphaerotheca pannosa* var. *rosae*). This disease is illustrated in Fig. 32 (see also Fig. 13). An early sysmptom is a tendency of the younger leaves to curl, exposing the lower surface. Such leaves are likely to be more purplish than normal leaves. If the tips of the canes of pole roses are infected, the leaves are dwarfed and deformed. Young canes may be infected downward from the tip for a foot or more. The ends of seriously infected canes are killed. Badly infected flower buds do not open. In some regions the fungus probably overwinters in the ascocarpic stage, but in a less severe climate it undoubtedly may live through the winter in infected buds or on leaves or branches that are not entirely killed.

Control: As soon as hybrid teas and hybrid perpetuals have been pruned in early spring, the dormant plants should be sprayed with commercial lime sulfur. During the growing season this disease may be curbed by using any one of the following materials: Actidione PM, Benlate, Karathane, or Phaltan. The last also controls black spot. Some of these materials cannot be used when the air temperature is over 85°F. Observe precautions on the container.

Infection by the mildew fungus occurs most readily when the air is saturated with moisture, but the spores of the parasite do not germinate well when the leaves are wet with dew or rain. This probably accounts for the fact that mildew, unlike black spot, is not favored by continuous rains.

Leaf Spots (*Alternaria circinans, Cercospora puderi, Mycosphaerella rosicola, Monochaetia compta,* and *Septoria rosae*). At least five species of fungi cause leaf spots of rose. These are all controlled with the sprays used to combat black spot.

Stem Cankers

A large number of fungi are known to cause cankers on rose canes. The identification of the particular fungus is not a matter of importance to the home gardener, for the same method of control is generally effective for all except the graft canker.

Brand Canker (*Coniothyrium wernsdorffiae*). The disease is so named because of the black sooty patches (suggesting a burn) which develop during the winter on the canes of climbing roses and other types which have been covered for winter protection. This disease is said not to be important in those parts of America where roses require no winter protection. The canker is at first merely a reddish spot. When mature, it is light buff at the center and very dark purplish brown at the margin. The small longitudinal slits in the bark of the diseased area caused by the necks of the protruding fruit-bodies are characteristic of this canker. (In brown canker, discussed below, the fruit bodies are more evenly distributed.) Brand canker usually occurs sporadically and then in epidemic form. It does not affect leaves and blossoms so often as the fungus that causes brown canker. The bark is smooth and not irregularly cracked, as it is by the common stem canker. On brand cankers that are somewhat sunken, the cracks are lengthwise, while the cracks that develop on common stem cankers extend in all directions.

Control: Infection occurs in late winter or early spring when rose canes are covered. Westcott says that unprotected canes (not covered for winter protection) do not contract the disease to any extent. Therefore the destruction of infected cames as soon as they are discovered, after the winter covering is removed, will usually control the disease. If this is not done, the cankers encircle the cane and the top wilts and dies back. In warmer climates where climbers and bush roses do not require winter protection, no other control is necessary.

Brown Canker (*Cryptosporella umbrina*). This is the most striking of rose cankers, with its light chestnut-brown center and deep purple margin (Fig. 211). Pycnidia, the asexual fruiting bodies of the fungus, extrude coils of

Fig. 211. Brown canker of rose caused by the fungus *Cryptosporella umbrina*.

light yellowish-brown spores in damp weather. This disease is likely to prove very serious in a rose garden where the plants have not been protected against other rose diseases by fungicides. The fungus also attacks leaves, causing small flecks and larger purplish spots. The young blooms of certain varieties are attacked. The petals turn brown and develop numerous dark brown fruiting bodies which appear to the eye as small specks.

Common Stem Canker (*Leptosphaeria coniothyrium*). This canker forms black pycnidial spots. It often develops at the point where the canes have been cut back in pruning. The fungus generally gains entrance through mechanical injuries caused by the whipping of thorny canes against each other or in other ways. The young cankers are at first pale yellowish or somewhat reddish; they become brown, sunken, and cracked with age. This fungus, which is ordinarily limited to the stems, will invade leaves already infected with *Diplocarpon rosae*. See below for control.

Dieback, Cane Blight Canker (*Botryosphaeria dothidea*). This blight is said to be caused by the same fungus that attacks currants and many trees. The leaves on the cane above the canker wilt, turn brown, and die.

Control: Cut out and destroy cankered canes. The black spot sprays will prevent new infections by this fungus.

Crown Canker (*Cylindrocladium scoparium*). This disease is confined largely to greenhouse roses. The bark is blackened and watersoaked at the union of the stock and scion, or on the cane just above. Often the cane is girdled, and fewer and inferior blooms are produced. In 1953 a commercial nurseryman in Delaware lost 500,000 rooted cuttings of *Rosa multiflora* after they were set in the field. This is the first severe epidemic reported on outdoor roses.

Control: Use steam-pasteurized soil because the fungus is soil-borne. Plant uninfected stock.

Rose Graft Canker (*Coniothyrium rosarum*). This canker is said to develop in forcing beds at the union of stock and scion. The infected canes die when the canker has entirely encircled the graft union.

Control: Growers find the "Manetti" stock is rather resistant. Wood to be grafted should be disease-free. Where the disease is serious, infected plants should be removed and destroyed.

Other Cankers. Among other fungi known to cause cankers of rose are *Cryptosporium minimum, Diplodia* sp., *Griphosphaeria corticola, Nectria cinnabarina,* and *Cytospora* sp.

Rust (*Phragmidium mucronatum*). Rusty spots appear on leaves and stems of cultivated roses. This is a serious disease in California and areas of similar climate. It occurs in the eastern United States but the climate is not favorable for its spread.

Control: Occasional applications of zineb or of a mixture of ferbam and sulfur provide control.

Other Rusts. Among other species of rust fungi found on cultivated roses are *Phragmidium americanum, P. rosae-pimpinellifoliae,* and *P. speciosum.*

Wild roses are subject to the following rust fungi: *Phragmidium montivagum, P. fusiforme, P. rosae-arkansanae, P. rosae-californicae,* and *P. rosicola.* These rusts are rarely serious enough to warrant control measures.

Other Diseases. Among other diseases reported on roses are: wilt caused by *Verticilium albo-atrum* and chlorosis due to a deficiency of iron.

The Control of Fungus Diseases

of Roses

The control of fungus diseases of roses in commercial greenhouses involves somewhat different procedures from those that are practical for the home gardener with outdoor roses. To control mildew some growers vaporize sulfur by either painting the heating pipes with a slurry of equal amounts of sulfur and lime, or they use a tin can vaporizer. Other growers use a spray made by dissolving 4 to 6 ounces of Karathane in 100 gallons of water. The Karathane should be applied on good drying days so that the spray will dry on the leaves before evening. It should never be applied when the temperature is above 85°F. A spreader used with this fungicide will give better control.

Sulfur should not be used with oil insecticides.

In a commercial greenhouse that is properly managed, there is little excuse for black spot. This disease is spread by splashing water during syringing. Hence, if water is kept off the leaves, the black spot fungus cannot infect them. Keeping the humidity low also helps to curb this fungus. Commercial growers formerly syringed the roses frequently to curb the spider mites. This practice is rarely followed today, because of the discovery of efficient mite-killers such as Aramite, chlorobenzilate, Kelthane, or Tedion.

Black spot control in commercial plantings of roses outdoors is a very important phase of rose culture, since water cannot be kept off the leaves. Commercial growers resort to the use of any one of several fungicides, including Fore, ferbam, maneb, Phaltan, sulfur-copper mixtures, and zineb. These are usually combined with an insecticide or miticide and a sticker-spreader. Many of the same materials are available to amateur rose growers. These can be purchased separately and mixed as directed, or they may be had in so-called combination sprays mixed with insecticides and miticides.

Some amateur growers with half a dozen or so roses rarely resort to the use of sprays. Where larger numbers are grown, with new kinds introduced into the garden each year, the chances of growing roses without resorting to sprays decrease sharply. In such situations the gardener must turn to sprays to protect the roses from infection by fungi or damage by insects.

The following procedure is suggested for amateur rosarians to assure a minimum of diseases with a minimum of sprays.

Purchase only top quality plants and plant them properly. Observe the plants carefully from time to time and prune out weak or canker-infected canes and remove and dispose of any black-spotted leaves. Spray weekly with a good combination spray. If aphids become prevalent, spray the plants with either malathion or Sevin.

If mites become prevalent and the combination spray does not contain a mite-killer, use Aramite, Dimite, Kelthane, or Ovotran.

If mildew develops, and the combination spray does not contain Phaltan or Karathane, then use one of these or Acti-dione PM dissolved in water as directed on the container.

Combination sprays containing sulfur or Karathane should never be used when the temperature is above 85°F. Rose sprays containing copper should not be used when the weather is cool and wet.

A good combination spray for roses is made with the following ingredients.

Phaltan, 50% wettable powder	4 teaspoonfuls
Sevin, 50% W P	2 Tablespoonfuls
Malathion, 25% W P	4 Tablespoonfuls
Kelthane, 35% W P	3 Teaspoonfuls
Water	1 gallon

Mix the four ingredients dry, then add enough water to make a very thin paste. Pour this mixture into the spray tank, preferably through a fine screen or cheesecloth, add water, and stir.

There are many combination sprays on the market that include other ingredients. These are practical for relatively small plantings but are expensive for large acreages.

Benlate, 1 tablespoonful per 2 gallons of water, is the newest and most effective control for black spot and powdery mildew of roses. The first application is made when the leaves unfold and repeated at 10-14 day intervals through the growing season. A spreader-sticker increases the effectiveness of the spray.

Another good combination spray for controlling diseases of rose leaves is ¹/₂ tablespoon of Benlate per gallon of water added to either Manzate 80 per cent wettable powder or Phaltan 75 per cent wettable powder at ¹/₂ tablespoon per gallon. Include an insecticide in this mixture 3 or 4 times a year as needed.

Recent tests have revealed that Funginex is extremely effective in controlling black spot, powdery mildew and rust of rose.

Virus Diseases

Mosaic (Rose mosaic virus). Rose mosaic occurs on greenhouse roses in the eastern and midwestern states. Chlorotic areas along the midribs of the leaflets and localized distortion are the principal symptoms. At times there are ring, oakleaf, and watermark patterns. There is a yellow strain of this virus which makes brighter and lighter yellow patterns (Fig. 212).

Control: Diseased plants should not be used for propagation. They should be destroyed. Mosaic-infected roses were almost

Fig. 212. Briarcliff rose leaves infected with rose mosaic virus. (U.S. Department of Agriculture)

completely freed of the virus after being held at 38°C. for 4 weeks.

Streak (Rose streak virus). Brown rings and brown vein-banding appear in fully expanded leaves, and brownish or greenish rings in the canes. Necrotic areas develop in the vicinity of grafted buds, resulting in stem-girdling and wilting of the leaves. This virus is transmitted by grafting.

Control: Same as for mosaic.

Other Diseases

Rose Leaf Curl. A graft-transmissible disease characterized by epinasty and premature dehiscence of leaves followed by shoot dieback, was recently reported from California.

Control: Effective controls have not been developed.

Rose Spring Dwarf. Yet another graft-transmissible disease characterized by "balled" or rosetted growth in spring has also recently been found in California.

Control: Control measures are unavailable.

Mercury Injury. Roses may be injured if grown in greenhouses where mercury-containing paints have been used recently. The mercury vapor released from such paints causes flowers to be off-color and prevents young buds from opening.

Control: Avoid using paints containing mercury. The mercury vapors in already-painted greenhouses can be trapped by applying over the paint a mixture of 5 parts dry lime sulfur in a paste of 10 parts wheat flour in 100 parts of water. Special sealing paints are also available.

Insects and Other Animal Pests

Aphids. Four species of aphids infest roses: green peach, melon, potato, and rose, These appear on garden roses in May and June, and are common in greenhouses. Most of them are greenish, but pink or reddish broods are often present on roses, especially early in the season. They multiply so rapidly that infested flower buds and stalks become covered with them. They are also found feeding on the under sides of the leaves. The oblong, shining black eggs are laid in the fall here and there on the bark and tip ends of the branches of canes and survive the winter there even though the temperature may fall to 10°F. or lower. In the western states, the small green aphid, *Myzaphis rosarum,* often becomes a serious pest of roses.

Control: For many years the standard spray for aphid control was 2 teaspoons of nicotine sulfate in a gallon of soapy water. This mixture is still effective provided it is applied on a warm day (above 80°F.). More commonly used materials for controlling aphids are Cygon, Meta-Systox R, malathion and Sevin.

Asiatic Garden Beetle (*Maladera castanea*). This beetle has habits similar to the Japanese beetle but feeds only at night.

Control: Thorough cultivation of the soil of the rose garden and of other ground where the eggs have been laid destroys many insects in the pupal stage. The Diazinon soil treatment recommended for Japanese beetles also helps to control the larval stage of this pest.

Rose Budworm (*Pyrrhia umbra*). The buds of roses and other garden flowers are chewed by two kinds of caterpillars. One is green with prominent dark longitudinal spots and black tubercles; the other has whitish-orange markings on its back.

Control: Spray with Sevin, when the caterpillars begin to feed.

Raspberry Cane Borer (*Oberea maculata*). This borer attacks uninjured canes of hybrid perpetuals and other roses, 6 or 8 inches below the tip ends, causing them to droop and the leaves above to wilt. The larvae bore downward in the cane to the base below ground, where they pupate.

Control: Prune away wilted tips well below the infested region.

Another borer invades the pith of rose stems after pruning. This pest may be controlled by painting the pruning cuts in spring with orange shellac or tree paint to prevent the adult female from inserting eggs on the exposed surface.

Rose Chafer (*Macrodactylus subspinosus*). This beetle can be readily distinguished from other beetles infesting roses by the grayish or fawn color of its elongated body (1/2 inch long) and by its sluggish movements. The adults feed not only on roses but on other garden plants such as peony and hollyhock. The leaves of grapes, elms, and several other shrubs and trees are also occasionally badly infested. The season of flower infestation lasts about 4 weeks. The eggs are laid in the soil and hatch within 2 weeks, after which the grubs feed on roots of lawn grasses, to which they may do considerable damage; they may be mistaken for the larvae of the Japanese beetle.

Control: Spray with methoxychlor or Sevin when the insects first appear, and repeat as often as required.

Rose Curculio (*Rhynchites bicolor*). This insect is about 1/4 inch long, reddish on the back and black underneath. With its long snout it can eat deep holes in buds of roses and some other garden plants. Infested buds usually fail to open. Examination of the buds will show that the petals are full of holes made by the feeding of the insects.

Control: Daily hand-picking of infested buds is helpful, and collecting and destroying the fruits or hips will lessen the infestation for the coming year, for this destroys the larvae. Since these weevils are likely to be still abundant after the blooming season, the plants may be sprayed with Sevin mixed with Kelthane. Although this pest is usually not troublesome on hybrid teas, it has been known to cause serious damage to cultivated roses grown near wild roses.

Mossy-Rose Gall Wasp (*Diplopepis rosae*). Greenish or reddish moss-like balls about an inch in diameter are sometimes found on the stems of bush roses (Fig. 14). These are caused by the sting of the mossy-rose gall wasp. Very little damage is usually done.

Control: Prune canes harboring the galls and destroy them.

Rose Stem Girdler (*Agrilus aurichalceus*). The larvae of the beetle work in the sapwood particularly of *Rosa hugonis;* they usually bore the stem in a close spiral. Swellings from 1 to 3 inches long are induced on the cane, which may crack or break off if the burrowing is rather extensive. The beetles lay their eggs singly on the stems in June and July. The larvae are active until October or even later and overwinter in the woody gall.

Control: Infested canes should be cut out below the point of attack and destroyed as soon as discovered.

Japanese Beetle (*Popillia japonica*). In regions where the Japanese beetle has become established, the foliage of bush roses and pole roses is subject to serious damage by the adult beetles. The characteristic work of the beetles is shown in Fig. 38. The leaves of hybrid tea roses are not damaged so long as there are blooms on the plants. The adults gather on the blooms after they are open, often in large numbers, and quickly destroy them entirely; they usually do not feed on the unopened buds. If the ground around hybrid tea roses is thoroughly worked over, the grubs do little or no damage. Many eggs are laid in grassy places about the garden. When the foliage is attacked the adult beetles may be controlled by spraying with methoxychlor or Sevin. It has been found that in the home garden it is advisable to hand-pick the beetles by knocking them into a can containing kerosene and water. The use of beetle traps is not advised because the geraniol bait attracts more beetles into the rose garden than the traps catch; if traps are to be used, they should be placed outside the garden and baited with a mixture of geraniol and eugenol. Apply Diazinon to grass plots or borders in the rose garden to control the larval stage of the Japanese beetle. "Milky disease" spore dust, sold under the trade name "Doom," can also be distributed over large areas of grass bordering a rose planting. This material, though acting more slowly than chemical substances, eventually reduces the beetle population. It should not be used in areas treated with insecticides.

Rose Leafhopper (*Edwardsiana rosae*). This insect overwinters in the egg stage in the bark of bush roses and climbers. The eggs hatch in May and the young insects feed on the under sides of the leaves, sucking out the sap and causing the appearance of white stippling similar to that caused by the two-spotted mite and the lace bug on rhododendron. When disturbed the young move about rather rapidly, while the adults fly away.

Control: Sevin sprays are very effective in combating this pest. Unfortunately, repeated applications of this insecticide will result in a heavy build-up of red spider mite. Should this occur, spray with a mite killer such as Aramite, Dimite or Kelthane. It is possible to mix Sevin with Aramite or Kelthane and thus prevent the build-up of mites. Diazinon sprays are also effective.

Oblique-Banded Leaf Roller (*Choristoneura rosaceana*). This pale green, black-headed larva, also known as the rose leaf tier, chews holes in rosebuds and rolls up the leaves and ties them together. It feeds on a wide variety of herbaceous and woody plants.

Control: Spray with Sevin as soon as the larvae begin to feed and before they roll up the leaves.

Rose Midge (*Dasineura rhodophaga*). Long known as a greenhouse pest, this insect now causes considerable damage to garden roses in the eastern states. There are two periods during which it is serious on garden roses, one during the June blooming season and another in the autumn blooming season of hybrid tea roses. The leaf buds and young tender branches are attacked, and the upper ends of the leafy shoots become deformed, turn brown or black, and die. Flower buds are infested so that they do not open normally; 15 or 20 maggots may be found in a single bud. The little whitish or light orange-colored larvae or maggots, $1/12$ inch long, drop from the infested parts to the ground and spin their cocoons in the soil. The midges emerge within a week or ten days, so that several new broods are developed during each blooming season.

Control: In the greenhouse, control of this pest is obtained with the standard malathion sprays or aerosols. On outdoor roses, Diazinon sprays are effective.

Scales. A great number of scale insects infest roses in the greenhouse and in the garden. The following have been reported: black, California red, camphor, cottony maple, European fruit lecanium, Florida red, greedy, green shield, latania, olive, oystershell, peach, rose, San Jose, and walnut.

Control: In addition to the pruning required by good cultural practice, varieties liable to infestation should be sprayed with commercial lime sulfur early in spring while the plants are still dormant. As the canes of certain varieties of climbing roses are rather susceptible to oil spray injury, avoid using this type of spray. Use a Cygon, malathion or Sevin spray in May and June for a complete clean-up.

Bristly Rose-Slug (*Cladius isomerus*). The leaves of climbing roses, especially, may be skeletonized at first, later entirely eaten away at blooming time by brown-headed, pale green caterpillars from $1/2$ to $3/4$ inch in length; these later become sparsely beset with fine hairs. They feed principally at night. In northern latitudes there are only two generations a year, but at Washington, D.C., there are six generations a year. The insects overwinter in cocoons concealed in rubbish.

Another rose-slug (*Endelomyia aethiops*),

is also common on roses in the eastern United States.

Control: Prevent infestation by cleaning up and destroying all rubbish. Spray infested plants with Diazinon or Sevin in June.

Thrips. Six species of thrips attack roses: Florida flower, flower, greenhouse, onion, tobacco, and western flower. The flower thrips, *Frankliniella tritici,* causes buds to ball without opening and the petals to turn brown. When infestation is heavy, few flowers open normally.

Control: Prevention of early infestations is very necessary in the control of thrips, as it is impossible to reach the insects with sprays once they have penetrated between the petals, where the pests are well protected. Plants likely to be infested should be sprayed in spring before the buds have developed to any

extent. Infested buds and open flowers should be picked off and destroyed (the insects mature in the refuse pile and fly back to the rose garden). Sprays containing malathion or Cygon are effective provided they are applied frequently.

Some commercial growers use Thimet on the soil around greenhouse roses. This systemic substance is absorbed by the roots and transported to the leaves, where it kills thrips and some other sucking pests. It is very poisonous and malodorous, and is not recommended for home gardeners.

Fall Webworm (*Hyphantria cunea*). This worm can be distinguished from the tent caterpillar most readily by the character of the tent or web. That of the webworm is more compact and encloses the ends of the leaves of individual branches (Fig. 213). Roses and

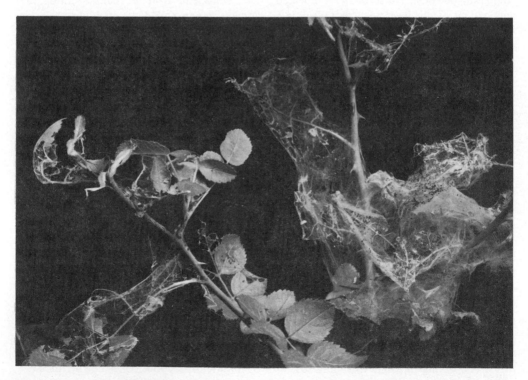

Fig. 213. Fall webworm *(Hyphantria cunea)* on rose.

other shrubs are attacked some time in August.

Control: See *Fraxinus.*

Two-Spotted Mite (*Tetranychus urticae*). This is a greenhouse pest of roses, but it can also do much damage to garden roses. Some polyantha and floribunda roses are so susceptible to mites that they lose their leaves prematurely.

Control: Frequent applications of sulfur either alone or in combination sprays help to control this mite. When sulfur sprays fail to provide adequate control, the gardener can use any one of several excellent mite killers. Among these are chlorobenzilate, Kelthane, or Tedion. Most of these materials are compatible with fungicides. Follow the manufacturer's directions on compatibility and dilutions.

Root-Knot Nemas (*Meloidogyne hapla* and *M. incognita*). The former infests outdoor roses in the North, the latter greenhouse roses in the North and outdoor ones in the South. See Fig. 214.

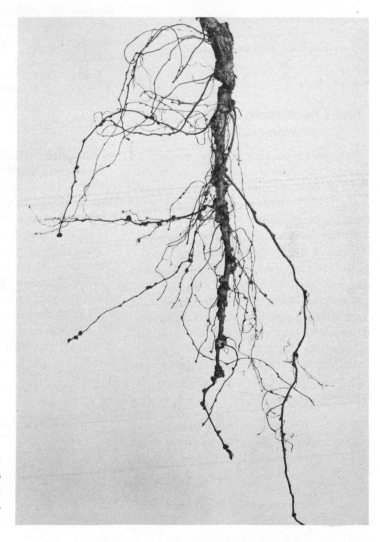

Fig. 214. Root-knot galls on rose roots caused by the nema *Meliodogyne incognita.*

Control: See Chapter 3.

Other Nemas. Several other species of nemas are associated with poor growth in roses. In southern California the most common ones are the root lesion nema, *Pratylenchus vulnus,* and the stubby root, *Trichodorus christiei.* Affected plants are stunted and chlorotic and have necrotic root systems that are smaller than normal. Leaves from infested plants are lower in iron, copper, and potassium than those of uninfested plants. *Control:* See Chapter 3.

Japanese Weevil. See *Ligustrum.*

Surinam Cockroaches. See *Filices.*

RUBUS (FLOWERING RASPBERRY AND SALMONBERRY)

Ornamental raspberries are subject to many of the diseases and insect pests that affect the furiting varieties of *Rubus.* The following are a few diseases that are common on the ornamental kinds.

Rubus odoratus, the flowering raspberry, is attacked by the powdery mildew fungus *Sphaerotheca humuli* and the rust *Phragmidium rubi-odorati.* They do little damage. The systemic orange rust, *Gymnoconia peckiana,* which is common on many species of *Rubus* grown for fruit, is not known to attack the flowering raspberry. In the northwestern states, *Rubus spectabilis,* the salmonberry, is very susceptible to a leaf spot caused by the fungus *Mycosphaerella rubi.*

Mosaic. This disease, more common on fruiting raspberries, is caused by a virus complex and is transmitted by the aphid *Amphorophora rubi.* Infection delays leaf development, and the canes become stunted and rosetted. The leaves exhibit chlorotic mottling, especially in cool weather.

RUDBECKIA (GOLDENGLOW)

Diseases

Downy Mildew (*Plasmopara halstedii*). This disease may cause wilting and death of seedlings. Older plants may not die but the foliage is mottled a light yellow. *Control:* Set plants in clean soil. Spray with Bordeaux mixture during summer to prevent severe outbreaks of the disease.

Leaf Spots (*Cercospora rudbeckiae, Phyllosticta rudbeckiae, Ramularia rudbeckiae,* and *Septoria rudbeckiae*). Leaf spots of goldenglow are seldom serious enough to require control measures. Picking off and destroying the first spotted leaves is usually sufficient.

Rusts (*Puccinia dioicae, Uromyces perigynius,* and *U. rudbeckiae*). Brown or yellow pustules on the leaves are caused by one of the three rust fungi. *Control:* Rusts on this host are rarely serious enough to warrant control measures.

Powdery Mildew (*Erysiphe cichoracearum*). This is perhaps the most common disease of this host. The leaves are coated white by the fungus in late summer. *Control:* Spray with Karathane or Benlate as soon as the mildew appears. Repeat a few times at 2-week intervals.

Other Diseases. This host is also subject to a crown rot caused by *Pellicularia rolfsii,* a leaf gall by *Synchytrium aureum,* a stem rot by *Sclerotinia sclerotiorum,* and a smut by *Entyloma compositarum.* The aster yellows disease has also been recorded on goldenglow.

Insects

Brown Ambrosia Aphid (*Dactynotus ambrosiae*). This bright red aphid with long legs is very common on goldenglow. It also infests delphinium, chrysanthemums, sunflower, and other plants.

Control: Spray with malathion, Meta-Systox R, or Sevin.

Goldenglow Sawfly (*Macrophya intermedia*). This gray larva with dark stripes may completely defoliate goldenglow.

Control: Spray with Diazinon, malathion, or Sevin when the young larvae begin to feed.

Other Pests. Goldenglow may also be infested by the asiatic garden and Fuller rose beetles; burdock and stalk borers; and the tarnished and four-lined plant bugs. These are discussed under more favored hosts.

SABAL (COMMON PALMETTO)—see PALMACEAE

SAGITTARIA (ARROWHEAD)

The only problems recorded on this host, which is grown in ponds and aquaria, are a leaf spot caused by the fungus *Cercospora alismatis* and the cotton aphid, *Aphis gossypii*.

Corky Spot. This disease of unknown cause appears as dead patches on the tips of leaves. The patches are light gray or brown with definite margins sunken on the upper sides and raised on the lower. Corky growth appears on the leaf stalk near the blade. Many small black dots like pinpoints are also present, but these may be the result of the feeding of sucking insects.

SAINTPAULIA (AFRICAN-VIOLET)

Diseases

Blight (*Botrytis cinerea*). Leaves are blighted and decayed by this fungus when plants are grown in the greenhouse under condition of high humidity.

Control: Improve ventilation, avoid overhead watering, and control mites with a miticide, for mites seem to increase the amount of this blight.

Crown Rot (*Pythium ultimum*). This disease occurs on greenhouse and homegrown African-violets when the plants are overwatered and the soil drainage is unsatisfactory. The crown and roots of plants turn soft and mushy, and the leaves wilt.

Control: Do not take leaf cuttings from infected plants. Destroy badly diseased plants. Set healthy rooted cuttings in steam-pasteurized soil. Do not overwater. A Dexon drench is effective as a spot treatment in commercial greenhouses. "Supreme" varieties are most frequently affected.

Petiole Rot. Rot of the petiole may occur at the point where the petiole touches the rim of the pot. This may be caused by fertilizer salts which are absorbed by the porous pot. A strip of aluminum foil placed over the rim of the pot will prevent contact between the petiole and the pot.

This trouble should not be mistaken for the crown rot disease caused by the fungus *Pythium ultimum*.

Powdery Mildew (*Oidium* sp.). *Saintpaulia ionantha* grown in commercial greenhouses is frequently subject to this air-borne fungus.

Control: Benlate sprays should provide control.

Physiological Diseases

Bud Drop. The buds of African-violets sometimes shrivel, turn brown, and drop prematurely in the home. Several factors are responsible, including low temperatures, low humidity, overwatering, and extreme fluctuations in soil moisture, temperature, and light intensity.

Chlorosis. Odd, yellow, ring, and line patterns frequently appear on the leaves. The condition is said to be due to some unfavorable cultural practice such as sudden chilling of the leaves with cold water in sunlight. Plants should be watered from the soil surface and should be kept out of direct sunlight. Failure to provide sufficient heat on cool nights is also believed to be a contributing factor. African-violets should be shaded from bright sun but should get as much indirect light as possible during the winter months.

Insects and Other Animal Pests

Mealybugs (*Planococcus citri*). This insect is especially troublesome on African violets.

Control: Use Cythion spray from time to time as needed. Do not over-dose with this material.

Mites. Two species of mites, the broad and the cyclamen, frequently infest *Saintpaulia.* The former causes leaves to take on a glassy appearance; the latter deforms leaves, makes them very hairy, and deforms stems.

Control: A hot-water dip of the plant, pot and all, was formerly recommended. Home gardeners should spray with Kelthane.

Springtails (*Collembola*). These small white, slender, very active insects ¹/₅ inch long are found in the soil, around the bottom of pots, and in water that drains from the pots after the plants are watered. They are most obvious when the soil surface is watered and frequently cause much concern to house plant owners.

Control: Water the soil with a weak solution of malathion, prepared from the emulsifiable concentrate, or methoxychlor.

Nemas. Two kinds of nemas infest African-violets, the fern, *Aphelenchoides olesistus,* and the southern root-knot, *Meloidogyne incognita.* The former causes the leaves to turn brown along the veins and spots to appear on the lower surfaces; the latter makes galls or swellings on the roots in addition to stunting and weakening the aboveground parts.

Control: See Chapter 3 for the standard control measures.

SALIX (WILLOW)

Bacterial and Fungus Diseases

Bacterial Twig Blight (*Pseudomonas saliciperda*). The leaves brown and wilt, and blighted branches die back for some distance. Brown streaks can be seen in sections of the wood. The parasite winters in the cankers, so that the young leaves are infected as soon as they unfold. The disease has so far been serious only in New England. There it has caused the death of a large number of trees by serious defoliation. The damage has been confused with frost injury.

Control: Pruning as many infected twigs as possible and spraying as suggested below for leaf blight are the recommended control measures.

Crown Gall (*Agrobacterium tumefaciens*). See *Rosa.*

Leaf Blight (*Venturia saliciperda*). This is the most destructive disease of willows. Soon after growth starts in spring, a few small leaves turn black and die. Later, all the remaining leaves on the tree suddenly wilt and blacken, as if they had been burned by fire. Cankers on twigs may result from the leaf infections. After rainy periods, olive-brown fruiting structures of the causal fungus appear on the under sides of blighted leaves, principally along the veins and midribs. The asexual stage of the fungus, *Pollaccia saliciperda,* is responsible for the heavy summer infections.

Control: Pruning of dead twigs and branches will eliminate the most important source of inoculum for early-season infections. Spraying 3 or 4 times with Fore, maneb, or zineb, starting when the leaves begin to emerge in the spring, will usually give control. These practices are recommended only for valuable specimens. A number of species, including weeping, bay-leaved, osier, purple, and the pussy willows, appear resistant to blight. These should be planted in place of the more susceptible species, such as the crack and the heart-leaved willow. Golden willow has been reported by some investigators to be susceptible, by others to be resistant.

Black Canker (*Physalospora miyabeana*). The symptoms of this disease resemble those of leaf blight but usually appear later in summer. Dark brown spots, many of which show concentric markings, appear on the upper leaf surfaces. Whitish-gray or gray elliptical lesions with black borders appear subsequently on the twigs and stems. Clusters of minute black fruiting bodies develop in the stem lesions. Successive attacks over a 2- or 3-year period usually result in the death of the entire tree.

Control: Pruning and spraying as suggested for leaf blight are recommended. The use of resistant varieties also offers a means of avoiding this destructive disease. The bay-leaved, the osier, and the weeping willow appear to be resistant, whereas the crack, the heart-leaved, the white, the purple, and the almond willow appear to be susceptible. As with blight, golden willow has been reported by some observers to be extremely susceptible, by others to be resistant.

Cytospora Canker (*Cytospora chrysosperma*). The sexual stage of this fungus is *Valsa sordida*. It affects willows in much the same way as poplars. The control measures listed under *Populus* hold also for this host. In addition the use of resistant varieties offers a means of avoiding serious trouble. One investigator has observed that the disease occurs rarely on black willow or on peach-leaf willow, whereas crack and golden willows appear to be extremely susceptible.

Other Cankers. Willows are susceptible to other dieback or canker diseases caused by *Botryosphaeria dothidea*, *Cryptodiaporthe salicina*, *Cryptomyces maximus*, *Discella carbonacea*, *Diplodina* sp., and *Macrophoma* sp.

Gray Scab (*Sphaceloma murrayae*). This disease affects many species of willow including *Salix fragilis*, S. *lasiandra*, and S. *lasiolepis*. Round, irregular, somewhat raised, grayish-white spots with narrow, dark brown margins appear on the leaves. Affected portions of the leaves frequently drop away.

Control: Same as for leaf spots described below.

Leaf Spots. At least ten species of leaf spots—*Ascochyta salicis*, *Asteroma capreae*, *Cercospora salicina*, *Cylindrosporium salicinum*, *Marssonina kriegeriana*, *Myriconium comitatum*, *Phyllosticta apicalis*, *Ramularia rosea*, *Septogloeum salicinum*, and *Septoria didyma*—cause leaf spots on willows. Some may also cause premature defoliation.

Control: Because most leaf spot fungi overwinter on diseased fallen leaves, gathering and destroying the leaves is a recommended practice. Valuable specimens should be sprayed with ferbam, zineb, or copper fungicides when leaf spots cause considerable defoliation annually.

Powdery Mildew (*Unicinula salicis*). Leaves infected with this mildew are covered with a whitish felt-like mold. This develops chains of white spores which are shed in clouds. The little black fruiting bodies formed later in the season are characterized by microscopic appendages curled at the end like a shepherd's crook (see Fig. 51). This is not a serious disease of willows, but may cause some loss of leaves.

Control: Valuable willows infected with this fungus can be protected by an occasional application of Karathane spray. Sprays containing wettable sulfur also can be used to control this mildew. Bordeaux mixture, recommended for several other diseases of willow, is also helpful.

Rust (*Melampsora* spp.). Three or four species of rust attack willow leaves, causing lemon-yellow spots on the lower surfaces. Later in the season the spore-bearing pustules are dark-colored. The disease may be severe enough to cause dropping of the leaves. Of the rust-causing fungi, one species, *M. paradoxa,* has the larch as the alternate host; *M. abieti-capraearum* has the balsam fir; and *M. arctica* lives a part of the year on a saxifrage.

Control: Although rust infections are not considered serious, they may result in heavy defoliation of young trees. Gathering and destroying fallen leaves will help to prevent serious outbreaks. The use of copper or sulfur fungicides as preventives is suggested only in rare instances.

Tar Spot (*Rhytisma salicinum*). These spots are usually jet black, very definitely bounded, about 1/4 inch in diameter, somewhat raised about the surface of the leaf. They are more common on maple.

Control: Since this fungus winters on the old leaves, care should be taken, where the disease is serious, to rake up and destroy dead leaves. Spray the shrubs or trees early in May with Bordeaux mixture or wettable sulfur.

Witches' Broom (Mycoplasma-like organism). Early breaking of auxillary buds and subsequent growth of numerous, spindly, erect branches with stunted leaves on *Salix rigida* are characteristic symptoms of this disease. The witches' brooms die the winter after they are formed.

Control: Ways of preventing this disease have yet to be developed.

Insects

Aphids. Several species of aphids infest willows, the most common being the giant bark, *Longistigma caryae.*

Control: Spray valuable specimens with Meta-Systox R, Sevin, or malathion.

Imported Willow Leaf Beetle (*Plagiodera versicolora*). These beautiful metallic-blue beetles, about 1/8 inch long, live through the winter under the bark scales and in the rubbish about the tree. They emerge and lay their lemon-yellow eggs some time in early June. The ugly larvae or grubs feed on the under sides of the foliage, leaving only a network of veins. The adult beetle develops during July and produces a second brood in August. This beetle is so much smaller than the Japanese beetle, *Popillia japonica,* that it can scarcely be mistaken for it. In the vicinity of New York both beetles cause rather serious damage.

Control: Spraying with methoxychlor or Sevin in late May will control this pest. A second spraying in late June may be necessary for the second brood.

Pine Cone Gall (*Rhabdophaga strobiliodes*). Cone-shaped galls at the branch tips that hinder bud development are produced by small maggots. The adult, a small fly, deposits eggs in the opening buds. The larvae hibernate in cocoons inside the galls.

Control: Remove and destroy galls in the fall, or spray thoroughly with malathion when the buds are swelling in the spring.

Willowbeaked Gall Midge (*Mayetiola rigidae*). Swollen, distorted twigs may be produced by yellowish, jumping maggots of the willowbeaked gall midge. The adults appear in early spring.

Control: Prune and destroy infested twigs.

Willow Lace Bug (*Corythucha mollicula*). Willow leaves may be severely mottled and yellowed by this sucking insect.

Control: Malathion, Diazinon, or Sevin sprays in late spring provide excellent control.

Willow Flea Weevil (*Rhynchaenus rufipes*). The overwintering adult beetle emerges in the middle of April. During the latter part of May it excavates a circular mine on the under side of the leaf and in it deposits its eggs. The adults feed on the foliage, causing it to become brown and dry. The larvae begin to mine the leaves about the middle of June. By the end of July, where infestation is heavy, the trees appear as if scorched by fires.

Control: To control the adult weevil, spray in late May with Sevin.

Mottled Willow Borer (*Cryptorhynchus lapathi*). This borer causes a rough, swollen, abnormal growth of the branches that are attacked. The borer is about ½ inch long and works near the surface of the stem. The adult is a black beetle about ⅓ inch long.

Control: Spray the trunk thoroughly in late August with methoxychlor.

Poplar Borer (*Saperda calcarata*). This borer penetrates deeply into the wood and may be distinguished from the willow borer by the excelsior-like frass. See also under *Populus.*

Control: If their tunnels are visible, the borers can be killed by inserting a flexible wire, or by using a preparation containing nicotine sulfate in jelly form, then sealing the hole with wax or chewing gum. Badly infested willows should be cut down and destroyed.

Satin Moth (*Stilpnotia salicis*). See *Populus.*

Willow Shoot Sawfly (*Janus abbreviatus*). The female lays its eggs in the shoots in early spring. It then girdles the stem, preventing further growth of the twig, which wilts and dies. The young borers feed in the pith of the shoots, which die eventually.

Control: Prune and destroy infested twigs. Spray with Sevin when the larvae are small.

Willow Scurfy Scale (*Chionaspis salicis-nigrae*). Branches and even small trees may be killed by heavy infestations of this pest, a pear-shaped white scale ⅛ inch long. The pest passes the winter in the egg stage underneath the scale of the female.

Other scale insects that attack willows are black, California red, cottony-cushion, cottony maple, European fruit, greedy, lecanium, obscure, oystershell, Putnam, soft, and terrapin.

Control: Spray with lime sulfur or a dormant oil in spring when trees are still dormant, then with malathion or Sevin in May and again in June to control the crawler stage.

Other Insects. Willows may also be infested by bagworm, California tent caterpillar, eastern tent caterpillar, hemlock looper, omnivorous looper, orange tortrix, red-humped caterpillar, walnut caterpillar, giant hornet, and several species of thrips.

SALPIGLOSSIS (PAINTED-TONGUE)

This old garden ornamental of the potato family is relatively free of pests. Two wilts caused by a species of *Fusarium* and by *Verticillium albo-atrum*, and aster yellows by a mycoplasma-like organism are the only diseases recorded.

The De Man's meadow nema, *Pratylenchus pratensis*, and the southern root-knot nema, *Meloidogyne incognita*, also infest this host. Controls for the nemas are discussed in Chapter 3.

SALVIA (SAGE)

Diseases

Damping-off (*Pythium debaryanum* and *Pellicularia filamentosa*). In seed beds where plants are rather crowded and under moist conditions some killing of seedlings may follow attacks by these fungi.

Control: See Chapter 4 under Soil-pasteurization.

Leaf Spots (*Cercospora salviicola* and *Ramularia salviicola*). These leaf spots are usually unimportant in garden plantings. Picking off and destroying the first spotted leaves usually provide control.

Rusts. Many species of rust fungi occur primarily on the wild species of *Salvia*. Among the more common ones are *Puccinia caulicola, P. farinacea,* and *P. salviicola.* Control measures are rarely practical.

Other Diseases. Among other diseases found on this host are downy mildew caused by *Peronospora swinglei,* powdery mildew by

Erysiphe cichoracearum, stem rot by *Sphaeropsis salviae,* wilt by *Verticillium albo-atrum,* and aster yellows by a mycoplasma-like organism.

Insects and Other Animal Pests

Salvias are subject to a number of pests that more frequently infest other hosts. Among these are the foxglove aphid, *Acyrthosiphon solani;* Asiatic garden beetle, *Maladera castanea;* stalk borer, *Papaipema nebris;* grape leafhopper, *Erythroneura comes;* greenhouse leaf tier, *Udea rubigalis;* greenhouse orthezia, *Orthezia insignis;* tarnished plant bug, *Lygus lineolaris;* greenhouse whitefly, *Trialeurodes vaporariorum;* and the yellow woollybear, *Diacrisia virginica.* The fern nema, *Aphelenchoides olesistus,* and the southern rootknot nema, *Meloidogyne incognita,* also affect salvia. All the animal pests listed above are discussed under more favored hosts in other parts of this book.

SAMBUCUS (ELDER)

Diseases

Cankers (*Cytospora sambucicola, C. chrysosperma, Diplodia* sp., *Nectria cinnabarina, N. coccinea,* and *Sphaeropsis sambucina*). Cankers on twigs and branches may be caused by any of the fungi listed. When the canker girdles the affected member, the distal portion dies.

Control: Prune and destroy stems and twigs showing cankers.

Leaf Spots (*Ascochyta wisconsina, Cercospora catenospora, C. depazoides, Cercosporella prolificans, Phyllosticta sambuci, Ramularia sambucina, Mycosphaerella* sp., and *Septoria sambucina*). Many fungi cause leaf spots on *Sambucus.* They are rarely important enough to warrant control measures.

Powdery Mildews (*Microsphaera alni, M. grossulariae, Phyllactinia corylea,* and *Sphaerotheca humuli*). Four species of powdery mildew fungi affect *Sambucus,* producing the typical white coating of the leaves.

Control: Valuable specimens can be protected with Benlate or Karathane sprays.

Other Fungus Diseases. *Sambucus* is also subject to thread blight caused by *Pellicularia koleroga;* root rots by *Helicobasidium purpureum, Phymatotrichum omnivorum,* and *Xylaria multiplex;* and wilt by *Verticillium albo-atrum.*

Insects

Borers. Several borers are important pests of this host. The currant borer, *Synanthedon tipuliformis,* attacks the black elder as well as currant. The elder borer, *Desmocerus palliatus,* riddles the base of the stems, causing dieback of branches and sometimes of the entire shrub. The elder shoot borer, *Achatodes zeae,* occasionally infests young shoots.

Control: Prune and destroy infested parts as soon as they are noted.

Other Insects. Among the insects of minor importance which infest elders are potato flea beetle, green stink bug, omnivorous looper, grape mealybug, San Jose scale, and madrona thrips.

SANSEVIERIA (BOWSTRING-HEMP)

Diseases

Bacterial Soft Rot (*Erwinia carotovora* var. *aroideae*). This bacterium may cause a soft mushy rot at the base of the stems, particularly when plants are overwatered.

Control: Keep plants on the dry side. Do not propagate from diseased plants. Use steam-pasteurized soil for growing new plants.

Leaf Spot (*Fusarium moniliforme*). This fungus causes sunken reddish-brown spots with yellowish borders, up to ½ inch in diameter. The spots may appear on only one side of the leaf or they may extend through it. They usually dry and fall out. If numerous, the spots may run together and encircle the leaf, in which case the part above dies. The sexual stage of this fungus is known as *Gibberella fujikuroi*. This species, or a closely related strain, causes a disease of rice in the Orient. It is the fungus which produces the growth-promoting substance, gibberellic acid.

Another leaf spot, caused by the fungus *Gloeosporium sansevieriae,* has been reported from Florida and Washington State.

Control: Cut out and destroy spotted leaves. Avoid wetting the foliage when watering.

SASSAFRAS

Diseases

Cankers (*Nectria galligena* and *Physalospora obtusa*). These fungi are associated with branch cankers and dieback of sassafras.

Control: Prune affected branches to sound wood.

Leaf Spots (*Actinopelte dryina, Diplopeltis sassafrasicola, Glomerella cingulata, Metasphaeria sassafrasicola, Phyllosticta illinoisensis,* and *Stigmatophragmia sassafrasicola*). Six species of fungi cause leaf spots on sassafras. They are rarely serious enough to warrant control measures.

Other Diseases. Powdery mildew caused by the fungus *Phyllactinia corylea,* wilt by a species of *Verticillium,* shoestring root rot by *Armillaria mellea,* and a disease of the yellows type have also been recorded on sassafras. The last causes bunching and fasciation of the branch tips, leaf rolling and leaf dwarfing.

This host is also subject to curly top caused by the beet curly top virus and to aster yellows caused by a mycoplasma-like organism. The controls of these diseases are discussed under more favored hosts.

Insects

Japanese Beetle (*Popillia japonica*). Sassafras is a favorite host of this beetle. The topmost leaves, exposed to the bright sun, are the first to be attacked.

Control: Sassafras trees used in ornamental plantings can be protected by spraying with Diazinon, methoxychlor, or Sevin, first when the beetles begin feeding on the leaves and then with 2 repetitions at weekly intervals.

Promethea Moth (*Callosamia promethea*). The leaves are chewed by the promethea moth larva, a bluish-green caterpillar that grows to 2 inches in length. The adult female has reddish-brown wings, near the tips of which eye-like spots are visible; the wingspread is nearly 3 inches. The cocoons of this pest are suspended in the trees.

The caterpillars of the hickory horned devil, (*Citheronia regalis*), the io (*Automeris io*), and the polyphemus moth (*Antheraea polyphemus*), also chew sassafras leaves.

Control: Spray with *Bacillus thuringiensis,* Imidan, or Sevin when the caterpillars are small.

Sassafras Weevil (*Odontopus calceatus*). This small snout weevil begins to feed as soon as the buds break and before the leaves have expanded, making numerous holes in the leaves. The female adults then deposit eggs on the midribs of the leaves, and the larvae which hatch from these mine into the leaves to cause blotches. Tulip-tree and magnolia are also susceptible.

Control: Sevin sprays applied in early June when the adults begin to feed, or after the eggs hatch, should provide control.

Scales. The oystershell and San Jose scales occasionally infest this host. Valuable specimens can be protected from these pests with two applications of malathion or Sevin sprays, one in May and the other in June.

Other Scales. In addition to the two scales mentioned above, sassafras is occasionally infested by the European fruit lecanium (*Lecanium corni*), Florida wax (*Ceroplastis floridensis*), and pyriform (*Protopulvinaria pyriformis*).

SAXIFRAGA (SAXIFRAGE)

Diseases

Leaf Spots. Four fungi (*Cercosporella saxifragae, Phyllosticta saxifragarum, Septoria albicans*, and *Ramularia* sp.) cause leaf spotting of *Saxifraga*.
Control: These fungi are rarely destructive enough to warrant control measures.

Powdery Mildew (*Sphaerotheca macularis*). A white powdery coating develops on the leaves.
Control: Sulfur or Karathane sprays will control powdery mildew.

Rusts. Three species and one variety of rust fungi – *Melampsora artica, Puccinia heucherae, P. pazschkei* and *P. pazschkei* var. *tricuspidatae* – may infect *Saxifraga*.
Control: Measures to control rusts are rarely adopted.

Insects

Grape Rootworm (*Fidia viticida*). Although primarily a pest on grape, the grub stage of this pest feeds on the roots of saxifrage and some other wild plants. The adult stage feeds on the leaves, leaving small holes.
Control: Spray leaves with Sevin as soon as the first punctures are noticed.

Other Pest. The spotted garden slug, *Limax maximus*, occasionally feeds on *Saxifraga*.
Control: See slugs and snails, in Chapter 3.

SCABIOSA

Diseases

Four fungus diseases occur on scabiosa: blight caused by *Pellicularia rolfsii*, powdery mildew by *Erysiphe polygoni*, root rot by *Phymatotrichum omnivorum*, and stem rot by *Sclerotinia sclerotiorum*.

This host is also subject to a virus disease, curly top caused by the beet curly top virus, and to aster yellows, caused by a mycoplasma-like organism.

The controls for these diseases are discussed under more favored hosts.

Insects

The Fuller rose beetle, *Pantomorus cervinus*); the aster leafhopper, *Macrosteles fascifrons;* and the chrysanthemum lace bug, *Corythucha marmorata* infest scabiosa. The leafhopper spreads the aster yellows disease.
Control: Spray frequently with Diazinon, malathion, or Sevin.

SCHEFFLERA—see BRASSAIA

SCHIZANTHUS (BUTTERFLY-FLOWER)

Diseases

Anthracnose (*Colletotrichum schizanthi*). Water-soaked areas first appear on stems and leaf stalks. Wilting of the upper part of the plant occurs later. Young, rapidly growing parts are more susceptible to infection than older, woody structures. Black acervuli, spore-producing structures, develop on the light brown dying parts. Older infected plants have canker-like lesions on the stems and main branches. Girdling of the stems is followed by the death of the parts above the canker. The leaves turn yellow, and the branch dies, from the tip downward. Light brown spots 1/8 inch in diameter may also develop on the leaves but cause little damage.
Control: Remove and destroy infected parts. Bordeaux mixture or other copper fungicides will prevent serious outbreaks of this disease.

Damping-off (*Pellicularia filamentosa* and *Pythium ultimum*). These fungi cause damping-off of seedlings.

Control: Drenching infested soil with a mixture of Dexon and PCNB (Terraclor) will control these fungi. Sowing seeds in milled sphagnum moss will also prevent damping-off.

Other Diseases. A stem rot caused by *Sclerotinia sclerotiorum*, spotted wilt by the tomato spotted wilt virus, and aster yellows by a mycoplasma-like organism also occur on *Schizanthus*.

Insect

The aster leafhopper, *Macrosteles fascifrons*, is the only insect reported on this host.
Control: See *Callistephus*.

SCIADOPITYS (UMBRELLA-PINE)

Umbrella-pine is susceptible to a fungus leaf spot caused by a species of *Phyllosticta*, a twig blight by *Sphaeropsis* sp., and root rot by *Pellicularia filamentosa*. Controls are rarely necessary.

SCILLA (SQUILL)

Diseases

Crown Rot (*Sclerotium delphinii*). This most destructive root and crown rot causes yellowing and drying of the leaves, wilting of the blossoms, and finally the death of the entire plant.
Control: See *Delphinium*.

Other Diseases. A blue-mold rot caused by *Penicillium gladioli* which occurs on imported bulbs, a flower smut caused by *Ustilago vaillantii*, a rust by *Uromyces scillarum*, and a mosaic by the ornithogalum mosaic virus are other diseases reported on *Scilla*.

Insect

Tulip Bulb Aphid (*Dysaphis tulipae*). A single species of aphids may become serious on *Scilla*.
Control: See *Tulipa*.

SCINDAPSUS (IVY-ARUM)

Ivy-arum, sometimes called Pothos, is susceptible to two leaf spots caused by *Phyllosticta aricola* and *P. pothicola*, root rots by *Pythium splendens* and *Pellicularia* sp., and four species of nemas: *Meloidogyne arenaria* var. *thamesii*, *M. incognita* var. *acrita*, *Radopholus similis*, and *Pratylenchus* sp.

The leaf spots are rarely serious enough to warrant control measures. The root rots are discussed under more favored hosts, and the control of nemas in Chapter 3.

SEDUM

Diseases

Crown Rot (*Pellicularia rolfsii*). Plants decay at the soil line when infected by this fungus.
Control: Set plants in clean soil or steam-pasteurize infested soil before re-use. Drenching infested soil with Benlate will also control the *Pellicularia* fungus.

Leaf Blotch (*Septoria sedi*). Dark circular blotches develop on the leaves, which quickly fall. Spores of the parasite develop on the fallen leaves, which should therefore be gathered and destroyed.

Leaf Spot (*Stemphylium bolicki*). In Florida a leaf spot (Fig. 215) occurs on several species of *Sedum*. This spotting strongly resembles oedema due to non-parasitic causes. It also occurs on *Kalanchöe* and *Echeveria*.
Control: Control measures have not been developed.

Stem Rot (*Colletotrichum* sp., *Phytophthora* sp., and *Pellicularia filamentosa*).

Fig. 215. Leaf spot of *Sedum* sp., caused by the fungus *Stemphylium bolicki.* (E. K. Sobers, Florida Department of Agriculture)

The stems of rock garden sedums may be infected by these fungi.

Control: Set plants in clean soil or steam-pasteurize infested soil before re-use.

Rusts (*Puccinia rydbergii* and *P. umbilici*). These rusts occur on *Sedum* in the Rocky Mountain states. Controls are unnecessary.

Insects

Aphid. Three species of aphids, green peach, melon, and sedum, infest this host.

The greedy scale, *Hemiberlesia rapax,* also infests Sedum.

Control: Spray with nicotine sulfate, rotenone, or Sevin.

Southern Root-Knot Nema (*Meloidogyne incognita*). This nema occasionally infests the roots of sedums. For control see Chapter 3.

SEMPERVIVUM (HOUSELEEK)

Diseases

Rust (*Endophyllum sempervivi*). Many species of *Sempervivum* are subject to attack by a systemic rust. The mycelium of the parasite gains entrance through the young leaves and growing points, penetrates the crown, and grows down into the roots.

Control: Remove and destroy all infected plants.

Other Diseases. A leaf and stem rot caused by *Phytophthora parasitica* and a root rot by a species of *Pythium* are other fungus diseases reported on *Sempervivum.*

SENECIO CRUENTUS—see CINERARIA

SEQUOIADENDRON (REDWOOD)

Diseases

Canker (*Dermatea livida*). Cankers develop on the bark in which brown to black fruiting bodies develop. These contain one-celled colorless spores. The fungus *Botryosphaeria dothidea* also causes cankers on *Sequoiadendron*.

Control: No satisfactory control measures have been developed.

Needle Blight (*Chloroscypha chloramela* and *Mycosphaerella sequoiae*). Redwood leaves may be blighted by these fungi. The giant sequoia, *Sequoiadendron giganteum*, is susceptible to two other leaf blighting fungi, *Cercospora sequoiae* and *Pestalotia funerea* and to twig blight by *Phomopsis juniperovora*.

Control: Small, importantly placed trees infected with these fungi should be sprayed with a copper or a dithiocarbamate fungicide.

Insects

Cedar Tree Borer (*Semanotus ligneus*). The larvae of this beetle make winding burrows in the inner bark and sapwood of redwood, cedars, arbor-vitae, Douglas-fir, and Monterey pine, occasionally girdling and killing the trees. The adult beetle is ½ inch long, black with orange and red markings on its wing covers.

Control: Young trees should be kept in good vigor by feeding and watering when necessary. Sprays containing methoxychlor on the trunk and branches, when the adult beetles emerge, should provide control.

Sequoia Pitch Moth (*Vespamima sequoiae*). The cambial region of the redwoods and many other conifers in the West is mined by an opaque, dirty white larva. The adult moth resembles a yellow-jacket wasp because it is black and has a bright yellow segment at its lower abdomen.

Control: This pest is rarely abundant enough to warrant control measures.

Mealybugs. Three species of mealybugs may infest redwoods: citrus, *Planococcus citri;* cypress, *Pseudococcus ryani;* and yucca, *Puto yuccae.*

Control: Spray young, valuable trees with malathion or Sevin. Repeat after a few weeks if the first spray does not provide good control.

Scales. Two scale insects have been reported on this host: greedy, *Hemiberlesia rapax,* and oleander, *Aspidiotus nerii.*

Control: Spray with malathion or Sevin when the young scales are crawling about.

SHEPHERDIA (BUFFALO-BERRY)

Diseases

Two leaf spots caused by *Cylindrosporium shepherdiae* and *Septoria shepherdiae,* two powdery mildews by *Sphaerotheca castagnei* and *S. humuli,* and a rust by *Puccinia caricis-shepherdiae* are among the fungus diseases reported on buffalo-berry. These are unimportant.

SHORTIA

This rare and interesting plant, a native of the hills of North Carolina and Tennessee, is subject in nature to infection by a fungus, *Pezizella oenotherae,* which appears to be very destructive to it. The spots, at first ⅛ inch or so in diameter, spread rapidly and become irregularly lobed, frequently occupying half the leaf. The center of the spots is light gray, the margin brown or blackish. When this host is brought into cultivation as a curiosity, the leaf spot should be controlled by spraying with a copper fungicide.

A species of *Sclerotium* is said to cause a rot of this host in South Carolina.

SIDALCEA[32]

Diseases

Leaf Spots (*Cercospora sidicola, Colletotrichum malvarum, Phyllosticta spinosa,* and *Ramularia sidarum*). Four fungi cause leaf spots of this malvaceous host. They are rarely severe enough to warrant control measures.

Rusts (*Puccinia heterospora, P. lobata,* and *P. schedonnardi*). These rust fungi occur primarily on wild hosts.

Other Diseases. *Sidalcea* is also subject to a blight caused by the fungus *Pellicularia rolfsii*, mosaic by the abutilon infectious mosaic virus, and root-knot by the nema *Meloidogyne incognita*.

SINNINGIA (GLOXINIA)

Diseases

Corm Rots (*Pythium debaryanum* and *Thielaviopsis basicola*). A soft, wet, internal decay of corms is caused by these fungi.

Control: Discard diseased corms.

Stem and Crown Rot (*Myrothecium roridum, Phytophthora cryptogea, Pythium ultimum,* and *Sclerotinia sclerotiorum*). Four soil-inhabiting fungi can cause serious decay of roots and stems of gloxinias.

Control: Once soils become infested with these fungi it is necessary to treat with heat or chemicals as described in Chapter 4.

Virus (Tomato spotted wilt virus). This virus disease appears as brown-ringed, spotlike markings of dead tissue, the centers of which remain green. Thrips spread this virus in nature.

The tobacco mosaic virus may also be present in greenhouse-grown gloxinias. It causes elongated shoots, and narrowed, downward-cupped leaves.

Control: Remove infected plants and de-

stroy them. Spray with Cygon, Diazinon or Sevin to control thrips.

Insects and Other Animal Pests

Aphids (*Myzus persicae* and *Neomyzus circumflexus*). The green peach and the crescent-marked lily aphids infest *Sinningia.*

Control: Spray with Meta-Systox R, Sevin, or malathion.

Thrips. The greenhouse and onion thrips cause rough or rusty brown spots bounded more or less by the larger veins. Infested leaves and blooms also have a characteristic silvery appearance and are somewhat deformed.

Control: Cygon, Diazinon, or Sevin sprays will control thrips.

Black Vine Weevil (*Otiorhynchus sulcatus*). The thick, whitish larvae of this weevil feed on the roots and crowns of gloxinia, causing much damage.

Control: Steam-pasteurize any sod used in composted soil. Screen greenhouse vents to prevent entrance of adult weevils.

Foliar Nemas (*Aphelenchoides* spp.). Necrotic lesions which ultimately destroy the entire leaf result from infestations by nemas. Spraying the leaves with Diazinon may provide control.

SMILAX[33]

Diseases

Four species of rust fungi and more than a dozen species of leaf spot fungi occur on wild *Smilax,* but are unimportant on the few cultivated, ornamental varieties.

Leaf Spot (*Cercospora smilacis*). The spots are more or less circular, up to 1/4 inch in diameter. At first they are dark purplish-red; they fade with age but the margins re-

---

[32] This genus was formerly known as *Sida.*

[33] Not to be confused with florists' smilax, for which see under *Asparagus.*

main very definite and dark-colored. The cinnamon-brown sporophores, which bear the long, many-celled, colorless spores, emerge in clusters from the stomata.

Control: Valuable ornamental specimens should be sprayed with Bordeaux mixture or other copper fungicides where this disease is troublesome.

Insects

Scales. Ten species of scales infest *Smilax:* chaff, Cyanophyllum, green, green shield, dictyospermum, latania, parlatoria-like, pustule, red bay, and smilax.

SOLANUM PSEUDO-CAPSICUM (JERUSALEM-CHERRY)

Fungus Diseases

Leaf Spots (*Alternaria solani, Mycosphaerella solani, Ascochyta lycopersici, Cercospora dulcamarae, Phyllosticta pseudocapsici,* and *Stemphylium solani*). Many of the fungi that cause leaf spots on this host also affect other members of the Solanaceae.

Control: Pick off and destroy spotted leaves. Copper fungicides may be used where these leaf spots are serious.

Other Diseases. In humid weather and in places where the false Jerusalem-cherry, *S. capsicastrum,* is overcrowded, heavy defoliation may be caused by a species of *Phytophthora.* No control is known but copper fungicide should be helpful.

Solanum pseudo-capsicum is also subject to crown gall caused by the bacterium *Agrobacterium tumefaciens;* wilt by the fungus *Verticillium albo-atrum;* and two viruses, spotted wilt by the tomato spotted wilt virus, and an unidentified mosaic probably caused by the tobacco mosaic virus.

Insects and Other Animal Pests

The potato aphid, the orange tortrix caterpillar, flower and onion thrips, and the citrus whitefly infest Jerusalem-cherry. All can be controlled with malathion or Sevin sprays. The latter is more readily controlled with synthetic pyrethroid sprays.

The southern root-knot nema, *Meloidogyne incognita,* and the Javanese root-knot nema, *M. javanica,* also infest this host.

SOLIDAGO (GOLDENROD)

Diseases

Only a few of more than a hundred species of *Solidago* are used as ornamental plants. The following are some of the more important diseases and pests of the cultivated sorts.

Scab (*Elsinoë solidaginis*). Young plants are killed, or dwarfed and stunted, when attacked by this fungus. Leaves that are attacked become covered with a fungus growth that causes them to wither and die as they unfurl. Infected stems become rusty.

Control: Remove and destroy infected plants. Sprays are rarely required.

Rust (*Coleosporium asterum*). This fungus attacks young goldenrods in the rosette stage. The alternate stage is on the pine.

Control: Remove and destroy infected plants.

Insects

Chrysanthemum Lace Bug (*Corythucha marmorata*). This pest breeds on the leaves of goldenrod and then moves to chrysanthemum, aster and scabiosa.

Control: Diazinon, malathion, or Sevin sprays control lace bugs.

Orange Tortrix (*Argyrotaenia citrana*). This dirty white, brown-headed caterpillar rolls and webs the leaves on which it feeds.

Control: Spray with Diazinon or Imidan when the caterpillars begin to feed.

SOPHORA JAPONICA (JAPANESE PAGODA-TREE)

Diseases

Canker (*Fusarium lateritium*). Oval, 1- to 2-inch cankers, with definite, slightly raised, dark red-brown margins and light tan centers, occasionally appear on this host. When the cankers completely girdle the stem, the distal portion dies. The perfect stage of this fungus is *Gibberella baccata.* Another fungus, *Cytospora sophorae,* is also found on dead branches. Both fungi are usually associated with frost damage in late fall or early spring.

Control: Prune diseased or dead branch tips to sound wood and apply a copper fungicide several times during the growing season.

Damping-off (*Pellicularia filamentosa*). In Connecticut and the southern states this fungus causes a damping-off of seedlings.

Control: Use steam-pasteurized soil, or soil treated with Benlate.

Twig Blight (*Nectria cinnabarina* and *Diplodia sophorae*). Two fungi cause cankers and dieback of twigs of this host.

Control: Same as for canker.

Other Fungus Diseases. Japanese pagoda-tree is also subject to powdery mildew caused by *Microsphaera alni,* and root rot by *Phymatotrichum omnivorum.*

SORBUS (MOUNTAIN-ASH)

Bacterial and Fungus Diseases

Fire Blight (*Erwinia amylovora*). This is one of the most serious diseases of Mountain-ash.

Control: See *Crataegus.*

Crown Gall (*Agrobacterium tumefaciens*). This is the second most prevalent disease of this host.

Control: See *Rosa.*

Canker. Four fungi, *Cytospora chrysosperma, C. massariana,* and *C. microspora,* and *Fusicoccum* sp., occur occasionally on mountain-ash, especially on weakened trees.

Control: Prune severely affected branches, and fertilize. The latter practice may increase the tree's susceptibility to fire blight, however, if high nitrogenous fertilizers are used.

Leaf Rusts. The alternate stages of the rust fungi *Gymnosporangium aurantiacum, G. cornutum, G. globosum, G. tremelloides, G. nelsoni, G. nootkatense,* and *G. libocedri* occur on *Juniperus* or *Librocedrus* species. On mountain-ash leaves, circular, light yellow, thickened spots first appear during the summer. Later, orange cups develop on the lower surface of these spots.

Control: Where mountain-ashes are highly prized, and where it is practicable, remove the alternate hosts. If such removal is impracticable, valuable trees can be protected by sprays recommended for rust control of flowering crab-apples (*Malus*).

Scab (*Venturia inaequalis*). See *Malus.*

Other Diseases. Mountain-ash is subject to many other diseases. These are discussed under rosaceous hosts in other parts of this book.

Insects

Aphids. The rosy apple and wooly apple aphids frequently infest this host.

Control: Spray with Meta-Systox R, Sevin, or malathion.

Roundheaded Borer (*Saperda candida*). Trees are weakened and may be killed by the roundheaded borer, a light yellow, black-headed, legless larva 1 inch long. Galleries in the trunk near the soil level, frass at the base of the tree, and round holes of the diameter of a lead pencil in the bark are typical signs of this pest. The adult is a beetle 3/4 inch long, brown with two white longitudinal stripes on the back. It emerges in April and deposits eggs on the bark.

Control: Spray trunk and branches thoroughly with methoxychlor starting in mid-May and repeating 3 times at 2-week intervals.

Pear Leaf Blister Mite (*Eriophyes pyri*). Tiny brownish blisters on the lower leaf surface and premature defoliation result from infestations of the pear leaf blister mite, a tiny, elongated, eight-legged pest, $1/125$ inch long. The pests overwinter beneath the outer bud scales. Eggs are deposited in spring in leaf galls, which develop as a result of feeding and irritation by the adult.

Control: Spray the trees with lime sulfur in late fall or early spring.

Japanese Leafhopper (*Orientus ishidae*). This insect causes a characteristic brown blotching bordered by a bright yellow margin, the yellow zone merging into the color of the leaf.

Control: Spray with Cygon, Sevin, or malathion in late May or early June.

Mountain-ash Sawfly (*Pristiphora geniculata*). Green larvae with black dots feed on mountain-ash leaves from early June to mid-July, leaving only the larger veins and midribs. The adults, yellow with black spots, deposit eggs on the leaves in late May.

Control: Spray with methoxychlor or Sevin when the leaves are fully expanded.

Scales. Five species of scale insects infest mountain-ash: black, cottony maple, oystershell, San Jose, and scurfy.

Control: Dormant oil or lime sulfur sprays, followed by malathion or Sevin sprays during the growing season, will control these insects.

SPIRAEA

Diseases

Spiraeas are subject to many of the diseases and pests that affect other members of the Rosaceae. Among these are fire blight caused by the bacterium *Erwinia amylovora*, bacterial hairy root by *Agrobacterium rhizogenes*, leaf spot by the fungus *Cylindrosporium filipendulae*, powdery mildews by *Microsphaera alni* and *Podospharea oxyacanthae*, and root rot by *Phymatotrichum omnivorum*. The controls for these diseases are discussed under other rosaceous hosts.

Insects

Spirea Aphid (*Aphis spiraecola*). Growth is checked in late June or early July by heavy infestation of the tender shoot-tips up to and including the flower-cluster.

Control: Spray with malathion or Sevin. Rotenone or pyrethrum sprays also provide control.

Oblique-Banded Leaf Roller (*Choristoneura rosaceana*). The leaf edges are drawn together with silk threads in summer. This caterpillar also infests roses, pyracantha, and many other plants.

Control: Spray with Sevin when the caterpillars begin to feed.

Scales. Three species of scale insects attack spiraea: cottony maple, oystershell, and spiraea.

Control: Spray with malathion or Sevin in mid-May and again in early June to control the crawler stage of these pests.

Other Pests. This host may also be infested by the saddled prominent caterpillar, *Heterocampa guttivitta*, and the southern root-knot nema, *Meloidogyne incognita*.

STAPHYLEA (BLADDERNUT)

Two fungi cause twig blight of bladdernut: *Hypomyces ipomoeae* and *Coryneum microstictum*. These species cause leaf spots: *Mycosphaerella staphylina*, *Ovularia isarioides*, and *Septoria cirrhosa*.

Control: These diseases are rarely serious enough to require control measures.

STATICE—see LIMONIUM

STELLARIA HOLOSTEA (EASTER BELLS)

Downy Mildew (*Peronospora* sp.). The fungus winters in the stems as a mycelium. The inflorescence and stems are distorted and shrunken.

Control: Destroy all infected plants and plant debris at the end of the season. Change the location of the plantings. Spray with Bordeaux mixture or any other copper fungicide during the growing season.

STRETLITZIA
(BIRD-OF-PARADISE FLOWER)

Diseases

Bacterial Wilt (*Pseudomonas solanacearum*). The first symptom is a yellow to orange discoloration of the leaf margin. The discoloration gradually extends toward the midrib. A slow wilting and death of the entire plant follow.

Control: Controls have not been developed.

Root Rot (*Fusarium moniliforme*). This fungus causes a root rot of *Strelitzia reginae*. It is seed-borne.

Control: Presoak seed one day in water at room temperature. Then treat in hot water at 135°F. for 30 minutes. Cool, dry, and plant in clean soil.

Insects

Mealybugs (*Planococcus citri* and *Pseudococcus longispinus*). The citrus and long-tailed mealybugs infest this host.

Control: Spray with malathion.

Scale. (*Hemiberlesia rapax*). The greedy scale, so common on many other trees, shrubs, and herbaceous ornamentals, also infests *Strelitzia*.

Control: Spray with malathion or Sevin to control the young crawlers.

SYMPHORICARPOS (SNOWBERRY)

Diseases

Anthracnose (*Glomerella cingulata* and *Sphaceloma symphoricarpi*). Two diseases of snowberry are referred to as anthracnose. The anthracnose ascribed to *Glomerella* appears as cinnamon-colored spots on the fruit. Flesh-colored spore-producing bodies, acervuli, develop in considerable numbers. Large numbers of infected berries become black, rough, and mummified before they drop off prematurely.

The disease caused by *Sphaceloma* first appears on the leaves in the spring as small, dark, purplish or blackish spots with gray centers. Leaves, flowers, fruit, and stems may become distorted and abnormal. Fruits especially may become pink and shrunken and dry up.

Control: Prune out diseased twigs down to the ground and discard the prunings. Spraying with zineb might help to prevent new infections.

Berry Rot (*Alternaria* sp. and *Botrytis cinerea*). The berries turn yellowish or brown and are affected by a soft, watery rot. Bud scales and bark also become infected. The gray mold, *Botrytis*, is often found with *Alternaria*. It causes a browning of the leaves and ochre-yellowing of the berries.

The three diseases, anthracnose, *Alternaria*, and *Botrytis* berry-rot, often occur together, and the symptoms become confused.

Control: Prune as for anthracnose. Spray several times during the growing season with Bordeaux mixture or any ready-made copper fungicide.

Leaf Spots (*Ascochyta symphoricarpophila, Cercospora symphoricarpi, Phyllosticta symphoricarpi, Septoria signalensis,* and *S. symphoricarpi*). Five species of fungi cause leaf spots of this host. *S. symphoricarpi* is sometimes highly destructive in the western states.

Control: Pick and destroy spotted leaves as they appear. Spray periodically during the growing season with a copper or dithiocarbamate fungicide if leaf spots were prevalent the previous year.

Powdery Mildews (*Microsphaera diffusa* and *Podosphaera oxyacanthae*). While not common diseases, these mildews may disfigure the leaves and fruit of snowberry.

Control: Important specimens can be protected with Karathane or wettable sulfur sprays.

Rusts (*Puccinia crandallii* and *P. symphoricarpi*). In the midwestern and western parts of the United States, *P. crandallii* is the more common of these two rusts. The two species are closely related.

Control: These two rusts are of no great importance in the eastern states. Control measures have not been worked out or thought necessary.

Stem Gall (*Phomopsis* sp.). Numerous small galls on the stems of *Symphoricarpos orbiculatus* have been reported from the state of Washington. Stems were frequently girdled and part of the plant killed.

Control: Prune and destroy infected stems.

Insects

Aphids. Three species of aphids may infest *Symphoricarpos:* honeysuckle, crescent-marked, and the snowberry.

Control: These species are easily controlled with malathion, Meta-Systox R, or Sevin sprays.

Snowberry Clearwing (*Hemaris diffinis*). The larvae, which chew the leaves of snowberry and bush honeysuckle, are green to brown or purplish and up to 2 inches in length at maturity.

Control: If only a few bushes are infested, pick off and destroy the worms. Sevin sprays will also control these pests.

Other Pests. The San Jose scale, and the glacial whitefly, *Trialeurodes glacialis,* also infest this host.

SYMPLOCOS (SWEETLEAF)

A bud gall caused by the fungus *Exobasidium symploci* occurs from North Carolina to Indiana and the Gulf States. Three leaf spots caused by *Septoria symploci, S. stigma,* and *S. tinctoria* also occur in the South. None of these diseases is serious enough to warrant control measures.

SYNGONIUM[34]

Diseases

Leaf Spot (*Cephalosporium cinnamomeum*). Irregular water-soaked areas about $1/8$ inch in diameter develop on the leaves. They become reddish-brown with pale yellow borders, and may increase somewhat in size with age. The centers became grayish and papery. In severe infections the leaves may turn yellow and die.

Control: Keep the temperature of the greenhouse as low as possible and avoid unnecessary syringing of the plants.

Cane Rot (*Ceratocystis* sp.). Stems of *Syngonium auritum* may be blackened by this fungus.

Control: In California infected plants are dipped, bare-root, in hot water at 120°F. for 3 minutes. The plants are then cooled and set in pasteurized soil. Some injury to leaves occurs but the plants usually recover quickly.

Insect

Thrips (*Heliothrips haemorrhoidalis*). Under dry atmospheric conditions this pest may attack *Syngonium.* Characteristic glistening blotches spotted with dark dots of excrement

---

[34] This is "Nephthytis" of the florist trade.

are seen on the undersides of the leaves, while on the upper surfaces the leaves are discolored yellowish brown.

Control: Spray with malathion.

SYRINGA (LILAC)

Bacterial and Fungus Diseases

Bacterial Blight (*Pseudomonas syringae*). The white-flowered varieties seem to be more susceptible than those with colored flowers to attack by this bacterium. The blight resembles fire blight of pears in general appearance. Young shoots are marked by black stripes, or one side of the entire shoot may be black. Spots may occur on the leaves and may run together, forming a blotch which may appear watersoaked. Immature leaves turn black and die quickly; on the older leaves the spots enlarge slowly. The inflorescence becomes limp and dark brown; the flower buds may be completely blackened. The bacteria may enter the young stems from the leaves or may attack them directly through the stomata and lenticels. They penetrate the intercellular spaces, where great masses are visible through a microscope. This disease is usually evident in rainy seasons and in the spring as the young shoots develop. It is strictly a disease of moist, mild weather. The organism that causes this blight has been shown to be very similar to or identical with that which infects plums and cherries and causes cankers on these plants.

Control: The plants should be thinned out and the young shoots cut to provide good air circulation. Destroy diseased shoots by pruning with sterilized shears. Spraying with a copper fungicide as soon as the disease is detected, has been found very helpful. Avoid excessive manuring or application of high-nitrogenous fertilizers. This disease may be confused with that caused by the fungus *Botrytis cinerea*, which also causes young shoots to wilt.

Phytophthora Blight (*Phytophthora cactorum*). This disease has much the same symptoms as those of the bacterial disease, except that the lesions are dark brown rather than black and the extent of killing is much greater. An attack by this fungus often kills shoots to the ground. Root sprouts that have come up under the bush often have leaves blackened and are extensively killed. If one cuts off small sections of shoots that have turned dark brown and places them in a glass dish for a day, he can see the hyphae or mycelium of the fungus growing out into the water. The characteristic fruiting structures that develop the zoöspores can be seen under the microscope. While this disease is presumed to be a wet-weather disease, it is known to have been severe under the driest conditions. Both the bacterial disease and this fungus disease should be distinguished from injury caused by excessive fertilizing with manure or other nitrogenous fertilizers.

A related species, *P. syringae*, has been reported from New York and Maryland.

Control: Cut out and destroy the blighted twigs and shoots well below the point showing infection. Prune out all excessive growths at the top and underneath the plants. Spray with a copper fungicide or with wettable sulfur. This will help to control the disease. Since the same fungus attacks rhododendrons, the two ornamentals should not be interplanted.

Leaf Blights (*Cladosporium herbarum* and *Heterosporium syringae*). These two fungi frequently occur together on lilac leaves in large brown zonate spots. The spores of *Heterosporium* appear brown and form a velvety layer with an olive bloom. The diseased areas dry out and become cracked along the margins so that they fall away, leaving an irregular shot-hole appearance.

Control: Spray plants with a copper fungicide beginning about mid-June in the Northeast. If the season is rainy, several other applications at weekly intervals should be sufficient.

Leaf Spots (*Cercospora lilacis, Macrophoma halstedii, Phyllosticta porteri, P. syringae, P. syringella,* and *Pleospora herbarum*). At least six species of fungi cause leaf spots on lilacs.

Control: Same as for leaf blights.

Powdery Mildew (*Microsphaera alni*). One of the more common fungus diseases of lilac is the powdery mildew, which covers the leaves with whitish, felt-like patches of mycelium. See Fig. 216. In the eastern states it seems to occur more frequently late in the season. This is a rather superficial disease; the fungus does not extend beyond the epidermal layer. The little black spherical fruiting bodies of the sexual stage are ornamented with beautiful appendages (Fig. 51c); each di-

vides into two parts, each of the branches again divides into two, and so on.

Control: If this mildew is likely to be very prevalent, spray with Acti-dione PM, Benlate, or Karathane.

A number of small animals, the larvae of *Chaetopsis* and other small insects, play an important part in preventing the spread of fungus diseases by feeding on the spores. Some of these organisms are rather small, invisible without the aid of a hand lens. An example of larger animals that destroy many fungus spores is the snail, which devours many spores of the powdery mildew of lilac. Fig. 217 shows a lilac leaf badly infected with powdery mildew. The beautiful etching marks represent the places where the snails have fed on the spores and superficial cells of the fungus.

Wilt (*Verticillium albo-atrum*). This fungus invades the water-conducting vessels, cutting off the water supply. Infected leaves lose their glossiness and appear pale and wilted; they fall prematurely, leaving the branches bare during the latter part of the summer. The branches of infected plants die during the winter.

Control: Infected plants should be dug up and discarded. Change the propagating location for a few years until the fungus has been eliminated from the soil.

Other Diseases. Lilacs are also subject to a shoot blight caused by the fungus *Gloeosporium syringage,* crown gall by the bacterium *Agrobacterium tumefaciens,* thread blight by the fungus *Pellicularia koleroga,* stem girdle by *Hymenochaete agglutinans,* and a dieback by *Physalospora obtusa.*

Virus Diseases

Ring Spot (Virus). An unidentified virus produces light green wavy lines or ringlike patterns in the leaves. It is also spread by grafting infected scions onto healthy understock.

Fig. 216. Powdery mildew of lilac. (Pennsylvania State University)

Fig. 217. Tracks left in lilac leaves by a snail *(Polygyra thyroides)* which feeds upon the powdery mildew fungus *Microsphaera alni*. (F. A. Wolf)

Witches' Broom. Lateral buds form two to six slender shoots which branch freely and bear small leaves, one-fourth the normal length (Fig. 218). This disease is graft-transmissible from lilac to lilac. No control is known except to destroy infected plants.

Physiological Diseases

Frost Injury. In late spring young leaves may be injured by near-freezing temperatures. The damaged leaves become torn along the veins in an irregular pattern.

Graft Blight (Incompatibility disease). This is a disease of practically all kinds of lilacs that are grafted on privet *(Ligustrum)*. The symptoms are those of nutritional deficiency. The leaves become yellow at the margins and in the spaces between the veins. They are reduced in size, irregular, curled, or otherwise abnormal in appearance, and most of them are brittle. The plants become stunted. Recovery is seldom complete unless the scion can establish its own root system.

Control: The use of lilac on privet *(Ligustrum)* as understock must be avoided. Propagate by own-root methods.

Leaf Roll Necrosis. Lilacs in urban areas occasionally develop a foliar disorder characterized by leaf roll, interveinal and marginal necrosis, chlorosis, bronzing, and early leaf drop. Research workers at the Brooklyn Botanic Garden observed it on "own-root" propagated plants; hence it was not the same as Graft Blight, discussed above. It was concluded that air pollutants, including ozone, are involved in the leaf roll necrosis complex.

Insects and Other Animal Pests

Lilac Borer *(Podosesia syringae syringae)*. Infested branches often wilt because of the

Fig. 218. Witches' broom virus disease of lilac. Upper foliage is normal. (U.S. Department of Agriculture)

destruction of the sapwood, which is eaten by the larvae before they enter the heatwood. The branches are frequently so weakened by the boring that they break. Sawdust-like material hangs at the openings made by the borers. When full grown, the borer is pure white, ³/₄ to 1¹/₂ inches long, with a brown head. The adult moth resembles a wasp and is a very active flyer. One effect of the borer is to open the way for the wood-destroying fungus *Polyporus versicolor*, whose fruiting bodies are beautifully zoned on the upper surface with soft hairs of various colors.

Control: Since the partly grown insects pass the winter in the stems of lilacs, the infested branches should be cut out and destroyed. These branches are marked by swollen areas with cracked bark that is broken away from the wood. Numerous holes are visible in the bark and wood. Spray or paint the trunks and limbs at the end of April and again 3 more times at 10-day intervals (in the latitude of New York City) with methoxychlor. Borers inside stems can be crushed in early summer by inserting a flexible wire or by squeezing Bortox into the burrows and sealing with putty or chewing gum.

Leopard Moth Borer (*Zeuzera pyrina*). In certain plantings in the vicinity of New York this leopard moth borer is more common on lilacs than the lilac borer. The larvae are pale yellowish or cream-colored and marked with numerous black spots. This borer invades the heartwood, tunneling up and down for some distance. The tunnel is much larger than that of the lilac borer and more regular. Damp sawdust-like frass is pushed out of the openings and falls to the ground. The presence of the borer can be detected by these little piles of sawdust. The common name is derived from the black markings on the white wings and body. The moths are feeble flyers and very sluggish. They are often found attached to the bark of trees. The adult females lay about 800 eggs each, a few at each place of deposit, throughout the summer. They also attack elms, maples, and a number of other deciduous ornamental trees.

Control: Cut and destroy all infested branches and trees during the fall and winter months. An injection with Bortox or some other preparation that contains nicotine sulfate has been found effective. A few drops of carbon disulfide may be injected into the burrows, the holes being plugged with chewing gum or putty.

Caterpillars. The larvae of three other moths feed on lilac leaves: cynthia, polyphemus, and promethea.

Control: Spray with *Bacillus thuringiensis*, Imidan, or Sevin.

Giant Hornet (*Vespa crabro germana*). This very large hornet, 1 inch or more in length, is black with dark orange markings. It removes a strip of bark about 1/8 inch wide around one side of the trunk or completely around branches 1 inch or so in diameter. The girdling is frequently sufficiently deep to kill

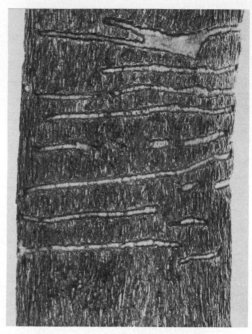

Fig. 219. Rhododendron stem girdled by the giant hornet *Vespa crabro germana.*

branches that are completely encircled (Fig. 219). The insects feed on the sap that flows from the bushes as a result of wounds. The bark is used in the construction of their nests, which are hidden in tree cavities, between the rafters of buildings, or sometimes in underground cavities.

Among other susceptible hosts are birch, boxwood, franklinia, lilac, poplar, rhododendron, and willow.

Control: Locate the nests and blow Diazinon dust into the openings. Apply a Sevin spray in July and again in early August to the trunk and branches of trees and shrubs subject to bark tearing by this pest.

Lilac Leaf Miner (*Gracillaria syringella*). This insect begins as a leaf miner in early June; later the caterpillars emerge, spin webs around the curled leaves, and further skeletonize the leaves. The foliage is badly disfigured by this process. There are two or three generations a year, the last one in September. Privet and ash are also attacked by this insect.

Control: Spray with Diazinon or malathion. The insecticide, however, must be applied before the leaves are rolled. Soil or branch applications of Cygon also give control.

Scales. Seven species of scale insects infest lilac: cottony maple, euonymus, olive parlatoria, oystershell, San Jose, scurfy, and white peach.

Certain Chinese lilacs are more subject to scale injury than our commoner lilacs. Of the seven scales listed above, the oystershell (Fig. 220) is probably the most common.

Control: Spray the plants early in spring, while they are in a dormant condition, with lime sulfur. This also controls mildew and other fungus diseases. For the San Jose scale a miscible oil is more effective. Unless the scale insects are present the plants should not be sprayed every year with oil, since injury is likely to follow its repeated use. If dormant sprays are not applied, or if the scale infestations are particularly heavy, spray with Diazinon or Sevin in early June and repeat twice at 2-week intervals.

Other Insects. Lilacs are occasionally infested by the melon aphid, the hickory horned devil caterpillar, the Japanese weevil, the oblique-banded leaf roller, and the citrus whitefly. The larval stage of the rhinoceros beetle, *Xyloryctes jamaicensis,* girdles lilac stems below ground, often causing death of the parts above.

Fig. 220. Oystershell scale *(Lepidosaphes ulmi)* on lilac stem.

Control: Pick off and destroy blighted and browned flowers as soon as they are seen.

Collar Rot and Root Rot. Four soil-inhabiting fungi—*Pellicularia filamentosa, P. rolfsii, Pythium ultimum,* and *Sclerotinia sclerotiorum*—may cause a rotting of the crowns or the roots.

Control: See Chapter 4 for methods of disinfesting soils that harbor these fungi.

Fusarium Wilt (*Fusarium* sp.). A severe wilting occurs in beds of the dwarf and French varieties which are reported to be immune to the *Phytophthora* wilt. This wilt has been referred to a species of *Fusarium;* cultures of this fungus can be easily isolated from the stems of dying plants. It is possible, however, that the *Phytophthora* may be the primary parasite and that the *Fusarium* follows secondarily.

TAGETES (MARIGOLD)

Fungus Diseases

Blight (*Botrytis cinerea*). During wet weather this fungus causes browning and decay of the flowers.

Control: The same as for *Phytophthora cryptogea,* discussed below under wilt and stem rot.

Leaf Spot (*Septoria tageticola*). Oval to irregular, smoky-gray to black spots speckled with minute black fruiting bodies develop on the leaflets. Infections start on the lower leaves and progress upward. Horticultural varieties of the African marigold, *Tagetes erecta,* are very susceptible, while the French marigold varieties, *T. patula,* are either resistant or immune.

Other leaf spots are caused by species of *Alternaria* and *Cercospora.*

Control: Severe outbreaks can be prevented by an occasional application of a copper or dithiocarbamate spray.

Wilt and Stem Rot (*Phytophthora cryptogea*). Infected stems become brown and shrivel near the soil line (Fig. 221). The parasite attacks the roots, causing much decay. Seeds also are rotted. The foliage wilts badly and the whole plant finally dies. Guinea Gold and African types are the most susceptible. The

Fig. 221. Marigold stems infected with the fungus *Phytophthora cryptogea.* (Cornell University)

author was the first to report this disease in the United States. He found that the French marigold, *T. patula,* and dwarf varieties are not susceptible.

Control: Remove and destroy all infected plants. Steam-pasteurize soil that is to be used in seedbeds or for later plantings.

Rust (*Coleosporium madiae*). African marigolds grown in California have been reported to be infected with this rust, which is said to be new on this host. Another rust fungus, *Puccinia tageticola,* occurs on *Tagetes* in Texas.

Control: Remove and destroy infected plants.

Other Diseases. Marigolds are subject to other diseases including wilt caused by the bacterium *Pseudomonas solanacearum,* charcoal rot by the fungus *Macrophomina phaseoli,* wilt by *Verticillium albo-atrum,* mosaic by the cucumber mosaic virus, and aster yellows by a mycoplasma-like organism. The controls for these are discussed under more favored hosts.

Insects and Other Animal Pests

Japanese Beetle (*Popillia japonica*). The African marigold, *Tagetes erecta,* is especially attractive to the Japanese beetle, which will feed on the open blossoms and upper leaves.

Control: See *Aesculus.*

Tarnished Plant Bug (*Lygus lineolaris*). Marigold is one of the many ornamentals attacked by this sucking insect. The poison that results from the feeding of the insects causes distortion of flowers and leaves.

Control: Spray with Cygon or with a mixture of Sevin and Kelthane.

Leafhoppers (*Empoascus fabae* and *Macrosteles fascifrons*). A characteristic symptom is a cupping or inrolling of the leaves at the margins, which fold over the midrib. This is accompanied by a twisting of the petioles. Some infested leaves, especially those ex-

posed to the sun, turn purplish-red on the under sides. Another symptom is a complete wilting of branch tips and leaflets; these leaves become yellow and dry. New shoots develop below the point of attack. The dwarf varieties are more severely injured than the tall. Flowering is delayed because of the repeated killing of the branch tips.

Control: See *Callistephus.*

Greenhouse Leaf Tier (*Udea rubigalis*). These caterpillars attack not only greenhouse plants but numerous plants grown in the garden. They tie the leaves or flower buds together with a web and feed on the under sides of the leaves.

Control: Young plants should be sprayed with Sevin before webbing occurs. Nicotine fumigation also works well with greenhouse plants.

Slugs (*Limax maximus* and *Milax gagates*). The spotted garden slug and the greenhouse slug feed on marigold foliage.

Control: Dust infested area with 15 per cent metaldehyde powder, or spray with liquid metaldehyde diluted as directed by the manufacturer. Mesurol and Zectran also control slugs. Use these as directed by the manufacturer. Spraying the foliage with Sevin might also help.

Other Pests. Occasionally marigolds are infested by the blister beetle, stalk borer, yellow woollybear, and three species of mites: broad, cyclamen, and two-spotted.

The root nema, *Aphelenchoides tagetae,* and the northern root-knot nema, *Meloidogyne hapla,* also infest this host.

TAMARIX (TAMARISK)

Diseases

Cankers (*Botryosphaeria tamaricis, Diplodia tamarascina,* and *Leptosphaeria tamaricis*). Three species of fungi form cankers and cause branch dieback of this host.

Control: Prune to sound wood and destroy the prunings.

Other Fungus Diseases. Tamarisk is also susceptible to powdery mildew caused by *Sphaerotheca humuli,* root rot by *Phymatotrichum omnivorum,* and a wood rot by *Polyporus sulphureus.*

Insects

Scales (*Hemiberlesia lataniae* and *Lepidosaphes ulmi*). The latania and oystershell scales frequently infest *Tamarix.*

Control: Spray in late spring with malathion or Sevin to control the crawler stage. Where the infestation is heavy, spray with concentrated lime sulfur in early spring just before growth begins.

TAXODIUM (BALD CYPRESS)

Diseases

Twig Blight (*Pestalotia funerea*). This disease appears as a spotting of the leaves, cones, and bark, and, in very wet seasons, a twig blight. The causal fungus is not considered a vigorous parasite but becomes mildly pathogenic on trees weakened by dry weather, sunscald, or low temperatures.

Control: Control measures are rarely applied, although a copper fungicide would probably be effective.

Wood Decay. A number of fungi belonging to the genera *Fomes, Lenzites, Poria,* and *Polyporus* are associated with wood decay of bald cypress. The last is sometimes found on living trees.

Control: Avoid wounding the trunk base of valuable trees. Keep trees in good vigor by watering and, if needed, by feeding.

Insects

Cypress Moth (*Recurvaria apicitripunctella*). The larval stage of this moth mines the leaves of bald cypress and hemlock, then webs them together in late summer. The female adult is a small yellow moth with black markings and fringed wings.

Control: Spray with Sevin when the larvae begin to mine the leaves in late spring and before they web the leaves together.

TAXUS (YEW)

Diseases

Needle Blight (*Herpotrichia nigra* and *Sphaerulina taxi*). Blighting of needles of this host in the western United States may be caused by these fungi.

Control: This disease is rarely destructive enough to warrant control measures.

Twig Blight. Several fungi are associated with a twig blight of yew during rainy seasons. One of the most common is *Phyllostictina hysterella,* whose perfect stage is *Physalospora gregaria.* Others are *Pestalotia funerea* and a species of *Sphaeropsis.*

Control: Prune out diseased twigs and destroy them. Spray with a copper fungicide several times at 2-week intervals during rainy springs.

Root Rot (*Armillaria mellea*). This disease appears in soil formerly occupied by apple or oak trees. Affected plants wilt and die; white wefts of fungus mycelium are present beneath the bark at the base of the plant.

Control: Diseased plants cannot be saved. Remove and replace them with narrow-leaved evergreens other than yews, or replace the soil to a depth of 12 inches before replanting yews.

Other Fungus Diseases. Among other fungus diseases of yews are a dieback and root rot caused by *Phytophthora cinnamomi,* a root rot by *Pythium* sp., and premature leaf drop in which a species of *Alternaria* is implicated.

Physiological Diseases

The most prevalent trouble on yews is die-back. The plants first turn yellow at the growing tips; this is followed by general yellowing, wilting, and death. Several months may elapse from the time the first symptoms appear to the complete wilting and death of the plant. The below-ground symptoms are a decay of the bark on the deeper roots; the affected bark sloughs off readily.

This trouble is not caused by parasitic organisms. Studies by author showed that it is associated with unfavorable soil conditions. In nearly every case investigated, the soil was very acid, pH 4.7 to 5.4, in addition to being heavy and poorly drained. Research at Rutgers University revealed that yews could be killed by immersing their roots in water for 32 to 64 hours and then drying out the soil.

Control: Improve drainage by embedding tile in the soil, or move plants to a more favorable area. Add ground limestone, according to the recommendation of a soil specialist, to increase the pH to about 6.5.

Twig Browning. This condition is not caused by fungus parasites but is due to snow and winter damage. The combined effect of heavy snow cover and low temperatures causes many small twigs at the end of branches to turn brown in late winter and early spring.

Control: Shake off heavy snow covers with a bamboo rake as soon as the snowfall stops. Prune browned branches in late spring.

Insects and Other Animal Pests

Black Vine Weevil (*Otiorhynchus sulcatus*). This pest, also known as the Taxus weevil, is by far the most serious one on yews. It is so named because of its color and because it attacks grapes in Europe. In the United States, it also attacks retinospora, hemlocks, and such broad-leaved plants as rhododendrons and azaleas. See Figs. 206,

207, and 208. The leaves of yew turn yellow, and whole branches or even the entire plant may die when the roots are chewed by the larval stage, a white-bodied, brown-headed pest, ³⁄₈ inch long. As few as eight larvae are capable of killing a large-sized yew. The adult, a snout beetle, ³⁄₈ inch long, feeds on the foliage of yews and other hosts at night. The edges of such leaves are scalloped (Fig. 222). Eggs deposited in the soil during July and August hatch into larvae which feed on the roots of susceptible hosts.

Control: The use of chlordane, long recommended as a control for the black vine and strawberry weevils, is presently restricted in some states and eventually may be completely banned by the Environmental Protection Agency (EPA) because of its suspected carcinogenic properties. In restricted states, homeowners are permitted to purchase small quantities for such specific uses as ant and termite control, control of the taxus and

Fig. 222. Yew leaves chewed by the black vine weevil. (George Runge, Jr.)

strawberry weevil, and the Japanese weevil.

In New York State homeowners are permitted to use the 45-50% emulsifiable chlordane concentrate at the rate of 1 ounce in 2 gallons of water per 1000 sq. ft. as a soil drench to control the larval stage of the black vine and strawberry weevil.

There are indications that some colonies of the taxus and strawberry weevils have developed resistance to chlordane. Resistant colonies should be treated with Thiodan, a highly toxic pesticide whose use is restricted in New York State to registered pesticide applicators. In States where its use is permitted, Furadan, as a soil drench will control strawberry and black vine weevils.

Strawberry Root Weevil (*Otiorhynchus ovatus*). This insect is related to the black vine weevil and has similar habits, but is smaller, measuring ⅕ to ¼ inch in length. It feeds on hemlock, spruce, and arborvitae in addition to *Taxus*. It often wanders into homes in search of hibernating quarters and thus may become a nuisance.

Control: See black vine weevil, above.

Taxus Mealybug (*Dysmicoccus wistariae*). First reported from a New Jersey nursery in 1915, this pest has become increasingly prevalent in the northern United States. The ⅜-inch-long bug, covered with white wax, may completely cover the trunk and branches of yews. Young mealybugs overwinter in bark crevices and mature in June. Although all species of *Taxus* are susceptible, those with dense foliage such as *Taxus cuspidata* var. *nana* and *T. wardii* are preferred hosts. This pest has also been seen on apple, basswood, and rhododendron, but probably does not breed on these plants.

Control: Good control is obtainable by spraying with malathion, Sevin, or Cygon when the young stage is crawling about. In the area of Long Island and Connecticut, the latter part of May is the proper time; in cooler regions the application should be made a week or two later.

Grape Mealybug (*Pseudococcus maritimus*). This pest occasionally infests the Japanese yew.

Control: Where it infests aboveground parts of yews, spray with malathion or Cygon.

Scales. Five species of scale insects infest yews: cottony taxus, California red, Fletcher, oleander, and purple. The first-mentioned, *Pulvinaria floccifera*, is ⅛ inch long, light brown, hemispherical. In the spring it produces long, narrow, fluted, cottony egg-masses.

Control: Apply a "superior" type dormant oil spray while the plants are dormant in early spring when the temperature is well above freezing. In July and again September spray with Cygon, Diazinon, Meta-Systox R, or Sevin.

Taxus Bud Mite (*Cecidophyopsis psilaspis*). The growing tips of yews is enlarged and may be killed. New growth is distorted. As many as a thousand mites can be found in a single infested bud.

Control: Spray with Kelthane in early May and repeat within 2 weeks if necessary.

Ants and Termites. The black carpenter ant, *Camponotus pennsylvanicus,* and the eastern subterranean termite, *Reticulitermes flavipes,* occasionally infest the trunks of older yews. Both are capable of excavating the trunk and making their nests therein.

Control: Apply Diazinon or Dursban in liquid form around the trunk base and soil surface.

Nemas (*Criconemoides* and *Rotylenchus* spp.). Several species of nemas attack the roots of *Taxus.*

Control: See Chapters 3 and 4.

TEUCRIUM (GERMANDER)

In northern greenhouses, and in the southern states where *Teucrium* is grown outdoors, the following fungus diseases may be present: downy mildew caused by a species of *Peronospora,* leaf spots by *Cercospora teucrii* and *Phyllosticta decidua,* powdery mildew by *Erysiphe cichoracearum,* and rust by *Puccinia menthae.* None of these diseases is serious enough to warrant control measures.

Leaf Crinkle (*Aculus teucrii*). Leaves of germander are crinkled as a result of feeding by a mite. The damage is only moderate, and hence miticides are rarely used.

THALICTRUM (MEADOW-RUE)

Only a few of nearly 100 species of *Thalictrum* are grown for ornament. Among the fungus diseases of wild species which may also affect the cultivated kinds are powdery mildew caused by *Erysiphe polygoni,* rusts by *Puccinia recondita* and *Tranzschelia prunispinosae,* and smuts by *Entyloma thalictri* and *Urocystis sorosporioides.* None of these diseases is serious enough to require special control measures.

THUJA (ARBOR-VITAE)

Diseases

Leaf Blight (*Fabrella thujina*). Although this disease is most destructive to giant arbor-vitae of the Northwest, it occasionally appears on ordinary arbor-vitae. From one to more than three irregularly circular brown to black cushions appear on the tiny leaves in late spring. The leaves then turn brown, and the affected areas appear as though scorched by fire. Toward fall the leaves drop, leaving the branches bare.

Control: Small trees or nursery stock can be protected by several applications of Bordeaux mixture or other copper sprays in midsummer and early autumn.

Juniper Blight (*Phomopsis juniperovora*). This blight, more common on redcedar and other species of *Juniperus,* also affects arbor-vitae. See *Juniperus.*

Tip Blight (*Coryneum berckmanii*). This disease resembles leaf blight but occurs primarily on varieties of *Thuja orientalis,* the golden biota or golden arbor-vitae being most susceptible. The leaves near the branch tips turn brown in late spring or early summer. Tiny black bodies, visible through a magnifying lens, occur on infected leaves. Several other fungi including *Cercospora thujina, Pestalotia funerea,* and *Phacidium infestans* are also associated with tip and twig blights.

Control: Spray with a copper fungicide before rainy periods.

Physiological Diseases

Leaf Browning and Shedding. The older, inner leaves of arbor-vitae turn brown and drop in fall. When this condition develops within a few days or a week, as it does in some seasons, many persons feel that a destructive disease is involved. Actually it is a natural phenomenon similar to the dropping of leaves of deciduous trees. When the previous growing season has been favorable for growth, or when pests, such as red spider mite, have not been abundant, the shedding occurs over a relatively long period through fall and consequently is not so noticeable.

Winter Browning. Rapid changes in temperature, rather than drying, in late winter and early spring are responsible for browning of arbor-vitae leaves.

Insects and Related Pests

Arbor-Vitae Aphid (*Cinara tujafilina*). This reddish-brown aphid with a white bloom infests roots, stems, and leaves of arbor-vitae, Italian cypress, and retinospora.

Control: Spray with malathion, Cygon or Diazinon to control pests above ground. Those below ground are difficult to control.

Cedar Tree Borer (*Semanotis ligneus*). This pest attacks the bark and wood of cedars, redwood, Douglas-fir, and Monterey pine. The adult beetle is ¹/₂ inch long, black with orange or red markings on the wing-cover. The larval stage bores into the inner bark and wood, frequently girdling the trees.

Control: Spray with methoxychlor when the beetles emerge from the tree.

Arbor-Vitae Leaf Miner (*Argyresthia thuiella*). The leaf tips turn brown as a result of the feeding within the leaves of the small leaf miner maggot. The adult stage is a tiny gray moth with a wingspread of ¹/₃ inch. The maggots overwinter in the leaves.

Control: Trim and destroy infested leaves. Spray with Diazinon in early June when eggs are hatching.

Arbor-Vitae Weevil (*Phyllobius intruscus*). White to pink larvae with brown heads feed on the roots of arbor-vitae and junipers. The adult, covered with greenish scales, feeds on the upper parts of the plants from May to July.

Control: Spray with Sevin in late May and repeat in mid-June to control the adult stage.

Mealybugs (*Pseudococcus ryani*). This pest also attacks incense-cedar, Norfold Island pine, and redwood.

Control: Spray with malathion or Sevin.

Scales. Four species of scale insects infest *Thuja:* European fruit lecanium, Fletcher, juniper, and San Jose.

Control: Spray with malathion or Sevin in late spring and early summer when the crawler stage is about.

Other Pests. Arbor-vitae is also subject to bagworm and mites. These are discussed under *Abies.*

THUNBERGIA (CLOCK-VINE)

Clock-vine is subject to crown gall caused by the bacterium *Agrobacterium tumefaciens,* the southern root-knot nema, *Meloidogyne incognita,* and the lesser snow scale insect, *Pinnaspis strachani.* Controls for these are given under more favored hosts.

THYMUS (THYME)

The only problems recorded on this host are root rot caused by *Pellicularia filamentosa,* and the ground mealybug, *Rhizoecus falcifer.* Methods of control for these are described in other parts of this book.

TIGRIDIA (TIGER-FLOWER)

Since *Tigridia* is related to *Gladiolus,* it is subject to some of the same diseases. The following are the more common diseases and pests of tiger-flower: scab caused by the bacterium *Pseudomonas marginata;* corm rot by the fungus *Fusarium orthoceras* var. *gladioli;* storage rot by *Penicillium gladioli;* mosaic by the iris mosaic virus; and the stem and bulb nema, *Ditylenchus dipsaci.* Most of these diseases and pests are discussed under *Gladiolus.*

TILIA (LINDEN)

Diseases

Anthracnose (*Gnomonia tiliae*). European lindens are occasionally affected by this disease. Elongated, light brown spots occur along the veins in various parts of the leaf but chiefly near the tip. A conspicuous, narrow black band appears between the dead and the healthy tissue. In severe infections, the tree may be completely defoliated.

Control: See anthracnose under *Quercus.*

Leaf Blight (*Cercospora microsora*). Circular brown spots with dark borders characterize this disease. The spots are very numerous, sometimes causing the entire leaf to turn brown and fall off. Young trees are most seriously affected. The sexual stage of the causal fungus is *Mycosphaerella microspora.*

Control: Same as for anthracnose.

Canker (*Nectria cinnabarina*). Twigs and larger branches bear cinnabar-colored fruiting bodies of the fungus, each body about the size of a pinhead. These ascocarps break through the bark and are readily seen without a hand lens. The same or similar fungi attack apples, oaks, and other trees.

Other cankers on *Tilia* are caused by *Aleurodiscus griseo-canus,* and *Strumella coryneoidea.*

Control: Cut out and destroy all cankered branches and remove and destroy twigs and branches that have fallen to the ground. Cover wounds with a good tree paint.

Leaf Spots (*Phlyctaena tiliae* and *Phyllosticta praetervisa*). These leaf spots are relatively rare and hence control measures are unnecessary.

Powdery Mildews (*Microsphaera alni, Phyllactinia corylea,* and *Uncinula clintonii*). Lindens are quite susceptible to powdery mildew fungi. They rarely cause enough damage to require control measures.

Control: Valuable specimens may be sprayed with Acti-dione PM, Karathane, or Benlate when the mildew appears.

Other Diseases. Other diseases reported on lindens include dieback caused by *Botryosphaeria dothidea,* and wilt by *Verticillium albo-atrum.*

Insects and Related Pests

Linden Aphid (*Eucallipterus tiliae*). Sap is sucked from the leaves and a sticky substance is exuded by a yellow-and-black aphid with clouded wings.

Control: Spray with malathion or Sevin when the young aphids appear on the leaves in spring.

Japanese Beetle (*Popillia japonica*). This beetle is attracted to certain trees in a planting, feeding high up on a sunny side.

Control: See *Aesculus.*

Linden Leaf Beetle (*Calligrapha scalaris*). Ragged holes remain in leaves chewed by creamy-white larvae with yellow heads. The adult beetle is ³/₈ inch long, oval, yellow, with green spots on the wing-covers and a broad, irregular, coppery-geeen stripe down the back. Lemon-yellow eggs are deposited on the lower leaf surfaces in late June or early July. The beetles hibernate in the ground. This pest is also known as elm calligrapha.

Control: Spray the foliage with Sevin as the larvae appear.

Linden Borer (*Saperda vestita*). Broad tunnels beneath the bark near the trunk base or in roots are made by the linden borer, a slender, white larva 1 inch long. The adult, a yellowish-brown beetle ³/₄ inch long, with three dark spots on each wing-cover, feeds on green bark. Eggs are deposited in small bark crevices made by the beetle.

Other borers that attack lindens are the flatheaded apple tree and the brown wood.

Control: Dig out the borers with a flexible wire, or inject a nicotine paste such as Bortox into the tunnels and seal the openings. Spraying the trunk base with methoxychlor may control many of the young larvae after they hatch out of their eggs.

Walnut Lace Bug (*Corythucha juglandis*). This pest also infests ash, hickory, and mulberry.

Control: Spray valuable specimens with Diazinon, malathion, or Sevin.

Caterpillars. Among the many caterpillars that chew the leaves of this host are cankerworms, the variable oak leaf caterpillar, and the larvae of the gypsy, cynthia, cecropia, and white-marked tussock moths.

Control: Spray with *Bacillus thuringiensis,* Imidan, or Sevin when the caterpillars are young.

Basswood Leaf Miner (*Baliosus ruber*). The beetles feed on the under sides of the leaves, eating out all tissues except the veins. The larvae also work on the undersides, making large blister-like mines. The foliage turns brown, withers, and falls off.

Control: See leaf miner under *Robinia.*

Elm Sawfly (*Cimbex americana*). These smooth caterpillars, pale green with a black stripe down the middle of the back, are about 1 inch long. They curl up tightly when at rest. Elm, willow, maple, and poplar are other hosts frequented.

Control: The standard methoxychlor spray used to control this pest on elms will also work on linden. Straight methoxychlor sprays may bring on an outbreak of mites, and it is therefore wise to include a mite-killer in the mixture.

Linden Looper (*Erannis tiliaria*). This pest, also known as the basswood looper, infests birch, elm, hickory, and maple. The caterpillars are 1¹/₂ inch long at maturity, bright yellow, with 10 longitudinal wavy black lines down the back. The moth, buff colored with a 1³/₄ inch wingspread, deposits its eggs from October to November.

Control: Sevin or methoxychlor sprays applied when the young caterpillars begin to feed will provide control.

Scales. Nine species of scale insects infest this host: cottony maple, European fruit lecanium, oystershell, Putnam, San Jose, terrapin, tuliptree, walnut, and willow.

Control: Valuable specimens should be sprayed from time to time with malathion or Sevin.

Carmine Spider Mite (*Tetranychus cinnabarinus*). In midsummer, especially in dry weather, the leaves become infested with this mite, which causes them to turn brown and dry up.

Control: Lindens are especially susceptible to mite damage when straight methoxychlor sprays are used. Hence valuable trees should be sprayed with a good miticide such as Kelthane. A good preventive is to use this material with the methoxyclor from the start.

TOLMIEA (PIGGY-BACK PLANT)

The only disease recorded on this host is powdery mildew caused by the fungus *Sphaerotheca mors-uvae.* Spraying with Ben-late or Karathane will control it. Mites and mealybugs also may infest *Tolmiea.* The former are controlled with Kelthane sprays and the latter with malathion sprays.

TRACHYMENE (BLUE LACE-FLOWER)

Diseases

Basal Rot (*Pellicularia filamentosa*). Occasionally in the propagating house the roots and lower parts of the stem may be attacked by this fungus. The first noticeable symptoms are the sudden wilting and collapsing of the plant.

Control: Discard infected plants and debris, and sow seeds in steam-pasteurized soil or soil treated with Benlate.

Other Diseases. A root rot caused by a species of *Fusarium* and root-knot by the name *Meloidogyne incognita* are other problems on this host.

TRADESCANTIA (SPIDERWORT)

Diseases

Leaf Spots (*Colletotrichum* sp., *Septoria tradescantiae*). Occasionally these fungi cause spotting of the leaves. Picking off and destroying infected leaves is usually sufficient to keep them in check.

Other Diseases. A rust caused by *Uromyces commelinae* and a blight by *Botrytis cinerea* are the other fungus diseases of *Tradescantia.*

Insects and Other Animal Pests

Three leaf-eating insects infest this host: greenhouse leaf tier, *Udea rubigalis;* the morning-glory leaf cutter, *Loxostege obliteralis;* and the orange tortrix caterpillar, *Argyrotaenia citrana.*

Sucking insects that may infest spiderwort include the citrus mealybug and chaff scale.

Sevin sprays will control all these chewing and sucking insects.

The southern root-knot nema *Meloidogyne incognita* also infests this host.

TRILLIUM (WAKE-ROBIN)

This host is subject to leaf spots caused by *Colletotrichum peckii, Gloeosporium trillii, Heterosporium trillii, Phyllosticta trillii,* and *Septoria trillii;* to stem rots by *Pellicularia rolfsii* and *Ciborinia trillii;* and to rust by *Uromyces halstedii.*

TRITONIA

Several blights caused by species of *Alternaria* and *Heterosporium* and by *Pellicularia rolfsii* occur on this host. Yellows caused by *Fusarium orthoceras* var. *gladioli* is common in California and on commercial stocks. This fungus also causes a rot of corms, as does *Stromatinia gladioli,* which is common in commercial stocks. The iris mosaic virus is also found on this host on the West Coast.

TROLLIUS (GLOBE-FLOWER)

Species of this group that are used in border plantings may occasionally be spotted by *Phyllosticta trollii, Cylindrosporium montenegrinum,* and *Ascochyta* sp. A smut caused by *Urocystis anemones* is occasionally found.

TROPAEOLUM (NASTURTIUM)

Diseases

Bacterial Leaf Spot (*Pseudomonas aptata*). This bacterium spots the leaves and then rots them. Some investigators believe that the causal organism is actually *P. syringae,* which causes lilac blight.

Control: Pick off and destroy spotted leaves.

Bacterial Wilt (*Pseudomonas solanacearum*). Plants attacked by this bacterium turn yellow, wilt, and die. The stems are more or less water-soaked and the water-conducting vessels appear as black streaks beneath the epidermis. Decayed roots also are black. If one cuts the stems or branches of infected plants, masses of gray slime ooze out and turn brown. The plants die without blossoming. Infection takes place through roots damaged in cultivation. Bacteria may also gain entrance through the water pores and stomata.

Control: Avoid planting nasturtiums near potatoes, tomatoes, eggplants, and other plants subject to the same disease. Do not plant nasturtiums in soil that harbors the bacteria unless it is first steam-pasteurized.

Leaf Spots (*Heterosporium tropaeoli, Cercospora tropaeoli,* and *Pleospora* sp.). The first-mentioned causes serious losses after midsummer to nasturtiums grown for seed and as a garden ornamental in coastal California. Because the *Heterosporium* fungus is seed-borne, hot-water treatment is standard practice among seedsmen.

Control: Most leaf spots can be curbed by an occasional application of a copper fungicide. This is rarely done except in large-scale commercial plantings.

Viruses. Two virus diseases are known to occur on this host: curly top caused by the beet curly top virus, and spotted wilt by the tomato spotted wilt virus.

Control: Rogue out and destroy infected plants. Control sucking insects with malathion.

Aster Yellows. This disease also occurs on nasturtiums.

Control: Same as for viruses.

Insects and Other Animal Pests

Aphids (*Aphis fabae*). The black bean aphid is usually very destructive to garden nasturtiums. They gather on the under sides of the leaves in large numbers and escape notice until the leaves turn pale yellowish-green and the plant begins to droop. If the leaves are lifted, the under sides can be seen covered completely with these black insects. They sometimes feed on the leafstalks near the blade.

Other species of aphids which attack nasturtiums are the green peach, *Myzus persicae,* and the crescent-marked lily, *Neomyzus circumflexus.*

Control: Malathion, Meta-Systox R, or Sevin sprays are very effective in combating all species of aphids. Other sprays, such as nicotine sulfate and soap, pyrethrum, derris, and rotenone, are also effective. An angled nozzle should be used to reach the under sides of the leaves.

Cabbage Looper (*Trichoplusia ni*). These green caterpillars, about $1^1/_4$ inches long, feed on the leaves and blossoms and often completely strip the plants of all their leaves. The moths' wings vary from grayish to dark brown mottled with lighter brown, with a silver-colored figure in the center of each wing.

Pieris rapae is an imported cabbage looper which also attacks nasturtiums. The caterpillars are grayish-green; the adult butterflies are white.

Control: Spray with Sevin when the worms begin to feed.

Corn Earworm (*Heliothis zea*). This common pest of corn also attacks many ornamentals, among them nasturtiums.

Control: Spray with Sevin.

Western Black Flea Beetle (*Phyllotreta pusilla*). These small beetles feed in great numbers on the leaves and often completely riddle them. They jump about vigorously when disturbed.

Control: Spray with a mixture of Sevin and Kelthane, or Cygon.

Thrips (*Heliothrips haemorrhoidalis*). Characteristic circular or irregular white spots up to $1/_8$ inch in diameter mark the upper surfaces of the leaves of *T. majus;* on the opposite sides larger and more irregular spots are found, marked by the dark, greenish-black excreta of the yellowish young thrips which feed at their margins. Infestation in the greenhouse appears to be more or less confined to the lower leaves. The adults are black with characteristic wings.

Control: Same as for flea beetle.

Two-Spotted Mite (*Tetranychus urticae*). This pest occasionally is serious on nasturtiums.

Control: Spray with Kelthane, chlorobenzilate, Meta-Systox R, or Tedion in early June, and repeat 2 or 3 times at 10-day intervals.

Other Insects. Nasturtiums may also be infested by the tarnished plant bug, the serpentine leaf miner, and the greenhouse leaf tier.

The southern root-knot nema, *Meloidogyne incognita,* and the root gall nema, *M. schachtii,* also infest this host.

TSUGA (HEMLOCK)

Diseases

Leaf Blight (*Fabrella tsugae*). In late summer, leaves of Eastern hemlock turn brown and drop prematurely when attacked by this fungus. Small, black fruiting bodies of the fungus occur on the fallen leaves. These produce spores the following spring, which initiate new infections.

Control: Leaf blight rarely damages the trees sufficiently to necessitate measures other than gathering and destroying fallen infected leaves in the autumn.

Cankers. At least 5 species of fungi—*Botryosphaeria tsugae, Cytospora* sp., *Dermatea balsamea, Hymenochaete agglutinans,* and *Phacidiopycnis pseudotsugae*—are known to cause cankers on hemlock.

Control: Prune affected branches and spray with a copper fungicide if affected trees are particularly valuable.

Blister Rust (*Pucciniastrum vaccinii* and *P. hydrangeae*). Young hemlocks and the lower leaves of older trees have yellowish blisters or pustules, from which the spores sift out during June and July. Rhododendron is an alternate host of *P. vaccinii,* which causes a rusty-brown leaf spot, more or less injurious in nurseries. Wild and cultivated hydrangeas are alternate hosts of *P. hydrangeae.*

Control: The only control known for these rusts is to be sure that neither of the alternate hosts is then planted in any given region. Spraying with ferbam may help.

Needle Rust (*Melampsora farlowii*). Eastern hemlock and, to a lesser extent, Carolina hemlock are attacked by this fungus. In late May or early June some of the new leaves turn yellow. Within 2 weeks, the shoots to which these leaves are attached turn yellow, become flaccid, and droop. Most of the needles then drop from the affected shoots. Severely rusted trees appear as though their branch tips had been scorched by fire. Red, waxy, linear fungus bodies occur on the lower leaf surfaces, on the shoots, and on the cones.

Control: A spray consisting of 4 pounds of dry lime sulfur in 50 gallons of water applied at weekly intervals in May has given good control of the disease on small trees in nursery plantings. The use of this material for large trees may be justified in unusual circumstances.

Sapwood Rot (*Ganoderma lucidum* and *Coniophora puteana*). These fungi frequently cause decay of the tissues immediately beneath the bark at the base of the trunk; this results in the death of the tree.

Control: No effective control measures are known. Avoid wounding the bark, and feed and water the trees to keep them in good vigor.

Physiological Disease

Sunscorch (nonparasitic). Ornamental hemlocks are frequently subject to severe burning or scorching when the temperature reaches 95°F. The ends of the branches may be killed for several inches back so that the affected tops may appear as if injured by a strong solution of nicotine sulfate.

Drought Injury. Hemlocks are more sensitive to prolonged periods of drought than most other narrow-leaved evergreens. The damage is most severe on sites with southern exposures or on rocky slopes where the roots cannot penetrate deeply into the soil. Thousands of hemlocks died in the northeastern United States as a result of severe droughts in the years 1960–66.

Insects and Related Pests

Hemlock Woolly Aphid (*Adelges tsugae*). This pest appears as white tufts on the bark and needles. It is capable of killing young ornamental hemlocks.

Control: When the pest becomes prevalent, spray with malathion, Dylox, Diazinon, or Meta-Systox R.

Hemlock Borer (*Melanophila fulvoguttata*). Wide, shallow galleries in the inner bark and sapwood result from boring by a white larva ½ inch long. The adult, a flat, metallic-colored beetle with three circular, reddish-yellow spots on each wing cover, deposits eggs in bark crevices.

Control: Prune and destroy severely infested branches. Keep the tree in good vigor by fertilizing and watering.

Hemlock Looper (*Lambdina fiscellaria*). Hemlocks may be completely defoliated by a pale yellow caterpillar with a double row of small black dots along the body, which is more than an inch long at maturity. The adult moth has tan to gray wings, which expand to more than 1 inch. Another species, *L. atha-*

saria athasaria, occurs less frequently but also defoliates hemlocks.

Control: Spray with Sevin and a miticide when the larvae are small.

Spruce Leaf Miner (*Taniva albolineana*). This species, more common on spruce, occasionally mines the leaves of hemlock.

Control: Spray with malathion when the pests begin to feed in late May.

Hemlock Fiorinia Scale (*Fiorinia externa*). This scale may infest hemlock leaves, and occasionally those of spruce, causing them to turn yellow and drop prematurely. Both male and female scales are elongated. The females are pale yellow to brown and are almost completely covered with their own cast skins. There are two generations a year in the New England states.

Control: Cygon sprays are very effective against this scale. In the Northeastern United States, a foliar spray in mid-May using one quart of the 23.4 per cent emulsifiable concentrate in 100 gallons of water gives adequate control of this pest. An additional application in late June is necessary for complete control.

Grape Scale (*Diaspidiotus uvae*). Hemlock hedges can be destroyed by infestations of this small, dingy white scale which has yellowish nipples or exuviae.

Control: Malathion or Sevin sprays, when applied from mid- to late June, provide good control.

Hemlock Scale (*Abgrallaspis ithacae*). The adult female, circular and nearly black, infests the lower surfaces of hemlock leaves, causing premature leaf fall. In heavy infestations it may move to the twigs and branches.

Control: Spray with a "superior" type dormant oil or a combination of the oil and ethion in April before new growth emerges. A Cygon spray during the growing season is also effective.

Hemlock Eriophyid Mite (*Nalepella tsugifoliae*). The unthrifty look of some hemlocks may be due to infestations of this mite.

Control: Kelthane or Meta-Systox R sprays applied in early April will control this pest.

Spider Mites. Hemlocks in ornamental plantings are extremely susceptible to several other species of mites. One, the spruce spider mite, *Oligonychus ununguis,* is most prevalent on spruces and junipers in addition to hemlock. The other, the two-spotted mite *Tetranychus urticae,* is discussed under *Althaea.*

Control: Mites can be controlled on this host by spraying with chlorobenzilate, Kelthane, Meta-Systox R, or Tedion. These should not be applied to tender foliage during the hottest part of the day, for the foliage of ornamental hemlocks is liable to be burned, even without spraying, during intense heat.

Other Pests. Hemlocks are also subject to the bagworm, fir flat-headed borer, spruce budworm, gypsy moth, hemlock sawfly, and Japanese weevil.

TULIPA (TULIP)

Diseases

Blight, or Fire (*Botrytis tulipae*). The leaves become flecked with small brown spots; flowers also are attacked (see Figs. 223 and 224). The spots are most noticeable on the light-colored varieties. When the bulb is attacked the whole plant becomes dwarfed and turns a pale yellowish-green, and the flower is blasted. The rot as it develops on the leaves and flower stalks may cause a light gray discoloration bordered by brown margins. Large areas of the leaves may be involved. The stems may rot off completely. In moist weather the diseased parts may be covered with a gray mold which produces large numbers of conidia; these are spread by air currents and other agents to other plants. At the base of the stem and on the outer scales of the bulbs one finds many blackish or dark-

Fig. 223. *Botrytis* blight infection on a tulip leaf. (Dr. C. J. Gould)

Fig. 224. Tulip flowers infected by the *Botrytis* fungus. (Dr. C. J. Gould)

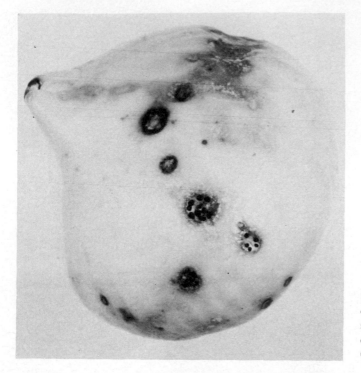

Fig. 225. *Botrytis* fungus on tulip bulb. Note the black sclerotia of the fungus in the diseased areas. (Dr. C. J. Gould)

brown sclerotia (Fig. 225). These bodies carry the fungus through the winter or other unfavorable conditions.

Control: A careful inspection of bulbs should be made before they are planted, and all bulbs that show infection should be discarded. The outer husks should be removed to disclose any diseased spots on scales beneath. Early removal of infected plants is essential. As soon as the disease appears in a bed, individual plants should be removed in such a way as to avoid scattering the spores or leaving parts of infected bulb scales in the soil. Destroy all blossoms and leaves that show infection. If bulbs are to be planted where diseased plants have been grown, the soil should be replaced, steam-pasteurized, or treated with an appropriate chemical as described in Chapter 4.

Good protection of outdoor plants can be achieved by frequent applications of Botran.

In rainy springs the applications must be thorough and frequent as often as every 3 days. They should be discontinued as soon as the blooms begin to open, or the flowers will be spotted with spray residue. Botran and Fore are also effective against *Botrytis.* As a rule it is advisable to change the location of plantings; in other words practice "rotation of crops." In greenhouse plantings the air should be kept as dry as possible. Do not shower the plants with water, and avoid the application of too much nitrogenous fertilizer.

Basal Rot (*Fusarium oxysporum* var. *tulipae*). Diseased bulbs produce leaves that turn red, wilt, and may die. Few roots are formed, and the bases of the bulbs are rotted. Infected bulbs in storage are dull white, and the basal decay is firm, shrunken, and sometimes zonate (Fig. 226). This disease occurs in the Pacific Northwest.

Fig. 226. Basal rot of tulip caused by the fungus *Fusarium oxysporum* var. *tulipae*. (Dr. Walter Apt)

Control: Dig bulbs as early as practicable and in dry weather. Avoid sunburning, bruising, and other injuries. Store bulbs in thin layers under cool, well-ventilated conditions. Soaking the bulb for 15 to 30 minutes in Benlate within 48 hours after digging will help to control the causal fungus. The dilution rate is two tablespoonfuls of Benlate per gallon of warm water (80-85°F.) or 1²/₃ pounds per 100 gallons of warm water. The bulbs should be dried after treatment.

Blue Mold Rot (*Penicillium* sp.). Bulbs infested with mites are often further damaged by blue mold which comes in as a secondary organism. Other fungi also associated with rotting bulbs are species of *Aspergillus* and *Rhizopus stolonifer.*

Control: Dipping bulbs in Benlate, as suggested for basal rot mentioned above, should also reduce the number of blue mold infections.

Crown Rot (*Pellicularia rolfsii* and *Sclerotium delphinii*). The bulb and stem below ground are rotted by these fungi. Leaves of affected plants then turn red, wilt, and die. This disease is worldwide and rarely becomes serious on tulips, but is highly destructive to many herbaceous plants.

Control: Remove and destroy infected plants together with nearby soil. Plant healthy bulbs in clean soil or treat infested soil with steam.

Gray Bulb Rot (*Pellicularia* [*Rhizoctonia*] *tuliparum*). The presence of this fungus in the soil of tulip beds is made evident by the bare areas. Plants that have succeeded in emerging from the ground wither away and die. The fungus enters the roots and progresses upward to destroy the bases of the leaves and the bulb, which become more or less rotted. The upper parts of the bulb are rotted more quickly than the lower parts; the rotted bulbs become covered with a heavy growth of gray mold. The roots themselves may be perfectly healthy. The rot is dry rather than soft and wet.

No spores are produced by this fungus. Sclerotia, at first white and later black, are the only means by which it persists in the soil from season to season; these may live 2 or 3 years.

Control: Remove and destroy all infected plants, using a "bulb sticker." Select clean bulbs and plant in soil that has been steam-pasteurized or treated with Benlate. Avoid poorly drained planting sites.

Stem Rot, Flower Spot (*Phytophthora cactorum*). Double varieties of tulips growing in moist shady places with poor circulation of air are subject to attack by this fungus. The flower stalks shrivel below or near the leaf axils; this causes the flowers to fall over.

Control: No practical method of control has been worked out except to avoid growing tulips in poorly ventilated situations.

Other Diseases. Tulips are also susceptible to anthracnose caused by the fungus *Gloeosporium theumenii* and soft rot by the bacterium *Erwinia carotovora*.

Virus Diseases

Tulip Breaking (Tulip breaking virus). This virus disease appears as a striping and somewhat irregular spotting of flowers, vary-

Fig. 227. Breaking of flower color in virus-infected tulip. (U.S. Department of Agriculture)

ing from yellowish to white (Fig. 227); such variegation is known as "breaks." The depigmentation is effected after the original color of the flower has developed. The foliage may be distinctly mottled and the plants are reduced in size and vigor of growth. Some reduction in the development of bulbs and offsets may result. It has been proved that two viruses may occur together to cause symptoms which are more or less confused. One virus removes the color of the flower and the other adds color to the light-colored flowers. The color-destroying virus retards plant growth; the color-adding virus has little effect on growth. Double-flowered varieties are more susceptible than single ones. Several species of aphids are known to spread the tulip breaking virus.

Control: Rogue out and destroy infected

plants. Spray frequently with malathion or Meta-Systox R to control aphids.

Mosaic (Cucumber mosaic virus). This virus causes a yellow streaking or fleck-like spotting of the leaves and dark colorations in flowers, unlike the breaking virus.

Control: Commercial plantings of tulips should not be made in areas where cucumber mosaic is abundant.

Necrosis (Tobacco necrosis virus). Severe necrotic lesions are produced on tulip leaves. The whitish dead areas on poorly formed leaves are usually surrounded by purple lines. Affected plants die early and rarely produce bulbs.

Control: Since this virus is soil-borne, roguing out of infected plants is useless. Where tulips die in patches and no fungus is associated with their demise, an expert on viruses should be consulted.

Physiological Diseases

Sunscald. Drying and shriveling of flower parts especially along the upper edges has been found to be caused by sunlight under dry conditions.

Control: Shading the flowering plants in the greenhouse is effective.

Frost Injury. Among unfavorable conditions frost has been reported as a cause of a disease. Oblong or oval spots develop along the veins. This injury is not common.

Flower Stalk and Stem Collapse, "Topple." Certain varieties of tulips develop weak watersoaked spots, with an exudation of liquid either on the upper half of the flower stalk or on the lower parts, or even on the neck near the bulb. Flower stalks soon shrivel and collapse. Some stems may topple without first showing water-soaked spots. The plants otherwise appear to be in excellent condition. The disease is said to be caused by insufficient ripening of the bulb after wet, cool summer weather and by forcing of tulips in clay soil or at excessive temperatures.

Control: Avoid high temperatures and high humidity in forcing. See that bulbs used for forcing ripen thoroughly. Spreading out the bulbs in the forcing house for 2 to 3 weeks is recommended as a secondary ripening period. Do not force the bulbs too early especially after wet, cold years. The varieties susceptible to this disease should be put in pots early to establish a strong root system. They may then be forced later. Some varieties are less susceptible and are to be preferred if this disease gives trouble.

Retarded Growth. If bulbs are stored or heeled-in under excessively warm conditions or are insufficiently ripened, the shoots are greatly retarded or are suppressed entirely.

Winter Injury. When bulbs are planted late in the fall in heavy clay soil or where drainage is not adequate, roots fail to grow and shoots are distorted and abnormal. Bulb decay follows.

Leaf-Flower Fusion. The author observed an abnormal fusion of the leaves and flower petals (Fig. 228). The cause of this condition has not been determined, but the use of hormone-type weed killers during the previous growing season are possible causes.

Insects and Other Animal Pests

Tulip Bulb Aphid (*Dysaphis tulipae*). This aphid also attacks iris, freesia, gladiolus, and crocus. It is gray with a waxy appearance and clusters under bulb coats. It may also infest aboveground parts.

Control: If aphids are present before planting dip bulbs in Diazinon, 1 ounce. in 3 gallons of water. Aphids that later appear on the foliage can be controlled with malathion sprays.

Crescent-Marked Lily Aphid (*Neomyzus circumflexus*). This aphid is yellowish-green with black markings on the body. It occasionally attacks tulips grown in greenhouses. The

Fig. 228. Fusing of leaves and flower petals of tulip due to some unknown factor.

green peach aphid, *Myzus persicae,* is not it-self very troublesome to tulips, but it is a vector (carrier) of virus disease.

The tulip leaf aphid *Rhopalosiphoninus tulipaella* infests tulips and iris leaves and may develop on the bulbs in storage as does the tulip bulb aphid.

Control: Same as the bulb aphid.

Narcissus Bulb Fly (*Merodon equestris*). Tulip bulbs are only occasionally destroyed by the larvae of these flies. See *Narcissus.*

Stem and Bulb Nema. See *Hyacinthus.*

Bulb Mite (*Rhizoglyphus echinopus*). These mites are colored yellowish-white with a pink tinge, are bead-like, shining, and slow-moving. They are large enough to be readily seen even without a hand lens. Bulbs that are infested by these mites before they are dug deteriorate rapidly. The mites are most active

at 60° to 80°F. and at high humidity. If infested bulbs are stored at a low temperature, so that the mites remain inactive and thus escape detection, they will be planted for uninfested bulbs; the mites then continue their work, causing the leaves to turn yellow and blasting the flowers. They move from one bulb to another in a planting, attaching themselves to some other insect or soil organism. The outer crust of the bulb scales becomes hardened and light chocolate-brown. The pulp of the scale is dry and broken up into fine more or less corky fragments. Hundreds of mites can be found working in this pulpy mass. The damage done by mites opens the way for rots caused by fungi and bacteria and to infestation by other organisms.

Control: Discard all bulbs in which heavy infestation is evident. Avoid planting clean bulbs in ground previously infested unless the soil has been steam-pasteurized. Bulbs may be freed of mites by dipping them in hot water at 122°F. for a few minutes. Hot-water treatments cannot be used safely if the roots have started to develop. No effective soil treatments are known.

Other Pests. Millipedes, wireworms, and the root-knot nema are other pests that infest tulips.

ULMUS (ELM)

Bacterial and Fungus Diseases

Wetwood (*Enterobacter* sp.). This bacterial disease appears as a wilt, branch dieback, and internal and external fluxing of elms. It occurs in American, Moline, Littleford, English, Siberian, and slippery elms. Trees affected by wetwood have dark, water-soaked, malodorous wood. The condition is usually confined to the inner sapwood and heartwood in trunks and large branches. Little or no streaking occurs in the outer sapwood, and no discoloration is seen in the cambial region or phloem.

Control: Injection of such chemical substances as mercuric chloride, copper sulfate, silver nitrate, and 8-hydroxyquinoline benzoate into infected trees have failed to control the disease. Although no effective control has been found, some relief to fluxing trees is possible through the installation of drainpipes in the trunk. Such drainpipes do not reduce the infection but provide a way for the sap and toxic gas to escape. Semirigid plastic pipes are more satisfactory than metal ones.

Cankers. At least 8 species of fungi— *Apioporthe apiospora, Botryosphaeria dothidea, Coniothyrium* sp., *Cytospora ludibunda, Nectria cinnabarina, N. coccinea, Phomopsis* sp., and *Sphaeropsis ulmicola*—cause cankers and dieback of twigs and branches of elms.

Control: Many small cankers can be eradicated by surgical means. The cuts should extend well beyond the visibly infected area to ensure complete removal of fungus-infected tissue. The edge of the wound should be painted with shellac and the entire exposed area finally dressed with a good tree paint. If the canker has completely girdled the stem, prune well below the affected area, and destroy the prunings.

Dutch Elm Disease (*Ceratocystis ulmi*). The first symptoms consist in a yellowing, wilting, and browning of leaves on individual branches, which eventually die. Stripping the bark from such branches reveals brown streaks in the sapwood. Cross sections show circles or rings of brown spots (Fig. 229). The spread of the parasite up and down from the point of infection is sometimes very rapid; the trees may die in one season. Other trees may live several years after having been infected in a number of different places. The *Pesotum* stage of the fungus (Fig. 230) develops underneath the dead bark, the minute spores being held together in mucilaginous masses. The elm bark beetles, *Scolytus multistriatus* and *Hylurgopinus rufipes*, and perhaps other beetles that develop on the dead wood beneath the bark carry the fungus to the young growth of other elm trees and by feeding in the crotches spread the disease. The female beetles deposit their eggs in furrows in the sapwood of limbs or trunks. The larvae boring out from both sides of the furrow make a characteristic pattern, shown in Fig. 33. They pupate and the young beetles bore out through the bark to spread infection to healthy trees. Recent research has revealed that automobiles may be important factors in the long-distance spread of infested bark beetles.

Control: Despite much research, no perfectly satisfactory control has been discovered. At present the disease is kept somewhat in check by strict sanitation (that is, by removing and destroying diseased or weak

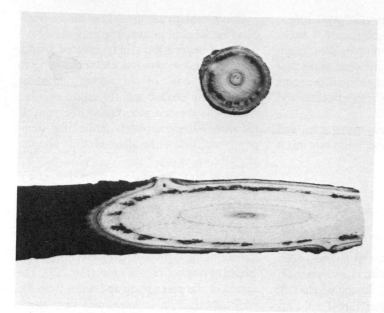

Fig. 229. Discoloration of the sapwood caused by the Dutch elm disease fungus, *Ceratocystis ulmi.*

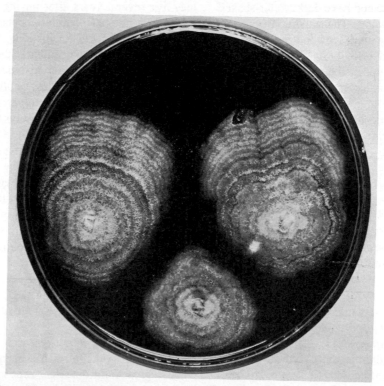

Fig. 230. The asexual stage of the Dutch elm disease fungus as it appears when grown in agar plates in the laboratory.

trees) and by a highly specialized spraying program. The trees should be removed by May 1, and those that are to be protected sprayed before May 15 with a special methoxychlor spray. A second application of methoxychlor mixed with Kelthane or some other mite-killer, should be made about July 1. Best results are achieved when this program is adopted on a community-wide basis.

It has been observed that healthy trees that are prunned in late July, August, and September are more apt to contract the disease than those pruned at other times of the year.

Pruning diseased branches has often been suggested as a means of checking this disease. However, J. H. Hart of the Michigan Agricultural Experiment Station found that this practice was effective in only 23 per cent of the cases. Because of the low percentage of success and the high cost of trimming large trees, he concluded that this method of control is neither effective nor practical.

More recently, however, Dr. R. J. Campana found that elimination of disease was inversely related to depth of infection. The infected tree had a better chance of survival if the infection in the excised branch had not penetrated too far down in the branch. He found that 87 per cent of the trees survived where the removed branch had 10 linear feet of apparent disease-free wood; 42 per cent with 5 to 10 feet; and 12 per cent with less than 5 feet.

Some spread of the disease may occur via root grafts between a diseased and a healthy tree. Vapam soil treatments will kill roots of diseased trees and thus prevent transmission via root grafts.

Recent tests have revealed that Benlate can be applied in a foliar spray or injected into the trunk as an aid in the control of Dutch elm disease. The treatments are made by trained arborists in conjunction with sanitation and insect control programs.

The foliar spray is applied in spring after the trees reach full leaf. Two pounds of Benlate per 100 gallons of water is the rate for hydraulic sprayers. A mature tree should receive 10 to 20 gallons of spray. A surfactant may be added to improve wetting of the leaves. The trunk injections can be made either via injection tubes or applied under pressure with special apparatus, anytime during the growing season but preferably in spring when the trees reach full leaf. Details are available from the manufacturer.

A report released early in 1976 stated that the fungicide LIGNASAN BLP injected into 7000 mature healthy elms by 1500 co-operators in 30 States indicated that the elms had a 99 percent chance of survival. Only the proper use of the chemical and time will tell whether this practice will help to save old elms from the ravages of this disease.

In late spring of 1977, the Merck Company, Rahway, New Jersey, introduced the systemic fungicide "Arbotect" 20-S for use as a dutch elm disease preventive and as a therapeutic treatment for mildly infected trees. The active ingredient in "Arbotect" 20-S is thiabendazole.

The greatest hope for eventual control lies in the discovery of American elms that have natural immunity to the disease. A number of such individuals are being watched carefully by scientists of the United States Department of Agriculture.

Perhaps the most promising news is the development by scientists at the Agricultural Research Service Shade Tree and Ornamental Plants Laboratory, Delaware, Ohio of a hybrid elm, named "Urban Elm" which is resistant to the Dutch elm disease. "Urban Elm" is a cross between an elm from the Netherlands (*Ulmus hollandica* var. *vegeta* X. *U. carpinifolia*) and a Siberian elm. The new tree will grow to moderate size, making it more suitable for urban planting than the American elm. It has an upright branching form as compared with the well recognized umbrella shape of the American elm.

"Urban Elm" will not be available for several years, when ample quantities will have been propagated by commercial nurseries.

Another disease-resistant hybrid clone, "Sapporo Autumn Gold," was developed by tree breeders at the University of Wisconsin. Several commercial nurseries are now propagating it, and as with the "Urban Elm," it should be available in 1979 or 1980.

The Hansen Manchurian elm, like most Asiatic elms, is decidedly resistant to the disease. A close relative of the American elm, Japanese keaki, *Zelkova serrata,* is somewhat more resistant to the disease than is the American elm. It is vase-shaped and has bark resembling beech and elm-like foliage that turns red in the fall.

The tiny wasp *Dentrosoter protuberans* from France was introduced into the United States by the Forest Service in the late 1960's with the hope that it would help to control the insect that spreads this disease. The wasp is a parasite on the fungus-carrying European bark beetle. The female wasp locates hidden beetle larvae and deposits eggs beside them. When the eggs hatch, the wasp larvae attack and kill the bark beetle larvae by sucking their body juices. If and when the wasps become established in large enough quantities, they may be an important factor in reducing the bark beetle population and thus reducing the spread of the causal fungus.

Scientists in the United States Department of Agriculture have extracted several sex lures from natural organisms. One, from virgin bark beetles, attracts adult elm bark beetles from both sexes. When the lure is synthesized in sufficient amounts, it will be subjected to large scale tests to control the beetles which disseminate the Dutch elm disease fungus.

Bleeding Canker (*Phytophthora cactorum*). This disease also affects maples.

Control: See *Acer.*

Leaf Curl (*Taphrina ulmi*). Small blisters which lead to abnormal leaf development follow an attack by this fungus. Infection usually takes place soon after the leaves unfold.

Control: Valuable specimens subject to this disease should be sprayed with concentrated lime sulfur in spring just before growth starts.

Leaf Spots (*Cercospora sphaeriaeformis, Cylindrosporium tenuisporium, Coryneum tumoricola, Gloeosporium inconspicuum, G. ulmicolum, Gnomonia ulmea, Monochaetia monochaeta, Phyllosticta confertissima, P. melaleuca, Mycosphaerella ulmi, Septogloeum profusum,* and *Coniothyrium ulmi*). There are so many fungi that cause leaf spots of elms that only an expert can distinguish one from another. Probably the most prevalent leaf spot however, is that caused by *Gnomonia ulmea,* the first symptom of which appears early in spring as small white or yellow flecks on the upper leaf surface. The flecks then increase in size, and their centers turn black (Fig. 231). If infections occur early and are heavy, the leaves may drop prematurely. Usually, however, the disease becomes prevalent in late fall about the time the leaves drop normally, and consequently little damage to the tree occurs.

Control: Gather and place the fallen leaves into the trash can in autumn. Ferbam or zineb applied 3 times at 10- to 12-day intervals starting when the leaves are half-grown, will give good control of leaf spots.

Powdery Mildews. Three species of powdery mildew fungi—*Microsphaera alni, Phyllactinia corylea,* and *Uncinula macrospora*—develop their mycelia on both sides of the leaves and cause a yellowish spotting. Damage is so slight that spraying is usually unnecessary.

Cephalosporium Wilt (*Deuterophoma ulmi*). The disease was once called *Dothiorella* wilt. Early symptoms are the drooping and yellowing of the leaves, which are more or less mottled and which later become

Fig. 231. Fungus leaf spot of elm. (Oxford University Press)

brownish and rolled. The foliage on trees whose trunk is infected is much dwarfed. Much dieback of twigs and branches occurs. This fungus is spread by wind, rain, insects, and birds. The parasite enters through wounds and develops in the water-conducting system, and also invades the medullary rays, pith, cambium, and other living tissues.

Control: Severely infected trees should be removed and destroyed. Mildly infected ones should be pruned heavily to remove as much of the diseased wood as possible. Because the fungus may develop internally well beyond the area of the external symptoms, pruning does not always produce the desired

results. Heavy fertilization may help mildly diseased trees to recover. The number of leaf infections can be reduced by applying combination sprays containing a fungicide and an insecticide. Fertilization is suggested as a general precautionary measure, despite the fact that there seems to be no correlation between the vigor of the tree and its susceptibility to the disease.

Verticillium Wilt (*Verticillium albo-atrum*). The symptoms of this disease are so much like those of the Dutch elm disease and *Cephalosporium* wilt that culturing of the fungus is necessary to distinguish them. This wilt may in time cause the death of large elms but usually does not become epidemic. The fungus usually spreads upward from the roots, but some recent research by scientists in the United States Department of Agriculture has revealed that air-borne spores can cause infection of aboveground parts.

Control: When infected trees wilt extensively, they should be cut down and destroyed, and as many of the roots as possible also destroyed. Fertilizing mildly infected trees may aid recovery.

Wood Decay. A number of fungi are associated with decay of elm wood. They cannot be checked once they have invaded large areas of the trunk. Many can be prevented from gaining access to the interior of the tree, however, by avoiding bark injuries, by properly treating injuries that do occur, and by keeping the tree in good vigor by fertilizing and watering.

Virus and Related Diseases

Phloem Necrosis (Mycoplasma-like organism). This disease is even more deadly than the Dutch elm disease caused by a fungus. Thousands of elms in the Middle West have died from its effects during the last 25 years. At present the disease has spread as far East as western New York State. The earliest symptoms appear in the extreme top of the tree at the outer tips of the branches. Here the foliage becomes sparse, and the leaves droop because of downward curvature of the leaf stalks. Individual leaves curl upward at the margin, producing a trough-like effect that makes them appear narrow and grayish-green. They are often stiff and brittle. The leaves then turn yellow and fall prematurely. These symptoms appear throughout the tree and are not confined to one or several branches as are wilt disease infections.

In advanced stages of the disease, the small fibrous roots and eventually the larger ones die. One of the most typical signs is the discoloration of the phloem tissue that precedes the death of the larger roots. The discoloration frequently extends into the trunk and branches. The cambial region becomes light to deep yellow, and the adjacent phloem tissue turns yellow, then brown, with small black flecks scattered throughout. After this, the phloem tissues are browned and killed. Moderately discolored phloem has an odor resembling wintergreen. In chronic cases of phloem necrosis, there is a gradual decline over a 12- to 18-month period before the tree dies. In acute cases, an apparently healthy and vigorous tree may wilt and die within 3 to 4 weeks.

The phloem necrosis organism can be transmitted experimentally by grafting patches of diseased bark, scions, or roots on healthy trees. In nature the infectious principle is transmitted by the elm leafhopper *Scaphoideus luteolus*. Actually there are two strains of this insect in the central states where the disease is most concentrated, but only one is capable of transmitting the infectious agent.

Control: Methoxychlor sprays will control the insect vector. Unfortunately even with nearly perfect control of the insect, only a few mycoplasma-bearing ones that are missed by the spray may spread the disease.

It may be possible to control phloem necrosis with sprays containing the anti-biotic tetracycline but the cost of such treatments would be prohibitive.

Mosaic (Elm mosaic virus). This virus disease, which causes yellow mottling of leaves, is rather rare and relatively harmless. It can be transmitted from diseased to healthy trees through both pollen and pistils. No control is known.

Scorch, another virus disease, occurs in the vicinity of Washington, D.C. Foliar necrosis and a gradual crown deterioration and eventual death are the principal symptoms. The causal virus has been transmitted by grafting.

Control: As with mosaic, no control is known.

Insects and Other Animal Pests

Woolly Apple Aphid (*Eriosoma lanigerum*). Stunting and curling of the terminal leaves result from infestations of bluish-white aphids. The growing tips may be killed back for several inches. The pest overwinters in the egg stage in bark crevices.

Control: In spring just after the buds burst, spray with Diazinon, malathion, or Meta-Systox R. Repeat in 10 days to 2 weeks.

Elm Leaf Curl Aphid (*Eriosoma americanum*). This insect may become injurious to elms at times. Another species of leaf-infesting aphid is *Tinocallis ulmifolii*.

Control: Same as for the woolly apple aphid.

Japanese Beetle (*Popillia japonica*). See *Aesculus.*

Smaller European Elm Bark Beetle (*Scolytus multistriatus*). Trees in weakened condition are most subject to infestation by the smaller European elm bark beetle. The adult female, a reddish-black beetle 1/10 inch long, deposits eggs along a gallery in the sapwood. The small white larvae that hatch from the eggs tunnel out at right angles to the main gallery. Tiny holes are visible in the bark when the adult beetles finally emerge. The beetle is of interest because it is one of the principal vectors of the Dutch elm disease fungus. Adult beetles will feed to a slight extent on buds and bark of twigs during the summer.

Control: Remove and destroy severely infested branches or trees, and fertilize and water weakened trees. High concentrations of methoxychlor should be applied in late April or early May to control this pest and thus prevent it from spreading the Dutch elm disease fungus.

Elm Leaf Beetle (*Pyrrhalta luteola*). Two distinct types of injury are produced by this pest. Soon after the leaves unfurl in spring, rectangular areas are chewed in them by the adult beetles, brownish-yellow insects 1/4 inch long (Fig. 232). Later in the season, the leaves are skeletonized and curl and dry up as a result of the feeding on the lower surface by the larvae, black grubs with yellow markings. The eggs (Fig. 233) are deposited on the lower leaf surface by the beetles.

Control: Spray with methoxychlor after the leaves are partly out, and again about 3 weeks later. Mites may increase on leaves sprayed too often with this material. The masses of grubs or pupae around the base of the tree can be destroyed by wetting the soil with a dilute solution of malathion, prepared from the emulsifiable concentrate.

Elm Borer (*Saperda tridentata*). Weakened trees are also subject to attack by the elm borer, a white grub 1 inch long, which burrows into the bark and sapwood and pushes sawdust out through the bark crevices. The adult is a grayish-brown beetle 1/2 inch long, with brick-red bands and black spots. Eggs are deposited on the bark in June. The larvae overwinter in tunnels beneath the bark.

Control: Spray the bark of the trunk and branches in late June and mid-July with methoxychlor.

Spring Cankerworm (*Paleacrita vernata*). Spring cankerworms, also called inch worms or measuring worms, are looping worms of various colors and about 1 inch in length, that chew the leaves. The adult female moth, which is 1/2 inch long and is wingless, climbs up the trunk to deposit eggs in early spring.

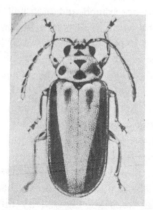

Fig. 232. Adult stage of elm leaf beetle. (U.S. Department of Agriculture)

Fig. 233. Eggs of leaf beetle. Notice that some have already hatched.

Control: Spray the leaves with *Bacillus thuringiensis* (Dipel, Thuricide), Imidan, or Sevin while the worms are small. In spring the trunk may be banded with a sticky material (Tree Tanglefoot) to trap the adult females as they crawl up the tree to deposit their eggs.

Fall Cankerworm (*Alsophila pometaria*). The leaves are chewed by the fall cankerworm, a black worm about 1 inch in length. The adult female is a wingless moth that deposits eggs in late fall on the twigs and branches.

Control: The same spray recommended for spring cankerworm will control this pest. Bands of sticky material should be applied by late September to trap the adult females as they climb the trees.

Elm Case Bearer (*Coleophora ulmifoliella*). When elms are infested by the case bearer, small holes are chewed in the leaves and angular spots mined between the leaf veins by a tiny larva. The adult is a small moth with a 1/2-inch wingspread. The pest overwinters in the larval stage in small cigar-shaped cases made from leaf tissue.

Control: Malathion or Sevin sprays in May, or a dormant spray before growth starts in spring, will control this pest.

Elm Lace Bug (*Corythucha ulmi*). In eastern states this insect may do considerable damage to elms. It first infests the tender foliage in spring, later causing a characteristic spotting of the leaves, which turn brown and die. Black specks of the excreta on the under side of the leaves are also characteristic.

Control: Spray with Diazinon malathion, or Sevin, when the young bugs appear in the spring.

Mourning-Cloak Butterfly (*Nymphalis antiopa*). The leaves are chewed by the caterpillar stage of this butterfly, which is 2 inches long, spiny, with a row of red spots on its back. The adult has yellow-bordered, purplish-brown wings. It overwinters in bark cavities and other protected places and deposits masses of eggs around small twigs in May.

Control: Spray with Sevin when the caterpillars are small. Prune and destroy infested twigs and small branches.

Elm Cockscomb Gall (*Colopha ulmicola*). Elongated galls which resemble the comb of a rooster are formed on the leaves as a result of feeding and irritation by wingless, yellow-green aphids. Eggs are deposited in bark crevices in fall.

Control: A malathion or Diazinon spray applied as the buds open in spring will destroy the so-called "stem-mother" stage.

Dogwood Twig Borer (*Oberea tripunctata*). This girdler causes the dropping of many small twigs of the elm in May and June. The female partially girdles branches up to 1/2 inch in diameter. When the eggs hatch, the grubs bore 4 or 5 inches down the center of the twig, which may have broken off at the girdled point. The grubs are dull yellow, 3/4 inch long; they winter in the twigs. The adult beetles appear in the spring.

Control: To destroy the larvae, gather and discard all fallen twigs as soon as they are noticed; to destroy the adults, spray the trees with methoxychlor or Sevin in June.

Elm Leaf Miner (*Fenusa ulmi*). Leaves of American, English, Scots, and Camperdown elms are mined and blotched in May and June by white, legless larvae, sometimes as many as 20 in a single leaf. Adult females are shining black sawflies which deposit eggs in slits in the upper leaf surfaces. The damage is shown in Fig. 86.

Control: Spray the leaves about May 1 with Diazinon, malathion, or Sevin. Repeat once in June to control the second generation.

Gypsy Moth (*Porthetria dispar*). The leaves of a large number of forest, shade, and ornamental trees are chewed by the gypsy moth larva, a hairy, dark gray caterpillar with pairs of blue and red dots down its back, and ranging up to 3 inches in length. Among the most susceptible trees are apple, speckled alder, gray, paper, and red birches, hawthorn, linden, oaks, poplars, and willows. Trees that are also favored as food include ash, balsam fir, butternut, black walnut, catalpa, redcedar, flowering dogwood, sycamore, and tuliptree. The average annual damage caused by feeding of this insect amounts to nearly 2 million dollars. More than 800,000 acres of woodlands have been 25 to 100 per cent defoliated in a single year.

Control: Bacillus thuringiensis, Imidan, methoxychlor, and Sevin and Sevimol sprays all control this pest. They are most effective on young caterpillars.

Destroying the egg masses during winter or early spring also helps to protect valuable ornamental trees.

A synthetic sex lure, Diparlure, has recently been developed by United States Department of Agriculture scientists. Male gypsy moths are lured into special traps by this material which enables Federal and State officials to determine the presence and density of gypsy moths in any particular area.

Leopard Moth Borer (*Zeuzera pyrina*). The young caterpillars enter the twigs at the base of the buds and wilting results. The borers work downward, making large burrows in the larger limbs and trunks. Borers are whitish or light pink, marked with a number of dark spots. They are 2 to 3 inches long.

Control: Cut out and destroy infested twigs of small trees. Destroy the borer in larger branches by inserting a flexible wire into their tunnels to crush them, or inject a nicotine paste such as Bortox and then seal the openings with putty or chewing gum. The females, which are unable to fly, may be collected and destroyed before they have laid their eggs.

White-Marked Tussock Moth (*Hemerocampa leucostigma*). The leaves are chewed by the tussock moth larva, a hairy caterpillar 1½ inches long, with a red head, longitudinal black and yellow stripes along the body, and a tussock of hair on the head in the form of a Y. The adult female is a wingless, gray, hairy moth which deposits white egg masses on the trunk and branches.

On the West Coast, the larvae of the western tussock moth, *H. vetusta,* feed on almond, apricot, cherry, hawthorn, oaks, pear, plum, prune, walnut, and willows in addition to elms.

Control: See *Aesculus.*

Scales. Eleven species of scales infest elms: brown elm, calico, camphor, citricola, cottony maple, elm scurfy, European elm, European fruit lecanium, oystershell, Putnam, and scurfy. The European elm scale, *Gossyparia spuria* (Fig. 234), is a soft scale not protected by a waxy covering.

Fig. 234. European scale *(Gossyparia spuria)* on an elm branch.

Control: Spray all surfaces with a "superior" type miscible oil before the buds open in spring, or with malathion plus methoxychlor or Sevin in late May and again in mid-June.

Linden Leaf Beetle (*Calligrapha scalaris*). See *Tilia.*

Elm Sawfly. See *Tilia.*

Linden Looper. See *Tilia.*

Forest Tent Caterpillar. See *Acer.*

Mites (*Tetranychus canadensis* and *Panonychus ulmi*). These pests infest elms, causing the leaves to turn yellow prematurely.

Control: The inclusion of a miticide such as Aramite, chlorobenzilate, or Kelthane in the regular insecticide spray will curb these pests.

UMBRELLULARIA (CALIFORNIA-LAUREL)

Diseases

Leaf Blight. At least three organisms are responsible for this disease: *Pseudomonas lauracearum, Kabatiella phoradendri* var. *umbellulariae,* and *Colletotrichum gloeosporioides.* The bacterium causes black angular spots; the fungi, large, irregular, brown spots. These symptoms may be followed by dieback and blackening of the branch tips associated with a species of *Botryosphaeria.*

Control: Copper fungicides should control leaf blight.

Other Diseases. This host is also susceptible to black mildew caused by *Asterina anomola,* and canker by *Nectria cinnabarina* or *N. coccinea.* Several wood decay fungi also occur.

Insects

The crescent-marked lily aphid, omnivorous looper, soft scale, onion and pear thrips, and the inconspicuous and iridescent whiteflies are the insects known to infest this plant. Whiteflies can be controlled with the synthetic pyrethroid, Resmethrin. The control for the others is given under more favored hosts in other parts of this book.

VACCINIUM (BLUEBERRY)

Diseases

The species of *Vaccinium* cultivated for their fruits are subject to many diseases and insects. Fortunately varieties grown as ornamentals are relatively free of pests. Among the common troubles of such ornamentals as the highbush blueberry are a leaf and stem fleck caused by *Gloeosporium minus,* cankers by *Coryneum microstictum, Fusicoccum putrefaciens;* dieback by *Botryosphaeria dothidea;* two leaf spots by *Rhytisma vaccinii* and *Dothichi·.a caroliniana;* a root and crown rot by *Phytophthora cinnamomi;* and two virus diseases, red ringspot and stunt.

Insects

The stem-gall wasp, *Hemadas nubilipennis,* causes conspicuous kidney-shaped (pepperbox) galls on the stems, as shown in Fig. 235.

Other Insects. Ornamental blueberries are also infested by the azalea stem borer, forest tent caterpillar, fall webworm, and four kinds of scales: oystershell, Florida wax, Putnam, and European fruit lecanium.

Nutrient Deficiencies

Chlorosis. Ornamental *Vaccinium* species are subject to iron chlorosis, especially when planted near cement walls where the lime from such walls leaches into the surrounding soil. The leaf yellowing can be corrected either by spraying iron chelates onto the leaves or applying the chelates to the soil. Three ounces of iron chelate worked into the soil around an average sized plant will usually restore the normal green color in the leaves

Fig. 235. Pepperbox gall, caused by *Hemadas nubilipennis*, on *Vacinium*. On the right, galls split open to show the larvae within; in the gall, below, the holes through which they have emerged are visible.

within a month, if lack of iron or excessive alkalinity is involved.

In Washington State, *Vaccinium* may also suffer from a deficiency of boron. This can be corrected by applying fertilizers containing traces of this essential element.

VERBENA

Bacterial and Fungus Diseases

Bacterial Wilt (*Pseudomonas solanacearum*). Leaves of infected plants turn yellow, wilt, and die. The water-conducting vessels become dark-colored. Plants often die without blooming. The bacteria gain entrance to the plant through the roots.

Control: Set plants in clean soil, or steam-pasteurize infested soil.

Other Diseases. Among the fungus diseases of the common garden verbena, *Verbena hybrida,* are a flower blight caused by *Botrytis cinerea,* powdery mildew by *Erysiphe cichoracearum,* a stem rot by *Macrophomina phaseoli,* and root rots by three soil-inhabiting fungi: *Pellicularia filamentosa, Phymatotrichum omnivorum,* and *Thielaviopsis basicola.* The controls for these are given under more popular hosts.

Insects and Other Animal Pests

Aphids. The foxglove, green peach, and melon aphids infest *Verbena.*

Control: Spray with Sevin, Meta-Systox R, or malathion.

Clematis Blister Beetle (*Epicauta cinerea*). This beetle, gray with a yellowish tinge, may feed on leaves of verbenas.

Control: Sprays containing Sevin will control this pest.

Caterpillars. The yellow woollybear, *Diacrisia virginica,* with yellow, bristly hairs, feeds on the foliage of verbena. The oblique-banded leaf roller, *Choristoneura rosaceana,* folds the leaves over and then ties them together. The garden webworm, *Loxostege similalis,* may feed on scarlet verbena.

Control: Spray with *Bacillus thuringiensis,* Imidan, or Sevin when the caterpillars are young.

Verbena Leaf Miner (*Agromyza artemisiae*). This pest makes rather extensive blotch mines along the margins of the leaves.

Control: Pick off and destroy infested leaves. Spray with Cygon. This will kill the young larvae. Destroy other debris in the fall or early spring.

Verbena Bud Moth (*Endothenia hebesana*). The larvae feed on the buds and flower stalks, and later on the seed capsules. For additional details, see *Iris.*

Greenhouse Whitefly (*Trialeurodes vaporariorum*). Certain varieties are much more susceptible to attack than others, and on these the whitefly becomes a serious pest. Leaves become bronzed on the upper surfaces; all stages of the insect may be seen crowded on the lower surfaces; the black stationary stages or nymphs resemble small scale insects.

Control: See *Fuchsia.*

Other Insects. This host is also infested by the snapdragon lace bug, tarnished plant bug, morning-glory leaf cutter, greenhouse orthezia, cottony-cushion scale, and two species of thrips—the flower and the greenhouse.

Mites. The broad, cyclamen, and two-spotted mites also infest verbenas. These are discussed in other parts of this book.

Nemas (*Aphelenchoides olesistus* and *Meloidogyne hapla*). The fern nema and the northern root-knot nema also infest verbena. Their control is discussed in Chapter 3.

VERONICA[35] (SPEEDWELL)

Diseases

Downy Mildew (*Peronospora grisea*). Pale spots develop on the upper side of the leaves, the corresponding regions on the lower side being covered with a grayish mildew.

Control: Spray with a copper fungicide.

Leaf Spot (*Septoria veronicae*). Numerous small circular spots which vary in color from violet to brown appear on the upper sides of the leaves. On the under sides the spots are yellowish-brown and occasionally dark-zonate. As the spots run together the leaves present a scorched, ragged, and "shot-hole" appearance; defoliation occurs later. Other leaf spots of this host are caused by *Cercospora tortipes* and *Gloeosporium veronicae.*

Control: Destroy all fallen or spotted leaves. Important plantings can be protected with a copper fungicide.

Other Diseases. *Veronica* is occasionally affected by leaf galls caused by *Sorosphaera veronicae* and *Synchytrium globosum;* root rots by species of *Fusarium, Pellicularia filamentosa,* and *Phymatotrichum omnivorum;* a stem rot by *Pellicularia rolfsii;* powdery mildew by *Sphaerotheca humuli;* and leaf smut by *Entyloma veronicae.*

Insects and Other Animal Pests

The checkerspot butterfly, *Euphydryas chalcedona,* the Japanese weevil, *Pseudocneorhinus bifasciatus,* and the southern root-knot nema, *Meloidogyne incognita,* also infest this host.

VIBURNUM

Bacterial Diseases

Bacterial Leaf Spot (*Pseudomonas viburni*). Circular, water-soaked spots on the

---

[35]Some species of *Veronica* are now listed under *Hebe.*

leaves and young stems develop into irregular sunken brown areas $1/8$ inch in diameter. The disease is widely spread. The organism is said to live through the winter in cankers or on buds and young stems.

Control: Pick off and destroy all spotted leaves. To prevent new infections spray 3 times at weekly intervals with Bordeaux mixture or some ready-made copper fungicide.

Crown Gall (*Agrobacterium tumefaciens*). This disease occasionally affects viburnums.

Control: See *Rosa.*

Fungus Diseases

Shoot Blight (*Botrytis cinerea*). This disease causes grayish, brown decayed spots on the leaves, which begin at the margin and gradually envelop the entire leaf. The inflorescence may become blighted and the twigs killed. The sclerotia develop in the inflorescences and occasionally on the leaves. The disease is not common.

Control: Spray with captan.

Leaf Spots (*Cercospora tinea, C. varia, C. viburnicola, Hendersonia foliorum, Helminthosporium beaumontii, Phyllosticta lantanoides, P. punctata,* and *Ramularia viburni*). Most of the fungus leaf spots of viburnum occur on wild rather than on cultivated kinds.

Control: Valuable specimens can be protected by spraying with a copper fungicide.

Powdery Mildew (*Microsphaera alni*). Late in summer bushes in shaded places may be badly infected, the leaves being completely covered with this mildew (see Fig. 236).

Control: Spray with Karathane or Benlate.

Rusts (*Coleosporium viburni* and *Puccinia linkii*). Two species of rust fungi occur on *Viburnum.* They are rarely serious enough to require control measures.

Other Diseases. *Viburnum opulus* is subject to three other fungus diseases: downy leaf spot caused by *Plasmopara viburni,* leaf spot by *Cercospora viburnicola,* and spot anthracnose by *Sphaceloma viburni.* These are rarely serious enough to warrant control measures.

Fig. 236. Powdery mildew *(Microsphaera alni)* on *Viburnum lentago.*

Physiological Disease

Spray Burn. Since sulfur sprays applied to ornamental viburnums cause black spots on the leaves and defoliation within a few days, such materials should never be used on this host. Viburnums should not be planted near roses or other plants that are sprayed frequently with sulfur because the fungicide may drift over to the more sensitive host and cause severe damage.

Insects and Other Animal Pests

Viburnum Aphid (*Brachycaudus viburnicola*). These insects cluster together in great numbers at the tips of branches, causing the leaves to curl over and become deformed. This curling of the leaves gives the aphids protection against contact sprays. The aphids vary from ash-gray to dark green. The damage is done before the middle of June, when the aphids leave this host. Other species of aphids which infest this host are bean, currant, grapevine, and ivy.

Control: Spray with malathion, Meta-Systox R, or Sevin. For the viburnum aphid, the spray must be applied before the leaves are curled.

Asiatic Garden Beetle (*Maladera castanea*). These night-feeders can be controlled by spraying with methoxychlor.

Citrus Flatid Planthopper (*Metcalfa pruinosa*). These jumping, sucking insects are about 1/4 inch or more long. They are covered with a whitish powder which extends to the dark-colored wings. A woolly matter is scattered on the twigs of the infested plants.

Control: Spray forcefully with pyrethrum or rotenone, or a combination of the two, so as to thoroughly wet the insects. Malathion or Sevin sprays also control this pest.

Tarnished Plant Bug (*Lygus lineolaris*). These bugs feed on the blossoms, young shoots, and especially on the inflorescence. Brown spotting with much discoloration follows.

Control: Best control is obtained with a Sevin-Kelthane mixture.

Thrips. Two species of thrips, the flower and the greenhouse, infest viburnums. These can be controlled with the spray recommended for tarnished plant bug.

Other Pests. This host is occasionally infested by the potato flea beetle, dogwood twig borer, and seven species of scales: chaff, cottony-cushion, cottony maple, olive parlatoria, oystershell, San Jose, and Putnam.

The southern root-knot nema, *Meloidogyne incognita,* is also an important pest of this host.

VICIA (VETCH)

Leaf Spot (*Erostrotheca multiformis*). Certain ornamental greenhouse vetches are attacked by this fungus, especially when the humidity and temperature are high. The spots that develop on the leaves are gray in color. Complete defoliation may occur. This fungus also attacks sweet peas grown in greenhouses. Its asexual stage is known as *Cladosporium album.*

Control: Spraying with wettable sulfur has been found effective, but entails some danger of burning the flowers. The spray may be safely used on young plants.

VINCA (PERIWINKLE)

Fungus Diseases

Blight (*Botrytis cinerea*). Brown or black spots extend from the margin of the leaf inward and eventually cover the entire leaf. The disease is of local importance. Spacing the plants somewhat farther apart and spraying with a copper fungicide such as Bordeaux mixture, captan, or zineb will be helpful.

Canker and Dieback (*Phoma exigua* var. *exigua*). The shoot tips become dark brown, wilt, and die back to the surface of the soil. Some affected stems are nearly black. The sexual stage of this fungus is known as *Diaporthe vincae*. The disease is always most prevalent during very rainy seasons.

Control: Remove infected plants or prune out diseased parts of plants and discard this material. Drench the soil 2 or 3 times at monthly intervals during the growing season with Benlate or thiabendazole, 1/2 to 1 pound of the formulation per 1000 square feet.

Leaf Spots (*Alternaria* sp., *Colletotrichum* sp., *Macrophoma vincae, Phyllosticta* sp., *P. minor,* and *P. vincae-majoris*). Several species of fungi cause leaf spots on periwinkle.

Control: Spray with a copper fungicide.

Root Rot (*Pellicularia filamentosa*). The roots and stems of this host may be decayed by this soil-inhabiting fungus. This disease may be mistaken for canker. It does not, however, have the tiny black fruiting bodies of the *Phomopsis* that contain colorless spores.

Control: Control of this disease is difficult in established beds of periwinkle. Benlate is very effective in ridding infested soils of this particular fungus.

Insects and Other Animal Pests

Several species of scale insects and the northern root-knot nema *Meloidogyne hapla* infest *Vinca minor*. Another nema *Xiphinema americanum* was found to be associated with severe decline of *V. minor* in Wisconsin in 1966. Root systems of declining plants were stunted and had few viable root tips.

VIOLA (VIOLET, PANSY)

Diseases

Anthracnose (*Colletotrichum violae-tricoloris*). This fungus attacks violets and pansies, causing a browning or blotching of their leaves. The dead areas are marked by distinct black margins. Petals of attacked flowers develop abnormally. The plants may be killed by serious infection.

Another species, *C. violae-rotundifoliae,* infects this host in the Middle West and South.

Control: Spray twice at 5-day intervals with maneb, zineb, or Fore as soon as the first browning occurs.

Crown Rot (*Pellicularia rolfsii* and *Sclerotium delphinii*). These soil-inhabiting organisms are difficult to control once they infest soil. Drastic measures are necessary, such as steam-pasteurization, described in Chapter 4.

Downy Mildew (*Bremiella megasperma*). Affected leaves show irregular spotting and a light grayish, felt-like growth on the under sides. The leaves nearest the soil are attacked first and rapidly rot. The spores develop on diseased leaves and spread the infection quickly to other plants. The whole plant may droop and die without showing definite dead areas on the leaves.

Control: Provide adequate ventilation and destroy plants on which the disease appears. Downy mildew develops especially under damp conditions.

Gray Mold (*Botrytis cinerea*). During damp weather that continues for several days without much sunshine, the gray mold is apt to attack leaves and flower clusters of violets, causing a soft slimy decay. The disease is prevalent where the soil temperature is too low and especially where the plants are not well aired.

Control: This disease seldom appears under good cultural conditions. Captan or zineb sprays will, however, control it.

Leaf Spots (*Alternaria* sp., *A. violae, Ascochyta violicola, A. violae, Centrospora acerina, Cercospora granuliformis, C. violae, C. murina, Cryptostictis violae, Cylindrosporium violae, Gloeosporium violae, Heterosporium* sp., *Marssonina violae, Phyllosticta violae, P. nigrescens, Ramularia lactea, R. agrestis, R. ioniphila,* and *Septoria·violae*). More fungi cause leaf spots of *Viola* than of any other genus mentioned in this book. However, only a mycologist can distinguish one species from another.

Control: Large plantings where these fungi have become troublesome should be cleaned. Old leaves should be gathered in the fall and destroyed so as to eliminate the overwintering spores. Valuable plantings can be protected by spraying with either maneb or zineb.

Powdery Mildew (*Sphaerotheca macularis*). This mildew affects *Viola* grown in greenhouses and outdoors.

Control: Control measures are rarely applied for this fungus.

Root Rots. Six soil-inhabiting fungi—*Ciborinia violae, Fusarium oxysporum* var. *aurantiacum, Helicobasidium purpureum, Pellicularia filamentosa, Phymatotrichum omnivorum,* and *Thielaviopsis basicola*—cause root and stem rots of *Viola.*

Control: Same as for crown rot.

Rust (*Puccinia violae*). Pale green spots develop on the under surfaces of the leaves. The aecial rust pustules develop on the opposite sides; these contain yellowish spores. Petioles and stems also are susceptible to infection. Later in the season the brown uredospores are developed; these spread the rust during the growing season. Still later the dark brown or black teliospores develop. Little damage to cultivated violets is done by this rust, which is not uncommon on wild violets.

Control: Spray with maneb or zineb.

Other Rusts. Other species of rusts of *Viola* which require special control measures include: *Puccinia effusa, P. ellisiana, P. fergussonii,* and *Uromyces andropogonis.*

Scab (*Sphaceloma violae*). This very common disease affects all green parts of the plant, including the seed capsule. Elongated or nearly circular lesions up to 1/4 inch in their greatest dimension are formed. The infected areas or spots may be bright yellowish-brown, rose-colored, or whitish. Darker green zones may surround the spots. The diseased areas readily fall out, leaving "shot-holes." When stems or leaf stalks are completely girdled, the parts above die. The spores are from one- to three-celled. The disease, which has been reported as serious in certain localities, occurs also on pansy and wild species of violet.

Control: Spray with maneb or zineb. Do not gather seeds from diseased plants.

Smut (*Urocystis violae*). Wild and cultivated violets are sometimes attacked by this parasite. Ovaries, calyx, flower stalks, and offshoots—practically all parts of the plant—are subject to attack. More or less elongated blisters or callus-like pustules develop on the leaf stalks, which are considerably deformed. These break open and discharge dark spores in small spore balls. The outer layer of cells of these balls is colorless.

Control: Remove and destroy all infected plants early in the season. If possible, change the location of the planting.

Stem Rot (*Myrothecium roridum*). This fungus attacks pansy stems at soil level. The diseased tissues become dry and brittle and bear an abundance of black spore pustules of the fungus. Leaves inoculated with this fungus turn purplish-black in spots or streaks. Infected tissues dry up, shrivel, and turn brown. This same fungus attacks hollyhocks.

Control: Practice crop rotation and sanitation.

Curly Top (Beet curly top virus). Damping and rosetting of shoots of pansies, followed by a reduction in the size of flowers and in the amount of seed produced, are characteristic of this virus disease. Because the pansy is one of the hosts of the beet leafhopper, *Circulifer tenellus,* which spreads this disease, one should avoid extensive growing of pansies in the vicinity of beet fields. Plants grown from seed are disease-free.

Aster Yellows. Vein-clearing and bright yellow leaf chlorosis are symptoms of this disease on *Viola tricolor* caused by a mycoplasma-like organism.

Control: Remove and destroy infected plants. Spray with malathion to control the insect vectors.

Physiological Disease

Oedema, Wart Disease. Corky or wartlike growths ⅛ inch long develop on the leaves and flower stalks and cause these parts to become dry and brittle. Insect punctures are often followed by such growths. Ordinarily, improper water relations lead to oedema; either a soil kept too wet by over-mulching, or excessive humidity of the air due to faulty lighting conditions. Admit more air to the greenhouse and stir the soil to make it more porous. Avoid rapid changes of conditions, however.

Insects and Other Animal Pests

Aphids. Four species of aphids attack violets and pansies: foxglove, red violet, green peach, and violet.

Control: Spray with Sevin or malathion.

Cutworms (*Peridroma saucia* and others). Several species of cutworms attack pansies and violets in the spring.

Control: See *Asparagus.*

Violet Gall Midge (*Phytophaga violicola*). Small grubs or maggots attack the leaves at the growing point, causing them to become distorted through the development of galls. These distorted leaves are later subject to wet rot. Infested plants are usually much dwarfed and blossoming is limited. Handpick infested leaves as soon as possible. Gather all fallen leaves frequently and put them into the trash can. Plant new stalks in fresh soil after removing the lower leaves.

Greenhouse Leaf Tier (*Udea rubigalis*). The yellowish-green caterpillars, less than 1 inch long, draw the leaves and flower buds together and feed on the undersides of the leaves and occasionally on the flowers. They attack garden violets as well as greenhouse violets.

Control: Hand-picking is the most practical method of control where the infestation is limited. Spray the plants with Sevin before the leaves are tied together.

Mealybugs (*Planococcus citri* and *Pseudococcus solani*). These two mealybugs infest *Viola;* the former occurs on violet, the latter on pansies.

Control: Spray with malathion or Diazinon.

Violet Sawfly (*Ametastegia pallipes*). The leaves of garden pansies and violets as well as those grown in greenhouses are often eaten by bluish-black larvae of the sawfly, about ½ inch long. The young larvae merely skeletonize the leaves; later they eat out holes, causing a "shot-hole" effect.

Control: Spray with Sevin.

Slugs (*Milax* sp. and *Limax* sp.). These animals leave characteristic slimy tracks where they have crawled away after eating holes in the leaves. Damp weather and moist greenhouse conditions seem to favor their activity. Slug baits, such as Snarol, Slug-getta, or metaldehyde dust applied over infested areas, will control these pests.

Two-Spotted Mite (*Tetranychus urticae*). Dry weather and dry greenhouse conditions encourage mites on violets as on other plants. Pansies in outdoor beds are also extremely susceptible.

Control: An important point to bear in mind is that the mites should not be allowed to develop in such numbers as to cause the leaves to turn yellowish-tan in color. Control measures should be started as soon as the first stippling of the leaves is noticed. Chlorbenzilate, Kelthane, Meta-Systox R, or Tedion can be used. Syringing of plants also helps to keep mite infestations down, but this practice is difficult with violets and pansies because of their low-growing habit. Nicotine sulfate and soap should not be used on violets because they are sensitive to this mixture.

Root-Knot and Meadow Nemas (*Meloidogyne incognita, M. hapla,* and *Pratylenchus pratensis*). The first two species cause small wart-like swellings on the roots, while the last-named is responsible for brown sunken lesions on the roots. The latter species frequently causes serious damage.

Control: See Nemas, Chapter 3.

Fern Nema (*Aphelenchoides olesistus*). Certain varieties are subject to infestation by this nema, which attacks the young growth around the growing point. The leaves are dwarfed and distorted; flowers are often lacking. Stalks are much shortened and the leaves become stunted. The base of the leaf stalk is often swollen and has a "cauliflower" appearance.

Control: Change the location of the plants and do not use plants from infested plantings for propagation. If offshoots from infested plantings must be used, they can be freed from nemas by immersing them for ½ hour in water heated to 110°F.

VITEX (CHASTE-TREE)

Chaste-tree is subject to two leaf spots caused by *Cercospora viticis* and *C. weberi* and to root rot by *Phymatotrichum onnivorum.*

WATSONIA

The only disease recorded on this host are root rot caused by the fungus *Armillaria mel-*lea, and mosaic by the iris mosaic virus. The gladiolus thrips, *Taeniothrips simplex,* is its only insect pest.

WEIGELA

Diseases

Weigela is susceptible to the bacterial disease crown gall caused by *Agrobacterium tumefaciens,* twig blight by the fungus *Phoma weigelae,* leaf spot by *Cercospora weigelae,* and root rot by *Phymatotrichum omnivorum.*

Insects and Related Pests

The four-lined plant bug, Japanese weevil, Comstock mealybug, and three species of scale—barnacle, cottony-cushion, and latania —attack weigela. These are discussed under more favored hosts.

Two species of nemas also attack this host —root-knot (*Meloidogyne* sp.) and meadow (*Pratylenchus pratensis*). Controls are discussed in Chapter 3.

WISTERIA

Bacterial and Fungus Diseases

Crown Gall (*Agrobacterium tumefaciens*). This bacterial disease occasionally affects wisteria, causing galls or swellings on the main roots or stems.

Control: See Rosa.

Leaf Spots (*Phyllosticta wisteriae, Septoria wisteriae,* and *Phomatospora wisteriae*). Three species of fungi cause leaf spots on this host. Pick off and destroy spotted leaves as soon as they appear.

Other Fungus Diseases. This host is also subject to stem canker caused by *Nectria cinnabarina,* powdery mildew by *Erysiphe cichoracearum,* and root rot by *Phymatotrichum omnivorum.*

Virus Diseases

Mosaic. (Tobacco mosaic virus). Newly affected leaves have yellowish blotches with scattered green islands. Mature leaves exhibit a lateral twisting of their leaflets.

Control: Control measures have not been developed.

Insects

The following are the insects known to infest this host: sweet-potato leaf beetle, *Typophorus nigritis* var. *viridicyaneus;* silver-spotted skipper, *Epargyreus clarus;* Japanese mealybug, *Pseudococcus krauhniae;* citrus flata planthopper, *Metcalfa pruinosa;* fall webworm, *Hyphantria cunea;* black vine weevil, *Otiorhyncus sulcatus;* and two species of scale: lesser snow, *Pinnaspis strachani,* and mining, *Howardia biclavis.*

YUCCA

Diseases

The ornamental species of yucca are subject to relatively few diseases and insects. Among the more common diseases are a leaf blight caused by the fungi *Kellermannia anomala* and *Leptosphaeria filamentosa,* and a leaf spot by *Coniothyrium concentricum.* The latter appears as large circular light brown spots with purple margins, concentric zonation, and pale centers. Small black fruiting bodies (pycnidia) of the fungus are arranged more or less in concentric circles. The same fungus attacks *Agave* and related plants. The spores, characteristic of the fungus are small, light brown, one-celled.

Control: Cut off and destroy infected leaves. Spray with ammoniacal copper carbonate or Bordeaux mixture. Avoid syringing infected plants, since this spreads the disease to healthy plants.

Insects

Plant Bug. (*Halticotoma valida*). This small blue-black bug with a reddish head stipples leaves and causes them to turn yellow. A small weevil also infests the flowers.

Control: Sevin sprays will control these pests.

Mealybug (*Planococcus citri*). Certain varieties of *Yucca* are very susceptible to attacks by this mealybug, which masses along the veins and leaf stalks. Another species, *Puto yuccae,* not only infests yuccas but many other plants, including aster, lantana, and lemon in the far West.

Control: Malathion sprays diluted as directed are very effective in combating mealybugs.

Stalk Borer (*Papaipema nebris*). Yucca is one of the many hosts of this borer, which invades the stems. The borers can be killed by inserting a flexible wire into the tunnels in the stems.

Scales. Several species of scales, including California red, *Aonidiella aurantii;* oleander, *Aspidiotus nerii;* and oystershell, *Lepidosaphes ulmi,* occasionally infest yucca.

Control: Malathion or Sevin sprays will control the crawler stages of these pests.

Yucca Weevil (*Scyphophorus yuccae*). This small black weevil feeds on the sap of yucca in the dry regions of the Southwest.

Control: Control measures are usually unnecessary.

ZANTEDESCHIA AETHIOPICA (CALLA-LILY)

Diseases

Bacterial Soft Rot (*Erwinia carotovora* var. *aroideae*). This is a disease of the base of the stem and the corms rather than a rot of the feeding roots. Infected plants first suffer a soft rot at the base near the soil level. Corms becomes infected later, and as the bacteria travel upward the leaves become blighted.

The entire plant finally wilts and dies. In extreme cases the roots themselves are involved in a slimy decay.

Control: Discard all badly decayed corms at digging time. Valuable corms can be saved if the soil is removed from about the roots of infected plants and all decayed parts washed and scraped away. While the corms are still dormant they should be treated with formaldehyde as described below for root rot. In greenhouses where infection has been serious, care should be taken to wash down all exposed parts of benches and side walls with lime or formaldehyde, and to disinfest the bench soil with formaldehyde, steam, or heat.

Crown Rot (*Pellicularia filamentosa* and *Sclerotium delphinii*). A soft decay of the lower half of the main corm and of the thick feeding roots may be caused by these fungi. This disease is far less common than bacterial soft rot and root rot.

Control: Set corms in steam-pasteurized soil or soil treated with PCNB (Terraclor).

Leaf Spots (*Cercospora richardiaecola, Gloeosporium callae,* and *Phyllosticta richardiae*). Three species of fungi cause leaf spots of calla-lily. The last and most common causes small, roundish, ash-gray, discolored spots which run together as the disease progresses, producing irregular, decayed areas. Stalks and flowers are also subject to infection, although not seriously.

Control: Pick off badly infected leaves. Fungicidal sprays are rarely applied to this host to control leaf spots.

Root Rot (*Phytophthora richardiae*). Sysmptoms of the disease appear on the lower or outer leaves at about the time the plants should begin to flower. The leaves become yellowish more or less in streaks, lose their stiffness, finally wilt, turn brown, and die. If flowers open at all, they are likely to be malformed and soon turn brown at the tip; the discoloration may extend down to the stalk. This disease does not kill the whole plant suddenly, but as new leaves and flowers develop they quickly show its effects. If such infected plants are pulled up, it will be seen that much of the root system is decayed (Fig. 237). The remaining roots present a water-soaked appearance, evidence of soft rot, and the epidermis, as a hollow tube, may be all that remains. The corm itself is seldom affected.

Control: Clean dormant rhizomes, then dip them in hot water at 122°F. for 1 hour. Cool and dry. Dormant rhizomes can also be soaked for one hour in a formaldehyde solution, 1 pint in 6¼ gallons of water.

Storage Rot (*Pythium ultimum*). This disease causes a decay of pink calla, *Z. rehmannii,* and yellow calla, *Z. elliottiana,* in storage.

Virus Diseases

Virus (Tomato spotted wilt virus.) This virus affects white, yellow, and pink callas. Chlorotic to pale white streaks and circular lesions, some of which may later become necrotic, are distributed between the veins on the leaves. Leaves may also be wrinkled and distorted, and the margins may curl upward or downward. The color of infected spathes is usually bleached.

Control: Destroy affected plants. Never propagate from such material. Spray plants frequently with malathion to control insects which may play a part in transmitting this virus.

Insects

The yellow woollybear, the grape and long-tailed mealybugs, bulb mite, and the banded greenhouse and greenhouse thrips are among the pests reported on calla-lily. These are discussed under more popular hosts.

Fig. 237. Root rot of calla-lily (*Zantedeschia aethiopica*), caused by *Phytophthora richardiae*. On the left, a healthy root-cluster for comparison with the diseased mass on the right.

ZINNIA

Diseases

Bacterial Wilt (*Pseudomonas solanacearum*). This bacterium causes a wilt of zinnias in Florida.

Control: Use clean or treated seed in steam-pasteurized soil.

Blight (*Alternaria zinniae*). Small, reddish-brown spots with grayish centers are the first symptoms of this widespread and highly troublesome disease. Dark brown cankers also occur on the stems. Flowers are spotted and at times completely blighted.

Control: Because the causal fungus may be carried with the seed, treat the seed with hot water at 125 degrees F. for 30 minutes before planting. Then cool and dry. Seeds more than one year old may be severely injured by this treatment. Protection during the growing season can be provided by frequent spraying with ferbam, Fore, or maneb.

Powdery Mildew (*Erysiphe cichoracearum*). This ash-gray mold which covers the leaves is found wherever zinnias are grown. The fruiting bodies of the fungus are known to be carried with seed.

Control: Spray with Acti-dione PM, Benlate, wettable sulfur, or Karathane as soon as the mildew appears.

Root and Stem Rots (*Fusarium* sp., *Pellicularia rolfsii*, *Phytophthora cryptogea*, and *Sclerotinia sclerotiorum*). These soil-inhabiting fungi may cause severe losses in zinnia plantings.

Control: See Chapter 4, under steam-pasteurization.

Virus. Many virus diseases affect zinnias.

Among the most prevalent are curly top caused by the beet curly top virus, mosaic by the cucumber mosaic virus, and spotted wilt by the tomato spotted wilt virus.

Control: Remove and destroy infected plants. Spray with malathion every few weeks to control sucking insects which spread these viruses.

Other Diseases. Zinnias are subject to other diseases including a blossom blight caused by a species of *Choanephora,* stem canker by *Botrytis cinerea,* damping-off by *Pellicularia filamentosa,* leaf spot by *Cercospora zinniae,* and aster yellows caused by a mycoplasma-like organism.

Insects and Other Animal Pests

Among the sucking insects that infest zinnias are the bean aphid, *Aphis fabae;* the redbanded leafhopper, *Graphocephala coccinea;* the aster leafhopper, *Macrosteles fascifrons;* the tarnished plant bug, *Lygus lineo-*laris; the four-lined plant bug, *Poecilocapsus lineatus;* and the long-tailed mealybug, *Pseudococcus longispinus.*

Control: Diazinon or Sevin sprays will control all these pests.

Beetles. Among the chewing insects which infest this host are the following beetles: Asiatic garden, blister, flea, Japanese, and cucumber. The Japanese beetle is perhaps most destructive.

Control: Spray with a mixture of Sevin and Kelthane.

Other Insects. Among the chewing insects that feed on zinnias are the stalk borer and the morning-glory leaf cutter.

Mites. Three species of mites infest zinnias: broad, cyclamen, and two-spotted.

Control: Spray with Aramite, Dimite, or Kelthane as directed by the manufacturer.

Nemas. Two species of nemas infest this host: *Meloidogyne incognita,* which causes root-knot, and *Aphelenchoides ritzema-bosi,* which causes angular spots on the leaves.

Control: See Chapter 3.

Index